Economics of Agglomeration, Second Edition

Economic activities are not concentrated on the head of a pin, nor are they spread evenly over a featureless plain. On the contrary, they are distributed very unequally across locations, regions, and countries. Even though economic activities are, to some extent, spatially concentrated because of natural features, economic mechanisms that rely on the trade-off between various forms of increasing returns and different types of mobility costs are more fundamental. This book is a study of the economic reasons for the existence of a large variety of agglomerations arising from the global to the local.

This second edition combines a comprehensive analysis of the fundamentals of spatial economics and an in-depth discussion of the most recent theoretical developments in new economic geography and urban economics. It aims to highlight several of the major economic trends observed in modern societies.

Masahisa Fujita, a member of the Japan Academy and the president of Research Institute of Economy, Trade and Industry, has been a major contributor to spatial economic theory during his twenty-year tenure at the University of Pennsylvania and more recently at Kyoto University and Konan University. Professor Fujita is the author or co-author of three books: *Spatial Development Planning* (1978); *Urban Economic Theory* (Cambridge University Press, 1989), which remains to this day the most authoritative graduate textbook on urban economics; and *The Spatial Economy* (1999, co-authored with Paul Krugman and A. J. Venables), which defines the field of new economic geography.

Jacques-François Thisse, a Fellow of the Econometric Society and of the Regional Science Association International, is professor of economics at the Université catholique de Louvain (Belgium) and the Higher School of Economics (Russia). He has published in numerous journals, including *American Economic Review*, *Econometrica*, *Journal of Political Economy*, *International Economic Review*, *Management Science*, *Exploration in Economic History*, and *Journal of Economic Geography*. He is the co-author of *Discrete Choice Theory of Product Differentiation* (1992; co-authored with S. P. Anderson and A. de Palma), *Economic Geography* (2008; co-authored with P.-P. Combes and T. Mayer), and *Economic Geography and the Unequal Development of Regions* (2012, co-authored with J.-C. Prager).

Professors Fujita and Thisse co-authored the first edition of *Economics of Agglomeration: Cities, Industrial Location, and Regional Growth* (Cambridge University Press, 2002).

Economics of Agglomeration

Cities, Industrial Location, and Globalization

Second Edition

MASAHISA FUJITA
Research Institute of Economy, Trade and Industry, Japan

JACQUES-FRANÇOIS THISSE
Catholic University of Louvain

CAMBRIDGE
UNIVERSITY PRESS

32 Avenue of the Americas, New York NY 10013-2473, USA

Cambridge University Press is part of the University of Cambridge.

It furthers the University's mission by disseminating knowledge in the pursuit of education, learning and research at the highest international levels of excellence.

www.cambridge.org
Information on this title: www.cambridge.org/9780521171960

First published 2002
Second edition 2013

A catalogue record for this publication is available from the British Library

Library of Congress Cataloguing in Publication data
Fujita, Masahisa.
Economics of agglomeration : cities, industrial location, and globalization / by Masahisa Fujita, Jacques-François Thisse.
pages cm
Includes bibliographical references and index.
ISBN 978-1-107-00141-1 (hardback) – ISBN 978-0-521-17196-0 (paperback)
1. Space in economics 2. Regional economics. 3. Urban economics. 4. Industrial location.
I. Thisse, Jacques François. II. Title.
HT388.F84 2013
330.9173′2–dc23 2012049385

ISBN 978-1-107-00141-1 Hardback
ISBN 978-0-521-17196-0 Paperback

Primitive though it may be, every stable society feels the need of providing its members with centers of assembly, or meeting places. Observance of religious rites, maintenance of markets, and political and judicial gatherings necessarily bring about the designation of localities intended for the assembly of those who wish to or who must participate therein.

Henri Pirenne, *Medieval Cities*, 1925

Contents

Acknowledgments

In preparing the second edition of this book, we have benefited from comments and remarks made by colleagues and friends. We wish to thank Steven Brakman, Gilles Duranton, Carl Gaigné, Florian Mayneris, Yasusada Murata, Antonella Nocco, Mitsuru Ota, Daisuke Oyama, Dominique Peeters, Takatoshi Tabuchi, Hajime Takatsuka, Suminori Tokunaga, Eric Toulemonde, Philip Ushchev, Yves Zenou, and Evgeny Zhelobodko. We are especially grateful to Toshihiro Gokan, who read all the new chapters and offered several suggestions. We also thank those who wrote reviews of the first edition, in particular Ed Glaeser and Bob Helsley. Their criticisms have been very useful in developing this second edition. Over the last years, we had very insightful discussions on topics covered in this book with Marcus Berliant, Ronald Davis, Vernon Henderson, and David Weinstein. We have received many comments from students who attended classes at the Ecole nationale des ponts et chaussées (Paris), New Economic School (Moscow), and Zhejiang University (China). Last, but not least, we wish to acknowledge the work of Yuki Nakamura who performed wonderfully in composing all the figures.

Preface to the Second Edition

Ever since we completed the first edition of this book, the fields of economic geography and urban economics have grown at a fast pace. The abundance of new and insightful results called for an updating of the first edition. Given this state of affairs, Scott Parris from Cambridge University Press kindly offered us the opportunity to prepare a second edition. The revision is not a minor one. Even though we have chosen to keep the same general organization of the book, all chapters have been rewritten, admittedly to various extents. As a consequence, by reflecting the rapid evolution of the discipline, our book is more comprehensive. However, we want to stress the fact that a large number of recent contributions keep relying on a few basic principles that are sometimes lost in long and sophisticated econometric developments.

Understanding these principles is necessary for our discipline to progress. They also make us realize that seemingly different issues are just the same ones operating at different spatial scales. Although links with empirical works are stressed in many places, the emphasis of the book is still on spatial economic theory. In what follows, we restrict ourselves to highlighting the main changes made in the second edition.

Although a good deal of the material devoted to the Fundamentals of Spatial Economics (Part I) has kept its relevance, the corresponding four chapters involve a fair amount of new material. They also have been revised in the hope of showing how the general principles we want to stress can be applied to a wide range of issues. The Structure of Metropolitan Areas (Part II) did not change much because no major progress took place during the last decade. We have highlighted the relationships between the material presented there and new strands of literature. Some sections have been redrafted to make them more reader-friendly.

By contrast, Factor Mobility and Industrial Location (Part III) has been almost completely rewritten. This is where most of the action has taken place during the last ten years. This part explicitly focuses on the developments that have opened new perspectives and led to new sets of predictions. Chapter 8 focuses on labor mobility. In addition to the basic core-periphery model, we discuss in great detail new issues, such as the potential function approach, the welfare analysis of the core-periphery model, the role played by land in regional development, the coagglomeration of industries, and the bell-shaped curve of spatial development.

Chapter 9 is new. It covers issues and methodological advances in economic geography that have been studied during the last decade. We use both the linear and constant elasticity of substitution (CES) models of monopolistic competition to revisit classical topics and to explore new ones. In particular, we provide a full and systematic analysis of the home market effect. We also address the case of heterogeneous firms as well as the endogenous determination of the wage structure in settings where capital is footloose and labor sticky. Last, combining monopolistic competition and Marshallian externalities, we study the emergence of industrial clusters.

In the last part, Urban Systems, Regional Growth, and the Multinationalization of Firms (Part IV), we have added some material to Chapter 10, whereas Chapter 11 is essentially new. Chapter 10 has been supplemented with a discussion of how the number and size of cities vary with the level of transport cost. By contrast, Chapter 11 deals with a much broader range of issues than its original counterpart. The sections on regional growth focus on sticky innovations, that is, the case where barriers to technological transfers prevent new goods and services from being produced in territories other than the ones where they have been developed. The remaining part of the chapter explores the international fragmentation of the firm bolstered by the integration of markets as well as the development of containerization and new information and communication technologies. By using a unifying framework, we show how homogeneous firms implement different strategies in conducting their business on foreign markets.

1

Agglomeration and Economic Theory

1.1 INTRODUCTION

This book is an attempt to uncover the main economic reasons for the existence of peaks and troughs in the spatial distributions of population and wealth. Economic activities are not concentrated on the head of a pin, nor are they spread evenly over a featureless plain. On the contrary, they are distributed very unequally across locations, regions, and countries, generating contour lines that vary with time and place. Just as matter in the solar system is concentrated in a small number of bodies (the planets and their satellites), economic life is concentrated in a fairly limited number of human settlements. Furthermore, paralleling large and small planets, there are large and small settlements with very different combinations of firms and households. Though universal, these phenomena are still in search of a general theory.

The common belief, however, is that we now live in a world where the tyranny of distance, which has been such a powerful force in human history, no longer exists. The spectacular and steady drop in transport costs since the mid-nineteenth century, compounded by the decline of protectionism and, more recently, by the near disappearance of communication costs, is said to have freed economic agents from the need to be located near one another, suggesting that our economies are entering an age that will culminate in the "death of distance." If so, locational difference would gradually fade because agglomeration forces would vanish. In other words, the combined impact of technology and globalization would make the traditional geography of economic activity obsolete and yesterday's world of peaks and troughs would miraculously become "flat."

Recent empirical and theoretical work in new economic geography and urban economics shows a very different reality. While it is true that the importance of proximity to natural resources has declined considerably, thus giving firms and households more freedom to locate where they wish, this does not mean that distance and location have disappeared from economic life. Quite the contrary, economic geography points to new forces, hitherto outweighed by natural factors, which are shaping an economic landscape that, with its many barriers and large inequalities, is anything but a "flat world." For example, the simplistic view that improvements in communication technologies will render financial centers obsolete is as misplaced as the opposite view that we will see ever-increasing concentration. As is seen throughout this book, the huge drop in transport and communication costs is precisely what allowed these new forces to emerge and subsequently fostered the greater productivity that now characterizes large cities.

Ever since the emergence of civilization, human activities and standards of living have been unevenly distributed among both the continents and their territories. According to the famous historian Braudel (1979, 39), a "world-economy" is the combination of three types of space:

> The centre or core contains everything that is most advanced and diversified. The next zone possesses only some of these benefits, although it has some share in them: it is the "runner-up" zone. The huge periphery, with its scattered population, represents on the contrary backwardness, archaism, and exploitation by others.

Even though economic activities are, to some extent, spatially concentrated because of natural features (think of rivers and harbors), it is our contention that economic mechanisms yielding agglomeration (or dispersion) of activities are more fundamental. As is discussed in this book, most of these mechanisms rely on the fundamental *trade-off* between various forms of *increasing returns* and different types of *mobility costs*. It applies to different types of scale economies and to the costs generated by the transfer of people, goods, and information. In addition, this trade-off is valid on all spatial scales (cities, regions, countries, or continents), which makes it a valuable analytic tool.

Although referring to agglomeration as a generic term is convenient, one should keep in mind that the concept of economic agglomeration refers to very distinct real-world situations.[1] At one extreme lies the core-periphery structure corresponding to the North-South divide. High-income nations are still clustered in small industrial cores in the Northern Hemisphere whereas productivity per capita steadily declines with distance from these cores.

Economic growth has always been and still is geographically unequal and very localized. This is especially well illustrated by the emergence of a core-periphery structure in Europe during the nineteenth century (Bairoch 1997). From 1800 to 1913, European countries experienced a high rate of growth. Yet, while the initial levels of economic development were roughly the same, varying by about 10 percent around the European average, countries were affected quite differently by the Industrial Revolution and its concomitant decrease in transport costs. Indeed, international differences grew progressively and

[1] The term "agglomeration" is less ambiguous than "concentration," which is used to describe different economic phenomena.

reached a ratio of 1 to 4 between the richest and poorest nations by 1913. While the average European GDP per capita increased gradually by a factor slightly greater than 2.5, the standard deviation increased even faster, going from 24 in 1800 to 229 in 1913. In other words, disparities between nations grew more than proportionally, the coefficient of variation increasing from 0.12 in 1800 to 0.42 in 1913. As usual, such aggregate measures hide even stronger contrasts between countries: while the GDP per capita of the United Kingdom increased by a factor exceeding 4, that of the Balkans (Bulgaria, Greece, and Serbia) barely rose by 50 percent.

A more recent example of such a phenomenon is provided by the evolution of world production during the last two decades of the twentieth century. We focus on the three biggest regional blocks, that is, the European Union (EU), the North American Free Trade Agreement (NAFTA), and East Asia.[2] At the global scale, in 1980 the EU-15 accounted for 29 percent of world gross domestic product (GDP), NAFTA for 27 percent, and East Asia for 14 percent. These three blocks thus produced 70 percent of world GDP. Twenty years later, the share of the EU-15 had fallen to 25 percent, while that of NAFTA had increased to 35 percent and that of East Asia to 23 percent. Together, they accounted for 83 percent of world GDP in 2000, a much larger share than in 1980. Throughout this period, we saw more agglomeration and rapid growth of the world economy with significant reductions in transport and communication costs, which fostered the international division of labor. In particular, East Asia has emerged as the world's manufacturing center (e.g., it provided 100 percent of digital cameras and hard disk drives, 99.8 percent of personal computers, and 71.5 percent of cell phones in 2008).

At the national level, a few large cities produce a sizable share of their country's GDP. For example, in the Republic of Korea, the capital region, which covers 11.8 percent of the country's surface area and includes 48.6 percent of the population, produced 47.8 percent of Korea's GDP in 2008. In France, the metropolitan area of Paris, which accounts for 2.2 percent of the country's area and 18.2 percent of its population, produced 28.3 percent of its GDP. Similarly, in Brazil, the world's fifth-largest country in surface area, 33.9 percent of GDP is produced by 21.6 percent of the population in the state of São Paulo, which occupies only 2.9 percent of the country's area. In 2000, the thirty-eight largest cities of the EU-15 accounted for 27 percent of its jobs and produced 29 percent of its GDP.

Highly diverse size and activity arrangements also exist at the regional and urban levels. Cities may be specialized in a very small number of industries, as are many medium-size cities. However, large metropolises such as New York or Tokyo are highly diversified in that they nest several industries that are not

[2] East Asia here is formed by China, Indonesia, Japan, Hong Kong, the Republic of Korea, Malaysia, the Philippines, Singapore, Thailand, and Taiwan.

related through direct linkages. Industrial districts involving firms with strong technological or informational linkages, or both (e.g., the Silicon Valley or Italian districts engaged in more traditional activities), as well as factory towns (e.g., Toyota City), manifest various types of local specialization.

At a very detailed extreme of the spectrum, agglomeration arises under the form of large commercial districts set up in the inner city itself (think of Soho in London, Montparnasse in Paris, or Ginza in Tokyo). At the lowest level, restaurants, movie theaters, or shops selling similar products are clustered within the same neighborhood, not to say on the same street, or the clustering may take the form of a large shopping mall. Understanding such phenomena is critical for the design of effective regional or urban policies. What distinguishes these various types of agglomeration is the *spatial scale*, or the spatial unit of reference, chosen in conducting one's research, just as there are different levels of aggregation of economic agents.

The economic reasons that stand behind strong geographical concentrations of consumption and production are precisely what we aim to investigate in this book. To achieve this objective, we appeal to the concepts and tools of modern microeconomics. Even though clusters appear at different geographical scales, it would be futile to look for *the* model explaining different types of economic agglomerations, the reason being these clusters involve distinct and contrasting details. This should not come as a surprise, for geographers have long known that spatial scale matters: What is true at a certain spatial scale is not necessarily true at another – the "ecological fallacy." In this respect, Martin (1999, 387) is right in his criticism of economists' proclivity to use the same models "to explain the tendency for economic activity to agglomerate at various spatial scales, from the international, through the regional, to the urban and the local."

To study issues arising at, say, the interregional and intra-urban levels, different models encapsulating specific spatial features are developed in this book, the reason being that *the nature and balance of the system of forces at work at different spatial scales need not be the same*. Or, in the words of Anas, Arnott, and Small (1998, 1440): "It may be that the patterns that occur at different distance scales are influenced by different types of agglomeration economies, each based on interaction mechanisms with particular requirements for spatial proximity."

However, as is seen, working with different models will not prevent us from deriving a few general principles that seem to govern the formation of distinct agglomerations. The main thrust of the book is that a few basic ideas and concepts lie at the foundations of the still needed general theory of location.

In particular, a major principle holds true regardless of the scale of analysis retained: The emergence of economic agglomerations is associated with the emergence of spatial inequalities. Such inequalities are often at the origin of strong tensions between different political bodies or jurisdictions, or even social, religious, or ethnic groups when they are geographically concentrated.

Understanding how spatial inequalities in economic activities and living standards arise is thus a fundamental challenge for economists, regional scientists, and geographers alike.

1.2 DO TRANSPORT COSTS STILL MATTER?

By its very nature, transport is linked to trade. Trade being one of the oldest human activities, the transport of commodities is, therefore, a fundamental ingredient of any society. People get involved in trade because they want to consume goods that are not produced within reach. The Silk Road provides evidence that shipping high-valued goods over long distances has been undertaken because of this precise reason.

The transportation sector underwent the most stunning changes during the Industrial Revolution. According to Bairoch (1997, volume 2, 26), "On the whole, between 1800 and 1910, it can be estimated that the lowering of the real (weighted) average prices of transportation was on the order of 10 to 1." For example, prior to the Industrial Revolution the average cost of ground transportation of grains per ton–kilometer was equal to the average cost of buying 4 or 5 kg of grain, but this cost fell to 0.1 kg per ton–kilometer in 1910 because of long-distance transportation by rail. Once we account for the decrease in the price of grain generated by technological innovations in agriculture, the decrease in transport costs is even larger: they are divided by a factor close to 50 (Bairoch 1997, chap. 4). It is, therefore, legitimate to ask whether it is still relevant to pay attention to transport costs in economic models.

Our answer involves two pieces of argument that are very different in nature. First, even though transport costs must be positive for space to matter, one should not infer from this observation that location matters less when transport costs decrease. Quite the opposite, by making them more footloose, new economic geography and urban economics show that lower transport costs make firms more sensitive to minor differences between locations. As a result, *a tiny difference across places may have a big impact on the spatial distribution of economic activity*. Such effects cannot be understood under the assumption of zero transport costs.

Second, transport (or trade or shipment) costs must be defined broadly enough to include all impediments to trade and movements. Spulber (2007) refers to them as "the four Ts": (i) Transport costs per se because goods have to reach their consumption place, whereas many services remain nontradable and various exchanges still require face-to-face contacts; (ii) Time costs as, despite Internet and video conferences, there are still communication impediments across dispersed distribution and manufacturing facilities that slow down reactions to changes in market conditions, whereas the time needed to ship certain types of goods has a high value; (iii) Transaction costs that result from doing business at a distance because of differences in customs, business practices, and political and legal climates; and (iv) Tariff and non-tariff costs such as different anti-pollution standards, anti-dumping practices, and the massive regulations that still restrict trade and foreign investments.

Furthermore, distribution costs, because of wholesalers and retailers, may be added to transport costs. Anderson and van Wincoop (2004) estimate that, for developed countries, average trade costs represent 170 percent of the produce price of manufactured goods. Trade costs consist of 55 percent internal costs and 74 percent international costs ($2.7 = 1.55 \times 1.74$). The international costs are in turn broken down into 21 percent transport costs and 44 percent costs connected with border effects ($1.74 = 1.21 \times 1.44$). Such results clash with Glaeser and Kohlhase (2004), who observe that the average cost of moving a ton a mile in 1890 was 18.5 cents, as opposed to 2.3 cents today (in 2001 dollars). It should be stressed, however, that Glaeser and Kohlhase focus on the sole transport sector within the United States, whereas Anderson and van Wincoop adopt a much broader perspective. Furthermore, the variance in trade costs across goods is large. Thus, although shipping certain goods is almost costless, trading some others remains very expensive.

Evidently, the relative importance of the four Ts varies enormously from one sector to another, from one activity to another, and from one commodity to another. Understanding the relative evolution of these components is, therefore, needed to figure out how transport costs evolve. Regardless of the elements accounted for, the intensification of competition, which has been caused in part by the secular decrease of transport costs, has made logistics an increasingly important issue in a world where firms are in search of flexibility. Being the inherent attribute of exchanges across places, transportation costs remain central to the formation of trade flows and the location of economic activity.

At a very different spatial scale, commuting is far more costly than what is commonly believed. Twenty kilometers a day to work costs thousands of euros a year (Glaeser 2011). That said, although we acknowledge the importance of understanding the evolution of the elements that determine the level of various types of transport costs, we are content with treating these costs and the transport industry as black boxes.[3]

1.3 CITIES: PAST AND FUTURE

Urbanization is probably the most extreme form of geographical unevenness. Indeed, casual observation reveals the extreme variation in the intensity of

[3] There is a need for a stronger connection between, on the one hand, transport economics and, on the other, new economic geography and urban economics. The state of the art in transport economics is provided by de Palma et al. (2011).

human settlements and land use – a fact that has culminated in the existence of *cities* in which population densities are very high.[4]

From a historical perspective, cities emerged in several parts of the world about 7,000 years ago as the consequence of the rise in agricultural surplus. The mere existence of cities may be viewed as a universal phenomenon whose importance slowly but steadily increased during the centuries preceding the sudden urban growth that appeared during the nineteenth century in a small corner of Europe. Technological development was necessary to generate the agricultural surplus without which cities would have been inconceivable at the time, as they would be today. In addition to technological innovations, a fundamental change in social and economic structure was also necessary: the division of labor into specialized activities. In this respect, there seems to be a large agreement among economists, geographers, and historians to consider "increasing returns" as the most critical factor in the emergence of towns and cities. Historical evidence shows that the existence of cities has increased the efficiency of trade, industry, and government, raising it to a level unattainable with a scattered population. Adam Smith's example of farmers in the Scottish Highlands, who had to work at a large number of different activities to survive, provides a contrary illustration of the validity of this assertion. Once the impact of increasing returns is recognized, cities may be viewed as "economic multipliers" magnifying individual decisions.

Although the sources are dispersed, not always trustworthy, and hardly comparable, data clearly converge to show the existence of an urban revolution, which started with the Industrial Revolution. In Europe, the proportion of the population living in cities increased very slowly from 10 percent in 1300 to 12 percent in 1800 (Bairoch 1988). It was approximately 20 percent in 1850, 38 percent in 1900, 52 percent in 1950, and is now close to 75 percent, thus showing an explosive growth in the urban population. In the United States, the rate of urbanization increased from 5 percent in 1800 to more than 60 percent in 1950 and is now nearly 77 percent. In Japan, the rate of urbanization was about 15 percent in 1800, 50 percent in 1950, and is now about 78 percent. The proportion of the urban population in the world increased from 30 percent in 1950 to 45 percent in 1995. According to the United Nations Population Fund, "In 2008, the world reaches an invisible but momentous milestone: For the first time in history, more than half its human population, 3.3 billion people, will be living in urban areas." Furthermore, concentration in very big cities keeps rising. In 1950, only two cities had populations greater than 10 million: New York and Greater London. In 1995, fifteen cities belonged to this category. In 2012, 26 cities exceed 10 million in population, the top five being in Asia.

[4] Throughout this book, the word *city* refers to a whole urban region; we use city, metropolitan area, and urban area interchangeably.

The largest one, Tokyo, with 37 million, exceeds the second one, Jakarta, by 11 million.

The first towns came into existence in different parts of the world with the creation of an agricultural surplus. Once this had been achieved, the effects of the social division of labor began to be felt and became finer when the geographical concentration of some people arose. Scale economies are always found in one form or another behind the process of urbanization, whether in business activities or in the supply of public goods and services (courts, hospitals, or universities). The pre-industrial town was dominated by the big landowners living there, as well as by the activity of the merchants and artisans. For example, according to Cantillon (1755), the origin of cities is to be found in the concentration of land ownership, which allows landowners to live at a distance from their estates in places where they "enjoy agreeable society," and in the landowners' demand, which attracts craftsmen, who produce nontradable consumption goods and services, and merchants, who buy and carry luxury goods produced in distant places. However, the pre-industrial town was also, and perhaps above all, a marketplace as well as a provider of services for the surrounding countryside.

Towns multiplied and their development undertook a profound change with the Industrial Revolution. Scale economies at the plant level played a fundamental role in this renewal of the urbanization process. The industrial town is typically the location where the means of production are combined under the same roof to take advantage of the division of labor. Initially, these new towns accommodated both workers and the owners of production means. However, the owners of capital increasingly left them for the conveniences of the big cities (as did the landowners before them), which were also both financial and political centers. Beyond the city fringe spreads what Lewis Mumford called the "invisible city," which symbolizes the influence that the visible city exerts over consumption, culture, and life styles, even in the smallest villages, because of dramatic advances in transportation and telecommunications.

Today, the big city is the result of a richer causality, which includes the specialization and diversification of tasks, the widening of the range of choices of consumption goods and production factors, as well as the various communication externalities. The post-industrial city (which may have played a major role in earlier periods; think of London, Milan, and Paris) is associated with the growth in services and, more recently, with its role as a node in communication networks. It is more diversified than the industrial town and thus better able to resist sectoral shocks. Finally, it is the source of most technological and social innovations. While scale economies within firms still play a role, increasing returns in the post-industrial city are perhaps to be found elsewhere, in the form of pecuniary and technological externalities.

One of the general principles derived from our analysis is that the relationship between the decrease in transport costs and the degree of agglomeration of economic activities is not that expected by many analysts: *Agglomeration happens provided that transport costs are below some critical threshold*, although further decreases may yield dispersion of some activities owing to factor price differentials. In addition, technological progress keeps bringing new types of innovative activities that benefit most from being agglomerated and, therefore, tend to arise in developed and rich areas. Consequently, the wealth or poverty of nations and regions seems to be more and more related to the development of prosperous and competitive clusters of industries as well as to the existence of large and diversified metropolitan areas. As Lucas (1988, 39) neatly put it, "What can people be paying Manhattan or downtown Chicago rents for, if not for being near other people?" But Lucas did not explain why people want, or need, to be near other people, especially in the Age of the Internet. Economists, regional scientists, and geographers must explain why firms and households concentrate in large metropolitan areas where housing and commuting costs are higher than in smaller urban areas.

In this book, we intend to address the main causes for the formation of the various types of economic agglomerations previously described. As discussed in the next sections, this includes increasing returns to scale, externalities, and imperfectly competitive markets with general and strategic interdependencies. From this list, it should be clear that the economics of agglomeration is fraught with most of the difficulties encountered in economic theory. Moreover, as will be seen in various chapters of this book, models of agglomeration involve both *complementarity* and *substitution* effects. For a long time, economists had problems handling complementarity effects, which can hardly be taken in account in the general competitive framework. This observation leads us to survey the rather complex history of the relationship between space and economic theory. Although space has not been ignored by some prominent economists, it has seldom been mentioned in economics texts. Thus, it is interesting to determine why this important ingredient of social life has been put aside for so long.

1.4 WHY DO WE OBSERVE ECONOMIC AGGLOMERATIONS?

The main principles that govern the organization of the space-economy and the emergence of agglomerations have been understood for a long time. First, the observed spatial configuration of economic activities is the result of a complicated balance of forces that push and pull consumers and firms. These forces may be organized in two main categories: agglomeration (or centripetal) forces and dispersion (or centrifugal) forces. This view agrees with very early work in economic geography. For example, in his *Principes de géographie humaine* published posthumously in 1921, the famous French geographer Vidal de la Blache argued that all societies, rudimentary or developed, face the same dilemma: "Individuals must get together to benefit from the advantages of the division of labor, but various difficulties restrict the gathering of many individuals" (our translation). Specifically, the location of human activity can be viewed as *the interplay between the need for proximity and a crowding-out effect*: agents benefit from a better proximity to one another or to some place, but face tougher competition in the use of scarce resources such as land and a green environment. As a consequence, production and consumption are locationally interdependent: consumption patterns are determined by the spatial distribution of consumer income, which in turn depends on the location of production, and vice versa.

1.4.1 Agglomeration and Increasing Returns

The most natural way to think of increasing returns is to recognize that firms must build a facility or a plant before starting production. This gives rise to overhead and fixed costs, which are typically associated with mass production. In other words, scale economies are *internal* to firms as in standard location theory.

One would expect trade theory to be the branch of economics that has paid most attention to the spatial dimension. The reason is that changes in the conditions under which commodities are shipped, as well as changes in the mobility of factors, affect the location of industry, the geography of demand, and eventually, the pattern of trade. The opposite has been true, for neoclassical trade theory has treated each country as dimensionless and has given little attention to the impact of transport costs. Yet, some predominant contributors in the field have long argued that location and trade are closely related topics. For example, Ohlin (1933; 1968, 97) has challenged the common wisdom that considers international trade theory as separate from location theory:[5]

> international trade theory cannot be understood except in relation to and as part of the general location theory, to which the lack of mobility of goods and factors has equal relevance.

Natural resources, and more generally production factors, are not uniformly distributed across locations, and it is on this unevenness that most of trade theory has been built. The standard model of trade considers a setting formed by two countries producing two goods by means of two factors (labor and capital) under identical technologies subject to constant returns to scale and strictly diminishing marginal products. When factors are spatially immobile and goods can be costlessly moved from one country to the other, this model

[5] That trade and location theories are two sides of the same coin was explicitly recognized by the Royal Swedish Academy of Sciences in the press release announcing the 1977 Nobel Prize in Economic Sciences: "Ohlin has also demonstrated similarities and differences between interregional (intra-national) and international trade, and the connection between international trade and the location of industries."

predicts the equalization of factor prices when the ratios of factor endowments are not too different.

Similarly, regional economics has long been dominated by the dual version of the neoclassical trade model. It is assumed that a single good is produced and that (at least) one production factor can *freely* move between regions. According to this model, capital flows from regions where it is abundant to regions where it is scarce until capital rents are the same across regions, or regional wage differences push and pull workers until the equalization of wages between regions is reached. Because the production function is linear homogeneous and has strictly diminishing marginal product in each factor, the marginal productivity of the mobile factor depends only on the capital–labor ratio. This implies that the mobile factor moves from regions with low returns toward regions with high returns up to the point at which the capital–labor ratio is equalized across all regions. In other words, the perfect mobility of one factor would be sufficient to guarantee the equalization of wages and capital rents in the interregional marketplace.[6]

Thus, it would seem that either costless trade or the perfect mobility of one factor would be sufficient to guarantee the convergence of labor income across various places. Ignoring unevenness in the spatial distribution of natural resources, Mills (1972a, 4) very suggestively described this strange "world without cities" that would characterize an economy operating under constant returns and perfect competition as follows:

> Each acre of land would contain the same number of people and the same mix of productive activities. The crucial point in establishing this result is that constant returns permit each productive activity to be carried on at an arbitrary level without loss of efficiency. Furthermore, all land is equally productive and equilibrium requires that the value of the marginal product, and hence its rent, be the same everywhere. Therefore, in equilibrium, all the inputs and outputs necessary directly and indirectly to meet the demands of consumers can be located in a small area near where consumers live. In that way, each small area can be autarkic and transportation of people and goods can be avoided.

Such an economic space is the quintessence of self-sufficiency: If the distribution of endowments is uniform the economy reduces to a Robinson Crusoe–type economy where each person produces for his own consumption (backyard capitalism). More precisely, each location would become an autarky in which exchanges took place, except possibly, as in the neoclassical theory of international trade, that trade between locations might occur if the geographic distribution of natural resources was nonuniform. This suggests that the constant

[6] It has recently been argued that capital does not necessarily flow from rich to poor regions (Lucas 1990), whereas persistent regional wage differences seem to be frequent within modern economies (Magrini 2004). In this respect, the empirical evidence that per capita income would converge across countries, or even between regions of the same country, is not conclusive.

returns perfect competition paradigm is unable to cope with the emergence and growth of large economic agglomerations.

Under the extreme assumption of zero transport costs, it is clearly desirable to concentrate all production in a few facilities, the number of which depends mostly on the ratio of market size to the optimal size for production facilities at the existing state of technology. Such a configuration makes it possible to reap the full benefits of scale economies. Conversely, if returns to scale are constant or diminishing, it is to firms' advantage to disperse production to bring it closer to customers, as this reduces transport costs without lowering productive efficiency. In this case, only different endowments of immobile production factors can explain the marked differences observed within the economic space, and hence explain the need for interregional and international trade.

According to Diamond (1997), spatial differences in edible plants, with abundant nutrients, and wild animals, capable of being domesticated to help man in his agricultural and transport activities, explain why only a few regions have become independent centers of food production at the dawn of civilization. In this book, we refer to the (uneven) distribution of natural resources, climate differences, or proximity to coasts and rivers, as being the "first nature geography," by contrast to the "second nature geography," which emerges as the outcome of human beings' actions to improve upon the first one. Though relevant for explaining the emergence of civilization in a few areas, first nature geography seems weak as the main explanation for second nature geography, which involves big agglomerations of activities and large trade flows.

When supplying (or sourcing from) a market, a firm can choose between shipments from (or to) some pre-existing distant plant or sales from (or to) a new local plant. The choice is not trivial when transportation is costly and there are increasing returns to scale at the plant level. Increasing returns and transport costs are, therefore, two fundamental ingredients to take on board when we aim to explain the space-economy. Although it has been rediscovered many times (including in recent periods), the trade-off between these two forces has been at the heart of the work developed by early location theorists such as Launhardt ([1885] 1993), Lösch (1940 [1954]), and Hoover (1948).

A simple example will serve to illustrate this fundamental idea. Suppose that a policy maker has to decide where to locate a facility or facilities to provide a certain good, the consumers of which are evenly distributed between two different places. The inhabitants of either place can be supplied free of cost if a facility is built in that place, but supplying them from the other place entails a delivery cost of T dollars. The cost of building a facility is equal to F dollars in each place. If the policy-makers seek to minimize the sum of construction and delivery costs, which amounts to maximizing efficiency, they will choose to build facilities in both places if and only if $2F$ is less than $F + T$, i.e., if T is greater than F. Otherwise, it will be less expensive to build a single facility that supplies all users in both places. In other words, *high transport costs promote the scattering of sources, whereas low transport costs foster their spatial concentration.*[7]

In more concrete terms, before the Industrial Revolution, in the steel industry it was possible for a firm to have a competitive position with a very small size. The narrowness of the market, due to high transport costs, made it even easier to operate at a very low scale. Things changed after the first half of the nineteenth century. The minimal size of a firm grew because of the use of increasingly specialized equipment, which then required many more workers. This growth in the size of firms was sustained by the expansion of markets areas, which in turn was possible because of the strong decline in transport costs. In brief, the interactions between these changes led to a gradual reduction in the number of firms, whose size increased. Take, for example, the case of Belgian steel enterprises: while their average workforce in 1845 was 26 people, it reached 446 people in 1930 (Bairoch 1997).

1.4.2 Agglomeration and Externalities

Ever since Marshall (1890; 1920, chap. X), externalities have been viewed as crucial in the formation of economic agglomerations because they generate something like a lock-in effect:

> When an industry has thus chosen a location for itself, it is likely to stay there long: so great are the advantages which people following the same skilled trade get from near neighbourhood to one another. The mysteries of the trade become no mysteries; but are as it were in the air, and children learn many of them unconsciously. Good work is rightly appreciated, inventions and improvements in machinery, in processes and the general organization of the business have their merits promptly discussed: if one man starts a new idea, it is taken up by others and combined with suggestions of their own; and thus it becomes the source of further new ideas. (Marshall 1920, 224)

For Alfred Marshall, relevant externalities for the formation of clusters involve the following: (i) the availability of specialized input providers, (ii) the access to a large pool of similar and specialized workers, and (iii) the production of new ideas based on the exchange of information and face-to-face communications. All together, they form what is called scale economies *external* to firms.[8]

Despite its relative vagueness, the concept of Marshallian externalities has been much used in the economics and regional science literature devoted to the location of economic activities because it captures the idea that an agglomeration is the outcome of a "snowball effect" in which a growing number of

[7] The remarkable regularity observed in the spatial pattern of provincial capitals in the Delta of ancient Egypt seems to be the consequence of the trade-off between the central storage of grain, one of the very first examples of increasing returns, and the high cost of shipping grain over distance exceeding ten miles.

[8] An attempt to clarify the concept of Marshallian externalities is made in Section 4.2.

agents want to congregate to benefit from a larger diversity of activities and a higher specialization. Note that cumulative processes are also associated with the interplay of pecuniary externalities in models combining increasing returns and monopolistic competition.[9]

In fact, the concept of externality has been used to describe a great variety of situations. Following Scitovsky (1954), it is now customary to consider two categories: "technological externalities" (also called spillovers) and "pecuniary externalities." The former deals with the effects of nonmarket interactions that are realized through processes directly affecting the utility of an individual or the production function of a firm; they take place in the small. In contrast, pecuniary externalities are by-products of market interactions: They affect firms or consumers and workers only insofar as they are involved in exchanges mediated by the price mechanism. Pecuniary externalities are relevant when markets are imperfectly competitive, for when an agent's decision affects prices, it also affects the well-being of others.

The main distinctive feature of Marshallian externalities is that they affect only the agents belonging to the same geographical area. They do not spread over other regions or, more precisely, their impact on distant regions may be considered negligible. According to Anas et al. (1998), cities would be replete with technological externalities. The same would hold in local production systems. In fact, much of the competitiveness of individuals and firms is due to their creativity, and thus economic life is creative in the same way as are the arts and sciences. Of particular interest for creativity are "communication externalities." This idea accords with the view of Lucas (1988, 38) when he writes that "New York City's garment district, financial district, diamond district, advertising district and many more are as much intellectual centers as is Columbia or New York University." Thus, to explain geographical clusters of somewhat limited spatial dimension such as cities and highly specialized industrial districts and scientific parks, it seems reasonable to appeal to technological externalities, which, in terms of modeling, have the additional advantage of being compatible with the competitive paradigm. To some extent, this compatibility explains why this road has been explored by the pioneers of urban economics (Mills 1967; Henderson 1974) and of growth theory (Romer 1986; Lucas 1988).

The advantages of proximity for production have their counterpart on the consumption side as some actions necessarily have a collective nature. For example, the propensity to interact with others is a fundamental human attribute, as is the tendency to derive pleasure in discussing and exchanging ideas with

[9] This corresponds to a revival of ideas advocated by early development theorists who used various related concepts such as the "big push" of Rosenstein-Rodan (1943), the "growth poles" of Perroux (1955), the "circular and cumulative causation" of Myrdal (1957), and the "backward and forward linkages" of Hirschman (1958). Recent additions to this cornucopia include the "dynamic economies of scale" of Kaldor (1985), the "positive feedbacks" of Arthur (1994, chapter 1) and the "complementarities" of Matsuyama (1995).

others. Distance is an impediment to such interactions, and thus cities are the ideal institution for the development of social contacts. Along the same line, Zenou (2009) argues that the inner city is often the substratum for the development of social norms such as conformity and status seeking that govern the behavior of groups of agents. However, it is hard to identify such external effects from the econometric standpoint, whereas the causality link is often difficult to assess (Manski 2000). The role of herd behavior therefore should not be exaggerated.

To a large extent, technological externalities are too often black boxes that aim at capturing the crucial role of complex nonmarket institutions whose role and importance are strongly stressed by geographers and spatial analysts. The study of micro-spatial interactions is a very active area of research (Ioannides 2012). But in spite of these efforts, we still know very little about the forces that are involved in such processes and how they interact to lead to those aggregate external effects that are central to urban models. By contrast, because pecuniary externalities focus on economic interactions mediated by the market, their origin is clearer. In particular, their impact can be traced back to the values of fundamental microeconomic parameters such as the intensity of returns to scale, the strength of firms' market power, the level of barriers to goods, and factor mobility.

However, when we consider a large geographical area, it seems reasonable to think that direct physical contact provides a weak explanation of interregional agglomerations such as the "Manufacturing Belt" in the United States and the "Blue Banana" in Europe (an area that stretches from London to northern Italy and goes through part of western Germany and the Benelux countries). This is the realm of pecuniary externalities that arise from imperfect competition in the presence of market-mediated linkages between firms and consumers and workers. Such externalities lie at the heart of models of monopolistic competition recently developed to explain the agglomeration of economic activities. They also have one major intellectual advantage: we can trace back their very origin.

Whatever externalities are at work, prices do not fully reflect the social values of goods and services, and thus market outcomes are inefficient. The dominant feeling in the economics profession is that most cities and agglomerations are just too big. The prevalence of big and gloomy slums in Third World megalopolises gives the impression that the laissez-faire policy has led to an excessive concentration of human beings in excessively large agglomerations all over the world. Likewise, most regional policy debates in industrialized countries implicitly assume that there is too much spatial concentration. In this respect, Hotelling (1929, 57) stated more than eighty years ago what probably remains the conventional wisdom of economists regarding cities and the spatial organization of economic activities: "Our cites become uneconomically large and the business districts within them are too concentrated." We see in this book that things are not that simple. Urban externalities are not necessarily negative, and increasing returns might be a strong force in favor of geographical concentration. Hence, it seems fair to say that there is no presumption regarding the direction in which governments should move in their regional and urban policies.[10]

Before proceeding, a warning is in order. For centuries, many activities needed for people to live in large settlements were plagued with strong *agglomeration diseconomies*. Apart from a few exceptions such as Rome, Beijing, Edo, London, or Paris, diseases, rubbish, and crime prevented the growth of cities. Besides spectacular decreases in commuting costs, technological progress and medical innovations brought about by the Scientific and Industrial Revolutions have vastly reduced the costs of city size. For example, the understanding of the causes of disease with consequent sanitation has been critical to permit the supply of clean water to a large population. The same holds with the revolution in public health, which has permitted a large number of people to live in densely populated areas. Strong reductions in costs associated with city size have allowed the previously mentioned scale economies to deliver their positive effects. In other words, it is not just agglomeration economies that have been causing cities to grow and prosper; *it is also reductions in costs of city size.*

1.4.3 Thünen as a Forerunner of Krugman

At this stage, it is worth noting that the economics profession has ignored the previous availability in Thünen's work of most of the factors explaining economic agglomerations.[11] When asking whether industrial firms are better off located in major cities (especially in the capital), Thünen ([1826] 1966) started by describing the main centrifugal forces at work:

> 1. Raw materials are more expensive than in the country towns on account of the higher cost of transport. 2. Manufactured articles incur the cost of haulage to the provincial towns when they are distributed to the rural consumers. 3. All necessities, especially firewood, are much more expensive in the large town. So is rent for flats and houses, for two reasons (1) construction costs are higher because raw materials have to be brought from a distance and are consequently more expensive, and (2) sites that may be bought for a few thalers in a small town are very dear. Since food, as well as fuel and housing, cost so much more in the large town, the wage expressed in money, must be much higher than in the small one. This adds appreciably to production costs. (pp. 286–7 of the English translation)

[10] The idea that cities have an optimal size is old and goes back at least to Plato, for whom the ideal city has 5,040 citizens. This number does not include women, children, slaves, and foreigners, thus making the total number of residents significantly larger (we thank Yorgos Papageorgiou for having pointed out this reference to us).

[11] See section 2 of part II of *The Isolated State*, which contains the extracts of posthumous papers on location theory written by Thünen between 1826 and 1842 and edited by Hermann Schumacher in 1863. The reader is referred to Fujita (2012) for more details.

This list is surprisingly comprehensive. In particular, the impact of high land rents on production costs in large cities is explicitly spelled out.

Thünen then turned to the centripetal forces that, according to him, stand behind industrial agglomerations.

> 1. Only in large-scale industrial plants is it profitable to install labour-saving machinery and equipment, which economise on manual labour and make for cheaper and more efficient production. 2. The scale of an industrial plant depends on the demand for its products. . . . 4. For all these reasons, large scale plants are viable only in the capital in many branches of industry. But the division of labour (and Adam Smith has shown the immense influence this has on the size of the labour product and on economies of production) is closely connected with the scale of an industrial plant. This explains why, quite regardless of economies of machine-production, the labour product per head is far higher in large than in small factories. . . . 5. the capital attracts outstanding talents – among businessmen, artisans and labourers as well as among scholars and civil servants – and in this way is able to obtain a significant advantage over the provinces. . . . 7. Since it takes machines to produce machines, and these are themselves the product of many different factories and workshops, machinery is produced efficiently only in a place where factories and workshops are close enough together to help each other work in unison, i.e. in large towns. . . . Economic theory has failed to adequately appreciate this factor. Yet it is this which explains why factories are generally found communally, why, even when in all other respects conditions appear suitable, those set up by themselves, in isolated places, so often come to grief. Technical innovations are continually increasing the complexity of machinery; and the more complicated the machines, the more the factor of association will enter into operation. (pp. 287–90 of the English translation)

Observe that the combination of Thünen's agglomeration factors 1, 2, and 4 almost coincides with Krugman's "basic story" for the emergence of a core-periphery structure (see Chapter 8). Furthermore, if we combine these factors with the last one (7), which is about interindustry linkages and technological spillovers, we get another fundamental explanation for the emergence of manufacturing or retailing agglomerations (see Chapters 7, 8, and 9). Last, as shown by factor 5, Thünen understood that large cities are magnets that attract skilled people.

Even though Thünen's work took place at the very beginning of the Industrial Revolution in Germany, it would be hard to imagine a more explicit description of the forces shaping the industrial landscape.

1.5 ON THE RELATIONSHIPS BETWEEN SPACE AND ECONOMICS

It is rare to find an economics text in which space is studied as an important subject – if it is even mentioned. As argued by Krugman (1995), this is probably because economists lacked a model embracing both increasing returns and imperfect competition, the two basic ingredients of the formation of the space-economy, as shown by the pioneering work of Harold Hotelling,

August Lösch, Walter Isard, Tjalling Koopmans, Edgar Hoover, and Melvin Greenhut.[12] Throughout this book, we use the word "space" instead of "geography" because the latter could suggest that we subscribe to some notion of physical determinism. Quite the opposite: one of our main points is that some places fare better than others for reasons that owe little to physical geography.

1.5.1 Space and the Competitive Paradigm

More than sixty years ago, when Isard (1949) critically discussed general equilibrium analysis, he was mainly concerned with Hicks's *Value and Capital* published in 1939. Isard concluded that Hicks confined himself to "a spatial wonderland of no dimensions." He further elaborated this point on page 477 in which he recorded a conversation he had with Schumpeter, who defended the Hicksian analysis, maintaining that "transport cost is implicitly contained in production cost, and thus Hicksian analysis is sufficiently comprehensive." Isard's point was that

> production theory . . . cannot justifiably treat certain production costs explicitly and other important ones implicitly in order to avoid the obstacles to analysis which the latter present. For a balanced treatment, the particular effects of transport and spatial costs in separating producers from each other must be considered. They are too vital to be sidestepped through implicit treatment, as Hicks and others may be interpreted as having done.

We believe that Isard was right.[13]

In fact, the debate about whether or not the general equilibrium model based on perfect competition is comprehensive enough to fully reflect the working of the spatial economy has a long history. On one side, general equilibrium theorists have maintained that the problem of space can be handled by defining each commodity by its physical characteristics as well as by the place (period) in which it is made available, and hence, once we have thus indexed commodities, we can essentially forget space (and time) in economic theory. This is the way Arrow and Debreu (1954) treated space (and time) in their seminal article.

On the other side, from the standpoint of the alternative view, supported by Lösch, Isard, and several others, the problem is not that simple. To capture the essential impact of space on the distribution of economic activities, new models are needed that are fundamentally different from those found in standard general equilibrium. In particular, Koopmans claimed in his *Three Essays on the State of Economic Science* that the vital effects of space become evident

[12] See Ponsard (1983) for a historical survey of spatial economic theory.

[13] It is not clear what Isard meant here by "the particular effects of transport and spatial costs in separating producers from each other." But, because Isard complained in the same paper about Hicks's rejection of monopolistic competition model in favor of perfect competition, we guess that "the particular effects" include the monopolistic elements that spatial costs introduce into price theory.

when our concern is the location of several economic activities and, hence, when the spatial distribution of activities itself becomes a variable. In this respect, Koopmans (1957, 154) maintained that

> without recognizing indivisibilities – in human person, in residences, plants, equipment, and in transportation – urban location problems, down to those of the smallest village, cannot be understood.

Thus, increasing returns are needed at the level of specific activities, either public or private, or in the aggregate for cities to emerge. The critical role played by increasing returns in city formation explains why this problem has been neglected for so long in mainstream economics. Yet, for a long time the introduction of increasing returns to scale into the general equilibrium model has generated much interest. Without denying that these attempts are interesting, they remain largely unsatisfactory because they do not answer the question posed by Sraffa (1926): to what extent is price-taking compatible with increasing returns to scale? Suppose the firm size that minimizes average production cost is "large" relative to the size of the market. A price-taking equilibrium could not have "many" firms, each operating at inefficiently small scale, because each such firm would have a profit incentive to increase its output. Hence the market can only accommodate a "few" firms of efficient size. But with only a few firms, how does one justify the hypothesis that firms treat prices as given, because firms must realize that their size permits them to influence prices to their own advantage?

In the long debate concerning the comprehensiveness of general equilibrium theory for the spatial economy, Starrett (1978) has made the fundamental contribution. The essential question is whether the competitive price mechanism is able to explain the endogenous formation of economic agglomerations and large trade flows. To check the ability of a spatial model to do so, the best approach is to consider the case of a space free of an exogenously given comparative advantage, in which economic agents are free to choose their locations. If any concentration of economic activities is to occur, it must be due to endogenous economic forces. Starrett has shown that if space is homogeneous and transport costly, then any competitive equilibrium is such that no transportation occurs. In other words, the economy degenerates into separated single-location groups of agents with all trades taking place within, rather than between, groups. Consequently, the perfectly competitive price mechanism alone is unable to deal simultaneously with cities and trade. This fact has a fundamental implication for the modeling of the spatial economy: If the purpose is to build a theory explaining the formation of economic agglomerations, then such a theory must depart from general competitive analysis.

Once it is recognized that the competitive equilibrium paradigm cannot be the right foundation for the space-economy, what theory is conceivable? The following is Isard's second major insight to which the alternative should be a general theory of spatial competition:[14]

> because of the monopoly elements which are almost invariably present in spatial relations, a broadly defined general theory of monopolistic competition can be conceived as identical with the general theory of location and space-economy. (Isard 1949, 504–5).

1.5.2 Urban Economics

Certainly many eminent economists have turned their attention to the subject at least in passing, and Samuelson (1983) places the subject's founder, Thünen, in the pantheon of great economists. Thünen ([1826] 1966) sought to explain the pattern of agricultural activities surrounding a typical city in pre-industrial Germany, and we see that his theory has proven to be very useful in studying land use when economic activities are perfectly divisible. In fact, the principles underlying his model are so general that Thünen can be considered the founder of marginalism (Samuelson 1983). Ekelund and Hébert (1999, 246) go one step further when they claim that "With uncommon brilliance and deftness Thünen virtually invented the modern economic 'model,' which integrates logical deduction with factual experiment." In addition, the import of Thünen's analysis for the development of spatial economics is twofold in that *space is considered as both an economic good and as the substratum for economic activities*, thus making his work more relevant and general than several later contributions.

Despite his monumental contribution to economic thought, Thünen's ideas languished for more than a century without attracting widespread attention. Why was this so? According to Ekelund and Hébert (1999, 245), the reason lies in the work and influence of Ricardo:

> The economics of David Ricardo constituted a negative watershed in the history of spatial theory. By reducing situational differences to differences in the fertility of land, Ricardo effectively eliminated spatial considerations from his analytical system. Moreover, he made transportation costs indistinguishable from other costs, and in international trade theory where spatial considerations had previously dominated, he substituted comparative costs as the crucial factor. The practical effect of Ricardo's method and of his analytical innovations was to dislodge space from mainstream economic theory, so that for a long period thereafter it came to be treated, if at all, outside the mainstream deductive models of British classical economics.

Blaug (1985, chapter 14) attributes the subject's neglect to Thünen's lack of clarity. Indeed, one had to wait for Launhardt (1885, chapter 30) to have a

[14] Later on, Isard did not try to provide the spatial model of imperfect competition he called for. Instead, he turned his attention to the "spatialization" of the competitive general equilibrium model.

formal and clear treatment of his ideas in the special case of two crops. The first model with an arbitrary number of crops is due to Dunn (1954).

Aside from such an unfortunate historical whim, Thünen's theory left a crucial issue unexplored: Why is there a city in Thünen's isolated state? As previously discussed and stressed by Thünen himself, a city is more likely to arise when increasing returns are at work in the design of trading places or in the production of some goods. In other words, one must appeal to "something" that is not in what became the Thünian model to understand what is going on.

There is an interesting analogy between Thünen's land use model and Solow's (1956) growth model. Both assume constant returns to scale and perfect competition. As in Thünen's, in which the city cannot be explained within the model, the main reason for growth, that is, technological progress, cannot be explained within the model of exogenous growth. This difficulty is well summarized by Romer (1992, 85–6) in the following paragraph:

> The paradox . . . was that the competitive theory that generated the evidence was inconsistent with any explanation of how technological change could arise as the result of the self-interested actions of individual economic actors. By definition, all of national output had to be paid as returns to capital and labor; none remained as possible compensation for technological innovations. . . . The assumption of convexity and perfect competition placed the accumulation of new technologies at the center of the growth process and simultaneously denied the possibility that economic analysis could have anything to say about this process.

Stated differently, explaining city formation in Thünian models is similar to explaining technological progress in the neoclassical growth model.

Despite this limitation, the Thünian model has proven its relevance lately for the development of spatial economics. Following a suggestion made by Walter Isard, Alonso (1964) succeeded in extending Thünen's central concept of bid rent curves to an urban context in which a marketplace is replaced by an employment center (the central business district). Urban economics aims to explain the internal structure of cities, that is, (i) how land is distributed among plants, offices, dwellings, and infrastructure, and (ii) why cities have one or several central business districts. The basic concept of what came to be known in 1970s as "New Urban Economics" is the land market, which serves to allocate both economic agents and activities across space. Alonso (1964), Mills (1967), and Muth (1969) may be considered as the founders of this field. Since that time urban economics has advanced rapidly. The reason for this success is that the canonical model can take leverage on the competitive paradigm.

1.5.3 Spatial Competition Theory

Combining space and economies of scale has a profound implication for economic theory. If production involves increasing returns, the economy accommodates only a small number of firms, which are *imperfect competitors*. Kaldor (1935) argued that space gives this competition a particular form. Because consumers buy from the firm with the lowest price augmented by transport cost, each firm competes directly with only a few neighboring firms regardless of the total number of firms in the industry. The very nature of spatial competition is, therefore, oligopolistic and should be studied within a framework of interactive decision making. This was one of the central messages conveyed by Hotelling's (1929) path-breaking paper "Stability in Competition," but ignored until economists became fully aware of the power of game theory for studying competition among the few. The value and importance of this contribution was brought to light in the 1980s by showing that its use exceeds the original geographical interpretation to accommodate various dimensions that differentiates firms and consumers in a given market. To be precise, the spatial framework proposed by Hotelling may serve as a powerful metaphor for dealing with issues involving heterogeneity and diversity across agents in a host of economic, political, and social domains. In Hotelling's (1929, 54) words: "distance, as we have used it for illustration, is only a figurative term for a great congeries of qualities." Examples include the specification of products by firms competing for customers in industrial organization and the choice of a political platform by parties competing for votes in political science.

But this is not yet the end of the story. Most of the contributions to location theory by industrial organization deal with partial equilibrium models. Although a comprehensive general equilibrium model with oligopolistic competition has so far been out of reach and is likely to remain so for a long time, specific models have been developed that, taken together, have significantly improved our understanding of how the spatial economy works.

1.5.4 New Economic Geography

In its simplest form, space may be regarded as the physical substratum of economic agents and activities. This structure is typically represented by a graph where agents are located at the vertices whereas goods flow along the arcs. The prototype of such an approach is the theory of international trade, where the reference unit is the *nation*, that is, a political concept that is not necessarily of economic relevance because it disregards local disparities. Hence, for a long time the only spatial aspect adopted in trade theory is the national border. This premise, which was not questioned by Adam Smith, was probably taken on board by British economists because domestic markets in England were more integrated than those on the continent. Trade between countries is supposed to be conducted in an even more surprising manner since transport costs are not included, at least in the basic models. Specifically, transport costs are implicitly nil for tradables and infinite for untradables. Once again, English economists probably based their ideas on maritime trade, which was fundamental to the English economy (linked as it was to its colonies) and relatively inexpensive. This tradition has been continued in international economics on the grounds that transport costs have fallen considerably further since the Industrial Revolution.

It was during the 1990s that Paul Krugman and some other trade theorists became aware that "they were doing geography without knowing it" and have turned their attention to spatial issues.[15] Their interest has been partially triggered by the integration of national economies within trading blocks, such as the EU-15 or NAFTA, that leads to the fading of national borders. Since then, scholars in trade theory have contributed significantly in promoting spatial economics through the use of models involving both monopolistic competition and increasing returns. The fundamental feature that makes new economic geography different from those developed in new trade theory (Helpman and Krugman 1985) is the interregional mobility of one production factor. How capital and labor are distributed across space determines the interregional distribution of economic activities and the intensity of spatial inequality. When production factors are evenly distributed, the global pattern of production is symmetric and there is no spatial inequality. If not, some regions accommodate a larger share of activities, and thus regional disparities arise. New economic geography (NEG) is thus the first body of economics that seeks to provide a detailed description of sizable and durable spatial inequalities that emerge as the equilibrium outcome of a full-fledged general equilibrium model.

The contributions to spatial economics made by economists have been long confined to a small circle of specialists. Whereas standard contributions to economic geography were often poorly related to mainstream economic theory, Krugman's work has drawn space from the periphery to the center stage of economic theory, making new and already existing ideas more amenable to both theoretical and empirical scrutiny. Whereas NEG is closely related to trade theory, it is also very much connected to industrial organization. It is, therefore, not totally surprising that the surge of NEG took place a few years after the revival of monopolistic competition and industrial organization, from which it borrows many ideas and concepts. There are also strong links to new growth theories, where many scholars see cities as the engine of growth. Thus, it is fair to say that NEG has contributed to the development of a new and large flow of high-quality research and to the gradual emergence of a unified field.

Yet, not everything was brand new in NEG. To be precise, several pieces of high-quality work were available in regional science, urban economics, and location theory. It is fair to say, however, that earlier contributions, such as Henderson (1974), Ogawa and Fujita (1980), Papageorgiou and Thisse (1985), or Fujita (1988) have not reached the level of visibility and interest achieved by

[15] In the 1970s, another prominent trade theorist, R.G. Lipsey, vastly contributed, with B.C. Eaton, to the development of spatial economic theory (see, e.g., Eaton and Lipsey 1977, 1997).

Krugman. These works as well as those developed under the heading of NEG are covered in this book. In doing so, we hope to provide the materials for a unified theory of economic agglomeration ranging from the small to the large.

1.6 PLAN OF THE BOOK

Before describing how the book is organized, we want to stress again the following point. Although it encompasses a large share of both, this book is not about NEG or urban economics. Instead, it aims at explaining one specific and well-defined issue, namely the emergence of economic agglomerations at various spatial scales. To this end, we borrow at will concepts and results from different fields of modern economic theory. For example, we use material stemming from industrial organization and trade theory. This has led us to start each chapter with a detailed, but nontechnical, introduction, which should help the reader understand the main results proven in the subsequent sections without having to go through to all the technicalities of microeconomic models.

That said, the organization of this book reflects what we have said in the foregoing sections. Although we have tried to make each chapter more or less self-contained, the reader may benefit from "agglomeration economies" in his or her reading. Thus the book has been organized into four parts. Part I deals with the fundamentals of spatial economics. After showing the insufficiency of the competitive paradigm for studying economic geography, we consider different issues such as the land rent formation, the formation of urban systems, the nature of competition between geographically separate firms, and the provision and financing of local public goods. Part II aims at explaining the structure of metropolitan areas and the clustering of firms selling similar products. In Part III, we shift to a different geographical scale and cope with the impact of factor mobility on the location of industry. In particular, we study the role of both technological and pecuniary externalities in the interregional distribution of firms. We also discuss the role of market size, a topic that has attracted a great deal of attention in the empirical literature. In the last part, Part IV, we offer a few syntheses of the different approaches taken in this book to shed light on new issues. By the same token, we hope to suggest new lines of research. First, we study land use and monopolistic competition in the product market can be combined with the aim of explaining the emergence of cities in an otherwise homogeneous setting. We then proceed by investigating the relationship between agglomeration and growth, once agents have forward-looking behavior. Last, by combining transport and communication costs, we investigate the impact of globalization on the way firms conduct their business across separated places.

One of the main distinctive features of our book is its strong connection to other recent developments in modern economics. First of all, we start with firms and consumers/workers pursuing their own interest. Our approach is, therefore, rooted in microeconomics. However, even though we do not appeal explicitly to economic geography proper, we find it important to say that we share many ideas and results with Jovanovic (2009) and Storper (2013). Second, whereas NEG is closely related to the new trade theory, it is also very much connected to industrial organization. In particular, the geography and economic performance of a territory appears to be more and more dependent on the way firms organize their activities. Likewise, modern growth theories highlight the importance of cities in the process of economic development. Ever since the first edition of this book, urban economics and NEG have undertaken a new development under the concrete form of a large flow of high-quality empirical research whose origin can be traced back to the pioneering contributions made by Ed Glaeser and Vernon Henderson.[16] Despite this methodological shift, the focus of this book remains on economic theory. We do not offer any apology for this because there is nothing more practical than a good theory. Yet, in many places we stress links between the results presented here and recent empirical studies. Furthermore, the topics covered in the book reflect our idiosyncrasies. Here, we owe our apologies to those who have contributed to the field but who might dislike our choice of menu. Finally, in a series of notes on the literature, we strive to track the evolution of the main ideas developed in spatial economics.

[16] Combes et al. (2012) epitomizes what has been accomplished during the last 10 years.

PART I

FUNDAMENTALS OF SPATIAL ECONOMICS

2

The Breakdown of the Price Mechanism in a Spatial Economy

2.1 INTRODUCTION

As a start, it is natural to ask the following question: To what extent is the competitive paradigm useful in understanding the main features of the economic landscape described in Chapter 1? The general competitive equilibrium model is indeed the benchmark used by economists when they want to study the market properties of an economic issue. Before proceeding, we should remind the reader that the essence of this model is that all trades are impersonal: When making their production or consumption decisions, economic agents need to know the price system only, which they take as given. At a competitive equilibrium, prices provide firms and consumers with all the information they need to know to maximize their profit and their utility.

The most elegant and general model of a competitive economy is undoubtedly that developed by Kenneth Arrow, Gérard Debreu, and Lionel McKenzie. According to this model, the economy is formed by agents (firms and households) and by commodities (goods and services). A firm is characterized by a set of production plans, each production plan describing a possible input–output relation. A household is identified by a relation of preference, by a bundle of initial resources, and by shares in firms' profits. When both consumers' preferences and firms' technologies are convex, a price system (one price per commodity), a production plan for each firm, and a consumption bundle for each household exist that satisfy the following conditions at the prevailing prices:

i. Supply equals demand for each commodity;
ii. Each firm maximizes its profit subject to its production set; and
iii. Each household maximizes her utility under her budget constraint defined by the value of her initial endowment and her shares in firms' profits. In other words, all markets clear while each agent chooses her most preferred action at the equilibrium prices.

In this model, a commodity is defined not only by its physical characteristics but also by the place it is made available.[1] By implication, the same good traded at different places is treated as different economic commodities, thus implying that the same good available in different places is supplied at different prices. Furthermore, within this framework, choosing a location is tantamount to choosing commodities. This approach integrates spatial interdependence of markets into general equilibrium in the same way as other forms of interdependence. Thus, the Arrow–Debreu model seems to obviate the need for a theory specific to the spatial context.

Unfortunately, however, matters are not that simple. As seen in Section 2.3, the competitive model cannot generate economic agglomerations unless strong spatial inhomogeneities are assumed. More precisely, we follow Starrett (1978) and show that introducing a homogeneous space (in a sense that will be made precise in the following paragraphs) in the Arrow–Debreu model implies that total transport costs in the economy must be zero at any spatial competitive equilibrium, and thus regional specialization, cities, and trade cannot be equilibrium outcomes. In other words, the competitive model per se cannot be used as the foundation for the study of a spatial economy. This is because we are interested in identifying purely economic mechanisms leading agents to agglomerate even in a featureless space.

Indeed, as argued by Lösch (1940, 105),

> We shall consider market areas that are not the result of any kind of natural or political inequalities but arise through the interplay of purely economic forces, some working toward concentration, and others toward dispersion. In the first group are the advantages of specialization and of large-scale production; in the second, those of shipping costs and of diversified production.

as well as by Hoover (1948, 3),

> Even in the absence of any initial differentiation at all, i.e., if natural resources were distributed uniformly over the globe, patterns of specialization and concentration of activities would inevitably appear in response to economic, social, and political principles.

Starrett's result has far-reaching implications for our purpose. Indeed, once it is recognized that economic agents use land, they cannot all be together at the same location. As a consequence, the only equilibrium compatible with the competitive setting and a homogeneous space involves a collection of local autarkies. It is thus impossible to consider a competitive economy embedded in a homogeneous space and to derive relevant and plausible results about the distribution of economic activities.

[1] This idea was put forward by Hotelling (1929) in a partial equilibrium context and by Allais (1943, 809) in general equilibrium.

Of course, the real world space is not homogeneous and trade may occur because the geographic distribution of resources is nonuniform, as in the neoclassical theory of international trade. Note that trade may also arise because exchange must occur at some given places, as in the Thünian model studied in Chapter 3. Although the unequal distribution of natural resources and amenities is obviously pertinent, it seems weak as the only explanation for agglomeration and trade. In particular, the spatial distribution of production factors should be endogenous instead of exogenous. Likewise, the formation of marketplaces is to be explained rather than assumed.

At this point, it is worth discussing the major assumptions made by Arrow and Debreu (1954), as well as their successors, to demonstrate the existence of prices that simultaneously equilibrate all markets. They suppose convexity of consumers' preferences and consumption sets as well as that of firms' production sets. These hypotheses are restrictive in themselves but in the context of a spatial economy become literally untenable. In particular, the convexity assumptions imply that consumers (producers) want to spread their consumption (production) activity over many locations as if they were ubiquitous. Because they are not, space therefore implies that some fundamental nonconvexities arise in the general equilibrium model.

Convexity of preferences is not really necessary for existence of a competitive equilibrium if there are a large number (a continuum) of consumers. Nevertheless, it is worth pointing out that convexity of preferences is contradicted by the evidence regarding consumers' choice of housing. As stressed by Mirrlees (1972), with convex preferences a consumer would purchase a small quantity of a large number of goods – in particular, a small quantity of housing in many different locations. This is not what consumers do.

Because each consumer resides in a small number of places (typically one), the residential choice also implies that parts of a consumer's initial endowment, especially labor force and skills, are available only at her residence. Since goods are differentiated by their location, a consumer's endowment changes with location as well and, therefore, with her consumption bundle. This leads to substitution patterns among goods that affect demand functions in complex ways.

Convex technologies are troubling in a more fundamental way.[2] Implicit in the hypothesis that production sets are convex is production that exhibits no increasing returns to scale – whatever its scale. Fragmenting a firm's operations into smaller units at different locations does not reduce the total output available from the same given inputs as transport costs decline. If the distribution of natural resources is uniform, the economy is such that each person produces

[2] More precisely, the proof of the existence of a competitive equilibrium assumes only the convexity of the production set of the economy, not the convexity of the production set of each firm, the latter being a sufficient condition for the former (Debreu 1959, chapter 6). This does not affect, however, the nature of the difficulty addressed here.

for her own consumption; we therefore have *backyard capitalism*. Although the number of firms is given, each firm prefers a small plant at each of many locations, which again differs from what we observe in the real world. Hence, increasing returns to scale are critical in explaining the geographical distribution of productive activities.

Although a competitive equilibrium does not in itself require many firms, they seem necessary to justify the behavioral hypothesis that agents are price-takers. Even if the economy is large, so that the total number of firms can be large, the geographic dispersion of consumption causes production to be dispersed and local markets to be "small." Thus, the combination of increasing returns and geographically dispersed consumption renders untenable the hypothesis that many firms compete in each market. If one returns to the suggestion of Arrow and Debreu to distinguish goods by their location, most markets are probably characterized by a small number of firms (if any) that, as a consequence, do not behave competitively.

The remainder of the chapter is organized as follows. The inadequacy of the competitive assumption for spatial economics is demonstrated by means of a simple example in Section 2.2. The robustness of the conclusions drawn from this example is then examined in Section 2.3 in which what we call the *spatial impossibility theorem* is proven: No competitive equilibrium involving trade across locations exists in a homogeneous space. Unlike the criticisms previously discussed, the point made here is internal to the theory, which makes it stronger. This leads us quite naturally to discuss in Section 2.4 the possible existence of a competitive equilibrium when (i) space is heterogeneous and (ii) spatial externalities in production are present. In Section 2.5, we survey the various modeling strategies that can be used to obviate the difficulty raised by the spatial impossibility theorem. Section 2.6 presents our conclusions.

2.2 THE ASSIGNMENT PROBLEM

We begin our discussion by considering the quadratic assignment problem introduced by Koopmans and Beckmann (1957). Assume that M firms are to be assigned to M locations. The *quadratic assignment problem* is defined by the following set of assumptions. Each firm is indivisible, and the amount of land available at each location is such that a single firm can be set up there. Hence, every firm must be assigned to a single location, and every location can accommodate only one firm. Each firm produces a fixed amount of goods and uses one unit of land as well as fixed amounts of the goods produced by the others. Suppose further that the technology used by each firm is not affected by the chosen location. Finally, shipping a good from a location to another location involves a positive cost.

To illustrate the nature of the difficulty, we consider the simplest case of two firms, denoted $i = 1, 2$, and two locations, denoted $r = A, B$. Without loss of generality, we assume that firm 1 is assigned to site A and firm 2 to site B. Firm i produces q_i units of good i and purchases q_j units of good j from firm $j \neq i$ regardless of its own location. Firm i also receives a revenue $a_i > 0$ from other sales to the rest of the world, which is independent from its locational choice. Finally, good i can be shipped from its place of production to the other locations at a unit cost $t_i > 0$.

To study the sustainability of the above assignment, we follow the suggestion of Arrow and Debreu by considering the same good at locations 1 and 2 as two different commodities, each with its own price. Let p_{ir} be the price of good i at location r and R_r be the rent to be paid by a firm for using one unit of land at location r. Firm 1's profit in location A is defined as follows:

$$\pi_{1A} = a_1 + p_{1A}q_1 - p_{2A}q_2 - R_A$$

where firm i receives a fixed revenue a_1 from its sales to the rest of the world. A similar expression holds for firm 2 at location B. If this price system sustains the foregoing configuration then, as shown by Samuelson (1952), the equilibrium prices p_{ir} must satisfy the following conditions:

$$p_{1B} = p_{1A} + t_1 > p_{1A} \tag{2.1}$$

$$p_{2A} = p_{2B} + t_2 > p_{2B}. \tag{2.2}$$

In other words, the price of good 1 (2) in location B (A) is equal to its price in location A (B) plus the corresponding transport cost $t_1(t_2)$.

We now show that it is impossible to find values for the rents R_A and R_B such that both firms 1 and 2 maximize their own profit at locations 1 and 2, respectively. Without loss of generality, assume that $R_A \geq R_B$. Then, if firms behave competitively, it is readily verified that firm 1 would earn a strictly higher profit by setting up at location B. Indeed, if firm 1 sets up at location B, its profit is

$$\pi_{1B} = a_1 + p_{1B}q_1 - p_{2B}q_2 - R_B.$$

Using (2.1) and (2.2), it is then readily verified that:

$$\begin{aligned} \pi_{1B} - \pi_{1A} &= (p_{1B} - p_{1A})q_1 - (p_{2B} - p_{2A})q_2 + R_A - R_B \\ &= t_1q_1 + t_2q_2 + R_A - R_B > 0. \end{aligned} \tag{2.3}$$

Hence, firm 1 always has an incentive to move. In other words, when locations have identical exogenous attributes, no feasible location pattern of firms can be sustained as a competitive equilibrium in the quadratic assignment problem. In deriving this surprising conclusion, it has been assumed that firms believe that "changing place" does not affect the prevailing prices of goods and land rents. The reader may find this assumption unrealistic, especially in the case of two firms. Such an assumption, however, is the essence of a competitive equilibrium.

The reader might believe that this negative result is an artifact of the two-location-two-firm setting. The answer is no: The nonexistence of an equilibrium carries over to the quadratic assignment problem with an arbitrary number of firms and locations when locations are a priori equally attractive from the viewpoint of firms. The proof is contained in the appendix. One might also think that this negative result is caused by the specifics of the quadratic assignment problem, especially the assumption that each firm consumes a fixed amount of land. In the next section, we show that such a breakdown of the competitive price mechanism does not rely on the specifics of the quadratic assignment problem because it holds for a general spatial economy.

2.3 THE SPATIAL IMPOSSIBILITY THEOREM

To gain more insights about the proof of the main result of this section, it is desirable to go one step further in the preceding example by computing firm 2's incentive to move as in (2.3), that is,

$$\pi_{2A} - \pi_{2B} = t_2 q_2 + t_1 q_1 + R_B - R_A. \tag{2.4}$$

Summing expressions (2.3) and (2.4) yields $2(t_1 q_1 + t_2 q_2)$. This means that the sum of firms' incentives to move is equal to twice the total transport costs. Because this sum must be nonpositive for a competitive equilibrium to exist, transportation cannot occur in such an equilibrium. This suggests that competitive pricing and positive transport costs are incompatible in a homogeneous spatial economy, for the incentive to change location is of the same order of magnitude as transport costs.

Our objective in this section is to show that this property, which we call the spatial impossibility theorem, holds in a general setting. To facilitate comparison, we use standard notation from general equilibrium theory. However, to make our point more transparent, we explicitly distinguish prices and goods by their location and separate land as well as transport services from the remaining goods.

2.3.1 Competitive Equilibrium in a Homogeneous Spatial Economy

Consider a spatial economy formed by two regions A and B that can both accommodate a large number of firms and households. Each region $r = A, B$ is endowed with the same positive amount of land $S > 0$. There are n goods (excluding land and transport-services) and each of them can be moved from one region to the other by using transport-services. There are M firms and N households; to ease the burden of notation, M and N denote also the sets of firms and households. The model being static, firms and households can choose at zero cost the region in which they want to conduct their activities.

When firm $f \in M$ sets up in region $r = A, B$, a production plan for this firm is given by a vector $\mathbf{y}_{fr}$ of n goods (outputs are positive and inputs are negative) and by a positive amount of land s_{fr} in region r. The firm's production set is denoted by $Y_{fr} \subset R^{n+1}$; this set may vary with the region in which the firm is established. Household $h \in N$ resides and works in the same region $r = A, B$ and its consumption plan is given by a vector $\mathbf{x}_{hr}$ of n goods (a positive component means that the household has a positive demand for the good whereas a negative component means that the household is a supplier of the good – such as labor) and by a positive amount of land s_{hr} in region r. The household's consumption set is given by $X_{hr} \subset R^{n+1}$. Household h has a utility function U_{hr} defined over X_{hr}, which may both change with the region in which the household is located, together with an initial endowment of goods $\boldsymbol{\omega}_h$ and a land endowment $\tilde{\mathbf{s}}_h = (\tilde{s}_{hA}, \tilde{s}_{hB})$. Because we consider location a separate attribute, we may assume that the same endowment in goods (e.g., labor) is available in any region in which the consumer resides and works; by contrast, the land endowment is immobile.

Transportation within each region is costless, but shipping goods from one region to the other requires resources. Without loss of generality, transportation between the two regions is accomplished by a profit-maximizing carrier (or broker) who purchases goods in a region at the market prices prevailing in this region and sells them in the other region at the corresponding market prices while using goods and land in each region as inputs. The carrier ships a (nonnegative) export plan $\mathbf{E}_{AB} \in R^n$ of goods from A to B and a (nonnegative) export plan $\mathbf{E}_{BA} \in R^n$ from B to A, using (nonpositive) vectors $\mathbf{y}_{tr} \in R^n$ of inputs and nonnegative amounts of land s_{tr} bought in both regions A and B. The set of feasible transportation plans for the carrier is denoted by $Z_t \subset R^{4n+2}$.

Let M_r be the set of firms and N_r the set of households located in region $r = A, B$ so that $M = M_A \cup M_B$ and $N = N_A \cup N_B$. An *allocation* is defined by the set N_r of households residing in region $r = A, B$, by the set M_r of firms located in region $r = A, B$, by N consumption plans $(\mathbf{x}_{hr}, s_{hr})$, by M production plans $(\mathbf{y}_{fr}, s_{fr})$, by two export plans $\mathbf{E}_{AB}, \mathbf{E}_{BA}$ together with the associated input vectors $\mathbf{y}_{tA}, \mathbf{y}_{tB}$ and land requirements s_{tA}, s_{tB}. Therefore, an allocation describes both the location and the consumption or production activities of each household or firm as well as the transportation activity conducted by the carrier.

For an allocation to be feasible, the following material balance conditions must be met:

i. for goods in region A

$$\sum_{h \in N_A} \mathbf{x}_{hA} + \mathbf{E}_{AB} - \mathbf{y}_{tA} = \sum_{h \in N_A} \boldsymbol{\omega}_h + \sum_{f \in M_A} \mathbf{y}_{fA} + \mathbf{E}_{BA} \tag{2.5}$$

ii. for goods in region B

$$\sum_{h\in N_B} \mathbf{x}_{hB} + \mathbf{E}_{BA} - \mathbf{y}_{tB} = \sum_{h\in N_B} \boldsymbol{\omega}_h + \sum_{f\in M_B} \mathbf{y}_{fB} + \mathbf{E}_{AB} \tag{2.6}$$

iii. for land in region $r = A, B$

$$\sum_{h\in N_r} s_{hr} + \sum_{f\in M_r} s_{fr} + s_{tr} \leq \sum_{h\in N_r} \widetilde{s}_{hr} \equiv S \tag{2.7}$$

where $(\mathbf{x}_{hr}, s_{hr}) \in X_{hr}$, $(\mathbf{y}_{fr}, s_{fr}) \in Y_{fr}$ and $(\mathbf{E}_{AB}, \mathbf{E}_{BA}, \mathbf{y}_{tA}, \mathbf{y}_{tB}, s_{tA}, s_{tB}) \in Z_t$.[3]

Finally, a *competitive equilibrium* for the economy is given by a price system – that is, two vectors $\mathbf{p}_A$ and $\mathbf{p}_B$ for the goods and a land rent pattern (R_A, R_B) – and a feasible allocation as previously discussed, such that:

i. all markets clear in each region r, that is, (2.5)–(2.7) hold;
ii. each firm $f \in M_r$ maximizes its profit at the chosen location and production plan:

$$\pi_{fr} \equiv \mathbf{p}_r \cdot \mathbf{y}_{fr} - R_r s_{fr} \geq \mathbf{p}_s \cdot \hat{\mathbf{y}}_{fs} - R_s \hat{s}_{fs}$$

for all $(\hat{\mathbf{y}}_{fs}, \hat{s}_{fs}) \in Y_{fs}$ and $s = A, B$;
iii. each household $h \in N_r$ maximizes its utility at the chosen location and consumption plan subject to the household's budget constraint:

$$U_{hr}(\mathbf{x}_{hr}, s_{hr}) \geq U_{hs}(\hat{\mathbf{x}}_{hs}, \hat{s}_{hs})$$

for all $(\hat{\mathbf{x}}_{hs}, \hat{s}_{hs}) \in X_{hs}$ and $s = A, B$ such that

$$\mathbf{p}_s \cdot \hat{\mathbf{x}}_{hs} + R_s \hat{s}_{hs} \leq \mathbf{p}_s \cdot \boldsymbol{\omega}_h + \sum_{r\in\{A,B\}} R_r s_{hr}$$
$$+ \sum_{r\in\{A,B\}} \sum_{f\in M_r} \theta_{hf} \pi_{fr} + \theta_{ht} \pi_t$$

where θ_{hf} is the share of household h in firm f's profits and θ_{ht} the household's share in the carrier's profit π^t; and
iv. the carrier maximizes its profit defined by:

$$\pi_t = (\mathbf{p}_B - \mathbf{p}_A) \cdot \mathbf{E}_{AB} + (\mathbf{p}_A - \mathbf{p}_B) \cdot \mathbf{E}_{BA} + \mathbf{p}_A \cdot \mathbf{y}_{tA}$$
$$+ \mathbf{p}_B \cdot \mathbf{y}_{tB} - R_A s_{tA} - R_B s_{tB} \tag{2.8}$$

subject to its transportation plan being in $Z_t \subset R^{4n+2}$.

Because they are not perfectly divisible, agents are not ubiquitous and, therefore, must choose an "address." Space is then said to be *homogeneous* when (i) the utility function U_h and the consumption set X_h are the same

[3] Replacing equalities by inequalities in (2.5) and (2.6) does not affect the result, whereas the inequality in (2.7) turns out to be essential.

regardless of the region where household h resides, and (ii) the production set Y_f is independent of the region elected by firm f. In other words, consumers and producers are of the type "putty," meaning that they are a priori indifferent across places. We want to stress that our disregard of first nature does not reflect any prejudice on our part. As mentioned in the introduction, this assumption is made because our wish is to uncover second nature mechanisms. We provide a more detailed discussion of this assumption in Section 2.2.4.

The proof involves three steps.

Step 1. The profit of firm f located in region A is given by the following expression:

$$\pi_{fA} = \mathbf{p}_A \cdot \mathbf{y}_{fA} - R_A s_{fA}.$$

Space being homogeneous, the production plan $(\mathbf{y}_{fA}, s_{fA})$ is also possible in region B. If firm f were to locate in region B while keeping the same production plan, its profit would become:

$$\pi_{fB} = \mathbf{p}_B \cdot \mathbf{y}_{fA} - R_B s_{fA}.$$

Hence, for firm f the incentive to move from A to B is defined by the difference in profit earned in each of the two regions:[4]

$$I_f(A, B) = \pi_{fB} - \pi_{fA} = (\mathbf{p}_B - \mathbf{p}_A) \cdot \mathbf{y}_{fA} - (R_B - R_A) s_{fA}. \tag{2.9}$$

Evidently, an expression similar to (2.9) holds for every firm set up in region B.

Step 2. Consider now a household h residing in region A. The household's residual income (neglecting its share in firms' profit and income from land that are independent of the place of residence) is defined by the expression:

$$B_{hA} = \mathbf{p}_A \cdot (\boldsymbol{\omega}_h - \mathbf{x}_{hA}) - R_A s_{hA}.$$

If this consumer were to locate in region B while keeping the same consumption plan, she would derive the same utility from $(\mathbf{x}_{hA}, s_{hA})$ and thus only the consumer's residual income in region B would matter:

$$B_{hB} = \mathbf{p}_B \cdot (\boldsymbol{\omega}_h - \mathbf{x}_{hA}) - R_B s_{hA}.$$

Hence, if there is no satiation, the consumer's incentive to move from A to B is given by the difference in her residual income in each of the two regions:

$$I_h(A, B) = B_{hB} - B_{hA} = (\mathbf{p}_B - \mathbf{p}_A) \cdot (\boldsymbol{\omega}_h - \mathbf{x}_{hA}) - (R_B - R_A) s_{hA}. \tag{2.10}$$

Again, an expression similar to (2.10) holds for a household residing in B.

[4] This expression underestimates the profit that firm f could make in region B by adjusting its production plan. The same holds for households. However, the argument used here is sufficient for the spatial impossibility theorem.

Step 3. Summing (2.9) and (2.10) for all firms and households across the two regions, we obtain:

$$
\begin{aligned}
I = {} & (\mathbf{p}_B - \mathbf{p}_A) \cdot \left(\sum_{f \in M_A} \mathbf{y}_{fA} + \sum_{h \in N_A} (\boldsymbol{\omega}_h - \mathbf{x}_{hA}) \right) \\
& + (\mathbf{p}_A - \mathbf{p}_B) \cdot \left(\sum_{f \in M_B} \mathbf{y}_{fB} + \sum_{h \in N_B} (\boldsymbol{\omega}_h - \mathbf{x}_{hB}) \right) \\
& - (R_B - R_A) \left(\sum_{f \in M_A} s_{fA} + \sum_{h \in N_A} s_{hA} \right) \\
& - (R_A - R_B) \left(\sum_{f \in M_B} s_{fB} + \sum_{h \in N_B} s_{hB} \right).
\end{aligned}
$$

Using the material balance conditions (2.5)–(2.7), we can rewrite this expression as follows:

$$
\begin{aligned}
I = {} & (\mathbf{p}_B - \mathbf{p}_A) \cdot (\mathbf{E}_{AB} - \mathbf{E}_{BA} - \mathbf{y}_{tA}) + (\mathbf{p}_A - \mathbf{p}_B) \cdot (\mathbf{E}_{BA} - \mathbf{E}_{AB} - \mathbf{y}_{tB}) \\
& + (R_B - R_A)(s_{tA} + \phi_A - S) + (R_A - R_B)(s_{tB} + \phi_B - S)
\end{aligned}
$$

where ϕ_r is the amount of land unused in region $r = A, B$. Adding $(\mathbf{p}_A + \mathbf{p}_B) \cdot (\mathbf{y}_{tA} + \mathbf{y}_{tB}) - 2(R_A s_{tA} + R_B s_{tB})$ to the first two terms, substracting the same expression from the last two terms, and regrouping them in the resulting expression yields

$$
\begin{aligned}
I = 2 & \left[\pi_t + \frac{\mathbf{p}_A + \mathbf{p}_B}{2} \cdot (-\mathbf{y}_{tA} - \mathbf{y}_{tB}) \right. \\
& \left. + \frac{R_A + R_B}{2} (s_{tA} + s_{tB}) \right] + (R_A + R_B)(\phi_A + \phi_B) \qquad (2.11)
\end{aligned}
$$

in which we have used (2.8) as well as $R_A \phi_A = R_B \phi_B = 0$ because the land rent is zero when all the land available in a region is not used.

In words, (2.11) means that the aggregate incentives for firms and households to move from one region to the other is equal to twice the carrier's profit $(2\pi_t)$ plus two terms that can be interpreted as twice the carrier's costs evaluated at the average prices $(\mathbf{p}_A + \mathbf{p}_B)/2$ and rent $(R_A + R_B)/2$ (they are called pseudo-transport costs) plus twice the value of vacant land evaluated at the average land rent $(R_A + R_B)/2$. Because the carrier maximizes its profit, π_t cannot be negative. In addition, unless the equilibrium involves no transportation, the pseudo-transport costs are strictly positive because shipping goods requires scarce resources: some components of the vectors y_{tr} must be negative, whereas no component is positive by assumption; similarly the quantities of land used must be nonnegative, whereas the land rents are nonnegative. Evidently, the last term in (2.11), $(R_A + R_B)(\phi_A + \phi_B)$, cannot be negative for land rents are nonnegative. Consequently, the global incentives to move are always strictly positive for any allocation involving costly trade between the two regions.

In a competitive equilibrium, no agent has a positive incentive to move. Therefore, we may conclude with the following theorem:

The Spatial Impossibility Theorem. *Assume a two-region economy with a finite number of consumers and firms. If space is homogeneous, transport is costly, and preferences are locally nonsatiated, there is no competitive equilibrium involving transportation.*

What does this theorem mean? If economic activities are perfectly divisible, a competitive equilibrium exists and is such that each location operates as an autarky. For example, when firms and households are identical, regions have the same relative prices and the same production structure (backyard capitalism). This is hardly a surprising outcome because, by assumption, there is no reason for economic agents to distinguish among locations and each activity can operate at an arbitrarily small level. Firms and households thus succeed in reducing transport costs at their absolute minimum, namely zero.

However, as observed by Starrett (1978, 27), when economic activities are *not* perfectly divisible (see Chapter 1) the transport of goods or people between some places becomes unavoidable:

> as long as there are some indivisibilities in the system (so that individual operations must take up space) then a sufficiently complicated set of interrelated activities will generate transport costs.

In this case, the spatial impossibility theorem tells us that no competitive equilibrium exists. This confirms what we have seen in the quadratic assignment problem, even though the individual land consumption is now endogenous.

This is clearly a surprising result that requires more explanation. When both regions are not in autarky, one should keep in mind that the price system must perform two different jobs simultaneously: (i) to support trade between regions (while clearing the markets in each region), and (ii) to prevent firms and households from relocating. The spatial impossibility theorem says that, in the case of a homogeneous space, it is impossible to hit two birds with one stone: the price gradients supporting trade bear wrong signals from the viewpoint of locational stability. Indeed, if a set of goods is exported from A to B, then the associated positive price gradients induce producers located in region A (who seek a higher revenue) to relocate in region B, whereas region B's buyers (who seek lower prices) want to relocate in A. Likewise, the export of another set of goods from B to A encourages such "cross-relocation." The land rent differential between the two regions can discourage the relocation in one direction only. Hence, as long as trade occurs at positive costs, some agents always want to relocate.[5]

To ascertain the fundamental cause for this nonexistence, it is helpful to illustrate the difficulty encountered by using a standard diagram approach. Depicting the whole trade pattern between two regions would require a diagram with six dimensions (two tradable goods and land at each location), which is a task beyond our capability. We thus focus on a suballocation formed by the feasible trade patterns of good i between A and B only and keep the other elements fixed. Because the availability of the same physical good at two distinct locations gives rise to two different commodities, this is equivalent to studying a standard transformation between two different economic goods.

Suppose that at most one unit of good i is produced by one firm at either location by using a fixed bundle of inputs. For simplicity, the cost of these inputs is assumed to be the same in both locations. The good is shipped according to an iceberg technology (Samuelson 1954a): when x_i units of the good are moved between A and B, only a fraction x_i/τ arrives at destination, where $\tau > 1$, whereas the rest melts away en route. In this context, if the firm is located in A, then the output is represented by point E on the vertical axis in Figure 2.1; if the entire output is shipped to B, then the fraction $1/\tau$ arrives at B, which is denoted by point F on the horizontal axis. Hence, when the firm is at A, the set of feasible allocations of the output between the two locations is given by the triangle OEF. Likewise, if the firm locates at B, the set of feasible allocations between the two places is given by the triangle $OE'F'$. Therefore, when the firm is not located, the set of feasible allocations is given by the union of the two triangles.

Let the firm be set up at A and assume that the demand conditions are such that good i is consumed in both locations so that trade occurs. To support any point belonging to the frontier EF, the price vector (p_{iA}, p_{iB}) must be such that $p_{iA}/p_{iB} = 1/\tau$, as shown in Figure 2.1. However, under these prices, it is clear that the firm can obtain a strictly higher profit by locating in B and choosing the production plan E' in Figure 2.1. This implies that there is no competitive price system that can support both trade and a profit-maximizing location for the firm.

This difficulty arises from the nonconvexity of the set of feasible allocations. If transportation were costless, this set would be given by the triangle OEE' in Figure 2.1, which is convex. In this case, the firm would face no incentive to relocate. Similarly, if the firm's production activity were perfectly divisible, the set of feasible allocations would again be equal to the triangle OEE', and no difficulty would arise.

[5] In the same spirit, Jones and Romer (2010, 228) observe that "a single price cannot simultaneously allocate goods to their most efficient uses *and* provide the appropriate incentives for innovation." Though unnoticed, the analogy between the two problems is striking.

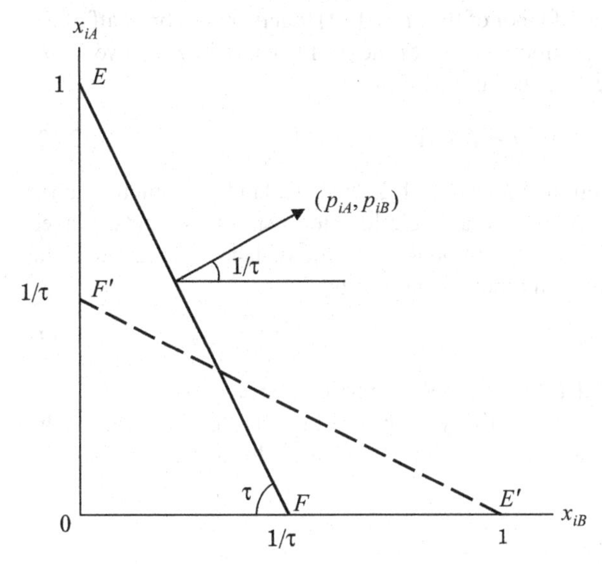

Figure 2.1. The set of feasible trade patterns in a homogeneous space.

Therefore, *the fundamental reason for the spatial impossibility theorem is the nonconvexity of the set of feasible allocations caused by the existence of transport costs and the fact that agents have an address in space.* In other words, we may safely conclude that ignoring transport costs in economic theory is far from being an innocuous assumption despite "the sanguine hope that if included they would not materially affect the results" (Deardorff 1984, 470).

To investigate the implications and meaning of the spatial impossibility theorem further, we find it illustrative to study in detail an example involving heterogeneous groups of agents.

Example. Consider an economy formed by two groups of agents such that the members of each group have strong internal linkages, whereas each group produces a distinct set of final goods indispensable to both groups. When the transport costs of the final goods are not too high, it is then natural to expect each group of agents to agglomerate into a separate region and to trade their net outputs across regions. We show in this example that if space is homogeneous (in the sense defined in Section 2.3.1), then there is no competitive price system that can support such a "natural" spatial configuration. We also show that locating both groups within one region (on the assumption that this is physically possible) is not an equilibrium either when the marginal utility of land is positive for at least one agent.

The economy has two locations A and B, two firms 1 and 2, and two workers a and b. The two locations have the same amount of land S. Worker $h = a$ (b)

is endowed with one unit of labor of type $i = 1$ (2) together with one half of the land available at each location and half of the profits earned by the two firms. Both workers share the same utility function,

$$U = x_1^{\beta/2} x_2^{\beta/2} s^{1-\beta} \qquad 0 < \beta < 1 \tag{2.12}$$

where x_i is the consumption of good $i = 1, 2$ and s the land consumption. Firm $f = 1, 2$ produces good $i = f$ at a single location using two inputs: a fixed amount $\bar{s}$ of land and a variable amount l_i of type of labor i acquired at the same location. Its production function is given by

$$Q_i = l_i^{\alpha} \qquad 0 < \alpha < 1. \tag{2.13}$$

Each good is transported according to the same iceberg technology.

Let p_{ir}, w_{ir}, and R_r be respectively the price of good i, the wage rate of the type of labor i, and the land rent at location r. If firm i locates at r, its profit is as follows:

$$\pi_{ir} = p_{ir} Q_i - w_{ir} l_i - R_r \bar{s}.$$

If this firm behaves competitively, maximizing π_{ir} yields

$$\alpha p_{ir} l_i^{\alpha-1} = w_{ir}. \tag{2.14}$$

Let Y_r be the total income of workers residing at r. Then, using (2.12), we obtain the demands as follows:

$$x_{ir} = \frac{\beta Y_r}{2} \frac{1}{p_{ir}} \tag{2.15}$$

$$s_r = (1 - \beta) Y_r \frac{1}{R_r}. \tag{2.16}$$

The land constraint $S = s_r + \bar{s}$ at r together with (2.16) yields

$$R_r = \frac{(1 - \beta)\, Y_r}{S - \bar{s}}. \tag{2.17}$$

Because firm f uses only the type of labor $i = f$, it is reasonable to expect firm f to locate with the worker of type i in equilibrium. Hence, because the two locations are identical, there are only two possible candidates as equilibrium configurations:

i. Dispersion: firm 1 and worker a locate together in A, whereas firm 2 and worker b are in B;
ii. Agglomeration: both firms and both workers locate together in, say, A.

We now consider each configuration in turn and examine whether it can be supported by a competitive price system. First, let us address the dispersed configuration. To begin, we fix locations of all agents as they are in this configuration and show the existence and uniqueness of a competitive equilibrium. Because the whole setting is symmetric, in equilibrium it must be that

$$w_{1A} = w_{2B} = 1 \tag{2.18}$$

where labor is chosen as the numéraire. Because the whole amount of labor is used in equilibrium, we may set $l_i = 1$ in (2.14) so that, using (2.18), we have

$$p_{1A} = p_{2B} = 1/\alpha \tag{2.19}$$

and, hence, from the iceberg transport technology with parameter $\tau > 1$

$$p_{1B} = p_{2A} = \tau/\alpha. \tag{2.20}$$

Setting $l_i = 1$ in (2.13), we also obtain

$$Q_A = Q_B = 1. \tag{2.21}$$

The total demand for good 1, say, is

$$D_1 = x_{1A} + \tau x_{1B}$$

where the last term represents the quantity of good 1 to be shipped from A for the quantity x_{1B} to be available for consumption in B. Substituting (2.15) into this equation and using (2.19) and (2.21), we get

$$D_1 = D_2 = \alpha\beta Y$$

where $Y = 1/\alpha\beta$ is the income common to each location. Then, by equating supply and demand ($D_i = Q_i$) and using the preceding equilibrium conditions, we obtain

$$\begin{aligned} R_A = R_B &= \frac{1}{\alpha\beta}\frac{1-\beta}{S-\overline{s}} \\ \pi_{1A} = \pi_{2B} &= \frac{\beta S - \overline{s}}{\alpha\beta(S-\overline{s})} - 1 \\ x_{1A} = x_{2B} &= \frac{1}{2} \\ x_{1B} = x_{2A} &= \frac{1}{2\tau}. \end{aligned} \tag{2.22}$$

Each firm's equilibrium profits are nonnegative ($\pi_{1A} = \pi_{2B} \geq 0$) if and only if

$$\alpha \leq \frac{S - \overline{s}/\beta}{S - \overline{s}}. \tag{2.23}$$

Therefore, if this condition holds, there exists a unique market equilibrium under the locations corresponding to dispersion. Condition (2.23) is satisfied when firms' land requirement is sufficiently small compared to S.

Let us evaluate the incentive to move of each agent in A. In doing so, we first note that w_{1B} (wage rate for type 1 at B) is not defined. In fact, we show next that, regardless of its value, at least one agent in region A has an incentive to move. To show this, let us set the value of w_{1B} at an arbitrarily level. Then, the incentive for firm 1 to move from A to B (defined under the same production plan) is such that

$$\begin{aligned} I_1(A, B) &= \pi_{1B} - \pi_{1A} \\ &= (p_{1B} - p_{1A})Q_1 - (w_{1B} - w_{1A}) \end{aligned}$$

because $R_A = R_B$. Similarly, the incentive for worker a to move from A to B (while keeping the same consumption plan) is defined as

$$\begin{aligned} I_a(A, B) &= B_{1B} - B_{1A} \\ &= (w_{1B} - p_{1B}x_{1A} - p_{2B}x_{2A} - R_B s_A) \\ &\quad - (w_{1A} - p_{2A}x_{1A} - p_{2A}x_{2A} - R_A s_A) \\ &= (w_{1B} - w_{1A}) - (p_{1B} - p_{1A})x_{1A} - (p_{2B} - p_{2A})x_{2A}. \end{aligned}$$

Summing these two expressions, we obtain

$$\begin{aligned} I(A, B) &= (p_{1B} - p_{1A})(Q_1 - x_{1A}) - (p_{2B} - p_{2A})x_{2A} \\ &= (p_{1B} - p_{1A})\tau x_{1B} - (p_{2B} - p_{2A})x_{2A} \\ &= p_{1A}(\tau - 1)\tau x_{1B} + p_{2B}(\tau - 1)x_{2A} > 0 \end{aligned}$$

in which we have used (2.19) and (2.20). Therefore, it must be that firm 1 or worker a has an incentive to move from A to B because $\tau > 1$, thus implying that dispersion is not a competitive equilibrium once agents can freely choose their location.

Consider now the agglomeration in which both firms and workers locate together in A. Using the equilibrium conditions (2.14)–(2.17), one can readily verify that the corresponding equilibrium prices are as follows:

$$\begin{aligned} & w_{1A} = w_{2A} = 1 \\ & p_{1A} = p_{2A} = 1/\alpha \\ & Q_1 = x_{1A} = Q_2 = x_{2A} = 1 \\ & R_A = \frac{4(1-\beta)}{\alpha\beta(S - 2\overline{s})} \qquad \text{and} \qquad R_B = 0 \\ & \pi_{1A} = \pi_{2A} = \frac{\beta(S + 2\overline{s}) - 4\overline{s}}{\alpha\beta(S - 2\overline{s})} - 1 \geq 0 \end{aligned} \tag{2.24}$$

when

$$\alpha \leq \frac{\beta(S + 2\overline{s}) - 4\overline{s}}{\beta(S - 2\overline{s})}.$$

Because all agents are located in A, they do not trade with B, and thus no good is consumed in transportation. Hence, given any wage rates and prices at B, summing the agents' incentives to move from A to B (while keeping the same production or consumption plan), all terms related to transactions between these locations cancel out, and thus the aggregate incentive for all agents to move from A to B is equal to the land cost saving:

$$\begin{aligned} I(A, B) &= (R_A - R_B)S \\ &= R_A S > 0. \end{aligned}$$

Accordingly, agglomeration is not a spatial equilibrium, either.

Before proceeding, some remarks are in order. First, using the same approach as Starrett (1978), we can extend the theorem to any finite number of regions at the expense of heavy notation. Second, we have assumed for notational simplicity that each firm locates in a single region. The argument could be generalized to permit firms to run two distinct plants, one plant per region. The aggregate incentives to move, I, would now be defined in relation to the activities performed by plants and households in each region because each plant amounts to a separate firm. Third, we have considered a closed economy. The model and the theorem can readily be extended to allow for trade with the rest of the world provided that each region has the same access to the world markets in order to satisfy the assumption of a homogeneous space. Last, the size of the economy is immaterial for the spatial impossibility theorem to hold, for assuming a "large economy," in which competitive equilibria often emerge as the outcome generated by several institutional mechanisms, does not affect the result because the value of total transport costs within the economy rises when agents are replicated. In other words, working with a large economy does not alleviate the difficulty.

2.3.2 The Land Rent in a Homogeneous Space

The spatial impossibility theorem per se does not preclude the agglomeration of all agents into a single region. However, we see that this is a very unlikely outcome. Indeed, if a competitive equilibrium exists, then the spatial impossibility theorem implies that there is no costly trade between regions. Hence, in the right-hand side of (2.11), the first three terms must be zero, so that

$$I = (R_A + R_B)(\phi_A + \phi_B)$$

thus implying that, if either $\phi_A > 0$ or $\phi_B > 0$, it must be that $R_A = R_B = 0$.

Corollary 2.1 *Assume that a competitive equilibrium exists in a spatial economy with a homogeneous space. If there is vacant land in one region, then the land rent must be zero in both regions.*

When all agents locate in region A, then region B is empty. Using Corollary 2.1, the equilibrium land rent must also be zero in region A. This is so only when no agent in the economy has a positive marginal utility/productivity for land – a situation that is very unlikely in practice.

In fact, Corollary 2.1 is a special case of a more general result that has farfetched implications. Summing (2.9) and (2.10) across firms and households in region A, and using (2.5)–(2.7), we obtain:

$$\begin{aligned} I(A, B) &= (\mathbf{p}_B - \mathbf{p}_A) \cdot (\mathbf{E}_{AB} - \mathbf{E}_{BA} - \mathbf{y}_{tA}) + (R_B - R_A)(s_{tA} + \phi_A - S) \\ &= (R_B - R_A)(\phi_A - S). \end{aligned}$$

Likewise, we get:

$$\begin{aligned} I(B, A) &= (\mathbf{p}_A - \mathbf{p}_B) \cdot (\mathbf{E}_{BA} - \mathbf{E}_{AB} - \mathbf{y}_{tB}) + (R_A - R_B)(s_{tB} + \phi_B - S) \\ &= (R_A - R_B)(\phi_B - S). \end{aligned}$$

At a competitive equilibrium, neither $I(A, B)$ nor $I(B, A)$ can be positive. As a consequence, if there is no vacant land in the economy ($\phi_A = \phi_B = 0$), it follows that

$$I(A, B) = (R_A - R_B)S \leq 0 \quad \text{and} \quad I(B, A) = (R_B - R_A)S \leq 0$$

thus implying that $R_A = R_B$. Alternatively, if there is some vacant land in, say, B, ($\phi_B > 0$), then $R_B = 0$ so that $I(A, B) = R_A(S - \phi_A) \leq 0$. This in turn implies that $R_A = 0$ and, hence, $R_A = R_B$.

Corollary 2.2 *If a competitive equilibrium exists in a spatial economy with a homogeneous space, then the land rent must be the same in all regions.*

This corollary has the following fundamental implication for us: *In a homogeneous space, the competitive price mechanism is unable to explain why the land rent is higher in an economic agglomeration* (such as a city, a central business district, or an industrial cluster) than in the surrounding area. Agents being a priori indifferent across places while the equilibrium (if any) involves no transportation, differences in accessibility among agents are immaterial, which explains why the land rent is equal across space. Finally, observe that, like the spatial impossibility theorem, Corollary 2.2 may be extended to the case of any finite number of locations.

2.3.3 Notes on the Literature

One of the first spatial competitive models is the spatial price equilibrium model formalized by Cournot (1838, chapter X). The sellers and buyers of a commodity are located at nodes of a transportation network. The issue is then to determine simultaneously the quantities supplied and demanded at each node and the local prices at which the commodity is supplied by the sellers and bought by the customers. The equilibrium is reached when the demand price equals the supply price plus the transport cost for all positive flows; if the demand price is less than the supply price plus the transport cost, then no trade flow occurs.

This problem has been revisited by Enke (1951), who found a formal connection with the theory of electric circuits and proposed a solution method based on this analogy. Soon after, Samuelson (1952) showed that the market equilibrium can be obtained as the solution to a mathematical program containing the celebrated Hitchcock–Koopmans transportation problem. This cross-fertilization between spatial economics and mathematical programming has generated many extensions dealing with different aspects of production and demand, which are summarized in Takayama and Judge (1971). Later on, Florian and Los (1982) demonstrated that spatial equilibrium models may also be solved by means of variational inequalities, thus opening the door to a new flow of contributions that are reviewed and extended in Nagurney (1993). A shorter synthesis may be found in Labys and Yang (1997). As shown by this vast literature, the general competitive model remains relevant for the study of commodity flows when both firms and households have fixed locations.

The quadratic assignment model introduced by Koopmans and Beckmann (1957) may be viewed as the first serious attempt made to capture the locational choices of agents when commodities are traded between them. The difficulties encountered by these authors have triggered a very limited number of articles. Heffley (1972, 1976) and Hamilton (1980) have provided useful complements to the work of Koopmans and Beckmann. A nice overview of the literature centered on the spatial price equilibrium and the quadratic assignment problem can be found in Schweizer (1986).

2.4 HETEROGENEOUS SPACE AND EXTERNALITIES

As is shown in this section, relaxing the assumption of a homogeneous space or introducing technological externalities may help to restore the existence of a competitive equilibrium involving transportation.

2.4.1 First Nature

Space is *heterogeneous* when locations have specific attributes that differentiate them. To illustrate, consider the example of Figure 2.1 in which we introduce inhomogeneities in space. More precisely, we assume that location A is endowed with an exogenous attribute that makes the firm more productive there. This exogenous attribute may correspond to a Ricardian comparative advantage, such as the presence of immobile inputs used by the firm or the vestige of a time where physical geography did matter. In any event, if the firm locates in B, the set of feasible allocations is given by the new triangle $OE'F'$, as depicted in Figure 2.2. We see that the set of feasible allocations is now convex. In this case, a competitive equilibrium exists because the firm has no incentive to leave A. This approach is extended in Chapter 3.

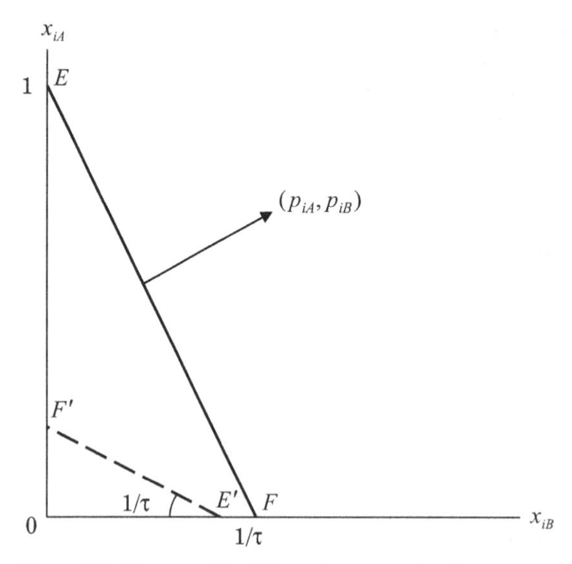

Figure 2.2. The set of feasible trade patterns in a heterogeneous space.

To gain more insights about the effect of given spatial inhomogeneities, consider one more time our 2 firm–2 location example with fixed lot size. We assume that location A has an *exogenous* attribute beneficial to firm 1 only (whereas firm 2 experiences a similar advantage in the sole location B). Whatever the reason for it, this attribute gives rise to a revenue a_{1A} exceeding a_{1B}. Then, firm 1's profit at location A is now defined as follows:

$$\pi_{1A} = a_{1A} + p_{1A}q_1 - p_{2A}q_2 - R_A$$

while π_{1B} is unchanged. Measuring again the incentive to move by the difference in profit at A and B, we obtain:

$$\pi_{1B} - \pi_{1A} = a_{1B} - a_{1A} + t_1q_1 + t_2q_2 + R_A - R_B$$

which is negative when $a_{1A} - a_{1B}$ is sufficiently large. Because the same argument holds for firm 2, we may conclude that *a competitive equilibrium involving trade may well exist if firms have strongly diverging preferences for location attributes*. Or, to put it differently, the market breaks down when inter-agent transportation costs outweigh other aspects of agents' preferences about locations.[6] As Hamilton (1980, 38) put it:

[6] Such a situation was typical of the manufacturing sector in the nineteenth century when plant locations were very much governed by the geographical distribution of raw materials, which was itself very uneven. This seems much less relevant in modern economies replete with footloose firms.

Stability is lent to the system by having plants differ from one another in their preferences for the sites *qua* sites, and instability arises from a large volume of trade among plants.

In other words, if firms interact and those interactions are costly, due to transportation or other transaction costs, each firm's profits depend on not just its own location, but also on the location decisions made by the other firms (Koopmans 1957). This creates a web of interdependencies that makes it difficult for competitive prices to clear markets, unless the interdependencies are sufficiently weak relative to the inherent "draw" of certain sites for particular activities. It is not clear, however, why firms should have a priori strong diverging preferences. On the contrary, first nature geography seems to be the outcome of processes in which agents have been driven by the supply of similar natural attributes such as raw material sites, coasts, or rivers. For example, in the nineteenth century, when firms' locations were more governed by natural factors than in modern economies, manufacturing firms had a strong proclivity to set up near raw material sites or transshipment points. That said, the following question comes naturally to mind: Is a market coping with the accessibility across agents missing when there are no strong external drivers?

Nevertheless, appealing to certain types of heterogeneity may help to solve the problem. First, specific spatial inhomogeneities may allow firms to produce at a lower cost (aluminum production where hydropower is cheap). Second, one can give Ricardian advantages to locations in natural transport means, such as rivers, large lakes, oceans, or flat areas. These advantages are magnified when they are combined with increasing returns in port facilities. Last, exogenous inhomogeneities may be useful to model the legacy of the past, that is, amenities that attract or repel modern firms and workers. Admittedly, assuming that space is heterogeneous seems to be sufficient to explain a nonuniform distribution of economic activities over space. More precisely, in some sectors, first nature may be more important than increasing returns to explain the specialization of some regions and cities. Even though we recognize the importance of first nature geography in the making of the spatial economy, we believe with Lösch and Hoover that building the economics of agglomeration upon exogenous spatial inhomogeneities *only* amounts to playing Hamlet without the prince. In saying this, we do not deny the usefulness of neoclassical trade theory based on constant returns to scale and comparative advantage. Rather, we mean that, by relying solely on the diversity of first nature, one puts aside the main endogenous socioeconomic forces that yield agglomeration and specialization.

Before proceeding, we find it worthy to stress the following point. Even though first nature may explain why *particular* locations nest agglomerations such as cities (see, e.g., Rappaport and Sachs 2003), it is not clear that natural advantages play a major role in the *emergence* of large agglomerations (see, e.g., Ellison and Glaeser 1999). It is our contention that first nature is *not* sufficient to explain why some cities become so large. Instead, their size must be explained through the interplay of economic and social interactions within economic models that encapsulate (external or internal) increasing returns.

2.4.2 Marshallian Externalities

We have seen that externalities generated by proximity are considered as one of the main engines of economic agglomerations. To illustrate the role of such externalities in an otherwise competitive setting, we go back to the example of Section 2.3.1 in which we now allow for M replicas of each of four agents, where M is an integer number. The $2M$ workers equally share the profit of each firm as well as the land rent at each location. When M is an even number and when land is abundant in each place, a competitive equilibrium exists with $M/2$ firms and workers of each type located in A and B, in which case there is autarky. This is not a very exciting outcome.

To obtain a competitive equilibrium with trade, we change the assumptions of the replicated economy as follows. First, for simplicity, we assume that workers are equally productive in either type of firm. Second, and this is more fundamental, the production function (2.13) of each firm of type i is now as follows:

$$Q_{ir} = E(M_{ir})l^{\alpha} \qquad i = 1, 2 \quad \text{and} \quad r = A, B \tag{2.25}$$

where l is the amount of labor used by a firm and $E(M_{ir})$ an increasing function of the number (M_{ir}) of type i firms at r. The function $E(M_{ir})$ represents the Marshallian externality associated with the local agglomeration of firms belonging to the same industry.[7]

Consider now the dispersed configuration in which M firms of type 1 and M workers locate together in A, whereas M firms of type 2 and M workers are at B, and find under which conditions this configuration is an equilibrium. Because each firm uses one unit of labor, the two locations are formally symmetric. Hence, we can readily obtain the following equilibrium values:

$$w_A = w_B \equiv 1 \tag{2.26}$$

$$\begin{aligned} p_{1A} &= p_{2B} = 1/[\alpha E(M)] \\ p_{1B} &= p_{2A} = \tau/[\alpha E(M)] \\ Q_{1A} &= Q_{2B} = E(M) \\ R_A &= R_B = \frac{M}{\alpha\beta}\frac{1-\beta}{S - M\bar{s}} \\ \pi_{1A} &= \pi_{2B} = \frac{1}{\alpha\beta}\frac{\beta S - M\bar{s}}{S - M\bar{s}} - 1. \end{aligned} \tag{2.27}$$

[7] The idea of modeling a firm's cost as a decreasing function of the number of firms belonging to the same industry goes back at least to Chipman (1970).

When the lot size $\bar{s}$ of each firm is sufficiently small, the profit of each firm is nonnegative because $\alpha < 1$, and thus a unique market equilibrium exists in which each region is fully specialized, and thus interregional trade occurs.[8]

Let us examine whether an agent has an incentive to relocate. All workers attain the same utility level and, therefore, have no reason to move. In considering the possible relocation of a firm, we assume that the number M is so large that each firm takes the externality levels, $E(M)$ and $E(0)$, as given when making its locational decision. In such a context, if a type 1 firm, say, moves from A to B, then its profit is

$$\pi_{1B} = p_{1B} E(0) l^{\alpha} - w_B l - R_B \bar{s}.$$

Using (2.26) and (2.27), the profit–maximizing labor input l_{1B} at B is equal to

$$l_{1B}^{\alpha-1} = \frac{1}{\tau}\frac{E(M)}{E(0)} \tag{2.28}$$

which yields

$$\pi_{1B} = \frac{1-\alpha}{\alpha} l_{1B} - R_B \bar{s}.$$

Because

$$\pi_{1A} = p_{1A} E(M) - w_A - R_{A\bar{s}} = (1/\alpha) - 1 - R_A \bar{s}$$

using $R_A = R_B$ yields

$$\pi_{1B} - \pi_{1A} = \frac{1-\alpha}{\alpha}(l_{1B} - 1)$$

which is nonpositive if and only if $l_{1B} \leq 1$, or

$$\frac{E(M)}{E(0)} \geq \tau > 1 \tag{2.29}$$

by (2.28). By symmetry, for a type 2 firm, the profit differential $\pi_{2A} - \pi_{2B}$ is nonpositive if and only if (2.29) holds.

Therefore, we may conclude that, when Marshallian externalities are sufficiently large in comparison with transport costs that (2.29) holds, the dispersed configuration involving the agglomeration of M firms of each type within the same region is a competitive equilibrium. Because of these externalities, the agglomeration of firms belonging to the same industry gives rise to *endogenous* spatial inhomogeneities, which allow for the existence of an equilibrium once such inhomogeneities are sufficiently strong. They generate new forces that are able to overcome the locational instability caused by the competitive price

[8] Like in the quadratic assignment problem, each firm is indivisible since $\bar{s}$ is fixed. Unlike what is assumed in this problem, however, the total supply of land is large enough here for each region to accommodate the whole industry ($S - M\bar{s} > 0$).

mechanism in a homogeneous space. In this case, *space is ex ante homogeneous but ex post heterogeneous*.

This example suffices to highlight the fact that the relationship between Marshallian externalities and transport costs is critical for the nature of the market outcome. We see in Chapters 6, 9, and 11 how externalities may lead to the emergence of city-centers and regional disparities.

2.5 HOW TO MODEL THE SPACE-ECONOMY?

Because our objective is to explain the geographical distribution of economic activities, especially the making of agglomerations and the process of regional specialization, the spatial impossibility theorem thus tells us that we must assume at least one of the following elements: (i) first nature differences; (ii) spatial externalities in production and/or consumption; or (iii) imperfectly competitive markets. Although in the real world, economic spaces are likely to be the result of the combination of these three elements, it is convenient to separate them so that we can grasp the effects of each of them better.

2.5.1 Comparative Advantage

In this case, the heterogeneity of space presupposes an uneven distribution of "givens" (technologies, natural resources, or amenities) or the existence of transport nodes and marketplaces. In the Ricardian model, a given country is assumed to have a more efficient technology than the others. Each country then specializes in the production of the good for which its relative opportunity cost is lower. In the Heckscher-Ohlin model, countries have access to the same technologies but have different endowments in production factors. The international immobility of production factors implies that the relative prices of goods are different under autarky, thus making trade desirable. As discussed in Section 2.4.1, the ex ante heterogeneity of space is an important element to take into account in the economics of agglomeration. However, it seems to us that understanding why a specific country (or region) is more efficient than others, or why, and which, production factors are immobile while goods are not, are fundamental questions to investigate. Likewise, the existence of transport nodes or marketplaces must be explained because they are often the results of human actions.

2.5.2 Externalities

It is widely recognized that agglomeration forces are generated endogenously through nonmarket interactions among firms and/or households (see

Section 2.4.2). According to Marshall and his successors, external effects are essential to understand the making of agglomerations. Marshallian economies aim to capture a fundamental idea: An agglomeration is the outcome of a snowball effect in which the concentration of a growing number of agents, who benefit from the advantages generated by a greater diversity and/or a greater specialization in activities, reinforces these advantages, thus attracting new agents, and so on. For a long time, Marshallian economies were used as black boxes hiding richer microeconomic mechanisms that lead to increasing returns at the aggregate level. Nowadays, these boxes have been opened and we have a much better understanding of these various mechanisms, though their relative importance remains an unsolved empirical question (Duranton and Puga 2004; Puga 2010).

2.5.3 Imperfect Competition

When maximizing their profits, firms no longer treat prices as given but are price-makers (Hotelling 1929; Kaldor 1935). Because the level of prices typically depends on the spatial distribution of firms and consumers, the resulting interdependence between firms and households may yield agglomerations. Two approaches must be distinguished.

(i) *Monopolistic competition.* This type of competition involves a modest departure from the competitive model while allowing firms to be price-makers because they produce differentiated goods under increasing returns. However, strategic interactions are either absent or weak because the number of firms is large.

(ii) *Oligopolistic competition.* We now have a small number of big agents (firms, local governments, or land developers) that interact strategically, as in spatial competition theory.

How to choose between oligopolistic and monopolistic competition to model competition in space is a more subtle issue than what is usually acknowledged in the literature. It is well known that the idea of monopolistic competition goes back to Chamberlin (1933). The Chamberlinian model relies on two main assumptions. First, each firm is free to choose its own price because it sells a differentiated product (*monopolistic*). Second, the number of competitors is sufficiently large for the action taken by any one firm to have a negligible impact upon the market (*competition*). As a consequence, the price level chosen by a particular firm does not impact the other firms, which, therefore, do not react. This idea is the cornerstone of the model of monopolistic competition developed much later on by Dixit and Stiglitz (1977), which has served as the workhorse of new trade and growth theories.

In his review of Chamberlin's book, Kaldor (1935) forcefully argued that, once it is recognized that firms operate in space, each one competes directly with only a few neighboring firms regardless of the total number of firms in the industry. The very nature of competition in space therefore would be oligopolistic, thus casting serious doubt on the relevance of monopolistic competition for the study of the space-economy. Independently, Lösch (1940) proposed a spatial version of monopolistic competition in which firms are located at the vertices of hexagons, and thus competition takes place among the few. Clearly, Lösch's setting bears some strong resemblance to Kaldor's ideas. Yet, one had to wait for Beckmann (1972a) to have a complete and rigorous analytical treatment of what came to be known as the "spatial model of monopolistic competition." Though extremely well executed, Beckmann's paper went unnoticed, perhaps because it was published in a journal that did not attract much attention in the economics profession. In this respect, it is worth noting that Beckmann's main results were independently rediscovered by Salop (1979) in a paper that became famous in industrial organization. The major accomplishment of these two papers is to show how the process of free entry and exit determines the equilibrium number of firms producing under increasing returns and competing oligopolistically with adjacent firms. Among other things, Beckmann and Salop highlighted in a very precise way how the market solves the trade-off between increasing returns (internal to firms) and transport costs, a fundamental problem that is tackled in great detail in Chapter 4.

Rather ironically, this is not the spatial model of monopolistic competition that Krugman (1991b) used in his pioneering paper on NEG. Instead, Krugman built on the Dixit-Stiglitz model in which every firm competes with every other firm. How to resolve this apparent paradox? It seems to us that the answer is to be found in the *spatial scale* at which the analysis is conducted. At the macro-spatial level, that is, the interregional or the international, using the Chamberlinian model makes sense because the international distance matters much more than the intraregional one. In such a market environment, it is indeed reasonable to think of competition as being global. By contrast, at the micro-spatial level, that is, a city or a region, using the spatial model is much more compelling for the reasons emphasized by Kaldor and Lösch: markets are predominantly local.

2.6 CONCLUDING REMARKS

The spatial impossibility theorem is important because the competitive price mechanism is the keystone of the economic theory of market equilibrium, and economic theory has long been dominated by this paradigm. This may partly explain why space has been neglected by the economics profession. Indeed, we have seen that, when a competitive equilibrium exists in a homogeneous spatial economy, no transportation can occur; hence, regions do not specialize and agglomerations of firms and households cannot be formed and sustained. This is not what we observe in the real world. Because land is essential and scarce and transportation is costly, the presence of some kinds of indivisibilities is crucial to understanding the emergence of economic agglomerations (see also our discussion in Chapter 1). The attempt made by economists to develop a rigorous theory of markets and prices has led them, through a series of simplifications and shortcuts taken long ago, to zero in on the combination "constant returns and perfect competition" with consequences for spatial economics that are comparable to those for growth theory (Warsh 2006). Whereas the lack of interest manifested by many economists about spatial issues is regrettable, the opposite attitude (disinterest in economic theory as a whole on the grounds that it is a-spatial) is untenable. This attitude long characterized traditional regional economists, and it largely explains the stagnation of this field. We see, however, that much can be achieved by appealing to noncompetitive theories of a market economy.

As shown in Chapter 3, we can appeal to the competitive framework when specific spatial inhomogeneities preexist. On the other hand, if we want to explain the emergence of economic agglomerations in an otherwise undifferentiated space, we must explicitly consider (i) market failures such as technological externalities (see Chapters 6 and 11) or public goods (see Chapter 5) and (ii) imperfect competition (see Chapters 7, 8, and 9).

APPENDIX

The quadratic assignment with M firms and locations. In the general case with M firms and M locations, when locations are appropriately situated (for example, locations are distributed along a circle) and when the input-output linkages among firms are appropriately chosen, a location assignment may seem supportable by a competitive price system. And, indeed, since the publication of Koopmans and Beckmann (1957), several "counter-examples" have been proposed. After close scrutiny, however, they turn out to be false. To prevent the reader from making such a vain attempt, we show here that no competitive equilibrium exists in the quadratic assignment problem when space is homogeneous.

There are M firms ($i = 1, \ldots, M$) and M homogeneous locations ($r = 1, \ldots, M$). Firm i produces good i using inputs $q_{ji} \geq 0$ ($j = 1, \ldots, M$) produced by each other firm j, where the q_{ji}'s are constants such that at least one q_{ji} is strictly positive. By convention, we set $q_{ii} = 0$ for all i. Each location can accommodate one firm only. Let $t_i(r, s) > 0$ be the cost of shipping one unit of good i from r to s ($r \neq s$).

Without loss of generality, we assume that firm i is assigned to location i. In this way, each location is characterized by the index of the firm that is assigned there. Let $\{p_i(r), R(r); i, r = 1, \ldots, M\}$ be the price system assumed to support this assignment. In this case, the profit of firm i at location i is given by

$$\pi_i(i) = a_i + p_i(i)\sum_{j=1}^{M} q_{ij} - \sum_{j=1}^{M} p_j(i) q_{ji} - R(i)$$

where a_i is a constant independent of the firm's location. If firm i relocates to location r and conducts the same activity, its profit is given by

$$\pi_i(r) = a_i + p_i(r)\sum_{j=1}^{M} q_{ij} - \sum_{j=1}^{M} p_j(r) q_{ji} - R(r).$$

Let us define the incentive for firm i to move from location i to location r by

$$I_i(i, r) = \pi_i(r) - \pi_i(i) \qquad r = 1, \ldots. M \quad \text{and} \quad r \neq i \tag{2A.1}$$

and define the aggregate incentive for all firms to move (to all other possible locations) as follows:

$$I = \sum_{i=1}^{M}\sum_{r=1}^{M} I_i(i, r). \tag{2A.2}$$

In equilibrium, because no $I_i(i, r)$ can be positive, the aggregate incentive I must be nonpositive. In fact, we show below that

$$I = M\sum_{i=1}^{M}\sum_{j=1}^{M} q_{ij} t_i(i, j) \tag{2A.3}$$

that is, the aggregate incentive for all firms to move is M times the total transport costs associated with the original assignment, which is strictly positive. This implies that no feasible assignment can be supported by a competitive price system.

To demonstrate (2A.3), we proceed as follows. First, observe that in calculating $I_i(i, r)$ in (2A.1), the constant a_i disappears. Second, in evaluating I as defined by (2A.2), when we compute the sum $I_i(i, r) + I_r(r, i)$ for each pair (i, r), the land rents $R(i)$ and $R(r)$ disappear. Therefore, we may focus on quantities q_{ij} and express the total incentive I as follows:

$$I = \sum_{i=1}^{M}\sum_{j=1}^{M} q_{ij} f_{ij}(P) \tag{2A.4}$$

where $f_{ij}(P)$ is a function of all prices $p_i(r)$. To determine these functions, let us focus on any one pair (i, j) such that $q_{ij} \neq 0$. Because q_{ij} is a part of the sales made by firm i whereas it is also an input of firm j, q_{ij} appears in each of the following incentive-to-move functions related to firm i and firm j:

$$\text{for firm } i : I_i(i,r) = \pi_i(r) - \pi_i(i) \qquad r \neq i,$$
$$\text{for firm } j : I_j(j,s) = \pi_j(s) - \pi_j(j) \qquad s \neq j.$$

Therefore, in calculating the aggregate incentive I, the quantity q_{ij} appears only in the following subtotal:

$$\sum_{r=1}^{M} I_i(i,r) + \sum_{s=1}^{M} I_j(j,s) \equiv I_i(i,j) + I_j(j,i) + \sum_{\substack{r=1 \\ r \neq i,j}}^{M} \{I_i(i,r) + I_j(j,r)\}.$$

In $I_i(i,j)$, using (2A.1) in which $r = j$, we see that the term related to q_{ij} appears as $q_{ij}[p_i(j) - p_i(i)]$. Similarly, in $I_j(j,i)$, the term related to q_{ij} appears as $q_{ij}[p_i(j) - p_i(i)]$; this stands for firm j's cost saving on input q_{ij} associated with firm j's relocation from j to i. Hence, in $I_i(i,j) + I_j(j,i)$, the term related to q_{ij} appears as $2q_{ij}[p_i(j) - p_i(i)]$.

Because, for each pair (i, j), the equilibrium prices must be such that

$$p_i(j) = p_i(i) + t_i(i,j) \qquad \text{when } q_{ij} > 0$$

in $I_i(i,j) + I_j(j,i)$, we have

$$2q_{ij}[p_i(j) - p_i(i)] = 2q_{ij}t_i(i,j). \tag{2A.5}$$

Finally, take any $r \neq i, j$. Then, in $I_i(i,r)$, the term related to q_{ij} appears as $q_{ij}[p_i(r) - p_i(i)]$, which represents the change in revenue for firm i from selling the quantity q_{ij} at location r instead of selling it at location i. On the other hand, in $I_j(j,r)$, the term related to q_{ij} appears as $q_{ij}[p_i(j) - p_i(r)]$, which represents a part of firm j's cost saving associated with the relocation from location j to r. Hence, in $I_i(i,r) + I_j(j,r)$, we have

$$q_{ij}[p_i(r) - p_i(i)] + q_{ij}[p_i(j) - p_i(r)] = q_{ij}[p_i(j) - p_i(i)] = q_{ij}t_i(i,j) \tag{2A.6}$$

thus implying that, if both firms i and j relocate to $r \neq i$ and j, they can save the transport cost $q_{ij}t_i(i,j)$.

Because we have $M - 2$ such locations $r \neq i, j$, we see from (2A.5) and (2A.6) that in the sum (2A.4), the term related to q_{ij} appears as

$$\begin{aligned} &2q_{ij}[p_i(j) - p_i(i)] + (M-2)q_{ij}[p_i(j) - p_i(i)] \\ &\quad = Mq_{ij}[p_i(j) - p_i(i)] = Mq_{ij}t_i(i, j) \end{aligned}$$

and thus, using (2A.4), we obtain

$$f_{ij}(P) = M[p_i(j) - p_i(i)] = Mt_i(i, j).$$

Because this result holds for any pair (i, j) such that $i \neq j$, we obtain (2A.3).

3

The von Thünen Model and Land Rent Formation

3.1 INTRODUCTION

Land use models explain the way various activities using land locate over a given area. This phenomenon can be studied from a different perspective by asking which activities are accommodated in specific locations. As seen in this chapter, these two approaches may be considered interchangeable, although they differ somewhat. The first is more in line with microeconomics in that the analysis focuses on where given agents chose to locate, whereas the second is more akin to the approach followed by many geographers, who put the emphasis on places and densities and not on agents.[1]

Because, in a market economy, land is allocated among activities through the price of land, the land use problem is equivalent to asking how the price of land is determined in a competitive economy. This does not seem to be a feasible task, for we have just seen that the price mechanism does not work in a spatial economy. The spatial impossibility theorem does not preclude, however, the possibility of uncovering particular, but relevant, economic situations in which the price mechanism is able to govern the allocation of activities over space. This is precisely what we try to do in this chapter.

The prototype of such particular situations has been put forward by Thünen (1826), who sought to explain the pattern of agricultural activities surrounding cities in preindustrial Germany. His model relies on the following basic idea: *each farmer faces a trade-off between land rents and transport costs.* The various models developed in his footsteps can be cast within the Arrow–Debreu framework because transactions must occur at a given marketplace (the town in Thünen's analysis), whereas activities (the crops in Thünen's analysis) and land are supposed to be perfectly divisible. Once markets are considered as perfectly competitive, it becomes easy to understand why the Thünian model

[1] Both approaches are used in this book. Roughly speaking, we can say that the former is followed in models with a finite number of agents to locate, while the latter is encountered in models with a continuum of agents.

has been extensively studied in both production theory and urban economics where it has proven to be a very powerful tool. That is, the Thünian model rests on the paradigmatic combination formed by the standard assumptions of constant returns and perfect competition, while assuming an exogenously located marketplace.

Each location in space is a bundle of characteristics such as soil conditions, relief, geographical position, and the like. Both land rent and land use vary across locations depending on these characteristics. Among them, the most important for location theorists is the transport-cost differential over space. Although Ricardo concentrated more on fertility differences in his explanation of the land rent, von Thünen constructed a theory focusing on the transport-cost differentials across locations. For that, he used a very simple and elegant setting in which space is represented by a plain on which land is homogeneous in all respects except for a marketplace in which all transactions regarding final goods must occur. We show that the price of land at any particular location reflects the proximity to the marketplace: the closer the marketplace, the higher the land rent.

More generally, the general principle holds that the distance to some specific places endowed with desirable attributes is the reason for having what is called a *differential land rent* ("differential" for differences in accessibility to some locations). Otherwise, how to explain why land rents are so high in cities? Indeed, in most habitable regions of the globe, the supply of land vastly exceeds the demand for land. Therefore, *absent the need for proximity, land should be* (almost) *a free good.*[2] This makes the case for proximity very strong. Several examples of this mechanism are studied later in this chapter and in subsequent ones.

We assume that a city exists where transactions take place, but the reasons for its existence are analyzed in subsequent chapters. This marketplace is a major spatial inhomogeneity that allows one to obviate the difficulties raised by the spatial impossibility theorem. Specifically, we see that very interesting results can be obtained with this model. In essence, the Thünen model shows how the existence of a center is sufficient for a competitive land market to structure the use of space by different activities. Not all transactions, however, need to occur at the market town. In particular, it seems reasonable to assume that intermediate inputs are traded on a local basis instead of being shipped to the marketplace. Therefore, we extend the basic model by integrating intermediate goods, which are also produced from land but locally traded. This allows us to shed light on the impact that technological linkages may have on the spatial distribution of activities under perfect competition. This is to be contrasted with the quadratic assignment problem in which technological linkages prevent the

[2] Land is also used for farming. However, the agricultural land rent is generally much lower than the urban land rent.

existence of a competitive equilibrium. The reason for this difference in results is that production activities are now assumed to be perfectly divisible, whereas the demand for the final goods comes from the marketplace, the location of which is fixed and given.

Our purpose in this chapter is not to provide a comprehensive survey of what has been accomplished in the large body of land use theory. Instead, we have chosen to focus on the main principles underlying Thünen's analysis. To this end, we discuss in Section 3.2.1 the properties of a simple, but suggestive, model formulated within the general competitive equilibrium framework. Specifically, we assume that (i) all agents are price-takers, (ii) producers operate under constant returns to scale, and (iii) there is free entry in each type of activity. The assumption of a competitive land market can be justified on the grounds that land in a small neighborhood of any location belonging to a continuous space is highly substitutable, thus making the competitive process for land very fierce.

However, because our main concern is to determine which agent occupies a particular location, it appears to be convenient, both here and in subsequent chapters in which we work with a land market, to determine the land use equilibrium from the *bid rent function* suggested by Thünen. The concept of bid rent function is probably what makes Thünen's analysis of land use so original and powerful. In a sense, it rests on the idea that land at a particular location corresponds to a single commodity whose price cannot be obtained by the textbook interplay between a large number of sellers and buyers, for as Alonso (1964, 41) put it, "land as space is a homogeneous good and land at a location is a continuously differentiated good."

Having said that, our aim is to find what kind of spatial distribution may arise in equilibrium as well as the features of the land rent profile sustaining such a distribution. Though the model is very simple, it shows that the spatial heterogeneity generated by a preexisting center is sufficient to obviate the negative conclusion of the spatial impossibility theorem. Two extensions of the basic model are considered, namely, the introduction of intermediate goods (Section 3.2.2) and the possibility of substitution between land and labor in production (Section 3.2.3).

In Section 3.3, we continue our exploration of the Thünian model by studying its applications to the formation of the urban land rent and the residential distribution of housing within a monocentric city. In this case, as suggested by Isard (1956, chapter 8) and formally developed by Alonso (1964), the Thünian town is reinterpreted as the city center (or central business district) to which individuals must commute in order to work, whereas housing is developed in the surrounding area. Our main focus here is on the tension between the desire for space and the desire to commute less. We see that this simple model provides a set of results consistent with the prominent feature of urban structures (Section 3.3.1). In particular, it explains the decrease in the urban land rent with distance away from the city center as well as the fall in the population density as one moves away from the center. As in the Thünian model, the city center plays a key role in the emergence of such a residential structure. Some comparative statics analysis is then performed on the residential equilibrium (Section 3.3.2). This analysis reveals several tendencies that agree with the main stylized facts suggested by urban economic history.[3] Among others, we note a spreading of the residential area corresponding to *suburbanization* when consumers get richer and commuting costs become lower, thus providing an explanation for what has been observed in many modern cities. We go on by showing that the market city is efficient in the absence of spatial externalities such as congestion in transport (Section 3.3.3).

In the foregoing analysis, the consumers are assumed to be identical in preferences and incomes. We go one step further by studying how the residential structure is affected when consumers are differentiated by their income (Section 3.3.4) and demonstrate that high-income consumers tend to settle far from the city center, which is left to the low-income ones. Such a pattern is commonly observed in North America, but not in Europe where the income gradient often slopes downward as the distance to the city center increases. We see how historical and cultural amenities located at the city center may reverse the social stratification within the city. A similar setting also allows us to shed light on the emergence of mixed urban-rural patterns (Section 3.3.4).

Finally, following the tradition of mainstream urban economics, we have assumed throughout this chapter a continuum of locations and consumers, thus working with a model in which *all* the unknowns are described by density functions. We show how the basic model of urban economics can be related to that of a city with a finite number of consumers located in a continuous urban space (Section 3.3.5). We conclude in Section 3.4 with a brief discussion of alternative, but related, urban models.

3.2 THE LOCATION OF DIVISIBLE ACTIVITIES

3.2.1 The Basic Model

By allocating an acre of land near the town to some crop, the costs of delivering all other crops are indirectly affected as they are forced to be grown farther away. Hence, determining which crops to grow where is not an easy task, thus making the work of Thünen very original. Though fairly abstract for the time, his treatment of the land use problem was not mathematical. One had to wait for the work of Launhardt ([1885], 1993, chapter 30) to have a formal treatment

[3] In this respect, the books by Bairoch (1988) and by Hohenberg and Lees (1985) offer both a great deal of relevant information.

of his ideas in the special case of two crops. The first model dealing with an arbitrary number of crops is due to Dunn (1954).

The model is based on the following premises. There is a town located at the center of a featureless plain. All the products of various agricultural activities established in the surrounding area are to be traded there. The state formed by the town and its hinterland has no economic connections with the rest of the world; it is thus referred to as an *isolated state.* This isolated state is formally described by a large set of the Euclidean plane in which the town, treated as a point, is at the origin of the plane, whereas the distance from any point to the town is measured by the Euclidean distance. Each location r is identified by its distance r to the town.[4]

There are n activities, each producing a different agricultural good, or crop, denoted $i = 1, \ldots, n$. One may think of an activity as a set of farmers selling the same crop and using the same technology. The production of one unit of good i requires only the use of a_i units of land, where a_i is a positive constant independent of location, so that the technology of activity i exhibits constant returns to scale.[5] Consequently, if a unit of land at distance r is allocated to activity i, the corresponding production $q_i(r)$ of good i is given by

$$q_i(r) = \frac{1}{a_i}. \tag{3.1}$$

The density of land at each location is unity, and thus land density at distance r equals $2\pi r$.

Because our focus is on land use, we put aside the determination of the prices of the agricultural goods in the town, which are supposed to be given and constant. Specifically, good i is sold at price p_i in the town to which it is shipped from its production place at a constant transport cost t_i per unit of good i and unit of distance. In other words, the product and transport markets are perfectly competitive.[6]

There is a perfectly competitive land market at every location in space, and the opportunity cost of land is assumed to be zero. However, as observed in the introduction, it is convenient to think that land at any point is allocated to an activity according to a bidding process in which the producer offering

[4] In general, a point is described by its radius and its angle, but we may omit the angle because space is featureless around the city.

[5] We treat a unit of land here as a given combination of land and labor. Alternatively, we may consider that the price p_i introduced below represents the crop i's price net of all input-costs other than land rent. The cost of labor is explicitly accounted for in Section 3.2.3.

[6] Note, in passing, that Thünen used a more general specification of the transport cost involving two components. The first component corresponds to a monetary cost proportional to the quantity shipped and the distance covered (like ours), whereas the second is given by a fraction of the initial shipment's melting during the transport. For example, Thünen supposed that the cost of shipping grain consists partially of the grain consumed on the way by the horses pulling the load. This anticipates the iceberg cost proposed by Samuelson (1954a) and used in NEG (see Chapter 8).

the highest bid secures the corresponding lot. In this regard, Thünen imagined a process in which each farmer makes an offer based on the surplus he can generate by using one unit of land available at any particular location. Because land is the only input and goods must be shipped to the market town, it should be clear that this surplus is given by $(p_i - t_i r)/a_i$. It varies with the activity but also with the location. Each activity i can then be characterized by a bid rent that is defined by the surplus per unit of land of any producer of good i at location r. Specifically, the *bid rent* of activity i at location r is here defined as follows:

$$\Psi_i(r) \equiv (p_i - t_i r)/a_i. \tag{3.2}$$

Since farmers are rational, they maximize profit per land unit. Being price-takers, the profit $\pi_i(r)$ made by a farmer in activity i per unit of land at location r is given by

$$\pi_i(r) = (p_i - t_i r)q_i(r) - R(r) = \Psi_i(r) - R(r)$$

using (3.1) and (3.2), where $R(r)$ is the rent per unit of land prevailing at distance r. Hence, a farmer's bid depends on both the transport rate of his output and the amount of land needed to produce one unit of the good. Because farmers compete for land until their profits are zero, the bid rent of those located at distance r coincides with the market land rent.

In the present setting, a competitive equilibrium is defined by a land rent function and by the areas in which each activity is undertaken such that no producer finds it profitable to change the location of its activity at the prevailing land rent. Because returns to scale are constant, it follows that any farmer with a positive output earns zero profits, whereas the equilibrium land rent cannot be negative. Consequently, (3.2) implies that the equilibrium land rent is such that

$$R^*(r) \equiv \max\left\{\max_{i=1,\ldots,n} \Psi_i(r), 0\right\} = \max\left\{\max_{i=1,\ldots,n} (p_i - t_i r)/a_i, 0\right\} \tag{3.3}$$

so that the *land rent function* $R^*(\cdot)$ emerges as the upper envelope of the bid rent functions $\Psi_i(\cdot)$. In other words, at the end of the bidding, each location is occupied by the agent who is able to offer the highest bid.[7]

[7] If the number of locations were finite, the land rent would be given by the outcome of an English auction in which the commodity is sold at the second highest reservation price. When the distance between adjacent locations along any ray goes to zero, the second highest reservation price tends to the highest reservation price at each location as given by Proposition 3.1 (Asami 1990). However, we must stress that, in more general settings in which the land use pattern is determined together with prices – wages or utility levels, say – this is no longer true. In such contexts, it is not clear how the bid rent function may emerge from a standard auctioning process.

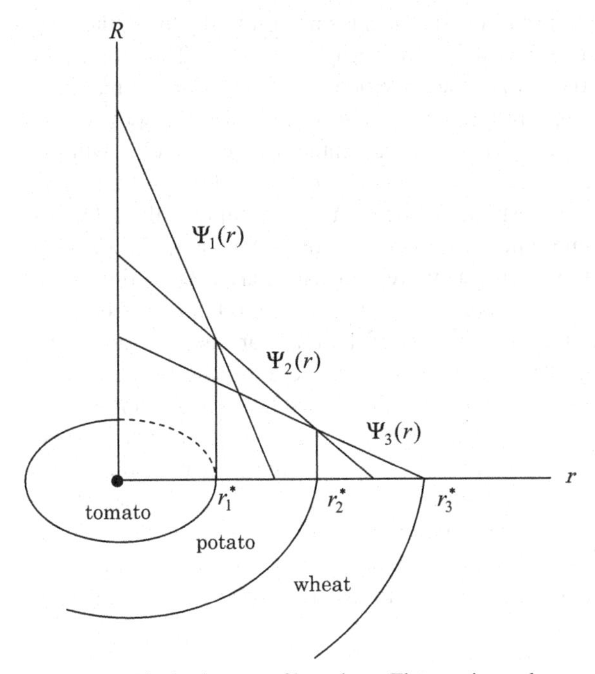

Figure 3.1. The land rent profile and von Thünen rings when $n = 3$.

Each bid rent function being decreasing and linear in distance, we may conclude as follows:

Proposition 3.1. *The equilibrium land rent function is the upper envelope of all bid rent functions, and each crop is raised where its bid rent equals the equilibrium land rent. If the transport cost function is linear in distance, then the equilibrium land rent is decreasing, piecewise linear, and convex.*

As suggested in the introduction, it appears that the land rent is given by the *differential* surplus corresponding to the resources saved in transport by the most profitable activity relative to the zero surplus obtained at the extensive margin of land use. It even turns out that, for each activity, land rent is equal to the saving in transport cost. This strict relationship should not be overemphasized, however, because it depends on the assumption of fixed technological coefficients (see Section 3.2.3). An illustration of a land rent profile in the case of three activities is provided in Figure 3.1 where each linear segment of the land rent represents the bid rent of the corresponding crop.

It follows from Proposition 3.1 that, in equilibrium, crops are distributed according to the famous pattern of concentric rings centered at the market town, each of them being specialized in one crop. Then, the crops, if they are raised, are ordered by the distance from the town in such a way that the crop having the steepest bid rent function locates nearest to the town, the crop with the second steepest locates in the next ring, and so on. Therefore, it is not true that zones near the market town are necessarily locations of intensive type of land use or are appropriated by activities producing transport costly goods. Instead, as one moves away from the center, it is the activity with the *steepest cost gradient*, defined here by the ratio t_i/a_i, that outbids the remaining activities, and secures the corresponding location. For example, if the activities use more or less the same amount of land per unit of output, the hard-to-transport goods, typically because they are perishable, are produced close to the market town, whereas the easier-to-ship goods are produced farther away from their consumption place. Conversely, if the transport rates are about the same across goods, land-intensive activities are located close to the market town, whereas land-extensive activities are developed far from the center.

Proposition 3.1 implies several other things. First, all activities are distributed around the center, which, therefore, appears to be the pivotal element in the spatial organization of production. Second, each location is specialized and activities are spatially segregated within rings of land. However, we see that, in other contexts (see Section 3.2.2), integrated configurations in which different activities are undertaken at the same locations may also arise in equilibrium. Last, any activity k such that

$$\Psi_k(r) < R^*(r) \qquad \text{for all } r \geq 0$$

has a zero output in equilibrium because it is unable to generate a surplus large enough to outbid the other activities anywhere in the plane.

Having this in mind, the following digression is in order. The market town may be viewed as the city-port of a small open economy. Once goods are gathered in the city-port, they may be sold within the country or exported to the rest of the world. In this case, the set of crops is primarily determined by the goods' prices that prevail on the international marketplace. Consequently, if the prices of the exported goods are sufficiently high, the goods consumed by the local population only may no longer be available because they generate too low surpluses. In other words, trade seems to be harmful to the local population since the inhabitants must pay higher prices to import the agricultural products they need. This argument must be qualified, however. As seen in the following discussion, the market distribution of crops generates the highest social surplus. Hence, the population is potentially better-off under trade because the surplus net of the costs of the imported goods is higher than the surplus made when the imported goods are locally produced. The key issue is the structure of property rights. If land is collectively owned, people are better-off. On the contrary, if the land rent is captured by absentee landlords or by an unproductive elite, people are worse-off. Therefore, trade per se is not harmful to the local population. What matters for the well-being of the local population is the ownership structure of land.

For notational simplicity, we assume from now on that all activities have a positive output in equilibrium. Without loss of generality, we can re-index the activities in decreasing order of the slope (in absolute value) of their bid rent functions:

$$t_1/a_1 \geq \ldots \geq t_n/a_n.$$

We now show how the land use equilibrium pattern can be determined by using the bid rent function. Because activity 1 generates the highest surplus in the immediate vicinity of the town, it uses a disk of land (that is, a ring with a zero inner radius) whose radius r_1^* must satisfy

$$\Psi_1(r_1^*) = \Psi_2(r_1^*)$$

that is,

$$r_1^* = \frac{p_1/a_1 - p_2/a_2}{t_1/a_1 - t_2/a_2}$$

beyond which activity 2 is undertaken because its surplus becomes higher than that of activity 1. Similarly, activity i $(= 2, \ldots, n-1)$ occupies a ring whose inner radius r_{i-1}^* is such that

$$\Psi_{i-1}(r_{i-1}^*) = \Psi_i(r_{i-1}^*)$$

whereas the outer radius r_i^* is the unique solution to

$$\Psi_i(r_i^*) = \Psi_{i+1}(r_i^*)$$

because the two bid rents are to be equal along the border between two adjacent rings. Solving this equation yields

$$r_i^* = \frac{p_i/a_i - p_{i+1}/a_{i+1}}{t_i/a_i - t_{i+1}/a_{i+1}}.$$

Finally, the external margin of land use is endogenously determined at the distance r_n^* from the market town at which

$$\Psi_n(r_n^*) = 0$$

because the opportunity cost of land is assumed to be zero:

$$r_n^* = p_n/t_n$$

so that land is used only within a bounded disk whose radius is given by r_n^*. Beyond this distance stands von Thünen's wilderness.

Because the equilibrium is competitive and there are no externalities, one expects the pattern of concentric rings to be socially optimal. That is, any other pattern in terms of size and shape would result in a lower *social surplus* S defined as the sum of crop surpluses minus transport costs:

$$S \equiv \sum_{i=1}^{n} p_i Q_i - \sum_{i=1}^{n} T_i \tag{3.4}$$

where Q_i is the output of activity i, and T_i is the corresponding transportation cost. Given (3.3), it is readily verified that the social surplus is here identical to the *aggregate land rent*.

Let $\theta_i(r) \geq 0$ denote the proportion of land used by activity i at distance r ($\sum_i \theta_i(r) \leq 1$). Then, because $2\pi r$ units of land are available at distance r, we have

$$Q_i = \int_0^{\infty} \theta_i(r) 2\pi r / a_i dr$$

and

$$T_i = \int_0^{\infty} [\theta_i(r) 2\pi r / a_i] t_i r dr.$$

Substituting Q_i and T_i into (3.4) and using (3.2), we obtain

$$S = 2\pi \int_0^{\infty} \left[\sum_{i=1}^{n} \theta_i(r) \Psi_i(r) \right] r dr.$$

Maximizing S with respect to $\theta_i(\cdot)$ is therefore equivalent to maximizing the bracketed term at each location r with respect to $\theta_i(r)$ subject to $\sum \theta_i(r) \leq 1$. Clearly, activity i is carried out at distance r if and only if $\Psi_i(r)$ is positive and the maximum of all bid rents. Therefore, both the optimum land use and market outcome are identical in the Thünen model, and both result in identical concentric rings.

Remark. It is worth mentioning that Koopmans and Beckmann (1957) also studied the *linear* assignment problem in which firm i receives revenue from its sales to the rest of the world, which is location-specific. In this setting, firms do not exchange goods directly. Instead, outputs and inputs are shipped to some preexisting marketplaces where they are sold and bought, as in the von Thünen model. By relaxing the integer constraints on firms, the linear assignment problem can be expressed as a linear program. von Neuman has showed that the solution of this linear program is given by integer numbers, which means that each firm is assigned to a single location. Because the shadow prices generated by the dual of this program are location-specific, these prices have the nature of land rents. Thus, a competitive equilibrium exists and the optimal solution may be decentralized through a competitive land market.

The preceding analysis can be readily extended to the case of several production factors if production functions are of the fixed coefficient variety and if the return of each factor other than land is the same across locations. The case of a neoclassical technology is more complex and is studied in Section 3.2.3.

The Thünen model can be closed by assuming that all agricultural activities need both land and labor whereas a $(n+1)$th manufactured good is produced in town by using labor alone, typically under the form of craftsmanship; such a specialization of tasks reflects the traditional division of labor between cities and the countryside. Workers are perfectly mobile between sectors and landlords reside in town; they all have identical (homothetic) preferences defined over the $(n+1)$ goods. The solution to such a general spatial equilibrium model, in which the real wage common to all workers as well as the prices of agricultural and manufactured goods are endogenous, has been studied by Samuelson (1983) when $n = 2$ and by Nerlove and Sadka (1991) when $n = 1$.

Thus, what remains to be explained is when a market town, which imports agricultural goods from and exports manufactured goods to its rural hinterland, emerges as an equilibrium outcome. To put it differently, *what binds together manufacturing firms and workers within a city?* This question has been at the heart of spatial economics for decades. In Chapter 10, we will answer this question by using a more general research strategy.

3.2.2 Technological Linkages and the Location of Activities

So far we have assumed that any produced good is shipped to the market town in which it is consumed. A well-known difficulty encountered in economics is to account for the existence of intermediate goods. It is interesting to figure out what the ring-shaped pattern obtained in the Thünian model becomes when some goods are used as inputs in the production of other goods. To the best of our knowledge, this problem was first modeled by Mills (1970; 1972a, chapter 5) and extended further by Goldstein and Moses (1975). These authors assumed that intra-area shipments go by the shortest route and need not be shipped through the town.

The main change in the spatial organization of production is that several goods may be produced simultaneously at the same location instead of being produced in separated locations, as in the preceding section. To illustrate the working of such an economy, we adopt a slightly modified version of Mills by assuming that only two goods are involved, good 2 being used only as an input for producing good 1, which is itself shipped to the market town to be sold at a given price p_1. We study this particular model in detail because it allows us to see how all the equilibrium conditions interact to determine the equilibrium configuration and why the assumption of complete markets is needed.

As before, the production of one unit of good i requires a fixed amount of land a_i. However, producing one unit of good 1 requires also b units of good 2.

Without loss of generality, the unit of good 2 is chosen for $b = 1$. Hence, it must be that $Q_1 = Q_2$.

It is worth noting that the equilibrium distance to the external land margin r_2 depends on the total production of good 1 but not on the way land is allocated between the two activities. Indeed, we have

$$a_1 Q_1 + a_2 Q_2 = (a_1 + a_2) Q_1 = \pi r_2^2$$

so that

$$r_2 = [(a_1 + a_2) Q_1 / \pi]^{1/2}.$$

An equilibrium configuration arises when no producer wants to change the location of his activity at the prevailing land rent and factor prices and when the market clearing conditions for the intermediate product hold. Because the model is linear, we may focus on the following two polar configurations: the integrated one, where both activities are undertaken together at each location, and the segregated one, where the two activities are separated as in Section 3.2.1. The spatial price equilibrium conditions imply that it is never profitable to transport good 2 when the configuration is integrated; when the configuration is segregated, they say that the price of good 2 at any location where good 1 is produced is equal to the cost for one unit of good 2 to be available at the border between the two areas plus the transport cost from the border point to the production point.

To identify the conditions under which each configuration emerges as an equilibrium, it is again useful to work with the bid rent function associated with each activity. If $p_2^*(r)$ stands for the equilibrium price of good 2 at r, the surplus per unit of land (or the bid rent) of activity i at each r is defined as follows:

$$\Psi_1(r) = \frac{p_1 - t_1 r - p_2^*(r)}{a_1} \tag{3.5}$$

$$\Psi_2(r) = \frac{p_2^*(r)}{a_2}. \tag{3.6}$$

First, consider an integrated configuration. For such a configuration to emerge, the two activities must have the *same* bid rent at each $r \leq r_2$, as illustrated in Figure 3.2. That is,

$$\frac{p_1 - t_1 r - p_2^*(r)}{a_1} = \frac{p_2^*(r)}{a_2}$$

or

$$p_2^*(r) = \frac{a_2}{a_1 + a_2}(p_1 - t_1 r). \tag{3.7}$$

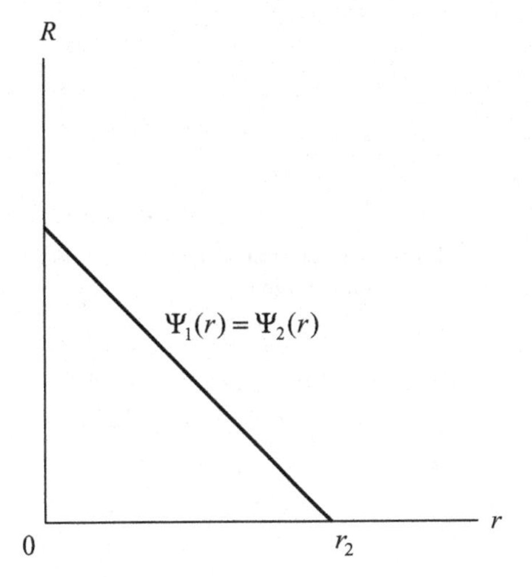

Figure 3.2. The rent profile for the integrated configuration.

Setting $\Psi_2(r) = 0$ (or $p_2^*(r) = 0$) at r_2, we obtain the fringe distance as follows:

$$r_2^* = p_1/t_1.$$

The integrated configuration is an equilibrium if and only if shipping good 2 must never be profitable. Since (3.7) is linear in distance, this amounts to

$$t_2 \geq \left| \frac{dp_2(r)}{dr} \right| = \frac{a_2 t_1}{a_1 + a_2}$$

or

$$\frac{t_2}{t_1} \geq \frac{a_2}{a_1 + a_2}. \tag{3.8}$$

This condition means that, given the relative intensity of land use in producing the two goods, shipping one unit of good 2 is more costly than shipping one unit of good 1, and thus it is preferable to save on the transport of 2 than on the transport of 1.

The case of a segregated configuration is more involved. Assume as in Figure 3.3 that good 1 is produced up to r_1, whereas good 2 is produced beyond r_1 up to r_2. Since the market for good 2 is competitive, everything works as if there were a marketplace for good 2 located in town, where this good is sold at some equilibrium price p_2^*. When good 2 is used at r, we have

$$p_2^*(r) = p_2^* - t_2 r. \tag{3.9}$$

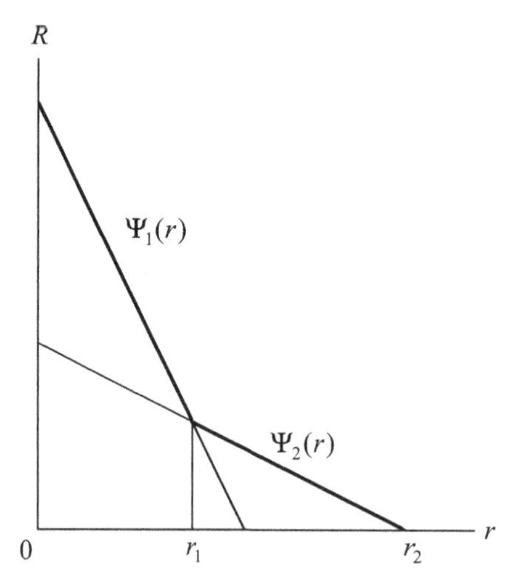

Figure 3.3. The rent profile for the segregated configuration.

Substituting (3.9) into (3.5) and (3.6) yields

$$\Psi_1(r) = \frac{p_1 - p_2^* - (t_1 - t_2)r}{a_1}$$

$$\Psi_2(r) = \frac{p_2^* - t_2 r}{a_2}.$$

The three unknowns, p_2^*, r_1, and r_2, can be determined by using the following equilibrium conditions. First, the two activities have the same bid rent at r_1:

$$\frac{p_1 - p_2^* - (t_1 - t_2)r_1}{a_1} = \frac{p_2^* - t_2 r_1}{a_2}.$$

Second, the bid rent of activity 2 is zero at r_2:

$$r_2 = p_2^*/t_2.$$

Third, $Q_1 = Q_2$ implies

$$\frac{\pi r_1^2}{a_1} = \frac{\pi(r_2^2 - r_1^2)}{a_2}$$

and thus

$$r_2 = \left(\frac{a_1 + a_2}{a_1}\right)^{1/2} r_1 \equiv k r_1$$

where $k > 1$. The three conditions above yield

$$r_1^* = \frac{a_2 p_1}{(k-1)(a_1 + a_2)t_2 + a_2 t_1}$$

$$r_2^* = \frac{a_2 k p_1}{(k-1)(a_1 + a_2)t_2 + a_2 t_1}$$

and

$$p_2^* = k t_2 r_1^*.$$

For the segregated configuration to be an equilibrium, as shown in Figure 3.3, the bid rent curve of crop 1 must intersect that of crop 2 from above at distance r_1^*, thus implying

$$-\frac{d\Psi_1(r)}{dr} \geq -\frac{d\Psi_2(r)}{dr}.$$

This amounts to

$$\frac{t_1 - t_2}{a_1} \geq \frac{t_2}{a_2}$$

or

$$\frac{t_2}{t_1} \leq \frac{a_2}{a_1 + a_2}. \tag{3.10}$$

To sum up, we have shown:

Proposition 3.2. *(i) If*

$$\frac{t_2}{t_1} \geq \frac{a_2}{a_1 + a_2}$$

holds, then the integrated configuration is an equilibrium.
(ii) If

$$\frac{t_2}{t_1} \leq \frac{a_2}{a_1 + a_2}$$

holds, then the segregated configuration is an equilibrium.

Though an equilibrium always exists, it involves positive transport costs. This does not contradict the spatial impossibility theorem because the existence of a center turns out to be a spatial inhomogeneity that facilitates coordinating producers' decisions. In addition, activities are perfectly divisible, which means that they do not have a restricted number of addresses. Furthermore, the equilibrium may involve positive interactivity transport costs as in the quadratic assignment problem studied in Chapter 2. This is so when the cost t_2 of shipping the intermediate good to the producers of good 1 is low relative to the cost t_1 of shipping the final product to the market town. In this case, the equilibrium involves specializing land in the production of good 1 in the vicinity of the center, whereas good 2 is produced farther away; the pattern of production is ring-shaped as in the Thünian model. Otherwise, the two activities are spatially integrated to save the interactivity transport costs because activities are perfectly divisible, unlike what was assumed in the quadratic assignment problem. Thus, in the presence of intermediate goods, the equilibrium does not necessarily involve spatial specialization.[8]

Consequently, when there are technological linkages, the type of spatial configuration emerging at the market solution varies with the relative value of the transportation rates. This has an important implication: The fall in transport costs observed since the beginning of the Industrial Revolution does not imply that activities become indifferent with respect to their location. Even though transport costs would decrease, what matters for the organization of space is their relative changes.

The set of equilibrium patterns becomes richer once we allow for a more general input-output structure and relax the assumption of an isolated state by permitting imports through the market town at given prices p_1 and p_2 (Goldstein and Moses 1975). For example, when each activity uses the output of the other, if there are no imports, the inner ring is specialized in activity 1 whereas the outer ring involves integration: good 2 is produced for use in the first ring, but also for producing locally good 1 in the second ring, which, in turn, is used as a local input for producing good 2. When they compare their approach to the quadratic assignment model, Goldstein and Moses (1975, 77) are right when they claim:

> By setting up a model with two goods, and a marketing center we are able to reach an equilibrium with complete interdependence and positive transport costs.

We may thus safely conclude that the continuous approach to land use combined with the existence of a marketplace for the final goods lead to important results with nontrivial equilibria. Unfortunately, determining the market outcome becomes quickly intractable when the number of goods increases, due to the large number of possible special cases involved in characterizing equilibria. However, we have seen that there is never outward shipment of goods in equilibrium: either good 2 is consumed on the spot (as in the case of an integrated configuration) or transported toward the inner ring (as in the case of a segregated configuration). Schweizer and Varaiya (1976) have shown that, in the general case of n goods under any Leontief technology in which goods may be used both in the final and intermediate sectors, the equilibrium always

[8] See Chapter 6 for a similar result in a different context.

involves one-way trade: goods are either shipped toward the marketplace or used locally.

As seen previously, the work by Koopmans and Beckmann (1957) has been at the origin of a long-standing debate about the (im)possibility of decentralizing the optimal configuration in a spatial economy. Of course, for this question to be addressed properly, one must work within a framework in which nontrivial competitive equilibria exist. In this perspective, Proposition 3.2 offers an interesting starting point. Furthermore, Mills (1970; 1972a, chapter 5) also showed that, in the model discussed above, the integrated solution is socially optimal if and only if (3.8) is verified, that is, when it pays to save on the transport of the intermediate good despite the need of shipping the final good to the center. On the contrary, when (3.10) holds, it is the segregated configuration that is socially desirable because it now pays to economize on the cost of shipping the final product. In both cases, the optimum can be sustained as an equilibrium. This turns out to be a fairly general property: Schweizer and Varaiya (1976) have shown that, in a monocentric economy, the optimal configuration can always be sustained by a decreasing and convex land rent in the general case of n goods. Therefore, in a monocentric economy with divisible activities and technological linkages, the second welfare theorem holds.

Accordingly, the existence of intermediate goods need not prevent the existence of a competitive equilibrium when activities are perfectly divisible and when there exists a single marketplace for the final goods. In addition, the analysis of Mills reveals that any equilibrium is an optimum, that is, the first welfare theorem also holds (Goldstein and Moses 1975). Again this seems to be fairly robust in the case of divisible activities, though a general result comparable to Schweizer and Varaiya is missing. The divisibility of activities makes the accessibility of an activity to the others potentially free since an integrated configuration is always feasible, whereas the existence of a single marketplace is a spatial inhomogeneity that plays the role of a coordination device among producers. In such a context, there is no market failure. We see an example of such a result in Section 3.3.3.

3.2.3 The Case of a Neoclassical Technology

Even though Thünen is considered the founder of marginalism, his model still belongs to the realm of classical economics to the extent that it assumes fixed technological coefficients. A more modern approach is obtained once substitution between land and labor is allowed. This problem was tackled by Beckmann (1972b), who considered the case of a neoclassical Cobb–Douglas production function, but more general well-behaved production functions could be similarly considered. Here we present a slightly more general analysis of this problem in that the parameter of this function may vary across activities. We assume that the assumptions of Section 3.2.1 are still valid, but (3.1) is now replaced by

$$q_i(r) = f[x_i(r)] = [x_i(r)]^{\alpha_i}$$

where $x_i(r)$ denotes the quantity of labor units used per unit of land, whereas $q_i(r)$ is the output of good i per unit of land. In this expression, $0 < \alpha_i < 1$ stands for the substitution parameter between land and labor for good i. Hence the marginal productivity of labor is positive and decreasing; the marginal productivity of land, given by $f(x_i) - x_i f'(x_i)$, is also positive and decreasing.

The profits $\pi_i(r)$ per unit of land earned by a producer at location r are then given by

$$\pi_i(r) = (p_i - t_i r)q_i - wx_i - R(r) \tag{3.11}$$

where w is the wage rate, which is assumed to be given and constant across locations. Therefore, the corresponding profit-maximizing demand for labor is

$$x_i^*(r) = \left[\frac{\alpha_i(p_i - t_i r)}{w}\right]^{\frac{1}{1-\alpha_i}} \qquad \text{for } r \leq \frac{p_i}{t_i}. \tag{3.12}$$

Accordingly, for each activity, less and less labor is used as one moves away from the market town so that the equilibrium output is decreasing and continuous in the distance to the market town. Plugging (3.12) into (3.11) and setting $\pi_i(r) = 0$ allows us to determine the maximum surplus that activity i may generate at location r. Consequently, the bid rent function associated with this activity is now defined by

$$\Psi_i(r) = (1 - \alpha_i)(\alpha_i/w)^{\beta_i}(p_i - t_i r)^{1+\beta_i} \qquad \text{for } r \leq \frac{p_i}{t_i}$$

where $\beta_i \equiv \alpha_i/(1 - \alpha_i) > 0$. Hence, each bid rent function is decreasing and strictly convex in distance.

Using the same argument as in Section 3.2.1, it may be shown that the equilibrium land rent is now given by

$$\begin{aligned} R^*(r) &\equiv \max\left\{\max_{i=1,\dots,n} \Psi_i(r), 0\right\} \\ &= \max\left\{\max_{i=1,\dots,n} (1 - \alpha_i)(\alpha_i/w)^{\beta_i}(p_i - t_i r)^{1+\beta_i}, 0\right\} \end{aligned}$$

and thus:

Proposition 3.3. *If production is described by a homogeneous linear Cobb-Douglas function and if the wage rate is constant across locations, then the* *equilibrium land rent is decreasing and strictly convex in distance to the market town.*

Hence, using a neoclassical production function does not affect the general pattern of location, which is still described by a set of specialized concentric rings, whereas the land rent keeps the same decreasing and convex shape, as in the Thünen model.

However, the simple and elegant condition describing the sequence of land use zones in the Thünen model does not hold anymore: the same crop may be raised within two different rings because Ψ_i and Ψ_j may intersect more than once. Furthermore, the employment level may not be a continuous and decreasing function across activities. We have seen that this function is continuous and decreasing within each ring but this does not necessarily hold at the border between two adjacent rings. Indeed, the equilibrium conditions imply that, at any distance r where activity i is undertaken, the land rent equals the marginal productivity of land whereas the wage equals the marginal productivity of labor, that is:

$$R(r) = (1 - \alpha_i)[x_i^*(r)]^{\alpha_i}(p_i - t_i r)$$

as well as

$$w = \alpha_i [x_i^*(r)]^{\alpha_i - 1}(p_i - t_i r).$$

Taking the ratio of these two expressions yields

$$\frac{R(r)}{w} = \frac{x_i^*(r)}{\beta_i}.$$

Because, at the border r_i^* between the i-th and $(i+1)$th rings, the same relationship holds for activity $i+1$ and since $R(r)/w$ is the same, it must be that

$$\frac{x_i^*(r_i^*)}{\beta_i} = \frac{x_{i+1}^*(r_i^*)}{\beta_{i+1}}.$$

Hence, the employment level is continuous across activities ($x_i^*(r_i^*) = x_{i+1}^*(r_i^*)$) if and only if the coefficients β_i are the same for all activities, that is, the production functions are identical for all activities. In this case, the equilibrium employment is a continuous and decreasing function of the distance to the market town across locations and activities.

On the other hand, if the coefficients α_i differ across activities there is a discontinuity in the employment level at the border between two adjacent rings. Nevertheless, this input might still be decreasing. Let us check when this is so. For $x_i^*(r_i^*) > x_{i+1}^*(r_i^*)$ to hold, it must be that $\beta_i < \beta_{i+1}$, that is, $\alpha_i > \alpha_{i+1}$. Therefore, in equilibrium, the labor input is decreasing (but not continuous) provided that the locations of activities are ordered by decreasing order of the share of labor in the production of goods. There is no reason to expect this condition to be satisfied at the equilibrium configuration. Though the consumption of land remains specialized and ring-shaped, it therefore appears that the employment level may jump up or down when land use shifts from one activity to the next once substitution between land and labor is allowed.

Note, finally, that the inspection of the market land rent $R^*(r)$ reveals that, for any given activity, the decrease in the land value no longer fully compensates for the corresponding increase of the transport cost. The change in land price now induces a substitution from labor to land as one moves away from the market town, thus making this relationship more involved. We return to this problem in Section 3.3.1.

3.2.4 Notes on the Literature

A lot of attention has been devoted to the possible re-switching of technologies as one moves away from the market town. The main results can be found Schweizer (1986).

3.3 THE URBAN LAND RENT

3.3.1 Residential Equilibrium in the Monocentric City

Two fundamental ideas lie at the heart of the economics of city structure: (i) people prefer shorter commuting trips to longer commuting trips and (ii) people prefer having more space than less space. Starting from these premises, the analysis of the internal structure of a monocentric city relies on the approach developed by Alonso (1964), Mills (1967), and Muth (1969), that is, *the households' trade-off between housing size and accessibility to the city center where jobs are available.*

To illustrate how this trade-off works, we consider a city with a prespecified center, called the central business district (CBD), where all jobs are located. For simplicity, the CBD is treated as a point, and space is assumed to be homogeneous except for the distance to the CBD. In this context, the only spatial characteristic of a location is its distance from the CBD, and thus the model is essentially one-dimensional. Compared with the Thünian model presented in Section 3.2.1, it therefore appears that the CBD replaces the market town, whereas the land available for raising crops is now used for housing. The land market works as if each household were to compare possible locations and evaluate, for each location, the maximum rent per unit of surface it would be willing to pay to live there. Each plot is then occupied by the household offering the highest bid. Competition for housing near the CBD where jobs are located leads households to pay a land rent that varies inversely with the distance between homes and jobs. Or, to put it differently, people trade bigger plots against higher commuting costs. Despite its simplicity, we see how the monocentric city model highlights a major principle of spatial economics, that is, *the land rent reflects the accessibility to a specific place endowed with features that economic agents value.*

Consider a continuum N of identical workers/consumers commuting directly to the CBD where they earn a given, fixed income Y. Each consumer has a utility U depending on the quantity z of a composite good, which is available everywhere at a price fixed by the world market, and the lot size s of housing.[9] It is assumed that U is strictly increasing in each good, twice continuously differentiable, strictly quasi-concave while both z and s are essential goods (every indifference curve has each axis as an asymptote). Furthermore, the lot size s is assumed to be a normal good. If a consumer is located at a distance r from the CBD, his budget constraint is then given by $z + R(r)s + T(r) = Y$ where $R(r)$ is the rent per unit of land at r and $T(r)$ is the commuting costs at r (the composite good is taken as numéraire). We suppose that there is no congestion in commuting while $T(r)$ is strictly increasing in distance and $0 \leq T(0) < Y < T(\infty)$.

The residential problem of the consumer can then be expressed as follows:

$$\max_{r,z,s} U(z, s) \qquad \text{s.t.} \quad z + sR(r) = Y - T(r) \tag{3.13}$$

where $Y - T(r)$ is the net income at r. The only difference from the standard consumer problem is that here the consumer must also choose a residential location $r \geq 0$, which affects the land rent he pays, his commuting cost and his consumption bundle. It should be clear that this problem encapsulates the trade-off between accessibility to the CBD, measured by $T(r)$, and the land consumption, measured by s.

Because consumers are identical in terms of preferences and income, at the *residential equilibrium* they reach the same utility level u^* regardless of their location. Observe the difference with the bid rent defined by (3.2) in the Thünian model in which it is implicitly assumed that the equilibrium profit level of activity i is zero. By contrast, the equilibrium utility level u is endogenous here because there are no in- or out-migrations. This makes the land market across locations interdependent. Yet, as in the Thünian model, we define the bid rent function $\Psi(r, u)$ of a consumer as the maximum rent per unit of land that he is willing to pay at distance r while enjoying the utility level u.[10]

[9] In order to focus on lot size and population density changes within the city, we use a simple utility with two arguments, z and s. However, the model can be extended to the case of several consumption goods as well as to nonland input for housing (Fujita 1989, 44).

[10] The bid rent function approach followed here is essentially the same as the indirect utility function approach used by Solow (1973) and is, therefore, closely related to duality theory as developed in microeconomics.

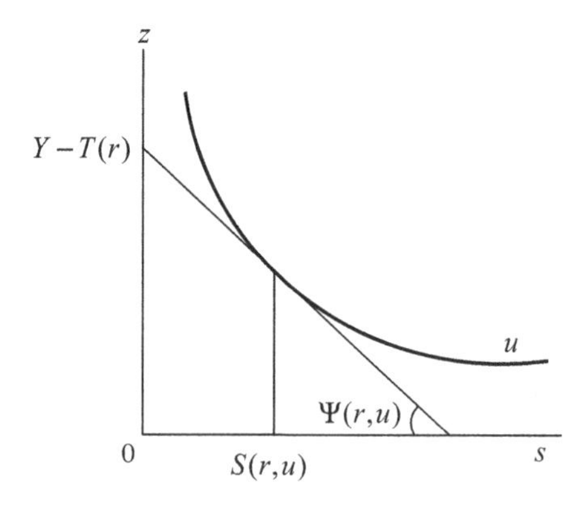

Figure 3.4. The equilibrium consumption bundle at r.

Given (3.13), we have

$$\Psi[Y - T(r), u] \equiv \Psi(r, u) = \max_{z,s} \left\{ \frac{Y - T(r) - z}{s} \quad \text{s.t.} \quad U(z, s) = u \right\}. \tag{3.14}$$

Indeed, for the consumer residing at distance r and selecting the consumption bundle (z, s), $Y - T(r) - z$ is the money available for land. As a result, $(Y - T(r) - z)/s$ represents the rent per unit of land at r. The bid rent $\Psi(r, u)$ is then obtained by choosing the utility-maximizing consumption bundle (z, s) subject to the constraint $U(z, s) = u$.[11]

Because U is strictly increasing in z, the equation $U(z, s) = u$ has a unique solution denoted by $Z(s, u)$. It is readily verified that the quantity $Z(s, u)$ of the composite good is strictly decreasing, strictly convex, strictly increasing in u, and such that $\lim_{s \to 0} Z(s, u) = \infty$. Consequently, (3.14) can be rewritten as follows:

$$\Psi(r, u) = \max_{s} \frac{Y - T(r) - Z(s, u)}{s}. \tag{3.15}$$

It follows from this expression that the equilibrium consumption bundle of a consumer located at r is obtained at the tangency point between the budget line whose slope equals $\Psi(r, u)$ and the indifference curve of level u in the positive orthant of the (z, s)-plane, as illustrated in Figure 3.4.

For each r at which the net income $Y - T(r)$ is positive, the unique solution to (3.15) is denoted by $S(r, u)$.

The price of the composite good being 1, the indirect utility when the land rent is R and the net income I is denoted $V(R, I)$. By definition of the bid rent,

[11] Because U is strictly quasi-concave, the utility-maximizing bundle (z, s) exists and is unique as long as the net income $Y - T(r)$ is positive.

we have the identity:

$$u \equiv V\left[\Psi(r,u), Y - T(r)\right]. \tag{3.16}$$

The land consumption $S(r,u)$ is given by the Marshallian demand $\hat{s}(R, I)$. Because consumers have the same utility level across space, $\hat{s}(R, I)$ is also equal to the Hicksian demand $\tilde{s}(R, u)$:

$$S(r,u) \equiv \hat{s}\left[\Psi(r,u), Y - T(r)\right] \equiv \tilde{s}\left[\Psi(r,u), u\right]. \tag{3.17}$$

In other words, when a consumer changes his location r, his bid rent is adjusted for his utility level to remain the same.

We are now prepared to characterize the bid rent and the lot size functions. Differentiating (3.15) and applying the envelope theorem, we obtain

$$\frac{d\Psi(r,u)}{dr} = -\frac{T'(r)}{S(r,u)} < 0 \tag{3.18}$$

because $T(r)$ is strictly increasing in r. Thus, using (3.17) yields

$$\frac{dS(r,u)}{dr} = \frac{\partial \tilde{s}}{\partial R}\frac{d\Psi(r,u)}{dr} = -\frac{\partial \tilde{s}}{\partial R}\frac{T'(r)}{S(r,u)} > 0 \tag{3.19}$$

because the Hicksian demand for land is strictly decreasing in land price.

Similarly, we have

$$\frac{d\Psi(r,u)}{du} = -\frac{1}{S(r,u)}\frac{\partial Z(s,u)}{\partial u} < 0 \tag{3.20}$$

because $Z(s,u)$ is strictly increasing in u. In other words, households' willingness-to-pay for one unit of land decreases when a higher utility level is sustainable, e.g., when the income Y rises. Indeed, when households are richer, the income share devoted to commuting decreases, and thus proximity to the CBD matters less. Note, however, that

$$\frac{dS(r,u)}{du} = \frac{\partial \tilde{s}}{\partial R}\frac{d\Psi(r,u)}{du} > 0 \tag{3.21}$$

which means that these households consume a larger land plot.

Thus, we have shown:

Proposition 3.4. *The bid rent function is continuously decreasing in both r and u (until it becomes zero). Furthermore, the lot size function is continuously increasing in both r and u.*

When $T(r)$ is linear or concave in distance, $\Psi(r,u)$ is strictly convex in r as shown by differentiating (3.18) with respect to r and using (3.19).

We now turn to the description of the equilibrium conditions for the monocentric city in which N homogeneous consumers have a given income Y earned at the CBD. Landowners are assumed to be absentee, and thus the land rent is not distributed to consumers. The equilibrium utility u^* is the maximum utility attainable in the city under the market land rent $R^*(r)$. Using (3.16), we obtain

$$u^* = \max_r V\left[R^*(r), Y - T(r)\right] \tag{3.22}$$

which is the common utility level in equilibrium.

If one differentiates (3.16) with respect to r and uses Roy's identity, the utility-maximizing choice of a location by a consumer at the residential equilibrium implies

$$S(r, u^*)\frac{dR^*(r)}{dr} + \frac{dT(r)}{dr} = 0. \tag{3.23}$$

That is, at the residential equilibrium, changes in *housing costs* evaluated at the utility-maximizing land consumption are balanced by the corresponding changes in *commuting costs*. In particular, when the lot size is fixed and normalized to 1 ($s = 1$), we get a "flat city" in which (3.23) becomes $dR^*(r)/dr + dT(r)/dr = 0$, and thus

$$R^*(r) + T(r) = \text{constant}. \tag{3.24}$$

In this case, as in the Thünian model, the shape of the land rent is the opposite of the shape of the commuting cost function, whereas the consumption of the composite good is the same across consumers. To put it differently, housing plus commuting costs are the same across the city. By contrast, when the lot size is variable, that mirror relationship ceases to hold. Unexpectedly, however, these two magnitudes remain closely related at the aggregate level: If commuting costs are linear in distance, then the aggregate differential land rent is just equal to total commuting costs when the city is linear, whereas it equals half the total commuting costs when the city is circular (Arnott 1979; 1981).

Let $n(r)$ be the consumer density at distance r in equilibrium. Then, we have

$$\begin{aligned} R^*(r) &= \Psi(r, u^*) \qquad \text{if} \quad n(r) > 0 \\ R^*(r) &> \Psi(r, u^*) \qquad \text{if} \quad n(r) = 0. \end{aligned}$$

If it is assumed that land not occupied by consumers is used for agriculture yielding a constant rent $R_A \geq 0$, the city fringe arises at distance r^* such that

$$\Psi(r^*, u^*) = R_A. \tag{3.25}$$

The bid rent being decreasing in r by Proposition 3.4, the residential area is given by a disk centered at the CBD having radius r^*. As a consequence, the market land rent is given by

$$R^*(r) = \begin{cases} \Psi(r, u^*) & \text{for} \quad r \leq r^* \\ R_A & \text{for} \quad r \geq r^* \end{cases}. \tag{3.26}$$

Because no land is vacant within the urban fringe, we must have

$$n(r) = 2\pi r / S(r, u^*) \qquad \text{for all } r \leq r^* \tag{3.27}$$

and thus the total population N within the urban area must satisfy

$$\int_0^{r^*} \frac{2\pi r}{S(r, u^*)} dr = N. \tag{3.28}$$

In summary, the residential equilibrium is described by $R^*(r)$, $n^*(r)$, u^* and r^* satisfying the conditions (3.25) through (3.28). Under the preceding assumptions made about preferences, income and commuting costs, the existence of a unique residential equilibrium can be shown to hold (Fujita 1989, Proposition 3.1).

Proposition 3.4 and (3.26) imply that within the urban area the market land rent is decreasing as one moves away from the CBD as in the Thünian model. Denoting the population density at r by $\delta(r) \equiv n^*(r)/2\pi r$, we see from (3.27) that

$$\delta(r) = 1/S(r, u^*).$$

We may then conclude from Proposition 3.4 that *the equilibrium population density is decreasing from the CBD to the urban fringe*, whereas the equilibrium land consumption simultaneously rises. In other words, consumers trade more (less) space for housing against a lower (higher) accessibility to the CBD in a way that allows them to reach the same highest utility level across locations. In monetary terms, a consumer paying a high (low) price for land bears low (high) commuting costs but the compensation is not necessarily exact because the consumption of the composite good also changes with r. Indeed, each consumer residing farther away from the city center has a larger consumption of land and a smaller consumption of the composite good for the utility level to be the same across the city.[12] Accordingly, *space is sufficient to render heterogeneous consumers who are otherwise homogeneous*.

Therefore, the equilibrium city accommodating a population of N consumers is described by a circular area centered at the CBD. The consumer density as well as the land rent fall as the distance to the city center rises. This provides an explanation for the fairly general empirical fact that the population density is higher near the city center (where housing costs are high) than at the city outskirts (where housing costs are low). In addition, the size of the residential area depends on the opportunity cost of land but also on the number of consumers, their income, and the value of their commuting costs to the CBD. These relations are used in Section 3.3.2 to explain another major fact about urban areas, namely suburbanization.

[12] As seen in the foregoing, there is exact compensation when the lot size is fixed.

3.3.2 Comparative Statics of the Residential Equilibrium

We can now perform some comparative statics that shed additional light on real world issues. First, an increase in the population size has fairly straightforward effects. Indeed, a rising population makes competition for land fiercer, which in turn leads to an increase in land rent everywhere and pushes the urban fringe outward. This corresponds to a well-documented fact stressed by economic historians. Examples include the growth of cities in Europe in the twelfth and nineteenth centuries as well as in North America and Japan in the twentieth century or since the 1960s in Third World countries. All were caused by demographic expansion and rural–urban migrations resulting from technological progress in agriculture, which freed some population from agricultural activity (Bairoch 1988, chapters 10 and 14; Hohenberg and Lees 1985, chapter 8). As a result, the inhabitants of a city facing an inflow of migrants bear higher housing and commuting costs, a force that limits the agglomeration of activities within a city. To see how this works, consider the simple case where the lot size is fixed. Using (3.24), we obtain $R^*(r) + T(r) = R_A + T(N/2)$, which is indeed an increasing function of the population size N.

We now investigate the impact of a rise in consumers' income Y. Using (3.25) and (3.28), we can readily verify that the residential area expands because the urban fringe moves outward. Although all consumers are clearly strictly better off, the impact on the land rent and the population density is less obvious. An increase in consumers' income raises demand for land everywhere. However, it also leads to a decrease in the relative value of commuting costs, thus making locations in the suburbs more desirable than before the income rise. Consequently, because enough land is available in the suburbs (recall that the additional land available between r and $r + dr$ is $2\pi r dr$), a substantial segment of the population moves from the center to the suburbs. This in turn decreases the land rent and the population density near the CBD but increases them in the suburbs. In other words, both the land rent and the population density become flatter. Because the locational decision of a consumer is governed by his net income, decreasing the commuting costs has exactly the same impact as increasing Y. We may then conclude that, since the development of modern transportation means (mass transportation and cars) that have followed the Industrial Revolution, income has increased and commuting costs have decreased, generating both suburbanization and a flattening of the urban population densities in many American and European cities (Bairoch 1988, chapter 19; Hohenberg and Lees 1985, chapter 9).

Finally, consider an increase in the opportunity cost of land as measured by the agricultural land rent R_A. Using (3.25) and (3.28), one can show that the urban fringe shrinks, whereas the equilibrium utility level falls as R_A rises. Then, Proposition 3.4 implies that both the market land rent and consumer density are higher at any distance within the new urban fringe. Hence a higher opportunity cost of land leads to a more compact city with more consumers at each location paying a higher land rent. Increasing the opportunity cost of land therefore leads to more concentrated populations and less well-being for consumers, as suggested by the current situation in many cities in Japan or other countries in East Asia. A high opportunity cost for land may be due to the relative scarcity of land, but it may also find its origin in public policies that maintain the prices of agricultural products far above the international level.[13] This also explains why, for centuries, the spatial extension of towns was limited by returns in agricultural activities as well as by the transport means available to ship produce (Bairoch 1988, chapter 1).

3.3.3 Efficiency of the Residential Equilibrium

It remains to discuss the efficiency of the residential equilibrium. Because this equilibrium is competitive (consumers are price-takers) and no externalities are involved, the first welfare theorem suggests that the equilibrium is efficient. However, we have here a continuum of commodities (land), and thus we need a more specific argument.

It is well known in urban economics that using a utilitarian welfare function leads to the unequal treatment of equals (Mirrlees 1972), whereas equals are equally treated in equilibrium. Such a difference is unexpected, and one might think that competition for space leads to strong social inefficiencies even though our economy is competitive. However, Wildasin (1986a) has shown that this pseudo-paradox arises because the marginal utility of income is different across consumers at different locations. Using a utilitarian approach is therefore unjustified. This fact invites us to consider an alternative approach in which the utility level is fixed across identical consumers.

Assume, then, that all consumers achieve the equilibrium utility level u^* and check whether there exists another feasible allocation $(n(r), z(r), s(r);$ $0 \leq r \leq \hat{r})$ that sustains u^* and reduces the social cost C. Note that such an allocation maximizes a Rawlsian welfare function (maximizing the minimum utility level in the economy) when the social planner cannot use lump-sum transfers. This has major implications that are be discussed in subsequent chapters.

[13] According to Ohmae (1995, 48), "within a 50-kilometer radius of Tokyo, 65 percent of land – nearly 330,000 hectares of some of the most expensive property in the world – is devoted to widely inefficient agriculture. If only one quarter of this land were sold for private housing, Tokyo-area families would be able to afford 120 to 150 square meters of living space, instead of today's average of 88 square meters. Moreover, cheaper – and more available – land would cut the cost of essential public work like providing better sewage, removing traffic bottlenecks, and double-tracking commuter trains." In the same spirit, restrictions on building height are also restrictions on the supply of living space. For example, Glaeser (2011) provides ample evidence of the perverse effects generated by the web of regulation prevailing in Manhattan that results in artificially high housing prices, which benefit the incumbents at the expense of newcomers who are relegated to distant neighborhoods.

In our model, the social cost for N consumers to enjoy the utility level u^* is obtained by summing the commuting costs, the composite good cost and the opportunity land cost borne by society for this to be possible. Let $Z(s(r), u^*)$ be the quantity of the composite good for which $U[Z(s(r), u^*), s(r)] = u^*$. In consequence, we want to minimize the function

$$C = \int_0^{\hat{r}} \left[T(r) + Z(s(r), u^*) + R_A s(r)\right] n(r)dr \tag{3.29}$$

subject to the land constraint

$$s(r)n(r) = 2\pi r \qquad \text{for all } r \leq \hat{r} \tag{3.30}$$

and the population constraint

$$\int_0^{\hat{r}} n(r)dr = N. \tag{3.31}$$

Using (3.30) and (3.31), we readily verify that minimizing (3.29) amounts to solving the following maximization problem:

$$\max_{\hat{r}, s(r)} S = 2\pi \int_0^{\hat{r}} \left[\frac{Y - T(r) - Z(s(r), u^*)}{s(r)} - R_A\right] r dr$$

subject to (3.31) in which $n(r) = 2\pi r/s(r)$.

Neglecting for the moment the population constraint, we may solve this problem by maximizing $[Y - T(r) - Z(s(r), u^*)]/s(r)$ with respect to $s(r)$ at each $r \leq \hat{r}$. By definition of $S(r, u^*)$, it must be that the efficient land consumption $s(r)$ is identical to the equilibrium land consumption for each $r \leq \hat{r}$, a condition which holds if and only if

$$\frac{Y - T(r) - Z[s(r), u^*]}{s(r)} = \Psi(r, u^*) \qquad \text{for all } r \leq \hat{r}$$

where $\Psi(r, u^*)$ is the bid rent given by (3.15). Therefore, in order to maximize S, $\hat{r}$ must satisfy

$$\Psi(r, u^*) = R_A$$

because $\Psi(r, u^*)$ is decreasing in r. Since this equation has a unique solution, it must be that $\hat{r} = r^*$. Given (3.28), it is easily seen that $(s(r), \hat{r})$ satisfies the population constraint (3.31) because $s(r) = S(r, u^*)$ and $\hat{r} = r^*$. Consequently, we may conclude as follows:

Proposition 3.5. *The residential equilibrium is efficient.*

3.3.4 Social Stratification and Amenities

In the Thünian model, we have seen that the presence of intermediate goods gives rise to two types of configurations, segregated or integrated (Section 3.2.2). A related question in understanding the working of a city is to determine how consumers with different incomes organize themselves within the city. As in the Thünian model, *each location is occupied by the consumers with the highest bid rent*. Therefore, land being a normal good, we do not observe an integrated configuration because consumers endowed with different incomes have different bid rent functions and there is no direct interaction among them (e.g., home services from the poor to the rich). Hence, the residential equilibrium involves segregation. What remains to be determined, however, is the shape of the corresponding *social stratification* at the residential equilibrium. However, we see in the last section that an integrated configuration involving households and farmers may emerge when the former value the rural amenities generated by the latter.

3.3.4.1 Why Is Downtown Detroit Poor?

Consider the simple case of a finite number m of income classes with N_i consumers in class i; without loss of generality, we assume that $Y_1 < Y_2 < \cdots < Y_m$. All consumers have the same preferences $U(s, z)$, face the same commuting costs $T(r)$, and are a priori indifferent about their residential location. Replacing Y with Y_i in (3.15), we denote by $\Psi_i(r, u_i^*)$ the bid rent function of the i-th income class and by $S_i(r, u_i^*)$ the associated land consumption. It then follows from (3.18) that

$$\frac{d\Psi_i(r, u_i^*)}{dr} = -\frac{T'(r)}{S_i(r, u_i^*)} < 0$$

for all $i = 1, \ldots, m$. Because a given group occupies the area of the city where it outbids the other groups, the social stratification results from the ranking of the bid rent functions in terms of their slope in a sense that is now defined.

If the social groups $j < k$ occupy adjacent plots, the land rent must the same for the two groups at the boundary $\bar{r}$ separating them. As a consequence, wherever the two bid rent curves $\Psi_j(r, u_j^*)$ and $\Psi_k(r, u_k^*)$ intersect at $\bar{r} \geq 0$, (3.17) and the normality of land imply the following inequality:

$$\begin{aligned} S_j(\bar{r}, u_j^*) &\equiv \hat{s}\left[\Psi_j(\bar{r}, u_j^*), Y_j - T(\bar{r})\right] < \hat{s}\left[\Psi_k(\bar{r}, u_k^*), Y_k - T(\bar{r})\right] \\ &\equiv S_k(\bar{r}, u_k^*). \end{aligned}$$

Hence, by (3.18), $\Psi_j(r, u_j^*)$ is steeper than $\Psi_k(r, u_k^*)$ at $\bar{r}$:[14]

$$\Delta = -\frac{T'(\bar{r})}{S_j(\bar{r}, u_j^*)} + \frac{T'(\bar{r})}{S_k(\bar{r}, u_k^*)} < 0.$$

In other words, consumers of class j (k) outbid those of class k (j) on the left (right) side of $\bar{r}$. Repeating the same argument for each pair (j, k) of income classes, we find that the N_1 consumers of the lowest income class occupy a disk of land centered at the CBD, the N_2 consumers with the second-lowest income occupy a ring surrounding this disk, . . . , and the N_m consumers belonging to the richest class are situated in the outermost ring. Thus, we have the following:

Proposition 3.6. *Assume that consumers have the same preferences and commuting cost function. Then, the social stratification of consumers within the city obeys the rule of concentric rings such that the consumer classes are ranked by increasing income as the distance from the CBD rises.*

Although some American central cities have rich enclaves, this result sheds light on the stylized fact that, in many U.S. cities, the poor live near the city center and the wealthy in the suburbs. Proposition 3.6 also offers a new perspective into the political economy of the city. An increase in the income of the rich consumers relaxes competition for land because these consumers move farther away from the center, making all income groups better off. On the other hand, raising the income of the poor consumers intensifies competition for land and pushes the rich farther away in the suburbs; eventually the poor people are better off but the rich ones are worse off. This suggests a potential conflict between the two classes: the poor have no objection to the rich class becoming richer, but the latter may find it better to keep the poor class poor. This agrees with the fact that shocks in the income distribution induce the development of particular urban sections at the expense of others, whereas the rich class members often try to lobby urban governments to implement restrictive zoning policies.

Having said this, we must acknowledge that this proposition is far from providing a complete answer to the stratification problem. Neglected factors governing the distribution of consumers over the urban space include the size of the family, the value of commuting time, and the financial support of the school system. Although we do not study these factors exhaustively, their impact can be summarized as follows:

1. A larger family has a stronger preference for space, which makes it live farther away from the CBD to benefit from the lower land rent prevailing there (Beckmann 1973).

[14] Note that the lot size is discontinuous at the border between two adjacent social areas. This corresponds to the discontinuity observed in the employment level at the border between two adjacent zones of production in the neoclassical model of land use of Section 3.2.2.

2. The previous proposition relies on the assumption that all consumers face the same commuting costs so that their share in consumers' expenditure falls with their income. If higher income workers place a higher value on their commuting time, they face a trade-off between a higher land demand (due to normality of land) and the extra value of commuting time. As a result, the low-income consumers reside near the center and the middle-class consumers in the suburbs; however, now the high-salary professionals and working couples choose to reside close to the CBD, because of their high value of time, in an urban section different from that of the poor consumers (Fujita 1989, chapter 2).

To illustrate, consider two income groups, the rich and the poor ($m = 2$ and $Y_1 < Y_2$). Rich households have a higher opportunity cost of time, and thus a higher commuting cost per mile, than the poor. Therefore, the rich value the accessibility to the CBD more than the poor. The net effect of these forces hinges on the behavior of the ratio of marginal commuting cost per mile and housing consumption. For example, if workers' commuting costs are proportional to their incomes, $T(r)Y_i$, we have

$$\Delta = -\frac{T'(\bar{r})Y_1}{S_1(\bar{r}, u_1^*)} + \frac{T'(\bar{r})Y_2}{S_2(\bar{r}, u_2^*)}$$

which is positive if the income share spent on housing at $\bar{r}$ by the poor exceeds that of the rich:

$$\frac{R(\bar{r})S_1(\bar{r}, u_1^*)}{Y_1} > \frac{R(\bar{r})S_2(\bar{r}, u_2^*)}{Y_2}.$$

In this case, the rich locate near the CBD and the poor in the outer ring.

3. Decentralizing the supply of local public goods within a city strengthens the spatial sorting of households based on income differences. Indeed, high-income consumers can afford to pay for high-quality public services provided in districts populated by households having similar socioeconomic characteristics, while low-income consumers can pay only for low-quality services (Henderson and Thisse 2001). In particular, when the financing of education is decentralized, families valuing more education (who are often those with higher incomes) similarly cluster in order to supply a better education to their offsprings. This results in higher human capital in the corresponding neighborhoods, thus perpetuating social and spatial segregation because the integrated equilibrium is unstable whereas the segregated one is stable (Bénabou 1994).

3.3.4.2 Why Is Central Paris Rich?

Many European cities, such as London, Paris, Barcelona, or Rome, display a social stratification that vastly differs from the one observed in the United States: the high-income people are located by the city center and the poor in the outer suburbs (Hohenberg and Lees 1985).[15] This difference may be explained by the fact that those cities have well-preserved historical centers (Bruekner, Thisse, and Zenou 1999).

Historical amenities are generated by monuments, buildings, parks, and other urban infrastructure from past eras that are pleasing to residents. Because these amenities are exogenous, they can be viewed as a causal factor in determining the pattern of location. In this case, households display a "love for the city center," and thus their preferences depend on housing consumption s and consumption of a composite good z, as well as on amenities $a(r)$, which is viewed as a local public good subject to a distance-decay effect. Thus, the indirect utillity is now given by $V(R, I, a(r))$.

Differentiating the spatial equilibrium condition and using the envelope theorem yields the expression:

$$-T'(r) - \frac{d\Psi_i(r, u_i^*)}{dr} S_i(r) + \frac{\partial V}{\partial a}\frac{da(r)}{dr} = 0$$

and thus

$$\frac{d\Psi_i(r, u_i^*)}{dr} = \frac{1}{S_i(r, u_i^*)}\left[-T'(r) + \frac{\partial V}{\partial a}\frac{da(r)}{dr}\right] \tag{3.32}$$

where the marginal value of amenities $\partial V/\partial a$ is evaluated *after* the optimal adjustment of housing consumption. Hence, when amenities decline with distance, the land rent must compensate for inferior amenities as well as the high cost of commuting.

Using (3.32), we readily verify that the difference Δ between the slopes of the bid rent functions at $\bar{r}$ for $j < k$ is given by

$$\Delta = -\frac{T'(\bar{r})}{S_j(\bar{r}, u_j^*)} + \frac{T'(\bar{r})}{S_k(\bar{r}, u_k^*)} + \frac{1}{S_j(\bar{r}, u_j^*)}\left.\frac{\partial V}{\partial a}\right|_{S_j}\frac{da(\bar{r})}{dr}$$
$$- \frac{1}{S_k(\bar{r}, u_k^*)}\left.\frac{\partial V}{\partial a}\right|_{S_k}\frac{da(\bar{r})}{dr}. \tag{3.33}$$

For the social stratification obtained in Proposition 3.6 to be reversed, this expression must be positive. This is so if historical landmarks appeal to high-income and educated households. For example, Glaeser (2011) observes that New Yorkers who live in the historic districts of Manhattan are on average 70 per cent wealthier than those who live outside such areas. With such numbers

[15] Ingram and Carroll (1981) observe that this pattern also exists in a number of Latin American cities

in mind, we find it reasonable to assume that the marginal valuation of historic amenities (after adjustment of s) rises with income faster than housing:[16]

$$\frac{1}{S_j(\bar{r}, u_j^*)} \left.\frac{\partial V}{\partial a}\right|_{S_j} - \frac{1}{S_k(\bar{r}, u_k^*)} \left.\frac{\partial V}{\partial a}\right|_{S_k} < 0.$$

If $da(r)/dr < 0$ is small in absolute value, then the entire amenity term in (3.33) is positive but close to zero. The negative sign of the first two terms of (3.33) (recall that $S_i(\bar{r}) < S_j(\bar{r})$) will then dominate. Thus, if the center's amenity advantage over the suburbs is weak, the United States location pattern holds: the poor live in the center and the rich live in the suburbs.

On the other hand, if $da(r)/dr$ is large in absolute value, then the amenity term dominates the conventional forces in determining the sign of Δ. In other words, if the center has a large amenity advantage, so that amenities fall rapidly with distance, then the United States pattern is reversed: the rich live in the city center and the poor live in the suburbs. This corresponds to the case of Paris, which has a steep amenity gradient and central location of the rich. In contrast, since an American urban area like Detroit lacks the rich history of Paris, the central-city's infrastructure does not offer appreciable aesthetic benefits. This means that no amenity force is working to reverse the conventional forces that draw the rich to the suburbs. As a result, central Detroit is poor.

Superior amenities make the central city rich, while weak amenities make it poor. Because location by income is now linked to a city's idiosyncratic features, the multiplicity of observed location patterns around the world becomes explicable. In particular, Europe's longer history provides an obvious reason why its central cities contain more buildings and monuments of historical significance than do cities in the United States. Many European cities were major metropolises at a time when much of the United States had not even been settled, and the legacy of urban development from this distant past provides an atmosphere in European city centers that appears to be highly valued by the residents. In addition to the effect of a longer history, government investment in central-city infrastructure appears in many cases to have been more extensive in European cities than in the United States.

Note also that the pattern of exogenous amenities differs across cities because a central city's historical amenities are determined mainly by past government decisions regarding investments in urban infrastructure. However, although the concept itself might suggest otherwise, historical amenities depreciate over time, which means that their maintenance requires ongoing investment. If such expenditures were withheld, the central city's amenities would decay, and high-income residents would be increasingly drawn to the suburbs (Bruekner et al., 1999).

[16] This assumption is consistent with familiar specifications of preferences. For example, Bruekner et al. (1999) shows that it holds under CES preferences when the elasticity of substitution between goods exceeds 1.

3.3.4.3 Why Live in the Sticks?

We turn to a different issue in which amenities also play a major role. In several countries, the last decades have witnessed the emergence of a new pattern of urban development called the "periurban belt," that is, a zone surrounding the city and occupied both by commuting workers and farmers. As a result, a periurban belt may be viewed as a rural space in the sense that the majority of its land is used for farming purposes, as well as an urban space with most of its working population commuting to the city. In 1999, periurban areas covered 33 percent of France and accommodated 21 percent of its population.

The main reason for the existence of such an integrated space is that *consumers value the rural amenities created by farmers as well as the greenness of the environment* (Cavailhès et al. 2004). For a periurban belt to arise, consumers' and farmers' bid rents must be the same over the belt. Such an equality is possible because the amenity level at a given location is determined through the interactions between consumers and farmers whose respective densities are endogenous.

Consumers share Cobb-Douglas preferences:

$$U(z, s, a) = z^{\alpha} s^{\beta} a^{\gamma} \qquad \alpha, \beta, \gamma > 0 \quad \text{and} \quad \alpha + \beta = 1 \tag{3.34}$$

where a is the amount of amenities available at the consumer's location. For simplicity, the level of urban amenities available within the city is assumed to be uniform and constant (a is normalized to 1). By contrast, the level of rural amenities available in the periurban belt is endogenous.

Farmers produce under constant returns and sell their product to the food processing industry, thus implying that the price of agricultural land R_A is positive. Because the distance to the food processing plants is immaterial for our purpose, we may assume that R_A is constant. Rural amenities $a(r)$ are a by-product of farming, the level of which is a linear function of the total area used for farming:

$$a(r) = \delta n_f(r) s_f(r) \qquad \delta > 0 \tag{3.35}$$

where n_f is the density of farmers and s_f the individual surface they use.

The total amount of space occupied by consumers and farmers at r is equal to the supply of land (which is normalized to 1):

$$n_c(r) s_c(r) + n_f(r) s_f(r) = 1 \tag{3.36}$$

where n_c is the density of residents and s_c the size of a residential plot.

For r to belong to a periurban area, it must be that $a(r) > 1$; otherwise consumers would prefer living in the city. Given (3.36) and (3.35), this condition requires $\delta > 1$. In other words, farming must produce a sufficiently large amount of rural amenities for a periurban area to exist.

To simplify the expressions of consumers' bid rent functions, we assume that the utility level is given by the outside option households face ($u = 1$) while allowing the population size to be variable (the open city model discussed in the concluding section). It is then readily verified that the bid rent function of a consumer residing in a periurban belt is as follows:

$$\Psi_p(r) = (Y - tr)^{1/\beta} [a(r)]^{\gamma/\beta}$$

whereas the bid rent of a city consumer is given by

$$\Psi_c(r) = (Y - tr)^{1/\beta} . \tag{3.37}$$

For farmers and consumers to share land at r, their bid rents must be the same:[17]

$$\Psi_p(r) = R_A$$

which implies that the equilibrium amount of rural amenities available at r is such that

$$a^*(r) = \left[\frac{R_A}{\Psi_c(r)} \right]^{\beta/\gamma} .$$

Rural amenities thus shift upward consumers' bid rent to the level of farmers' bid rent. The previous expression also implies that $a^*(r)$ increases with r, which means that the size of the farming area must increase with the distance to the city center. This is because consumers need a higher level of rural amenities to be compensated for their longer commuting. This in turn implies that the size of the residential area decreases with the distance to the CBD. The periurban belt vanishes when all the land is used for farming.

When the income Y is sufficiently large, (3.37) implies that $\Psi_c(0) > R_A$. Because $\Psi_c(r)$ is strictly decreasing with $\Psi_c(Y/t) = 0$, $a^*(r)$ is increasing and the equation $a^*(r) = 1$ has a unique solution $r_u > 0$. Therefore, $[0, r_u]$ is occupied by households only, whereas the periurban belt starts from r_u and ends at r_p where land is used for agricultural activities only, i.e., $a^*(r_p) = \delta$ (see Figure 3.5 for an illustration).

A few remarks are in order. First, at the same distance r from the city center, the residential plot is smaller in the periurban belt than in the city that does not possess such a belt. Indeed, because the land rent in the periurban belt capitalizes the rural amenities, it is higher than in a purely urban area, thus reducing the consumption of land. Furthermore, whereas the lot size increases within the city as one moves away from the center, it decreases inside the periurban belt, because households bear higher commuting costs and pay a land rent that remains constant and equal to R_A. These results do not contradict what we have seen above because households are compensated by more rural amenities as the distance to the CBD rises. Last, rural amenities having the nature of a local public good available at r, their Lindhal price $P(r)$

[17] See Section 3.2.2 for a similar case.

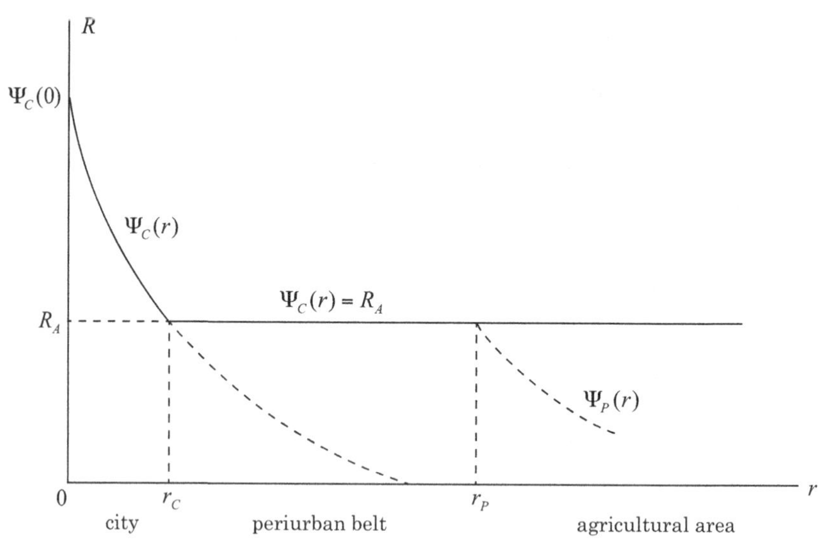

Figure 3.5. The equilibrium land rent under rural amenities.

is given by the marginal rate of substitution between rural amenities and the composite good z, times the number of consumers residing there:

$$P(r) = \frac{\partial U/\partial a}{\partial U/\partial z} n_c^*(r) = \frac{\gamma}{\beta} \Psi_p(x) \left[\frac{1}{A_p^*(x)} - \frac{1}{\delta} \right].$$

As expected, the equilibrium price of the rural amenities depends positively on the land rent in the periurban belt and negatively on the amount of available amenities. Everything else being equal, the higher γ/β, the higher the amenity price. Observe also that $P(r) = 0$ when $\gamma = 0$, i.e., when consumers do not value rural amenities.

3.3.5 Discrete Foundations of Continuous Land Use Theory

The monocentric city model differs from standard microeconomics in that all the unknowns are described by *density* functions. Instead, one might want to develop a discrete model with a finite number of households each consuming a positive amount of the composite good as well as a positive amount of land. Though Alonso himself has proposed two alternative formulations of such a discrete model, very little work has been devoted to this issue.[18] In this section, we follow Asami, Fujita, and Smith (1990) as well as Berliant and Fujita (1992), and study a simple one-dimensional model in which consumers are identical.

[18] By contrast, the connection between the Arrow-Debreu model and the continuous approach to general equilibrium developed by Aumann has attracted a lot of attention in microeconomics (Hildenbrand 1974).

Space is described by the interval $X = [0, \infty)$ with a unit density of land everywhere and the CBD located at the origin; the opportunity cost of land R_A is constant and positive. A finite number n of consumers may be accommodated in this area. The utility of a consumer is $U(z, s)$ where z is the quantity of the composite good, but now $s > 0$ is the size of a lot defined by an interval $[r, r + s) \subset X$. If a consumer occupies the lot $[r, r + s)$, r describes his location, and the commuting cost is defined by tr where t is a positive constant. All consumers have the same income Y and the same utility function U, which satisfies all the properties stated in Section 3.3.1. As in Section 3.3.1, let $Z(s, u)$ be the positive quantity of the composite good that yields utility level u when a consumer occupies a lot of size $s > 0$. Recall that $Z(s, u)$ is strictly decreasing, strictly convex, and such that $\lim_{s \to 0} Z(s, u) = \infty$.

An allocation $(z_i, s_i, r_i;\ i = 1, \ldots, n)$ is defined by a consumption bundle and a location for each consumer. It is feasible if and only if no pair of lots overlap. Without loss of generality, we may rank consumers such that $r_1 < r_2 < \cdots < r_n$.

Let $R(r)$ be the land price function defined on X such that a consumer choosing a lot $[r, r + s)$ pays $R(r)s$ for the lot. Then the consumer problem is given by

$$\max_{r,z,s} U(z, s) \qquad \text{s.t.} \quad z + R(r)s = Y - tr.$$

This is formally identical to (3.13) where $T(r) = tr$. Therefore, if this consumer chooses location r and achieves the utility level u, then he must choose a lot size $S(r, u)$ which maximizes the bid rent function (3.15).

A residential equilibrium with n consumers is given by a utility level u^*, a land price function $R^*(r)$ together with a feasible allocation $(z_i^*, s_i^*, r_i^*;\ i = 1, \ldots, n)$ such that the following conditions hold:

$$R^*(r) \geq \max\{\Psi(r, u^*), R_A\} \tag{3.38}$$

$$R^*(r_i^*) = \Psi(r_i^*, u^*) \qquad i = 1, \ldots, n \tag{3.39}$$

$$R^*(r_n^*) = R_A \tag{3.40}$$

$$s_i^* = S(r_i^*, u^*) \qquad i = 1, \ldots, n \tag{3.41}$$

$$r_1^* = 0 \quad \text{and} \quad r_{i+1}^* = r_i^* + s_i^* \qquad i = 1, \ldots, n - 1 \tag{3.42}$$

where the bid rent function $\Psi(r, u^*)$ is defined by (3.15) for all $r \geq 0$. The condition (3.40) on the land rent for the last consumer allows us to avoid unnecessary technical difficulties;[19] condition (3.42) states that there is no vacant land within the city.

[19] When this condition is replaced by the inequalities $\Psi(r_n, u^*) \geq R_A$ and $\Psi(r_n + s_n, u^*) \leq R_A$, there is a continuum of equilibria (Asami et al. 1990, Theorem 2).

Evidently, since the bid rent function decreases with distance, the equilibrium rents R_i^* satisfy $R_1^* > R_2^* > \cdots > R_n^* = R_A$. Furthermore, since $S(r, u^*)$ is strictly increasing in r (Proposition 3.4.(ii)) $i < j$ implies that $s_i^* < s_j^*$. So, we have shown:[20]

Proposition 3.7. *Consider any finite number of consumers and assume that a residential equilibrium exists. Then, this residential equilibrium is such that the land rent decreases as one moves away from the CBD whereas consumers with larger lots locate farther from the CBD than consumers with smaller lots.*

This means that the residential equilibrium with a finite number of consumers displays the same basic features as the continuous standard model of urban economics. However, the preceding discrete model suffers from a serious defect, namely, each consumer pays the same price for each unit of his lot, and thus the landowner may want to extract more from the consumer or a consumer may buy more land for resale to the next one. To avoid this difficulty, one may either assume that arbitrage is prohibitively costly or that a consumer located at r pays a price given by

$$\int_r^{r+s} R(y)dy$$

for the lot $[r, r + s)$, which is also suggested by Alonso. Proposition 3.7 remains essentially the same in this alternative model, but the analysis is more complex (Berliant and Fujita 1992).

Note, finally, that Asami et al. (1990) have shown that the standard continuous model provides a good approximation of the discrete model considered in this section when n is large enough. In particular, they show that the two sequences of normalized (by the population size) distributions have the same limit when $n = N$.

3.3.6 Notes on the Literature

The urban land use model has been developed independently by Beckmann (1957; 1969), Mohring (1961), Alonso (1960; 1964), Muth (1961; 1969), Mills (1967; 1972b), Casetti (1971), and Solow (1973).[21]

Definitions of closed and open cities were introduced by Wheaton (1974), whereas the public ownership model is credited to Solow (1973). The existence of a residential equilibrium with a continuum of locations and a single marketplace for heterogeneous consumers has been established by Fujita and Smith

[20] Standard tools of general equilibrium analysis are not applicable here due to nonconvexities. However, existence, uniqueness, and optimality have been shown by Asami et al. (1990).

[21] Note that Beckmann (1969) assumes that households are heterogeneous in income. This led him to propose a different solution method to determine the residential equilibrium.

(1987). The study of the monocentric model when consumers have heterogeneous tastes as described by the logit can be found in Anas (1990), whereas the extension of the standard model to several prespecified centers was considered by Papageorgiou and Casetti (1971).

The comparative statics of the residential equilibrium was first studied by Wheaton (1974) in the case of homogeneous consumers. The optimal city was studied by Mirrlees (1972), who used a utilitarian welfare function. The approach taken in Section 3.3.3 is based on Herbert and Stevens (1970), who retained a discrete space and used the duality theorem of linear programming. The general analysis of the residential equilibrium with several income classes has been presented by Hartwick, Schweizer, and Varaiya (1976) as well as Fujita and Tokunaga (1993). Finally, the discrete foundations of the continuous urban model have been criticized by Berliant (1985). Possible solutions have been investigated by Asami et al. (1990), Papageorgiou and Pines (1990), and Berliant and Fujita (1992).

The state of the art in urban economics is summarized in the three complementary books by Fujita (1989), Papageorgiou and Pines (1999), and Zenou (2009). A historical and methodological outlook of the field is provided by Baumont and Huriot (2000).

3.4 CONCLUDING REMARKS

We have seen how land use patterns and land rent profiles can be determined in competitive land markets once it is assumed that a center exists where (some or all) tradable goods have to be shipped. As in Chapter 2, we have assumed that there are no physical differences in land at different locations. The differences in land rents can therefore be attributed to the relative advantage of each location compared with the extensive margin of land use. In other words, the land rent at a given location corresponds to a *locational rent*.[22] Since the city is the reason for this locational rent to come into being, it should be clear that the critical issue is now to figure out why cities, or central business districts, exist. This question has haunted spatial economics for decades. We see in different chapters of this book how various economic and non-economic reasons may explain why people choose to form a city.

In the Thünian model, the land rent is equal to the excess of revenues obtained from the sale of goods produced by using land over payments to non-land factors used in production and transportation. This is why the bid rent function is obtained from a condition of zero profits, which can be interpreted

[22] The concept of locational rent is to be contrasted to the more standard concept of scarcity rent, which could be integrated into the Thünian model by assuming that the "isolated state" is replaced by a "small circular island." At the border of the island, the land rent would be positive, and this value would express the global scarcity of land, whereas the difference in the value of the land rent inside the island would still have the nature of a locational rent.

as a free-entry condition of producers in each activity considered. When consumers (instead of producers) are the land-users, the mechanism leading to the formation of the bid rents is similar to the one uncovered by Thünen provided that the utility level is given by the reservation utility and the population size is variable (this amounts to a condition of free entry). This is called the *open city* model, an example of which is discussed in the next chapter. By contrast, in the *closed city* model in which the population size is fixed, the utility level is endogenous. This requires a more general approach to the formation of bid rents such as that studied in Section 3.3.1. Though both types of models (closed city and open city) lead to similar results, they are useful because they correspond to different situations.

In addition, we have implicitly assumed absentee landlords. That is, the land rent earned within the city goes to landlords who do not reside within the city; hence, the rent does not feed back into consumers' incomes. Both the closed city and open city models can be extended to cope with public ownership of land in which the aggregate land rent is first collected by a public agency and then equally shared among consumers. The analysis remains essentially the same. The choice of a particular specification (open versus closed, absentee landlords versus public property) is dictated by the main features of the problem under consideration. In this chapter, we have chosen to present the most popular model, and we refer to Fujita (1989) for more details regarding the other approaches. Last, the market town in Section 3.2 and the CBD in Section 3.3 are exogenously given. We see in Chapters 6 and 10 how they can be determined endogenously.

A word, before closing. We have seen that housing and commuting costs increase with the city size. Everything else being equal, this reduces the level of consumers' real income, and thus makes the city less attractive. In other words, *land use appears to be a major dispersion force in the making of the space-economy*. The intensity of this force varies inversely with the efficiency of the technology used by commuters and the supply of transportation infrastructures. We see in Chapters 6 and 8 how land use interacts with various agglomeration forces to shape the economic landscape.

4

Increasing Returns and Transport Costs

The Fundamental Trade-off of a Spatial Economy

4.1 INTRODUCTION

A higher density of economic activity typically means higher land rent and commuting costs for which workers must be compensated. For firms to pay them higher wages, they must derive some advantages from being agglomerated, e.g., within the CBD. The source of these advantages lies in the presence of various types of scale economies. As they take very different forms, they are likely to elude a superficial analysis. Increasing returns may be "internal" or "external" to firms. Internal scale economies are found in a wide variety of sectors. For example, they are characteristic of certain public services (e.g., large general hospitals and universities) as well as many private businesses in a range of sectors extending far beyond the heavy industries of the nineteenth century. These cases all involve firms' internal economies of scale, which, thanks to costly but efficiency-raising investments, provide incentive to concentrate production in a small number of plants or facilities. Increasing returns at the firm level are central to NEG (see Chapter 8) as well as to spatial competition theory (see Section 4.5).

As seen in Chapter 2, a homogeneous space together with the competitive mechanism is not compatible with the existence of economic agglomerations such as cities. This is why we broached the assumption of homogeneity in Chapter 3 by assuming the existence of a prespecified center to which workers must commute. We did not, however, provide any justification for the existence of such a center. The standard explanation has been to appeal to Marshallian externalities. As argued in Chapter 1, this often amounts to using a black box. More interesting is a recent and growing literature that explores the specific factors that can generate such social scale economies, especially when firms co-locate. Alternative (but not exclusive) explanations have emerged that all focus on what is usually called "external scale economies," which allow firms to be more productive. These scale effects being external to firms, all markets may be assumed to be perfectly competitive and firms to be price-takers, thus providing a way out to the spatial impossibility theorem. Unlike Ricardian comparative advantage, external scale economies are endogenous and are often the unintentional outcome of a myriad of decisions made by economic agents pursuing their own interests. For these scale effects to deliver on their promises, the employment density must be sufficiently high, a necessary but not sufficient condition.

It is not our intention to provide a full survey of this new literature, especially the many contributions aiming to measure the relative magnitude of the various density economies. Instead, we build on Duranton and Puga's (2004) trilogy – sharing, matching, and learning – and discuss their main implications for the economics of agglomeration. *Sharing* refers to the variety of goods and services that firms benefit from when they set up within the same area. This ranges from the existence of specialized intermediate services used by firms to the supply of sophisticated infrastructure and local public goods that contribute to enhancing their productivity. Sharing such aggregated inputs is possible only when the extent of the market is sufficiently large to permit the entry of many intermediates, the financing of high-quality infrastructures, or both. *Matching* means that the quality of matches between workers and jobs (firms) on the labor market is better in a thick market than in a thin one because of the larger number of opportunities each agent faces when it operates in a denser area. The same applies to suppliers and customers, to retailers and consumers. For example, a firm is more likely to find the intermediate inputs it needs in a denser area because the corresponding market is able to sustain a wider array of specialized suppliers.

Learning asserts that different agents own different bits of information so that their gathering yields a higher level of knowledge; this in turn improves their productivity. More generally, the level of non-market interactions across agents increases with the density of activity and the population size, thus facilitating the process of learning and the spreading of new ideas. Interactions also lie at the origin of new ideas because a new idea is often a new combination of old ideas.

The common denominator of these three approaches is that they yield similar "reduced forms" linking wage and productivity to the size of the labor force. In this sense, they are very much in the spirit of Adam Smith ([1776] 1965, 17) when he wrote the following:

> There are some sorts of industry, even of the lowest kind, which can be carried on no where but in a great town. A porter, for example, can find employment and subsistence in no other place. A village is by much too narrow a sphere for him; even an ordinary market town is scarce large enough to afford him constant occupation.

In a nutshell, Adam Smith and Alfred Marshall hold that "the whole, here the city or the industrial district, is more than the sum of its parts." Those ideas are both old and new. They are old because they were spelled out by Smith and

Marshall, but they are new because their ideas had been ignored for a long time and were developed by using microeconomic tools only recently. In particular, each of the above concepts lies at the origin of a finer division of labor and provides a foundation for increasing returns in the aggregate.

We start this chapter by showing how a larger population permits additional gains generated by the magnification of effects arising from sharing, matching, and learning. To achieve our goal, we use simple settings, which rely on (i) the Smithian idea of market size, (ii) the Chamberlinian idea of diversity, and (iii) the Marshallian idea of informational spillovers.

Having done this, we note that the degree of increasing returns may be so high that a single firm operates at the CBD. Such a situation is reminiscent of the "factory town" in which workers are hired by a single firm that also holds the land leased to its workers. Besides production activity, the firm therefore assumes the tasks of a *developer*. In such a context, housing and the composite consumption good may be viewed as "intermediate inputs" used by the firm to attract workers who move in to produce the final goods in the firm *and* to live in the city. In this sense, it is fair to say that the factory town resembles a vertically integrated structure. Furthermore, this approach allows regarding a city as a firm maximizing some objective. Specifically, the land-development company, owned by Arrow-Debreu shareholders, seeks to maximize land rents net of any cost.

What makes this setting interesting for our purpose is that the firm must take actions to attract workers from the rest of the economy, which has powerful implications. Indeed, the firm must meet two requirements. First, it must pay the migrants a wage high enough to compensate them for the extra costs they incur while residing in the city (land rent plus commuting costs). Second, the firm must give the workers a utility level at least as high as the best alternative they can secure in the rest of the economy, which means that firms behave as utility-takers. In addition, it is possible to describe an entry-exit process similar to that encountered in the Marshallian theory of competition in which the free-entry, zero-profit equilibrium involves a system of factory towns, each accommodating the optimum population of workers. At this equilibrium, there are positive transport costs within cities. Note that this result does not contradict the spatial impossibility theorem because firms are not wage-takers.

There are two main results. The first one states that, at the zero-profit equilibrium, each firm must select an output, or equivalently an employment level, arising in the domain where it faces increasing returns. Roughly speaking, the essence of the argument is as follows. The average total (production plus transport) cost of each firm must be minimized at the long-run output and is, therefore, equal to the corresponding marginal total cost. Furthermore, as long as increasing the number of workers causes transportation costs to rise more than proportionally, the marginal transport cost exceeds the average transport cost. Hence, the marginal production cost of each firm must be lower than its average production cost. This means that *the optimal firm size must be in the phase of increasing returns*.

The second result has unexpected implications. Although workers are paid at their marginal productivity, increasing returns do not prevent the emergence of a market outcome in which profit-maximizing firms break even and supply the first-best quantities. This is so because, at the zero-profit equilibrium, the losses incurred by each firm are exactly compensated by the aggregated differential rent within each city. Indeed, when firms (or, more generally, any group of agents forming a production coalition) capitalize the land rent they create by their activity, everything works as if firms were able to capture the whole consumer surplus, when firms do the socially optimal things when maximizing profit, as they do under perfect price discrimination. This should not come as a surprise, for we have seen that a competitive land market leads residents to pay the highest surplus they can afford in order to occupy a particular location (see Section 3.3.1); thus, *land capitalization can be viewed as a way of extracting the whole consumer surplus*. Or, as Vickrey (1977, 343) put it in a very neat and transparent way:

> Urban land rents are, fundamentally, a reflection of the economies of scale of the activities that are carried on within the city, and that efficient organization of a city, or even of the urban life of a nation as a whole, requires that these land rents, or their equivalent, be devoted primarily to the financing of the intramarginal residues that represent the difference between revenues derived from prices set at marginal costs and the total cost of the activities characterized by increasing returns.

This is important because the presence of increasing returns is known to make it very unlikely for producers to respond optimally to a central message (e.g., a price system in a competitive setting). Here, optimality is obtained by introducing three main changes in the competitive model: (i) firms are wage-makers (instead of wage-takers); (ii) they are utility-takers, that is, firms do not assume they can manipulate the utility level of consumers; and (iii) they are able to capitalize the differential land rent they create into their payoffs. Though the first two assumptions are not related to space per se, the third one does require an explicit accounting for land and transportation.

These results are probably the most distinctive contribution of urban economics to general economic theory because they show how spatial friction costs go hand in hand with the presence of increasing returns in production as well as how site rents play an essential role in the emergence of the optimum in an economy involving increasing returns in production.

From the spatial point of view, these results confirm Mills' (1967) view that *cities form in the economy because there are scale economies in production*. Nevertheless, despite the presence of increasing returns in production, the profit-maximizing population of workers is finite, and the corresponding urban area is bounded. It turns out, therefore, that scale economies in production are dampened by scale diseconomies arising in transportation (even when the individual commuting cost displays long-haul economies). As also acknowledged by Mills (1967), the size of a city is determined by a trade-off between increasing returns and commuting costs. Stated differently, in the absence of scale economies in production, there would be no city (backyard capitalism), whereas, with no commuting costs, there would be a single city in the economy (the world megalopolis). Thus, it is not too much to say that this trade-off is central to the understanding of a city.[1]

An alternative institutional system is obtained by assuming that a group of workers decides to form a cooperative producing the final good. They do so because they understand that, by joining efforts, they may enjoy the benefits of increasing returns (at least up to some employment level). To this end, they cluster within a small area and form a *community*, which then establishes a local government. This government is entitled with the objective of maximizing the well-being of the community members by choosing the optimum community size. This problem is related to the previous one in that each community's behavior encapsulates a developer's problem, and competition among communities yields the same long-run equilibrium. In fact, both approaches amount to assuming a "market for cities" (Henderson) in which cities are created until no opportunity exists for a developer or a community to build a new one.[2] This leads to a simple theory of the urban system, which can in turn be extended to explain why different types of cities emerge.

Better known is the classical trade-off between goods' transportation costs and increasing returns at the firm's level. Though rediscovered several times, it goes back at least to Kaldor (1935) and Lösch ([1940] 1954). Despite the difference in settings, this trade-off is similar to those discussed above. However, its description involves a particular form of imperfect competition known as *spatial competition*.

When production entails increasing returns at the firm's level and demand is spatially dispersed, the economy accommodates only a finite number of firms, which are imperfect competitors because they can derive monopoly power from their geographic isolation. Treading in Hotelling's footsteps, Kaldor argued that space gives this competition a particular form. Because consumers buy from the firm with the lowest "full price," which is defined as the posted price plus

[1] When mentioning scale economies, we mean "gross increasing returns to scale." The balance of agglomeration and congestion effects, which the literature refers to as "net increasing returns to scale" is a different concept. Net increasing returns of 0 percent at the city level does not mean that gross agglomeration effects do not exist. On the contrary, we see in this chapter that congestion effects emerge because agglomeration effects exist.

[2] Both approaches have much to share with club theory à la Buchanan (1964). This literature is surveyed in Scotchmer (2002).

the transportation cost to the corresponding firm, each firm competes directly with only a few neighboring firms regardless of the total number of firms in the economy. Or, as Kaldor (1935, 391) put it:

> Looked at from the point of view of any seller, a change of price by any other particular seller (the prices of the rest being assumed as given) is less and less important for him, the further away that particular seller is situated.

Therefore, the process of spatial competition takes place among the few and should be studied within a framework of non-cooperative game theory. This is the other main contribution of location theory to economics in that it shows the importance of strategic considerations in the formation of prices in spatial markets. However, it was ignored until economists became fully aware of the power of game theory for studying competition in modern market economies. Following the outburst of industrial organization theory since the late 1970s, it became natural to study the implications of space for competition. New tools and concepts are now available to revisit and formalize the questions raised by early location theorists.

In that context, scale economies in production have another far-reaching implication: the number of marketplaces open in the space-economy is likely to be suboptimal. Or, to put it differently, spatial markets being incomplete because of nonconvexities in technologies, an equilibrium allocation is generally not efficient. This sheds additional light on the trade-off between increasing returns and transportation costs in a spatial economy in which firms compete strategically to attract consumers. As is seen, large-scale economies yield a sparse production pattern, whereas high transportation costs lead to a dense spatial configuration of firms. And it is only when both become negligible that the market equilibrium approaches the competitive outcome and so gets close to the optimum.

Spatial competition models can be referred to as "location without land" models because no land market exists. Yet, they can be extended to integrate a land market when it is recognized that consumers are mobile. Introducing a land market and consumer mobility into spatial competition models has at least two important consequences. It permits the location decisions of firms and consumers to be jointly endogenous, and it permits allocation mechanisms based on land capitalization, as in the literature on local public goods. Indeed, a differential land rent is generated by the relative proximity to the stores. When each firm is allowed to collect the extra rent that its activity creates, the discrepancy between the market equilibrium and the optimum vanishes, thus extending the results obtained in the foregoing sections inasmuch as firms now behave strategically.

The organization of this chapter reflects what has been previously said. The microeconomic underpinnings for increasing returns at the city level are spelled out in Section 4.2. In Section 4.3, we study the trade-off between scale economies and commuting costs in the context of city formation. The factory town model (Section 4.3.1) and the community model (Section 4.3.2) are successively discussed and compared. These models then serve as a basis for the analysis of urban systems (Section 4.3.3). In Section 4.4, we extend the framework in order to figure out how the interplay between increasing returns and transport costs between cities explains why cities are specialized in the production of a very small number of goods or, instead, are diversified because they nest a wide array of activities. After that, we turn in Section 4.5 to the study of the trade-off between increasing returns and transport costs in the context of spatial competition. Specifically, we first consider the market equilibrium (Section 4.5.1) and then the social optimum (Section 4.5.2). The two solutions are different, but we see how they can be reconciled once firms are allowed to capitalize the differential land rent they create into their profits (Section 4.5.3). Our conclusions are presented in Section 4.4.6.

4.2 MICRO-FOUNDATIONS OF EXTERNAL INCREASING RETURNS

In this section, the three main lines of research developed to explain the existence of external increasing returns are discussed.

1. Sharing. The (Smithian) approach rests on the popular idea that a large market (think of a metropolitan area) allows for a finer division of labor through a larger number of intermediate commodities, final goods or public facilities. In particular, the access to a wider range of intermediate services and goods enhances the productivity of the final sector,[3] thus resulting in wages that increase with the size of the urban labor force. In the same vein, consumers are better-off because they have a direct access to a broader set of locally produced goods and services.

2. Matching. The (Chamberlinian) idea of diversity is applied to the urban labor market to show that a large city allows for a better average match between heterogeneous workers and firms' job requirements.[4] Hence, something like an agglomeration economy is at work when new firms, workers, or both enter the city labor market, which induces firms to pay higher wages. Likewise, a large city allows for a better matching between customers and vendors, especially those supplying untradable services.

3. Learning. The (Marshallian) approach asserts that "the secrets of the industry are in the air" once workers and producers are gathered in an area that facilitates the transmission of information. It builds on the idea that heterogeneous workers and firms may improve their productivity by sharing their own

[3] This echoes the idea that trade generates gains by expanding the assortment of intermediate goods available to domestic firms. The difference between the two channels is that cities may provide untradables and customized services.

[4] In the same vein, once it is recognized that bilateral search often arises on the labor market, cities reduce search costs, and thus workers invest more in human capital.

knowledge through repeated face-to-face communications, thereby creating new knowledge that benefits all. That knowledge is shared by a larger pool of agents, which permits the use of more sophisticated and efficient technologies. This in turn improved the actions taken by better trained workers.

For our purpose, it is convenient to retain three simple, specific models, each illustrating one of the previously mentioned ideas. Note that another reason for our choice of menu is that two of these models rely on the canonical models used in spatial economics, namely the CES and the circular city models, respectively. In this way, they serve as an introduction to topics that are discussed in subsequent chapters.

As is seen, aggregate increasing returns do not emerge from a vacuum: certain types of indivisibilities must exist within the city. What is shown is that *such indivisibilities translate into wages increasing with the size of the labor force.* In the first model, it is argued that a large market permits workers to become more specialized and, therefore, to be more efficient when they are gathered within cities. In the second, it is shown how a large city allows for a better average match between heterogeneous workers and firms' job requirements. In the last one, we see how a denser population of workers may achieve a higher average level of knowledge, whence a higher productivity.[5]

4.2.1 Sharing: The Intermediate Sector

Assume that the final sector produces a homogeneous good under constant returns and perfect competition (we take this good as the numéraire). Without loss of generality, this sector may then be represented by a firm whose production function is assumed to be as follows:

$$X = \left(\int_0^M q_i^\rho \, \mathrm{d}i \right)^{1/\rho} \tag{4.1}$$

where ρ takes a value strictly between 0 and 1. In this expression, X is the output of the firm, q_i the quantity of input i used, and M the number (or mass) of intermediate goods available in the city.

As observed by Ethier (1982), (4.1) can be interpreted as the production function of a competitive firm that has constant returns with respect to a given number M of specialized inputs q_i. However, this function exhibits increasing returns in the number M of intermediate goods. Suppose, indeed, that each intermediate good is sold at the same price $\bar{p}$, and let E denote the expense of the firm on all the intermediate goods. Then, the consumption of each variety

[5] The preceding three approaches have much in common with the Marshallian externalities of type (ii) and (iii) discussed in Section 1.3. Externalities of type (i) are at the heart of spatial competition and new economic geography, which are covered in Section 4.5 as well as in Chapters 8 and 9. Externalities of type (iv) correspond to local public goods, which will be discussed in the next chapter. Finally, we study the sharing of information in Chapter 6.

by a firm of the final sector is such that $q_i = E/M\bar{p}$ for all $i \in [0, M]$. Plugging this expression into (4.1), we obtain

$$X = \frac{EM^{(1-\rho)/\rho}}{\bar{p}}.$$

Hence, for any given value of E, production strictly increases with the mass of intermediate goods as long as $\rho < 1$. The more specialized the intermediate goods, the stronger this effect, that is the smaller ρ. Therefore, the working of the final sector depends on the way the intermediate sector operates.

Consider a monocentric city with a final goods industry and an intermediate goods industry. The latter supplies specialized services to the former. The production function of a firm belonging to the final sector is given by (4.1), whereas the production function of the service firms is described in the following paragraphs. Both types of firms are located in the CBD. The city has a population of N workers, each supplying one unit of effective labor.

Because of specialization in production, each variety is produced by a single firm according to an identical technology for which the only input is labor. The total amount of labor required to produce the quantity q_i of the intermediate good i is given by

$$l_i = f + cq_i, \tag{4.2}$$

where f is the fixed labor requirement and c the marginal labor requirement; f may arise from developing and/or setting the production line of a variety. Evidently, this technology exhibits increasing returns to scale.

Let w denote the common wage prevailing in the city. If p_i denotes the price of the intermediate good i, the representative firm selling the final good chooses q_i so as to maximize its profit given by

$$X - \int_0^M p_i q_i \mathrm{d}i$$

subject to the production function (4.1). The first-order conditions yield the input demands as

$$q_i^* = Xp_i^{-\sigma} P^{\sigma} \quad i \in [0, M] \tag{4.3}$$

and the total expenditure as

$$\int_0^M p_i q_i^* \mathrm{d}i = PX$$

where P is the price index for the intermediate sector defined as follows:

$$P \equiv \left(\int_0^M p_j^{-(\sigma-1)} \mathrm{d}j \right)^{-1/(\sigma-1)} \tag{4.4}$$

where

$$\sigma \equiv \frac{1}{1-\rho}$$

is the elasticity of substitution between any two varieties that varies between 1 and ∞. Because the profit function of the representative firm, given by $X - PX = (1 - P)X$, is linear in X, the equilibrium price index P^* must satisfy

$$P^* = 1 \tag{4.5}$$

for the equilibrium output to be positive and finite.

Therefore, we follow Abdel-Rahman and Fujita (1990) and assume that the intermediate sector is described by a market structure in which (i) each firm produces one intermediate good (monopolistic) and (ii) profits are just sufficient to cover average costs (competition). That is, we use Dixit and Stiglitz' (1977) monopolistic competition model in which the representative consumer is replaced by the representative firm of the final sector. Since there is a continuum of firms in the intermediate sector, each one is negligible in the sense that its action has no impact on the market. Hence, when choosing its price, a firm accurately neglects the impact of its decision over the aggregated magnitudes X and P. In addition, because firms sell differentiated intermediate goods, each one has some monopoly power in that it faces an isoelastic demand function, the elasticity of which is σ.

The profit of firm i is

$$p_i q_i^* - w l_i.$$

Because demands (4.3) are symmetric and isoelastic, the equilibrium price is the same across firms and is equal to the common marginal production cost times a positive relative markup

$$p^* \equiv p_i^* = cw/\rho \qquad i \in [0, M] \tag{4.6}$$

common to all firms.

Firms enter the intermediate goods industry until profits are zero, that is, $p^* q^* - wl^* = 0$. Substituting (4.2) and (4.6) into this equality yields the equilibrium output common to all firms of the intermediate sector as follows:

$$q^* \equiv q_i^* = \frac{f}{c}\frac{\rho}{1-\rho} \tag{4.7}$$

which in turn yields the equilibrium labor consumption:

$$l^* \equiv l_i^* = \frac{f}{1-\rho}. \tag{4.8}$$

Thus, a firm size is independent from the market size.

Assuming that each worker supplies one unit of labor, full employment prevails in the city when

$$N = Ml^*. \tag{4.9}$$

Using (4.8), (4.9) may be rewritten so as

$$M^* = (1 - \rho)N/f \tag{4.10}$$

which means that *the equilibrium number of intermediate goods is increasing in the labor force* but decreasing in its own fixed cost. In other words, the process of specialization is limited by the size of the labor market (N) as well as by the presence of fixed costs in the intermediate sector (f). The equilibrium number of intermediate goods also rises with the degree of product differentiation characterizing this sector (ρ is small).

We now determine the unknowns X and w as functions of the mass of intermediate goods M. Using (4.1) and (4.7), we obtain the following relationships:

$$X = K_1 M^{1/\rho} \tag{4.11}$$

where $K_1 \equiv \rho f/(1 - \rho)c > 0$ because $f > 0$ and $\rho < 1$. Furthermore, using (4.4)–(4.6) leads to

$$w = K_2 M^{(1-\rho)/\rho} \tag{4.12}$$

where $K_2 \equiv \rho/c$. In other words, both the equilibrium output of the final sector and the equilibrium city wage increase with the mass of the intermediate goods.

As a consequence, (4.10) and (4.11) allow us to rewrite the city production function (4.1), built here from individual components, as follows:

$$X = AN^{1/\rho} \tag{4.13}$$

where $A \equiv f^{-(1-\rho)/\rho}\rho(1 - \rho)^{(1-\rho)/\rho}/c$ is a positive constant, the value of which is determined by the parameters of the intermediate sector.

Thus, *in the aggregate, production in the final sector exhibits increasing returns in labor* (the exponent of N in (4.13) is greater than 1 when $\rho < 1$) even though the production function in the final sector displays a priori constant returns to scale. This is because the number of specialized firms in the intermediate sector rises with the population size, thus permitting a higher degree of specialization. The concept of city production function is not obvious because the city is not an agent per se but a collection of agents, each with her own interest. Hence, aggregate production functions should be built inside the model. This is precisely what we have achieved above. Interestingly, though any individual firm belonging to the final sector operates under the perception of constant returns, this sector as a whole exhibits increasing returns. Note also that the elasticity of the output with respect to the population size is independent of f, whereas A decreases with f. As a result, weaker increasing returns in the intermediate sector translates into a higher productivity of labor in the final sector through a wider range of intermediate goods.

Depending on the value of ρ, the degree of increasing returns might be high enough for a "large" number of workers to reside within the same city. In particular, when $\rho < 1/2$, the marginal product of labor rises at an increasing rate with the population size. This does not strike us as a realistic outcome, and we find it more reasonable to assume that the increase in the marginal productivity falls with N. Thus, provided that $\rho > 1/2$, the process of specialization cannot be pursued indefinitely. Still, even in this case, the economy displays what may be called "returns to scale at the city level."

The equilibrium wage may be obtained from (4.10) and (4.12):

$$w^* = AN^{(1-\rho)/\rho}$$

which also increases with the size of the labor force. Indeed, *when more workers are available in the city, more firms can enter the intermediate sector, generating higher wages*. However, when $\rho > 1/2$, the equilibrium wage rises at a decreasing rate.

As discussed in Section 3.3, an increasing population leads to an expansion of the residential area, which yields in turn higher land rents and longer commuting. Consequently, the city size is determined endogenously at the solution to the trade-off between increasing returns in the intermediate sector and workers' commuting costs to the CBD. Of course, cities specialized in different final goods will have different production functions, yielding different sizes.

In sum, a city involving a larger labor force has (i) more intermediate inputs, (ii) higher productivity in the final sector, and (iii) higher wages. Loosely speaking, we may thus conclude as follows: As in Adam Smith, the division of labor within the city is limited by the supply of labor but, as in Young (1928), the extent of the labor market is itself limited by the existence of alternative jobs available in other places as well as by workers' commuting costs within the city.

4.2.2 Matching: The Labor Market

We now follow a different path by assuming a population of workers who are heterogeneous in the type of work they are best suited for. For example, think of a big city (such as London or New York) that accommodates a large number of lawyers with specific training. Once it is recognized that the labor force is heterogeneous in the skill space, it should be clear that firms have incentives to differentiate their technologies in much the same way as firms have incentives to locate at different places when consumers are dispersed over space (see Section 4.5). Indeed, firms are then able to obtain monopsony power in the labor market that allows them to set wages below the productivity of workers. The approach taken here relies on Helsley and Strange (1990).[6]

Consider a monocentric city with M firms located in the CBD. As in the foregoing section, we assume that firms sell their output at a given market price (we take this output as the numéraire). For simplicity, a firm is fully described by the type of worker it needs. Specifically, firm i's skill requirement is denoted by r_i ($i = 1, \ldots M$) in some skill space. Production involves constant returns to scale once some fixed entry cost measured in terms of the numéraire has been paid.

There is a continuum of workers of size N with heterogeneous skills, each worker supplying one unit of labor. Workers are heterogeneous in the type of work they are best suited for, but there is no ranking in any sense of these types of work. In the skill space described by the unit circle $\mathbf{C}$, skills are continuously and uniformly distributed along this circle with a density equal to the labor force N. We also assume that firms' job requirements r_i are equally spaced along the unit circle so that $1/M$ is the distance between two adjacent firms in the skill space.[7] Because workers are heterogeneous, they have different matches with the firm's job offer. Thus, if firm i hires a worker whose skill differs from r_i, the worker must get trained. Her cost of training to meet the firm's requirement is a function of the difference between worker's skill r and the skill requirements r_i: $s|r - r_i|$ where $s > 0$ may be viewed as an index for various frictions and idiosyncrasies. After training, all workers are identical from the firm's viewpoint and their ex post productivity is equal to α units of the good. Firm i offers the same wage to all workers conditional on the workers having been trained to the skill r_i. Each worker then compares the wage offers of firms and the required training costs; she simply chooses to work for the firm offering the highest wage net of training costs.

The wage-setting game proceeds as follows. First, firms simultaneously choose their gross wage offers. Workers then observe all wage offers and choose to work for the firm that yields the highest net wage. Because each firm anticipates workers' choices, it will hire all workers who prefer to work for it. In equilibrium, there are no quits or layoffs because both employers and workers have no incentive to deviate. The allocation of workers among firms is based entirely on individual competitive advantage.

Consider firm i. If the firms on each side of it offer wages w_{i-1} and w_{i+1}, respectively, then firm i's labor pool consists of two subsegments whose outer boundaries are $\bar{r}_i$ and $\bar{r}_{i+1}$. The worker at $\bar{r}_i$ receives the same net wage from firm i and firm $i - 1$, whereas the worker at $\bar{r}_{i+1}$ receives the same net wage from firm i and firm $i + 1$. Because firm i knows the training cost function and

[6] The model used here is the labor market counterpart of the spatial competition model discussed in detail later (Section 4.5).

[7] The assumption of equidistant firms is the spatial counterpart of that of symmetric and equally weighted varieties in the Dixit-Stiglitz model.

all firms' job requirements, it can determine $\bar{r}_i$ and $\bar{r}_{i+1}$. Specifically, $\bar{r}_i$ is the solution to the equation: $w_i - s(r_i - \bar{r}_i) = w_{i-1} - s(\bar{r}_i - r_{i-1})$, so that

$$\bar{r}_i = \frac{w_{i-1} - w_i + s(r_i + r_{i-1})}{2s}. \tag{4.14}$$

Firm i attracts workers whose skill type lies in the interval $(\bar{r}_i, r_i]$ because they obtain a higher net wage from firm i than from firm $i - 1$. Workers with skill types in $[r_{i-1}, \bar{r}_i)$ prefer to work for firm $i - 1$. Similarly, we can show that

$$\bar{r}_{i+1} = \frac{w_i - w_{i+1} + s(r_i + r_{i+1})}{2s}. \tag{4.15}$$

The firm's labor pool thus consists of all workers with skill types in the interval $(\bar{r}_i, \bar{r}_{i+1}]$, which expands when w_i rises. Everything else being equal, workers are more responsive to a wage hike, hence firms have less monopsony power, in a thicker labor market.

Firm i's profits gross of fixed cost are given by

$$\Pi_i = \int_{\bar{r}_i}^{\bar{r}_{i+1}} N(\alpha - w_i)\mathrm{d}r = N(\alpha - w_i)(\bar{r}_{i+1} - \bar{r}_i).$$

For a given number of firms, wages and profits at the Nash equilibrium can be determined as follows. It can be readily verified that a Nash equilibrium exists in wages. We find the Nash equilibrium wages by taking the first-order condition for Π_i with respect to w_i:

$$\frac{\partial \Pi_i}{\partial w_i} = -N(\bar{r}_{i+1} - \bar{r}_i) + N(\alpha - w_i)\left(\frac{\partial \bar{r}_{i+1}}{\partial w_i} - \frac{\partial \bar{r}_i}{\partial w_i}\right) = 0. \tag{4.16}$$

Using (4.14), (4.15), and (4.16) and $r_i - r_{i-1} = 1/M$, and setting equilibrium wages equal to each other, we obtain

$$w^*(M) = \alpha - s/M. \tag{4.17}$$

Assume now that there is free entry whereas firms remain equidistant. The agglomeration of firms in the CBD has the nature of an externality for the workers because the entry of a new firm leads to a wage increase (recall that $w^*(M)$ given by (4.17) is increasing in M). This is because an additional firm improves the quality of the average match between skills and job requirements. As the number of firms keeps increasing, firms have to pay higher wages because adjacent firms compete for workers who have better matches. In the limit, when the number of firms becomes arbitrarily large, the wage approaches the competitive level α, whereas profits go to zero. However, each firm that enters the market must pay a positive fixed cost f. Therefore, at the free-entry equilibrium, the number of firms is limited.

Because profits per firm gross of entry costs are equal to $\Pi(M) = sN/M^2$, the equilibrium number of firms is determined by the zero-profit condition:

$$M^* = \sqrt{sN/f} \tag{4.18}$$

and thus a firm's equilibrium size is given by its workforce:

$$l_i^* = l^* = \frac{N}{M^*} = \sqrt{\frac{Nf}{s}}$$

which increases with the population size.

Using (4.18), we readily verify that the city production function is obtained by subtracting the sum of training costs from the gross output:

$$X = \alpha N - 2NM^* \int_0^{1/2M^*} sx\mathrm{d}x = N\left(\alpha - \frac{1}{4}\sqrt{\frac{sf}{N}}\right) \tag{4.19}$$

which increases at a decreasing rate with the size of the labor force (see also [4.13]). The upshot is that *a better match between jobs and workers gives rise to increasing returns in the aggregate.* Surprisingly enough, the source of aggregate increasing returns is here competition between firms on the labor market. As N grows, the number of firms increases less than proportionally due to greater labor market competition (see [4.18]). Consequently, firms end up with a larger number of employees. In the presence of fixed production costs, this increases output per worker.

Substituting (4.18) into (4.17) yields the long-run equilibrium wage:

$$w^* = \alpha - \sqrt{\frac{sf}{N}}.$$

Because the quality of the average match improves, *the long-run equilibrium wage rises at a decreasing rate with the thickness of the labor market.* Thus, as it is now expected, denser urban labor reduces firms' monoposony power. Note also that w^* does not equal the marginal productivity of labor obtained from (4.19) because firms are wage-setters.

To sum up, a city involving a larger population of heterogeneous workers has (i) higher productivity, (ii) higher wages, and (iii) larger firm size. As in Section 4.2.1, the city size is determined endogenously according to the trade-off between increasing returns in the final sector and workers' commuting costs to the CBD. In other words, although the microeconomic mechanism vastly differs from the one investigated above, we arrive at the same conclusion when we look at what happens at the city level.

4.2.3 Learning from (or Interacting with) Others

It should be clear that what matters for a city to be productive is the total amount of effective labor available therein, not the total number of workers per se. As a result, one should not be deluded with the sole scale effect. "Small places" may be very productive if they accommodate workers embodying a large amount of effective labor. After all, at the height of the Renaissance, Florence accommodated only 40,000 inhabitants. To be precise, the productivity of a city is the compound of two different effects: a scale effect and a human capital effect.[8] Therefore, it is important to understand how the gathering of firms and workers may help them learn from each other.

The concept of *knowledge spillover* is widespread in growth theory (Romer 1986; Lucas 1988) and has a much longer history in urban economics starting with Alfred Marshall. The role of information in modern cities has long been emphasized by economic historians. As Hohenberg and Lees (1985) put it: "Urban development is a dynamic process whose driving force is the ability to put information to work. After 1850, the large cities became the nurseries as well as the chief beneficiaries of an explosion in knowledge-centered economic growth." Cities are the places where people talk. Undoubtedly, much of this talk does not generate productivity gains. However, the larger the number of people, the more likely the talk leads to innovations increasing productivity. As Glaeser (2011, 24) noted: "cities, and the face-to-face interactions that they engender, are tools for reducing the complex-communication curse." The idea seems compelling: a larger number of agents owning different bits of information allows for the emergence of a wider range of combinations, which in turn fosters the emergence of a higher level of information and knowledge. As Jones and Romer (2010, 42) put it, "there are powerful incentives for connecting as many people as possible into trading networks that make all ideas available to everyone." This is precisely what cities do: *they connect people*. We see in Chapter 6 how *learning from others* fosters the agglomeration of firms and workers.[9]

4.3 CITY SIZE UNDER SCALE ECONOMIES

The setting we explore in this section deals with a large firm endowed with a production function displaying internal scale economies, while facing world

[8] See Acemoglu (1998) for a study of the microfoundation of social increasing returns in human capital accumulation.

[9] Note that the connectivity argument disregards the fact that the exchange of information may also be deliberate and reciprocal. In this case, the transfer of knowledge is endogenous and determined as the equilibrium outcome of a repeated game between agents. Helsley and Strange (2004) observe that efficient knowledge exchange may not be sustainable in very large cities because defection in exchange barter is more difficult to detect. Under these circumstances, the relationship between knowledge and agglomeration need not be monotone.

competitive markets. These conditions are typical of what is known to be a factory town. More realistically, perhaps, we have just seen that several mechanisms operating at the level of individual agents may generate increasing returns at the city level. Building on this observation, we may assume that the city's production function exhibits increasing returns, at least over some range of output values. The latter case is known to be compatible with a perfectly competitive market. We show that the same holds in the former case when firms can internalize the land rent.

In the presence of external economies, the market may suffer from coordination failures that prevent the realization of undertakings that are advantageous to stakeholders. Note also that transaction costs are often too large for the potential stakeholders to bargain and reach the optimum, thus preventing the Coase Theorem to hold. In the absence of such bargaining, no single firm has an incentive to internalize the spillovers. This is why Henderson and others assume the existence of a "large agent" whose job is precisely to solve the assembly problem through land taxation and labor subsidies. The "market for cities" differs from a standard market in that there is no price for cities. It emerges as a result of profit or welfare opportunities associated with the existence of potential agglomeration economies, which materialize when particular agents coordinate firms' and workers' action.

In this section, our purpose is to explore, for different institutional arrangements, the implications of this assumption for the process of city formation. Specifically, we consider two types of institutions. In the first one, the city is viewed as the outcome of decisions made by a developer that internalizes the benefits of amalgamating workers within a factory. In Henderson's words, the developer plays "an entrepreneurial role which facilitates large movements of people, so that a new city can form en masse" (1987, 84). In the second, the city is formed by a community of workers who choose to combine efforts in order to enjoy the surplus generated by the presence of increasing returns.

4.3.1 The City as a Firm

Consider a monocentric city with a single profit-maximizing firm located at the center (a factory town). This firm produces one homogeneous good, using one production factor, *labor*. This good, which is both locally consumed and sold on the world competitive market, is the numéraire. The firm's production function is

$$X = F(N)$$

where X is the amount of the consumption good and N the mass of workers (see, e.g., (4.13) and (4.19)). This function is such that $F(0) = 0$, it is strictly increasing in N, and there exists $N_a > 0$ such that

$$\frac{dF}{dN} \equiv F'(N) \gtreqless F(N)/N \quad \text{as} \quad N \lesseqgtr N_a. \tag{4.20}$$

Thus, production involves increasing returns for $N < N_a$ and decreasing returns for $N > N_a$. Alternatively, (4.20) may be viewed as the aggregate production function stemming from the internalization of the external scale economies studied in Section 4.2.

Potential employees of the firm, who have the same preferences as the consumers studied in Section 3.3.1, enjoy a reservation utility level $\bar{u}$ in the rest of the economy. In order to be able to produce, the firm must attract workers from the rest of the world. To this end, it must pay them a wage w high enough for these workers to be compensated for the urban rent determined on a competitive land market as well as for the commuting cost to the firm. Indeed, when some workers choose to reside within this city they anticipate that they will be organized according to a residential equilibrium as that described in Section 3.3.1, whereas their income is now given by the wage w, which is endogenous.[10] Given this wage rate, workers migrate into the new city as long as the utility level they can reach there is higher than or equal to their reservation utility. As seen in Section 3.3.2, the equilibrium utility level in the city decreases when the population size rises. Consequently, workers stop migrating just when the utility level they can reach within the factory town is equal to $\bar{u}$. Clearly, such a problem belongs to the family of open city models.

When the wage rate is w, the city fringe $r^*(w, \bar{u})$ is determined by the unique solution to the equation

$$\Psi\left[w - T(r), \bar{u}\right] = R_A. \tag{4.21}$$

Using (3.27) and (3.28), we thus obtain the equilibrium mass of workers residing in the city as given by the following function of the wage rate:

$$N(w, \bar{u}) = \int_0^{r^*(w,\bar{u})} \frac{2\pi r}{S[w - T(r), \bar{u}]} \mathrm{d}r \tag{4.22}$$

which is called the *population supply function* (from the rest of the economy to the city). When w increases, (4.21) implies that the bid rent curve of each worker moves upward and, hence, the urban fringe expands. Furthermore, since their (reservation) utility is fixed, their Hicksian demand for land $S[w - T(r), \bar{u}]$ falls. Consequently, (4.22) implies that *the population supply rises with the wage offered by the firm*. When w becomes arbitrarily large, $N(w, \bar{u})$ goes to infinity. It is easy to show that an increase in the reservation utility $\bar{u}$ leads to a decrease in the labor supply to the city. As a result, more workers are attracted

[10] We assume that each firm is equally shared by all the individuals in the economy. Since profits are zero in equilibrium, the residents of each city have no income other than wages.

to the factory town when w increases, but fewer workers move in when the level of utility in the rest of the economy rises.

Conversely, we may define the *wage function* $w(N, \bar{u})$ as the wage the firm must pay in order to attract exactly N workers when the reservation utility level is $\bar{u}$. Evidently, $w(N, \bar{u})$ is the inverse of $N(w, \bar{u})$. It is readily verified that this function is strictly increasing in both N and $\bar{u}$, while $N \to \infty$ implies that $w \to \infty$.

Denote by $C(N, \bar{u})$ the value of the urban cost (3.29) evaluated at the efficient allocation when the population is equal to N and the utility level $\bar{u}$ with $C(0, \bar{u}) = 0$. Let also

$$ADR(w, \bar{u}) = \int_0^{r^*(w,\bar{u})} [\Psi(w - T(r), \bar{u}) - R_A] 2\pi r \mathrm{d}r \tag{4.23}$$

be the *aggregate differential land rent* (that is, the sum across locations of the difference between the urban land rent and the agricultural land rent) when the income is w and the common utility level $\bar{u}$.

At the residential equilibrium, total income equals total expenditures for all values of N:

$$Nw(N, \bar{u}) = C(N, \bar{u}) + ADR(w(N, \bar{u}), \bar{u}). \tag{4.24}$$

Differentiating this expression with respect to N yields

$$w(N, \bar{u}) + N \frac{\partial w(N, \bar{u})}{\partial N} = \frac{\partial C(N, \bar{u})}{\partial N} + \frac{\partial ADR[w(N, \bar{u}), \bar{u}]}{\partial N}. \tag{4.25}$$

Since the integrand of (4.23) is zero at $r^*(w, \bar{u})$ by (3.26), we have

$$\begin{aligned}\frac{\partial ADR(w(N, \bar{u}), \bar{u})}{\partial N} &= \int_0^{r^*(w,\bar{u})} \left(\frac{\partial \Psi}{\partial w}\right) \left(\frac{\partial w(N, \bar{u})}{\partial N}\right) 2\pi r \mathrm{d}r \\ &= \frac{\partial w(N, \bar{u})}{\partial N} \int_0^{r^*(w,\bar{u})} \frac{2\pi r}{S[w(N, \bar{u}) - T(r), \bar{u}]} \mathrm{d}r \\ &= \frac{\partial w(N, \bar{u})}{\partial N} N\end{aligned}$$

where (3.15), (3.28), and (4.22) have been used. Therefore, (4.25) becomes:

$$w(N, \bar{u}) = \frac{\partial C(N, \bar{u})}{\partial N}. \tag{4.26}$$

This means that the wage the firm has to pay to attract one additional worker is equal to the marginal urban cost. Since $\partial w / \partial N = \partial^2 C(N, \bar{u}) / \partial N^2$ and since $w(N, \bar{u})$ is strictly increasing in N, we see that C is strictly convex in N. We may similarly show that C is strictly increasing in $\bar{u}$. In summary, we have:

Proposition 4.1. *The urban cost is strictly increasing and strictly convex in N as well as strictly increasing in $\bar{u}$.*

Intuitively, the reason lies in the fact that, due to increase in the distances to travel, the total commuting costs within the city increases more than proportionally with the population size. In other words, given the monocentric structure, *there are diseconomies in urban transportation when the population rises.*[11] This result coincides with another well-documented fact in economic history that high commuting costs placed an upper limit on the growth of cities for fairly long time periods (Bairoch 1988).

This result has another important implication: *the cost of living in larger cities is higher* because of the higher commuting costs workers have to pay. This does not mean, however, that people residing in cities are worse-off than others. As seen in Section 4.2, individuals living in larger cities earn higher wages. The increase in urban costs is the response of the market to this wage premium.

There are two equivalent ways to look at the factory town problem. Consider the first one. The firm buys some land from farmers at the price R_A; it then plans and manages every aspect of the formation of the city, including the allocation of housing to workers, subject to the fact that workers have the reservation utility level $\bar{u}$. The cost borne by the firm is then given by $C(N, \bar{u})$ since the urban cost is minimized at the residential allocation. In this event, the firm chooses a population size N so as to maximize its profit given by

$$\Pi(N) = F(N) - C(N, \bar{u}).$$

If the firm were to do so, however, it would involve a tremendous amount of action and require even more information. Fortunately, there is an alternative and simpler way for the developer to maximize its profit. The firm still buys the land from farmers at R_A, but it now lets the competitive market for land determine the residential allocation. In this case, the firm sets a wage w and, hence, the corresponding $N(w, \bar{u})$ workers migrate into the city and organize themselves on the residential area as described in Section 3.3.1. In particular, the urban land is leased at the competitive market rent. The firm then chooses a wage w so as to maximize its profit in which the aggregate differential rent is capitalized as follows:

$$\Pi(w) = F\left[N(w, \bar{u})\right] - wN(w, \bar{u}) + ADR(w, \bar{u}).$$

In fact, the alternatives above yield the same outcome. Indeed, the first problem

$$\max_{N} F(N) - C(N, \bar{u})$$

is equivalent to

$$\max_{w} F\left[N(w, \bar{u})\right] - C[N(w, \bar{u}), \bar{u}] \tag{4.27}$$

[11] Note that there is no congestion in commuting. Adding congestion would make the commuting cost even more convex.

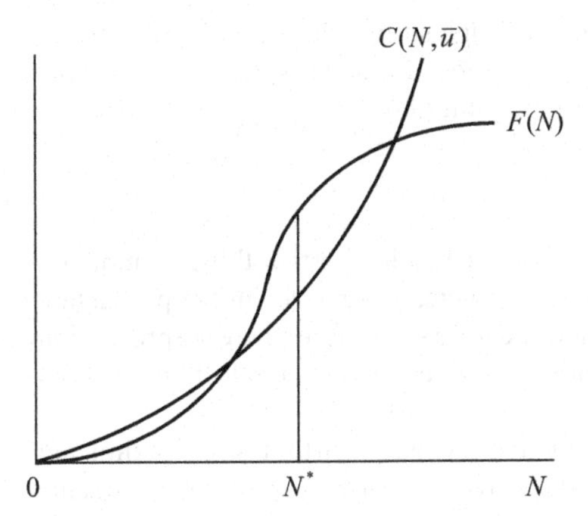

Figure 4.1. The determination of the population size in the factory town.

since $N(w, \bar{u})$ increases from zero to infinity when w varies from zero to infinity. In turn, by (4.24), (4.27) amounts to the second problem

$$\max_{w} F\left[N(w, \bar{u})\right] - wN(w, \bar{u}) + ADR(w, \bar{u}).$$

Consider the first problem. Differentiating Π with respect to N and using (4.26) yields the following equilibrium condition

$$F^{'}(N^*) = w(N^*, \bar{u}) \tag{4.28}$$

which states that the profit-maximizing employment level is such that the equilibrium wage equals the value marginal product of labor, even though the firm is not a wage taker on the labor market. For the second order condition to be met, it must be that

$$F^{''}(N^*) - \frac{\partial^2 C(N^*, \bar{u})}{\partial N^2} < 0 \tag{4.29}$$

so that both $F^{''}(N^*) > 0$ and $F^{''}(N^*) < 0$ are consistent with the second order condition since $C(N, \bar{u})$ is strictly convex.

Graphically, it is seen in Figure 4.1 that the profit-maximizing employment arises at the point N^* when the tangents to $F(N)$ and $C(N, \bar{u})$ are parallel.

Furthermore, it is easy to see that the equilibrium population size rises when the output price increases. More interesting is the impact of the transportation costs. In order to simplify the argument, suppose that $T(r) = tr$ and, for the city to continue to exist when t rises, that $\Pi(N^*) > 0$. Then, it is easily checked that an increase in t leads to a higher urban cost for each given value of N. Simultaneously, the wage function moves upward so that the marginal urban cost also shifts upward because of (4.26). As a consequence, the equilibrium mass of workers as well as the urban fringe shrink. Stated differently, *lower commuting costs lead to a larger population size and a spreading out of the urban area*. This is the other side of the same coin.

4.3.2 The City as a Community

Assume now that a group of workers choose to join efforts within a community in order to benefit from the presence of increasing returns in the production activity. For that purpose, they must work at the same place where the production function, which is now to be interpreted as the community production function, is given by $F(N)$ as described by (4.20).

These workers elect a *local government* endowed with the task of maximizing their well-being. Since all these workers are identical, they are to enjoy the same utility level so that the objective of the local government is to maximize this common utility level. In so doing, of course, the local government must meet some budget constraint, which is defined in the following discussion.

As usual, it is assumed that the community buys the land from farmers at R_A. In order to maximize the utility level of the community members, the local government chooses a certain population size N^o. Again, from now on, two approaches are possible. In the first one, the local government plans and manages all the aspects of city formation. Consequently, its budget constraint is expressed as follows:

$$F(N) - C(N, u) \geq 0.$$

This implies that the problem of the local government is to achieve the highest utility for the community members by choosing the community size while satisfying the budget constraint, that is,

$$\max_N u \quad \text{s.t.} \quad F(N) - C(N, u) \geq 0$$

where N must be strictly positive for the problem to be meaningful.

Since $C(N, u)$ is strictly increasing in u, the budget constraint is binding at the optimum. Therefore, the following two conditions must hold in optimum:[12]

$$F'(N^o) = \frac{\partial C(N^o, u)}{\partial N} \tag{4.30}$$

$$F(N^o) = C(N^o, u). \tag{4.31}$$

[12] Observe that this optimization problem does not necessarily have a solution. For that, some fairly mild assumptions must be imposed on preferences and the production function (Fujita 1989, Proposition 5.8).

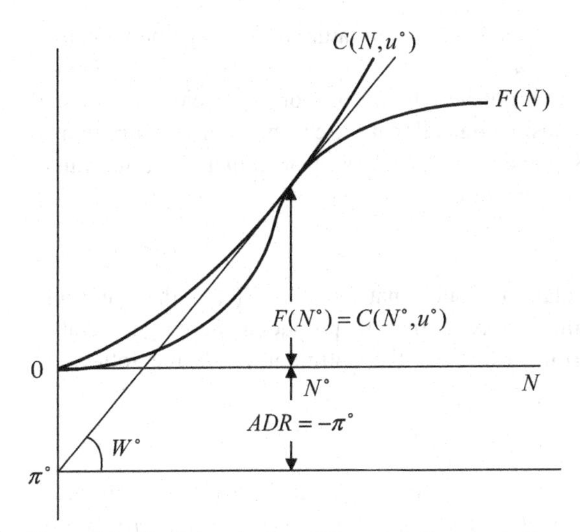

Figure 4.2. The determination of the population size in the community.

The strict convexity of the urban cost function implies that

$$\frac{\partial C(N^o, u)}{\partial N} > \frac{C(N^o, u)}{N^o}$$

so that (4.30) and (4.31) yield

$$F'(N^o) > \frac{F(N^o)}{N^o}.$$

Thus,

Proposition 4.2. *The utility-maximizing population size occurs in the phase of increasing returns to scale.*

Hence, *for a group of workers to agglomerate in a community and engage together in production, there must be increasing returns*; otherwise no community would emerge. This shows how increasing returns operate to create an agglomeration of workers around the center of production. Yet, the corresponding urban area will accommodate a finite mass of workers. This is because the benefit of increasing returns will be more than compensated by the extra cost generated by an additional worker once the optimum population size is reached. In addition, when the output domain over which increasing returns prevail is narrow, the equilibrium population size is small.

Graphically, it is seen in Figure 4.2 that the optimum population N^o arises for the value of u^o at which $F(N)$ and $C(N, u^o)$ are tangent.

If $T(r) = tr$, an increase in t leads to a decrease in u^o because the urban cost curve $C(N, u)$ moves upward with t. However, the impact on the population size is ambiguous in that it depends on the curvature of $F(N)$ at the tangency point between $F(N)$ and $C(N, u)$.

Suppose now that the optimum population of workers decides to form a community. As usual, the residential allocation can be achieved through a competitive land market. Suppose that workers are paid at their marginal value product so that their common income is

$$w^o = F'(N^o).$$

Because the optimum population is such that $N^o w^o > F(N^o)$, the wage bill exceeds the output value, thus implying that the production activity generates a loss. Nevertheless, rewriting (4.24) at the optimum yields the following relationship:

$$ADR(N^o, u^o) = -[F(N^o) - N^o w^o]. \tag{4.32}$$

Accordingly, *at the optimum the aggregate differential land rent capitalized by the community just compensates for the loss incurred in the production activity once workers received the marginal value product of labor*. This is an important result suggesting how the loss incurred in the production under increasing returns may be compensated through the capitalization of the differential land rent, and so without introducing any distortive tax. This is a version of a more general relationship named the *Henry George Theorem* by Stiglitz (1977).[13]

We are now able to compare the two institutional systems studied in the foregoing sections. It is straightforward from (4.28) through (4.31) that *the factory town and the community models yield the same outcome if and only if the firm's profit is zero*. Stated differently, the profit-maximizing size equals the optimum size if and only if the reservation utility level is the same as the optimum utility level.

This is no longer true when firms' profits are positive. The two outcomes differ in the following way: the profit-maximizing firm chooses a labor force strictly larger than the optimum size when the reservation utility level $\bar{u}$ is lower than the optimum utility level u^o. Indeed, if $\bar{u} < u^o$ the firm is able to pay its workers a wage high enough to attract more than N^o workers. This induces the firm to hire a population larger than the optimum one. On the other hand, when $\bar{u} < u^o$ the firm cannot break even and, hence, the factory town is not formed.

4.3.3 System of Cities: A Simple Framework

The foregoing results suggest an interesting entry/exit process, which leads to the formation of a *system of cities*. To this end, suppose the economy consists of an urban sector with many potential cities and a rural sector with an insignificant

[13] The most popular version of the Henry George Theorem is associated with local public goods, as discussed in Chapter 5.

population (like in most developed countries). For simplicity, we assume that the total population of the urban sector is exogenously given by a constant **N**. Because the economy under consideration is closely tied with the world economy, both the output price of the urban sector and that of the rural sector are assumed to be given and fixed. Whenever a city is to be developed, the production function is the same and expressed by (4.20). The economy has enough land for each developer to buy the land needed at the fixed agricultural land rent R_A and for all the created cities not to overlap.

The process of city formation works as follows. We have seen that u^o is the highest utility a firm-developer may sustain without losses while w^o is the highest wage it can pay to its workers. Suppose that the optimum number of cities in the economy, given by $\mathbf{N}/N^o$, is large enough to be safely treated as a real number. Because the size of each city is small compared to the population **N**, each developer considers the utility level in the other cities as given. As long as $u^* < u^o$, each existing developer can earn a strictly positive profit, for example by hiring N^o workers at a wage lower than w^o, thus inviting the entry of new developers. Eventually, profits earned from the formation of new cities become zero and entry stops. At this zero profit equilibrium $u^* = u^o$, and each firm will hire exactly N^o workers and pay them w^o. By implication, workers enjoy the optimum utility level u^o in each city and the number of cities developed is optimal.

Clearly, the same results hold if competition takes place among utility-maximizing communities. Furthermore, since all cities are identical, (4.32) holds in each one of them. We may summarize these results as follows:

Proposition 4.3.

(i) *The equilibrium city system resulting from competition between profit-maximizing firms-developers is identical to the optimum system in which the common utility level is maximized, and conversely.*

(ii) *In every city of the equilibrium/optimum city system, the aggregate differential rent just covers the loss from production activity when goods and labor are priced at their competitive level (Henry George Theorem).*

It follows from the first part of the proposition that the optimum city system may be obtained through competition among profit-maximizing firms or utility-maximizing communities. This is interesting because, for factory towns to exist in the zero profit equilibrium, it must be that the firms' production function exhibits increasing returns. *Although workers are paid at their marginal productivity, which exceeds the average productivity, the corresponding loss incurred in production is exactly compensated by the aggregate differential land rent capitalized within each factory town.* This result, suggested by Vickrey (1977), shows how the land market may provide a solution to a well-known problem in economic theory due to increasing returns, which is usually solved by adding constraints that lead to second best solutions.

Furthermore, in equilibrium all individuals enjoy the same utility level regardless of the city where she resides. This implies that the corresponding allocation is *fair* in the sense of Rawls. This is an intrinsic property of the spatial equilibrium that suggests that a market economy is not necessarily characterized by excessive spatial inequalities, as often claimed by the proponents of regional planning. Within the present simple setting, there is no reason for the government to interfere with the market system, when such an intervention is motivated by redistributive considerations because the market outcome maximizes the Rawlsian welfare function.

However, all cities are identical and do not trade among themselves. The city system obtained here looks like a collection of isolated cities while one would expect to get cities of different types trading goods. We return to this question in Section 4.4.

4.3.4 Notes on the Literature

As already mentioned, in the presence of externalities there can be aggregate increasing returns without the need to introduce a noncompetitive market structure. This is what Mills (1967) and Henderson (1974) assumed in their pioneering papers: firms behave competitively while the city displays increasing returns through Marshallian externalities. It is worth noting that spatial economists and regional scientists have understood the importance of externalities for the formation of cities far before growth theorists came across the idea that externalities matter for growth. Early attempts made to measure the magnitude of spatial externalities go back at least to Hoover (1936), who proposed the concepts of "localization economies" (intra-industry externalities) and "urbanization economies" (inter-industry externalities). The renewal of interest in measuring agglomeration economies started in the 1990s with Glaeser et al. (1992), Henderson, Kuncoro, and Turner (1995), and Ciccone and Hall (1996). Since then, the literature has grown at a fast pace. See Rosenthal and Strange (2004) and Puga (2010) for surveys. Recent contributions finding evidence of all three agglomeration mechanisms include Ellison, Glaeser, and Kerr (2010) as well as Jofre-Monseny, Marín-López, and Viladecans-Marsal (2011).

The work of Mills has also served as a basis for many developments in urban economics, regarding especially the role of developers and the creation of communities. In this respect, our approach to the formation of a system of cities owes much to Mirrlees (1972, 1995), Henderson (1974), Eaton and Lipsey (1977), Kanemoto (1980, chapter 2), Berglas and Pines (1981), Hochman (1981), and Fujita (1989, chapter 5). Schweizer (1986) provides a discrete treatment of city numbers.

In *Progress and Poverty* published in 1879, Henry George forcefully argued that the land rent should be shared by society rather than being owned privately; see Laurent (2005) for a recent discussion of George's work. The Henry George rule, as applied to the financing of the loss incurred under perfect competition and increasing returns, corresponds to an old conjecture stated by Hotelling in a series of papers published in the late thirties, and available in Darnell (1990). It has been studied independently by Serk-Hanssen (1969) and Starrett (1974), whereas Vickrey (1977) did the same but within a system of competing cities.

Last, note that there is a formal analogy between the results presented in this section and those obtained in another strand of the economics literature: labor-management versus entrepreneurial management. Specifically, Meade (1972) has shown that both institutional systems yield the same long run equilibria when there is free mobility of factors and perfect competition. Labor-management eliminates both profits and wages as guides to business decisions and assumes that firms maximize their value added per worker. This setting is therefore similar to the community model when members' utilities are replaced with workers' income.

4.4 INTERCITY TRADE

4.4.1 Specialization and Trade

The urban system previously described looks like a system of isolated city-states, which produce the same good and have the same size. These are major limitations because trade is one of the main features of the space-economy, while urban systems typically involve cities having different sizes. A comprehensive theory of a system of cities is an essential component to understand interregional and international trade. As seen, the preceding approach can be extended to the case of several goods that are traded within the urban system formed by different types of cities. The main question to be answered is similar to the one raised in international trade theory: Why do cities trade goods instead of each city producing all of them? The reason is that cities, like countries, are specialized in the production of certain products.

We know from the spatial impossibility theorem that some market failures are necessary for trade to arise when production factors are mobile. Here, perfect competition and trade are consistent because scale economies are external to firms but internal to the industry.[14] On the other hand, we have seen that adding a new worker to the city generates a higher average urban cost (see Proposition 4.1). As a result, when external economies are confined within each industry, *specialization will lead to a better exploitation of scale effects*. Indeed,

[14] New trade theories have underscored the fact that countries may specialize in activities displaying increasing returns (Helpman and Krugman 1985).

for the same degree of global efficiency in any two sectors, when workers residing within a city are engaged in the production of two different tradables, the average commuting cost is higher than when they are located in two separate cities producing each tradable good as long as the transport costs of these goods are sufficiently low (here they are assumed to be zero). Under these circumstances, it is more efficient for each city to supply a single tradable good that is both locally consumed and exported to the rest of the economy, whereas other tradable items are imported from other cities.[15]

But why should such an efficient outcome occur in a market economy? In the presence of external effects that are industry-specific, the coordination problem mentioned in the previous section is particularly acute. One way out, suggested by Henderson (1974) and discussed in Section 4.3, is to be found in the existence of large economic agents who understand that they may benefit from organizing cities in a way that maximizes the utility level of residents, while internalizing the external effects generated by the agglomeration of firms and workers belonging to the same industry. These agents also collect the land rent prevailing in the city, and incorporate the resulting aggregate land rent into their payoffs or redistribute it to the residents (for notational simplicity, the opportunity cost of land is assumed to be zero). As previously discussed, examples of such agents include *land developers* and *local governments* who compete on the market for cities. These agents are assumed to be many, whereas the total population $\mathbf{N}$ of workers is sufficiently large for many cities of each type to exist. In order to see how Henderson's argument works, we present here a simplified version of the general equilibrium model developed by Henderson (1974; 1977; 1985; 1987; 1988).

The economy involves n sectors producing tradable goods, whereas labor is the only production factor; good 1 is the numéraire. For reasons already discussed, it is never profitable for a city to provide more than one tradable good. Because cities specialized in producing the same good are identical, a city may be identified with the tradable good i produced therein. This city also provides their residents with a bundle of untradable goods (such as housing, retailing, schools) that cannot be shipped between cities because of prohibitive transportation costs. As in Chapter 3, these goods are compounded into the amount of space a worker consumes. For simplicity, we assume a fixed lot size. Commuting over a unit distance requires $t > 0$ units of the numéraire. In this case, as seen in Section 3.1.1, the urban cost borne by the worker living in a type i-city is equal to $tN_i/2$, where N_i the mass of workers/residents.

Workers share the same Cobb-Douglas preferences:

$$U = x_1^{\alpha_1} \cdots x_n^{\alpha_n} s$$

[15] Henderson (1987, 1997a) argues that there is a substantial amount of empirical evidence showing that small and medium-sized cities tend to be specialized.

where x_i stands for the consumption of good i and $s = 1$ for the fixed lot size. Without loss of generality, we assume that the expenditure shares α_i sum up to 1. Workers now choose the industry in which they work as well as the place where they live. This in turn implies that the size of each industry, not just the size of each city, is endogenous. Let w_i be the wage paid in a type i-city. Because a worker residing in this city bears an urban cost equal to $tN_i/2$ while her share in the city aggregate land rent is $tN_i/4$, the income available to buy the tradable goods is equal to $w_i - tN_i/4$.

Let p_i be the price of good $i = 1, \ldots, n$. It is standard to show that individual demands for each tradable good are as follows:

$$x_j = \frac{\alpha_j}{p_j}\left(w_i - \frac{tN_i}{4}\right) \qquad j = 1, \ldots, n$$

so that the indirect utility of a worker living in a type i-city is given by

$$V_i = \left(w_i - \frac{tN_i}{4}\right)\prod_{j=1}^{n}\left(\frac{\alpha_j}{p_j}\right)^{\alpha_j} \qquad i = 1, \ldots, n. \tag{4.33}$$

Note that goods' prices are the same across the urban system because shipping these goods between cities is costless.

Technology in industry i exhibits constant returns to scale at the firm level. However, firms benefit from external scale economies when they are located together at what becomes the city's CBD (see also Chapter 6). Specifically, the aggregate production function of this sector is as follows (see Section 4.2):

$$X_i = F_i(N_i) = E_i(N_i)N_i \tag{4.34}$$

where $E_i(N_i)$ is a Hicksian shift factor taken by each firm as given, with $E_i' > 0$ and $E_i'' < 0$. Because this scale effect is external to firms, firms treat $E_i(N_i)$ parametrically, and thus product markets may be assumed to be perfectly competitive and firms to be price-takers.

Because labor is perfectly mobile across cities and sectors, workers enjoy the same utility level in equilibrium, whatever the type of city in which they live. However, because the production functions are not the same, the wages paid in cities of different types are not the same, thus generating different population sizes, which in turn implies different urban costs. Specifically, it follows from (4.33) that

$$w_i - \frac{tN_i}{4} = w_j - \frac{tN_j}{4} \tag{4.35}$$

must hold in equilibrium. In words, *the equilibrium wage net of the urban cost is the same across city types*. This has an important implication from the policy standpoint: nominal wages may be bad proxies of workers' well-being when they are not corrected for the urban cost prevailing in the city where workers live. It also follows from (4.33) and (4.35) that workers consume the same quantity of each tradable good.

Because each firm operates under constant returns to scale, the number of firms is immaterial for the market outcome. It is, therefore, more convenient to describe variables at the industry level. In particular, firms' aggregate profits in a type i-city are given by

$$p_i X_i - w_i N_i = p_i E_i(N_i) N_i - w_i N_i.$$

Because each firm treats the externality E_i and the market price p_i parametrically, workers are paid their private marginal value product. For N_i to be positive and finite, the equilibrium wage and city size must be related through the following wage function:

$$w_i = p_i E_i(N_i). \tag{4.36}$$

Everything else equal, the wage increases at a decreasing rate with N_i. In equilibrium, firms earn zero profits because they operate under constant returns.

City development is undertaken by local governments that aim to maximize the utility of their residents. To achieve its goal, a local government chooses a tradable good to be produced while letting competitive product, labor, and land markets to determine production activities as well as residential locations. As in Section 4.3.2, it also chooses the population size that maximizes the residents' indirect utility V_i in which prices p_j are treated parametrically because the number of cities is large. In doing so, the local government *internalizes* the external effects associated with the agglomeration of firms within the CBD. In other words, unlike firms, it takes into account the externality $E_i(N_i)$ when choosing N_i. This is precisely the role of the "large agent" to do so.

To fix ideas, assume that

$$E_i(N_i) = N_i^{\gamma_i} \tag{4.37}$$

where $0 < \gamma_i < 1$ measures the degree of increasing returns in sector i (see Section 4.2). Without loss of generality, we may re-index the goods for $\gamma_1 < \gamma_2 < \cdots < \gamma_n$.

Rewriting (4.36) for (4.37) and plugging the resulting expression in (4.33), the maximization of V_i with respect to N_i yields the equilibrium size of a type i-city:

$$N_i^* = \left(\frac{4p_i}{t}\gamma_i\right)^{\frac{1}{1-\gamma_i}} \qquad i = 1, \ldots, n. \tag{4.38}$$

The equilibrium size of a city thus increases with the price of the good produced therein because a higher price allows firms to pay higher wages. Market prices, however, are endogenous.

Using (4.36) and (4.38), we readily verify that

$$w_i^* - \frac{tN_i^*}{4} = p_i^{\frac{1}{1-\gamma_i}} k_i \qquad i = 1, \ldots, n \tag{4.39}$$

where

$$k_i \equiv \left(\frac{4\gamma_i}{t}\right)^{\frac{\gamma_i}{1-\gamma_i}} (1 - \gamma_i)$$

decreases with t. Therefore, (4.35) is equivalent to

$$p_i^{\frac{1}{1-\gamma_i}} k_i = k_1 \qquad i = 2, \ldots, n$$

since $p_1 = 1$. This equation has a single solution, which is the equilibrium price of good i:

$$p_i^* = \left(\frac{k_1}{k_i}\right)^{1-\gamma_i} \qquad i = 2, \ldots, n. \tag{4.40}$$

Substituting (4.40) into (4.38) and simplifying, we obtain the equilibrium city size:

$$N_i^* = \frac{4k_1\gamma_i}{(1-\gamma_i)\,t} > 0 \tag{4.41}$$

since $\gamma_i > 0$ and $1 - \gamma_i > 0$.

Type i-cities vanish when γ_i is arbitrarily small, that is, when there are no external economies at the city level. Specifically, when $\gamma_i = 0$, there are constant returns and good i is produced everywhere at an arbitrarily low scale, while commuting costs are zero. This shows once more that increasing returns are needed for cities to exist. Moreover, because $k_i = 1$ when $\gamma_i = 0$, we have $p_i^* = 1$: all goods are equally priced because they are produced under the same technology. As γ_i becomes positive, type i-cities are created. Moreover, the size of a city increases with the degree of increasing returns (γ_i) of the industry in which it is specialized. That is, we have $N_1^* < N_2^* < \cdots < N_n^*$.

Furthermore, all cities grow when commuting costs (t) fall because k_1 also decreases as t rises. Hence, low commuting costs associated with the emergence of mass transport means and the use of cars permit the coexistence of cities having very different sizes. By way of contrast, when commuting costs were very high with people getting around on foot as before the Industrial Revolution, urban systems were predominantly formed by small cities (Bairoch 1988). Since $\gamma_1 < \gamma_i$, lower commuting costs lead to lower market prices, hence to higher welfare levels. Indeed, because there are increasing returns, cities are formed and commuting is inevitable. In such a context, lowering t implies that more resources are available for producing good 1, thus all tradable goods.

What is more, because the degree of increasing returns varies with the good produced, *cities specializing in the production of different goods have different sizes*. In particular, large (small) cities are those specialized in the production of tradable goods with high (low) degrees of increasing returns. In other words:

> City sizes vary because cities of different types specialize in the production of different traded goods, exported by cities to other cities or economies. If these goods involve different degrees of scale economies, cities will be of different sizes because they can support different levels of commuting and congestion costs. (Henderson 1974, 640)

Accordingly, through free entry and exit in the market for cities, *the benefits of agglomeration are eventually transferred to workers in order to make up for the higher urban costs they bear in more productive but larger cities*. Thus, though some cities seem to fare better than others through the payment of higher wages, the utility level is the same across all cities.

Plugging (4.40) into (4.39) yields the disposable income of any worker:

$$w_i^* - \frac{tN_i^*}{4} = k_1 \qquad i = 1, \ldots, n \tag{4.42}$$

which shows the existence of a positive relationship between city size and wage. It should be clear that this relationship hinges on the interaction between general equilibrium effects. In other words, both variables are interdependent. This implies *a bidirectional and circular causality between wage and city size*: the city attracts workers because firms can pay a high wage, and the local firms can do so because the local labor force is large enough to exploit scale economies.

Using (4.41), we obtain the equilibrium wage paid to city-i's workers:

$$w_i^* = \frac{k_1}{1 - \gamma_i}$$

which increases with γ_i. Finally, adding individual net wages (4.42) across all workers yields the total disposable income that consumers spend on consumption goods:

$$\mathbf{Y} = k_1 \mathbf{N}. \tag{4.43}$$

Thus, the relationship between **Y** and **N** being linear, we may conclude that, at the equilibrium outcome, increasing returns in production are just compensated by decreasing returns in commuting.

It remains to determine the number of cities of each type. The number of cities providing a certain good is adjusted for the quantity of this good demanded in the whole economy to equal its supply. The argument involves two steps.

1. The demand for good i is given by $\alpha_i \mathbf{Y}/p_i^*$, for $i = 2, \ldots, n$, whereas the demand for good 1 is given by workers' consumption plus commuting consumption:

$$\alpha_1 \mathbf{Y} + \sum_{i=1}^{n} m_i \frac{tN_i^2}{4}$$

where m_i denotes the number of type i-cities. The supply of good $i = 1, 2, \ldots, n$ is equal to $m_i X_i^*$. Market clearing for good i implies

$$\alpha_1 \mathbf{Y} + \sum_{j=1}^{n} m_j \frac{tN_j^2}{4} = m_1 X_1^* \tag{4.44}$$

$$\frac{\alpha_i \mathbf{Y}}{p_i^*} = m_i X_i^* \qquad i = 2, \ldots, n. \tag{4.45}$$

Using (4.40), (4.43), and (4.45), the number of type i-cities

$$m_i^* = \frac{\alpha_i}{k_1} \frac{(1 - \gamma_i)^2}{\gamma_i} \frac{t}{4} \mathbf{N}. \qquad i = 2, \ldots, n \tag{4.46}$$

which is proportional to the consumption share α_i: a higher demand for good i leads to a larger number of type i-cities whose size remains the same. This number also decreases with the degree of increasing returns γ_i, the reason being that a smaller number of larger cities allows for a better exploitation of scale economies. Note also that higher commuting costs generate a larger number of all types of cities $i = 2, \ldots, n$ because this increase reduces urban costs within each type of city.

Last, an increase in total population triggers a proportional increase in the number of cities ($i = 2, \ldots, n$). This proportionality rule is the counterpart of (4.43), which states that the equilibrium disposable income increases proportionally with the population size. This result implies that a growing population translates into a larger number of cities that keep the same size. In other words, the model cannot explain why a growing population also feeds urban growth through the expansion of existing cities.

2. Let us now consider cities of type 1, which produce the numéraire. Using (4.43), (4.44) and (4.46), we get

$$m_1^* = \frac{\alpha_1 k_1 \mathbf{N} + \sum_{j=2}^{n} \frac{t}{4} m_j^* \left(N_j^*\right)^2}{\left[1 - \frac{t}{4}(N_1^*)^{1-\gamma_1}\right] (N_1^*)^{1+\gamma_1}}$$

which is less than proportional to the whole population size and to the consumption share of good 1. Indeed, since good 1 is also used in commuting activity, a relatively smaller number of type 1-cities permits other types of cities to benefit more from scale economies. Using (4.41) and (4.46), we may readily verify that m_1^* also increases with t.

In sum, the trade-off between scale economies and commuting costs takes here the following form: (i) *as increasing returns get stronger in the production of good i, the number of type i-cities decreases, while these cities become larger*; and (ii) when commuting costs fall, all cities get bigger, while the number of each type of cities decreases. For the same reasons as those discussed in the previous section, the number and size of each city-type resulting from the action of developers and local governments is socially optimal.

Another important finding of the model is that wages paid in large cities are higher than those paid in small cities. However, this difference is offset by higher land rent and commuting costs, which means that real wages are equal across all cities.[16] In equilibrium, workers are indifferent about the city in which they live. This result may be extended to cope with non-pecuniary elements. If, for whatever reasons, type j-cities are endowed with higher (lower) amenities than the other types of cites, they offer workers lower (higher) wages and/or higher (lower) land rents. In other words, *there are pecuniary compensations that result in equal utility in all cities*. Finally, the model can be extended to cope with final and intermediate goods. Under the assumption of zero transport costs, cities specialize in producing either the final good or the intermediate good because producing the two goods within the same city causes only higher urban costs with no offsetting benefits.

It is fair to say that Henderson's canonical model provides a compelling and original approach to the existence of an urban system with different types of cities and intercity trade. It also sheds new light on the trade-off between increasing returns and commuting costs. However, as in the previous section, the model critically depends on the existence of large agents who run the cities. Under external increasing returns, the role of these agents is even more important because, in the presence of externalities, the market is unlikely to be able to coordinate the individual decisions needed for cities to exist. Note also that Mirrlees (1995) revisited the previous setting using the approach of Section 4.3. In equilibrium, each city specializes in one particular good produced under increasing returns by a single wage-setting firm. In this alternative context, Mirrlees reached conclusions similar to Henderson.

Admittedly, many North American cities started as communities of immigrants (e.g., the Puritans in New England). William Penn, who launched the city of Philadelphia, epitomizes the kind of agent Henderson probably has in mind. Similarly, factory towns emerged in nineteenth-century Europe in places endowed with coal or other raw material deposits; some of them were even launched by paternalistic businessmen who aimed to improve upon the living conditions of their workers. In today's China many city governments act as competitive firms that do not differ much from factory towns. Even though

[16] Preliminary empirical studies seem to confirm this result. See Glaeser and Gottlieb (2009) for the United States and Rice and Venables (2003) for the United Kingdom.

historically large agents may also be responsible for the creation of several cities – think of landlords, monasteries or temples, royal courts, or large profit-maximizing factories – many settlements around the world also have emerged as the outcome of self-organizing mechanisms.[17] This is precisely what models in NEG, such as those studied in Chapter 8, aim to achieve.

Another limitation of the model is that local governments or land developers are able to control the population size of cities. Yet, as observed by Alonso (1994), "from Moscow to London and Paris and from Lagos to Jakarta, policies to stop growth have proved ineffective."[18] Furthermore, cities are like floating islands because intercity transport costs are zero. A complete theory of urban systems should explicitly account for city location. Rich soil, a safe harbor, fresh water, easy defense were often the start of many small towns (first nature); increasing returns and labor specialization made the urban system (second nature). This question is investigated in Chapter 10. Last, Henderson's model does not explain the existence of large, diversified cities such as Tokyo, New York, or London. In what follows, we turn our attention to this question.

4.4.2 Specialized or Diversified Cities

Many cities are *specialized* in the production of few goods and services, while a few others are *diversified* in that they supply several goods, but not necessarily all of them. In the real world, both types of cities coexist. From the historical viewpoint, most cities were small and diversified because intercity trade was very costly. Indeed, despite the presence of increasing returns, it was desirable to provide locally a wide array of goods in order to save on their transport costs. Nowadays, transport costs are much lower, and it thus seems desirable to take advantage of increasing returns. In other words, cities should become specialized to reduce workers' commuting costs. Yet, though many cities are specialized, we observe a growing number of large and diversified metropolises.

(i) One reason for diversification is the possibility of exploiting economies of scope in the production of business-to-business services and local public goods (Goldstein and Gronberg 1984). If the demand for the final output of a city-industry is not perfectly elastic as in Henderson, then it is not profitable for

[17] Glaeser (2011) provides ample evidence that urban growth in the American Sunbelt owes a lot to the action of developers. It is less clear, however, that developers play a significant role in determining the activities in which cities are specialized.

[18] Note, however, that the *Hukou system*, initiated in China at the time of the planned economy, seems to have been effective in restricting rural-urban migrations. Migrants must acquire different permits in order to access health care, schools, and housing. In order to get those permits they must pass various hurdles, and may still have to pay taxes to their home village for public services they do not consume. Typically, rural-urban migrants face total fees that can be equivalent up to several months' wages. While most of these fees were abolished in 2001, various administrative barriers still restrict labor mobility in China. All of this could explain why Chinese cities could be "too small" (Au and Henderson 2004).

this industry to grow beyond some limit. If different industries co-locate within the same city, they may enjoy a larger range of intermediate goods and public services, especially those that cannot be traded, thus making each industry more productive. On the other hand, this co-location requires more workers within the same city and, therefore, longer commuting. As a consequence, firms must pay a higher wage. In this case, the balance is between the productivity gains of the final industries and the higher commuting costs within the diversified city. The same type of argument may be applied to consumption (Abdel-Rahman 2000). More generally, Abdel-Rahman and Anas (2004) highlight the importance of the trade-off between the *trading-economy effect* and the *crowing-out effect* for the formation of both types of cities. In particular, as more intermediate goods and services are tradable, cities tend to become specialized.

(ii) Abdel-Rahman and Fujita (1993) provides a simple illustration of a similar trade-off in a setting with two cities and two final goods. Let $C_i = F_i + c_i X_i$ be the production cost in industry $i = 1, 2$. There are economies of scope, meaning that total fixed costs are lower when both industries co-locate: $F < F_1 + F_2$. The cost of producing both goods in a diversified city is then given by $F + c_1 X_1 + c_2 X_2$. Assuming zero transport costs for the goods, these authors show that the urban system involves one large and diversified city producing the two goods and one small city specialized in the production of good 1, say, when $F_1 < F < F_2$. Otherwise, the saving on fixed costs is not sufficient to compensate the crowding out of the land market, and the two cities are specialized.

(iii) Abdel-Rahman and Fujita have identified a channel that goes through production. Tabuchi and Thisse (2006) have identified a different channel in which the interaction between the two industries goes through the range of varieties they supply. The two differentiated goods are produced under the same production costs $F + cX_i$. However, whereas good 1's transport costs are zero, shipping good 2 is costly. Tabuchi and Thisse then show that the market outcome displays *regional specialization*. More precisely, good 1 is produced in the two cities but good 2 is produced in, say, city A only. Workers who choose to live in the larger city bear higher urban costs but consume the whole range of good 2-varieties at lower prices. In contrast, workers living in city B bear lower urban costs but the price they pay good 2 is higher because all varieties of this good are imported from A.

This may be explained as follows. As shipping good 1 is costless, sector 1(2)–firms (workers) are a priori indifferent about their location. By contrast, sector 2-firms seek to minimize their transport costs and do so by being located together in city A. Some workers produce good 1 in this city. Would all sector 1-workers reside in city B, they would have to pay for shipping good 2 from city A and bear fairly high urban costs. Furthermore, as long as good 2's transport costs are not too high relative to commuting costs, the agglomeration of sector

2 in city A implies that some workers produce good 1 in city B. Otherwise both sectors would be agglomerated in city A where urban costs would be very high.[19] Thus, city A is larger and diversified, whereas city B is smaller and specialized. The space-economy thus involves one large city and one small city with different industrial combinations. Observe that workers residing in cities A and B have different consumption structures but reach the same utility level. *The mobility of workers yields utility equalization but not factor price equalization*. Once more, difference in urban costs between cities is crucial to explain those results.

These authors also show that the existence of a nontradable consumption good (other than housing) is sufficient to generate an *urban hierarchy*. Because good 2 is nontradable, it is now produced in both cities. When commuting costs are not too large, the market outcome is such that a larger array of each good's varieties is produced in city A than in city B. This result, which agrees with Christaller's (1933) central place theory, is the outcome of a bidirectional process. On the one hand, a larger export sector boosts urban growth by attracting services. On the other hand, a larger service sector leads to the expansion of the export sector, which can serve as another engine of urban development. As usual, high commuting costs and land rents put a break on city A's growth.

Though both cities are diversified, sector 2 is more agglomerated than sector 1. Therefore, city A has a larger labor share in sector 2 whereas city B has a larger labor share in sector 1. Each city is thus *partially* specialized: city A has a comparative advantage in the nontradables because it has a larger market, whereas city B has a comparative advantage in terms of urban costs, which makes it attractive to people working in the manufacturing sector. This is consistent with Ricardo's comparative advantage theory. Comparative advantages here are endogenous because they are generated by market interactions.

The previous two contributions could convey the wrong impression that a city is either specialized or completely diversified. In an economy involving only two industries, a diversified city is necessarily completely diversified. When the number of industries exceeds two, this need not be true. We see in Chapter 10 that cities hosting several but not all industries may arise in equilibrium.

(iv) Another advantage of having diversified cities is that such cities are able to smooth out shocks affecting specific industries. In this case, a diversified city is to be viewed as a portfolio of activities: when one activity is adversely affected, workers have the opportunity to move to other sectors. The expected wage is then higher than in a specialized city (Krugman 1991a). This bears

[19] Note that what distinguishes those two contributions from Henderson's is that the formation of the space-economy results from market interactions only because there is no large agent who chooses cities' industrial mix.

some resemblance with portfolio theory, which recommends spreading risks over several assets. Although one may extend Henderson's approach and assume that city corporations behave like financial investors, it is hard to believe that they have the capability to develop and run large cities such as New York or Tokyo. The insurance benefits generated by diversification must be viewed as an additional attribute that makes large cities more attractive to workers, and that may compensate them for the higher urban costs they bear in such big cities.

In addition, specialization weakens a city's ability to adapt to technical change. All industries must one day decline, and thus a specialized city may turn into a "negative cluster" when the implicit collusion between firm managers, trade unions, and local politicians leads them to lobby the national government or other political bodies to extract resources that permit the survival of firms specialized in declining activities. Examples abound in Europe of old industrialized cities and regions that have succeeded in attracting sizable subsidies to finance inefficient firms, with the consequence of delaying even further the possibility for the corresponding area to find a new niche (Polèse 2010).

(v) Finally, Jacobs (1969) has argued that urban diversity facilitates innovation because it allows new producers to observe and borrow ideas initiated by firms belonging to other industrial sectors. And, indeed, Feldman and Audretsch (1999) report that innovation is fostered by a more diversified productive environment. Charlot and Duranton (2004) find that, in larger and more educated cities, workers communicate more, which in turn has a positive effect on their wages. In the same spirit, Bacolod, Bull, and Strange (2009) observe that the productivity gains in large and diversified cities are higher for skilled workers than for others. Therefore, it is no real surprise that Duranton and Puga (2001) find that uncertainty about the production process in the initial phases of the product cycle may lead to the coexistence of different sectors within the same city. When firms master their production processes, they relocate to more specialized areas, so that diversified cities are viewed here as "nurseries." Therefore, the coexistence of the two types of cities would be explained by the fact that firms need different environments and benefit from different types of externalities in the product cycle and the supply chain. More generally, the city of Jane Jacobs is the place that enables people to cooperate through *learning by doing* and *learning from others*.

Though seemingly different, intra- and intersectoral agglomeration economies are unlikely to be orthogonal to one another. Therefore, it seems reasonable to believe that large and diversified cities enjoy both types of economies, as well as insurance benefits against asymmetric shocks. Medium-sized and small cities are likely to benefit only from the intrasectoral agglomeration economies, while facing the prospect of idiosyncratic shocks. There would thus be additional size effects caused by the combination of different types of externalities within large metropolitan areas.

4.5 COMPETITION AND THE SPATIAL ORGANIZATION OF MARKETS

We now come to quite a different tradition, which is deeply rooted in classical location theory. If firms and consumers are geographically dispersed and the number of firms is small relative to the mass of consumers owing to indivisibilities in production, each firm has some monopoly power over the consumers in its immediate vicinity. In other words, the presence of increasing returns at the plant level prevents spatial markets from being perfectly competitive because differences in consumer locations, and hence transport costs, are a source of market power. Competition in space is, therefore, imperfect and should be studied according to the relevant theories. Once this is recognized, the trade-off between increasing returns and transport costs turns out to be crucial for determining the number of firms competing within a given area whose population size is given. The present setting may be viewed as the product-counterpart of that studied in Section 4.2.2.

4.5.1 Equilibrium and the Number of Firms in Space

The prototype of spatial competition is generally attributed to Hotelling (1929), who studied firms' price decisions assuming that consumers' locations are fixed. Hotelling's main purpose was to model competition in a way to ensure that each firm's demand is continuous, while permitting consumers to react discontinuously at the individual level. The heterogeneity across consumers, introduced through transportation costs, is to make sure that individual discontinuities, stemming from the fact that consumers make mutually exclusive purchases, are distributed such that they are not noticeable to the firm.

Yet, the essence of spatial competition was probably better described by Kaldor (1935). According to this author, locations in space mold the nature of competition between firms in a very specific way. Whatever the number of firms participating in the aggregate, *competition is localized: each firm competes more vigorously with its immediate neighbors than with more distant neighbors.* Spatial competition is therefore inherently strategic in that each firm is only concerned with a small number of direct competitors regardless of the total number of firms in the industry. This does not imply, however, that the industry is formed by independent clusters of sellers. Because a chain connects firms such that any two subsequent firms in the chain are direct competitors, all of them are interrelated within a complex network of interactions. Some "chain effect" linking of apparently independent firms seems to be inherent to the spatial framework. The whole demand system must then be inspected to delineate the extent of a spatial market.

In order to gain more insights about the working of competition in such a context, we suppose a simple setting in which M firms supplying the same good are distributed equidistantly along a circle $\mathbf{C}$ of unit length. There is a continuum of workers of size N who are uniformly distributed along the same circle (maybe because the lot size is fixed and the same across locations). Then, firm i has two *direct competitors*, firms $i-1$ and $i+1$. The market situated between firms $i-1$ and $i+1$ is segmented according to the principle stated above: each consumer patronizes the firm with the lowest full price, which is defined as the posted price plus the transportation cost to the corresponding firm. Hence, for a vector of prices (p_{i-1}, p_i, p_{i+1}), there are three groups of consumers in this local market: the customers of firm $i-1$, of firm $i+1$, and of firm i. Under these circumstances, a unilateral price cut by firm i extends its own market only at the expense of firms $i-1$ and $i+1$, while the other firms are not directly affected. Therefore, the cross-price elasticity between firm i and firm $j \neq i-1, i+1$ is zero.

Because each consumer purchases from the firm that, for her, has the lowest full price, consumers are divided into different segments, and each firm's demand is the sum of consumers' demands in one particular segment. The boundary between two firms' markets is given by the location of the consumer indifferent between them known as the *marginal consumer*. This boundary is endogenous because it depends on the prices set by the firms. Given the continuous dispersion of consumers, a marginal variation in price changes the boundary and each firm's demand by the same order.

Each consumer buys one unit of the product.[20] As a result, a consumer at location $r \in \mathbf{C}$ has an indirect utility given by

$$V_i(r) = u + Y - p_i - t\,|r - r_i| \tag{4.47}$$

when she patronizes the shop located at $r_i \in \mathbf{C}$. In this expression, u described the gross utility a consumer derives from the product, Y her income, p_i the price posted by firm i, and $t\,|r - r_i|$ the transportation cost the consumer must bear when visiting firm i, with $t > 0$ and $|r - r_i|$ the length of the shortest arc connecting r and r_i. The net income $Y - t\,|r - r_i|$ is supposed to be high enough for each consumer to be able to buy the good. All firms have the same production cost given by $C(q) = f + cq$ where $f > 0$ and $c > 0$ (see also [4.2]). A price vector is denoted by $\mathbf{p} = (p_1, \ldots, p_n)$ while $\mathbf{p}_{-i}$ stands for the price vector $\mathbf{p}$ from which the i-th component has been deleted.

Our first task is to determine the position of the marginal consumer between firm i and each of its two neighbors. Consider the case of firm $i-1$. The corresponding marginal consumer is located at $\bar{r}_i \in [r_{i-1}, r_i]$, which must satisfy $V_{i-1}(\bar{r}_i) = V_i(\bar{r}_i)$ so that

$$\bar{r}_i = \frac{-p_{i-1} + p_i + t(r_i + r_{i-1})}{2t}.$$

[20] The assumption of a perfectly inelastic demand could be removed without affecting our main results but at the expense of longer analytical developments.

Because a similar expression holds for $\bar{r}_{i+1}$, it follows that the demand for firm i when prices are given by p_{i-1}, p_i and p_{i+1} is

$$D_i(p_{i-1}, p_i, p_{i+1}) = N\frac{p_{i-1} - 2p_i + p_{i+1} + 2t/M}{2t}. \quad (4.48)$$

This expression reflects the *localized* nature of competition since, besides its own price, firm i's demand D_i depends only upon the prices charged by its two neighbors.

Consequently, firm i's profit, contingent on the prices p_{i-1} and p_{i+1} set by its two neighbors, can be written as follows:

$$\pi_i(\mathbf{p}) = (p_i - c)D_i(p_{i-1}, p_i, p_{i+1}) - f. \quad (4.49)$$

We consider a Nash price equilibrium in pure strategies, that is, a price vector $\mathbf{p}^*$ such that each firm $i = 1, \ldots, M$, anticipating correctly the prices charged by the other firms, maximizes its profit $\pi_i(p_1^*, \ldots, p_i, \ldots, p_n^*)$ at p_i^*. If such an equilibrium exists, it must solve the first order condition applied to (4.49):

$$p_{i-1} - 4p_i + p_{i+1} + 2t/M + 2c = 0 \qquad i = 1, \ldots, M.$$

This is a system of M linear equations that has a unique solution given by

$$p^* = p_i^* = c + t/M. \quad (4.50)$$

This solution is a Nash equilibrium. Indeed, the second order condition is locally satisfied, while any unilateral deviation that prices firms $i - 1$ and $i + 1$ out of business leads to negative profit.

Inspecting (4.50) reveals that firms apply an absolute markup t/M that increases with the transportation rate t as well as with the distance $1/M$ between two adjacent firms. In other words, geographical isolation, economically expressed by the value of the transportation cost, allows each firm to have market power. However, this market power is restricted by the market power exercised by the closest competitors, as measured by the distance between two successive firms along **C**. This shows how space acts as a barrier to competition: higher transportation costs, fewer firms, or both yield higher equilibrium price and profit.

On the contrary, when the number of firms becomes arbitrarily large, the equilibrium price converges toward the marginal production cost, that is, the competitive outcome. But the existence of a fixed cost prevents the number of firms from rising indefinitely. In fact, firms are confronted by a trade-off when deciding whether or not to enter. A firm will only enter if it can locate sufficiently far from other firms (in terms of economic distance, not physical distance) so that it can serve enough consumers and charge a high enough price to cover its fixed costs.

Under free entry, the equilibrium number of firms M^* is obtained when firms' equilibrium profit is equal to zero (disregarding again the integer problem), that is, when $(t/M)(N/M) - f = 0$ so that

$$M^* = \sqrt{\frac{Nt}{f}}. \tag{4.51}$$

Consequently, *the equilibrium number of firms increases with the unit transportation cost but decreases with the fixed production cost.* The intuition is the same as presented in Section 4.2.2. This is the spatial competition version of the now classical trade-off between increasing returns and transportation costs: Whereas the former reduces the average production cost, it also increases the cost of transportation for those traveling to the firm. This trade-off determines the number of firms in space.

This result can be given an interesting interpretation from the historical point of view. In preindustrial societies, production involved low investments while traveling was very costly; there was a large number of firms operating at small scales. Since the beginning of the Industrial Revolution, however, one has faced a dramatic fall in transport costs while production has involved larger and larger overhead costs (Bairoch 1997). Consequently, we may safely conclude that *the type of technological progress observed for many decades in developed countries has led to a substantial reduction in the number of operating plants as well as to an expansion of their size and market area.* On the other hand, a rise in the population size, through an increase of N, leads to a larger number of plants.

A word, in closing. The previous discussion shows that price competition is a strong dispersion force that leads firms to seek geographical isolation in order to relax competition. So one may wonder what brings firms together within a city or an industrial cluster. In Chapters 7–9, we discussed how the combination of product differentiation and agglomeration economies, generated by external effects, may offset the competition effect and induce firms to congregate.

4.5.2 The Optimum Spatial Distribution of Firms

Consider now the efficient configuration. How many firms should there be in the market? Or, equivalently, how many markets should be open? In the setting considered in the preceding section in which each consumer buys one unit of the product, there is no dead-weight loss associated with a discrepancy between price and marginal cost. Because consumers' indirect utility (4.47) is linear in income and each consumer buys one unit of the good produced at a constant unit cost c, the optimal number of firms minimizes the firms' fixed production costs plus consumers' total transport costs. Hence, the problem involves a trade-off, for increasing the number of firms, hence fixed costs, reduces the aggregate transport costs and vice versa.

It is readily verified that the social cost to be minimized is defined as follows:

$$C(M) = Mf + 2M \int_0^{1/2M} Ntr\mathrm{d}r$$
$$= Mf + Nt/4M.$$

Treating M as a real number and differentiating this expression with respect to M yields the optimum number of firms (the second order condition is met since C is strictly convex):

$$M^o = \frac{1}{2}\sqrt{\frac{Nt}{f}} = M^*/2. \tag{4.52}$$

Using (4.51), we thus have shown:

Proposition 4.4. *In the spatial competition model, the equilibrium number of firms is larger than the optimal number.*

This is a fairly general result suggesting that the market tends to provide too many small firms, thus leading to a denser pattern of production than the one chosen by a benevolent and informed planner. The reason is that, although there are M firms in the industry, each firm competes with its two neighbors only, thus leading to high market prices, which, in turn, invite more entry. Proposition 4.4 can be viewed as the spatial counterpart of Chamberlin's excess capacity theorem in that the total capacity built by the market, expressed by the number of plants, is too high. This is interesting because proponents of regional planning often argue that the market works poorly in fighting against regional imbalances and "desertification." After all, the market seems to generate denser patterns of production than what is optimum – a result that invites us to be careful in evaluating the relevance of some criticisms of a spatial market economy's organization.

The search for spatial equity may lead the planner to locate a larger number of firms because this gives consumers a better access to the service. In such a context, it is natural to ask what the Rawlsian configuration is, i.e., the configuration that maximizes the utility of the worst-off consumer. Assuming that fixed costs are equally shared across consumers, the worst-off consumer is the one who is the farthest away from a firm. Her utility is given by

$$\frac{Mf}{N} + t\frac{1}{2M}.$$

Differentiating this expression with respect to M and solving yields the equitable number M^R of firms:

$$M^o < M^R = \sqrt{\frac{Nt}{2f}} = \frac{M^*}{\sqrt{2}} < M^*.$$

As expected, a Rawlsian planner provides more firms than an efficiency-maximizing planner. In other words, the pursuit of spatial equity, or of other considerations such as political acceptability, is detrimental to efficiency. Less expected, perhaps, it appears that *a Rawlsian planner chooses a number of firms that is smaller than what the market selects*. Indeed, unlike profit-maximizing firms, the Rawlsian planner cares about the total investment cost Mf, which leads her to launch fewer firms.

4.5.3 Land Capitalization

Space has an important consequence that is ignored in spatial competition models but is central to urban economics, namely *land capitalization*. Capitalization means here that the land rent reflects both the price paid and the transport cost incurred by the occupant when patronizing the cheapest store. There is no capitalization in the standard spatial competition model because land is not involved. Yet, the model can be extended to cope explicitly with consumers simultaneously choosing location and consumption. The basic framework has been laid down by Asami, Fujita, and Thisse (1993).

We suppose that firms and households make their decisions sequentially. In the first stage, M equidistant firms choose prices in a noncooperative way. In the second stage, given the decisions made by firms, households consume one unit of land (the lot size is fixed) in addition to one unit of firms' output. Hence, households have to choose a location and the firm to patronize. To ease the burden of notation, we assume that the mass N of consumers is equal to 1. Consumers compete for land and pay the land rent. Besides land rent, the income of each household is spent on the firms' output, transport cost, and the numéraire. A consumer at location $r \in \mathbf{C}$ now has an indirect utility given by

$$V_i(r) = u + Y - p_i - t\,|r - r_i| - R(r) \tag{4.53}$$

when she patronizes the shop located at $r_i \in \mathbf{C}$ and pays the market land rent $R(r)$ at location r. Hence, in equilibrium consumers enjoy the same utility level because they pay a land rent that reflects the difference in the accessibility to firms.

When choosing their prices firms anticipate consumers' responses, thus reflecting the fact that the firms have more market power than consumers. Our equilibrium concept can then be summarized as follows. Given a price configuration of firms, consumers decide on their location and shopping place at the corresponding residential equilibrium, which is of the competitive type. With respect to firms, consumers could be viewed as the followers of a Stackelberg game in which firms would be the leaders. Firms choose prices at the Nash equilibrium of a noncooperative game whose players are the firms and in this way anticipate consumers' residential equilibrium.

To show how spatial competition may yield the first best outcome, we propose an institutional system in which the firms' payoff functions are modified through land capitalization. Specifically, we assume that firm i's payoff is defined by the sum of the operating profit made from selling its product and the added land value as a result of its presence in the urban area. The added land value ($\Delta_i(\mathbf{p})$) is obtained by subtracting the aggregate land rent when firm i does not operate ($ADR(\mathbf{p}_{-i})$) from the aggregate land rent when firm i operates with the other $M-1$ firms ($ADR(\mathbf{p})$):

$$\Delta_i(\mathbf{p}) \equiv ADR(\mathbf{p}) - ADR(\mathbf{p}_{-i})$$

so that firm i's payoff is

$$\Pi_i(\mathbf{p}) = \pi_i(\mathbf{p}) + \Delta_i(\mathbf{p}).$$

Given what we said in Section 4.4.3, this means that firm i behaves like a land developer within its market area, which corresponds to a segment of the urban area.

If M equidistant firms have entered the urban market and incurred the fixed cost f, each of them is active in the price equilibrium. At the resulting residential equilibrium, all consumers must reach the same utility level, so that (4.53) implies that there exists a constant $\bar{R}$, which equals the common urban cost borne by consumers:

$$R(r) + \min_{j=1,\ldots,M} \{p_j + t\,|r - r_j|\} = \bar{R} \tag{4.54}$$

for all $r \in \mathbf{C}$. In what follows, it is supposed that all firms consider the common urban cost $\bar{R}$ as a given constant.[21]

When firm i is the only inactive firm, we have

$$R_{-i}(r) + \min_{j \neq i} \{p_j + t\,|r - r_j|\} = \bar{R}$$

where $R_{-i}(r)$ is the land rent prevailing at r when firm i is inactive. Then the added land value of firm i, $\Delta_i(\mathbf{p})$, is given by the shaded area in Figure 4.3, which can be shown to be equal to:

$$\Delta_i(\mathbf{p}) = \frac{(p_{i-1} - p_i + t/M)(p_{i+1} - p_i + t/M)}{2t}$$

so that firm i's payoff is given by

$$\Pi_i(\mathbf{p}) = (p_i - c)D_i(p_{i-1}, p_i, p_{i+1}) + \Delta_i(\mathbf{p}) \tag{4.55}$$

where $M = 1$ in (4.48).

[21] Note that this constant cannot be determined within the model because of our assumptions of a fixed lot size and of no vacant land. When there is an arbitrarily small amount of vacant land, this constant is given by $\bar{R} = \max_{r \in C} \min_{j=1,\ldots,m} \{p_j + t|r - r_j|\}$. In any case, the value of this constant does not affect the results of this section.

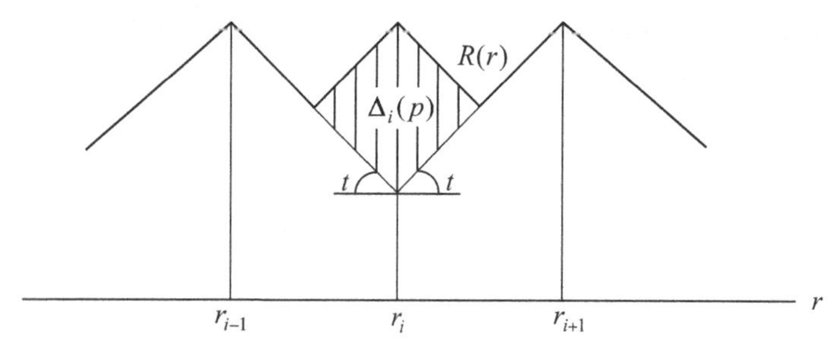

Figure 4.3. Firm i's added land value.

Differentiating (4.55) with respect to p_i and equating the resulting expression to zero yields:

$$\begin{aligned}\frac{\partial \Pi_i}{\partial p_i} &= D_i + (p_i - c)\frac{\partial D_i}{\partial p_i} + \frac{\partial \Delta_i(\mathbf{p})}{\partial p_i} \\ &= D_i + (p_i - c)\frac{\partial D_i}{\partial p_i} - D_i \\ &= -\frac{p_i - c}{t} = 0\end{aligned}$$

which implies that $p_i^* = c$. Clearly, $\Pi_i(\mathbf{p})$ is concave in p_i so that the unique solution to the first order condition is the price equilibrium. In fact, since $p_i^* = c$ is the optimal strategy for firm i *regardless* of the prices charged by all other firms, we have the following result:

Proposition 4.5. *Assume that firms capitalize the added land value on their market area into their payoffs. If firms consider the common urban cost as a constant, then marginal cost pricing is the equilibrium in strongly dominant strategies of the price game.*

The intuition behind this somewhat surprising result is that land capitalization is equivalent to first-degree price discrimination, up to a constant that is the same across firms because the consumer surplus is identical to the land rent (up to the same constant for all firms), which is now captured by the agent who creates it. Therefore, making the socially optimal decision is a Nash equilibrium. We have, however, a stronger result because our equilibrium is in dominant strategies.

Marginal cost pricing implies that operating profits are zero for all firms so that their payoff is equal to their added land value net of fixed cost. In the entry process, the number of firms are such that the added land value Δ of the last firm is equal to the fixed entry cost f (neglecting the integer problem). Because the added land value by a firm is equal to the corresponding reduction in total transport costs, the free-entry condition means that the last entrant must balance the social gain and the social entry cost. Hence, we have the following:

Proposition 4.6. *Assume that firms capitalize the added land value on their market area into their payoffs. If firms consider the common urban cost as a constant, then the free entry equilibrium leads to the efficient number of firms.*

The equilibrium number of firms is now given by (4.52). Indeed, Proposition 4.6 implies that the social value of an additional firm is identical to its added land value. Hence, when land rents are accurately accounted for, there is no excess capacity in a spatial economy, thus "proving" the following conjecture stated by Hotelling (1938, 242) more than seventy years ago:

> all taxes on commodities, including sales taxes, are more objectionable than taxes on incomes, inheritances, and the site value of land; and . . . the latter might be applied to cover the fixed costs of electric power plants, waterworks, railroads, and other industries in which the fixed costs are large, so as to reduce to the level of marginal cost the prices charged for the services and products of these industries.

Proposition 4.6 also implies that we have obtained a Henry George rule in an environment in which firms behave strategically. In other words, allowing firms to capitalize the added land rent they create by their activities leads to the first best outcome even though firms behave strategically on the product market. Note, however, that they are not supposed to be able to manipulate the urban cost borne by the consumers. This behavioral assumption is acceptable as long as no firm is dominant within the economy. Lastly, all consumers reach the same utility level because the differential land rent washes out the differences in accessibility.

4.5.4 Notes on the Literature

Hotelling's analysis had been anticipated in several respects by Launhardt (1885, chapter 29) who questioned the validity of the price-taking assumption by observing that firms dispersed over space have some market power over the customers situated in their vicinity, thus allowing them to manipulate their prices to their own advantage. His analysis was, however, ignored outside the German-speaking community (see Dos Santos Ferreira and Thisse, 1996, for a modern presentation of Launhardt's ideas).

Beckmann (1972b) and Stern (1972) were the first who formalized in a precise way the trade-off between increasing returns and transportation costs under spatial competition, while the circular model was developed independently and later on by Salop (1979). Interestingly, Beckmann has shown that the equilibrium price is lower when firms compete in a two-dimensional space rather than in one-dimensional space. This is because each firm now has six direct competitors (located at the vertices of a hexagon) instead of two, thus making price competition fiercer.

Since the path-breaking paper of Hotelling (1929), it is well known that the framework used to describe a spatial industry permits one to study the working of a differentiated industry. The power of this analogy has been exploited extensively in industrial organization (Eaton and Lipsey 1977; Gabszewicz and Thisse 1986). There is a substantial amount of literature in industrial organization that addresses the issue of whether the market under- or overprovides differentiated products, which is of direct relevance for spatial competition. Surveys can be found in Eaton and Lipsey (1988), Gabszewicz and Thisse (1992), and Anderson, de Palma, and Thisse (1992, chapter 6). Finally, it is worth noting that several results obtained in using the spatial competition model in industrial organization were anticipated by Vickrey in his *Microstatics* published in 1964. The main extracts have been reproduced in Anderson and Braid (1999).

Observe that the forces at work in Section 4.4 are not tied to the particular spatial price policy used in the foregoing developments and called mill pricing. For example, the ability to price discriminate (see Chapters 7 and 9 for more details) implies that a firm can cut its prices in one part of its market without the need to change its prices elsewhere. This effectively reduces the power of the firm to commit to a set of prices and so strengthens price competition. But fiercer price competition will not necessarily work to the benefit of consumers. On the one hand, for a given number of firms stronger price competition will, indeed, reduce the prices charged by incumbent firms. On the other hand, stronger price competition can also be expected to act as an entry deterrent, and so may benefit incumbent firms (Norman and Thisse 1996).

4.6 CONCLUDING REMARKS

We have seen that the trade-off between increasing returns and transportation costs may take very different forms and explain a wide range of issues in a spatial economy. First, this trade-off lies at the source of the mechanism governing the size of a city in either context of the city as a firm or a community. Though admittedly the description of a city system provided here is very simple, it is interesting that the first best outcome is achieved in a setting with increasing returns and perfect competition. This is due to the Henry George rule, which states how the loss incurred in production may be financed by the differential land rent once all goods are sold on competitive markets.

A similar trade-off may also be utilized to understand the connections between the two main settings discussed in this chapter, which otherwise seem to be largely unrelated. While the urban economics approach presented in Section 4.3 allows competitive firms to enjoy the benefits of external increasing returns, the spatial competition model of Section 4.5 assumes that increasing returns are internal to firms operating on imperfectly competitive markets. It is thus fair to say that this chapter has illustrated the two modeling strategies which can be employed to obviate the difficulties raised by the spatial impossibility theorem. As discussed in Chapter 1, the choice of a particular model must be grounded in an in-depth discussion of the spatial scale at which the economic analysis is conducted. Nevertheless, we have also seen that accounting explicitly for a land market permits a reconciliation of the above two approaches through the land capitalization mechanism. This suggests that a comprehensive model encompassing different spatial scales need not be out of reach.

High overhead costs in production leads to a sparse distribution of firms whereas high transportation costs have the opposite effect. These are the elements considered (implicitly) by Christaller ([1933] 1960) and (explicitly) by Lösch ([1940] 1954) in their explanation of a one-commodity spatial market. The presence of increasing returns prevent spatial markets from being complete and, as previously seen, the number of active firms depends on the trade-off between increasing returns and transportation costs. In general, the two systems lead to a different number of markets. However, when firms are allowed to capitalize the land rent they create over their market area, the market yields one more time the first best outcome. This shows the power of the urban land rent in a market economy and provides a reconciliation of Hotelling (1929) with Hotelling (1938). This result constitutes a superb illustration of the contributions made by this author to the development of modern economics through the use of space as a specific economic category.

More fundamental, perhaps, the same trade-off is encountered in planning the number and location of all sorts of private or public facilities such as schools, recreational facilities, fire stations, and the like. The corresponding optimization problem is at the heart of facility location analysis in Operations Research. It was originally formulated by Manne (1964) and Stollsteimer (1963). Since then it has served as a basis for several developments in integer programming and been used in many applications.[22] Last, the same trade-off has been once more "rediscovered" in the new economic geography that started with the work of Krugman (1991a, 1991b). It operates in a still different way and is studied in Chapter 8. So it does not seem an exaggeration to say that *the trade-off between increasing returns and transportation cost is fundamental for the operation of a spatial economy.*

From the methodological viewpoint, this chapter has illustrated the modeling power of the CES and circular city models to apprehend the idea of heterogeneity. We know that two identical agents located at two different places are heterogeneous, while their (dis)similarity is measured by the geographical distance that separates them: the shorter the distance, the more similar the two

[22] See Labbé, Peeters, and Thisse (1995) for an Operation Research–based survey of the main models developed in facility location analysis.

agents. Evidently, other types of proximity may be studied by means of these two models. They are not equivalent, however. In the CES, any two agents are equally distant from one another (Anderson et al. 1992, chapter 4). In the circular city, an agent has two neighbors, who have neighbors, and so on. In other words, the distance between two agents varies with their relative position.

Two more comments are in order. First, in this chapter, we have focused on what are probably the two main existing spatial models. The first one (Sections 4.3 and 4.4) involves land and consumer location, but it does not deal with the relative position of cities. The second one (Section 4.5) involves the location of firms but often neglects land. One of the fundamental challenges for future research is to merge these two structures to study the location of cities using land. In this perspective, one may wonder what the efficiency result of Proposition 4.3 becomes when the choice of locations by developers becomes critical.

Second, Section 4.2 shows how detailed economic analyses are able to uncover some of the forces leading to workers' agglomeration around a CBD. In particular, as argued in Chapter 1, appealing explicitly to imperfect competition has allowed a sharper grasp of the mechanisms at work. In such disaggregate models, instead of using ad hoc expressions, it is possible to evaluate the impact of a particular policy on all the agents and to design better corrective public policies. We believe that this kind of approach may also lead to better empirical models because they suggest what could be the relevant variables to consider. Conversely, recent and impressive progress made in the empirics of agglomeration economies should help theorists to focus on more relevant issues (Henderson 2003a; Rosenthal and Strange 2004; Puga 2010; Combes, Duranton, and Gobillon 2011). Although it is likely that black box models will remain useful in urban economics, not all black boxes are alike. We paraphrase George Orwell in *Animal Farm* by observing that all black boxes are black but some boxes are more black than others.

5

Cities and the Public Sector

5.1 INTRODUCTION

When seeking a reason for the existence of cities, the one that comes most naturally to mind is the supply of public services. In large measure, this is dictated by historical considerations. For example, in medieval Europe cities were signified in two ways: a physical boundary (*the walled city*) and a legal status (*the democratized city*). Clearly, walling a city exhibits increasing returns and corresponds to a local public good whose supply is governed by size effects: the length of a circular wall is $2\pi r$, whereas the size of the corresponding area is πr^2; the ratio of the circumference to the area falls as the radius r increases, and thus a larger number of individuals may be defended at a lower average cost. In addition to its defensive purpose, the wall was also the symbol of the city's political autonomy, and the corporate freedom of the towns brought emancipation to individuals.[1] Historians agree that the specific legal status, which may itself be interpreted as a local public good, was a major criterion for identifying the city at least until the end of the Middle Ages (Bairoch 1988, chapter 1), if not later on. This clear-cut separation no longer exists. The legal status has been homogenized, except for minor exceptions, in most nations. Urban activities have gradually extended beyond the physical boundaries of the city to create suburbs, which are now very much part of the city considered as an economic agglomeration. As a result, the modern city is more dispersed and has fuzzy boundaries. However, the availability of local public goods remains a major ingredient of modern cities because the congregation of a large number of people facilitates the mutual provision of collective services that could not be obtained in isolation.[2]

[1] For example, the German emperor Henry V affirmed the principle "City air brings freedom" in charters for Speyer and Worms.

[2] Other examples of local public goods that have played a major role in the history of cities are religious temples and shrines, royal palaces, and public places such as the agora or the forum.

A *pure public good* is collectively consumed by all members of a community such as a city or a nation (Samuelson 1954b). Its consumption is *nonrivalrous* in the sense that each individual's consumption does not subtract from any other individual's consumption of that good. A pure public good's benefits are also *nonexcludable* because, once the good is provided, it is virtually impossible to exclude any member of the community from the benefits. Hence, unlike private goods, public goods can serve unlimited numbers of consumers without having quantity or quality degraded through congestion or increased costs. In contrast to this somewhat extreme model, most public services suffer from congestion (e.g., too many people attending an exhibit). Furthermore, consuming the public good often involves traveling. If a public good is located in space, there is competition for the limited land close to the public good. Hence, the social cost increases with the number of users because higher travel costs are required to use the public good. The literature following Tiebout (1956) and Buchanan (1965) has argued that both these effects compromise the "purity" of public goods and make them more similar to private goods. In this chapter, we consider this broader class of "impure" public goods.

It is well known that consumers have incentives not to reveal their true preferences regarding pure public goods because they cannot be excluded from their consumption. In this respect, it was Tiebout's merit to observe that many public services, such as police and fire protection, schools, hospitals, and stadiums, are "local." By migrating to the jurisdictions that respect their tastes in terms of goods and tax schemes, consumers reveal their preferences. According to Tiebout (1956, 420),

> Moving or failing to move replaces the usual market test of willingness to buy a good and reveals the consumer–voter's demand for public goods. Thus each locality has a revenue and an expenditure pattern that reflects the desires of its residents.

Thus, if each locality competes for consumers by providing its own package of public goods and taxes, competition among communities and "foot voting" by consumers may lead to the efficient provision of local public goods.

For this to work, consumer mobility is necessary. However, there is another aspect that has been neglected in the standard literature on local public goods. That is, the choice of a particular community implies the choice of residence, which, in turn, involves land consumption. This fact has an important consequence for local public goods models, namely, *land capitalization*. Capitalization means that the price of land embodies the benefits and costs of public services incurred by the residents. Hence, capitalization provides a natural measure of social surplus or willingness to pay for an increase in local public goods. In fact, capitalization and consumer mobility are inextricably linked: because consumers can move from unattractive locations to attractive locations, land prices will adjust to compensate for the differences in attractiveness.

In other words, through capitalization and consumer mobility, populations are endogenous to local policies.

Although the traditional spatial competition model has "location without land" (see Section 4.5), new local public goods models have "land without location" in the sense that travelling within the community is costless. In Tiebout's local public goods model, consumers are mobile in the sense that they choose what jurisdiction or location to occupy, but once there, their accessibility to public goods is irrelevant. Consumers cannot use the public goods of a neighboring locality even if those public goods are closer. The tying of consumer benefits to residency in the jurisdiction is essential to the success of the model; without it, the land value would not capture all the benefits of its policies. This assumption is most vividly met in the "islands" model of Stiglitz (1977) in which it is infeasible for a consumer on one island to consume the public goods of another.

In the context of local public goods, it is generally not desirable to increase the size of the city population indefinitely even though the per capita cost of the public good is decreasing with the number of users. Indeed, even when the public good is pure, the marginal social cost of a consumer, which is identical to the additional commuting cost, increases. Therefore, in the same spirit as in Chapter 4, *there is a trade-off between transport costs and the cost of supplying the public good*. In general, the city has a finite optimal size, which is determined by maximizing the utility level of the residents.

In pointing out the analogy between private goods and local public goods, however, Tiebout did not specify the objective function of the jurisdictions. Much of the debate following his work has revolved around this question. According to several authors, including Arnott (1979), Kanemoto (1980, chapter 3), and Henderson (1977, chapters 3 and 10; 1985), there is a missing agent in Tiebout's local public good setting, namely, a land developer who capitalizes the benefits of the public good in the land rent. In such an institutional context, competition between land developers may lead to the efficient provision of local public goods in a spatial economy. Indeed, jurisdictions, which are now identified with land developers, can profit by respecting their residents' tastes when the provision of public goods is capitalized into land prices. Thus, if capitalized land values are included in profits, jurisdictions have an incentive to organize their affairs efficiently.

In the real world, local public goods are often provided under the form of a public facility designed to provide a bundle of services to a community of consumers (Tiebout 1961; Teitz 1968). From the practical point of view, the importance of public infrastructure in shaping cities as well as the quality of life within them has been emphasized, with humor, by Teitz (1968, 36):

> Modern urban man is born in a publicly financed hospital, receives his education in a publicly supported school and university, spends a good part of his time travelling

on publicly built transportation facilities, communicating through the post office or the quasi-public telephone system, drinks its public water, disposes of his garbage through the public removal system, reads his public library books, picnics in his public parks, is protected by its public police, fire, and health systems; eventually he dies, again in a hospital, and may even be buried in a public cemetery.

In an otherwise homogeneous space, the location of a public facility becomes the center of the city. This is because consumers must travel to this facility to enjoy the public services made available there.[3]

In Section 5.2, we study the optimal provision of local public goods in a system of cities populated with identical consumers. We show that, when the population size is such that the residents' common utility level is maximized, the cost of the public good is equal to the aggregate differential land rent within each city. Furthermore, if land developers take the common utility level in the economy as given, the first best optimum can be sustained as a free-entry equilibrium among land developers. In each city, the cost of the local public good is financed by the aggregate differential land rent. These results suggest that the rules governing the supply of local public goods are similar to those applicable to private goods, as discussed in Chapter 4. In other words, we have "Tiebout without politics," or, as Henderson (1977, 72) put it:

The existence of land developers seeking to maximize profits ensures that scale economy benefits of increasing city size versus commuting cost increases are traded off implicitly or explicitly to achieve optimal city size.

In the preceding approach it is assumed that there is enough land for each city to be developed as an "isolated city state." At this point, it is therefore natural to ask *where* a local public good should be supplied when consumers are dispersed over the entire territory. Furthermore, we are also interested in checking what happens when the provision of public services is decided through a political process such as voting. This is a topic that has recently attracted attention in political economics. In Section 5.3, we consider a voting procedure in which consumers vote first for the number of facilities and then for their locations. As expected, each facility is set up at the middle point of its service area. Less expected is the result that, when the construction of these facilities is financed through a proportional income tax, voters tend to choose a number of facilities exceeding the efficient one. This suggests that the recourse to voting for choosing the system of public facilities fosters a proliferation of public infrastructure.

However, using more sophisticated taxation schemes enables one to sustain the optimum as a voting equilibrium. Specifically, we show that the optimal

[3] The distinction between *traveled-for goods* and *delivered goods* is not essential for our purpose. It is indeed reasonable to believe that the quality of a delivered good often decreases as the distance increases. So, in both cases, users' benefits are subject to a distant-decay effect.

tax scheme has the same profile as the land rent. More precisely, voting yields the optimum when the benefits associated with the proximity of facilities is capitalized in the land rent and when consumers are aware that they have to pay the corresponding rent.

5.2 THE CITY AS A PUBLIC GOOD

Into the urban land use model considered in Section 3.3, we now introduce a third commodity in the consumers' utility function, that is, a *local public good*. This good is made available to consumers through a facility located in the city. For simplicity, each city is to be formed within a one-dimensional space with unit land density. Consumers must bear some travel costs $T(r)$ to have access to the public service. In their attempt to reduce the access costs, consumers agglomerate around the place where the public facility is built in the same way as they do around the business district. Let $g = g(G, N)$ be the quantity of public good, where G stands for public expenditure and N for the mass of users. If the local public good is *pure*, then g is independent of N and, without loss of generality, we may assume that $g = G$. If the local public good is *congestible*, then an additional consumer has a negative impact on the welfare of others, in which case g is a strictly decreasing function of the mass N of users.

The whole population in the economy is formed by N identical consumers whose income is Y. This income is earned in a perfectly competitive industry operating under constant returns to scale. The utility function of a consumer is

$$U[s, z, g(G, N)].$$

When the consumer resides at distance r from the city center, his budget constraint is given by

$$z + sR(r) = Y - T(r) - \theta(r)$$

in which $R(r)$ denotes the land rent prevailing at distance r and $\theta(r)$ any tax paid (or subsidy received) by a consumer at distance r. This tax depends only upon the consumer's location because consumers are identical up to their distance to the facility.

Suppose that the local public good is pure. Although the results we present in the following discussion can be generalized to the case in which the lot size is variable, we find it convenient to assume that the lot size used by each consumer is fixed and normalized to one. Therefore, if N consumers live in the city, at the corresponding residential equilibrium they are evenly distributed around the city center over the interval $[-N/2, N/2]$. Let G be the level of public expenditure. Then, from the equality of the utility level across consumers and from the consumer budget constraint in which we set $s = 1$, a common level of consumption of the composite good z^*, and an equilibrium land rent $R^*(r)$

exist such that

$$z^* = Y - R^*(r) - T(r) - \theta(r) \qquad r \in [-N/2, N/2]. \tag{5.1}$$

Thus, given G and $R^*(r)$, maximizing the utility of a consumer amounts to maximizing the consumption z^* as given by (5.1). In this case, evaluating the land rent at the urban fringe, we obtain

$$R^*(r) = T(N/2) + \theta(N/2) - T(r) - \theta(r) + R_A \qquad r \in [-N/2, N/2] \tag{5.2}$$

where R_A is the agricultural land rent (or land opportunity cost).

In what follows, we first analyze the case of a single city and identify conditions under which confiscating the aggregate differential land rent is sufficient to finance the public good. We then consider the centralized provision of a local public good in a system of cities and discuss how the optimum can be decentralized by appealing to competition among land developers. Throughout this section, the amount of land available in the whole economy is assumed to be sufficiently large for the numbers of cities determined to be feasible.

5.2.1 The Henry George Theorem

Consider a group of individuals who choose to form an urban community to benefit from a local public good. In this section, the quantity of public good G is assumed to be fixed. Because individuals are identical, they delegate to a city government the task of maximizing their common utility level. To this end, the government first buys the land for the city from farmers at the agricultural rent R_A. Because the government knows that the competitive residential equilibrium is efficient (see Proposition 3.5), it may allow for a competitive land market to determine the consumer residential allocation and the consumption of the composite good within the city. Nevertheless, the government must find resources that allow it to finance the public good. To achieve its goal, the city government can confiscate the differential land rent created by the establishment of the public facility. In addition, the government may levy a tax $\theta(r) \geq 0$ that may vary with consumers' locations. The government is also entitled to choose the city population size N.

The city government understands that it is wasteful to have vacant land within the city and that the consumers must be symmetrically distributed about the public facility. Focusing on the right-hand side of the city, this implies that

$$R^*(r) - R_A \geq 0 \qquad r \in [0, N/2] \tag{5.3}$$

and

$$R^*(N/2) = R_A. \tag{5.4}$$

Because each consumer's budget constraint is given by $Y = z^* + R^*(r) + T(r) + \theta(r)$, the equilibrium land rent must be such that

$$R^*(r) = Y - z^* - T(r) - \theta(r) \qquad r \in [0, N/2]. \tag{5.5}$$

The city government has to solve the following problem:

$$\max_{N,\theta(\cdot)} z^*$$

subject to the city budget constraint

$$2\int_0^{N/2} \theta(r)dr + 2\int_0^{N/2} [R^*(r) - R_{\mathrm{A}}]\mathrm{d}r \geq G \tag{5.6}$$

as well as to (5.3), (5.4), and (5.5).

Let $ADR(N)$ be the aggregate differential land rent when there are N consumers

$$ADR(N) \equiv 2\int_0^{N/2} [R^*(r) - R_{\mathrm{A}}]\mathrm{d}r \tag{5.7}$$

and denote by $TTC(N)$ the total commuting costs incurred by the N consumers

$$TTC(N) = 2\int_0^{N/2} T(r)\mathrm{d}r.$$

Substituting (5.5) into (5.6) and using the resource constraint yields

$$NY = Nz^* + TTC(N) + G + NR_{\mathrm{A}}$$

and thus

$$z^* = Y - \frac{TTC(N) + G + NR_{\mathrm{A}}}{N}. \tag{5.8}$$

Accordingly, the optimal utility level corresponding to G is reached when the per capita cost $G/N + TTC(N)/N + R_{\mathrm{A}}$ is minimized with respect to N. The trade-off discussed in the introduction should now be clear: if the population size rises, the per capita cost of the public good G/N decreases, but the per capita commuting cost $TTC(N)/N$ increases because the cost TTC is strictly increasing and strictly convex in N by Proposition 4.1.

Because (5.8) does not involve $\theta(\cdot)$, without loss of generality $\theta(r)$ may be set equal to zero for all r as long as (5.3) and (5.4) are met. Indeed, any positive or negative transfer is automatically reflected in the equilibrium land rent defined by (5.5). In this case, using (5.4), (5.5) becomes

$$R^*(r) = T(N/2) - T(r) + R_{\mathrm{A}}$$

and, hence, ADR depends only upon N:

$$ADR(N) = 2\int_0^{N/2} [T(N/2) - T(r)]\,\mathrm{d}r$$

which is strictly increasing in N.

Furthermore, evaluating (5.5) at the urban fringe shows that

$$z^*(N) = Y - T(N/2) - R_A$$

which strictly decreases with N. Consequently, maximizing $z^*(N)$ under the budget constraint (5.6), which is now rewritten $ADR(N) \geq G$, implies that the optimal population size $N^o(G)$ must satisfy the condition

$$ADR[N^o(G)] = G.$$

Thus, we have shown the following:

Proposition 5.1. *Given any level of expenditure on a pure public good in a city, the aggregate differential land rent equals public expenditure if and only if the population size maximizes the utility level of the city's residents.*

In urban public finance, this result is known as the Henry George theorem based on the proposal for a confiscatory tax on pure land rents made in 1879 by the American activist Henry George in his book *Progress and Poverty*.[4] It is worth stressing that Proposition 5.1 does not depend on the structure of preferences and holds regardless of the quantity of public good supplied within a city. This is to be contrasted to the standard equilibrium conditions for the efficient supply of a pure public good identified by Samuelson (1954b), which requires knowing the marginal utility of the supplied public good across all consumers. Further, because $\theta(r) = 0$ for all r, *a single tax on land rent is sufficient to finance the public expenditure.* The land tax proposed by Henry George also has the advantage of being levied on land, which is supplied inelastically so that no distortion is introduced in the price system. In practice, however, implementing such a taxation policy might be a difficult task.[5] Nevertheless, the idea is both provocative and stimulating, and we have already seen in Section 4.3.3 that similar mechanisms can be applied to firms providing private goods.

Furthermore, it follows from Proposition 5.1 and because $ADR(N)$ is a strictly increasing function of N that

$$ADR(N) \lesseqgtr G \quad \text{if and only if} \quad N \lesseqgtr N^o(G).$$

[4] A brief overview of the work of George is provided by Whitaker (1998).

[5] This question has generated harsh political debates in the United States. See Mills (1972b, chapter 3) for a critical appraisal of the welfare and ethical aspects of the single tax.

Stated differently, the aggregate differential land rent exceeds expenditure on the public good in a city with a population above the optimal size: too large a number of consumers leads to increasing land rent at each urban location. By contrast, expenditure on the public good exceeds the aggregate land rent in a city with a population below the optimal size: too small a number of consumers makes the land rent too low at each urban location. In this case, a tax is needed to finance the public good.

It can be shown that the Henry George theorem remains valid when the lot size is variable (hence, the population density now decreases as one moves away from the public facility) as well as in the presence of locational amenities (see Arnott and Stiglitz 1979 and Fujita 1989, chapter 6, for more details).

5.2.2 Should Land Be Collectively Owned?

The Henry George theorem and the results presented in Chapter 4 show that a perfectly competitive land market is a powerful device to achieve and sustain the first best optimum. This has led several economists to argue that *land should not be privatized*. To illustrate their argument, we provide an extract from a letter sent to the Soviet president Mikhaïl Gorbachev in 1990. This letter was drafted by Nicolaus Tideman, Mason Gaffney, and William Vickrey; the list of signatories includes William Baumol, Zvi Griliches, Franco Modigliani, Richard Musgrave, Tibor Scitovsky, Robert Solow, and James Tobin.[6]

It is important that the rent of land be retained as a source of government revenue. While the governments of developed nations with market economies collect some of the rent of land in taxes, they do not collect nearly as much as they could, and they therefore make unnecessarily great use of taxes that impede their economies – taxes on such things as incomes, sales and the value of capital.

The rental value of land arises from three sources. The first is the inherent natural productivity of land, combined with the fact that land is limited. The second source of land value is the growth of communities; the third is the provision of public services. All citizens have equal claims on the component of land value that arises from nature. The component of land value that arises from community growth and provision of services is the most sensible source of revenue for financing public services that raise the rental value of surrounding land. These services include roads, urban transit networks, parks, and public utility networks for such services as electricity, telephones, water, and sewers. A public revenue system should strive to collect as much of the rent of land as possible, allocating the part of rent derived from nature to all citizens equally, and the part derived from public services to the governmental units that provide those services. When governments collect the increase in land value that results from the provision of services, they are able to offer services at prices that represent the marginal social

[6] The full letter is available at http://course.earthrights.net/book/export/html/87.

cost of these services, promoting efficient use of the services and enhancing the rental value of the land where the services are available. Government agencies that use land should be charged the same rentals as others for the land they use, or services will not be adequately financed and agencies will not have adequate incentive or guidance for economizing on their use of land.

A balance should be kept between allowing the managers of property to retain value derived from their own efforts to maintain and improve property, and securing for public use the naturally inherent and socially created value of land. Users of land should not be allowed to acquire rights of indefinite duration for single payments. For efficiency, for adequate revenue and for justice, every user of land should be required to make an annual payment to the local government, equal to the current rental value of the land that he or she prevents others from using.

5.2.3 The Centralized Provision of a Local Public Good

Consider an economy-wide planner whose objective is to maximize the common individual utility level among the whole population $\mathbf{N}$ in the economy. The role of the planner is to determine the number of cities, their population size and corresponding residential area, the supply of public good in each city and the corresponding tax scheme, the allocation of consumers within each city, and their consumption of the composite good. Because all cities are identical, it is sufficient to focus on the representative city. As seen in the foregoing section, the planner allows for a competitive land market to determine the allocation of residential land to consumers and the consumption of the composite good within each city, whereas confiscating the aggregate differential land rent permits the financing of the public good.[7] In order to do so, he acquires the land needed for each city at the prevailing agricultural rent R_A. If N consumers choose to reside within the city, the planner knows that land will be used only for residential purposes and that consumers distribute themselves over the segment $[-N/2, N/2]$. As a result, the planner has only to choose the population size N per city (or, equivalently, the number of cities $\mathbf{N}/N$) as well as the public expenditure G and the taxation scheme $\theta(\cdot)$ in each city. In the case of a pure local public good, the planner problem may then be written as follows:

$$\max_{G,N,\theta(\cdot)} u = U(1, z, G)$$

subject to (5.3), (5.4), (5.5), and (5.6). Except for the choice of G, this problem is equivalent to the one considered in the previous section.

[7] In a planning approach without a land market, we should account for the land availability constraint at each r. The corresponding multipliers would then correspond to the equilibrium land rent used here.

Let $Z(u, G)$ be the unique solution to the equation $U(1, z, G) = u$. Then, using consumers' budget constraints, the city budget constraint (5.6) becomes

$$2\int_0^{N/2} [Y - Z(u, G) - T(r) - R_{\text{A}}]\text{d}r \geq G$$

in which the tax $\theta(\cdot)$ cancels out. The planner problem may then be rewritten as follows:

$$\max_{G,N,\theta(\cdot)} u = U(1, z, G)$$

subject to (5.3), (5.4), (5.5), and

$$2\int_0^{N/2} [Y - Z(u, G) - T(r) - R_{\text{A}}]\text{d}r \geq G. \tag{5.9}$$

As before, the value of $\theta(r)$ has no impact on the solution as long as the residential area is given by $[0, N/2]$, and thus we may choose $\theta(r) = 0$ for all r without loss of generality. Hence, the planner's problem reduces to

$$\max_{N,G} u = U(1, z, G)$$

subject to (5.3), (5.4), (5.5), and (5.9). Let (u^o, N^o, G^o) be the optimal solution.[8]

To investigate what the solution to this problem is, we first note that, when the reservation utility is u^o and when $G = G^o$, if the migration to the city were free, the equilibrium population of the representative city would be

$$N^*(u^o, G^o) = 2\mu\left\{r \geq 0; Y - Z(u^o, G^o) - T(r) - R_{\text{A}} \geq 0\right\}$$

where $\mu(\cdot)$ is the size (i.e., Lebesgue measure) of the corresponding residential area. Set

$$\varepsilon \equiv N^*(u^o, G^o)/2 - N^o/2.$$

Since $T(r)$ is strictly increasing in distance and $Y - Z(u^o, G^o) - T(r) - R_{\text{A}} = 0$ when it is evaluated at $r = N^*(u^o, G^o)/2$, it can be readily verified that $\varepsilon \neq 0$ and (5.9) imply that

$$2\int_0^{N^*(u^o,G^o)/2} [Y - Z(u^o, G^o) - T(r) - R_{\text{A}}]\text{d}r$$

$$> 2\int_0^{N^o/2} [Y - Z(u^o, G^o) - T(r) - R_{\text{A}}]\text{d}r \geq G^o.$$

Therefore, since $Z(u, G^o)$ is continuous in u, there would exist $u' > u^o$ and $\delta > 0$ such that

$$2\int_0^{N^*(u',G^o)/2-\delta} [Y - Z(u', G^o) - T(r) - R_{\text{A}}]\text{d}r \geq G^o$$

8 If this optimization problem has several solutions, there exist several optimal urban systems. In this case, the following discussion applies to each one of them.

and

$$Y - Z(u', G^o) - T(r) \geq R_A \qquad r \in [0, N^*(u', N^o)/2 - \delta]$$

with the equality holding at the urban fringe $N^*(u', G^o)/2 - \delta$. This would contradict the optimality of (u^o, N^o, G^o), and thus $\varepsilon = 0$. This means that the optimal population size N^o equals the equilibrium population size of the open city model in which $G = G^o$, and the reservation utility level is u^o.[9] Stated differently, we have

$$N^o = N^*(u^o, G^o). \tag{5.10}$$

Since ε must be 0 at the optimal solution, we have

$$2\int_0^{N^o/2} [Y - Z(u^o, G^o) - T(r) - R_A]\mathrm{d}r = ADR^*(u^o, G^o).$$

Consequently, at the optimum, it must be that

$$ADR^*(u^o, G^o) = G^o. \tag{5.11}$$

More generally, when the reservation utility is u and G is a public good supplied in the city, the aggregate differential land rent corresponding to the residential equilibrium of the open city model is such that

$$ADR^*(u, G) = 2\int_0^{N^*(u,G)/2} [Y - Z(u, G) - T(r) - R_A]\mathrm{d}r \tag{5.12}$$

where $N^*(u, G)$ denotes the equilibrium population size associated with u and G. Assume now that there exists G' such that

$$ADR^*(u^o, G') > G'.$$

It then follows from (5.12) that

$$ADR^*(u^o, G') \equiv 2\int_0^{N^*(u^o,G')/2} [Y - Z(u^o, G') - T(r) - R_A]\mathrm{d}r > G'.$$

Again, $u' > u^*$ would exist such that

$$ADR^*(u', G') > G'$$

thus contradicting the optimality of (u^o, N^o, G^o). Therefore, it must be that

$$ADR^*(u^o, G) \leq G \qquad \text{for all } G \geq 0. \tag{5.13}$$

To sum up, if (u^o, N^o, G^o) is an optimal solution, the three conditions (5.10), (5.11), and (5.13) must be satisfied. Conversely, it is readily verified that these

[9] Using the notation introduced in the previous section, we also have $N^o = N^o(G^o)$.

three conditions are also sufficient for (u^o, N^o, G^o) to be an optimal solution to the planner's problem. In addition, (5.11) and (5.13) imply that

$$\frac{\mathrm{d}ADR^*(u^o, G^o)}{\mathrm{d}G} = 1. \tag{5.14}$$

Furthermore, using (5.12) and the envelope theorem shows that

$$\frac{\mathrm{d}ADR^*(u^o, G^o)}{\mathrm{d}G} = -2\int_0^{N^*(u^o,G^o)/2} \frac{\partial Z(u^o, G^o)}{\partial G}\mathrm{d}r$$
$$= -N^o \frac{\partial Z(u^o, G^o)}{\partial G}$$

and thus

$$\frac{\mathrm{d}ADR^*(u^o, G^o)}{\mathrm{d}G} = -N^o \frac{\partial Z(u^o, G^o)}{\partial G} = 1. \tag{5.15}$$

This is equivalent to the standard Samuelsonian condition, which states that the optimal quantity of a public good is such that the sum of the marginal rates of substitution between the public good and the numéraire is equal to its marginal production cost (which is here equal to 1). In addition, (5.15) also implies that the marginal social value of the local public good is equal to the marginal increase in the aggregate differential land rent. This is a land capitalization rule (Starrett 1988, chapter 13).

Finally, provided that the optimal city size is sufficiently small relative to the whole population **N**, the integer problem may be neglected and the optimal number of cities is given by $\mathbf{N}/N^o$ where $N^o \equiv N^o(G^o)$.

5.2.4 The Supply of Local Public Goods by Land Developers

Following a well-established tradition in urban economics, we now assume a different institutional setting in which each city is developed by a profit-maximizing land developer. We now consider a market mechanism in which consumers are free to move into any city (N is endogenous to the city developer) and to choose the location they find appealing to them in the corresponding city (the residential equilibrium is also endogenous). Furthermore, consumers being identical, they must achieve the same utility level regardless of the city in which they live. Because many cities exist, each developer treats the utility level prevailing in the economy as given. Clearly, the assumption according to which the utility level is exogenous to each developer has a "competitive" flavor. It is reasonable, provided that the number of developers (cities) is large enough, for each consumer to consider his impact on consumers' welfare as negligible. Note that this assumption does not necessarily mean that a developer is able to observe the prevailing utility level. It just means that the developer believes (for whatever reason) that he cannot manipulate the reservation utility.

In such a context, the developer's policy is, therefore, to attract some consumers by supplying them with a local public good, taking their utility level as given. When consumers decide to reside in a city, its developer may charge them a fee (which may be positive or negative) $\theta(r)$ that may vary with the distance to the facility (here the city center). As in Chapter 4, it is assumed that the developer is able to anticipate the residential equilibrium corresponding to his policy on G and $\theta(\cdot)$, taking the utility level u as given.

The developer's profit is equal to the aggregate differential land rent plus the total fee collected from the residents minus the expenditure on the local public good. Hence, the maximization problem of a developer can be written as follows:

$$\max_{G,\theta(\cdot)} \Pi[G, \theta(\cdot); u] = 2\int_{X_R^*} [R^*(r) - R_A]dr + 2\int_{X^*} \theta(r)dr - G \quad (5.16)$$

where $X_R^* = \{r \geq 0; R^*(r) \geq R_A\}$ denotes the equilibrium residential area, whereas the corresponding equilibrium land rent $R^*(r)$ is given by

$$R^*(r) = Y - Z(u, G) - T(r) - \theta(r). \quad (5.17)$$

Substituting (5.17) into (5.16), we obtain

$$\begin{aligned} \Pi[G, \theta(\cdot); u] &= 2\int_{X_R^*} [Y - Z(u, G) - T(r) - \theta(r) - R_A]dr \quad (5.18) \\ &\quad + 2\int_{X_R^*} \theta(r)dr - G \\ &= 2\int_{X_R^*} [Y - Z(u, G) - T(r) - R_A]dr - G. \end{aligned}$$

For a given value of G, it follows from (5.18) that choosing $\theta(r)$ is equivalent to choosing the residential area X_R^*. Evidently, the profit-maximizing residential area X^* is the domain over which the willingness to pay for land exceeds its opportunity cost, that is,

$$X_R^* = \{r \geq 0; Y - Z(u, G) - T(r) \geq R_A\}. \quad (5.19)$$

Hence, as before, the profit-maximizing value of $\theta(r)$ can be set equal to zero.

Because consumers maximize utility, they move to the developer's city up to the point in which the utility prevailing there is equal to u. Let $N^*(u, G)$ be the equilibrium population corresponding to G (as defined in Section 5.2.2) so that $X_R^* = [0, N^*(G; u)/2]$. Using (5.12), a developers' profit may be rewritten as follows:

$$\begin{aligned} \Pi(G; u) &= 2\int_0^{N^*(u,G)/2} [Y - Z(u, G) - T(r) - R_A]dr - G \quad (5.20) \\ &= ADR[u, N^*(G; u)] - G. \end{aligned}$$

Consequently, each developer maximizes $\Pi(G;u)$ with respect to G when the utility level is u.

If there is free entry and exit (see also Section 4.3.3), then developers enter (leave) the city market as long as potential profits obtained by developing a city are positive (negative). During this process, the utility level u, the quantity of local public good G, and the population N of each city vary. When the long-run equilibrium is reached, profits (5.20) are zero:

$$ADR[u^*, N^*(G^*;u^*)] = G^* \tag{5.21}$$

so that profit-maximizing behavior also implies that

$$ADR[u^*, N^*(G;u^*)] \leq G \qquad \text{for all } G \geq 0. \tag{5.22}$$

Finally, the equilibrium population N^* satisfies

$$N^* = N^*(G^*;u^*). \tag{5.23}$$

Conditions (5.21), (5.22), and (5.23) are necessary and sufficient for the market outcome (u^*, N^*, G^*). They are identical to the equations (5.10), (5.11), and (5.13) determining the optimum. Hence, it must be that $u^* = u^o$, $G^* = G^o$, and $N^* = N^o$. Consequently, the number of cities arising at the market equilibrium $\mathbf{N}/N^*$ is also equal to the optimal number of cities $\mathbf{N}/N^o$.

Because the Henry George theorem holds in each city, the aggregate differential land rent collected by each developer allows him to finance exactly the efficient provision of local public good, which is a result comparable to that obtained in Section 4.3.3 for private goods.

In addition, we have the condition

$$\frac{\mathrm{d}ADR^*(u^*, G^*)}{\mathrm{d}G} = 1$$

which is similar to (5.14).

All this analysis may be summarized as follows:

Proposition 5.2. *An urban system is efficient if and only if it is a free entry equilibrium of the city market. In both cases, the public good is solely financed by the aggregate differential land rent.*

Thus, if the entrepreneur is brought back under the form of a land developer, the supply of a local public good seems to obey rules similar to those governing the production of a private good. This process is reminiscent of that described in Section 4.3.3, although the reasons for the emergence of urban agglomerations differ.

5.2.5 The Case of a Congestible Public Good

Consider now a public good such that an additional resident has a negative impact on the consumption of this good by the incumbents. This is probably more realistic than the case studied in the preceding section because most public facilities have a maximum capacity. According to Buchanan (1965) and Berglas (1976), congestion would be sufficient to foster the decentralized provision of public services by clubs, internalizing the trade-off between financing and congestion. For this to occur, each club must be able to charge a fee equal to the congestion cost generated by an additional user and imposed to all users. Charging such a fee then allows financing a congestible public good and provides the right incentives to choose the optimal quantity for the users of the good. In this context, a city can be viewed as a "consumption club" in much the same way as a city is considered a "production club" in Section 4.3.

In each city, the land developer (or the local jurisdiction) now maximizes the aggregate differential land rent plus the total fee charged to all users of the congestible public good made available by the developer minus the cost of this good (see Fujita 1989, chapter 6, for more details). In particular, it can be shown that $\theta(r)$ is no longer equal to zero but to an admission fee $\theta^o(N^o) > 0$ for all r. Both types of tax must be combined to finance the public good, implying that the Henry George theorem is amended in the following way: When the city size is optimal (N^o), public expenditure equals the aggregate differential land rent plus the optimal user fee $\theta(N^o)$ collected from all the users:

$$G = ADR(N^o) + N^o\theta(N^o).$$

Hence, once we account for the spatial setting, a Pigovian tax falls short of the provision cost, but the deficit is just equal to the differential land rent. Consequently, the decentralization of a local, but congested, public good is still possible. Observe, finally, that the optimal fee depends here only upon the mass of consumers patronizing a facility and not upon their residential locations.

5.2.6 The Limits of Land Capitalization

Appealing as the capitalization argument seems, it needs qualification.

(i) The most serious criticism of the land capitalization process is probably due to Roback (1982): *the value of the public good need not be fully internalized in land rents because it may affect other economic variables*. The argument goes as follows. Consider a large number of cities endowed with exogenous quantities of a public good. Firms use land and labor. They operate under constant returns and perfect competition on the world markets, which implies that firms earn zero profits in equilibrium. Therefore, when the price of their product is fixed, their unit production cost $c(Y, R) = c^*$ must be the same across all occupied locations. Consumers have identical preferences and choose the

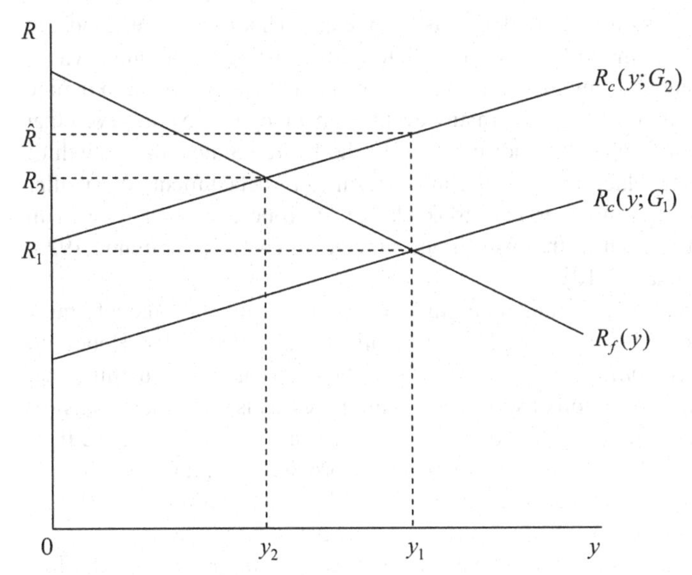

Figure 5.1. Equilibrium wage and land rent.

quantities of product and land (there is no commuting); they treat parametrically the quantity G of the public good available in the city where they live. In equilibrium, incomes and land rents must adjust to equalize the indirect utility $V(Y, R; G) = u^*$ across all occupied locations. In sum, the equilibrium incomes and land rents in occupied locations are determined simultaneously by equal utility and equal cost conditions. These conditions imply that, for any given value of G, the inverse function $R_f(Y) \equiv c^{-1}(Y; c^*)$ decreases with Y for the unit cost to remain equal to c^*, whereas the inverse function $R_c(Y; G) \equiv V^{-1}(Y; G, u^*)$ increases with Y for the indirect utility to be equal to u^*.

Consider any two cities 1 and 2 such that $G_1 < G_2$. At every given income, workers must pay a higher rent in city 2 than in city 1 to be indifferent between the two cities. In other words, the curve R_c is shifted upward when G increases from G_1 to G_2. Because the curve R_f is the same in both cities, Figure 5.1 shows that the land rent is higher in city 2 than city 1 but the income is lower in city 2 than in city 1. Indeed, as more workers want to reside in city 2, competition in the corresponding labor market is intensified. As a result, city 2's workers have a lower income, thus a lower bid rent. For this reason, the land rent R_2 prevailing in city 2 is smaller than the land rent $\hat{R}$ that would prevail if the income were constant and equal to Y_1. However, if firms do not use land as in the previous analysis, the unit production cost is independent of R. In this event, the income is constant and the land rent increases from R_1 to $\hat{R}$.

(ii) For Proposition 5.2 to hold, the city boundaries must be variable. Revising urban and regional borders certainly goes against the customary habit of regarding administrative boundaries as permanent. This rigidity responds, at least partly, to the individuals' need to belong to a lasting community whose geographic contours remain stable. Agents involved, therefore, need to handle a new socioeconomic trade-off. In any event, Henderson (1985) observed that such a process of revision is not unusual. In the United States, the growth of many cities took place through the annexation (and detachment) of smaller spatial entities. A similar process took place in Europe during the two main waves of urbanization in the twelfth and nineteenth centuries (Pirenne 1925; Bairoch 1988, chapter 10).

Furthermore, for land-value maximization to yield efficiency, the city must include all the beneficiaries of its fiscal policy within its border. Hence, to avoid uncounted *spillovers*, cities must be sufficiently large – something that may require the annexation of suburban communities. This might not be easy to do, for local governments and communities will resist precisely because their autonomy allows them to free ride on the city's provision of public goods.[10]

Finally, we also encounter neighborhood public goods within a city (Fujita 1989, chapter 6). These goods are to the city what local public goods are to the nation in the sense that they have a utility only to the residents who live in a particular urban neighborhood of the city. The land rent prevailing in a neighborhood increases with the provision of such goods, and the principles described above remain valid provided that the supplier can recover the increment in the land rent created by his decision to offer a particular neighborhood public good. However, implementing such a policy at a low spatial level seems to be fairly problematic because the service areas tend to be fuzzy and spillovers are likely to be important.

(iii) Each city must be small relative to the total population. In this case, the prices of land in other cities, hence utility, are almost unresponsive to one city's change in fiscal policy. If the city is large relative to the economy, the competitive hypothesis may fail to hold. Indeed, as pointed out in Section 5.1, capitalization and consumer mobility go hand in hand. Land prices rise in a city because more public goods attract residents from elsewhere, which pushes up demand for land and increases the population of the city. Meanwhile, as residents leave the other cities, the land prices there fall, providing the remaining residents more utility than they had before. In this way, utility is "exported" from the city that increased its public goods to the other cities. As a result, with a small number of cities, the utility-taking assumption is no longer tenable, thus making competition among land developers strategic.

Because of this utility effect, the increase in land value in the city that has increased its supply of public goods may underestimate willingness to pay for the public goods, and in equilibrium public goods may be underprovided. When

[10] See also Helsley and Strange (1997) as well as Henderson and Thisse (2001) for related limitations of the land development process when strategic considerations are taken into account.

the utility effect described in the preceding paragraph is strong enough, under-provision arises because firms compete by using only public goods. However, as Scotchmer (1986) has shown, a city can do potentially better if it has two instruments to govern these two effects. If cities can charge a head tax to control migration $\theta(N)$, public goods are provided efficiently within each city, but the allocation of population among cities may not be optimal.

(iv) We have assumed so far that a single facility is able to supply all public services to the city's residents. Instead, one should expect different local (pure) public goods to be supplied by different facilities that are not necessarily located together. Indeed, the efficient number and locations of facilities generally differ across goods and services. As a result, each consumer patronizes different public facilities and, therefore, belongs to different service areas. Hence, the problem is now to find a way to distribute the differential land rent among the various local public goods consumed by the residents. Because each type of facility is likely to have a specific service area, the relative position of a consumer with respect to the nearest facility supplying each type of good varies with this consumer's location. In other words, the "contribution" of a particular facility to the differential land rent changes with the residential location.

This is not the end of the story. The problem of giving the right incentives to each supplier to make the efficient decisions regarding the location and size of his facility remains. In the aggregate, the Henry George theorem holds true. But the rent-sharing rule must relate the proceeds to the actions taken by each supplier of a local public good. More precisely, the supplier's revenue must exactly reflect the net social benefit of his decision for all his patrons operating within the various facilities. For example, if some fixed rule is applied, each supplier receives a certain fraction of the differential land rent, but then his marginal profit generally differs from the net social marginal benefit.

As shown by Hochman, Pines, and Thisse (1995), space has a major implication for the socially desirable institutional structure of local governments: the efficient provision of local public goods must be decentralized through metropolitan governments that supply the whole range of local public goods over some appropriate territories.

For this to hold, the area monitored by the metropolitan government must be sufficiently large. To avoid the degenerate situation in which the whole economy is used as a reference, one may assume that the metropolitan region should be small enough that all trips made within this territory to consume public services both originate and end there. This permits the corresponding territory to include an integral number of each service area. In this way, the rent-sharing problem is solved because the metropolitan government internalizes all the benefits generated by the facilities under its control.

But practically, this implies that the corresponding units will often be large. One then runs the risk that the metropolitan governments will behave strategically. This would invalidate the extension of Proposition 5.2 to the multiservice case. Furthermore, the setting of large local governments could generate other well-known inefficiencies.

(v) Finally, the assumption of identical consumers is obviously very strong. When there are several types of consumers, different types of cities, involving different mixtures of individual types, are likely to emerge (Scotchmer 2002). Hence, in this case, even when the economy is large, it is far from being obvious that land developers will be utility-takers. Indeed, it is likely that they will know that the change in one particular city has a direct and significant impact only upon a few other cities. In other words, competition among land developers becomes localized as in Section 4.5.

5.3 THE NUMBER AND SIZE OF JURISDICTIONS UNDER POLITICS

The preceding section shows that consumers want to be organized into communities whose number is governed by the existence of a trade-off between transportation costs and the cost of the public good. Furthermore, this trade-off is solved optimally when the provision of the public services is capitalized into the land rent and when developers are able to collect the differential land rent they create. However, in this setting, a city's area is not constrained by the other cities, and each one freely chooses how much land to use. One may wonder what our results become when consumers are continuously dispersed over the entire space within a given territory while their locations are fixed. As in Section 5.2, the number and size of cities/jurisdictions are endogenous, but they occupy the whole territory whose size is fixed; hence, jurisdictions are connected through endogenous borders. It seems reasonable to think of this problem as one in which consumers are asked to express their preferences about local public goods through a political process such as voting.[11]

Because legal factors may prevent the use of other taxes or political difficulties may prevent the implementation of specific taxes,[12] the public good is assumed to be financed through an income tax. Thus, consumers voting on the number and location of public facilities are aware that they are both users of public goods and taxpayers. As users, they would like to have a public facility as close as possible to their residence, thus fostering the proliferation of such facilities. However, as taxpayers, they also understand that their tax bill will increase with the number of facilities, thus leading to the reduction in the supply of facilities. Hence, each voter internalizes the trade-off but does not take into account the impact of his decision upon the others.

[11] In this section, we follow Cremer, de Kerchove, and Thisse (1985). Note that Alesina and Spolaore (1997) have developed independently a similar analysis.

[12] As an example, think of the many difficulties faced by public authorities when they try to implement urban tolls or peak-load pricing within cities.

5.3.1 The Political Economy of Community Formation

Voting is modeled as a two-stage process in which consumers first vote on the number of facilities and then on their locations. This division into stages is dictated by the fact that the choice on the number of facilities (the first stage) is prior to the decisions regarding their locations (the second stage). When choosing the number of facilities, voters anticipate the locations of the corresponding facilities. For simplicity, we make the following assumptions: (i) the local public good is pure and supplied in a fixed quantity so that its cost is given and equal to G for each facility and (ii) transport costs are linear in distance, that is, $T(r) = tr$.

Space is described by a linear segment with unit length (working with a space whose size is arbitrary amounts to rescaling the parameter t). Consumers are evenly distributed over this segment, perhaps because they consume a fixed lot size, and the uniform density is equal to a constant n. Thus, the total mass of consumers is also equal to n. If M facilities are built, the global budget constraint under a proportional income tax $0 < \theta < 1$ is given by[13]

$$n\theta Y = MG. \tag{5.24}$$

Consider a locational configuration of M facilities $\mathbf{y}_M = (y_1, \ldots, y_M)$ such that facilities are placed at $0 \leq y_1 < \cdots < y_M \leq 1$. If a consumer at $x \in [0, 1]$ patronizes the facility located at y_i, his budget constraint is

$$Y = z + t\,|x - y_i| + \theta Y.$$

Note that consumers' locations are fixed so that there is no land market and hence no land rent. Because the quantity of public good is the same at each facility, each consumer patronizes the nearest facility. Because G is also fixed, a consumer located at x maximizes his utility $U(1, z, G)$ (see Section 5.2) if and only if the consumer at x maximizes consumption of the composite good, which is given by

$$\begin{aligned} z(x; M, \mathbf{y}_M) &= Y(1-\theta) - \min_{i=1,\ldots,M} t\,|x - y_i| \\ &= Y - \min_{i=1,\ldots,M} t\,|x - y_i| - \frac{MG}{n} \end{aligned} \tag{5.25}$$

in which we have used (5.24). A consumer's utility therefore depends on the number of jurisdictions and the locations of the corresponding public facilities.

Let us now describe the voting procedure. In the second stage, the number of jurisdictions is known to the voters as the outcome of the first-stage voting game. The utility of a consumer, therefore, depends only on the location of the nearest facility, and the utility level decreases as the distance to this

[13] Because the income Y is fixed, this is equivalent to the lump sum tax scheme used in the previous section.

facility increases. This yields a voting subgame whose outcome is defined as a *Condorcet equilibrium* (i.e., a locational configuration such that no other locational configuration with the same number of facilities is strictly preferred by a strict majority of voters). When the number of facilities is M, the Condorcet equilibrium is denoted by $\mathbf{y}_M^* = (y_1^*, \ldots, y_M^*)$.

To illustrate how this works, consider two configurations $\mathbf{y}_1$ and $\mathbf{y}_2$ with M facilities each. Then, if the mass of consumers who strictly prefer $\mathbf{y}_1$ to $\mathbf{y}_2$ exceeds the mass of consumers who strictly prefer $\mathbf{y}_2$ to $\mathbf{y}_1$, then $\mathbf{y}_1$ is collectively chosen. Because the population density is uniform, this means that the size of the area in which consumers strictly prefer $\mathbf{y}_1$ to $\mathbf{y}_2$, is larger than or equal to the size of the area in which consumers strictly prefer $\mathbf{y}_2$ to $\mathbf{y}_1$:

$$\mu\left\{x; z(x; M, \mathbf{y}_1) > z(x; M, \mathbf{y}_2)\right\} \geq \mu\left\{x; z(x; M, \mathbf{y}_1) < z(x; M, \mathbf{y}_2)\right\}$$

where μ is the length (i.e., Lebesgue measure) of the corresponding area.

We can now study the first-stage voting game in which consumers choose the number of jurisdictions. In doing so, they anticipate the outcome of the voting subgame induced by their choice. Hence, the utility of a consumer at x is given by the utility achieved in the second stage, that is, by (5.25) in which $\mathbf{y}_M$ is replaced by the Condorcet equilibrium $\mathbf{y}_M^*$. This game is solved at the number of facilities such that no other (integer) number is strictly preferred by a strict majority of voters. This works as follows. If two numbers of facilities, M_1 and M_2, are proposed, M_1 is chosen if the mass of consumers who strictly prefer M_1 to M_2 is larger than or equal to the mass of consumers who strictly prefer M_2 to M_1. Formally,

$$\mu\left\{x; z(x; M_1, \mathbf{y}_{M_1}^*) > z(x; M_2, \mathbf{y}_{M_2}^*)\right\} \geq \mu\left\{x; z(x; M_1, \mathbf{y}_{M_1}^*) < z(x; M_2, \mathbf{y}_{M_2}^*)\right\}.$$

The Condorcet equilibrium of the first-stage voting game is denoted M^*.

The final outcome of the voting procedure, called a *subgame perfect Condorcet equilibrium*, is such that the following two conditions are met: (i) for each integer M, there are more consumers who strictly prefer the configuration $\mathbf{y}_M^*$ to any other configuration $\mathbf{y}_M$ with M facilities, and (ii) for all $M \neq M^*$, there are more consumers who strictly prefer M^* to M than consumers who strictly prefer M to M^*. This is denoted by $(M^*, \mathbf{y}_{\bar{M}}^*)$.

As usual, the game is solved by backward induction. In the second stage, the utility of a consumer at x reduces to

$$z(x; M, \mathbf{y}_M) = Y - \min_{i=1,\ldots,M} t\,|x - y_i| - \frac{MG}{n}$$

which is single-peaked about x. This problem is, therefore, reminiscent of the median voter principle. However, this principle does not apply here because M items – the locations of facilities – instead of one are to be chosen by the voters.

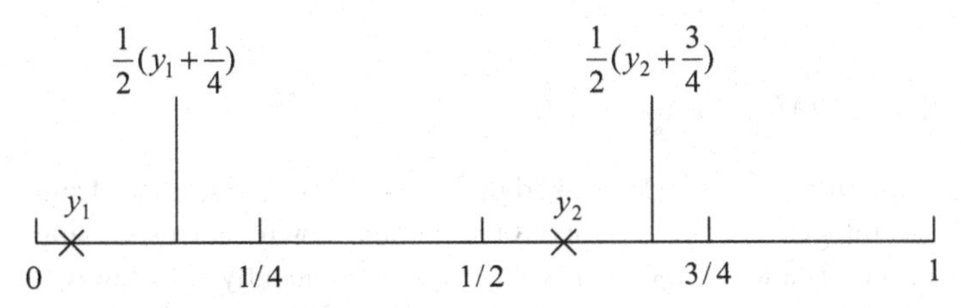

Figure 5.2. Comparing (y_1, y_2) to (1/4, 3/4).

This implies that we need a specific result, which we state in Proposition 5.3 (the proof is contained in appendix A).

Proposition 5.3. *Assume a proportional income tax. Then, for any given M, the equidistant configuration* $\mathbf{y}_M^* = (1/2M, \ldots, (2M-1)/2M)$ *is the unique Condorcet equilibrium of the second-stage voting game.*

The intuition behind this result is as follows. Because each facility is at the middle of its jurisdiction, its location is the median of its consumer distribution. It is as if the median voter principle had been applied to each facility conditional on his own jurisdiction. Let us show how the proof works when $M = 2$. If both facilities are located outside (inside) the first and third quartiles, then a majority of consumers are located on both sides of the center (in the two hinterlands generated by the facility's locations) who strictly prefer $(1/4, 3/4)$ to the status quo. Assume now that facility 1 (2) is located between 0 and $1/4$ ($1/2$ and $3/4$). Then, all consumers between $(y_1 + 1/4)/2$ and $1/2$ strictly prefer a configuration with a facility at $1/4$. Similarly, all consumers between $(y_2 + 3/4)/2$ and 1 strictly prefer a configuration with a facility at $3/4$ (see Figure 5.2 for an illustration). Adding these two numbers, we obtain

$$\frac{n}{2}\left(1 - y_1 - \frac{1}{4} + 2 - y_2 - \frac{3}{4}\right) = \frac{n}{2}\left(\frac{9}{4} - y_1 - y_2\right) > \frac{n}{2}$$

because $y_1 < 1/4$ and $y_2 < 3/4$.

It should be clear that the equidistant configuration is also the one that minimizes total transport costs (see appendix B for a proof). Hence, voting and planning yield the same outcome when the number of facilities is fixed, as in the case when individuals vote for a single item.

Consider now the first stage. Consumers now vote on the number of jurisdictions conditionally upon the locations obtained in the second stage. Therefore, the utility of a consumer at x becomes

$$z(x; M, \mathbf{y}_M^*) = Y - \min_{i=1,\ldots,M} t\left|x - y_i^*\right| - \frac{MG}{n}$$

where

$$y_i^* = (2i - 1)/2M \qquad i = 1, \ldots M.$$

This utility function is not single-peaked in M. Indeed, as M increases from 1 to some large integer, $z(x; M, \mathbf{y}_M^*)$ exhibits ups and downs corresponding to variations in the distance to the nearest facility. Consequently, a Condorcet equilibrium may not exist for some parameter configurations.

However, we have the following result whose proof is given in appendix C.

Proposition 5.4. *Assume a proportional income tax. Let* $\bar{M}$ *be the largest integer satisfying the inequality*

$$M(M-1) < \frac{nt}{2G}. \tag{5.26}$$

Then, if

$$G \geq \frac{nt}{40} \tag{5.27}$$

holds, there exists a unique Condorcet equilibrium of the first-stage voting game, which is given by $\bar{M}$.

Accordingly, a subgame perfect Condorcet equilibrium exists when the cost G of a public facility is sufficiently large compared with the transport cost t, the population size, n, or both. Stated differently, condition (5.27) is likely to be satisfied when the territory or the population is small.

One may wonder what happens when (5.27) does not hold. When $M = 5$, a simple calculation shows that $M = 3$ is strictly preferred to $M = 5$ by more than half of the voters. The same holds for any odd number M larger than 5, which can be shown to be defeated by $M - 2$. The reason is as follows. When M is odd, a facility is always established at the center of the segment, and consumers around it strictly prefer the equidistant configuration with $M - 2$ facilities to that with M facilities because the tax bill is lower. Consequently, there are only $M - 1$ groups of consumers located respectively around the remaining $M - 1$ facilities who strictly prefer M to $M - 2$. However, when $M \geq 5$, these groups are too small to form a majority in favor of M. Hence, in general, M is not a Condorcet equilibrium when M exceeds 4.

However, if we define a *local Condorcet equilibrium* for the first-stage voting game as a number defeating $M - 1$ and $M + 1$, we can obtain (see appendix D for a proof) the following:

Proposition 5.5. *Assume a proportional income tax. Then,* $\bar{M}$ *is the unique local Condorcet equilibrium of the first-stage voting game.*

The uniqueness of the local equilibrium endows the number $\bar{M}$ with some degree of stability. In addition, as shown by the proof of Proposition 5.5, the number $\bar{M}$ is also the single surviving outcome of the following sequential choice process. Consumers are first asked to vote between one or two jurisdictions. Then, they are asked to choose between the winner and three jurisdictions. The procedure is iterated until $\bar{M}$ is reached. Because $\bar{M}$ defeats any number $M > \bar{M}$, as shown in the proof of Proposition 5.5, it is indeed the only surviving outcome. Finally, when a Condorcet equilibrium of the first-stage voting game exists, it is also given by $\bar{M}$. All these results lead us to retain $(\bar{M}, \mathbf{y}^*_{\bar{M}})$ as the outcome of the voting procedure for all values of G.

Hence, given (5.26), we see that the voting number of jurisdictions increases as the cost of the public good (G) decreases, the transport cost (t) increases, and the population size (n) increases. Correspondingly, the size of each jurisdiction decreases.

5.3.2 Are There Too Many or Too Few Jurisdictions?

In the present setting, the efficient outcome is obtained by minimizing the social cost defined as the sum of fixed costs and transport costs. In view of the discussion in the preceding section, we see that, for a given value of M, the voting configuration is identical to the efficient one: they are both equidistant.

However, the numbers of facilities generally differ according to the decision-making procedure selected. Indeed, given (5.25), the efficient number of jurisdictions minimizes the social cost defined as follows:

$$\begin{aligned} C(M) &= MG + 2M \int_0^{1/2M} ntx\,\mathrm{d}x \\ &= MG + nt/4M. \end{aligned} \tag{5.28}$$

Given the shape of $C(M)$, it can readily be verified that the efficient number of jurisdictions is the largest integer M^o that satisfies the condition (see also Section 4.5.2):

$$M(M-1) < \frac{nt}{2G}. \tag{5.29}$$

Comparing (5.26) and (5.29), we immediately obtain the following:

Proposition 5.6. *Assume a proportional income tax. Voting tends to set a number of facilities exceeding the number that a planner maximizing total welfare would choose.*

Hence, voting fosters an excessive number of jurisdictions as well as an oversupply in public infrastructure very much as the market does in the case of a private good (see Section 4.5.2). The discrepancy appears to be especially large when the public good cost is large and transport costs are low. In addition, each jurisdiction is too small.

In particular, the divergence between $\bar{M}$ and M^o can be made more visible when these numbers are large inasmuch as $M(M-1)$ is almost equal to M^2. In this case, $\bar{M}$ is approximately equal to $\sqrt{2}M^o$, which means an increase of 40 percent in the public budget.

Somewhat surprisingly, the voting procedure yields the number of jurisdictions that would be chosen by a Rawlsian planner who maximizes welfare of the worst-off consumer. Indeed, because the Rawlsian configuration is equidistant, the maximum distance covered by a consumer when there are M facilities equals $1/2M$. Hence, the social welfare function of such a planner is given by:

$$Y - \frac{t}{2M} - \frac{MG}{n}. \tag{5.30}$$

Evidently, this function is maximized when M is the largest integer satisfying inequality (5.26). Recall that the outcome of voting is generally associated with the preferences of the median voter. In the community formation problem, however, the pivotal voter is the most extreme voter (at least when the public good is financed by an income tax). This can be explained as follows. The preferences of the individuals in the hinterlands $[0, 1/2M]$ and $[(2M-1)/2M, 1]$ are decisive for the voting outcome. Furthermore, those individuals vote in the same manner. Accordingly, the voting number of jurisdictions must be such that the consumers at 0 (or at 1) strictly prefer $\bar{M}$ to $\bar{M}-1$ and $\bar{M}+1$. But these consumers belong to the set of worse-off ones in any equidistant configuration, and thus their best choice is socially desirable under Rawlsian optimality.

Hence, we have the following:

Proposition 5.7. *Assume a proportional income tax. The voting outcome coincides with the Rawlsian planning solution.*

This proposition may also be used to understand the intuition that stands behind Proposition 5.6. At the efficient number of jurisdictions M^o, consumers' average utility is maximized, and this utility level is reached by the consumers located at a distance $1/4M^o$ from their nearest facility. As a result, the utility of a consumer located at distance $1/2M^o$ is much lower because he has to cover twice the average distance, which gives him an incentive to vote for a larger number of facilities. Because we just saw that these consumers are critical for the outcome of the voting process, it becomes simple to understand why voting yields a number of jurisdictions exceeding the efficient one.

Finally, a more general approach can follow once it is understood that (5.28) and (5.30) are the two polar cases of the CES social welfare function given by

$$\left\{\int_0^1 \left[\min_{i=1,\dots,M} t\,|x-y_i| + \frac{MG}{n}\right]^\alpha \mathrm{d}x\right\}^{1/\alpha} \tag{5.31}$$

in which $\alpha \geq 1$ is a measure of the degree of aversion toward inequality. Minimizing this function can be shown to yield the following results: (i) for any given value of M, facilities are equidistant, and (ii) the socially optimal number of jurisdictions is a nondecreasing function of α (Cremer et al. 1985).

As a consequence, the answer to the question raised in the title of this section varies with the nature of the planner's objective. If α is small, so that efficiency considerations are predominant, then voting fosters excess capacity and overtaxing. However, the discrepancy narrows as the population density (n) increases, whereas it enlarges when the cost of the public good (G) or the transport rate (t) decreases. In other words, when the economy is large in terms of either its population (or physical size), the voting outcome is not very different from the efficient one. By contrast, the gap between the two outcomes becomes significant when the transport rate is sufficiently low.

On the contrary, if α is large, so that equity considerations drive the choice made by the planner, then voting is socially desirable because it yields the socially optimal number of jurisdictions. As a result, a trade-off exists between efficiency and spatial equity in the formation of public communities: spatial equity leads to a larger number of jurisdictions and a bigger public budget than efficiency.

In sum, when α increase from 1 to ∞, then the discrepancy between the voting outcome and the socially optimum one decreases.

5.3.3 The Role of Land Capitalization

Thus far, consumer locations have been assumed to be fixed so that there is no land market. In contrast, when consumers can move, they compete for land and pay a land rent. We want to reconsider the voting problem addressed in Section 5.3.1 in the presence of a land market. We assume that each consumer uses a unit lot size so that the equilibrium distribution of consumers is uniform. Consequently, without loss of generality, we may also assume that the total mass of consumers is 1.

The differential land rent arises here because of consumers' proximity to their nearest facility, as in Section 5.2. In other words, if M facilities are placed at $0 \leq y_1 < \cdots < y_M \leq 1$, the bid rent of a consumer at $x \in [0, 1]$ is given by

$$\Psi(x) = Y - z^* - \min_{i=1,\ldots,M} t\,|x - y_i| - \theta(x)$$

where z^* is the common equilibrium consumption of the composite good at the residential equilibrium corresponding to $(M, \mathbf{y}_M, \theta)$ and $\theta(x)$ the tax paid (or the subsidy received) by this consumer. The equilibrium land rent is such that

$$R^*(x) = Y - z^* - \min_{i=1,\ldots,M} t\,|x - y_i| - \theta(x) \geq 0 \qquad x \in [0, 1]. \quad (5.32)$$

Furthermore, the total budget constraint is such that

$$\int_0^1 R^*(x)dx + \int_0^1 \theta(x)\mathrm{d}x = MG.$$

Using (5.32), we can rewrite this constraint as follows:

$$\int_0^1 [Y - z^* - \min_{i=1,\dots,M} t\,|x - y_i|]\mathrm{d}x = MG \tag{5.33}$$

in which $\theta(x)$ cancels out. In turn, (5.33) yields

$$z^*(M, \mathbf{y}_M) \equiv z^* = Y - \frac{\int_0^1 \min_{i=1,\dots,M} t\,|x - y_i|\,\mathrm{d}x + MG}{N}.$$

As a result, consumers cast their votes in order to maximize z^* subject to (5.33). Therefore, following the same voting procedure as in Section 5.3.1, we see that, in the second-stage voting subgame induced by M, all consumers agree to select the equidistant configuration because it minimizes total transport costs, thus maximizing consumers' equilibrium consumption of the composite good. Similarly, in the first stage, given the equilibrium locations resulting from the second stage, consumers unanimously choose the number of jurisdictions minimizing total cost $C(M)$ given by (5.28).

Given (5.32), we have

$$R^*(x) + \theta(x) = Y - z^* - \min_{i=1,\dots,M} t|x - y_i|.$$

Setting

$$R^*(x; M, \mathbf{y}_M) \equiv R^*(x) + \theta(x)$$

we obtain

$$R^*(x; M, \mathbf{y}_M) = Y - z^* - \min_{i=1,\dots,M} t|x - y_i| \qquad x \in [0, 1].$$

For the foregoing analysis to hold, the respective share of the land rent, $R^*(x)$, and tax, $\theta(x)$, is immaterial. Consequently, we may focus on $R^*(x; M, \mathbf{y}_M)$ which we call the *land quasi-rent*.[14] Hence, in equilibrium, we have

$$\int_0^1 R^*(x; M^*, \mathbf{y}^*_{M^*})dx = M^*G$$

which means that the aggregate land quasi-rent is equal to the cost of the equilibrium number of facilities.

[14] By choosing $\theta(x)$ appropriately, we may guarantee that (5.32) always holds.

Thus, we have the following:

Proposition 5.8. *The voting equilibrium under a perfectly competitive land market is efficient. Furthermore, the efficient number of facilities is financed solely by the aggregate land quasi-rent.*

This result is reminiscent of Proposition 4.5 derived in a spatial competition model. Note that the same outcome could be reached by applying a tax scheme involving a location-based income tax given by

$$t(x) = \frac{1}{Y}\left[MG + \frac{1}{M} - \min_{i=1,\dots,M} t\,|x - y_i|\right].$$

One way to implement this tax is to fully subsidize transportation while levying a lump sum tax equal $(M^o G) + (t/4M^o)$.

5.3.4 Notes on the Literature

The process of competition between cities considered in Section 5.2 bears strong resemblances to the one analyzed in Section 4.3. Not surprisingly, therefore, the results are comparable and references overlap. These processes are, however, often cast within different frameworks. Indeed, despite the conceptual similarity between private and public goods in the spatial context, economists studying these subjects have made different modeling assumptions that have different intellectual origins. The literature on local public goods is huge and cannot be reviewed in this book. Distinct and complementary surveys may be found in Wildasin (1986; 1987) and Scotchmer (2002). Note that the role of the Henry George theorem in local public finance has been studied independently by Flatters, Henderson, and Mieszkowsi (1974) as well as by Stiglitz (1977) and Arnott and Stiglitz (1979).

A large body of literature also exists devoted to the location of public facilities that is more in the spirit of the material presented in Section 5.3. The aim of these models is to help the decision maker by giving him relevant information about the desirable configurations. Despite significant differences, facility location and local public goods are connected fields; both strands of literature are compared in Thisse and Zoller (1983).

5.4 CONCLUDING REMARKS

The analysis conducted in this chapter leads to fairly strong conclusions. Space blurs the distinction between public and private goods. Together with Chapter 4, this chapter suggests indeed that the supply of local public goods obeys principles that are not fundamentally different from those governing the efficient supply of private goods. In both cases, the working of a perfectly competitive land market seems to be able to improve the allocation of resources vastly in situations that are often described as typical market failures – a property that is overlooked by many in the economics profession. The underlying principle is simple: The differential land rent capitalizes the costs and advantages associated with a particular location, thus fostering the equalization of utility across similar individuals located at different places. Indeed, when the land market is perfectly competitive, the optimal system of cities is identical to the one emerging from competition among land developers. In the same spirit, when there are several public goods, the relevant decision-making entities should be consolidated and incorporated into areas sufficiently large to allow them to internalize the effects of local public policies as much as possible. Finally, even under a political process such as voting, accounting for the differential land rent allows for a reconciliation between the voting outcome and the optimum.

Such results are provocative enough for the problem of land property rights to receive more attention than it does nowadays. Despite the limitations discussed in Section 5.2.5, as well as the imperfections that characterize the housing markets in the real world (Arnott 1995), we may safely conclude that competition among land developers, local governments, or both in the presence of competitive land markets will significantly contribute to the efficient provision of local public goods. In the absence of better alternative mechanisms, land capitalization is worth serious consideration. At the very least, it seems wise to promote public interventions that are land market savvy. In particular, antitrust authorities should be invited to watch more carefully how land and housing markets and developers operate.

It is often forgotten that major debates about land property rights have arisen in the past precisely for the reasons discussed in this chapter. Considering the situation in Europe during the second half of the nineteenth century, Hohenberg and Lee (1985, 326) came to the following conclusion:[15]

> It was recognized that public purposes might require forced purchase of land, for example, for roads.... But only such land as would actually be used could be appropriated by the collectivity, and any regulation imposed on landowners must be the same for all, whatever their location in the city. Thus large-scale public projects could not recoup their cost by capturing the gains in land value they generated.

It is also worth stressing that the results derived in Section 5.3 suggest a stylized history of the formation of nations in Western Europe. The process of amalgamation of regions started under the Ancien Régime. As democracy developed in the nineteenth century, centralization of government services was pursued. This is likely because, at the same time, nationalism took a firm hold among the population while substantial technological progress developed in

[15] For example, Hausmann financed property acquisition and construction against future revenues obtained from the increased property values created by the planned improvements of Paris. Interestingly, the operation went bankrupt when the landowners recouped their property at the prices prevailing before the improvements (Marchand 1993).

transportation. Indeed, as observed by Alesina and Spolaore (1997), the rise in nationalism can be viewed in the present model as a decline in the parameter t that intensified the decrease generated by technological innovations. Ultimately, a large group of individuals came to favor a geographical concentration of government services. In other words, this was the time of the nation-state.

Around the middle of the twentieth century, a resurgence of regionalism occurred. In our setting, this means an increase in the parameter t. Not surprisingly, geographical decentralization was the answer of most national governments. Our analysis then suggests that the regional system chosen by the majority of the population has been inefficient, thus generating endless debates with those defending centralization of government activities.

As suggested by Alesina and Spolaore (1997), through an increased reliance on voting, the number of regions and countries may increase as the degree of economic integration and openness rises. Indeed, the benefits of a large home market become relatively less important if small countries can freely trade with each other as well as with the rest of the world. Small jurisdictions are also able to change existing rules and laws quickly in reaction to new environments and opportunities because they display a high degree of political homogeneity (Streeten 1993). Reforming existing laws or passing new ones takes much longer in big, diversified economies, where any change in the status quo implicates long negotiations involving a large variety of interest groups. Consequently, today's regional separatism might well replace yesterday's nationalism. In other words, "Tiebout with politics" would favor the long-term persistence of spatial inequality because interpersonal solidarity mechanisms would henceforth function only between or within certain areas. One should not, therefore, underestimate the risk that the rise in spatial inequality resulting from greater economic integration and deeper political decentralization could generate acute conflicts.

APPENDIX

To ease the burden of notation, we first divide (5.25) by t and then replace G/nt by G. Recall that μ is the Lebesgue measure defined on the interval [0, 1].

A Proof of Proposition 5.3. Consider the equidistant configuration with M facilities located at $y_i^* = (2i-1)/2M$ for $i = 1, \ldots, M$. Let $A_1, \ldots, A_i, \ldots, A_M$ be the M intervals of [0, 1] given by:

$$A_1 = [0, 1/M), \ldots, A_i = [(i-1)/M, i/M), \ldots, A_M = [(M-1)/M, 1]$$

which define the set of corresponding jurisdictions.

Consider now any other configuration $\mathbf{y}_M \neq \mathbf{y}_M^*$ with M facilities (without loss of generality, we assume that all the components of $\mathbf{y}_M$ are distinct). Let N be the number of locations such that $y_i = y_i^*$ with $N < M$, and I the set of consumers indifferent between the configurations $\mathbf{y}_M^*$ and $\mathbf{y}_M$. We denote by μ^* ($\bar{\mu}$) the measure of the set of consumers who strictly prefer $\mathbf{y}_M^*$ to $\mathbf{y}_M$ ($\mathbf{y}_M$ to $\mathbf{y}_M^*$) and show that μ^* always exceeds $\bar{\mu}$.

For any j such that $y_j = y_j^*$, $\mu\left(A_j\right) = 1/M$ implies

$$\mu\left(A_j \cap I\right) \leq \frac{1}{M}$$

and thus

$$\mu(I) \leq \frac{N}{M}. \tag{5A.1}$$

Let $B_1, \ldots, B_i, \ldots, B_{M+1}$ be the $M+1$ intervals of $[0, 1]$ defined as follows:

$$B_1 = [0, 1/2M), \ldots, B_i = [(2i-3)/2M, (2i-1)/2M), \ldots, B_{M+1} = [(2M-1)/2M, 1].$$

Denote by k_i the number of facilities in $\mathbf{y}_M$ belonging to B_i and by $\hat{\mu}_i$ the measure of the set of consumers located in B_i who strictly prefer $\mathbf{y}_M$ to $\mathbf{y}_M^*$.

For $i = 2, \ldots, M$, it is readily verified that $\hat{\mu}_i = 0$ if $k_i = 0$, $\hat{\mu}_i = 1/2M$ if $k_i = 1$, and $\hat{\mu}_i < 1/M$ if $k_i \geq 2$. Similarly, for $i = 1$ and $i = M+1$, we have $\hat{\mu}_i = 0$ if $k_i = 0$ and $\hat{\mu}_i < 1/2M$ if $k_i \geq 1$, respectively.

Let $\hat{M}$ be the number of intervals B_i for which $k_i \geq 2$. Then, the following three cases may arise.

i. $k_1 = k_{M+1} = 0$. Then, there are at most $(M - 2\hat{M} - N)$ intervals B_i containing one facility, and thus

$$\bar{\mu} \leq \frac{\hat{M}}{M} + \frac{M - 2\hat{M} - N}{2M}$$

the inequality being strict when $\hat{M} > 0$.

ii. $k_1 = 0$ and $k_{M+1} \geq 1$ (or, symmetrically, $k_1 \geq 1$ and $k_{M+1} = 0$). Then, we have

$$\hat{\mu} \leq \frac{1}{2M} + \frac{\hat{M}}{M} + \frac{M - 1 - 2\hat{M} - N}{2M}.$$

iii. $k_1 \geq 1$ and $k_{M+1} \geq 1$. Then, we have

$$\hat{\mu} \leq \frac{1}{M} + \frac{\hat{M}}{M} + \frac{M - 2 - 2\hat{M} - N}{2M}.$$

The preceding three inequalities imply

$$\hat{\mu} \leq \frac{M - N}{2M}. \tag{5A.2}$$

Assume that the inequality is strict in (5A.2). Then, (5A.1) and (5A.2) imply that μ^* is strictly larger than $\hat{\mu}$, which means that $\mathbf{y}_M$ is defeated by $\mathbf{y}_M^*$.

Suppose now that the equality holds in (5A.2). In this event, it must be that $k_1 = k_{M+1} = 0$ and $\hat{M} = 0$. Consequently, there exists an interval B_j containing one facility and having one facility placed at one of its endpoints such that either

$$\mu\left(A_{j-1} \cap I\right) < 1/M$$

or

$$\mu\left(A_j \cap I\right) < 1/M$$

holds. This implies that $\mu^* > \hat{\mu}$, and thus $\mathbf{y}_M$ is again defeated by $\mathbf{y}_M^*$.

B The optimality of the equidistant configuration. When there are M facilities, total transportation costs are defined as follows:

$$\begin{aligned} TTC(y_1, \ldots, y_M) &= \int_0^{(y_1+y_2)/2} |x - y_1| \, dx \\ &\quad + \sum_{i=2}^{M-1} \int_{(y_{i-1}+y_i)/2}^{(y_i+y_{i+1})/2} |x - y_i| \, dx \\ &\quad + \int_{(y_{M-1}+y_M)/2}^{1} |x - y_M| \, dx \\ &= \frac{y_1^2}{2} + \sum_{i=1}^{M-1} \frac{(y_{i+1} - y_i)^2}{4} + \frac{(1 - y_M)^2}{2}. \end{aligned}$$

Applying the first order conditions yields the following system of linear equations:

$$3y_1 - y_2 = 0$$

$$-y_{i-1} + 2y_i - y_{i+1} = 0 \qquad \text{for } i = 2, \ldots, M - 1$$

$$-y_{M-1} + 3y_M = 2$$

which has a single solution given by $y_i^* = (2i - 1)/2M$. It is easily checked that the second order conditions are always satisfied.

C Proof of Proposition 5.4. Let $\bar{M}$ be the candidate equilibrium defined as in Proposition 5.4. First, some simple calculations show that $\bar{M}$ defeats any $M < \bar{M}$ when $\bar{M} \leq 4$. It then remains to prove that $\bar{M}$ defeats any $M > \bar{M}$ when (5.27) holds. Let $\bar{\mu}$ be the measure of the set of consumers who strictly prefer $\bar{M}$ to $M > \bar{M}$ and show that $\bar{\mu} > 1/2$.

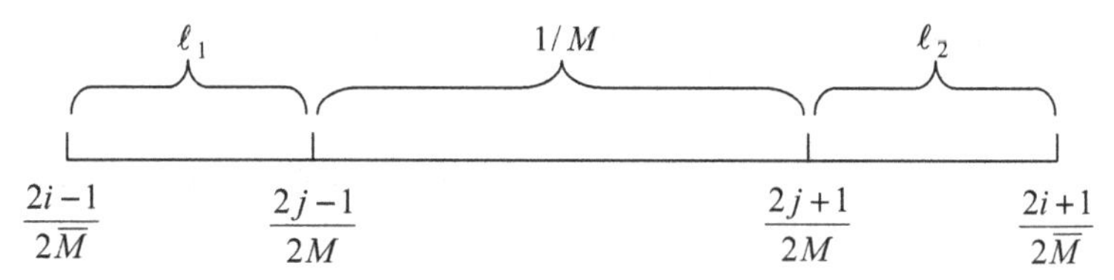

Figure 5.3. Population segmentation.

Assume first that $M > (3\bar{M} + 1)/2$. For each $i = 1, \ldots, \bar{M}$, a consumer located at

$$x \in \left[\frac{2i-1}{2M} - \frac{1}{2M}\min\left\{\frac{M-\bar{M}}{M+1}, 1\right\}, \frac{2i-1}{2M} + \frac{1}{2M}\min\left\{\frac{M-\bar{M}}{\bar{M}+1}, 1\right\}\right]$$

strictly prefers $\bar{M}$ to M because

$$\min_{i=1,\ldots,\bar{M}} \left|x - y_i^*(\bar{M})\right| - \min_{i=1,\ldots,M} \left|x - y_i^*(M)\right| < \frac{M-\bar{M}}{2(\bar{M}+1)\bar{M}}$$

where

$$y_i^*(M) = (2i-1)/2M \qquad i = 1, \ldots, M.$$

Therefore, $\hat{\mu}$ is larger than or equal to

$$\min\left\{\frac{M-\bar{M}}{\bar{M}+1}, 1\right\}$$

so that $\bar{\mu} > 1/2$ because $M > (3\bar{M} + 1)/2$.

Assume now that $\bar{M} < M \leq (3\bar{M} + 1)/2$. To start with, consider the interval $[0, 1/2M]$. We know that $1/2M < 1/2\bar{M} < 3/M$. Consequently, the consumers in $[0, 1/2M]$ strictly prefer $\bar{M}$ to M if and only if $1/M\bar{M} < 2G$, which follows from the definition of $\bar{M}$. The same holds for the interval $[(2\bar{M} - 1)/2\bar{M}, 1]$.

Consider now the $M - 2$ intervals given by

$$C_i = ((2i-1)/2\bar{M}, (2i+1)/2\bar{M})$$

for $i = 2, \ldots, M - 1$. Two subcases may arise. In the first one, there is one facility in the equidistant configuration with M facilities that belongs to C_i. Then, the measure of the set of consumers who strictly prefer $\bar{M}$ to M is larger than $1/2\bar{M}$. In the second one, there are two facilities located at l_1 and l_2 that belong to C_i (see Figure 5.3).

i. If both l_1 and l_2 are smaller than $G(M - \bar{M})$, then the consumers at locations $(2j - 1)/2M$ and $(2j + 1)/2M$, and, therefore, all consumers in C_i, strictly prefer $\bar{M}$ to M.

ii. If only l_1, say, is smaller $G(M - \bar{M})$, then the consumers located in

$$\left(\frac{2i-1}{2\bar{M}}, \frac{4j-1}{2M}\right]$$

and in

$$\left(\frac{2j+1}{4M} + \frac{2i+1}{4M}, \frac{2i+1}{2\bar{M}}\right]$$

strictly prefer $\bar{M}$ to M.

iii. Finally, observe that both l_1 and l_2 cannot exceed $G(M - \bar{M})$ because

$$l_1 + l_2 = \frac{1}{\bar{M}} - \frac{1}{M} < \frac{(M - \bar{M})}{(\bar{M}+1)\bar{M}} < 2G(M - \bar{M}).$$

Thus, in the three cases, the measure of the set of consumers in C_i who strictly prefer $\bar{M}$ to M is larger than $1/2\bar{M}$. Summing over all the intervals and using $M \leq \bar{M}$, we obtain

$$\bar{\mu} > \frac{1}{\bar{M}} + \frac{M-1}{2\bar{M}} > 1/2.$$

D Proof of Proposition 5.5. It is sufficient to show that M defeats $M - 1$ as long as $M \leq \bar{M}$. This, together with appendix C, implies that $\bar{M}$ is the unique value of M that simultaneously defeats $M - 1$ and $M + 1$.

The consumers who strictly prefer M to $M - 1$ are located either in the hinterlands or around the M facilities of the equidistant configuration. Consider the first group. The consumer at $1/2M$ strictly prefers M to $M - 1$ because of (5.25). This holds a fortiori for all the consumers in $[0, 1/2M)$. The same applies to consumers in $[(2M - 1)/2M, 1]$.

We now consider the second group. Focusing on the consumers located in the vicinity of the facility established at $(2i - 1)/2M$ for $i = 2, \ldots, M - 1$, we have

$$\frac{2i-3}{M-1} < \frac{2i-1}{M} < \frac{2i-1}{M-1}.$$

Let x_i^l be the location of the consumer situated on the left-hand side of the i-th facility and indifferent between M and $M - 1$. Because x_i^l must belong to the interval

$$\left(\frac{2i-3}{2(M-1)}, \frac{2i-1}{2M}\right]$$

it must be that x_i^l is the solution to

$$x_i^l - \frac{2i-3}{2(M-1)} - \left(\frac{2i-1}{2M} - x_i^l\right) = G$$

that is,

$$x_i^l = \frac{2i-3}{4(M-1)} + \frac{2i-1}{4M} + \frac{G}{2}. \tag{5A.3}$$

Similarly, if x_i^r is the location of the consumer situated on the right-hand side of the i-th facility and indifferent between M and $M-1$, we obtain

$$x_i^r = \frac{2i-1}{4(M-1)} + \frac{2i-1}{4M} - \frac{G}{2}. \tag{5A.4}$$

Thus, all consumers in (x_i^l, x_i^r) strictly prefer M to $M-1$. Denote by μ_M^* the measure of the set of consumers who strictly prefer M to $M-1$. It then follows from (5A.3) and (5A.4) and from the continuity of the utility functions that

$$\mu_M^* > \frac{1}{M} + (M-2)\left[\frac{1}{2(M-1)} - G\right].$$

Because $M \leq \bar{M}$, we have

$$\frac{1}{2(M-1)M} > G$$

so that $\mu_M^* > 1/2$.

PART II

THE STRUCTURE OF METROPOLITAN AREAS

6

The Spatial Structure of Cities under Communication Externalities

6.1 INTRODUCTION

The most distinctive feature of a city is its much higher population density than the surrounding nonurban areas. As a result, economic agents residing within a city are close to one another. But why do households and firms seek spatial proximity? Fundamentally, this occurs because economic agents need to interact and distance is an impediment to interaction. This need is gravitational in that its intensity is likely to increase with the number of agents set up in each location and to decrease with the distance between two locations. This need has been at the heart of the work of several geographers, and we encounter it on many occasions and with different economic meanings.

However, by crowding a few locations only, economic agents also decrease their satisfaction because they normally enjoy consuming more land, either as consumers or as producers. Therefore, *one can view the agglomeration process*, at least in the first order, *as the interplay between an interaction field among agents and competition on the land market.* In such a setting, the need to interact acts as a centripetal force, whereas competition for land has the nature of a centrifugal force. As is seen in this chapter, it is remarkable that the mere need to interact turns out to be sufficient to generate a single-peaked distribution of (homogeneous) agents across locations.

But this is not the end of the story. Indeed, one has to explain why economic agents want to interact. It should be clear that several explanations can be put forward. That human beings are "social animals" is perhaps the most basic justification of the need for interaction among individuals. Indeed personal relations are the essence of societies even though the consequences of relations are often double-edged. For example, according to Fisher (1982, 2–3),

> Our day-to-day lives are preoccupied with people, with seeking approval, providing affection, exchanging gossips, falling in love, soliciting advice, giving opinions, soothing anger, teaching manners, providing aids, making impressions, keeping in touch.... Although modern nations have elaborate arrays of institutions and organizations, daily

life proceeds through personal ties. . . . Those personal ties are also our greatest motives for action.

Psychologists also recognize that human beings have a pervasive drive to form and maintain lasting and positive relations with others. According to Baumeiter and Leary (1995, 497), who reviewed a vast literature, two conditions must be met for this drive to be satisfied:

First, there is a need for frequent, affectively pleasant interactions with a few other people, and, second, these interactions must take place in the context of a temporally stable and enduring framework of affective concern for each other's welfare.

To the best of our knowledge, the first economic model focusing on such a trade-off was proposed by Beckmann (1976). More precisely, Beckmann assumes that the utility of an individual depends on the average distance to all individuals with whom this person interacts as well as on the amount of land she buys on the market. Under such preferences, the city exhibits a bell-shaped population density distribution supported by a similarly shaped land rent curve. Thus, the city emerges here as a social magnet. Stated differently, the natural gregariousness of human beings leads to the spatial concentration of people within compact areas. This model is presented in Section 6.2.1.

Although the process of interaction goes both ways, individuals worry only about their role as "receivers" and tend to neglect their function as "transmitters" to others. Hence, the equilibrium distribution of agents within the city is unlikely to be an optimum. Indeed, a comparison of the equilibrium and optimum densities shows that the former is less concentrated than the latter. This suggests, from the social standpoint, that the need to interact may well result in an insufficient concentration of population around the city center. Contrary to general belief, therefore, it is not obvious that agents are too densely packed in cities. This concurs with the recent literature on network economics where the density of equilibrium networks is often too low. Indeed, building a link gives rise to an external effect that benefits the agents located in the vicinity of the two agents involving the new connection. However, when an agent decides whether to build a link with another, she does not account for this effect, and thus links that are socially desirable may not arise (Jackson and Wolinsky 1996; Jackson 2008; Ioannides 2012).

At this stage, it is natural to ask whether the principles uncovered by Beckmann for households also govern the locational decisions made by firms within an urban area. In raising such a question, one may wonder what is the nature of the interaction that would foster firms' concentration beyond the standard market transactions in which they are involved. The reason here is very different from the one we saw for consumers in that it refers to the role of information as a basic input in firms' activities. By this, we mean the kind of information related to products, technologies, and markets, which is difficult to codify because it is tacit, and thus it can typically be collected only through face-to-face communications that require travel by high-skilled people whose time is valuable.

The impact of information on locational decisions is not new. The decline of manufacturing employment and the growth of office employment in central cities has been a common trend observed in many countries that started after the Industrial Revolution.[1] For example, in their study of the urban making of Europe, Hohenberg and Lee (1985, 299) forcefully argue that:

> the common element of the tertiary or service activities of cities is information, an intangible and therefore bulkless commodity that manifests itself mainly in the act of being transferred or exchanged. Town centers were the natural location where those trafficking in knowledge congregated, and they displaced not only residents but also most activities dealing with visible commodities. The business center was taken over by an army of brokers, clerks, bankers, couriers, and other dealers in the quintessentially urban commodity, information.

Information (or knowledge) is a *nonrival* good: the use of a piece of information by a firm does not reduce the content of that information for other firms. Hence, the exchange of information through communication within a set of firms generates externality-like benefits for each of them (Stigler 1961; Romer 1986; Lucas 1988). Provided that firms own different types of information, the benefits of communication generally increase as the number of firms rises. The quality of the information is also better when firms are gathered in that the number of intermediates is smaller. However, even in the Age of the Internet information is subject to *distance-decay effects* because communications across distant agents often distort and reduce the content and quality of information, a fact well documented since the pioneering work of Hägerstrand (1953). As a result, the benefits are greater if firms are located closer to each other.

In this respect, it is well known that face-to-face communication is most effective for rapid product and process development when the access to information about new products and production processes turns out to be essential for the competitiveness of firms. Most likely, the origin of these spillovers lies in the existence of face-to-face contacts. And, indeed, in their survey of empirical evidence, Tauchen and Witte (1984) observed that much of the interaction among the employees of different firms consists of such contacts. For example, Saxenian (1994, 33) emphasized the importance of this factor in making the Silicon Valley an efficient productive system:

> By all accounts, these informal conversations were pervasive and served as an important source of up-to-date information about competitors, customers, markets, and

[1] Even before the Industrial Revolution, the exchange of information seems to have been the main cause for the emergence of a prominent center in the business community (think of Venice, Antwerp, and Amsterdam) in different time periods (Smith 1984).

technologies. Entrepreneurs came to see social relationships and even gossips as a crucial aspect of their business. In an industry characterized by rapid technological change and intense competition, such informal communication was often of more value than more conventional but less timely forums such as industry journals.

The key point here is that personal contacts within the agglomeration encourage a constant intercommunication of ideas. This might come as a surprise in the age for which futurists had predicted the decline of cities because people would use more and more telecommunications devices instead of face-to-face interaction. However, this argument overlooks the fact that a substantial amount of knowledge used by firms turns out to be tacit and difficult to transfer from one location to another. The difference between *tacit* and *codified* information (knowledge) is crucial here. The transfer of information through modern transmission devices requires its organization according to some prespecified patterns, and only formal information can be codified and sent to others in this way. For example, the initial steps in the development of a new technology require repeated contacts between the actors involved to develop a mutual way of communicating through some common codes, to figure out how to interpret personalized information, and to make them operational. Such a process is facilitated by spatial proximity. Moreover, face-to-face communications are often at the origin of new ideas, combining insights from each party that are crucial for innovations. Research and development also requires long periods of exchange and discussion, during which knowledge is gradually structured through repeated trial and error. Such exchanges of ideas are truly effective only in the form of frequent face-to-face meetings.

In essence, the explanation is that the transmission of knowledge and ideas is not a routine activity that can be performed through standardized procedures. It is a cognitive process (and uncertainty is therefore inherent to the exchange) that is made easier when the individuals involved are close to each other. As nicely summarized by Glaeser et al. (1992, 1127), even in the era of the Internet, "intellectual breakthroughs must cross hallways and streets more easily than oceans and continents." Furthermore, face-to-face communications are often at the origin of new ideas, combining insights from each party that are crucial for innovations.

The empirical evidence is fairly conclusive. Controlling for the geographical concentration of sectors affecting the location of patent use, Jaffe, Trajtenberg, and Henderson (1993) found that, in the United States, citations of patents are more likely to be domestic and to come from the same states and metropolitan statistical areas, thus suggesting that the diffusion of knowledge is spatially concentrated (at least at the early stages of the diffusion process). In the same vein, using a sample of 147 regions in 18 countries, Peri (2005) shows that crossing one regional border reduces the flow of patent citations by 80 percent. This conclusion is strengthened by several other empirical studies, such as those surveyed by Audretsch and Feldman (2004), who observed that spillovers are likely to be geographically bounded within the region where the new knowledge was created. Developing a very detailed and advanced econometric analysis, Combes et al. (2012) confirm the prevalence of spillover effects in large French cities.

Furthermore, the historical evidence regarding the impact of the telephone on urbanization suggests a positive correlation between city size and telephone use. Although telecommunications may be a substitute for face-to-face meetings, these two forms of communications may also be complementary. For example, Gaspar and Glaeser (1998) reported on some suggestive evidence that an increase in business trips has occurred despite (or because of) recent improvements in telecommunications technologies. Thus, contrary to the opinions of futurists, the development of such technologies does not (necessarily) imply the death of cities as information centers. Would new information technologies change this state of affairs? Probably not. As argued by Glaeser (2011, 38),

> Better information technology has made the world more information intensive, which in turn has made knowledge more valuable than ever, and that has increased the value of learning from other people in cities.

In two independent articles, Borukhov and Hochman (1977) and O'Hara (1977) have shown how face-to-face communications may induce (office) firms to congregate and to form a central business district, even though clustering results in higher land rents. This topic is discussed in Section 6.2.2.

Diversity is another fundamental distinctive feature of cities. In other words, cities are concentrations of different agents (mainly firms and households). The mere recognition of this simple fact should lead to a new and richer set of results. The next step is, then, to mix consumers and firms within broader models of applied general equilibrium in order to study what the interplay between the two groups of agents may result in. The centripetal force in this interplay is the communications among firms permitting the exchange of information: other things being equal, each firm has an incentive to establish itself near other firms, thus fostering agglomeration. The centrifugal force goes through the land and labor markets. The clustering of many firms in a single area increases the average commuting distance for their workers, which, in turn, increases the wage rate and land rent in the area surrounding the cluster. Such high wages and land rents tend to discourage further agglomeration of firms in the same area. The equilibrium distribution of firms and households is thus the balance between these opposing forces. In Section 6.3, we focus on the direct interaction between firms because we believe that they are even more fundamental in modern societies for the shaping of cities than social interactions among individuals. One distinguishing feature of this approach is that consumers now choose both a residential place and a working site.

The interplay between those two types of forces has been studied in a series of articles by Fujita, Imai, and Ogawa.[2] These authors have shown that different equilibrium patterns may emerge according to the values of the economy's basic parameters, thus affecting the balance of the two opposite forces. More surprising, perhaps, is that the shape of the interaction field also influences the types of equilibria that arise. We consider in Section 6.4 a linear accessibility field and study how the market outcome changes with the level of commuting costs. The equilibrium city need not be monocentric. When commuting costs are high in relation to the accessibility parameter measuring the importance of the distance-decay effect in the interaction field, the equilibrium involves a complete mixture of business and residential activities. As the commuting cost falls, two business districts, which are themselves flanked by a residential area, are formed around the integrated section that shrinks. Eventually, *when commuting costs are low enough, the city becomes monocentric with the emergence of a single business district surrounded by two residential sections.* This evolution seems to accord with what we have observed since the beginning of the technological revolution in transportation.

Furthermore, the monocentric configuration is socially desirable for a larger domain of parameters than for the equilibrium outcome. In other words, the market may lead to a more dispersed configuration of firms than would be socially optimal.

As examined in Section 6.5, the possible equilibrium patterns are much more complex in the case of an exponential distance-decay function. In addition to the configurations just mentioned, we see that intermediate values for the commuting costs may lead to a duocentric configuration, or to a configuration involving a primary business center and two secondary business centers, or to three more or less identical centers. In these last three cases, the equilibrium pattern may also be viewed as describing a system of two or three cities.

Even more interesting is the nature of the transition from one equilibrium to another when some parameters slightly change. For example, one may observe catastrophic modifications in the urban configuration when the equilibrium city moves from a monocentric configuration to a duocentric one in which the interior residential area is quite large although the distance-decay parameter changes only slightly. All these results show how nonlinearities in accessibility may lead to a vast set of different outcomes and, by the same token, may explain why it is often hard to make reliable predictions about urban development.

Finally, in Section 6.6, we briefly discuss the case in which a firm splits its activities between two units located far apart. In this way, we may capture the

[2] In two later, but independent, papers, Lucas (2001) and Lucas and Rossi-Hansberg (2002) also appeal to spillovers to explain the existence of a monocentric city in a two-dimensional space. It is worth noting the analogy with Lucas' (1988) work in growth theory where externalities are the main driver of economic development.

idea that some activities are crucially dependent on the information obtained from other firms, whereas more routine activities require communication with the firm's headquarters only. The typical configuration associated with low intrafirm communication costs is the agglomeration of front offices at the city center and the dispersion of back offices together with their workers in the suburbs.

In all models studied in this chapter, a city emerges in an otherwise homogeneous space as the collective outcome of the interplay between individual decision makers. Cities are not the result of the actions taken by land developers or local governments. Furthermore, we focus on the formation and spatial structure of a city but do not address the issue of its size. Thus, all the results derived in this chapter are to be understood relative to given populations of households and firms.

Before proceeding, we want to stress that, although we work with a continuum of agents, we assume that each agent is indivisible. The implications of this assumption are important for the models examined in this chapter as well as in subsequent ones because the results are partly determined by the indivisibility of firms and households over several locations (even in the case of the multiunit firms, units cannot be subdivided). In other words, agents have an address.

6.2 AGGLOMERATION AND SPATIAL EXTERNALITIES

Ever since the pioneering work of Jackson and Wolinsky (1996), there exists a new and growing economic literature that shows how agents interact within social networks (Ioannides 2012). This literature stresses the importance of physical proximity for the formation of social ties between agents. Simultaneously, it recognizes that proximity may well be a black box that hides more subtle microeconomic phenomena. In what follows, we show by means of two simple models of urban economics how nonmarket interactions across agents of the same type lead to the emergence of a single cluster characterized by a unimodal distribution.

6.2.1 The City as the Outcome of Interaction between Consumers

The propensity to interact with others is a fundamental human attribute. People like to be close to each other to maximize social interaction. However, they also care about the quantity of space they consume. In other words, we consider a population of individuals who are social animals driven by their own interest. The following simple model demonstrates how the preference for social life leads to the emergence of a center through a unimodal and symmetric distribution of individuals. This distribution is dispersed around the center because competition for land leads to higher land rents near the center.

The self-organizing city. Consider a continuum N of identical consumers and a one-dimensional space $X = (-\infty, \infty)$ in which the land density is 1 everywhere and the opportunity cost of land is $R_A > 0$. Land is owned by absentee landlords. A consumer residing at x is endowed with the preferences

$$U = u(z, s) + I_x$$

where, as usual, z and s denote the composite good and the lot size, respectively, and I_x stands for the *interaction field* of a consumer located at x whose budget constraint is

$$z + sR(x) = Y - T(x).$$

Here $T(x)$ is the associated travel cost borne by the consumer when she interacts with other people. Because trips are costly, the occupied area must be bounded. Without loss of generality, the urban area is denoted by $[-b, b]$, where b is the agglomeration boundary determined at the equilibrium. As in Section 3.2, the quantity of the composite good is obtained by solving $u(z, s) = U - I_x$ for z, which is represented by $z = Z(s, U - I_x)$; thus, the consumer's bid rent function is given by

$$\Psi(x, U) = \max_s \frac{Y - Z(s, U - I_x) - T(x)}{s}. \tag{6.1}$$

In analyzing this model, Beckmann (1976) made several simplifying assumptions to derive a closed-form solution. First, the utility u is expressed as

$$u(z, s) = z + \alpha \log s$$

in which $\alpha > 0$ is a parameter indicating the weight of land in consumer preferences. Second, the interaction field is supposed to be such that each consumer interacts once with each and every other consumer in the area, which represents the extreme view that the individual network of personal ties is formed by the whole population residing in the urban area. Hence, the utility of I_x is constant across locations:

$$I_x = I.$$

Finally, maintaining a bond requires time, money, and attention. It is assumed that this takes the form of a trip whose cost is linear in distance, and thus the total travel cost borne by a consumer at x while interacting with others is given by

$$T(x) \equiv \int_{-b}^{b} t|x - y|n(y)\mathrm{d}y \tag{6.2}$$

where $n(y)$ is the density of consumers at location y and $t > 0$ the unit travel cost. It is worth noting that, in $T(x)$, the travel cost from x to y is weighted by the number (formally the density) of individuals located at the destination y, which means that there is one trip per individual at y. Evidently, we have

$$T(x) = \int_{-b}^{x} t(x-y)n(y)\mathrm{d}y + \int_{x}^{b} t(y-x)n(y)\mathrm{d}y \tag{6.3}$$

and thus $T(x)$ varies with the consumer's location as well as with the entire population density. It should be clear that the cost borne by a consumer when interacting with others is very different from what it was in Chapter 3, where all activities were supposed to take place at the city center.

Because all consumers must reach the same utility level U^* in equilibrium, (6.1) may be rewritten as

$$\Psi(x, U^*) = \max_{s} \frac{Y - U^* + I + \alpha \log s - T(x)}{s}. \tag{6.4}$$

The first order condition with respect to s gives the following equilibrium condition:

$$Y - U^* + I - \alpha + \alpha \log s - T(x) = 0. \tag{6.5}$$

Let

$$\zeta \equiv Y - U^* + I - \alpha$$

be a constant whose value is unknown because the value of U^* is endogenous. Solving (6.5) for s and using the definition of ζ, we obtain

$$s^*(x) = \exp\left(\frac{-\zeta + T(x)}{\alpha}\right) \tag{6.6}$$

so that

$$n^*(x) = \exp\left(\frac{\zeta - T(x)}{\alpha}\right) \tag{6.7}$$

where $n^*(x) \equiv 1/s^*(x)$ is the equilibrium population density. Substituting (6.6) into (6.4) leads to

$$\Psi(x, U^*) = \frac{\alpha}{s^*(x)}. \tag{6.8}$$

Because $\Psi(x, U^*) = R_{\mathrm{A}}$ at the equilibrium fringe b^*, we must have

$$\frac{R_{\mathrm{A}}}{\alpha} = n^*(b^*) = \exp\left(\frac{\zeta - T(b^*)}{\alpha}\right). \tag{6.9}$$

Differentiating (6.3) twice yields

$$\frac{\mathrm{d}^2 T}{\mathrm{d}x^2} = 2tn^*(x)$$

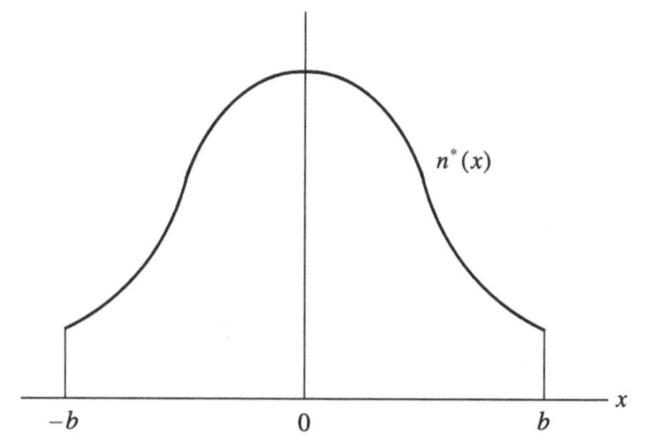

Figure 6.1. The equilibrium population density when consumers like to interact.

and thus $T(x)$ is strictly convex in x. It then follows from (6.7) that

$$\frac{d^2 T}{dx^2} = 2t \exp\left(\frac{\zeta - T(x)}{\alpha}\right). \tag{6.10}$$

Solving this differential equation yields

$$T(x) = -\alpha \log\left[\frac{\alpha}{t}\exp\left(-\frac{\zeta}{\alpha}\right)\frac{k^2 \exp(k\,|x\,|)}{(1+\exp(k\,|x\,|))^2}\right] \tag{6.11}$$

where k is an unknown positive constant of integration (see appendix A for detailed calculations). Substituting (6.11) into (6.7), we obtain

$$n^*(x) = \frac{\alpha}{t}\frac{k^2 \exp(k|x\,|)}{(1+\exp(k|x\,|))^2} \tag{6.12}$$

which gives the equilibrium population density as a function of the constant k.

Clearly, this function is symmetric about the origin. Furthermore, differentiating (6.12) with respect to x shows that $n^*(x)$ has a unique maximum at $x = 0$. The equilibrium consumer density is therefore unimodal. Taking the second derivative shows that $n^*(x)$ is concave over the interval

$$\left[-\log\left(2+\sqrt{3}\right)/k, \log\left(2+\sqrt{3}\right)/k\right]$$

and convex outside. A typical pattern of the population density is depicted in Figure 6.1.

Accordingly, a preference for social life is sufficient to form an agglomeration around an endogenous center and, therefore, to preclude the flat distribution of individuals from being an equilibrium. This center is the place where the interaction among people is most convenient and individual land consumption is the lowest. And, indeed, the population is more concentrated around the center because the population density falls when the distance from the center rises, thus confirming the intuition that being at the center of the urban area gives the individuals located there the highest accessibility to others. By implication, the center emerging here plays the same role as the CBD in the urban economics models of Chapter 3. The crucial difference is that the center is endogenous here, whereas the CBD considered in Chapter 3 is exogenous.

Using (6.9) and (6.12), we see that the following condition must hold at the urban fringe:

$$\frac{R_A}{\alpha} = \frac{\alpha}{t}\frac{k^2 \exp(kb)}{(1+\exp(kb))^2}. \tag{6.13}$$

Furthermore, integrating the population density over the interval $[-b, b]$ must be equal to N:

$$\begin{aligned} N &= 2\int_0^b n^*(x)\mathrm{d}x = 2\frac{\alpha}{t}\int_0^b \frac{k^2 \exp(kx)}{(1+\exp(kx))^2}\mathrm{d}x \\ &= \frac{\alpha}{t}k\frac{\exp(kb)-1}{\exp(kb)+1}. \end{aligned} \tag{6.14}$$

These two expressions give the equilibrium values of the constant of integration k and of the agglomeration boundary b. Setting $y = \exp(kb)$ in (6.13) and (6.14), solving (6.14) for y, and replacing the value thus obtained in (6.13), we obtain

$$k^2 = \frac{t}{\alpha^2}(tN^2 + 4R_A). \tag{6.15}$$

Hence, by (6.7) we have

$$n^*(0) = \frac{1}{\alpha}\left(\frac{tN^2}{4} + R_A\right). \tag{6.16}$$

Therefore the peak of the population distribution moves upward (and the population density is more concentrated) when the population size N is larger, when the unit cost of traveling t rises, and when the opportunity land cost R_A increases; the peak of the population distribution moves downward when the preference for land α gets stronger. This shows how a bigger population tends to be more agglomerated because individuals are willing to trade less space against a higher level of interaction. These results are similar to those derived in Section 3.3, but the center is no longer exogenously given.

Similarly, the urban fringe may be obtained by replacing k in (6.14) with the positive root of (6.15). Using this root then permits the complete determination of the equilibrium population density, which, in turn, is used to find $T(x)$ by (6.3), thus yielding the equilibrium value of ζ by (6.11).

Setting $R^*(x) = \Psi(x, U^*)$ and $1/s^*(x) = n^*(x)$ in (6.8) implies

$$R^*(x) = \alpha n^*(x)$$

and thus the market land rent supporting the residential equilibrium mirrors the population density. Both densities are bell-shaped and vary in the same way with the parameters of the economy. In particular, a rise (fall) in the population (the cost of trips) is reflected in higher (lower) land rents near the urban center. Again, this agrees with what we saw in Chapter 3.[3]

We may summarize these results as follows:

Proposition 6.1. *Assume that consumers value land and interaction with others. Then, if consumers' utility is given by*

$$U = \alpha \log s + I - T(x)$$

both the equilibrium population distribution and the equilibrium land rent are unimodal and symmetric.

The indivisibility of human beings is fundamental for this proposition to hold. Indeed, if each individual were to be perfectly divisible, spatial equilibrium would involve a uniform distribution of people and a flat land rent.

The optimal city. We now study the optimal distribution of consumers using the same approach as in Section 3.3.3. Though our equilibrium is competitive, it is not socially optimal. The explanation for this market failure is that, although the location of each individual directly affects the travel costs of all others, the consumer considers only her own travel costs in making a locational decision. That the interaction among individuals goes both ways and does not transit through the market implies an externality preventing the equilibrium from being at an optimum. However, it is interesting to know whether the equilibrium is excessively or insufficiently concentrated around the center.

To answer this question, we have to provide a fairly detailed analysis of the optimum density. Because they are identical, all consumers at the same location x must have the same consumption bundle (z, s). Consequently, if U^*

[3] In the same vein, Papageorgiou and Smith (1983) consider a trade-off between the need for social contacts, which is negatively affected by distance, and the need for land, which is negatively affected by crowding. Space is circular (a circle or a taurus) so that the uniform distribution of individuals is always a spatial equilibrium. When the propensity to interact with others is large enough, this equilibrium becomes unstable: any marginal perturbation is sufficient for the population to evolve toward an irregular distribution. In this model, cities are considered as the outcome of a social process combining basic human needs, which are not (necessarily) expressed through the market. It is probably fair to say that this model captures much of the intuition of early geographers interested in the spatial structure of human settlements in that the key variables are independent of the economic system. However, from the economic standpoint, it is important to consider less abstract formulations and, rather, to study models based on specific economic interactions.

denotes the equilibrium utility level obtained above, the optimal distribution must minimize the total cost as defined by (3.29) with respect to $s(x)$ and b:

$$C \equiv \int_{-b}^{b} \{T(x) + Z[s(x), U^*] + R_A s(x)\} n(x) \mathrm{d}x$$

where $Z[s(x), U^*]$ is equal to $U^* - \alpha \log s(x) - I$ and $T(x)$ is given by (6.3) subject to the land constraint

$$s(x)n(x) = 1 \quad -b \leq x \leq b \tag{6.17}$$

the population constraint

$$\int_{-b}^{b} n(x)\mathrm{d}x = N \tag{6.18}$$

and the nonnegativity constraints on s and n.

As in Section 3.3.3, one can show that solving this minimization problem is equivalent to solving the following maximization problem:

$$S \equiv NY - C = \int_{-b}^{b} \{[Y - U^* + I + \alpha \log s(x) - T(x)]n(x) - R_A\} \mathrm{d}x$$

subject to the aforementioned constraints.

We present here an intuitive argument showing how the optimality conditions are obtained.[4] For that, we use (6.17) in order to rewrite our optimization problem as the maximization of the expression

$$S = \int_{-b}^{b} \{[Y - U^* + I - \alpha \log n(x) - T(x)]n(x) - R_A\} \mathrm{d}x$$

subject to (6.18), that is, we want maximize the Lagrangian function

$$\begin{aligned} \mathcal{L} &= \int_{-b}^{b} \{[Y - U^* + I - \alpha \log n(x) - T(x)]n(x) - R_A\} \mathrm{d}x \\ &\quad + \lambda \left[\int_{-b}^{b} n(x)\mathrm{d}x - N \right] \\ &= \int_{-b}^{b} \{[Y - U^* + I + \lambda - \alpha \log n(x) - T(x)]n(x) - R_A\} \mathrm{d}x - \lambda N \end{aligned} \tag{6.19}$$

where λ is the multiplier associated with the population constraint and U^* is supposed to be given.

[4] A formal derivation of these conditions is provided in appendix B.

We first choose $n(x)$ at every location x inside the city to maximize $\mathcal{L}$. If we neglect for the moment the impact of the choice of $n(x)$ on $T(x)$, the marginal benefit of increasing the population at x is measured by

$$Y - U^* + I + \lambda - \alpha \log n(x) - T(x) - \alpha.$$

However, by increasing the number of consumers at x by one unit, we increase the travel costs of the other consumers by $T(x)$ owing to the symmetry in transport cost between any two locations, and thus the net benefit generated by one more consumer at x is equal to

$$Y - U^* + I + \lambda - \alpha \log n(x) - T(x) - \alpha - T(x).$$

The optimum is therefore reached when this magnitude equals zero:

$$Y - U^* + I - \alpha + \lambda + \alpha \log s(x) - 2T(x) = 0. \tag{6.20}$$

This condition states that, when the number of consumers at x increases by one, the transport cost at this location increases by the amount $T(x)$. However, the transport cost of the other consumers at x also rises by the same amount. Therefore, in the optimum problem, one must account for both costs in choosing the location of a consumer. By contrast, in the equilibrium problem, in choosing a location at x, a consumer only accounts for her travel cost to the others but neglects the impact of this choice over the travel costs borne by the others (which is also given by $T(x)$).

Setting

$$\zeta^o \equiv -\alpha + Y - U^* + I + \lambda$$

we obtain from (6.20) the optimal distribution:

$$n^o(x) = 1/s^o(x) = \exp\left(\frac{\zeta^o - 2T(x)}{\alpha}\right) \tag{6.21}$$

which is identical to (6.7) except that the total travel cost $T(x)$ enters with the factor 2 instead of 1.

It remains to determine the optimal city boundary. As previously if we neglect the impact of a marginal increase in b on $T(x)$ and assume symmetry of the distribution, the Lagrangian function (6.19) is maximized when the city expands up to the point b at which the marginal benefit from both sides given by

$$2\{[Y - U^* + I + \lambda - \alpha \log n^o(b) - T(b)]n^o(b) - R_A\}$$

becomes zero. However, in so doing, we have not accounted for the fact that a marginal increase in b (respectively in $-b$) leads to an increase in the population by $n^o(b)$ at b (respectively at $-b$), which, in turn increases the travel costs for the other consumers by an amount equal to $n^o(b)T(b)$. Hence, the net benefit from expanding the city fringe is given by

$$2\{[Y - U^* + I + \lambda - \alpha \log n^o(b) - T(b)]n^o(b) - R_A\} - 2n^o(b)T(b).$$

Setting this expression equal to zero and using the optimality condition (6.20) evaluated at b, we obtain

$$\alpha n^o(b^o) - R_A = 0$$

so that

$$n^o(b^o) = \exp\left(\frac{\zeta^o - 2T(b^o)}{\alpha}\right) = \frac{R_A}{\alpha} \tag{6.22}$$

which is again identical to (6.9) except that $T(b^o)$ is now multiplied by 2.

Therefore, we may conclude that the equilibrium conditions become identical to the optimality conditions when $T(x)$ is replaced by $2T(x)$.

Using the same technique as in the equilibrium case, we can see that the optimum population density is given by

$$n^o(x) = \frac{\alpha}{2t} \frac{h^2 \exp(h|x|)}{(1 + \exp(h|x|))^2}$$

where h is a constant of integration that can be computed as k in the equilibrium case:

$$h^2 = \frac{t}{\alpha^2}(4tN^2 + 8R_A).$$

It can then be readily verified that the optimum population density at the center is such that

$$n^o(0) = \frac{1}{\alpha}\left(\frac{tN^2}{2} + R_A\right).$$

Observe that the equilibrium and optimum solutions are identical when t is replaced by $2t$ in the former, that is, when consumers internalize the others' interaction costs. Because consumers have no incentives to do so, it appears that the optimum distribution is more concentrated than the equilibrium one. This result may come as a surprise because the conventional wisdom is that market cities are too crowded near the center. The reason for this surprising result is that consumers do not account for the locational externality they generate and, therefore, use a larger land plot. Of course, we have not considered negative externalities (such as transport congestion or pollution) in the present model. Still, it is interesting to observe that *a preference for social life is sufficient to foster the emergence of an agglomeration of individuals* and that *the optimal agglomeration requires an even stronger concentration of people.* This is a fairly robust result, for we encounter it in very different settings.

In fact, it always holds provided that the individual benefit of interaction is additive across the whole population of agents (Fujita and Smith 1990).

By replacing $\log s$ with $1/s$ in individual preferences, Mossay and Picard (2011) show that multiple-city configurations may emerge along a circular geographical space. These spatial equilibria involve the existence of empty hinterlands between identical and evenly spaced cities. Furthermore, total welfare decreases with the number of cities. As in the foregoing, under a linear space, the spatial equilibrium is unique and involves a single city.

6.2.2 The CBD as the Outcome of Interaction between Firms

In the same spirit, we now characterize the equilibrium distribution of firms interacting together and using floor space. This topic has been addressed by Borukov and Hochman (1977) as well as by O'Hara (1977). We consider a continuum M of identical firms and a linear space for which the land density is 1, whereas the opportunity (presumably housing) land cost is $R_A > 0$. Each firm produces the same output Q, which is sold on a competitive market at a unit price. To do so, firms must interact with all other firms, thus bearing the corresponding interaction cost $T(x)$, and use one unit of floor space. This competition for proximity leads to the building of *offices* for firms. O'Hara (1977, 1196) put it this way:

> One firm's use of land near the center imposes higher travel costs on other firms which are precluded from using that land, and these costs are reflected in its rent. This provides an incentive to economize on these costs by substituting other inputs for land, especially by building taller buildings in the center than on the periphery of the CBD.

In addition, each firm also uses one unit of floor space acquired on the market at the prevailing *office rent* $R_o(x)$. Therefore, the profit of a firm at location $x \in [-b, b]$ is defined as follows:

$$\pi(x) = Q - T(x) - R_o(x)$$

where the interaction cost borne by the same firm is

$$T(x) \equiv \int_{-b}^{b} t\,|x - y|\, m(y)\mathrm{d}y \tag{6.23}$$

with $m(y)$ denoting the endogenous firm density at y. Because each firm uses one unit of floor space, $m(y)$ also describes the number of floors built at y. As is seen, the centrifugal force is expressed by the office rent, which is an increasing and strictly convex function of the number of offices supplied at a given location.

Suppose that offices are supplied by the construction sector formed by a large number of competitive firms. If $s(x)$ denotes the amount of floor space provided by a developer per unit of land at location x, the developer's profit is given by

$$\pi_c(x) = R_o(x)s(x) - [s(x)]^2 - R(x)$$

where s^2 stands for the construction cost of s units of floor space per unit of land and $R(x)$ is the land rent prevailing at x. Assuming that this cost is quadratic captures the idea that construction exhibits decreasing returns with respect to office height at the same place.

The equilibrium condition for construction firms implies that the density of floor space supplied at x is such that

$$s^*(x) = R_o(x)/2.$$

So the supply of offices rises with the office rent. In turn, the market clearing condition for offices implies that $m(x) = s^*(x)$ for all locations x occupied by firms, thus showing that the equilibrium office rent must be such that

$$R_o(x) = 2m(x). \tag{6.24}$$

As a result, at the free entry equilibrium for the construction sector, it must be that

$$\pi_c = R_o(x)m(x) - [m(x)]^2 - R(x) = 0$$

so that, using (6.24),

$$R^*(x) = [m(x)]^2 \tag{6.25}$$

which means that the land rent prevailing at a particular location increases at an increasing rate with the number of firms set up there.

Because business firms are identical, in equilibrium each firm earns the same profit π^*, which is unknown but such that

$$\pi^* = Q - T(x) - R_0^*(x)$$

holds for all x in $[-b, b]$. Using (6.24), we obtain

$$2m(x) = Q - T(x) - \pi^*.$$

Differentiating this expression and using the relation $\mathrm{d}^2T/\mathrm{d}x^2 = 2tm(x)$ leads to the following differential equation:

$$\frac{\mathrm{d}^2 m}{\mathrm{d}x^2} + tm(x) = 0$$

whose solution, that is the equilibrium firm density, is

$$m^*(x) = k \cos\left(t^{1/2}\,|x|\right)$$

where k is a positive constant of integration, which is determined below. In words, the equilibrium office firm density is therefore bell-shaped (as in Figure 6.1) with a maximum arising at $x = 0$, which is equal to k. Consequently, the presence of an information field is sufficient to explain the formation of a CBD despite the fact that the technology of the construction sector exhibits decreasing returns. Furthermore, the density of firms, or the building height, decreases with the distance from the center inside the CBD, thus showing that the concentration of firms is the highest at the center.

Using (6.25), the equilibrium land rent is

$$R^*(x) = k^2 \left[\cos\left(t^{1/2} |x|\right)\right]^2$$

which is described by a bell-shaped curve as is the office rent obtained from (6.24):

$$R_0^*(x) = 2k \cos\left(t^{1/2} |x|\right).$$

It remains to determine the extent of the CBD. At the fringe b of the business area, $R^*(b)$ must be equal to R_A, yielding:

$$\sqrt{R_{\mathrm{A}}} = k \cos\left(t^{1/2} b\right). \tag{6.26}$$

Furthermore, the business firm population constraint implies that

$$M = \int_{-b}^{b} m(x)\mathrm{d}x = 2k \int_{0}^{b} \cos\left(t^{1/2} x\right) \mathrm{d}x$$

which, after some manipulations, becomes

$$M = 2kt^{1/2} \sin\left(t^{1/2} b\right). \tag{6.27}$$

From (6.26) and (6.27), it then follows that

$$b^* = t^{-1/2} \arctan\left(\frac{M}{2}\sqrt{\frac{t}{R_{\mathrm{A}}}}\right)$$

whereas k can be obtained by replacing b^* in (6.26):

$$k = \frac{(R_{\mathrm{A}})^{1/2}}{\cos \arctan\left(\frac{M}{2}\sqrt{\frac{t}{R_{\mathrm{A}}}}\right)}.$$

Consequently, interaction among firms leads to the same kind of pattern within the CBD as interaction among consumers within the city. For exactly the same reason as the one discussed in the preceding section, the optimum density of firms is more concentrated than the equilibrium density.

6.3 THE CITY AS SPATIAL INTERDEPENDENCE BETWEEN FIRMS AND WORKERS

In the previous section, we have considered consumers' and firms' agglomeration separately. Here, we study how the interaction between both types of agents shapes the spatial structure of the entire city. Our discussion is based on a model in which the agglomeration force is generated, as in Section 6.2.2, through business externalities among firms, whereas social interaction among households is neglected for simplicity. Firms and households interact through perfectly competitive labor and land markets.

Specifically, the agglomeration force is due to the existence of communications among firms permitting the exchange of information. As long as the transmission of information requires direct communication between agents who typically incur specific distance-sensitive costs, the benefits of information are larger when firms locate closer to each other. Indeed, when a firm chooses to be close to another one, it is also close to its neighbors and, consequently, benefits from the information these ones own. Therefore, all other things being equal, each firm has an incentive to establish itself close to other firms. On the other hand, the clustering of many firms into a single area increases the average commuting distance for workers, which, in turn, gives rise to higher wages and land rent in the residential area around the cluster. Such high wages and land rents tend to discourage further agglomeration of firms within the same area and act as a dispersion force. Consequently, the equilibrium distributions of firms and households/workers are determined as the balance between these two opposite forces. What makes this approach especially original is that the wage and land rent paid by firms are endogenous and vary with the location choices made by the firms.

6.3.1 The Model

Consider a one-dimensional space $X = (-\infty, \infty)$. The amount of land at each location $x \in X$ is equal to 1. There is a continuum N of homogeneous households/workers who are to reside in the city as well as a continuum M of firms that operate in the city. Land is owned by absentee landlords, and firms by absentee shareholders. Firms produce the same good sold at a given price p and use the same technology. Specifically, each firm needs S_f units of land and some fixed amount of labor (L_f) to undertake its production activity. Furthermore, households use a fixed amount of land S_h. The total amount of land used in the city being fixed and equal to $MS_f + NS_h$, without loss of generality, we may choose the units of M and N for $S_f = S_h = 1$ to hold. Consequently, a large value of M (N) means that firms (workers) are numerous, firms (workers) use a large plot, or both. We also assume that the opportunity cost of land is equal to zero.

Land and labor markets are perfectly competitive at each and every location $x \in X$. The land rent prevailing at $x \in X$ is denoted by $R(x)$, and $W(x)$ stands for the wage at $x \in X$. Labor market clearing implies that the number of firms is

$$M = N/L_{\mathrm{f}}. \tag{6.28}$$

Consumers. As usual, the utility of a household is given by $U(z, s)$, where $s = 1$ represents the land consumption and z the consumption of a composite good. Furthermore, each household supplies one unit of labor, and the composite good is imported from outside the urban area at a constant price normalized to 1. Then, if a household chooses to reside at $x \in X$ and to work at $x_{\mathrm{w}} \in X$, its budget constraint is given by

$$z + R(x) + t|x - x_{\mathrm{w}}| = W(x_{\mathrm{w}})$$

where t is the unit commuting cost.[5] Because the lot size is fixed, the objective of a household is to choose a residential location and a job site that maximize the consumption of the composite good given by

$$z(x, x_{\mathrm{w}}) = W(x_{\mathrm{w}}) - R(x) - t|x - x_{\mathrm{w}}|.$$

It is convenient to define a mapping J from X to X associating a (potential) job site $J(x) = x_{\mathrm{w}}$ with a (potential) residential location x. This mapping describes the commuting pattern of workers and, for this reason, is called the *commuting function*. It follows that an individual residing at x must work at the location $J(x)$ that maximizes her net income:

$$W[J(x)] - t|x - J(x)| = \max_{y \in X} [W(y) - t|x - y|] \quad x \in X.$$

The associated *bid rent function* of a household at x is then defined as follows:

$$\Psi(x, u) = W[J(x)] - t|x - J(x)| - Z(u) \tag{6.29}$$

where, as usual, $Z(u)$ is the solution to the equation $U(z, 1) = u$. In this case, $\Psi(x, u)$ is the rent per unit of land that a household can bid at location x while working at $J(x)$ and enjoying the utility level u.

Firms. The output level Q of a firm depends on the amount of information this firm obtains from the other firms in the city. Firms are symmetric but heterogeneous in the type of information they own. As a result, each firm wants to engage actively in communications with all other firms. The intensity of communications is measured by the level of contact activity (e.g., the number of face-to-face contacts), and each firm chooses its optimal level

[5] Because land and firms are assumed to be owned by absentee landlords and shareholders, the income of each consumer equals her wage earned at the chosen job site.

of contact activity with others. When $\varphi(x, y)$ is the level of contact activity chosen by a firm at $x \in X$ with a firm at $y \in X$, $V[\varphi(x, y)]$ represents the total contribution of this contact level to the firm's revenue Q. This contribution, denoted by $V[\varphi(x, y)]$, is supposed to be the same across firms because of symmetry.

Communication from one firm to another is a pairwise activity that is time-consuming for both parties because of the need to organize, store, analyze, and communicate information. When a firm at x obtains information from a firm at y, the firm at x must bear a cost $c_1(x, y)$ per unit of contact, which is supposed to be a function of the location of the two firms. However, during this action, the firm at y also bears some cost c_2, which is typically independent of the firms' locations. For example, when a manager of a firm at x calls a manager of a firm at y, she imposes some cost on the manager contacted by consuming her time, and this cost does not depend on the interfirm distance. This means that each firm bears the additional cost generated by the communication activity taken by other firms.

Let $m(y)$ be the density of firms at location $y \in X$ and $\varphi(x, y)$ the level of contact activity chosen by a firm at $x \in X$ with each firm at y. Then, the revenue of a firm at x is given by

$$Q(x) = \int_X \{V[\varphi(x, y)]\} m(y) \mathrm{d}y$$

and thus its profit is

$$\begin{aligned}\pi(x) &= Q(x) - \int_X [c_1(x, y)\varphi(x, y) + c_2\varphi(y, x)] m(y) \mathrm{d}y \\ &\quad - R(x) - W(x)L_f \\ &= \int_X \{V[\varphi(x, y)] - c_1(x, y)\varphi(x, y) - c_2\varphi(y, x)\} m(y) \mathrm{d}y \\ &\quad - R(x) - W(x)L_f. \qquad (6.30)\end{aligned}$$

Each firm chooses its location x and its contact field $\varphi(x, y)$ so as to maximize its profit, taking the firm spatial distribution and contact field as given.[6]

The optimal contact level of a firm at x with any firm at y can be determined, independently of the whole distribution of firms, by choosing $\varphi(x, y)$ so as to maximize $V[\varphi(x, y)] - c_1(x, y)\varphi(x, y)$ in (6.30). If $c_1(x, y) = c_1(y, x)$, firms are symmetric in the process of communication so that the optimal level of contact between each pair of firms is the same for both of them: $\varphi^*(x, y) = \varphi^*(y, x)$.

[6] This means that no firm refuses a contact initiated by any other firm. This assumption seems natural because of the symmetry of the information environment.

We define the *local accessibility* between each location pair (x, y) by

$$a(x, y) \equiv V[\varphi^*(x, y)] - [c_1(x, y) + c_2]\varphi^*(x, y). \tag{6.31}$$

Then the profit function (6.30) can be rewritten as follows:

$$\pi(x) = A(x) - R(x) - W(x)L_f \tag{6.32}$$

where

$$A(x) \equiv \int_X a(x, y)m(y)dy \tag{6.33}$$

stands for the *aggregate accessibility* of each location $x \in X$. As a consequence, the global accessibility of a specific place depends on the location decisions made by all firms. As expected, the global accessibility of x increases when the density of firms is more concentrated around this point.

Note that $a(x, y)$ could alternatively be interpreted as the information spillover experienced by a firm at x from a firm set up at y. In this case, $A(x)$ would represent the information field having the nature of a spatial externality. The amount of information received by a firm is in itself exogenous; however, it depends on its location relative to the others.[7]

Observe that communications externalities may find their origin in previous innovations occurring in the same production sector or in innovations made in other sectors. Thus, they are consistent with intra-sectoral and inter-sectoral externalities. The literature on informational spillovers stresses the importance of interfirm mobility when knowledge and information is embodied in certain types of workers. The interfirm mobility being often confined to a small labor pool, the transmission of knowledge through interfirm mobility seems to be generated by spatial externalities. Whatever the reason for the transmission of knowledge or information, distance is good proxy to capture, at least in the first order, the main forces at work.

In association with (6.32), the *bid rent function* of a firm at x is defined as follows:

$$\Phi(x, \pi) = A(x) - W(x)L_f - \pi \tag{6.34}$$

which represents the highest price a firm is willing to pay for a unit piece of land at $x \in X$ while earning a profit equal to π.

The equilibrium configuration of the city is then determined through the interplay of the firms' and households' bid rent functions. More precisely, a *spatial equilibrium* is reached when all the firms achieve the same equilibrium profit π^*, all the households the same utility level given by u^*, and rents and wages clear the land and labor markets. The unknowns are the firm distribution

[7] In Chapter 11, we allow firms to benefit from variable spillovers through research and development.

$m(x)$, the household distribution $n(x)$, the land rent function $R(x)$, the wage function $W(x)$, the commuting function $J(x)$, and the equilibrium profit level π^* and utility level u^*.

6.3.2 The Market Outcome

In our setting, because (i) the mass N of households is fixed, (ii) each firm hires a fixed number of workers, and (iii) there is no unemployment, either the equilibrium profit π^*, or the equilibrium utility level u^*, is indeterminate. Here, we assume that profits are zero so that $\pi^* = 0$ is an additional equilibrium condition. To put it differently, potential entrepreneurs compete for land and labor until the profits earned are zero.

Let the opportunity costs of land be 0. Then, from the bid rent functions (6.29) and (6.34), the equilibrium conditions can be described as follows:

(i) land market equilibrium: at each $x \in X$,

$$R(x) = \max\left\{\Psi(x, u^*), \Phi(x, 0), 0\right\} \tag{6.35}$$

$$\Psi(x, u^*) = R(x) \qquad \text{if } n(x) > 0 \tag{6.36}$$

$$\Phi(x, 0) = R(x) \qquad \text{if } m(x) > 0 \tag{6.37}$$

$$n(x) + m(x) = 1 \qquad \text{if } R(x) > 0 \tag{6.38}$$

(ii) commuting equilibrium pattern: at each $x \in X$,

$$W[J(x)] - t\,|J(x) - x| = \max_{y \in X}\left[W(y) - t\,|y - x|\right] \tag{6.39}$$

(iii) labor market equilibrium: at each $x \in X$,

$$\int_I n(x)\mathrm{d}x = \int_{J(I)} L_f m(x)\mathrm{d}x \quad \text{for every interval } I \text{ of } X \tag{6.40}$$

(iv) firms' and households' population constraints:

$$\int_X m(x)\mathrm{d}x = M \tag{6.41}$$

$$\int_X n(x)\mathrm{d}x = N. \tag{6.42}$$

Conditions (6.35) through (6.38) together mean that each location is occupied by agents with the highest bid rent. Condition (6.39) says that, for each potential residential location x, the commuting destination $J(x)$ maximizes the net wage. Condition (6.40) ensures the equality of labor supply and demand under the commuting function J. The meaning of the population conditions is obvious.

It is worth noting one general property of any spatial equilibrium. Given a commuting function J, if there exist $x \in X$ and $x' \in X$ such that

$$(J(x) - x)(J(x') - x') < 0 \qquad (x - x')(J(x) - J(x')) < 0 \tag{6.43}$$

we say that *cross-commuting* occurs. The first inequality means that a resident at x and a resident at x' commute in the opposite directions, whereas the second one implies that their commuting paths have an overlapping section. Because (6.39) requires that each resident chooses a job site that maximizes her net income, the following result is intuitively obvious: in any spatial equilibrium configuration, cross-commuting does not occur. Indeed, if two groups of workers cross-commute, any household belonging to any of these groups would strictly increase its net income by choosing a job site in the area in which the other group works.

It turns out that the properties of the equilibrium urban configuration crucially depend on the shape of the local accessibility function $a(x, y)$. By specifying the analytical form of the benefit function $V(\varphi)$ and of the cost function $c_1(x, y)$, we can obtain a different expression for $a(x, y)$. In what follows, we focus on two special but meaningful cases:

$$a(x, y) = \beta - \tau|x - y| \tag{6.44}$$

and

$$a(x, y) = \beta \exp(-\tau|x - y|) \tag{6.45}$$

where τ and β are two positive constants, τ measuring the intensity of the distance-decay effect. The former equation corresponds to a *linear accessibility*, whereas the latter is a *spatially discounted accessibility*. Both expressions have been used extensively in models of spatial interaction.

For example, expression (6.45) can be justified on the following grounds. Let us assume that the benefit function is given by the *entropy-type function*

$$V(\varphi) == \begin{cases} -\varphi \log \varphi & \text{for } \varphi < 1/e \\ 1/e & \text{for } \varphi \geq 1/e \end{cases}$$

representing the firms' propensity to collect heterogeneous information in the context of (6.30). Then, for each location pair (x, y), by choosing $\varphi(x, y)$ so as to maximize $\{V[\varphi(x, y)] - c_1(x, y)\varphi(x, y)\}$, we obtain the optimal level of contact

$$\varphi^*(x, y) = \exp[-1 - c_1(x, y)].$$

Substituting this expression into (6.31) yields

$$a(x, y) = (1 - c_2)\exp[-1 - c_1(x, y)]$$

or, setting $\beta \equiv (1 - c_2)/e$, which is assumed to be positive, yields

$$a(x, y) = \beta \exp[-c_1(x, y)].$$

If $c_1(x, y) = \tau|x - y|$, we obtain (6.45).[8]

The case of linear accessibility has been studied independently by Ogawa and Fujita (1980) and Imai (1982), whereas Fujita and Ogawa (1982) have investigated the implications of the spatially discounted accessibility. In the following two sections, we examine each case in turn.

6.4 THE MONOCENTRIC CITY

When the local accessibility is linear, the aggregate accessibility of each location $x \in X$ is given by:

$$A(x) = \int_X [\beta - \tau\,|x - y|]\, m(y)\mathrm{d}y. \tag{6.46}$$

We may restrict ourselves to symmetric densities defined over an interval centered at the origin. Thus, we have

$$\frac{\mathrm{d}A(x)}{\mathrm{d}x} = -\tau \left\{ \int_{-\infty}^{x} m(y)\mathrm{d}y - \int_{x}^{\infty} m(y)\mathrm{d}y \right\} \gtreqqless 0 \quad \text{if } x \lesseqgtr 0. \tag{6.47}$$

Furthermore, the support of the density m, denoted $m_+ \equiv \{x \mid m(x) > 0\}$, is the *business area*. Therefore, we have

$$\frac{\mathrm{d}^2 A(x)}{\mathrm{d}x^2} = -2\tau m(x) \begin{cases} < 0 & x \in m_+ \\ = 0 & x \notin m_+ \end{cases} \tag{6.48}$$

implying that $A(x)$ is strictly concave over the business area and linear elsewhere. That $A(x)$ is concave with a maximum at $x = 0$ creates a strong agglomeration force, thus suggesting that firms do not want to be too far apart from one another.

In what follows, we determine each potential equilibrium configuration in turn and then examine under which conditions they are equilibria using the basic principles of land competition described in Chapter 3. As is seen, the bid rent functions are continuous with respect to x so that all the intervals presented may be considered as closed.

We first represent in Figure 6.2 the monocentric city case. The upper diagram depicts the corresponding land use pattern together with the associated wage curve $W(x)$. There is a CBD, defined by the interval $[-b_1, b_1]$, surrounded by two residential sections of equal size, $[-b_2, -b_1]$ and $[b_1, b_2]$. Because there

[8] Note that we obtain (6.44) when $c_1(x, y) = [\log(1 - \tau\,|x - y|)]^{-1}$, i.e., an increasing and convex function of distance.

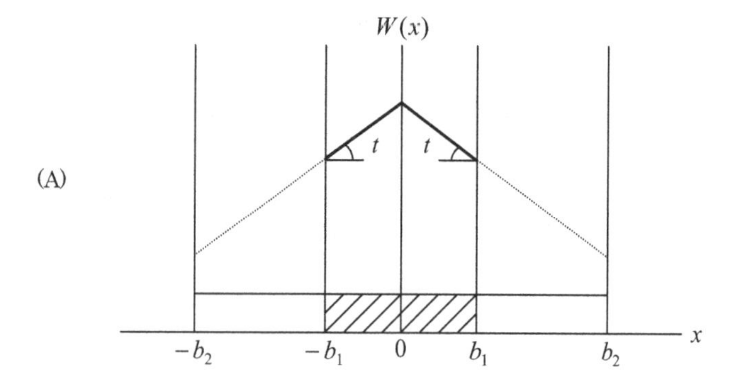

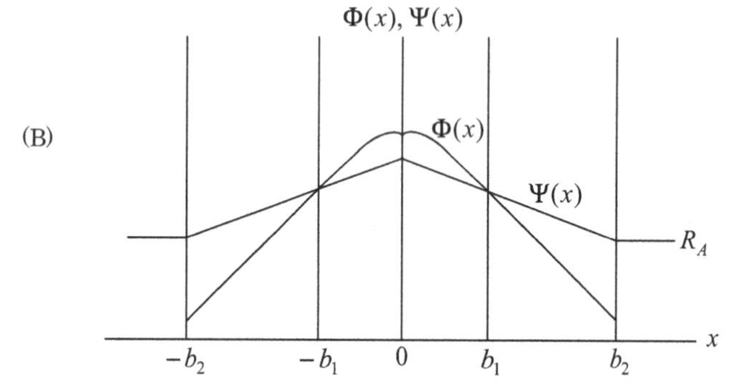

Figure 6.2. The monocentric configuration.

is no cross-commuting, the left (right) side half of the business area contains the job sites associated with the locations belonging to the left (right) side residential section. For all workers to have the same net wage, the wage curve must be linear on each side of the city center and must have a slope equal to the unit commuting cost t. This is an equilibrium if and only if the bid rent curves associated with the monocentric pattern are as those depicted in the lower diagram of Figure 6.2, that is, the households' bid rent curve dominates the firms' bid rent curve in the business area, whereas the converse holds in each section of the residential area.

In the monocentric configuration, the business area is completely separated from the residential area so that each worker must commute to her job site. At the other extreme, the completely integrated configuration is depicted in Figure 6.3, where both firms and households are uniformly distributed inside the urban area $[-b_2, b_2]$. In this case, the job site is identical to the residential location for all workers so that there is no commuting. For this to be a spatial equilibrium, the corresponding households' and firms' bid rents must be equal at each location.

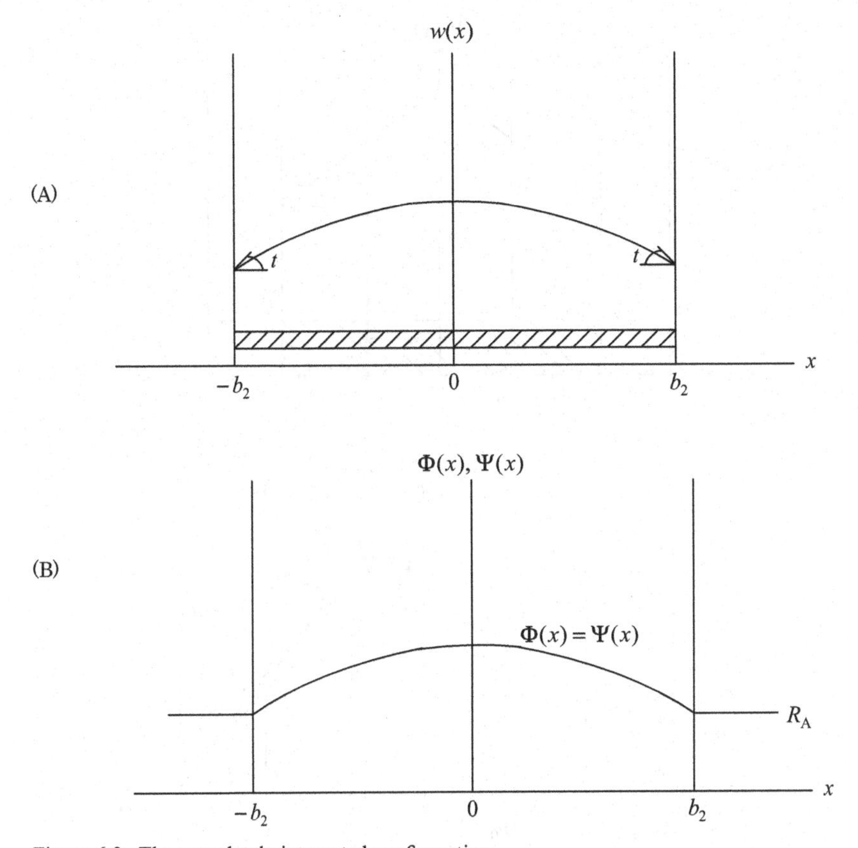

Figure 6.3. The completely integrated configuration.

The third case corresponds to the incompletely integrated configuration depicted in Figure 6.4 and is a mixture of the first two cases. As shown in the upper diagram, firms and households are uniformly mixed within the *integrated district*, $[-b_0, b_0]$, where no commuting arises. This area is surrounded by two business sections, $[-b_1, -b_0]$ and $[b_0, b_1]$, each of which is adjacent to a residential section, $[-b_2, -b_1]$ and $[b_1, b_2]$. The bid rent curves supporting such a configuration must resemble those given in the lower diagram of Figure 6.4.

The reader has probably noticed that the first two configurations are special cases of the third one. Indeed, if we set $b_0 = 0$ in Figure 6.4, we obtain the monocentric pattern; similarly, if we set $b_0 = b_2$ we get the completely integrated configuration. In other words, the incompletely integrated configuration corresponds to the generic pattern under linear accessibility. Consequently, in what follows, we first determine the set of parameters for the incompletely integrated configuration to be an equilibrium. The other two configurations

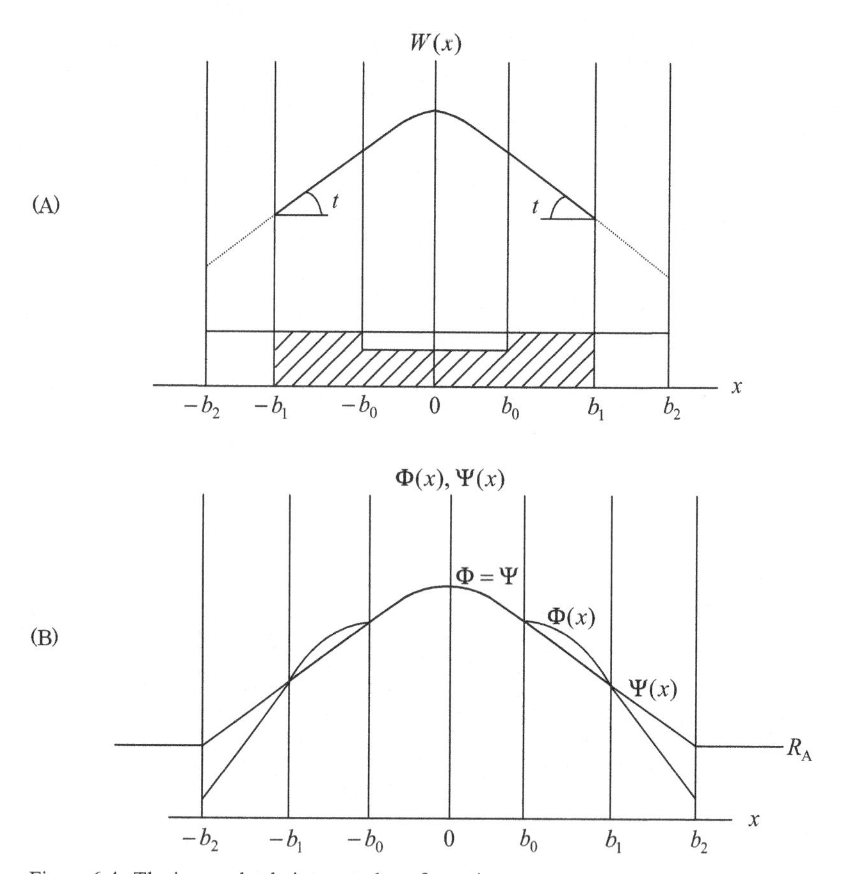

Figure 6.4. The incompletely integrated configuration.

may then be derived as special cases. In so doing, we see that the whole domain of admissible values for the parameters is fully covered.

Consider the configuration represented in Figure 6.4. Because the configuration is symmetric about $x = 0$, we may restrict ourselves to the nonnegative values of x. In the integrated area, $[0, b_0]$, all individuals work at their residential place, thus implying that $J(x) = x$ for all $x \in [0, b_0]$. The land constraint condition (6.38) and the labor market clearing condition (6.40) then imply:

$$m(x) = 1/(1 + L_f) \quad \text{and} \quad n(x) = L_f/(1 + L_f) \quad x \in [0, b_0]. \tag{6.49}$$

In each business section, it must be that:

$$m(x) = 1 \quad \text{and} \quad n(x) = 0 \quad x \in [b_0, b_1]. \tag{6.50}$$

Likewise, in each residential section, we must have:

$$n(x) = 1 \quad \text{and} \quad m(x) = 0 \qquad x \in [b_1, b_2]. \tag{6.51}$$

In addition, the firm population constraint (6.41) implies that

$$\frac{M}{2} = \int_0^{b_0} m(x)\mathrm{d}x + \int_{b_0}^{b_1} m(x)\mathrm{d}x = \frac{b_0}{1+L_\mathrm{f}} + b_1 - b_0$$

which yields the equilibrium boundary location as a function of b_0:

$$b_1^*(b_0) \equiv b_1^* = \frac{L_\mathrm{f}}{1+L_\mathrm{f}} b_0 + \frac{M}{2}. \tag{6.52}$$

Because there is no vacant land between $-b_2^*$ and b_2^*, it is readily verified that $M + N = 2b_2^*$ implies that the city fringe is given by

$$b_2^* = N(1+L_\mathrm{f})/2L_\mathrm{f} \tag{6.53}$$

which increases with the population size.

Since no cross-commuting occurs in the integrated district and since all the individuals residing in the section $\left[b_1^*, b_2^*\right]$ work in the business section $[b_0, b_1^*]$, we can assume without loss of generality that the commuting function $J(x)$ is as follows:

$$J(x) = \begin{cases} x & x \in [0, b_0] \\ \frac{b_1^*(x-b_1^*)+b_0(b_2^*-x)}{b_2^*-b_1^*} & x \in [b_0, b_2^*] \end{cases}. \tag{6.54}$$

This means that an individual living in the integrated district $[0, b_0]$ is assigned to her residential location, whereas one living in the residential section $[b_1^*, b_2^*]$ is assigned to a location belonging to the business section $[b_0, b_1^*]$ with x and $J(x)$ varying in the same direction. To support this commuting pattern, condition (6.39) requires:[9]

$$W^*(x) = W^*(b_0) - t\,(x - b_0) \qquad x \in [b_0, b_2^*]. \tag{6.55}$$

Next, substituting (6.49)–(6.51) into (6.46), we obtain the following description of the aggregate accessibility:

$$\begin{aligned} A^*(x) &= \beta M - \left\{\tau(b_1^2 - b_0^2) + \frac{\tau}{1+L_\mathrm{f}}(b_0^2 + x^2)\right\} & x \in [0, b_0] \quad (6.56)\\ &= \beta M - \left\{\tau(b_1^2 - 2b_0x + x^2) + \frac{2\tau}{1+L_\mathrm{f}} b_0 x\right\} & x \in [b_0, b_1^*] \\ &= \beta M - \left\{2\tau(b_1 - b_0x) + \frac{2\tau}{1+L_\mathrm{f}} b_0 x\right\} & x \in [b_1^*, b_2^*]. \end{aligned}$$

[9] Observe that the equilibrium wage rate is not unique in the interval $[b_1^*, b_2^*]$ because no firm is set up there. However, the expression (6.55) is sufficient to show that no firm wants to locate in this interval.

Setting $\pi^* = 0$ in (6.34), the equilibrium bid rent function of a firm is:

$$\Phi^*(x) = A^*(x) - W^*(x)L_f. \tag{6.57}$$

Similarly, setting $u = u^*$ in (6.29) and using the first part of (6.54) as well as (6.55), the equilibrium bid rent function of a household is:

$$\begin{aligned}\Psi^*(x) &= W^*(x) - Z(u^*) \qquad x \in [0, b_0] \\ &= W^*(b_0) - t(x - b_0) - Z(u^*) \qquad x \in [b_0, b_2^*].\end{aligned} \tag{6.58}$$

As shown by the lower diagram of Figure 6.4, the incompletely integrated configuration is a spatial equilibrium if and only if (i) the commuting condition (6.39) holds and (ii) the equilibrium bid rent functions satisfy the following conditions:[10]

$$\Phi^*(x) = \Psi^*(x) \qquad x \in [0, b_0] \tag{6.59}$$

$$\Phi^*(x) \geq \Psi^*(x) \qquad x \in [b_0, b_1^*] \tag{6.60}$$

$$\Phi^*(x) \leq \Psi^*(x) \qquad x \in [b_1^*, b_2^*] \tag{6.61}$$

$$\Psi^*(b_2^*) = 0 \tag{6.62}$$

with the commuting function given by (6.54).

The remainder of the argument involves five more steps.

(i) Using (6.53), we obtain from the second part of (6.58) and from (6.62):

$$W^*(b_0) = t\left[(1 + L_f)M - 2b_0\right]/2 + Z(u^*). \tag{6.63}$$

(ii) Using (6.59) together with (6.57) and (6.58) yields the equilibrium wage inside the integrated area:

$$W^*(x) = \frac{A^*(x) + Z(u^*)}{1 + L_f} \qquad x \in [0, b_0]. \tag{6.64}$$

We evaluate (6.64) by substituting $A^*(x)$ as defined by the first equality in (6.56) into (6.64) and using (6.52). The value of $W^*(x)$ at b_0 may then be equalized to (6.63) to determine u^* uniquely as a function of b_0, denoted $u^*(b_0)$. It follows from (6.55), (6.63), and (6.64) that the equilibrium wage $W^*(x)$ at each location $x \geq 0$ may be uniquely determined as a function of b_0.

(iii) To determine b_0, we observe that (6.59) implies:

$$\Phi^*(b_0) = \Psi^*(b_0) \tag{6.65}$$

whereas (6.60) and (6.61) lead to:

$$\Phi^*(b_1^*) = \Psi^*(b_1^*). \tag{6.66}$$

[10] As usual, one must also check that $\max\{\Phi^*(x), \Psi^*(x)\} \geq 0$ for $x \in [0, b_2^*]$ whereas $\max\{\Phi^*(x), \Psi^*(x)\} < 0$ for $x > b_2^*$.

These two conditions then yield:

$$\tau(b_1^* - b_0) + \frac{2\tau b_0}{1 + L_f} = (1 + L_f)t.$$

Substituting b_1^* given by (6.52) into this expression allows for the determination of the equilibrium value of b_0, which is given by:

$$b_0^* = \frac{t(1 + L_f)^2}{\tau} - \frac{N(1 + L_f)}{2L_f}. \tag{6.67}$$

This means that b_0^* is a linear and increasing function of t and N. Since b_0^* must belong to the interval $[0, b_2^*]$ where b_2^* is given by (6.53), the following inequalities must hold:

$$\frac{M}{2(1 + L_f)} \leq \frac{t}{\tau} \leq \frac{M}{1 + L_f}. \tag{6.68}$$

(iv) It is easy to check that $\Psi^*(x)$ is linear for $x \in [b_0^*, b_2^*]$, that $\Phi^*(x)$ is strictly concave for $x \in [b_0^*, b_1^*]$ and linear for $x \in [b_1^*, b_2^*]$ whereas the left-hand side and right-hand side derivatives of $\Phi^*(x)$ are equal at b_1^*. These properties together with (6.65) and (6.66) imply immediately that both (6.60) and (6.61) hold.

(v) It remains to check that the commuting function defined by (6.54) is sustainable. Because $W^*(x)$ is strictly concave on $[0, b_1^*]$ and linear on $[b_1^*, b_2^*]$ with slope $-t$, the commuting pattern is part of the equilibrium if and only if the absolute value of the left-hand side derivative of $W^*(x)$ at b_0^* does not exceed t. Using the first equality of (6.56) and (6.64), this means:

$$t \geq \frac{2\tau b_0^*}{(1 + L_f)^2} \tag{6.69}$$

or, using (6.67),

$$t \geq 2t - \frac{\tau N}{(1 + L_f)L_f}$$

which amounts to

$$\frac{t}{\tau} \leq \frac{N}{(1 + L_f)L_f}.$$

This condition is satisfied whenever (6.68) holds.

Consequently, using (6.28), we have shown the following result:

Proposition 6.2. *The incompletely integrated configuration is a spatial equilibrium if and only if*

$$\frac{N}{2(1 + L_f)L_f} \leq \frac{t}{\tau} \leq \frac{N}{(1 + L_f)L_f}.$$

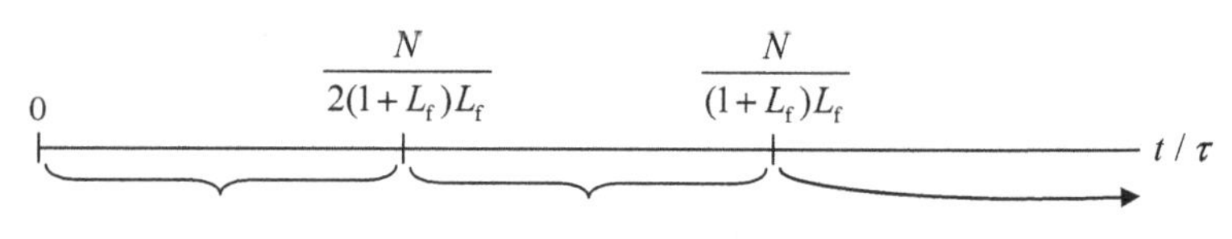

Figure 6.5. The parameter ranges for the three equilibrium configurations under linear accessibility.

As previously noted, the incompletely integrated configuration degenerates into the monocentric configuration represented in Figure 6.2 once $b_0^* = 0$. By setting $b_0 = 0$ in all the analyses above and by replacing (6.65) by

$$\Phi^*(b_0) \geq \Psi^*(b_0)$$

we obtain:[11]

Proposition 6.3. *The monocentric configuration is a spatial equilibrium if and only if*

$$\frac{t}{\tau} \leq \frac{N}{2\left(1+L_{\mathrm{f}}\right)L_{\mathrm{f}}}.$$

In the same manner, by setting $b_0 = b_2$ in the preceding developments and by replacing b_0^* in (6.69) by b_2^* given in (6.53), we get:[12]

Proposition 6.4. *The completely integrated configuration is a spatial equilibrium if and only if*

$$\frac{t}{\tau} \geq \frac{N}{\left(1+L_{\mathrm{f}}\right)L_{\mathrm{f}}}.$$

The preceding results are summarized in Figure 6.5 in which the whole domain of values for t/τ is covered. As this ratio steadily decreases, the economic landscape moves from a completely-integrated configuration to a monocentric one through an incompletely integrated configuration. In other words, when commuting is very costly, the economic landscape displays a pattern in which each location is essentially self-sufficient: workers live close to their jobs and firms have a low efficiency level because agglomeration economies are weak. This explains why land was less specialized in preindustrial cities where most people got around on foot than in modern cities, where workers

[11] The same type of externality has been further explored by Kanemoto (1990), who considered the case in which firms are engaged in transactions with others. Combining the exchange of intermediate inputs between firms with indivisibilities in their production creates externalities similar to those considered by Fijita, Imai, and Ogawa. If τ is the unit transportation cost of the intermediate goods, Kanemoto then showed that the monocentric configuration is an equilibrium when the ratio t/τ is small, which is a condition similar to Proposition 6.3.

[12] See Proposition 3.2 for a similar result.

have access to rapid transport means. Some form of land specialization emerges for intermediate values of t/τ under the form of specialized districts. Last, the modern monocentric configuration is an equilibrium when t, the unit commuting cost, is relatively small in comparison with τ, the distance-decay parameter in communication.[13]

As commuting costs fall while the intensity of communication between firms rises (two fairly general trends observed since the Industrial Revolution), one moves from backyard capitalism to a monocentric city with complete specialization of land. This means that the monocentric configuration is likely to emerge when commuting costs are low, when the spatial distance-decay effect is strong, or both. If the second result is fairly intuitive, the first is probably less apparent but appears on several occasions in subsequent chapters: low transportation costs foster agglomeration. On the other hand, high transportation costs lead to the completely mixed configuration, that is, a pattern with no land specialization and no commuting. All these results confirm and extend those we have found in Section 3.2.2. They also show that rural-urban migrations have not only fueled the growth of cities. They have triggered the process of land specialization and fostered the emergence of large monocentric cities by increasing the urban population.

Another interesting implication of the previous propositions is that the monocentric configuration is more likely to arise when land intensity in production is low. This is because firms may benefit from a better accessibility to each other while occupying a smaller district where the land rent is on average lower. In the same spirit, when labor intensity in production is low, more firms are in business. In this event, firms' benefits resulting from being agglomerated in the CBD are larger, and thus a monocentric city is again more likely to emerge. As a result, one may expect a CBD to involve a large number of small firms rather than a small number of large firms. In other words, large manufacturing plants are less likely to form a CBD than service firms using a small amount of floor space and a small number of workers. This pattern holds when firms' business need not be conducted under the same roof because intrafirm communication costs are low (see Section 6.6). Likewise, the development of communication infrastructure that lower the value of τ will favor the decentralization of jobs (e.g., e-work) within the city.

We are also equipped to briefly discuss the optimal configuration under linear accessibility. As in the models presented in Section 6.2, the competitive outcome is inefficient because a firm, when choosing a location, considers only its own communication costs and disregards the change in the same cost incurred

[13] Showing the uniqueness of these configurations involves fairly elaborate arguments (Ogawa and Fujita 1980). In appendix C, we restrict ourselves to the case of a duocentric configuration and will give an intuitive argument showing why it cannot be an equilibrium under linear accessibility.

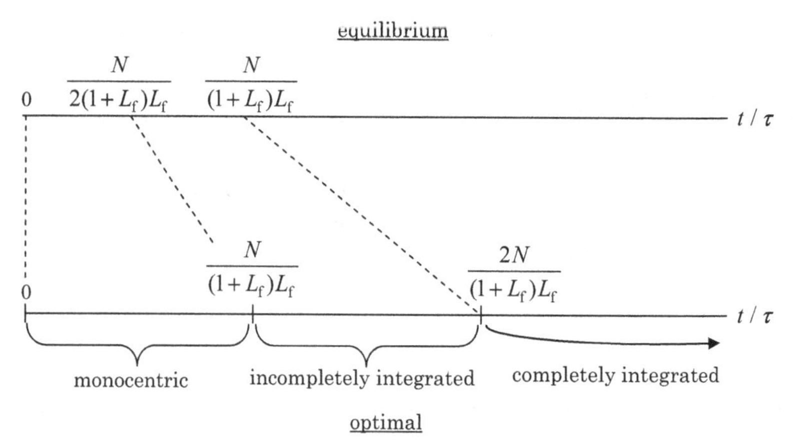

Figure 6.6. Parameter ranges of equilibrium and optimal configurations.

by the other firms.[14] For the optimal configuration to emerge as an equilibrium, each firm should internalize the communication costs of each other firm, that is, τ should be replaced by 2τ in all the formal developments previously presented. Thus, Figure 6.5 can be replaced by Figure 6.6, which specifies the parameter ranges corresponding to the different optimal configurations.

As a consequence, the domain of t/τ for which the monocentric configuration is socially optimal is twice as large as the domain for which it is an equilibrium. Again, as in the preceding section, firms tend to be less agglomerated in equilibrium than they should be at the optimum. Therefore, contrary to general belief (see Chapter 1), business districts are probably not too concentrated. As in Section 6.2, this market failure arises because firms do not internalize the whole social benefits they generate when they are more densely packed.

We argued in Chapter 4 that a larger pool of workers and firms boosts the exchange of information and the circulation of ideas, which in turn fosters the agglomeration of activities (see Section 4.2.3). The previous results provide a neat illustration of this idea. Indeed, when the labor force increases, so does the number of firms. Consequently, more information and knowledge becomes available in the urban economy, which leads firms to seek proximity, whence to get more concentrated. This can be understood as follows. For given b_0 and b_1, a larger number of firms fuels a larger number of contacts and, therefore, raises each urban location's accessibility, especially the central ones (see [6.56]). Therefore, profits increase, which in turn permits firms to pay a higher rent and to secure the whole amount of land in the central district where accessibility is

[14] For simplicity, we neglect the inefficiency arising from the cost c imposed by a firm on another when getting information from it.

the highest. To put it differently, a monocentric configuration is more likely to emerge when there is more information to share through a larger population.

As a result, learning from others fosters the emergence of a business district where the level of information and knowledge reaches its apex. This in turn increases the productivity of firms, which therefore are able to pay higher wages. Furthermore, as the population grows, the district expands through a larger number of firms, and thus the amount of information available to firms rises. All of this shows the existence of *a scale effect in the production of localized information and knowledge*. Note that the critical assumption here is that firms are heterogeneous in the information they own. Should firms belong to the same industry or not is immaterial for this result to hold. Informational heterogeneity may equally arise within and between industries, which could explain why empirical studies report the existence of both intra- and inter-industry urban spillovers.

Those three propositions may be used to explain the formation of local labor markets. In the case of a monocentric city, a single labor market is established in the CBD. When the equilibrium configuration is completely integrated, labor is traded in each location within the city. The pattern of labor markets is more involved in the case of an incompletely integrated configuration: labor is locally traded in the integrated district, which is surrounded by two labor pools attracting workers from the outskirts.

A word, in closing. We saw in Chapter 1 that Cantillon (1755) proposed one of one the first economic explanations for the existence of a city: the concentration of land ownership allows landowners to gather in order to "enjoy agreeable society." In such a context, the city center is the palatial area occupied by the landlords who interact as firms do in the foregoing; craftsmen form an integrated belt where they live and produce goods that are sold to the landlords.

6.5 THE POLYCENTRIC CITY

The set of market outcomes under spatially discounted accessibility is much richer, but also more complex, than under linear accessibility. Indeed, differentiating $A(x)$ twice, in which $a(x, y)$ is given by (6.45), leads to

$$\frac{\mathrm{d}^2 A(x)}{\mathrm{d}x^2} = -\beta\tau[2m(x) - \tau A(x)].$$

Given that $A(x) < 2/\tau$ at any x (see appendix D), it then follows that $A(x)$ is strictly convex on any residential section, because $m(x) = 0$, and strictly concave on any business section given that $m(x) = 1$. This implies that $A(x)$ may display several peaks and, in turn, opens the door to the possible emergence of several employment centers. Furthermore, the impact of the parameter τ on the agglomeration force is not monotone. Indeed, it is obvious that $A(x)$ is flat and equal to M when $\tau = 0$, and $A(x)$ is again flat but equal to 0 when $\tau \to \infty$.

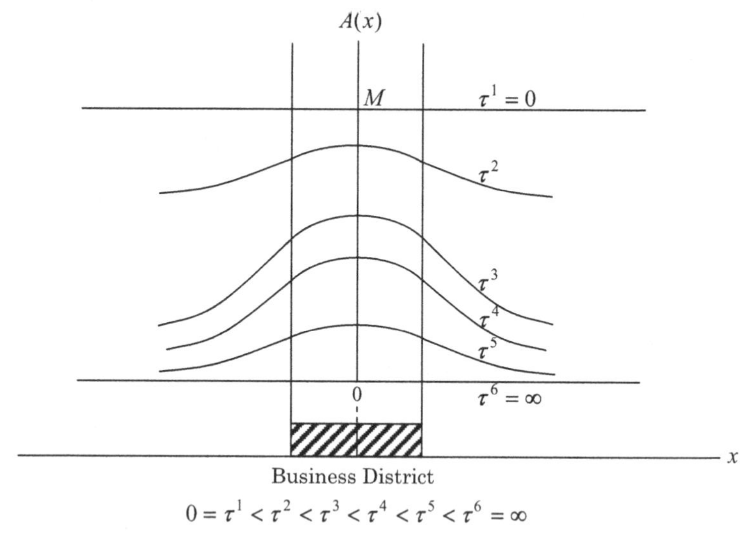

Figure 6.7. The impact of τ on the accessibility function $A(x)$.

The function $A(x)$ is depicted in Figure 6.7 for different values of τ in the case of a single business district. For example, differences in accessibility at the center and at the fringe of the business district are greatest for intermediate values of τ. The profit function (6.32) shows that such differences are critical in the choice of a location by a firm. Accordingly, we may expect to observe new results for the intermediate values of τ. However, the counterpart of the richness of the results is a much higher level of analytical complexity. As a result, we are content to appeal to numerical analysis when necessary.

When τ is very small, it should be obvious that the spatially discounted accessibility can be well approximated by the linear one, and thus the three possible configurations described in the preceding section still prevail in such cases.[15] As we just pointed out, the more involved situations occur when τ takes intermediate values. In such cases, the following may occur: (i) there exist configurations exhibiting several centers; (ii) there is multiplicity of equilibria; and (iii) the transition from an equilibrium to another may be catastrophic.

Consider first the emergence of a polycentric city. In addition to the three configurations provided in Figures 6.2 to 6.4, we describe in Figures 6.8 to 6.10 the most typical examples of what may be observed. In Figure 6.8, a duocentric city with two business districts of equal sizes is shown. This pattern may also be interpreted as two adjoining cities creating external economies for each other and, therefore, enjoying agglomeration economies within a system of cities.

[15] Observe that the same holds when the city size is small enough for the linear approximation to be acceptable.

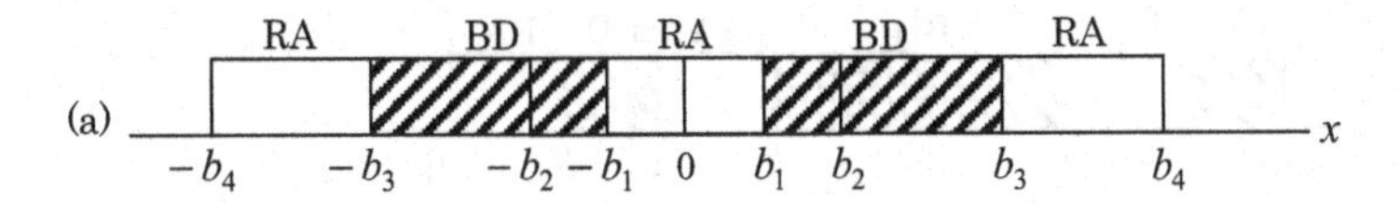

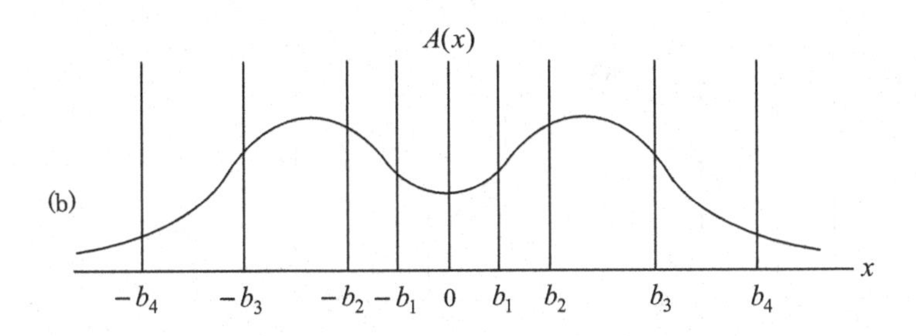

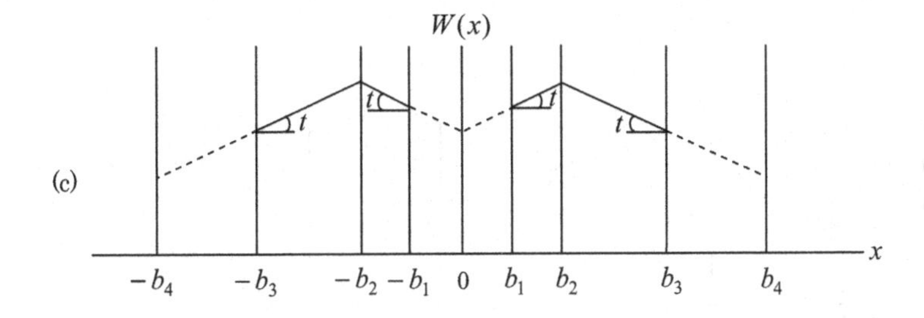

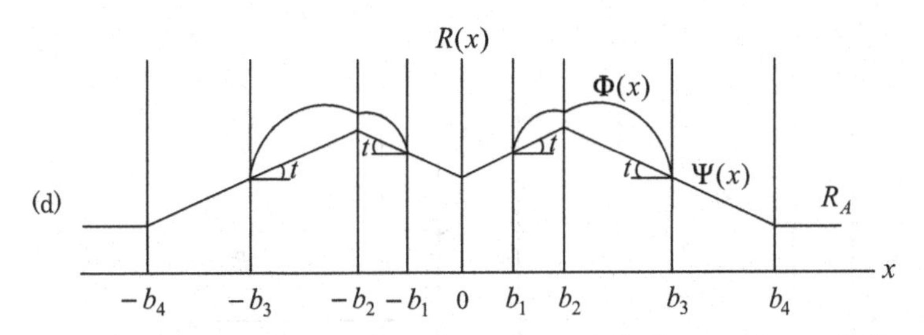

Figure 6.8. The duocentric configuration under spatially discounted accessibility.

In Figure 6.9, the equilibrium city has one primary center and two secondary centers of identical size. The arrows indicate the direction of the workers' commuting flows. Observe that some workers cross a secondary center because they work in the primary center. This is because firms located in a secondary center cannot be too far from those in the primary center to enjoy the external effects generated by this center. In terms of labor markets, this means that the primary center attracts workers from all the residential areas whereas each secondary center pulls people from its periphery only.

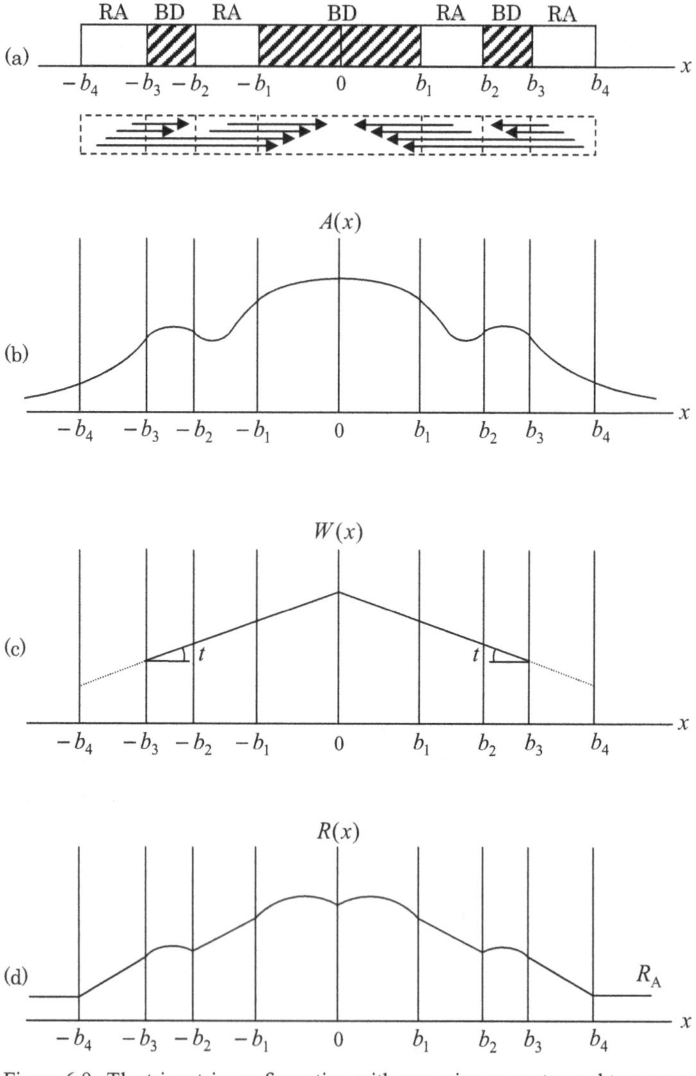

Figure 6.9. The tricentric configuration with one primary center and two secondary centers.

Finally, in Figure 6.10, there are three approximately identical centers surrounded by two residential sections each, which is a pattern akin to three connected small cities. The two internal residential sections are occupied by people who work in the middle business section or in one of the two peripheral business sections. Each center attracts workers from its two neighboring residential sections only.

(a)
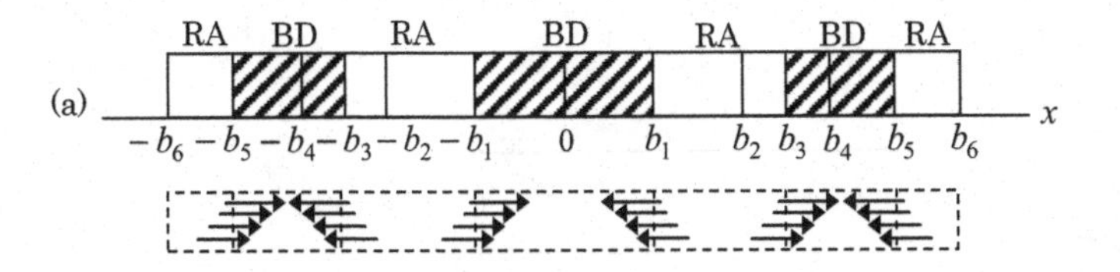

(b)
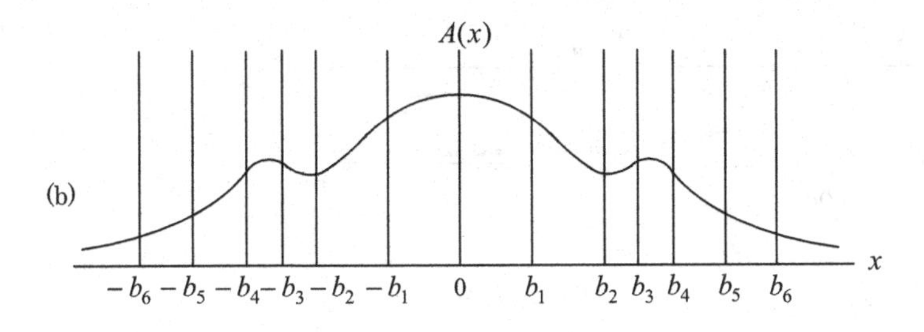

(c)
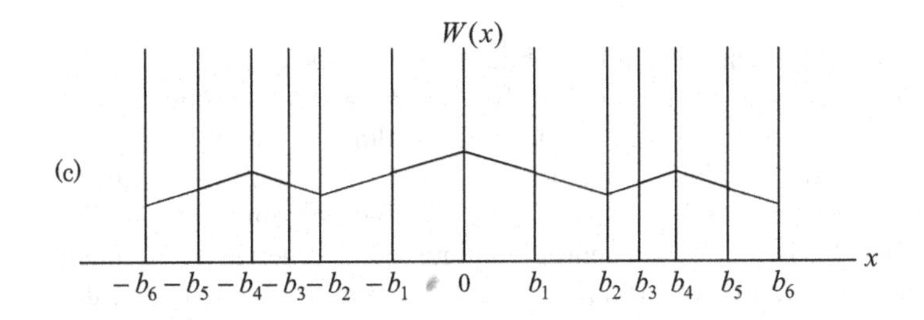

(d)
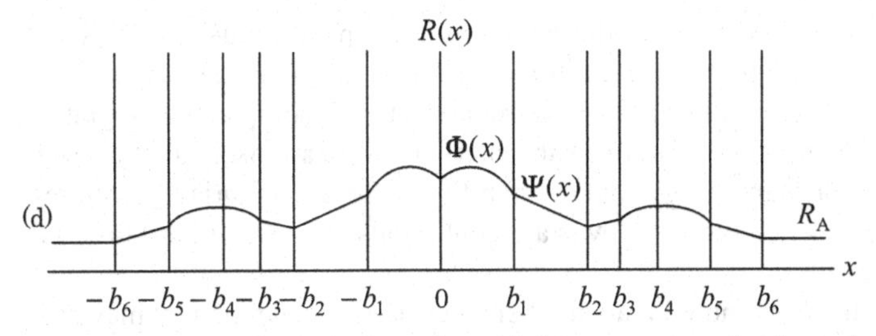

Figure 6.10. The tricentric configuration with three approximately identical centers.

It must be stressed that these configurations do not exhaust the set of equilibria. Because of the nonlinearities arising in the model, it is hard to provide a full characterization of this set.

We now come to the problem of multiplicity of equilibria. In Figure 6.11, borrowed from Fujita and Ogawa (1982), the regions in the parameter space

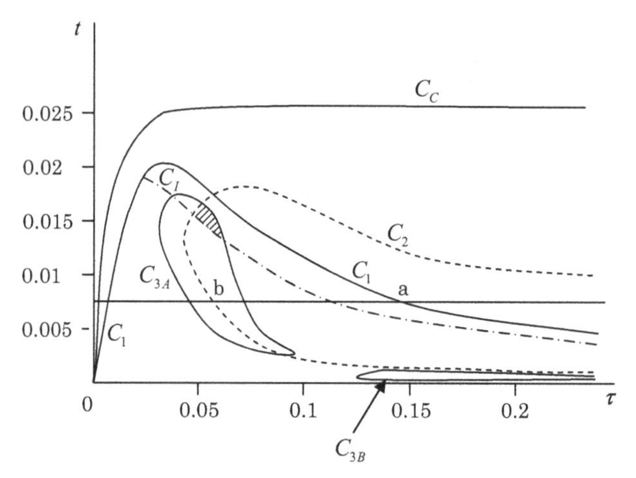

Figure 6.11. Parameter ranges for six equilibrium configurations.

(t, τ) corresponding to the various equilibria described earlier are depicted for the parameter values $(N, M, L_f) = (100, 100, 1)$. Below the locus denoted as C_1 lie the monocentric configurations; in the preceding, C_C is the domain of completely integrated configurations; the domain of incompletely integrated configurations can be found between C_I and C_C; the domain delineated by the broken line C_2 is that of duocentric configurations, whereas the domain delineated by the solid line C_{3A} (C_{3B}) corresponds to the cities with one center and two secondary centers of identical sizes (three approximately identical centers).

It is easily seen that some of these regions overlap, and thus, for the same parameter configuration, several equilibrium patterns may exist. For example, in the shaded area, four equilibria exist: the monocentric, incompletely integrated, duocentric, and tricentric (with two subcenters) configurations. Note, however, that we do not know anything about the stability of these equilibria. Performing such an analysis when the unknowns are continuous curves is a hard task left for future research.

Finally, it should be noted that small changes in some parameters may lead to dramatic modifications in the prevailing equilibrium pattern. For example, if $t = 0.007$ in Figure 6.11, the following path may well arise. When τ is very small, we have an integrated city because commuting costs are dominant; above some threshold, the city is incompletely integrated because the accessibility of each firm to the others now matters; when τ keeps rising, we reach the domain in which the city is monocentric. So far, the transition is smooth and similar to that observed under linear accessibility. The picture changes drastically when τ takes some intermediate values larger than a, as shown in Figure 6.10. The city becomes duocentric. At this point, the size of the central residential section is significantly large (≅50 units of land). Similarly, the aggregate differential rent drops down by a fairly large amount because a much lower degree of centrality now prevails within the city. The transition at point a is therefore catastrophic. Interestingly, the equilibrium is also path-dependent because it shows inertia. For example, decreasing τ from the right of a yields a duocentric pattern up to point b, where the size of the central residential section is approximately equal to 30 units of land. At this point, the city exhibits another catastrophic change, becoming monocentric.

Another important point to make is that diversity in agent types is crucial for the preceding patterns to arise. Considering firms only with the framework of interaction, Tabuchi (1986) obtained results similar to those derived in Section 6.2; that is, the equilibrium distribution of firms is always unimodal because the global accessibility function $A(x)$ remains concave over the whole urban area. On the contrary, with both firms and households, we typically observe an alternation of concavity and convexity. The standard assumption of a single class of agents is, therefore, not as innocuous as might be expected and may well prevent the emergence of more realistic urban patterns.

6.6 THE DECENTRALIZATION OF URBAN EMPLOYMENT

So far, a firm has been considered as a single-unit entity. Consequently, the model discussed in Section 6.3 is not able to explain a basic trend observed in the spatial organization of large cities, that is, the location of firm units in suburban areas. For example, many firms (e.g., banks or insurance companies, but also industrial firms a long time ago) have moved part of their activities (such as bookkeeping, planning, and employee training) to the suburbs; similar moves had been observed earlier in the case of industrial activities (Hohenberg and Lees 1985, chapter 6). In this case, a firm typically conducts some of its activities (such as communications with other firms) at the front office located in the CBD, whereas the rest of its activities are carried out at the back office set up in the suburbs.

This problem has been tackled by Ota and Fujita (1993). With the other assumptions of the model in Section 6.3 kept unchanged, it is now assumed that each firm consists of a front unit and a back unit. Each front unit is assumed to interact with all other front units for business communications, whereas each back unit exchanges information or management services only with the front unit belonging to the same firm. Each firm must choose the location of the front unit and back unit so as to maximize its profit. If a firm sets up its front unit at $x \in X$ and back unit at $z \in X$, the firm incurs an *intrafirm communication cost* $\Gamma(x, z)$ that depends only upon the locations x and z. Each front unit needs S_f units of land and L_f units of labor; each back unit requires S_b units of land and L_b units of labor.

In this context, the only change from the model presented in Section 6.3 is in the profit function (6.32). A firm having a front unit at x, a back unit at z, and choosing a level of contact activity $\varphi(x, y)$ with the front unit of each other firm at $y \in X$ has now a profit function defined as follows:

$$\pi(x, z) = A(x) - R(x)S_{\mathrm{f}} - W(x)L_{\mathrm{f}} - R(z)S_{\mathrm{b}} - W(z)L_{\mathrm{b}} - \Gamma(x, z)$$

where the first term is defined by (6.33). If local accessibility is linear (see [6.44]) and the intrafirm communication cost is linear in distance, Ota and Fujita (1993) have shown that no less than eleven different equilibrium configurations are possible, depending on the values of the various parameters. These configurations are the result of two basic effects: (i) as the commuting cost of workers decreases, the segregation of business and residential areas increases, and (ii) as the intrafirm communication cost gets smaller, back units separate from front units. The most typical configuration arising when intrafirm communication costs are low involves the agglomeration of the front units at the city center surrounded by a residential area, whereas back units are established at the outskirts of the city together with their employees. In other words, a primary labor market emerges at the city center (e.g., Manhattan), whereas secondary labor markets are created in the suburbs.

The advancement of intrafirm communications technologies has led to a transformation of the industrial structure of cities, which have shifted from specializing by sector to specializing mainly by function with headquarters and business services clustered in larger cities, and plants clustered in smaller cities (Duranton and Puga 2005). For example, Anas et al. (1998) observe that by the end of the nineteenth century telephones and trucks were making it possible for firms in the United States to decentralize jobs. In the same vein, Henderson (1997) argues that production plants have moved to medium-sized and specialized cities that are within reach from firms' headquarters located in city centers. The relocation of production plants from industrialized countries to developing countries where labor is much cheaper can be given a similar explanation (see Chapter 11). In all these cases, the relocation of some activities is driven by factor price differences. What differs between these various issues is the spatial scale of the problem under consideration.

6.7 CONCLUDING REMARKS

According to the conventional wisdom, externalities are at the root of economic agglomerations. And indeed, we have seen in this chapter how nonmarket interactions among economic agents may give rise to different types of agglomerations. In particular, appealing to externalities allows one to save the competitive paradigm in the economics of agglomeration and to use standard models. Thus, the mere social inclinations of people are sufficient for the formation of a settlement exhibiting the main features of a modern city with an endogenous center around which human beings organize themselves. The same type of spatial organization arises among firms benefiting from information spillovers. However, it does not seem easy to get several settlements, districts, or centers with a population of homogeneous agents. At least two groups of agents, such as firms and households, seem necessary for richer spatial patterns to emerge. In addition, nonlinear fields of interaction are required because linear fields tend to support monocentric structures only. Unfortunately, although the use of an exponential distance-decay function is a good approximation of many real-world patterns of interaction, it appears that such models very quickly become hard to manipulate. As is well known, nonlinearities tend to generate multiplicity of equilibria and discontinuous transitions. The contrast between the results obtained under linear and exponential distance-decay functions suggests that the form taken by the social process of interaction in the transmission of knowledge and information is crucial for the type of urban configuration that may emerge.

Not surprisingly, the first theorem of welfare does not apply because of the presence of externalities. Unlike the conventional wisdom, which stresses the negative externalities associated with the formation of cities more, we have singled out here one of the main benefits generated by agglomerations, that is, the spreading of information among close-knit agents. Such an external effect may explain why economic agents are prepared to pay high rents to live close to the centers of large cities where this effect is most intense. Consequently, we have shown that, in a market economy, agglomeration of firms or households is desirable from the social point of view. Even less expected, we have seen that it is socially optimal to have denser or more agglomerated patterns of agents than those generated by the market. This seems to be a fairly general principle inherent to the process of information dissemination: people account for their role as receivers but not as transmitters. In this case, equilibrium patterns are too spatially dispersed. Surely, this is not what most proponents of spatial planning would expect. Of course, the models discussed in this chapter focus upon specific aspects only, and other agglomeration and dispersion forces must also be studied. In particular, external effects like traffic congestion, urban pollution or crime tend to deter further urban growth and, therefore, favor the dispersion of human activities. In addition, as stated in Section 6.1, the population of households has been assumed to be given. Consequently, our welfare results are valid conditional upon some given population of workers who must reside in the city.

Finally, low commuting costs tend to foster a monocentric urban configuration. This occurs because such low costs allow the nonmarket interactions among firms to become the predominant location factor for firms. Once this fact is understood, it is no surprise that firms want to agglomerate in a single district. This is a general theme that we will encounter again in the next chapter.

APPENDIX

A The solution of the differential equation (6.10). Set $v' \equiv dv/dx$ and $v'' \equiv d^2v/dx^2$ where v is a function defined for $x \geq 0$. Given (6.10), we want to solve the following differential equation:

$$v'' = \frac{a}{2}\exp(-v) \tag{6A.1}$$

where $v(x) \equiv T(x)/\alpha$ and $a \equiv (\alpha/4t)\exp(\zeta/\alpha)$. Multiplying both sides of (6A.1) by v' and integrating yields

$$(v')^2 = -a\exp(-v) + c_1 \tag{6A.2}$$

where c_1 is a constant of integration. Set

$$w^2 = -a\exp(-v) + c_1 \tag{6A.3}$$

so that

$$2w\mathrm{d}w = a\exp(-v)\mathrm{d}v$$

from which it follows by (6A.2) that

$$\mathrm{d}v = \frac{2w\mathrm{d}w}{c_1 - w^2} \tag{6A.4}$$

Denoting $c_1 = k^2$ and using $\mathrm{d}v = w\mathrm{d}x$ in (6A.4), we obtain:

$$\frac{2\mathrm{d}w}{k^2 - w^2} = \mathrm{d}x. \tag{6A.5}$$

Observe that

$$\frac{2}{k^2 - w^2} = \frac{1}{k}\frac{1}{k+w} + \frac{1}{k}\frac{1}{k-w}.$$

Substituting the relation above in the left-hand side of (6A.5) and integrating the resulting expression, we have

$$\frac{1}{k}\log\frac{k+w}{k-w} = x + c_2 \tag{6A.6}$$

where c_2 is a constant of integration. Solving (6A.6) for w gives

$$w = k\frac{\exp k(x+c_2) - 1}{\exp k(x+c_2) + 1}.$$

Using (6A.3) and the definition of k, we obtain

$$\frac{k^2}{a} - \exp(-v) = \frac{k^2}{a}\left(\frac{\exp k(|x|+c_2) - 1}{\exp k(|x|+c_2) + 1}\right)^2$$

whose solution is

$$v(x) = -\log \frac{k^2}{a}\left[1 - \left(\frac{\exp k(|x| + c_2) - 1}{\exp k(|x| + c_2) + 1}\right)^2\right]. \tag{6A.7}$$

In order to determine c_2, we observe that $T(x)$ and, therefore, $v(x)$ are minimized at $x = 0$, thus implying that $c_2 = 0$. Consequently, (6A.7) may be rewritten as follows:

$$v(x) = -\log \frac{k^2}{a}\frac{4\exp k\,|x|}{(1 + \exp k\,|x|)^2}$$

which is equivalent to

$$T(x) = -\alpha \log\left[\frac{\alpha}{t}\exp\left(-\frac{\varsigma}{\alpha}\right)\frac{k^2\exp(k\,|x|)}{(1 + \exp(k\,|x|))^2}\right]$$

after having replaced a by its value.

B The Optimal Configuration in Section 6.2.1. We derive here the optimality conditions of Section 6.2.1 by expressing the optimization problem as an optimal control problem. However this turns out to be fairly involved because trips between locations go both ways. It is worth noting that we encounter here one of the main differences between time and space modeling in that interactions in space are essentially bidirectional.[16]

Differentiating (6.3), we obtain

$$\begin{aligned}\frac{\mathrm{d}T}{\mathrm{d}x} &= \int_{-b}^{x} tn(y)\mathrm{d}y - \int_{x}^{b} tn(y)\mathrm{d}y \\ &= tN(x) - t\left[N - N(x)\right] \\ &= 2tN(x) - tN\end{aligned}$$

where

$$N(x) \equiv \int_{-b}^{x} n(y)\mathrm{d}y$$

denotes the total population situated on the left of x. By definition of $N(x)$, we have

$$\frac{\mathrm{d}N}{\mathrm{d}x} = n(x)$$

together with the terminal conditions $N(-b) = 0$ and $N(b) = N$.

[16] Formally, this means that we have to solve a problem of calculus of variations with multiple integrals.

Specifying the initial condition on $T(x)$ appcars to bc especially complex here since the value of $T(-b)$ depends on the entire population distribution:

$$T(-b) = \Gamma(-b) + tbN$$

where

$$\Gamma(x) \equiv \int_x^b tyn(y)\mathrm{d}y$$

so that we have the new differential equation:

$$\frac{\mathrm{d}\Gamma}{\mathrm{d}x} = -txn(x)$$

with the corresponding terminal condition $\Gamma(b) = 0$.

Consequently, our optimization may now be rewritten as a standard optimal control problem under the form:

$$\max_{b,s(x)} S = \int_{-b}^{b} \{[Y - U^* - \alpha \log n(x) + I - T(x)]\, n(x) - R_A\}\,\mathrm{d}x$$

subject to the constraints

$$\frac{\mathrm{d}T(x)}{\mathrm{d}x} = 2tN(x) - tN$$

$$\frac{\mathrm{d}N(x)}{\mathrm{d}x} = n(x)$$

$$\frac{\mathrm{d}\Gamma(x)}{\mathrm{d}x} = -txn(x)$$

together with the terminal conditions

$$T(-b) = \Gamma(-b) + tbN \qquad N(-b) = 0 \quad \text{and} \quad N(b) = N \qquad \Gamma(b) = 0.$$

As a result, we have the following Hamiltonian:

$$\begin{aligned} H(x) = {} & [Y - U^* - \alpha \log n(x) + I - T(x)]\, n(x) - R_A \\ & + \lambda(x)\,[2tN(x) - tN] + \mu(x)n(x) - \nu(x)txn(x) \end{aligned}$$

where $\lambda(x)$, $\mu(x)$, and $\nu(x)$ are the costate variables (multipliers) associated respectively with the state variables $T(x)$, $N(x)$, and $\Gamma(x)$. By solving the motion equations of the costate variables, we get

$$\begin{aligned} \lambda(x) &= N(x) - N \\ \mu(x) &= -T(x) + txN + T(-b) + \mu(-b) \\ \nu(x) &= N. \end{aligned}$$

Setting

$$\zeta^o \equiv Y - U^* + I - \alpha + T(-b) + \mu(-b)$$

and substituting the costate variables by their values, the Hamiltonian may be rewritten as:

$$\begin{aligned} H(x) = [\alpha + \zeta^o - \alpha \log n(x) - 2T(x)]\, n(x) - R_A \\ + [N(x) - N]\,[2tN(x) - tN]\,. \end{aligned}$$

Applying the first order condition with respect to n leads to the solution (6.21).

Finally, since b is chosen without constraint, the Hamiltonian evaluated at b must be equal to zero, which means that (6.22) holds since $N(b) = N$.

C The duocentric configuration is not an equilibrium under linear accessibility. Consider the symmetric duocentric configuration depicted in Figure 6A.1 in which each of the business areas $[b_1, b_3]$ and $[-b_3, -b_1]$ is surrounded by two residential sections from which the required labor is supplied. To support such a commuting pattern, the wage function must take the following form:

$$W^*(x) = W^*(b_2) - t|b_2 - x| \quad x \in [0, b_4]$$

which shows a peak at some location b_2 between b_1 and b_3. By (6.29) and (6.34), this means that the equilibrium bid rent functions are now given by

$$\begin{aligned} \Phi(x, 0) &= \{A(x) - [W^*(b_2) - t|b_2 - x|]L_f \quad x \in [0, b_4] \\ \Psi(x, u^*) &= [W^*(b_2) - t|b_2 - x| - Z(u^*)] \quad x \in [0, b_4]. \end{aligned}$$

Furthermore, because b_1 is by definition the boundary between a business district and a residential section, it must be that

$$\Phi(b_1, 0) = \Psi(b_1, u^*).$$

Because $|b_2 - x| = b_2 - x$ for $x \in [0, b_1]$, the three previous expressions imply that

$$\begin{aligned} \Phi(x, 0) - \Psi(x, u^*) &= [\Phi(x, 0) - \Phi(b_1, 0)] - [\Psi(x, u^*) - \Psi(b_1, u^*)] \\ &= A^*(x) - A^*(b_1) + t(b_1 - x)(1 + L_f)/2. \end{aligned}$$

However, inasmuch as $\mathrm{d}A(x)/\mathrm{d}x = 0$ by (6.47) for $x \in [0, b_1]$, $A^*(x) = A^*(b_1)$ for $x \in [0, b_1]$, we have

$$\Phi(x, 0) > \Psi(x, u^*) \quad x \in [0, b_1]$$

a result contradicting the assumption that $[0, b_1]$ is part of a residential section. In other words, when the local accessibility is linear, the aggregate accessibility is *flat* on the central interval $[-b_1, b_1]$. Consequently, because the wage function

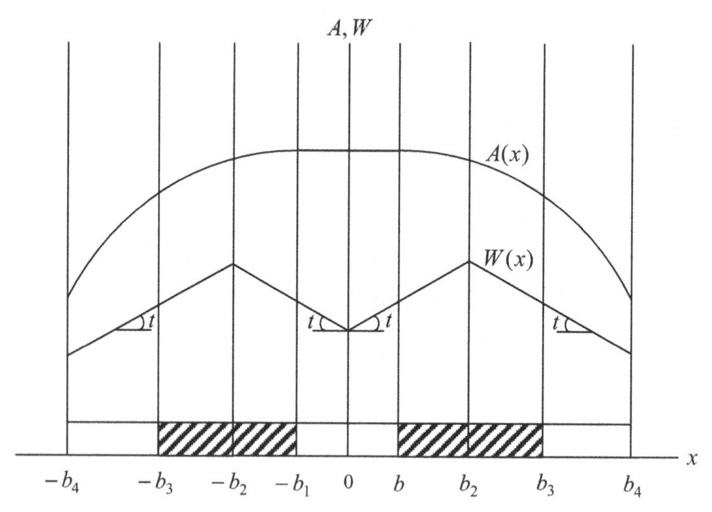

Figure 6A.1. The impossibility of a duocentric configuration under linear accessibility.

decreases from $x = b_1$ to $x = 0$, firms can afford to make higher bids inside this residential area than they do at b_1, whereas households can only make lower bids than they do at b_1. That the two bids are equal at b_1 implies firms would choose to be in $[-b_1, b_1]$.

Figure 6A.1 also shows that, for a duocentric configuration to be an equilibrium, the aggregate accessibility function $A(x)$ must exhibit a peak inside each business district as the wage function $W(x)$ does. This is possible provided that the local accessibility function $a(x, y)$ decreases sufficiently fast with the distance between x and y, which may occur with the spatially discounted accessibility (6.45).

D Proof of $A(x) < 2/\tau$ in Section 6.5. By the land constraint (6.38), we must have $m(y) \leq 1$ for all $y \in X$. Furthermore, the firm population constraint (6.41) implies that

$$\begin{aligned} A(x) &= \int_{-\infty}^{\infty} m(y) \exp(-\tau\,|x - y|)\mathrm{d}y \\ &< \int_{-\infty}^{\infty} \exp(-\tau\,|x - y|)\mathrm{d}y \\ &= 2\int_{0}^{\infty} \exp(-\tau z)\mathrm{d}z \\ &= \frac{2}{\tau} \end{aligned}$$

which gives us the desired inequality.

7

The Formation of Urban Centers under Imperfect Competition

7.1 INTRODUCTION

The analysis developed in the previous chapter sheds light on the emergence of centers within a city. There, the emergence of an urban center crucially depends on the existence of nonmarket interactions (externalities) among agents and is typical of the formation of a CBD involving high-level activities. However, in the real world, we also frequently observe the formation of *clusters of retailers* selling similar goods (fashion clothes, restaurants, movie theaters, antiquity shops, and so on) or of *employment centers* in which different kinds of jobs are performed. In such cases, the agglomeration forces are created through market interactions between firms and consumers or workers. As seen in Chapter 2, for this to occur, one must consider increasing returns and imperfect competition. In this chapter, our purpose is to show how urban centers of different types, such as commercial areas or employment centers, may emerge under imperfect competition in the product or labor market. We will consider different market structures. The common thread of the various models considered here is that monopoly (or monopsony) power on the product (labor) market is needed for such agglomerations to emerge in equilibrium.

In Section 7.2, we suppose monopolistic competition with a large number of firms selling a differentiated product to consumers who display a taste for variety (Fujita 1988). Firms no longer assume that they can sell whatever they want at given market prices. Instead, each firm is aware that its optimal choice (location and price) depends on the demand for the variety it supplies. This demand itself rests on the spatial consumer distribution, thus showing how firms' choices are directly affected by consumers' choices. In turn, the optimal choice of a consumer (location and consumption) depends on the entire firm distribution. This is so because firms sell a differentiated product and consumers like variety; hence, their purchases are distributed across locations and the distribution of their shopping trips varies with the number of varieties available at each location. This creates some form of spatial interdependence between the two distributions. We show that this interdependence leads firms and consumers to form a city where they share land.

It is worth stressing that, in such a context, the knowledge of prices alone does not allow firms and households to make their optimal location choices. As noted by Koopmans (1957, 154) in a different, but related context,

> the decisive difficulty is that transportation of intermediate commodities from one plant to another makes the relative advantage of a given location for a given plant dependent on the locations of other plants.

This difficulty was further highlighted by Papageorgiou and Thisse (1985, 29) in the case of consumption goods traded between land-using firms and households:

> The optimal behavior of a firm depends on what households and other firms do, while the optimal behavior of a household depends on what firms and other households do; space here binds everyone together.

When activities are not perfectly divisible, the relative advantage of a given location for an agent depends on the locations chosen by the others, thus making locations interdependent.

That firms sell differentiated varieties and therefore price above marginal cost allows them to compete for land with the aim of being close to consumers. In the absence of a positive markup, firms would lose their incentives to get close to their customers. Indeed, their operating profits being uniformly equal to zero, the agglomeration would vanish. This chapter shows how imperfect competition operates to generate agglomeration through market transactions and also sheds additional light on the meaning and implication of the spatial impossibility theorem discussed in Chapter 2.

The monopolistic competition model is easy to handle but fails to capture one of the basic ingredients of spatial competition, that is, the strategic nature of spatial competition, as discussed in Chapter 4. This problem was addressed by Hotelling (1929) in the special case of a homogeneous product, and since then it has been generally accepted that competition for market areas is a centripetal force that leads vendors to congregate – a result known in the literature as the "principle of minimum differentiation." This principle has generated controversies about the inefficiency of free competition, for, according to Hotelling (1929, 54) himself, it would suggest that "buyers are confronted everywhere with an excessive sameness."

The classical two ice-cream men problem provides a neat illustration of this principle. Two merchants selling the same ice cream at the same fixed price compete in location for consumers who are uniformly distributed along a bounded linear segment (Main Street). Each consumer purchases one ice cream from the nearer seller. The consumers are thus divided into two segments, and each firm's aggregate demand is represented by the length of its market segment. Since Lerner and Singer (1937), it has been well known that the unique Nash equilibrium of this game is given by the two firms located at the market center, and so regardless of the shape of the transport cost function. In other words, two firms competing for clients choose to minimize their spatial differentiation.[1] However, matters become more complex when (mill) prices are brought into the picture because price competition is so fierce under product homogeneity that firms always want to separate in order to benefit from the monopoly power generated by geographical isolation.

Spatial separation may cease to be profitable, however, when firms sell a differentiated product. This is so because demand for a firm's variety now arises at each and every consumer location. In addition, it is a well-established result in industrial organization that product differentiation relaxes price competition. It therefore becomes natural to investigate the possibility of an agglomeration of oligopolistic firms when there is a strong preference for variety.

Using a framework similar to the one in the preceding section, we show in Section 7.3.1 that, despite the presence of strategic price competition, the agglomeration of firms at the market center is a Nash equilibrium of the corresponding noncooperative game when firms supply sufficiently differentiated varieties, assuming that the consumer distribution is given. By putting together all these results, we may conclude that, regardless of the market structure, *a commercial area involving a large number of retailers, restaurants, or theaters is likely to emerge when it offers sufficiently differentiated products, when the transport costs borne by consumers are low enough, or both.* This echoes Launhardt (1885, p. 150 of the English translation) for whom "the most effective of all protective tariffs [is] the protection through poor roads." Furthermore, although the conventional wisdom sees such clusters as socially wasteful, we show that they are often socially desirable once their ability to supply differentiated goods is taken into account.

The foregoing models can be referred to as *shopping* models because consumers visit firms and bear the entire transportation costs. Instead, we have *shipping* models when firms deliver the product and take advantage of the fact that the customers' locations are observable to price discriminate across locations. Shopping models seem to be appropriate for studying competition among sellers of consumption goods, whereas shipping models better describe competition among sellers of industrial goods. However, the possibility of ordering through such communications technologies as the telephone and Internet and the existence of mail-order firms make these settings increasingly relevant for the study of consumption goods too. Despite significant differences in the

[1] Contrary to a widespread opinion, this result is not driven by the existence of boundaries. To see this, consider a continuous distribution over the real line. Then, both firms are located back to back at the median of the distribution.

process of competition, the tendency toward agglomeration is shown in Section 7.3.3 to be governed by principles similar to those uncovered for shopping models. As seen, strategic interaction is at the heart of these two families of models, and space is the reason for it: competition is localized in shopping models whereas shipping models involve oligopolistic competition in spatially separated markets. Finally, we conclude in Section 7.3.4 with a brief survey of what has been accomplished in spatial competition when consumers make multipurpose trips.

Once it is recognized that consumers shop for the best price and variety opportunity on the purchasing day, it becomes sensible to assume that they have incomplete information about which firm offers which variety at which price. Although search theory grew rapidly in the early 1970s, it is fair to say that space brings about specific dimensions that have attracted the attention of only a few analysts. Indeed, because trading arises in a number of places much smaller than where consumers reside, they experience different search costs, and the way consumers conduct their search affects firms' strategies through their demand. This in turn implies that search costs are influenced by firms' strategic decisions such as locations and prices. In such a context of comparison shopping, the clustering of shops is based on consumers' economizing on their search cost (Nelson 1970). More precisely, Stuart (1979, 19) has noted that "a seller who does locate as a spatial monopolist might have a hard time attracting search-conscious buyers in the first place." This observation has a major implication for our purpose in that "a spatial clustering of sellers can result from desires of buyers to search in marketplaces where there are relatively many sellers" (Stuart 1979, 17).

Indeed, consumers unaware of the characteristics of the varieties supplied in various places reduce their search costs by visiting the place with the largest number of retailers even though this place is located farther away. Hence, incomplete information on the consumer side is an agglomeration force. This problem has been tackled in the 1980s and 1990s. Common to all these contributions is that the expected utility from visiting a cluster of firms increases with its size, which is a result reminiscent of the gravity principle. Although each consumer buys a single variety, in the aggregate consumers exhibit a preference for a large number of retailers because of their lack of information about the available varieties. Furthermore, consumers are affected differentially according to their distances to the marketplaces. In Section 7.4, we show how the agglomeration force is generated from the aggregate behavior of individual consumers pursuing a search strategy. We first focus on a standard model of spatial competition in which prices are given. We briefly discuss what happens when the analysis is then extended to deal with price competition and variable total demand.

In all cases, if consumers have different tastes and are uncertain about the characteristics of the varieties on offer, the firms can manipulate the search cost structure by joining an existing market or by establishing a new one. The basic trade-off faced by a firm is as follows: a firm captures a small market share when setting up in a large market or monopolizes a small local market when opening a new one. When a firm chooses to join the cluster, it generates a *demand externality* in that more consumers benefit from economies of scope in searching, thus increasing the number of consumers visiting the cluster (that is, the extent of the product market is endogenous). Such an externality is obviously a centripetal force similar to the network externalities encountered in the consumption of goods whose utility increases with the number of users (e.g., telephone, e-mail, and so on). This externality is also akin to the agglomeration force that we encounter in Chapter 8.

After having studied the formation of commercial areas, it is natural to move to the creation of employment centers in Section 7.5. As we know, the CBD is a natural place in which employment may be concentrated. However, contrary to general beliefs, the suburbanization of jobs is not a new phenomenon. As noticed by Hohenberg and Lees (1985, 131), it arose, for example, in protoindustrial Europe:

> Big-city entrepreneurs took advantage of lower rural wages and of heightened division of labor in decentralizing parts of their production while reserving the more delicate operations to city artisans.

Today, the creation of suburbanized jobs seems to obey a similar logic, although it may take different forms such as the emergence of *edge cities* (Henderson and Mitra 1996). Thus, our research strategy is similar to that developed in the previous sections. We first assume that employers have no market power on the labor market (Section 7.5.1) and go on by analyzing the case of a firm having some monopsony power on the urban labor market (Section 7.5.2). From the formal point of view, the results obtained in this section can be viewed as the labor-market counterpart of those obtained in the previous ones.

Before proceeding, two remarks are in order. First, although the models presented in this chapter may look very different from one another, they are in essence analogous, address similar questions and lead to results that bear a strong resemblance. Second, this chapter does not intend to be a survey of the very rich literature on spatial competition theory and related topics. Instead, it aims to provide an overview of the results dealing with the agglomeration of firms selling similar products, which were available before the emergence of NEG.

7.2 THE FORMATION OF DOWNTOWN UNDER MONOPOLISTIC COMPETITION

Large cities include districts mixing dwellings and stores where consumers do their shopping: think of Soho in New York City, Montparnasse in Paris, or Shinjuku in Tokyo. For this to arise, households and shopkeepers must have the same bid rent in the locations they share (see Sections 3.2.2 and 3.3.4). To show how such a land use pattern emerges, we consider an economy endowed with three goods. The first one is homogeneous; it is supplied on a perfectly competitive market and serves as the numéraire. The second one is land. Space is linear and given by $X = (-\infty, \infty)$; the amount of land at each location is equal to 1, and land is owned by absentee landlords. The opportunity cost of land is zero.

The third good is a horizontally differentiated product supplied by a continuum M of firms. Each firm in this sector has a negligible impact on the market outcome in the sense that it can ignore its impact on, and hence reactions from, other firms. Additionally, each firm sells a variety of a differentiated product and therefore faces a downward sloping demand. There are no scope economies, and thus, owing to increasing returns to scale, there is a one-to-one relationship between firms and varieties, which implies that M is also the mass of varieties of the differentiated product. Consequently, our model is one of monopolistic competition.[2]

Each firm faces the same technology; it uses the fixed amount of land S_{f} and has a constant marginal cost c expressed in terms of the numéraire. Finally, firms are owned by absentee shareholders. Each variety can be traded at a positive cost of t units of the numéraire for each unit transported over one unit of distance, regardless of the variety. In other words, transportation costs are linear in distance and quantity.

There is a continuum N of consumers, each using the same fixed amount of land S_{h}. As in Section 6.3, we choose the units of M and N for $S_{\mathrm{f}} = S_{\mathrm{h}} = 1$ to hold. Hence, a large value of M (N) means that stores (households) are numerous, stores (households) use a large plot, or both.

Preferences are identical and are described by the following additive utility function, which is symmetric in all varieties:

$$U(z; q_i, i \in [0, M]) = \int_0^M u(q_i)\,\mathrm{d}i + z \tag{7.1}$$

where u is strictly concave and increasing with respect to q_i for $i \in [0, M]$ and z the quantity of the numéraire.[3]

Let $Q > 0$ be any given quantity of the differentiated good. If the consumption of a variety is given by Q/x on $[0, x]$ and zero on $(x, M]$ for any $x \in [0, M]$, the utility level is given by $xu(Q/x)$. Then, the utility u is strictly concave if and only if the function $xu(Q/x)$ strictly increases over the interval $[0, M]$.

[2] In game-theoretic terms, this means that we consider a large aggregative game in which each player is negligible.

[3] We assume that $u(0) = 0$. Indeed, $u(0) \neq 0$ implies that increasing the number of varieties affects the consumer's well-being even when he does not change the range of varieties he consumes. This does not strike us as being plausible.

In other words, the concavity of the utility function u means that consumers are variety-lovers: rather than concentrating their consumption over a small mass of varieties, they prefer to spread it over the whole range of available varieties. We appeal to the same property in the next two chapters.

There is no multipurpose trip, and each unit of each variety is bought on a single trip (think of restaurants, theaters, and so on). If the firm supplying variety i locates at $y_i \in X$, the budget constraint of a consumer located at $x \in X$ can be written as follows:

$$\int_0^M (p_i + t|x - y_i|) q_i \, \mathrm{d}i + R(x) + z = Y$$

where Y is the consumer's income, which is given and the same across consumers, p_i the price of variety i, and $R(x)$ the land rent at location x. The income Y is supposed to be large enough for the optimal consumption of the numéraire to be strictly positive for each individual.

Because of identical production functions, transportation costs, and symmetric preferences, in equilibrium all varieties provided at the same location y must be supplied at the same (mill) price $p(y)$. Hence, owing to the concavity of u, the quantity of each variety purchased at location y by any consumer at x is the same across varieties:

$$q_i(x; y_i = y) = q(x, y) \quad \text{for each variety available at } y.$$

Then, if $m(x)$ is the density of stores at $y \in X$, the indirect utility of a consumer at x is

$$V(x) = \int_X u[q(x, y)] m(y) \, \mathrm{d}y - \int_X [p(y) + t\,|x - y|] q(x, y) m(y) \, \mathrm{d}y \\ -R(x) + Y. \tag{7.2}$$

Regarding the supply side, if the number (formally, the density) of consumers at x is $n(x)$, the profit made by a store located at x and facing its demand field is

$$\pi(y) = [p(y) - c] \int_X q(x, y) n(x) \, \mathrm{d}x - R(y). \tag{7.3}$$

Given the firm and price densities $m(\cdot)$ and $p(\cdot)$ as well as the land rent $R(\cdot)$, each consumer chooses a location x and demand distribution $q(x, \cdot)$ so as to maximize his indirect utility (7.2). Given the densities $n(\cdot)$, $q(\cdot, \cdot)$, and $R(\cdot)$, each firm selects a location y and its price $p(y)$ to maximize its profits (7.3). As usual, the equilibrium is such that all consumers reach the same utility level across occupied locations and firms earn the same profits at each occupied location.

7.2.1 How Households and Stores Are Mixed in Downtown

To facilitate the comparison with the oligopolistic case dealt with in the next section, we suppose that the utility (7.1) has an entropy-like form:

$$\begin{aligned} u(q) &= \frac{q}{\alpha}(1 + \log \beta) - \frac{q}{\alpha} \log \frac{q}{\alpha} \qquad &\text{if } q < \alpha\beta \\ &= \beta &\text{if } q \geq \alpha\beta \end{aligned} \tag{7.4}$$

where α and β are two positive constants such that u is strictly concave over the interval $[0, \alpha\beta]$. In physics, the entropy measures the dispersion of particles: the higher the entropy, the stronger the dispersion. Here the entropy captures the idea that consumers like to disperse their consumption over the whole range of available varieties. Note also that the entropy function is a close relative of the CES, which will be used in Chapters 8 and 9 to describe consumers' love for variety (Anderson et al., 1992, chapters 3 and 4). Finally, the parameter α is an inverse measure of the degree of differentiation between varieties: the higher α is, the less differentiated are the varieties. The parameter β is the satiation level in consuming a variety.

Because preferences on the differentiated good are additive while the upper-tier utility is linear, each firm may choose its output as if it were a monopolist. Plugging (7.4) into (7.2) and maximizing the resulting expression with respect to $q(x, y)$ for each location pair (x, y), we obtain

$$q^*(x, y) = \alpha\beta \exp -\alpha(p(y) + t|x - y|) \quad x, y \in X. \tag{7.5}$$

Hence, the demand by a consumer at x for a variety supplied at y is described by the exponential distance-decay function considered in the previous chapter (when $\tau = \alpha t$). The main difference is that now the firm's price enters as a variable. This demand describes the "interaction" between a consumer at x and a firm at y, but the interaction now goes through the market because it results from the choices made by both firm and consumer in the market.

Plugging (7.5) into (7.3) and maximizing the resulting expression with respect to $p(y)$, we obtain the firm's profit-maximizing price under monopolistic competition:

$$p^* \equiv p^*(y) = c + 1/\alpha. \tag{7.6}$$

In words, the equilibrium (mill) price is equal to the marginal cost plus a markup that increases with $1/\alpha$; clearly the equilibrium converges toward marginal cost when $\alpha \to \infty$. This means that α plays exactly the role of a substitution parameter between varieties, although there is no direct substitution among varieties. Another way to say the same thing is that the price elasticity of (7.5) is equal to $\alpha p(y)$. Accordingly, a larger value for α implies a more elastic demand for each variety because they are closer substitutes.

Replacing $p(y)$ by p^* throughout and using (7.5), we obtain:

$$V(x) = \gamma \int_X m(y) \exp(-\alpha t|x-y|)\, dy - R(x) + Y \tag{7.7}$$

$$\pi(y) = \gamma \int_X n(x) \exp(-\alpha t|x-y|)\, dx - R(y) \tag{7.8}$$

where $\gamma \equiv \beta \exp[-(\alpha c + 1)]$.

These two expressions are very similar to the profit function obtained in Section 6.3 under spatially discounted accessibility. The fundamental difference is that here the interaction takes place between agents belonging to different groups, whereas in Section 6.3 interaction develops among firms only. This implies that *stores are attracted by consumers* and, likewise, that *consumers are attracted by stores*. However, because of land competition, *firms are repulsed by firms and households by households*. As a consequence, the spatial distribution of both classes of agents concerns everyone. In a nutshell, this says that the agents of a given group are attracted by those of the other group but repulsed by those of the same group. This mutual attraction of firms and households is the agglomeration force, whereas competition for land is the dispersion force.

The objective functions of consumers and firms are perfectly symmetric except that, in (7.7), the last two terms $Y - R(x)$ represent an income varying with the consumer's location, whereas the same terms in (7.8) corresponds to a fixed cost $R(x)$ changing with the firm's location.

As usual, we define the households' and firms' bid rent functions as follows:

$$\Psi(x, U^*) = \gamma \int_X m(y) \exp(-\alpha t|x-y|)\, dy + Y - U^* \tag{7.9}$$

$$\Phi(y, \pi^*) = \gamma \int_X n(x) \exp(-\alpha t|x-y|)\, dx - \pi^*. \tag{7.10}$$

The unknowns being $m^*(x)$, $n^*(x)$, $R^*(x)$, U^*, and π^*, the equilibrium conditions can be derived by following the same method as in Section 7.6.3. They are given by

$$R^*(x) = \max\{\Psi(x, U^*), \Phi(x, \pi^*), 0\} \tag{7.11}$$

$$\Psi(x, U^*) = R^*(x) \quad \text{if } n^*(x) > 0 \tag{7.12}$$

$$\Phi(x, \pi^*) = R^*(x) \quad \text{if } m^*(x) > 0 \tag{7.13}$$

$$n^*(x) + m^*(x) = 1 \quad \text{if } R^*(x) > 0 \tag{7.14}$$

$$\int_X m^*(y)\, dy = M \qquad \int_X n^*(y)\, dy = N. \tag{7.15}$$

The following properties are shown in appendix A: the bid rent curve $\Psi(x, U^*)$ is strictly concave on any business section ($m(x) = 1$) and strictly convex on any residential section ($n(x) = 1$); $\Phi(x, \pi^*)$ is strictly convex on any business section and strictly concave on any residential section. This prevents the emergence of any specialized section surrounded by two areas in which agents of the other group are (exclusively or partially) located. Suppose, indeed, that $[b, b']$ is a business area surrounded by residential or integrated sections, or both, thus implying that $\Phi(b, \pi^*) = \Psi(b, U^*)$ and $\Phi(b', \pi^*) = \Psi(b', U^*)$. Because $\Psi(x, U^*)$ is strictly concave and $\Phi(x, \pi^*)$ is strictly convex over this area, we must have $\Phi(x, \pi^*) < \Psi(x, U^*)$ for all $b < x < b'$, which contradicts the equilibrium condition $\Phi(x, \pi^*) \geq \Psi(x, U^*)$ for all $b < x < b'$. The same argument applies if $[b, b']$ is a residential area surrounded by two business or integrated sections, or both. Using a similar argument, one can readily show that there is no vacant land inside the city.

Consequently, focusing on symmetric patterns, we conclude that the city is formed by a single *integrated* district surrounded by two residential or business sections. A centrally integrated district is the consequence of the agglomeration force generated by the mutual attraction of firms and households. Only two configurations are then possible: (i) all stores are located with some consumers in the central district surrounded by two residential sections, or (ii) all consumers reside within the central district together with some firms whereas the remaining firms occupy the two adjacent areas. These two equilibrium patterns are depicted in Figure 7.1.

Consider first the case in which all stores, together with some consumers, locate in the central district $[-b_0, b_0]$ surrounded by two residential sections $[-b_1, -b_0]$ and $[b_0, b_1]$. We begin by showing that both densities are constant over $[-b_0, b_0]$. Because the district is integrated, it must be that $\Phi(x, \pi^*) = \Psi(x, U^*)$ for all $x \in [-b_0, b_0]$. Then, using (7.9) and (7.10), we obtain

$$\int_X [m^*(y) - n^*(y)] \exp(-\alpha t|x - y|)\, \mathrm{d}y = k, \quad x \in [-b_0, b_0]$$

where k is an unknown constant equal to $-(Y - U^* + \pi^*)/\gamma$. This expression can be rewritten as follows:

$$\begin{aligned} &\int_{-b_0}^{x} [m^*(y) - n^*(y)] \exp(-\alpha t(x - y))\, \mathrm{d}y \\ &\quad + \int_{x}^{b_0} [m^*(y) - n^*(y)] \exp(-\alpha t(y - x))\, \mathrm{d}y \\ &\qquad = k + \int_{-b_1}^{-b_0} \exp(-\alpha t(x - y))\, \mathrm{d}y + \int_{b_0}^{b_1} \exp(-\alpha t(y - x))\, \mathrm{d}y. \end{aligned} \tag{7.16}$$

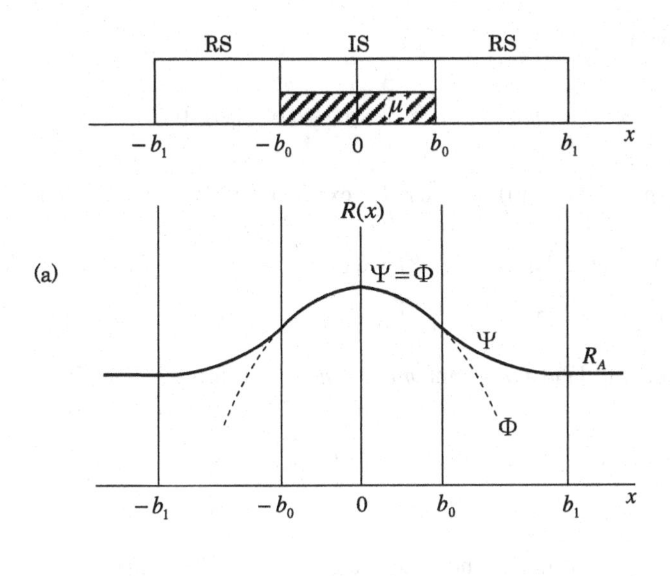

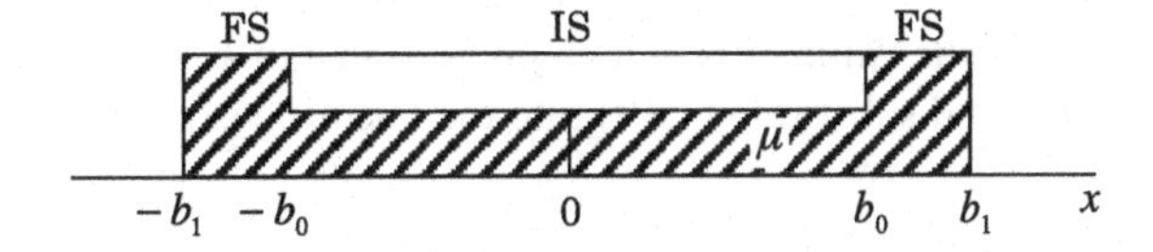

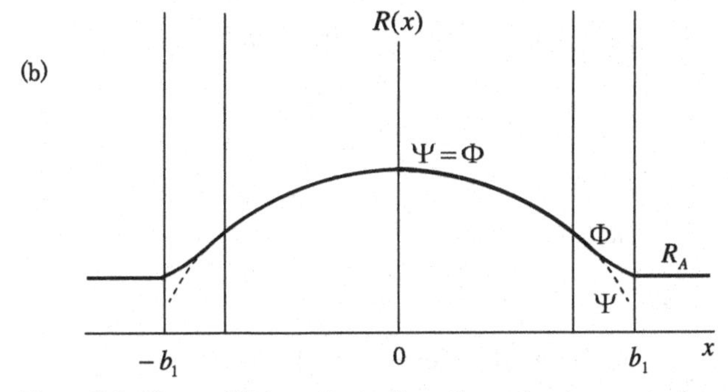

Figure 7.1. The equilibrium city configurations when consumers love variety.

Differentiating (7.16) with respect to x yields

$$\int_{-b_0}^{x} [m^*(y) - n^*(y)] \exp(-\alpha t(x - y)) \, dy$$

$$- \int_{x}^{b_0} [m^*(y) - n^*(y)] \exp(-\alpha t(y - x)) \, dy$$

$$= \int_{-b_1}^{-b_0} \exp(-\alpha t(x - y)) \, dy - \int_{b_0}^{b_1} \exp(-\alpha t(y - x)) \, dy. \quad (7.17)$$

Differentiating again yields

$$2[m^*(x) - n^*(x)] - \alpha t \int_{-b_0}^{b_0} [m^*(y) - n^*(y)] \exp(-\alpha t|x - y|) \, dy$$
$$= -\alpha t \int_{-b_1}^{-b_0} \exp(-\alpha t(x - y)) \, dy - \alpha t \int_{b_0}^{b_1} \exp(-\alpha t(y - x)) \, dy. \quad (7.18)$$

Multiplying (7.16) by αt and adding (7.18), we get

$$m^*(x) - n^*(x) = \alpha tk/2 \qquad x \in [-b_0, b_0]. \quad (7.19)$$

This, together with the land constraint $m(x) + n(x) = 1$ for $x \in [-b_0, b_0]$, implies that

$$m^*(x) = (1 + \alpha tk/2)/2 \equiv \mu \qquad x \in [-b_0, b_0]$$
$$n^*(x) = 1 - m^*(x) = (1 - \alpha tk/2)/2 \qquad x \in [-b_0, b_0]$$

which implies that both consumers and firms are uniformly distributed over the integrated district.

It remains to determine the value of μ, which gives us that of k. To this end, we add (7.16) and (7.17) and substitute (7.19) into the resulting expression:

$$\alpha tk \int_{-b_0}^{x} \exp(-\alpha t(x - y)) \, dy$$
$$= k + 2 \int_{-b_1}^{-b_0} \exp(-\alpha t(x - y)) \, dy \quad x \in [-b_0, b_0].$$

Integrating yields

$$\exp(-\alpha tx)[\alpha tk \exp(-\alpha tb_0) + 2\exp(-\alpha tb_0) - 2\exp(-\alpha tb_1)]$$
$$= 0, \qquad x \in [-b_0, b_0]$$

which holds provided that

$$\alpha tk \exp(-\alpha tb_0) + 2\exp(-\alpha tb_0) - 2\exp(-\alpha tb_1) = 0$$

or

$$\exp \alpha t(b_1 - b_0) = 1/2\mu. \quad (7.20)$$

Therefore, we must determine b_0^*, b_1^*, and μ simultaneously.

The population constraints imply that

$$M = 2b_0^* m^*(x) = 2b_0^* \mu \quad (7.21)$$
$$N = 2b_0^* n^*(x) + 2(b_1^* - b_0^*) = 2b_0^*(1 - \mu) + 2(b_1^* - b_0^*). \quad (7.22)$$

Taking the logarithm of (7.20) and solving for $b_1^* - b_0^*$, solving (7.21) for b_0^*, and substituting the results in (7.22), we obtain

$$-\frac{2}{\alpha t}\log 2\mu = N - \frac{1-\mu}{\mu}M$$

which is equivalent to

$$\frac{M}{\mu} = M + N + \frac{2}{\alpha t}\log 2\mu. \tag{7.23}$$

Because $b_1^* - b_0^* > 0$, it follows from (7.20) that μ must be positive and smaller than $1/2$. It can then readily be verified that (7.23) has a single solution less than $1/2$ if and only if $N > M$, that is, the total amount of land used by consumers exceeds the one used by firms. In this case, firms are agglomerated because this configuration offers the highest accessibility to consumers. Once μ is determined, one may obtain k, b_0^*, and b_1^*, and hence U^* and π^*.

When $N = M$, $\mu = 1/2$ is the only solution of (7.23), which means that all stores and households are integrated in a single district.

Finally, it is easy to see that the case in which all consumers are located in the central district $[-b_0, b_0]$ surrounded by the business sections arises when $M > N$. In other words, when the total amount of land used by consumers is smaller than the one used by stores, the former are agglomerated whereas the latter are distributed over a wider domain. The mass of varieties is large enough for all consumers to be located in the central locations together with some stores.

To sum up, we have shown the following:

Proposition 7.1. *There exists a unique spatial equilibrium. At this equilibrium, firms and households form an integrated city such that*

(i) When $M < N$, all stores are concentrated into a central district with a constant density smaller than $1/2$, whereas the remaining consumers reside in the two adjacent areas.
(ii) When $M > N$, all consumers are concentrated into a central district with a constant density smaller than $1/2$, whereas the remaining stores are located in the two surrounding segments.
(iii) When $M = N$, the city is formed by an integrated district where the common density is $1/2$.

In other words, the same area is occupied by both stores and households because of their mutual attraction.[4] Stores do not exclusively use the whole central district, for otherwise firms near the center ($x = 0$) would be (much) less attractive than stores situated at the district fringes ($x = -b$ and $x = b$)

[4] Observe that Papageorgiou and Thisse (1985) also show the emergence of the agglomeration of firms and households in a related model, but with a finite number of locations.

because of the sharp decrease in their own demand (see [7.5]). The area around the city center is very attractive for consumers like to distribute their purchases among stores, thus endowing these locations with the highest accessibility to symmetrically distributed retailers.

The share of each group inside the integrated district, however, varies with the parameters α and t. Specifically, it can be shown from (7.23) that the density of stores decreases as α or t rises. In other words, the packing of stores is denser when varieties are more differentiated, when transportation is cheaper, or both.[5] The reason is that, in both cases, the demand field $q^*(x, y)$ falls less sharply with distance, inducing firms to get closer to the center where the accessibility is the highest. By contrast, when varieties are very close substitutes, the equilibrium price is slightly above marginal cost and the land rent is almost flat and close to zero. Consumers now buy very little from stores not located in their close vicinity, so that total transportation costs in the economy are also very low. In the limit, when $\alpha \to \infty$ consumers buy only from stores located at the same place as them (backyard capitalism) or refrain from buying the differentiated product.

7.2.2 The Optimality of a Mixed Downtown

We now move to the characterization of the first best optimum where there are N consumers and M firms. As in Chapters 3 and 6, we consider the optimal solution in which the utility level U^* is achieved for the N consumers through minimizing social cost. The decision variables are the consumer density, $n(x)$, the firm density, $m(x)$, the demand density of a consumer at $x \in X$ for the differentiated product, $q(x, \cdot)$, and the consumption of the numéraire by a consumer, $z(x)$, at each x. Then, the corresponding total cost is:

$$C = \int_X \left[\int_X q(x, y)(c + t\,|x - y|)\, m(y)\, \mathrm{d}y \right] n(x)\, \mathrm{d}x + \int_X z(x) n(x)\, \mathrm{d}x \tag{7.24}$$

which is to be minimized subject to the constraints:

$$\int_X u[q(x, y)] m(y)\, \mathrm{d}y + z(x) = U^* \quad \text{for all } x \text{ such that } n(x) > 0 \tag{7.25}$$

$$m(x) + n(x) \leq 1 \qquad x \in X \tag{7.26}$$

$$\int_X n(x)\, \mathrm{d}x = N \qquad \int_X m(y)\, \mathrm{d}y = M \tag{7.27}$$

plus the standard nonnegativity constraints. This is equivalent to maximizing $S = NY - C$ subject to the same constraints. Solving (7.25) with respect to

[5] The latter result is in line with what we have seen in Chapter 6.

$z(x)$, substituting the solution in (7.24), and using (7.27), we may rewrite S as follows:

$$S = \int_X \left\{ \int_X [u[q(x,y)] - q(x,y)(c + t|x-y|)]\, m(y)\, dy \right\} n(x)\, dx + N(Y - U^*) \tag{7.28}$$

subject to (7.26)–(7.27).

The bracketed term in (7.28) may be maximized with respect to each $q(x, y)$. Under (7.4), this yields:

$$q^o(x,y) = \alpha\beta \exp -\alpha(c + t|x-y|) \qquad x, y \in X. \tag{7.29}$$

Comparing (7.4) and (7.29), as expected, we find that the optimal consumption is given by the equilibrium consumption when $p(y) = c$. Substituting (7.29) into (7.28), we obtain:

$$S = \gamma_1 \int_X \int_X m(y) n(x) \exp(-\alpha t|x-y|)\, dy dx + N(Y - U^*) \tag{7.30}$$

where $\gamma_1 \equiv \beta \exp(-\alpha c)$. The double integral stands for the sum across consumers of the indirect utility derived from the differentiated product priced at marginal cost. Since $N(Y - U^*)$ is a constant, our problem amounts to maximizing:

$$\gamma \int_X \int_X m(y) n(x) \exp(-\alpha|x-y|)\, dy dx$$

with respect to $m(\cdot)$ and $n(\cdot)$ subject to (7.26)–(7.27), where $\gamma \equiv \gamma_1 e$.

Applying the maximum principle of optimal control theory shows that a multiplier function $R^o(x)$ associated with (7.26) and two multipliers U^o and π^o associated with the constraints (7.27) exist such that the following conditions hold for the optimal densities $m^o(\cdot)$ and $n^o(\cdot)$:

$$R^o(x) = \max\left\{ \gamma \int_X m^o(y) \exp(-\alpha t|x-y|)\, dy - U^o, \; \gamma \int_X n^o(y) \exp(-\alpha t|x-y|)\, dy - \pi^o \right\} \tag{7.31}$$

$$\gamma \int_X n^o(y) \exp(-\alpha t|x-y|)\, dy - \pi^o = R^o(x) \quad \text{if } m^o(x) > 0 \tag{7.32}$$

$$\gamma \int_X m^o(y) \exp(-\alpha t|x-y|)\, dy - U^o = R^o(x) \quad \text{if } n^o(x) > 0 \tag{7.33}$$

$$m^o(x) + n^o(x) = 1 \quad \text{if } R^o(x) > 0 \tag{7.34}$$

in addition to (7.26) and (7.27).

Intuitively, these conditions can be explained as follows. In our setting, there are three activities: consumption, production, and agriculture. If we marginally increase the number of consumers at x, this leads to an increase in the objective function by an amount given by $\gamma \int_X m^o(y) \exp(-\alpha t|x - y|) \, dy$. However, this incremental benefit must be reduced by the value of the multiplier associated with the consumer population constraint. The same argument holds, mutatis mutandis, if we marginally increase the number of firms at x. Because one consumer or one firm uses one unit of land (7.31) means that $R^o(x)$ is equal to the highest marginal value of land at x. Condition (7.32) means that firms are located at x provided that their marginal value of land is the highest one; the same applies to (7.33). Finally, (7.34) says that all the land at x is used by firms, households, or both when their marginal value of land is positive.

Clearly, we do not change the optimal densities $n^o(x)$ and $m^o(x)$ when we replace U^o with $U^o - Y$ in (7.31)–(7.33). Then, we see that the optimality conditions (7.31)–(7.34) are identical to the equilibrium conditions (7.11)–(7.14) when U^o is replaced by U^* and π^o by π^*. Consequently, *the equilibrium land use pattern is identical to the optimum one.*

This is a rather surprising result because firms price above marginal cost. Note, however, that there is no substitution between land and the two consumption goods, and thus pricing the differentiated good above marginal cost generates no distortion in the relative consumption of these three goods. Furthermore, the markup $1/\alpha$ is constant. These two properties explain why the market and socially optimal land patterns are identical, up to a constant factor. However, this no longer holds when the densities of households and firms are endogenous through the number of floors made available at each location (Liu and Fujita 1991). Indeed, land and the other two consumption goods are now substitutable.

It is more surprising that the equilibrium land use pattern ceases to be efficient when firms are constrained to price at marginal cost. Indeed, because profits are now zero at all locations, firms are indifferent across locations, and thus their bid rent curve is flat and equal to zero. In this case, the equilibrium pattern involves a residential area integrated with some firms surrounded by two business sections. Regardless of the values of N and M, the density of firms in the integrated area is always lower than at the optimum. Accordingly, pricing at marginal cost results in a more dispersed configuration of firms.

That the land use pattern is not optimal when firms price at marginal cost does not contradict the first theorem of welfare economics. Indeed, although now all prices are given to the agents, our equilibrium concept is not competitive. To find his utility-maximizing location, each consumer must know what the entire distribution of shopping opportunities will be (see [7.7]). Similarly, to find its profit-maximizing location, each firm must know what will be its aggregate demand, which depends itself on the whole consumer distribution over space (see [7.8]). However, there is no price accounting for the difference in the accessibility of one agent to the rest of the economy. Therefore, the information needed by the agents to be able to *always* choose their optimal location goes beyond the usual type of information conveyed by the price system. What is here required on each agent's part has a game-theoretic flavor that brings us far away from the competitive paradigm. This shows, once more, that a spatial economy cannot be completely described by a system of competitive markets.

This negative conclusion has powerful implications. It is the discrepancy between price and marginal cost that allows firms to compete with other agents on the land market and to sustain the agglomeration of firms. When price equals marginal cost, the firms' incentive to locate close to consumers vanishes. Not surprisingly, therefore, the market outcome is too dispersed because there is no longer any agglomeration force. Put in a different way, firms' markup must be positive for their agglomeration to arise at the market outcome.

7.3 OLIGOPOLY AND THE AGGLOMERATION OF FIRMS

7.3.1 Spatial Competition with Preference for Variety

In the previous section, we have assumed a continuum of firms, thus implying that there is no strategic interaction on the product market. This turns out to be a convenient framework to study the working of the product market in relation to other markets such as the land market. However, the monopolistic competition model fails to account for the strategic aspects that spatial proximity brings about (see Section 7.4.5).

There is an old tradition in location theory, going back at least to Hotelling (1929), which suggests that spatial competition leads to the agglomeration of firms even when consumers are dispersed. In the typical example of two retailers selling a homogeneous product, each firm gains by establishing near its competitor on the more populated side of the market. The only equilibrium is then obtained when both firms are located at the median of the consumer distribution where no additional gains are possible provided that transport costs increase with distance. In the case of a uniform density, the median becomes the market center. Hence, two retailers competing for clients choose to minimize their spatial differentiation.[6]

The proponents of this approach, however, overlooked the fact that firms selling a homogeneous product always want to locate far apart to avoid the devastating effects of price war. Indeed, when (at least) two firms are located back to back, they get trapped into a Bertrand situation in which they find themselves with zero operating profits. This cannot be an equilibrium because

[6] Here, consumers' locations are fixed; hence, there is no mutual attraction through the interplay of consumers' and firms' locations. Introducing a land market would strengthen the tendency toward agglomeration (Fujita and Thisse 1991).

firms could restore positive profits by moving away unilaterally and exploiting the monopoly power each firm has on the consumers situated in its close vicinity. For example, when transport costs are quadratic in distance and consumers are evenly distributed over $X = [0, 1]$, the equilibrium prices of any second stage subgame decrease with the interfirm distance, whereas the equilibrium locations of the first stage game are given by $y_1^* = 0$ and $y_2^* = 1$ (d'Aspremont, Gabszewicz, and Thisse 1979).

This extreme spatial dispersion is the result of a trade-off in which price competition pushes retailers away from each other whereas competition for market area tends to pull them together. To illustrate how this trade-off works, let π_1^* be firm 1's profit evaluated at the equilibrium prices $p_i^*(y_1, y_2)$ corresponding to the location pair $y_1 < y_2$. Then, because $\partial\pi_1/\partial p_1 = 0$, we have

$$\frac{d\pi_1^*}{dy_1} = \frac{\partial\pi_1}{\partial p_2}\frac{\partial p_2^*}{\partial y_1} + \frac{\partial\pi_1^*}{\partial y_1}.$$

In general, the terms on the right-hand side of this expression can be signed as follows. The first one corresponds to the *strategic effect* (the desire to relax price competition) and is expressed by the impact that a change in firm 1's location has on price competition. Because goods are spatially differentiated, they are substitutes and thus $\partial\pi_1/\partial p_2$ is positive; because goods become closer substitutes when y_1 increases, $\partial p_2^*/\partial y_1$ is negative. Hence, the first term is negative. The second term, which corresponds to the *market area effect*, is positive. Consequently, the impact of reducing the interfirm distance upon firms' profits is undetermined. However, when firms are close enough, the first term always dominates the second, and thus firms always want to be separated in the geographical space. This implies that the principle of minimum differentiation ceases to hold when firms are allowed to compete in prices. The tendency for firms to choose distinct locations has been confirmed by many works, and has led Tirole (1988) to call it the *principle of differentiation*. This principle stresses the fact that price competition is a strong dispersion force sufficient to destroy agglomeration in standard models of spatial competition.

However, these negative results do not kill the subject. It should be kept in mind, indeed, that they are based on an extreme price sensitivity of consumers: if two retailers are located side by side with identical prices, a small price reduction of one firm will attract all the customers. Such extreme behavior seems unwarranted. When the product is differentiated and when consumers like product variety, the aggregate response to a price cut will not be so abrupt because the quality of product match matters to consumers. Product differentiation then alleviates price competition. This modification of the spatial competition model, which has been developed by de Palma et al. (1985), has two major implications. First, if consumers' preference for variety becomes sufficiently large, firms' demand functions are smoothed sufficiently even when they are located close together so that a price equilibrium in pure strategies exists. Second, under the same condition, retailers tend to agglomerate at the market center to have the best access to the market, as suggested by Hotelling. Price competition at the center is relaxed because of the differentiation among retailers, which gives them market power even when they are agglomerated. As we see, agglomeration can then be shown to be a Nash equilibrium when transportation costs are low with respect to product differentiation.

Hence, we follow the main idea of the previous section by assuming that firms sell a differentiated product and that consumers like variety. Nevertheless, unlike before, we consider a *finite* number M of firms behaving strategically. We will also follow the Hotelling tradition by assuming that the consumer distribution over the location space $X = [0, 1]$ is fixed. For example, when each consumer uses one unit of land, the consumer distribution is uniform over X. Like Hotelling again, it is supposed that firms do not consume land. As in Section 7.2, the utility of a consumer is additive:

$$U(z; q_i, i = 1, \ldots, M) = \sum_{i=1}^{M} u(q_i) + z.$$

The main difference with (7.1) is that we have here a finite number of firms instead of a continuum. We saw in Section 7.2 that there is no direct substitution among varieties. To introduce this effect explicitly in a simple way, we suppose that each consumer buys a fixed number $\overline{q} > 0$ of units of the differentiated product per unit of time (e.g., a given number of restaurant dinners per month):

$$\sum_{i=1}^{M} q_i = \overline{q}. \tag{7.35}$$

Such a constraint implies that firms compete for clients within a market of a given size. Here also, we suppose that the utility U has an entropy-form:[7]

$$\begin{aligned} U &= \sum_{i=1}^{M} q_i - \sum_{i=1}^{M} \frac{q_i}{\alpha} \log q_i + z \qquad && \text{if } \sum_{i=1}^{M} q_i = \overline{q} \\ &= -\infty && \text{otherwise.} \end{aligned} \tag{7.36}$$

As usual, the budget constraint of a consumer at $x \in X$ is:

$$\sum_{i=1}^{M} (p_i + t\,|x - y_i|)\, q_i + z = Y$$

[7] Because the total consumption of the differentiated product is constant and the same across consumers, we may set $\beta = 0$. Without loss of generality, the utility U is multiplied by α. It is then easy to see that (7.4) and (7.36) are equivalent.

where p_i is the (mill) price selected by firm i selling variety i and $y_i \in X$ the location chosen by this firm.

Using standard optimization techniques, we get:

$$q_i^*(x) = \frac{\exp -\alpha (p_i + t|x - y_i|)}{\sum_{j=1}^{M} \exp -\alpha \left(p_j + t\left|x - y_j\right|\right)} \bar{q} \qquad x, y_i \in X \tag{7.37}$$

which, unlike (7.5), depends not only upon the firm's price p_i and location y_i but also upon the prices and the locations chosen by all its rivals ($j \neq i$). Indeed, (7.35) imposes that the total consumption of the differentiated product is fixed so that, because the number of firms is finite, the consumption of a variety impacts on the consumption of the others.

Unlike the monopolistic competition model in which price elasticity is location independent and equal to αp_i, price elasticity is now location dependent because it equals $\alpha p_i[1 - P_i(x)]$, where

$$P_i(x) \equiv \frac{\exp -\alpha (p_i + t|x - y_i|)}{\sum_{j=1}^{M} \exp -\alpha \left(p_j + t\left|x - y_j\right|\right)}$$

is known as the *multinomial logit* (McFadden 1974). It is assumed here that each firm is aware of this fact when selecting its price and location. As a consequence, there is strategic interaction between firms in both prices and locations. As is seen, this leads to a more involved and richer pattern of interdependence among firms.

To develop some insights about this interaction pattern, we first discuss the special case of two firms ($M = 2$) located at $0 < y_1 < y_2 < 1$ and pricing at the same level p. Then, it can readily be verified that

$$\begin{aligned} q_1^*(x) &= \frac{\bar{q}}{1 + \exp - \alpha t(y_2 - y_1)} && x \in [0, y_1] \\ &= \frac{\bar{q}}{1 + \exp - \alpha t[y_2 - y_1 + 2(y_1 - x)]} && x \in [y_1, y_2] \\ &= \frac{\bar{q}}{1 + \exp \alpha t(y_2 - y_1)} && x \in [y_2, 1]. \end{aligned}$$

Consider Figure 7.2 in which $q_1^*(x)$ is described as a function of the consumer location. We see that the demand of variety 1 is continuous over the entire location space X, constant in the two hinterlands $[0, y_1]$ and $[y_2, 1]$, and decreasing in the contention segment $[y_1, y_2]$. Stated differently, the demand to retailer 1 is highest over its hinterland, decreasing as x moves away from y_1 to get closer to y_2, and lowest over its competitor's hinterland. Furthermore, it is easy to check that $q_1^*(x)$ is concave on $[y_1, \bar{y}]$ and convex on $[\bar{y}, y_2]$, where $\bar{y}$ is the middle point of the two suppliers. Finally, $q_1^*(x)$ exceeds $q_2^*(x)$ if and only if x is closer to retailer 1 than to retailer 2. At $x = \bar{y}$, both demands are equal to $\bar{q}/2$. The details of this demand pattern agree with intuition and experience.

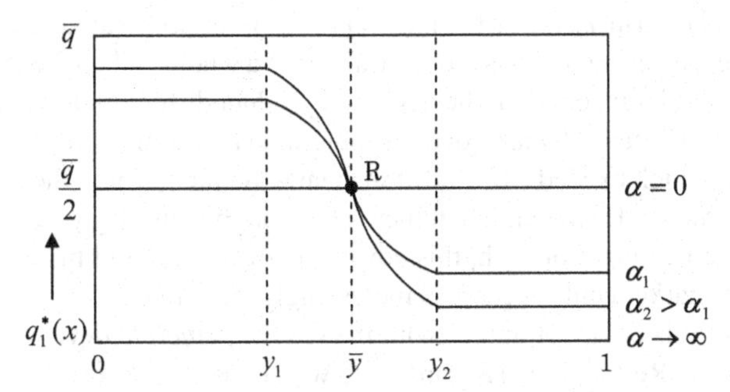

Figure 7.2. The equilibrium demand pattern for store 1 when consumers love variety.

When the degree of differentiation, measured by $1/\alpha$, increases, the quantity $q_1^*(x)$ shifts downward (upward) on the left (right) of $\bar{y}$. This occurs because consumers value more product diversity and are, therefore, less sensitive to spatial proximity. In the limit, when $\alpha = 0$, distance becomes inessential and $q_1^*(x) = 1/2$ for all $x \in X$. On the other hand, when $\alpha \to \infty$ (the product is homogeneous), $q_1^*(x) = 1$ for $x \in [0, \bar{y})$ and 0 for $x \in (\bar{y}, 1]$, that is, each consumer patronizes the closer retailer; we fall back on Hotelling's original model.

Consider now Figure 7.3 where a single firm locates at y_1 and $(M - 1)$ firms at y_2. It is straightforward to show that:

$$\begin{aligned} q_1^*(x) &= \frac{\overline{q}}{1 + (M-1)\exp -\alpha t(y_2 - y_1)} & x \in [0, y_1] \\ &= \frac{\overline{q}}{1 + (M-1)\exp -\alpha t[y_2 - y_1 + 2(y_1 - x)]} & x \in [y_1, y_2] \\ &= \frac{\overline{q}}{1 + (M-1)\exp \alpha t(y_2 - y_1)} & x \in [y_2, 1]. \end{aligned}$$

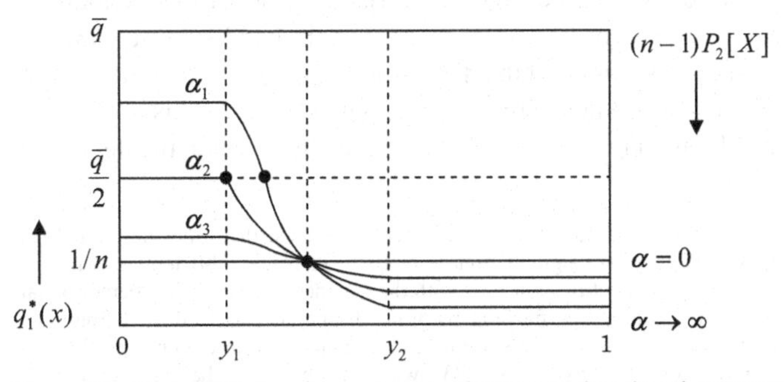

Figure 7.3. The equilibrium demand pattern for store 1 when the other stores are agglomerated at the market center.

Evidently, the demand to firm 1 falls as the number of firms agglomerated at y_2 rises, thus making the clustering of firms more attractive as a whole. When the number of firms at y_2 is not large, or when the degree of product differentiation is not high, or both, retailer 1 has a demand over its hinterland and some part of the contention segment, which exceeds the one at the market center (where the other firms are agglomerated). However, when there are enough firms at y_2, or varieties are differentiated enough, or both, this advantage of the isolated firm tends to vanish, and the market center becomes increasingly attractive.

It is worth noting that this behavior agrees with the *gravity principle* developed in retailing models by Reilly (1931) according to which distance between places is an impediment to interaction whereas the size of a marketplace makes it more attractive to consumers. This principle has been extended to the description of actual trip patterns by geographers and regional scientists and has generated a vast and rich literature known as *spatial interaction theory*.[8]

As usual, firm i's profits are:

$$\pi_i(\mathbf{p}; \mathbf{y}) = (p_i - c) \int_0^1 q_i^*(x) \mathrm{d}x$$

where $q_i^*(x)$ is given by (7.37). Assume for the moment that all prices p_i are equal and fixed. Clearly, in the present case maximizing profits amounts to maximizing demand. It can be shown that the agglomeration of M firms at $1/2$ is a Nash equilibrium if and only if

$$1/\alpha t \geq (1 - 2/M)/2. \tag{7.38}$$

Hence, for given values of α and t, increasing the number of firms makes the tendency toward central agglomeration weaker. Indeed, when M rises, the elasticity decreases at each point (since $P_i(x)$ decreases at all x) and the difference between elasticity at the agglomeration and elasticity at a noncentral location increases. As a result, the benefits of exploiting a local market may well exceed those associated with a central location.

However, such an effect can be offset by a rise in product differentiation, a fall in transportation cost, or both. Because the right-hand side of (7.38) is bounded above by $1/2$, it is apparent that the central agglomeration is always an equilibrium for any large number of retailers as long as $\alpha t \leq 2$. This is reminiscent of the results obtained in Section 6.4 for "small cities" when the degree of

[8] Very much like in Newtonian physics, it has long been recognized that cities and countries interact according to forces that have a gravitational nature: the intensity of bilateral interactions rises with the size of the spatial entities but falls with the distance that separates them. Spatial interaction theory aims to explain such movements of goods and people. To this end, regional scientists and geographers have developed several models, ranging from the entropy (Wilson 1967) to the gravity and logit models (Anas 1983), which has proven to be very effective in predicting different types of flows. By ignoring for a long time this body of research, spatial economists have missed a fundamental ingredient of the space-economy.

product differentiation plays the role of the intensity of communication between firms.

For agglomeration to arise, varieties must be differentiated enough. Consider, indeed, the extreme case in which all varieties are perfect substitutes. Then, if $M > 2$, any clustering of firms at the market center (or somewhere else) is not an equilibrium. This occurs because any firm can always substantially increase its sales by locating slightly away from the cluster (on the larger side of the market if the cluster is not established at the market center). Because the product is homogeneous, all consumers closer to the deviating firm than to the cluster will purchase from this firm so that this one can guarantee to itself a market share equal to $1/2 - \varepsilon$ instead of getting $1/M$ in the cluster. Nevertheless, the benefits of such a deviation decrease as varieties become increasingly differentiated because consumers ill-matched to the variety supplied by the deviating firm will find it advantageous to go their way as far as the cluster.

For the more general case in which firms compete in both prices and locations, we have the following:

Proposition 7.2. *Consider M firms competing in prices and locations. If $\alpha t \leq 2$, then $p_i^* = c + M/\alpha(M-1)$ and $y_i^* = 1/2$, $i = 1, \ldots, M$, is a Nash equilibrium of the simultaneous game.*

The structure of the proof is as follows (details are given in appendix B). When all firms are agglomerated, it is easy to see that there is a unique price equilibrium at which the common price is $p^* = c + M/\alpha(M-1)$. Assume now that $M - 1$ firms are set up at the market center and charge p^*, whereas firm 1 is located at $y_1 < 1/2$, and set $p_1 \geq c$. Whatever the value of p_1, if $\alpha t \leq 2$, firm 1's profit is increasing in y_1 over $[0, 1/2)$, and so firm 1 wants to join the others at the market center. Because p^* is the only price equilibrium when all firms are together, firm 1's profit is greatest when $p_1 = p^*$ and $y_1 = 1/2$. As in the preceding section, we therefore see that a high degree of product differentiation, a low transportation rate, or both, sustain the agglomeration of the M retailers at the market center. It can also be shown that the market center is the only agglomerated location equilibrium.[9]

To highlight the role of product differentiation, we show that a Nash equilibrium never exists when firms produce a homogeneous good and choose prices and locations simultaneously. Consider, indeed, any two firms and suppose that such an equilibrium exists. Whatever the market configuration, the firm earning (weakly) smaller profits could strictly increase its profits by locating at the same place as the other firm and slightly undercutting its price. By doing this,

[9] Assume that consumers are distributed over a finite set of loctions connected by a transportation network. Then, if αt is sufficiently large, all firms set up at the point minimizing the sum of distances to the locations, weighted by the number of consumers living at each vertex of the network (de Palma et al 1989). This confirms Hotelling's idea that firms are attracted by the location with the highest accessibility.

the undercutting firm captures its rival's clientele without losing its previous market segment. It is therefore strictly better off, a contradiction to the equilibrium condition. This shows how important is the assumption that firms supply differentiated products. Furthermore, Ben-Akiva, de Palma, and Thisse (1989) and De Fraja and Norman (1993) obtain results similar to Proposition 7.2 when consumers have alternative preferences for differentiated products. We may then safely conclude that the existence of an agglomerated equilibrium under sufficient product differentiation is robust against alternative specifications of demand.

When transport costs are low, the benefits of geographical separation are reduced and prices are lower. Firms might then choose to reconstruct their profit margins by differentiating their products in terms of some nongeographical characteristics that are tangible or intangible. Stated differently, product differentiation is substituted for geographical dispersion (this is shown in a model of spatial competition by Irmen and Thisse 1998). In this case, firms no longer fear the effects of price competition (the centrifugal force is weakened by product differentiation) and strive to be as close as possible to the consumers with whom the matching is the best. Because these consumers are spread all over the market space, firms set up at the market center and, therefore, minimize their geographical differentiation. Put differently, the principle of minimum differentiation holds under sufficient heterogeneity.

Consider now the implications of the logit model (7.37) for the sequential Hotelling duopoly model. Anderson et al. (1992, chapter 9) have shown the existence and the uniqueness of a price equilibrium for any location pair when αt is sufficiently small. Using this price equilibrium, these authors were then able to study the location game by appealing to numerical analysis. The following results emerge (they are depicted in Figure 7.4). As $1/\alpha t$ rises from 0 to 0.30, there is no location equilibrium (in pure strategies). For $0.30 < 1/\alpha t < 0.76$, there is a symmetric dispersed equilibrium that initially entails increasing geographical separation of firms. However, when $1/\alpha t$ goes beyond some threshold (around 0.50), the geographical separation starts to decrease. For $0.76 < 1/\alpha t < 1.47$, an agglomerated equilibrium exists along with the dispersed one; however, the former is unstable whereas the latter is stable. Finally, for $1/\alpha t \geq 1.47$, there is a unique equilibrium that involves central agglomeration.

The intuition behind these results is pretty straightforward. An arbitrarily small amount of differentiation is not sufficient to restore existence because consumers' shopping behavior, though smooth, remains very sharp (i.e., close to the standard $0 - 1$ behavior). When existence is guaranteed, firms' market areas overlap, thus making price competition so fierce that firms want to move apart. Beyond some threshold, the product differentiation effect tends to dominate the price competition effect, and firms set up closer to the market center because price competition is relaxed. Finally, for a sufficiently large degree of differentiation, the market area effect becomes predominant and the

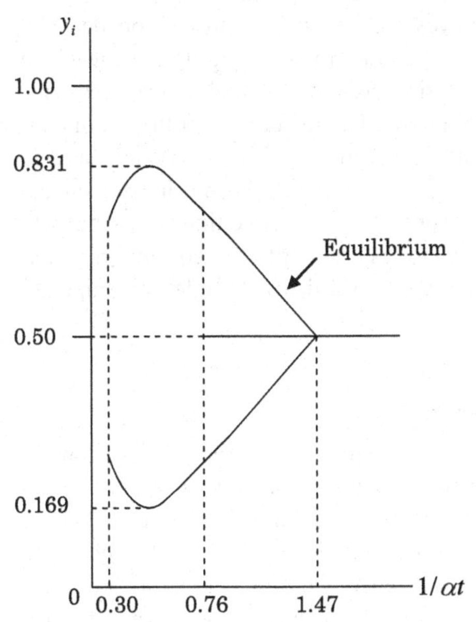

Figure 7.4. Firms' equilibrium locations when consumers love variety.

agglomeration of sellers is the market outcome, as in the nonprice competition context. In both the simultaneous and sequential games, the message is the same: agglomeration arises when price competition is relaxed through sufficient product differentiation.

Remark. Hotelling's paper is really a path-breaking contribution to general economic theory, not just to spatial economics. First, one of its main innovations is the use of a two-stage game to model the process of spatial competition: in the first stage, retailers choose their location non-cooperatively; in the second, these locations being publicly observed, firms select their selling price. The use of this sequential procedure means that firms anticipate the consequences of their locational choices on their subsequent choices of prices, thus conferring to the model an implicit dynamic structure. The game is solved by backward induction. For an arbitrary pair of locations, Hotelling started by solving the price subgame corresponding to the second stage. The resulting equilibrium prices are introduced into the profit functions, which then depend only upon the locations chosen by the firms. These functions are the payoffs that firms will maximize during the first-stage game. Such an approach anticipates by several decades the concept of subgame perfect Nash equilibrium introduced by Selten in the 1960s.

Even though the individual purchase decision is discontinuous – a consumer buying only from one firm – Hotelling finds it reasonable to suppose that firms' aggregated demands are continuous with respect to prices. Supposing that each consumer is negligible solves the apparent contradiction between discontinuity at the individual level and continuity at the aggregated level. In other words, when consumers are continuously distributed across locations, aggregated demands are "often" continuous. The hypothesis of the continuum that had been popularized much later by Aumann (1964) is found here to represent the idea that competitive agents have a negligible impact on the market outcome. However, Hotelling considers a richer setting involving both "small" agents whose individual behavior is competitive – consumers – and "big" agents whose behavior is strategic because firms are able to manipulate the market outcome.

7.3.2 Is the Agglomeration of Firms Efficient?

The welfare analysis reveals some unexpected results. Because consumers' locations are fixed, the utility level across locations may not be the same, and we cannot minimize total costs anymore. At the optimum, prices are set equal to the common marginal cost c so that consumers' well-being depends only upon the firms' locations ($\mathbf{y}$). In the homogeneous product case, total costs are simply given by aggregate transportation costs. However, once we introduce differentiation across varieties, consumers no longer patronize the nearest firm on each trip (recall that all prices are equal to c) because they now benefit from intrinsic differentiation between shops. In this context, one needs a more general approach accounting for both distance and product diversity effects. The appropriate measure is the indirect utility. For a consumer at x, it is obtained by introducing the quantities (7.37) in the utility (7.36):

$$V(x;\mathbf{y}) = \frac{\bar{q}}{\alpha} \ln \left[\sum_{i=1}^{M} \exp -\alpha \left(c + t \left| x - y_i \right| \right) \right].$$

Consumer surplus is defined by the sum of the individual indirect utilities:

$$S(\mathbf{y}) = \int_0^1 V(x;\mathbf{y}) \mathrm{d}x. \tag{7.39}$$

Somewhat surprisingly, the optimum involves the agglomeration of firms as long as $\alpha t \leq 2$. In what follows, we give a proof for the case in which $M = 2$. It is intuitively plausible (and it can be shown) that the pair of optimal locations is symmetric. Hence, we may set $y_1 = 1/2 - a$ and $y_2 = 1/2 + a$ and rewrite the consumer surplus (7.39) as follows:

$$\begin{aligned} S(a) = & \frac{2}{\alpha} \int_{1/2}^{1/2+a} \ln \left[\exp -\alpha t (x - 1/2 + a) + \exp -\alpha t (1/2 + a - x) \right] \mathrm{d}x \\ & + \frac{2}{\alpha} \int_{1/2+a}^{1} \ln \left[\exp -\alpha t (x - 1/2 + a) + \exp -\alpha t (x - 1/2 - a) \right] \mathrm{d}x. \end{aligned}$$

After some routine manipulations, we obtain:

$$S(a) = -t\,[1/4 - a(1-2a)] + \frac{2}{\alpha}\int_{1/2+a}^{1} \ln[1 + \exp -2\alpha t(x - 1/2)]\, \mathrm{d}x$$
$$+ \frac{2}{\alpha}(1/2 - a)\ln[1 + \exp 2\alpha t a]. \qquad (7.40)$$

Differentiating (7.40) with respect to a leads to

$$1 - 4a - \exp(-2\alpha t a) = 0. \qquad (7.41)$$

Evidently, $a = 0$ is always a root of this equation. A necessary and sufficient condition for (7.41) to have a strictly positive root is that the derivative of $\exp(-2\alpha t a)$ must be smaller than the derivative of $1 - 4a$, both evaluated at $a = 0$. This is equivalent to $\alpha t > 2$. Totally differentiating (7.41) with respect to a and alpha and using the second order condition, we get:

$$\frac{da^*}{d\alpha} > 0.$$

Hence, as the degree of product differentiation rises (α decreases), we see that the optimal distance $2a^*$ between the two retailers falls. Because distance matters less and less to consumers relative to preference for variety, moving the retailers toward more central locations becomes increasingly desirable; this allows one to increase the accessibility of consumers dispersed over the entire segment to more variety.

In contrast, when $\alpha t \leq 2$, the first derivative of $S(a)$ is negative for all admissible values of a, thus implying that $S(a)$ is maximized at $a = 0$. In other words, when the varieties are differentiated enough, the two retailers must be located at the market center to maximize the consumer surplus. This occurs because the retailer's attributes dominate the transportation factor sufficiently to render the market center desirable from the consumer's standpoint.

It remains to deal with profits. As usual, we assume free entry. Anderson et al. (1992, chapter 7) have shown that the optimal number of firms is equal to the equilibrium number minus 1. Therefore, we may conclude that the formation and size of the cluster of retailers at the market center are (almost) socially optimal when product differentiation is strong enough ($\alpha t \leq 2$).

As noticed by Eaton and Lipsey (1979, 21), "it is part of conventional wisdom of economists to refer to Hotelling and to the socially wasteful nature of clustering whenever local clusters are encountered in the real world." Our results do not confirm this view because we have just seen that the formation of clusters is socially desirable when varieties are differentiated enough, when transport costs are low enough, or both, that is, $\alpha t \leq 2$. The conventional wisdom is wrong here because it ignores the fact that firms sell differentiated products whereas consumers have heterogeneous tastes. However, when $\alpha t > 2$, it is not optimal to group firms anymore, and thus high transportation costs result in separate locations. In this case, Anderson et al. (1992, chapter 9) have provided several examples suggesting that the market may well provide insufficient geographical dispersion.

Note, finally, the following relationship with the model of Section 7.2. When firms' land consumption shrinks to zero, there is only one equilibrium involving the agglomeration of all firms at the city center. This opens the door to the possibility of extending the present model by adding a land market (as in Section 4.5.3). Furthermore, the common equilibrium price (given in Proposition 7.2) is identical to (7.6) when $M \to \infty$, suggesting that the monopolistic competition model of Section 7.2 can be viewed as the asymptotic version of the spatial competition model discussed here.

7.3.3 Shipping Goods and Agglomeration

Shipping models come from a different tradition that derives from the analysis of spatial price discrimination in an oligopolistic environment (local markets are segmented, whereas they are tied in shopping models). When products are delivered, the location of the customers is observable to the firms, which are then able to price discriminate across locations (this corresponds to third-degree price discrimination à la Pigou). Shipping models were initiated by Hoover (1937) and have been much developed in the 1980s and 1990s. Shopping and shipping models in spatial competition correspond to the standard distinction between integrated and segmented markets in international trade.

Consider the case in which firms compete in price schedules. This means that each firm announces for each location a *delivered price* at which it is willing to supply the corresponding customers (e.g., pizzerias). Then, discriminating firms always want to be located far apart when the product sold is homogeneous (Lederer and Hurter 1986). This is again because price competition at each consumer location is such a strong centrifugal force that firms are hurt by geographical proximity. However, for exactly the same reasons as those discussed in Section 7.3.1, discriminating oligopolists locate closer when they supply a product that is more differentiated (Anderson and de Palma 1988).

This tendency toward agglomeration is even stronger when firms compete in quantity schedules. Indeed, as shown by Anderson and Neven (1991), when the product is homogeneous, agglomeration at the market center is the unique equilibrium for any given number M of firms if $t \leq (1 - c)/M$, that is, if shipping costs are sufficiently low. Hence, although the product is homogeneous, firms do agglomerate because quantity-setting firms are less affected by competition, making the market area effect dominant.

However, when t goes beyond some threshold, the center is no longer an equilibrium: firms want to differentiate their locations in order to retain enough customers near the market endpoints. This new effect, called the market periphery effect, corresponds to a centrifugal force. It is present in any spatial competition model in which local demands are price sensitive. When transportation costs are low, this force is not strong enough to prevent the market area effect from dominating, thus leading to agglomeration. The opposite holds when transportation costs get higher: the market equilibrium involves gradual dispersion of producers. As in the shopping models both agglomerated and dispersed equilibria may coexist for some range of t (Gupta, Pal, and Sarkar 1997).

Accordingly, although shopping and shipping models have different aims and obey different incentive systems, it seems fair to say that they are governed by essentially the same centrifugal and centripetal forces, thus leading to similar locational patterns under similar conditions.

7.4 CONSUMERS' SEARCH AND THE CLUSTERING OF RETAILERS

When firms sell differentiated varieties, consumers are often unsure about which variety is offered where and at which price.[10] In many circumstances, the only way for consumers to find out which variety is on offer in a particular retailer is to visit this retailer and to pay the corresponding transportation cost. Indeed, it is hard to figure out how good the matching with a product is without seeing it. Collecting information by telephone may be helpful for prices but not for varieties. To compare alternatives before buying, consumers must undertake search among firms. Given the expense of gathering information, each consumer compares the cost of an additional bit of information with the expected gain in terms of expected surplus. In a spatial setting, both vary with the consumers' and firms' locations.[11]

Very much as consumers prefer a short commute to a long one, they prefer a short shopping trip to a long one, which introduces agglomeration effects among retailers. In such a context, when several retailers are located together, it is reasonable to assume that the typical consumer knows the location and the size of the shopping center formed by independent retailers but not its composition. Once the consumer arrives at the shopping center, the travel costs are sunk, and he can visit any retailer at a very low cost. In other words, each consumer visiting the cluster enjoys scope economies in search. On the other hand, the consumer must pay the transport cost to each isolated retailer he visits. Geographical clustering of retailers is therefore a particular means by which firms can facilitate consumer search. Indeed, a consumer is more likely to visit a cluster of retailers than an isolated one because of the higher probability he

[10] The model can be extended to the case in which consumers are also unsure about firms' prices when these are endogenous.

[11] One point needs clarification. We consider a static model in which consumers shop only once. This is of course a caricature of reality. Instead, one should think of an environment in which new consumers arise over time in different locations. Another interpretation is that shops change their goods from time to time, as in the case of fashion stores.

faces of finding a good match and a good price there. When firms realize this fact, each of them understands that it might be in its own interest to form a marketplace with others.

Matters are not that simple, however. As observed by Stahl (1982, 98),

> the aggregate demand observed at a market place increases with its size, as defined by the number of commodities offered there. Therefore, a seller, upon choosing a profit maximizing location, is confronted with the alternative either to establish a local monopoly with a small market area and a large share of consumers purchasing, by lack of variety, his variety; or to join other firms in a competitive marketplace with a large market area in which fetches the demand from only the small subset of consumers not substituting away towards the other alternatives available there.

In other words, when a firm considers the possibility of joining competitors within the same marketplace, it faces a trade-off between the following two effects: a negative competition effect and a positive market area effect, both being generated by the pooling of firms selling similar products.

In this section, we follow the analysis of Wolinsky (1983) and show how a cluster of firms may emerge as a Nash equilibrium when firms sell their varieties at a common fixed price. As in Section 7.3, the population of consumers is uniformly distributed along the segment $[0, 1]$. Product differentiation is modeled using a spatial setting à la Hotelling–Lancaster. More precisely, varieties of the same product are evenly distributed along a circle C of unit length, thus substituting a Lancasterian space of characteristics for the geographical space used in Section 4.5. The location r_i of firm i now stands for the position of its variety in the characteristic space C, the location r of a consumer for his ideal product, whereas the transportation cost $s|r - r_i|$ corresponds to the utility loss incurred for not consuming his ideal product, where $|r - r_i|$ stands for the length of the shorter arc between r and r_i. As a result, a consumer is now described by two parameters: his location x in the geographical space $[0, 1]$ and his ideal product r in the characteristics space C. The two distributions are supposed to be independent so that the distribution of consumer type (x, r) is uniform over the cylinder whose basis is C and height 1.

Nonconvexities in transportation are needed for the cluster to emerge here. The simplest form is to assume that consumers bear some positive fixed cost t_0 each time they make a separate trip because of the corresponding terminal conditions (e.g., parking, waiting time for a bus). This is certainly a reasonable assumption that we did not make earlier because the existence of a positive fixed cost in transportation has no impact on the results obtained so far inasmuch as consumers visit a *single* place each time they make a purchase. On the other hand, as is seen in Proposition 7.3, this cost turns out to be critical for the description of a consumer's search strategy. Furthermore, instead of considering $t|x - y|$ as the cost of a round trip between x and y, it now describes a one-way trip. This assumption is made because the return trip may differ from the initial trip. Hence, if consumers were to know which firm sells which variety, the indirect utility of a consumer of type (x, r) patronizing firm i would be given by

$$V_i(r, x) = Y - p + u - s|r - r_i| - 2(t_0 + t|x - y_i|)$$

where p is the common fixed price, s the marginal utility loss incurred for not consuming at one's ideal product (also called the matching cost), y_i firm i's endogenous location, and t_0 the fixed transport cost. However, although consumers are able to observe the location y_i of firm i, they do not observe the variety (r_i) it sells. For that, consumers must visit firm i and bear the corresponding travel cost.

Because we want a shopping center formed by all firms to be an equilibrium, it is sufficient to investigate the case in which $M - 1$ firms are located together at y_C, whereas the remaining firm (say firm M) is alone at $y_I \neq y_C$, and to show that this firm is better off by joining the cluster. For simplicity in notation, we set $\Delta \equiv |y_C - y_I| > 0$. In the case of such a configuration, the search plan of a consumer then consists of a decision made on the basis of two things: (i) where to start and (ii) when to stop the search.

A consumer has two possible plans: either he starts at the cluster and, possibly, continues to the isolated firm, or proceeds the other way round. In both cases, the consumer adopts a sequential search with a fixed stopping rule. Because prices are fixed and identical across retailers, the only element that matters in the consumers' decision whether to continue a search is the quality of the match between the searched varieties and the ideal product. The optimal search is therefore to keep on searching until a variety within the "reservation distance" in the characteristics space C is found. This means that the consumer buys from the *first* retailer offering the variety whose distance to the ideal product is less than, or equal to, the distance D at which the expected utility increase from sampling another retailer is just equal to the additional search cost (see the following discussion for the formal definition of the reservation distance). When the consumer visits a shop in which the variety does not fall within his reservation distance, the search is continued (McMillan and Rothschild 1994).

Suppose that the consumer (x, r) first visits the cluster. When visiting a new retailer within the cluster, this consumer must bear a cost k independent of his tastes and location. Because all consumers know that varieties are equidistantly located along the circle C, consumers behave approximately as if the distribution of varieties were uniform along C when the number M of varieties is large while evaluating the benefit of a further search.

When the consumer has already visited some retailers within the shopping center and the best-offered variety is at distance D from the ideal product, the expected utility gain from visiting another retailer in the cluster is defined by the following expression (recall that varieties are supposed to be uniformly distributed along C):

$$B(D) = \int_0^D [(Y - p + u - s\delta) - (Y - p + u - sD)]\,\mathrm{d}\delta$$
$$= \int_0^D (sD - s\delta)\,\mathrm{d}\delta.$$

The reservation distance is defined as the maximum distance along C beyond which a consumer at $x \in [0, 1]$ stops his search for a better opportunity among the varieties available at some location x. The reservation distance $D_C < 1$ associated with the cluster is then obtained by equalizing the expected utility gain to find a better opportunity outside the cluster and the additional search cost, that is, D_C is the unique solution to the equation:

$$B(D) = k$$

where k is the cost of sampling a new retailer in the cluster. The search is stopped when a variety at a distance smaller than, or equal to D_C is found in a retailer established in the cluster. In other words, the typical consumer has an "acceptance zone" centered at his or her ideal point whose size is $2D_C$. The reservation distance D_C increases with the search cost k and decreases with the matching cost s. Note that s and k must be such that $D_C = (2k/s)^{1/2} < 1/2$, for otherwise no search would be undertaken. Furthermore, a consumer buys from any retailer in the cluster he is going to visit with a probability equal to $1/2D_C$ because this is the probability that the variety supplied by this retailer falls in the consumer's acceptance zone. Because consumers have identical preferences (up to a rotation of their ideal product) and the same beliefs about the distribution of varieties, the value of D_C is the same across consumers.

Assuming that the isolated retailer carries the variety at distance D_I from his ideal product, a consumer first visiting this retailer buys from it if and only if the expected gain from buying in the cluster does not exceed the transportation cost to go there. The expected gain associated with a continued search at the cluster is

$$(Y - p + u - sD_C) - [s(D_I - D_C) + k](1 - 1/2D_C)^{M-1}$$
$$- (Y - p + u - sD_I)$$

where $1 - 1/2D_C$ is the probability that the consumer does not find a variety within his acceptance zone in a retailer sampled at cost k within the cluster. Hence, the reservation distance D_I at the isolated firm is given by the solution of

$$s(D_I - D_C) - [s(D_I - D_C) + k](1 - 1/2D_C)^{M-1} = t_0 + t\Delta$$

where $t_0 + t\Delta$ is the transport cost to the cluster. Note that a positive solution may not exist. If it does, then D_I increases with the transport cost parameters

(t_0 and t) as well as with the distance Δ between the isolated firm and the cluster. More important, it decreases with the matching cost s and the number of retailers established in the cluster. As a consequence, the attractiveness of a cluster increases with its size as well as with consumers' matching cost.

The expected match is always higher when the cluster is visited first because more varieties are available there. However, the transport costs to the cluster and to the isolated firm, denoted respectively by T_C and T_I, generally vary with the consumer's location x. The following result identifies a sufficient condition on M and Δ for the difference in transport costs $(T_I - T_C)$ to be positive for *all* consumers when the distance between the cluster and the isolated firm does not exceed the threshold $\Delta(M)$. Accordingly, when $\Delta \leq \Delta(M)$, there is no spatial search (the proof is given in appendix C).

Proposition 7.3. *Consider $M - 1$ firms located at y_C and one firm at y_I. If M is large enough, there exists a distance $\Delta(M)$ such that all consumers visit first the cluster if the distance between the cluster and the isolated firm does not exceed $\Delta(M)$. Furthermore, the distance $\Delta(M)$ is increasing in M.*

The rest of the argument is straightforward. Let $M > \tilde{M} \equiv \max\{\Delta(M), 1/2D_C\}$. Then, if one firm is located at most $\Delta(M)$ away from the cluster, all consumers choose to go to the cluster first. In addition, because $M > 1/2D_C$, each consumer finds in the cluster a variety below his reservation distance D_C. This implies that the isolated firm has no customers. As a result, this firm would be strictly better off by joining the cluster where it enjoys a market share equal to $1/M$. If the urban area is small enough for $\Delta(M) \geq 1/2$ to hold, all consumers therefore buy from the cluster. Accordingly, we have the following result.

Proposition 7.4. *Consider M firms selling differentiated varieties and a continuum of consumers who do not know which firm offers which variety. If $M > \tilde{M}$ and $\Delta(M) \geq 1/2$, then $y_i^* = y^* \in [\max\{0, 1 - \Delta(M)\}, \min\{\Delta(M) - 1/2, 1\}]$, for $i = 1, \ldots, M$, is a Nash equilibrium.*

In other words, the ignorance of consumers about the available varieties leads to the emergence of a cluster when the size of the urban area is small (or, equivalently, when variable transport costs as measured by t are low) and when there are enough retailers to make the cluster attractive to all consumers.

By now, the role played by the fixed transport cost t_0 should be clear. If this cost were equal to zero, all consumers located to the left of the isolated firm would always visit this firm before the cluster because this firm could be sampled at no cost. As a result, any single firm would have an incentive to locate close to the cluster on the larger side of the market inasmuch as it would be visited by a majority of consumers. That the emergence of a cluster is more likely when the number of firms increases agrees with the gravity principle developed in economic geography.

It is worth noting that *the shopping center may emerge away from the market center*. Indeed, Proposition 7.4 does not require the cluster to be at the point minimizing total transportation costs. Any point such that no single firm is able to find an alternative location far enough to induce some consumers to visit it before the cluster is an equilibrium even when most of the population is concentrated away from it (note that the proof of Proposition 7.3 does not use the assumption that the population is uniformly distributed along the unit interval [0, 1]). To illustrate the implications of this result, consider a cluster established in the middle of the urban area while this area starts expanding leftward. Then, the cluster still attracts new firms entering the market even though more consumers are now located to the left of the cluster. By its mere existence, a cluster generates a lock-in effect similar to those that we encounter in Chapters 8 and 10.

Of course, the cluster tends to be not too far from the market center because retailers need to offer good accessibility to all consumers. Once the urban area extends far away in the same direction, some firms want to create a new cluster to the left of the original one, thus leading to a (hierarchical) spatial structure of retailers within the expanding urban area.

The foregoing findings can be extended to the more general case in which firms also choose prices strategically and both prices and variants are not directly observable by consumers. Wolinsky (1983) has then shown the existence of a symmetric price equilibrium.

Schulz and Stahl (1989; 1996) have shown that it is possible to uncover additional and surprising results by considering a market of variable size. To this end, they consider an unbounded geographical space that allows them to capture the idea that *more competition within the shopping center may attract more customers coming from more distant locations, thus allowing the demand for each variety to increase*. In other words, the entry of a new variety may lead to an increase in the cluster's demand that outweighs the decrease in market share inflicted on existing varieties. Furthermore, prices may increase with the number of firms so that individual profits first rise and then fall with the number of firms in the cluster. Clearly, when the number of varieties is not too large, such positive effects associated with the gathering of firms strengthen the agglomeration force that lies behind the cluster.

Though several firms may collectively want to form a new market, it may not pay an individual firm to open a new market in the absence of a coordinating device. Consequently, a new firm entering the market will choose instead to join the incumbents, thus leading to a larger agglomeration. In such a setting, the entry of a new firm creates a positive externality for the existing firms by making total demand larger. Although price competition becomes fiercer, it appears here that firms take advantage of the extensive margin effect to increase their prices in equilibrium. In other words, the market size effect "transforms" goods that are substitutes in the consumers' eyes into complements competing in the same market. As observed by Eaton and Lipsey (1977), this might explain the common fact that malls encourage the location of competing firms within the shopping center.

A related idea is explored by Gehrig (1998) when two differentiated markets are separated. Unlike Schulz and Stahl, Gehrig supposes that the aggregate demand over the two local markets is fixed. The number of products available in a local market increases with the number of consumers visiting this place, thus reducing the average matching costs. The attractiveness of a market therefore depends on the size of its clientele. Gehrig then shows that, in such a setting, an entrant is likely to join one of the existing markets – especially when transportation costs are low.

Although the context differs from those considered in Chapters 4 and 5, the foregoing discussion illustrates once more the role that a land developer or a public authority, internalizing here the demand externality, may play in the emergence of a new commercial area such as shopping malls or large supermarkets supplying a wide array of goods. Coordination failure (or a missing agent) may prevent the emergence of a shopping center when the agglomeration rent is not internalized (Smith and Hay 2005). Thus, public policies restricting the entry of supermarkets to protect small businesses limit the extent of internalization.

7.5 THE FORMATION OF INPUT CENTERS

7.5.1 The Spatial Integration of Upstream and Downstream Firms

In Section 7.2, we focused on monopolistic competition on the product market. Here we want to show how the same principles can be applied to study how intermediate goods may affect the agglomeration of firms. In Section 4.2.1, we have analyzed the role of variety in intermediate goods under the assumption that all producers of such goods locate together in the CBD. Our purpose is to make this center endogenous by following an approach that is essentially identical to the one taken in Section 7.2 in that we replace consumers by firms producing the final good and firms supplying consumption goods by firms producing intermediate goods.

We consider again a linear space $X = (-\infty, \infty)$. The final sector involves a continuum M_e of firms producing a homogeneous good, using land and a continuum M_S of intermediate inputs; the final good is chosen as the numéraire. Each intermediate input is produced by one service-firm under a constant marginal cost c (measured in terms of the numéraire) while using some fixed requirement of land S_S.

The production function of a firm belonging to the final sector is given by

$$X = \int_0^{M_s} v(q_i)\, \mathrm{d}i \tag{7.42}$$

in addition to the use of some fixed requirement of land S_e. In (7.42), q_i is the quantity of the intermediate good i, and $v(\cdot)$ expresses the contribution of any intermediate good to the output of the final sector. As in Section 7.2, we assume that v is given by an entropy-type such as

$$v(q) = \begin{cases} \frac{q}{\alpha}(1 + \log \beta) - \frac{q}{\alpha} \log \frac{q}{\alpha} & q < \alpha\beta \\ \beta & q \geq \alpha\beta \end{cases}.$$

As in Section 4.2.1, the production function (7.42) exhibits increasing returns in the number of intermediate goods (the production counterpart of preference for variety in consumption). Last, the opportunity cost of land is zero whereas the units of M_e and M_s are chosen for $S_e = S_s = 1$. Thus, the numbers of firms operating in the final and intermediate sectors may differ.

Following the same approach as the one taken in Section 7.2, we may write the profit function of a firm producing the final good located at x as follows:

$$\pi_e(x) = \int_X \{v[q(x,y)] - [p(y) + t|x-y|]q(x,y)\} m_s(y)\, \mathrm{d}y \\ - R(x)$$

where $p(y)$ is the common price of the intermediates available at y, $q(x, y)$ the quantity of each input purchased by the firm at x from a service-firm at y, t the common transportation rate of the intermediate goods, and $m_s(y)$ the number of service-firms located at y.

Maximizing the term between curly brackets yields (7.5), and thus the profit function of a firm producing the final good at x becomes:

$$\pi_e(x) = \int_X \beta m_s(y) [\exp -\alpha(p(y) + t\,|x-y|)]\, \mathrm{d}y - R(x). \tag{7.43}$$

Similarly, the profit function of a service-firm at x is

$$\pi_s(x) = [p(x) - c] \int_X q(y,x) m_e(y)\, \mathrm{d}y - R(x).$$

Using (7.5) again:

$$\pi_s(x) = [p(x) - c] \int_X \alpha\beta m_e(y) [\exp -\alpha(p(y) + t\,|x-y|)]\, \mathrm{d}y - R(x). \tag{7.44}$$

The common price of the intermediate goods is again

$$p_s^*(x) \equiv p^*(x) = c + 1/\alpha$$

which is to be interpreted along the lines of (7.6). Substituting this result in (7.43) and (7.44), we obtain

$$\pi_{e}(x) = \gamma \int_X m_s(y) \exp(-\alpha t|x - y|)\,\mathrm{d}y - R(x) \tag{7.45}$$

$$\pi_{s}(x) = \gamma \int_X m_e(y) \exp(-\alpha t|x - y|)\,\mathrm{d}y - R(x) \tag{7.46}$$

where $\gamma \equiv \beta \exp -(\alpha c + 1)$.

Evidently, (7.45) and (7.46) are structurally identical to (7.7) and (7.8). Therefore, the analysis developed in Section 7.2 similarly applies so that Proposition 7.1 holds under some obvious modifications ($N \to M_e$ and $M \to M_s$). As a consequence, vertically related firms that are otherwise independent choose to be spatially integrated within the same district to benefit from a better accessibility to each other. In this event, *the coagglomeration of the two sectors may be viewed as a substitute to their vertical integration.*

When the amount of land used by the service-firms exceeds the one used by the final producers, the equilibrium involves the agglomeration of the latter located with some service-firms, whereas the remaining service-firms sandwich the integrated district. This result sheds some light on the internal structure of CBDs: the headquarters of large corporations agglomerate with some service-firms, forming the nucleus of the CBD, whereas other service-firms locate in the outer ring of the CBD.

7.5.2 The Formation of Secondary Employment Centers

In the previous section, firms were assumed to be "small" relative to the market size. This provides an incomplete picture of what we observe in the real world because small and medium-size cities are often molded by a few firms that are "large" relative to the urban labor market. Many examples may be found in the industrialized world in which cities welcome a large plant of a multinational firm (think of Toyota in Albany [Kentucky] or Michelin in Clermont-Ferrand [France], whereas NEC, one of the largest Japanese electronics firms, has decentralized its mass-production plant in medium-sized cities throughout Japan). The entry of such firms dramatically affects the nature of competition on both the labor and land markets in the city. Furthermore, by the choice of their location, such firms may create secondary employment centers. Finally, their entry may also attract workers from other regions and cities, thus expanding the local population. These issues have not yet been considered.

To study the impact of large firms on the urban spatial structure, we consider a simple setting developed by Fujita, Thisse, and Zenou (1997). A large firm considers locating a new plant in a city where none of the existing businesses have a significant share of the urban labor market. The city itself is considered to be a small open economy subject to inflow migrations. Because the entrant is large relative to the city size, its location can therefore be viewed as a *secondary employment center*. By choosing a particular location, the firm affects the process of competition on the labor market in a rather complex way; it also affects the land rent, especially through the migration of rural workers who are hired by the firm. Because it is large relative to the urban market size, the entrant anticipates the impact of its location on the residential equilibrium owing to the migration of new workers.

Because the firm pays lower wages in the neighboring rural area where the land rent is lower, competition for workers generates a dispersion force that pushes the entrant away from the city center. However, as previously explained, the existence of specialized firms located in the CBD, as well as the information flows generated by the CBD firms, acts as an agglomeration force that pulls the firm toward the city center. Consequently, the emergence of a secondary employment center appears as the outcome of the interplay of these two opposing forces.

To formalize this problem, we consider the now familiar model of the monocentric and linear city whose population size may increase with the migration of new workers. The existing firms are located in the CBD and behave competitively on the labor market. In setting up its plant in the city, the new firm competes with the incumbents in the labor market. If the entrant locates in the CBD, then it must compete with the existing firms to attract workers. This results in a higher wage that also pulls some workers from the neighboring rural areas who come in small numbers. If the firm locates at the outskirts of the city, its labor force is mainly constituted by new workers who choose to reside in the urban area, and, therefore, the firm brings new workers in the city in close proportion to its labor needs. In this case, the firm does not compete with the CBD firms and is able to offer a lower wage. This is possible because workers pay a lower rent on the land market and bear a lower commuting cost.

Consider a linear city in which all existing firms are small and located in the CBD, which is taken as the origin of the location space $X = (-\infty, \infty)$. In the spirit of the open-city model (see Chapter 3), the population N of workers is variable to allow for the migration of new workers. Workers are homogeneous, each consuming a fixed amount of land normalized to 1 and a variable amount of a composite good z (considered as the numéraire). Because the consumption of land is fixed, the workers' utility level can be expressed through the consumption z of the composite good. When they do not reside in the city, workers can guarantee themselves a given reservation utility level expressed in terms of the numéraire $\bar{z}$. Because the utility level decreases with the population size, workers migrate to the city until they reach the utility level $\bar{z}$. Let 0 be the city center and y_e the location chosen by the entrant. Then, the budget constraint of a new or incumbent consumer at x working at y_i $(i = 0, e)$

is as follows:

$$\bar{z} + t|x - y_i| + R(x) = w(y_i) \tag{7.47}$$

where t is the unit commuting cost, $R(x)$ the land rent at x, and $w(y_i)$ the wage rate at y_i. This implies that the CBD workers' bid rent is

$$\Psi(x; w) = w - \bar{z} - tx \tag{7.48}$$

where $w \equiv w(0)$.

Before the entry of the new firm, the city is in the following state. If each worker in the city receives a wage w, the residential equilibrium condition at $x \in X$ is

$$\bar{z} + tx + R(x) = w.$$

When the opportunity cost of land is normalized to zero, this implies that the city expands on both sides up to the distance:

$$b = \frac{w - \bar{z}}{t}.$$

Consequently, the labor supply function is

$$N^{\mathrm{s}}(w) = \frac{2(w - \bar{z})}{t}.$$

For simplicity, the optimizing behavior of the CBD firms is subsumed in the following linear demand function for labor:

$$N^{\mathrm{d}}(w) = \frac{1 - w}{\theta}$$

where θ is a positive constant; the higher θ, the less elastic the demand for labor.

The market clearing wage is then

$$w^* = \frac{t + 2\bar{z}\theta}{t + 2\theta}$$

whereas the corresponding equilibrium employment is denoted by $N^* \equiv 2(1 - \bar{z})/(t + 2\theta)$. It is easy to check that the labor demand function can be rewritten as follows:

$$N^{\mathrm{d}}(w) = N^* - \frac{w - w^*}{\theta}.$$

Given this monocentric city, we consider a new large firm, called e, entering the city. We assume this is a branch of a nationwide corporation that chooses the production target $\bar{Q}$ and product price for its subsidiary, which can be normalized to 1, as well as the region where it is to be located. The local manager selects a specific location within this region and the wage to be paid to the workers. The labor requirement of this firm is fixed and equal to $\bar{L}$, whereas its land consumption is assumed to be zero for simplicity. If firm e locates at y_e and pays a wage w_e, its profit function is

$$\Pi_e = \bar{Q} - w_e\bar{L} - ky_e\bar{Q} \tag{7.49}$$

where k stands for the accessibility cost to the CBD services per unit of output. Everything else being equal, decreasing the distance to the CBD leads to a lower unit cost for the firm.

Because the entrant is large relative to the city, it anticipates the impact of its location and wage choice on the labor market. Three types of equilibrium configurations may arise, which are depicted in Figure 7.5.

Case 1. The entrant locates at the CBD (or near the CBD). Then, firm e competes with the CBD firms in order to attract its whole labor force. Specifically, the labor demand curve is shifted to the right by an amount equal to $\bar{L}$ whereas the supply of labor is given by the existing population N^* augmented by some immigrants. The land rent is uniformly shifted upward (see Figure 7.5(a) where b_1 is the new boundary of the city). The new equilibrium wage is obtained by solving the labor market clearing condition:

$$N^d(w) + \bar{L} = N^s(w)$$

that is:

$$w_1^* = w^* + \frac{\bar{L}}{1/\theta + 2/t}. \tag{7.50}$$

In this case, the labor market is competitive and fully integrated because all people work in (or near) the CBD; the city employment increases by

$$\Delta N_1 = \frac{\bar{L}}{1 + t/2\theta}$$

which is always smaller than $\bar{L}$, that is, some workers hired by the entrant were employed by the incumbents before entry. Note that lowering commuting costs leads to a larger city labor force and to a lower wage.

The same results hold true if firm e locates at y_e smaller than

$$x^- \equiv \frac{N^*}{2} + \frac{\bar{L}}{t/\theta + 2} - \bar{L}$$

because the rise in population keeps the urban pattern symmetric.

Case 2. The entrant locates between x^- and x^+ where

$$x^+ = (N^* + \bar{L})/2.$$

The firm still competes with the CBD firms by attracting some workers who used to work for these firms (because $y_e < x^+$). However, its labor force is

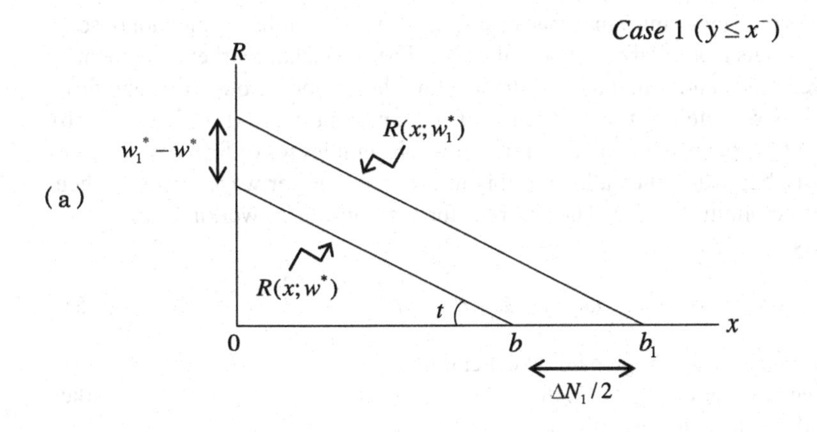

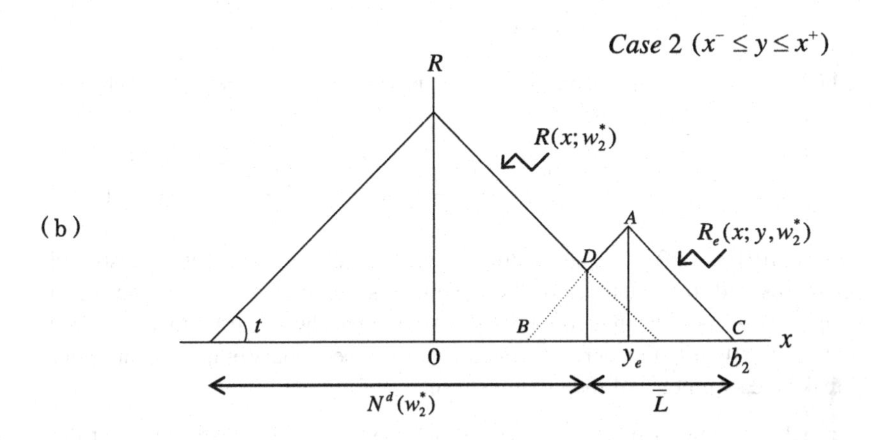

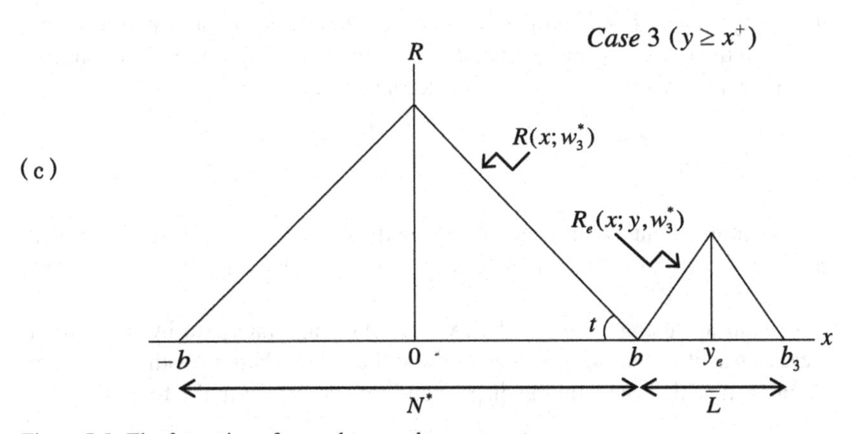

Figure 7.5. The formation of secondary employment centers.

also formed by immigrants (because $y_e > x^-$) so that it has some monopsony power on its labor market. By implication, the urban labor market is segmented between the central market and the local market formed around the new firm, which is reflected in the two peaks of the land rent curve (see Figure 7.5(b) where b_2 is the new boundary of the city). The employees of firm e reside near the city boundary, thus allowing this firm to pay a lower wage owing to their lower commuting costs. The bid rent for the consumers working in the new firm is

$$\Psi(x; y_e, w(y_e)) = w(y_e) - \bar{z} - t|x - y_e| \tag{7.51}$$

where $w(y_e)$ is the wage paid by the entrant.

Because the bid rents (7.48) and (7.51) must be equal at the labor market boundary, the equilibrium wage at the CBD is

$$w_2^*(0) = w_1^* - A(\theta)(y_e - x^-)$$

which decreases when the entrant locates farther away from the CBD, whereas the wage set by the entrant is

$$w_2^*(y_e) = \frac{w^* + 2\bar{z} + 2t\bar{L}}{3} + \frac{A(\theta)t(N^* + \bar{L})}{6} - \frac{[1 + A(\theta)]t}{3} y_e \tag{7.52}$$

where $A(\theta) \equiv 1/(2 + 3t/2\theta)$ decreases with the level of commuting costs and increases with the elasticity of the incumbents' demand for labor. The urban employment rises by an amount $\Delta N_2(y_e)$, which is always larger than $\Delta N_1(y_e)$ but smaller than $\bar{L}$. Furthermore, the creation of a secondary employment center breaks the symmetry of the urban pattern.

Case 3. The new firm establishes itself outside the city at a distance $\bar{L}/2$ from the initial city fringe b. It hires immigrants only, whereas all former residents keep working for the CBD firms (see Figure 7.5(c) where b_3 is the new boundary of the city). There is no competition between the two local labor markets, and thus both the pre-entry land rent and wage still prevail after entry in the initial urban area. Firm e is a monopsonist offering a wage given by

$$w_3^* = \bar{z} + \frac{t\bar{L}}{2}. \tag{7.53}$$

Urban employment is augmented by exactly $\bar{L}$, and a new center is created that interacts with the preexisting city only through services bought from firms located at the CBD.

To sum up: using (7.50)–(7.53), we see the wage rate paid by the entrant decreases as its location moves away from the CBD where the other firms are established. This is exactly the dispersion force described in the foregoing.

Given the profit function (7.49), the entrant must balance the advantages provided by the greater proximity to the center against the intensity of competition on the labor market as reflected by a downward-sloping wage gradient. Which pattern arises depends on the relative intensity of these two opposing forces. Because the profit function is piecewise linear in y_e, the equilibrium location is always at one extremity of the feasible interval associated with each case.

It is then easy to show the following:

Proposition 7.5. *When the profit function is given by (7.49), the equilibrium location of the entrant is such that:*

(i) *if* $k\bar{Q} > t\bar{L}$, *then* $y_e^* = 0$;
(ii) *if* $t\bar{L} \geq k\bar{Q} > t\bar{L}[1 + A(\theta)]/3$, *then* $y_e^* = x^-$;
(iii) *if* $t\bar{L}[1 + A(\theta)]/3 \geq k\bar{Q}$, *then* $y_e^* = x^+$.

When the intensity of communication with the service firms at the CBD is strong enough (Case 1), the new firm locates together with its competitors on the labor market. At the other extreme, when the intensity of communication is low, the firm will choose to create an edge city at the fringe of the existing city by appealing to immigrants only (Case 3). In between, there is interdependence between the two local labor markets (Case 2). When the distance to the CBD rises, the interdependence between these two markets weakens smoothly, as shown by the fact that the firm offers a continuously decreasing wage. It is in this case that the entry of a new firm gives rise to the creation of a secondary employment center within the city. The location of this center with respect to the CBD eventually depends on the basic parameters of the urban economy.[12]

7.6 CONCLUDING REMARKS

The main conclusion of this chapter is that the clustering of firms and the emergence of local labor markets within a city may correspond to equilibrium outcomes once it is admitted that markets are imperfectly competitive. Although externalities are likely to be crucial in the formation of such agglomerations in the real world, we believe that the results presented here support our claim that the presence of imperfectly competitive markets is another major reason for the existence of these agglomerations.

Even though we have used fairly specific models, a few general principles emerge from our analysis. First, a commercial (employment) center is likely to form when products (intermediate goods) are differentiated enough, transport costs are sufficiently low, or both. This is in accord with several of the results

[12] For further developments of the model, the reader is referred to Zenou (2009, chapter 6).

derived in Chapter 6 for which we assumed externalities to be at work in an otherwise competitive environment. Interestingly, in Part III we encounter again the same kind of logic in the formation of a core–periphery structure. In fact, the spatial monocentric structure obtained in Propositions 6.3, 7.2, and 7.4 can be interpreted as the urban counterpart of the core–periphery structure. We also notice that principles governing the working of spatial product markets are similar, mutatis mutandis, to those to be applied to spatial intermediate goods markets.

More surprising, perhaps, is that, when agglomeration occurs, it is often socially desirable. This is because consumers like to try each variety and, therefore, benefit from a spatial concentration of sellers at the center of the urban area. The need for agglomeration is even stronger when consumers have incomplete information about varieties and prices, for the grouping of firms allows a substantial reduction in consumers' search costs. Thus, besides the positive effects that agglomeration may have for firms (as discussed in Chapter 6), we have stressed here some of the positive effects of agglomeration for consumers/workers. However, we would certainly be the last ones to claim that agglomeration is always optimal. Quite the reverse is true. We have identified some major dispersion forces that may pull typical urban economic activities away from the city center. In addition, even when agglomerating firms is socially desirable, we have seen that the location selected by firms may not be socially optimal.

A word, in closing. We have mainly focused here on Hotelling-like spatial competition whereas NEG considers monopolistic competition (see Chapters 8 and 9). Each type seems to describe competition at two different spatial scales. The former fits well competition "in the small," which involves firms located within the same city; the latter provides a fairly good approximation of competition "in the large," that is, competition among firms supplying different regions and countries. In spite of this difference in market structure, we see that the results presented in this chapter are rather similar to those obtained in NEG.

APPENDIX

A $\Psi(x)$ is strictly concave and $\Phi(x)$ is strictly convex on business areas. Consider first any residential section $[a_1, a_2]$ in the urban area $[-l, l]$. By (7.9), we have:

$$\frac{\mathrm{d}^2\Psi(x)}{\mathrm{d}x^2} = \gamma\alpha^2 t^2 \left[\int_{-l}^{a_1} m(y)\exp(-\alpha t(x-y))\mathrm{d}y + \int_{a_2}^{l} m(y)\exp(-\alpha t(y-x))\mathrm{d}y\right]$$

since $m(y) = 0$ over $[a_1, a_2]$. Because this expression is strictly positive, $\Psi(x)$ is strictly convex over $[a_1, a_2]$.

Assume now that $[a_1, a_2]$ is a business section. Taking again the second derivative of (7.9) yields:

$$\begin{aligned}
\frac{\mathrm{d}^2\Psi(x)}{\mathrm{d}x^2} &= -\gamma\alpha t[\exp -\alpha t(x - a_1) + \exp -\alpha t(a_2 - x)] \\
&\quad + \gamma\alpha^2 t^2 [\int_{-l}^{a_1} m(y) \exp(-\alpha t(x - y))\mathrm{d}y \\
&\quad + \int_{a_2}^{l} m(y) \exp(-\alpha t(y - x))\mathrm{d}y] \\
&\leq -\gamma\alpha t[\exp(-\alpha t(x - a_1)) + \exp(-\alpha t(a_2 - x))] \\
&\quad + \gamma\alpha^2 t^2 [\int_{-l}^{a_1} \exp(-\alpha t(x - y))\mathrm{d}y + \int_{a_2}^{l} \exp(-\alpha t(y - x))\mathrm{d}y] \\
&= -\gamma\alpha t[\exp(-\alpha t(x + l)) + \exp(-\alpha t(l - x))]
\end{aligned}$$

which is always negative so that $\Psi(x)$ is strictly concave over $[a_1, a_2]$.

A similar argument applied to (7.10) shows that $\Phi(x)$ is strictly convex (concave) over any business (residential) section.

B Proof of Proposition 7.2. Assume that firm 1 is located at $y_1 < 1/2$ and quotes a price p_1 while the others are at $1/2$ and set $p^* = c + M/\alpha(M-1)$. Firm 1's profit is given by

$$\begin{aligned}
\pi_1(p_1, y_1) = (p_1 - c) &\left[\frac{y_1}{1 + (M-1)\exp(\Lambda - \Theta)} + \frac{1}{2} - y_1 \right. \\
&\left. - \frac{1}{\alpha\tau} \ln \frac{1 + (M-1)\exp(\Lambda + \Theta)}{1 + (M-1)\exp(\Lambda - \Theta)} + \frac{1/2}{1 + (M-1)\exp(\Lambda - \Theta)} \right]
\end{aligned}$$

where $\Theta \equiv \alpha t/(1/2 - y_1)$ and $\Lambda \equiv \alpha(p_1 - p^*)$. Therefore,

$$\begin{aligned}
\text{sign}\frac{\partial \pi_1}{\partial x_1} = \text{sign} &\left\{ te^{\Theta} \left[e^{\Theta} + (M-1)e^{\Lambda}\right]^2 + \frac{1}{\alpha}(e^{2\Theta} - 1)\left[e^{\Theta} + (M-1)e^{\Lambda}\right] \right. \\
&\left. \times \left[1 + (M-1)e^{\Theta}e^{\Lambda}\right] - 2ty_1 e^{\Theta}\left[1 + (M-1)e^{\Theta}e^{\Lambda}\right] \right\}.
\end{aligned}$$

When $\alpha t \leq 2$, a lower bound for the right-hand side of this expression is obtained by replacing $1/\alpha$ with $t/2$ and y_1 with $1/2$, which is positive regardless of Λ. Thus, firm 1 wants to join the others at $1/2$.

It remains to show that it is more profitable for firm 1 located at $l/2$ to charge p^*. Its profit is $\pi_1 = (p_1 - c)l\mathbf{P}_1$ where

$$\mathbf{P}_1 = \frac{\exp(-\alpha p_1)}{\exp(-\alpha p_1) + (M-1)\exp(-\alpha p^*)}.$$

It can then be readily verified that

$$\frac{\partial \pi_1}{\partial p_1} = (p_1 - c)\alpha l \mathbf{P}_1(\mathbf{P}_1 - 1) + l\mathbf{P}_1$$

and

$$\frac{\partial^2 \pi_1}{\partial p_1^2} = (p_1 - c)\alpha^2 l \mathbf{P}_1(\mathbf{P}_1 - 1)(2\mathbf{P}_1 - 1) + 2\alpha l \mathbf{P}_1(\mathbf{P}_1 - 1).$$

Evaluating $\partial^2 \pi_1/\partial p_1^2$ at any price for which $\partial \pi_1/\partial p_1 = 0$ gives $-\alpha l \mathbf{P}_1 < 0$. The profit function π_1 is therefore strictly quasi-concave, and thus the solution $p_1 = p^*$ of $\partial \pi_1/\partial p_1 = 0$ is a profit-maximizing price when firm 1 is with the others.

C Proof of Proposition 7.3. Let T_{C} be the expected transport costs when the consumer starts his search in the cluster and T_{I} the same cost when the search starts at the isolated firm. First, we have the following inequality:

$$\begin{aligned} T_{\mathrm{C}} \leq {} & [t_0 + t\,|x - y_{\mathrm{C}}|] + \left[(t_0 + t\,|x - y_{\mathrm{C}}|)[1 - (1 - D_{\mathrm{I}})(1 - D_{\mathrm{C}})^{M-2}]\right] \\ & + \left[(t_0 + t\Delta)(1 - D_{\mathrm{I}})(1 - D_{\mathrm{C}})^{M-2}\right] \\ & + \left[(t_0 + t\,|x - y_{\mathrm{I}}|)[(1 - D_{\mathrm{I}})(1 - D_{\mathrm{C}})^{M-2} - (1 - D_{\mathrm{I}})(1 - D_{\mathrm{C}})^{M-1}]\right] \\ & + \left[(t_0 + t\Delta + t_0 + t\,|x - y_{\mathrm{C}}|)(1 - D_{\mathrm{I}})(1 - D_{\mathrm{C}})^{M-1}\right] \end{aligned} \tag{7A.1}$$

where (i) the first (bracketed) term, $t_0 + t\,|x - y_{\mathrm{C}}|$, is the cost of visiting the cluster; (ii) the second term corresponds to the cost of returning home, $t_0 + t\,|x - y_{\mathrm{C}}|$, times the probability, $1 - (1 - D_{\mathrm{I}})(1 - D_{\mathrm{C}})^{M-2}$, that the consumer assigns to buying in the cluster; (iii) the third term stands for the cost of traveling from the cluster to the isolated firm, $t_0 + t\Delta$, times the probability, $(1 - D_{\mathrm{I}})(1 - D_{\mathrm{C}})^{M-2}$, the consumer wants to go there from the cluster; (iv) the fourth term represents the cost to go home from the isolated firm, $(t_0 + t\,|x - y_I|)$, weighted by the probability, $(1 - D_{\mathrm{I}})(1 - D_{\mathrm{C}})^{M-2} - (1 - D_{\mathrm{I}})(1 - D_{\mathrm{C}})^{M-1}$, that the consumer does not want to return to the cluster; and (v) the last term is the cost of going back to the cluster before returning home, $t_0 + t\Delta + t_0 + t\,|x - y_{\mathrm{C}}|$, weighted by $(1 - D_{\mathrm{I}})(1 - D_{\mathrm{C}})^{M-1}$. The inequality holds in (7A.1) because the last weight, $(1 - D_{\mathrm{I}})(1 - D_{\mathrm{C}})^{M-1}$, overestimates the probability that the consumer wants to return to the cluster, thus making the last term larger than what it should be.

Second, we also have

$$\begin{aligned} T_{\mathrm{I}} \geq {} & [t_0 + t\,|x - y_{\mathrm{I}}|] + [(t_0 + t\,|x - y_{\mathrm{I}}|)D_{\mathrm{I}}] \\ & + [(t_0 + t\Delta)(1 - D_{\mathrm{I}})] + [(t_0 + t\,|x - y_{\mathrm{C}}|)(1 - D_{\mathrm{I}})] \end{aligned} \tag{7A.2}$$

where (i) the first term, $t_0 + t\,|x - y_{\mathrm{I}}|$, is the cost of traveling to the isolated firm; (ii) the second term is the cost of returning home, $t_0 + t\,|x - y_{\mathrm{I}}|$, times the probability, D_{I}, of buying from this firm; (iii) the third term stands for the cost of going to the cluster from the isolated firm, $t_0 + t\Delta$, weighted by the probability, $1 - D_{\mathrm{I}}$, the consumer assigns to this event; and (iv) the last term represents the cost of going home from the cluster, $t_0 + t\,|x - y_{\mathrm{C}}|$, times the probability of being in the cluster, $1 - D_{\mathrm{I}}$. The inequality holds in (7A.2) because we do not account for the possibility that the consumer might want to return to the isolated firm after having visited the cluster.

Subtracting (7A.1) from (7A.2) and using the triangle inequality, we obtain after some manipulations:

$$\begin{aligned} T_{\mathrm{I}} - T_{\mathrm{C}} &\geq -2t\Delta + (1 - D_{\mathrm{I}})[t_0 + 2t\Delta - (1 - D_{\mathrm{C}})^{M-2} t_0 \\ &\quad - (t_0 + 2t\Delta)(1 - D_{\mathrm{C}})^{M-1}] \\ &\equiv f(\Delta). \end{aligned}$$

Let $\Delta = 0$ and choose $\hat{M}$ large enough for $(1 - D_{\mathrm{C}})^{M-1}$ to be smaller than $1/2$. Evidently, $f(0) > 0$ since $t_0 > 0$ and $D_{\mathrm{I}} < 1$ for otherwise a consumer would visit a single place, i.e., the cluster, and the problem would become trivial. On the other hand, $f(\Delta) < 0$ when Δ is large enough. Because $f(\Delta)$ is continuous, the intermediate value theorem implies that there exists a value $\Delta(M)$ such that $T_{\mathrm{I}} - T_{\mathrm{C}} > 0$ for $0 \leq \Delta \leq \Delta(M)$.

Since $\Delta(M)$ is the smallest solution of the equation

$$-2t\Delta + (1 - D_{\mathrm{I}})[t_0 + 2t\Delta - (1 - D_{\mathrm{C}})^{M-2} t_0 - (t_0 + 2t\Delta)(1 - D_{\mathrm{C}})^{M-1}] = 0$$

it is readily verified that $\Delta(M)$ increases with M.

PART III

FACTOR MOBILITY AND INDUSTRIAL LOCATION

8

Industrial Agglomeration under Monopolistic Competition

8.1 INTRODUCTION

At the interregional or international level, the spatial economy is replete with *pecuniary externalities*. For example, when workers choose to migrate, they bring with them both their production and consumption capabilities. As a result, their movements affect the size of labor and product markets in both the origin and destination regions. These effects have the nature of pecuniary externalities because migrating workers do not take them into account in their decisions. Pecuniary externalities are especially relevant when markets are imperfectly competitive because prices do not perfectly reflect the social values of individual decisions. The effects generated by migrations are better studied within a general equilibrium framework that accounts for the interactions between the product and labor markets. Among other things, this allows studying the dual role of individuals as workers and consumers. At first sight, this seems to be a formidable task. Yet, as shown by Krugman (1991b), several of these various effects can be combined and studied within a relatively simple general equilibrium model of monopolistic competition, which has come to be known as the *core–periphery* (CP) *model.*

Recall that monopolistic competition à la Chamberlin (1933) involves consumers with a preference for variety (*varietas delectat*), whereas firms producing these varieties compete for a limited amount of resources because they face increasing returns. The prototype that has emerged from the industrial organization literature is the constant elasticity of substitution (CES) model developed by Dixit and Stiglitz (1977). These authors assumed that each firm is negligible in the sense that it may ignore its impact on, and hence reactions from, other firms, but retains enough market power for pricing above marginal cost regardless of the total number of firms (like a monopolist). Moreover, the position of a firm's demand, which is obtained by maximizing a CES utility function, depends on the actions taken by all firms in the market (as in perfect competition).

In many applications, the Dixit–Stiglitz model has proven to be a very powerful instrument for studying the aggregate implications of monopoly power and increasing returns – especially so when these elements are the basic ingredients of self-sustaining processes such as those encountered in modern theories of growth and economic geography (Matsuyama 1995; Brakman and Heijdra 2004). This is so because of the following two main reasons: (i) each firm being negligible to the market, it accurately assumes that its action has no impact on the market outcome and behaves as a monopolist on the residual demands, thus making the existence of an equilibrium much less problematic than in general equilibrium under oligopolistic competition, and (ii) the assumption of free entry and exit leads to zero profit so that a worker's income is just equal to her wage, which is another major simplification.

The setting considered by Krugman, described in Section 8.2, is simple but rich enough to capture the major forces at work in the multiregional economy. It combines the Dixit–Stiglitz model with the iceberg-type transport cost in which only a fraction of the good shipped reaches its destination. This modeling strategy, due to Samuelson (1954a), may be viewed as a "trick" that avoids dealing with the transport sector explicitly. There are two sectors: (i) the agricultural sector producing a homogeneous good under constant returns to scale and (ii) the manufacturing sector supplying a differentiated good under increasing returns.

As usual, the market equilibrium is the outcome of the interplay between a dispersion force and an agglomeration force. The centrifugal force is simple. It lies in the following two sources: (i) the spatial immobility of farmers whose demands for the manufactured good are to be met and (ii) the increasing competition that arises when firms are more agglomerated. The centripetal force is more involved. If a larger number of manufactures is located in one region, the number of varieties locally produced is also larger, and thus the equilibrium price index of manufactured goods is lower in this region. This in turn, induces some workers living in the smaller region, to move toward the larger region, where they may enjoy a higher standard of living. The resulting increase in the numbers of workers creates a larger demand for the differentiated good, which, therefore, leads additional firms to locate in this region. This implies the availability of more varieties in the region in question but less in the other because there are scale economies at the firm's level. Consequently, as noticed by Krugman (1991b, 486), *circular causality* à la Myrdal is present because these two effects reinforce each other: "manufactures production will tend to concentrate where there is a large market, but the market will be large where manufactures production is concentrated." The great accomplishment of Krugman was to integrate all these effects within a unified framework and to determine precisely the conditions under which the cumulative process predicted by Myrdal occurs or not. To be precise, Krugman has shown that the value of transportation costs is the key determining factor.

When transportation costs (or, more generally, trade costs) are sufficiently low, Krugman (1991b) has shown that all manufactures are concentrated in a single region that becomes the *core* of the economy, whereas the other region, called the *periphery*, supplies only the agricultural good. Firms are able to exploit increasing returns by selling more in the larger market without losing much business in the smaller market. For exactly the opposite reason, the economy displays a symmetric regional pattern of production when transportation costs are high. Hence, the CP model allows for the possibility of divergence between regions, whereas the neoclassical model, based on constant returns and perfect competition in the two sectors, would predict convergence only. As in previous chapters, there is a monotone decreasing relationship between the degree of agglomeration and the level of transport costs. The process of circular causality, then, looks like a snowball effect that leads industrial firms to be locked in the same region for long periods: think of the Industrial Belt in the United States, the Pacific Industrial Belt in Japan, or the "Blue Banana" in Europe. This result also represents a neat formalization of an idea put forward by Myrdal (1957, 26–27) a long time ago:

> Within broad limits, the power of attraction of a centre has its origin mainly in the historical accident that something was once started there, and not in a number of other places where it could equally well have been started, and that start met success.

In such a context, it is well known that small initial differences between territories, minor changes in the socioeconomic environment, or both may eventually result in vastly different economic configurations. Because there are multiple equilibria, there is a need for some refinement. As before, instability is used to dismiss some equilibria, which has led Krugman and others to stress the existence of several stable equilibria. We build on the work of Oyama (2009a, b) to show that this emphasis is exaggerated.

Whether there is too much or too little agglomeration is unclear. Yet, speculation on this issue has never been in short supply and it is fair to say that this is one of the main questions that policy makers would like to address. The welfare properties of the CP model have been for long unexplored. There are, however, several good reasons to believe that the market outcome is not efficient. Indeed, besides the standard allocative inefficiencies generated by firms pricing above marginal costs, economic geography models contain new sources of inefficiency whose origin lies in the mobility of agents. Indeed, firms and workers move without taking into account the benefits and losses they bring about to the agents residing in their new region, nor the benefits or losses they impose on those left behind. Here the pecuniary externalities generated by the mobility of agents matter for welfare because competition on the product market is imperfect. In this event, there is a priori no general indication as to the social desirability of agglomeration or dispersion. In order to compare the two equilibrium market outcomes – agglomeration and dispersion – that most economic geography models yield, Charlot et al. (2006) use several tools of public economics, starting from the least controversial Pareto criterion to various social welfare functions. Even though the CP model involves no technological externalities, its welfare analysis does not deliver a simple and unambiguous message.

In Section 8.3, we show that neither agglomeration nor dispersion Pareto dominates the other: farmers living in the periphery always prefer dispersion, whereas farmers and workers living in the core always prefer agglomeration. This is hardly a surprising result, given the terminology (core and periphery) used to describe the interregional system in the agglomerated configuration. Turning to compensation mechanisms, we show that, *provided that transportation costs are sufficiently low, agglomeration is preferred to dispersion*: farmers and workers located in the core can compensate the farmers staying in the periphery, whereas the farmers staying in the periphery are unable to compensate the workers who choose to move in what becomes the core. For higher transport costs, there is indetermination: none of the two configurations is preferred to the other with respect to both the foregoing criteria. In a way, such an indetermination may be considered as the "synthesis" of the very contrasted views that prevail in a domain in which the two tenets have many good reasons to be right. These results are to be contrasted with those obtained in Sections 4.3 and 4.4 where the market outcome delivers the social optimum. This difference in results is easy to understand. There, cities emerge as the actions taken by some large agents who internalize the costs and benefits of urban agglomeration. Here, agglomeration is the unintended consequence of a myriad of decisions made by small agents who have no incentives to do the socially optimal thing.

By focusing on the interactions between the product and labor markets, Krugman's work remains in the tradition of international trade. As a consequence, the CP model has been subject to several criticisms, especially because regions are internally spaceless. Modern regional and urban economics holds that the difference in the economic performance of regions is, to some extent, explained by the behavior and interactions between households and firms that are located within them (Section 4.2). In this context, as suggested by Weber ([1909] 1927, p. 121), Helpman (1998), and Tabuchi (1998), the main dispersion force would lie in the urban costs borne by workers living in large agglomerations, and not in the agricultural sector whose share in employment and expenditure has sharply decreased in industrialized countries. Indeed, as discussed in Chapter 3, a sizable human settlement typically takes the form of a city in which workers compete for land and bear commuting costs. For example, in the United States, housing accounts on average for 20 percent of household budgets while 18 percent of total expenditures is spent on car purchases, gasoline, and other related expenses (Quigley and Raphael 2004). In Section 8.4, we therefore suppose that an agglomeration is structured as a monocentric city in which firms gather in a central business district. In the NEG-like city model of this section, competition for land among workers gives rise to land rent and commuting costs that both increase as the population expands. The space-economy is now the outcome of the interaction between two types of mobility costs: the transport costs of commodities and the commuting costs of workers. To be precise, these costs are associated with the following trade-off: concentrating people and firms in a reduced number of large cities minimizes commodity shipping among urban areas but yields a longer average commuting; dispersing people and firms across numerous small cities has the opposite effects.

As noted earlier, the main result obtained by Krugman is the monotone relationship between the degree of agglomeration and the transportation cost level. We build on Murata and Thisse (2005) to show that the symmetric configuration is stable for low transportation costs, whereas the core–periphery structure is a stable equilibrium when transportation costs are high. Simply put, *Krugman's scenario is reversed.* This difference in results is simple to explain. In the NEG-like city model, when workers gather in the core, urban costs rise, which strengthens the dispersion force. Furthermore, lower transportation costs facilitate intercity trade. By contrast, in the CP model the dispersion force gets weaker because there are fewer people to be supplied in the periphery, and they are so at a lower delivery cost; in addition, there are no urban costs in the CP model. Among other things, this shows that the interplay between agglomeration and dispersion forces changes with the nature of the forces at work.

This is not yet the end of the story, however. Agglomeration is always a stable equilibrium when commuting costs are sufficiently low, whereas dispersion prevails when these costs are high. Interestingly, what "low" and "high" mean depends on the level of transportation costs. For example, when transportation costs take on low values, agglomeration may emerge if commuting costs are themselves sufficiently low. Thus, it is *the relative evolution of interregional transport costs and intra-urban commuting costs that determines the structure of the space-economy*. This has the following interesting implication: what matters for the global economy is not just the evolution of transportation costs, as suggested by the CP model; what goes on inside the different regions is also crucial. This draws attention to two facts that policy makers often neglect: on the one hand, local factors may change the global organization of the economy and, on the other, global forces may affect the local/urban organization of production and employment. This calls for better coordination of transport policies at the urban and global levels.

That two models based on the combination of monopolistic competition and iceberg costs yield opposite predictions may cast doubt on the relevance of NEG. In fact, the situation is not as bad as it might seem at first glance. If economic integration is indeed capable of initially fostering a more intensive agglomeration of economic activities, its continuation is liable to generate a redeployment of activities that could lead to a kind of geographical evening-out. In short, one may expect the process of spatial development to unfold according to a *bell-shaped curve*. If true, the bell-shaped curve would provide a reconciliation of the above two extreme approaches, as this curve encapsulates these two complementary factors. Whereas Krugman concentrates on the right-hand side of the bell, Helpman focuses on its left-hand side.

In Section 8.5, we follow Pflüger and Tabuchi (2010) who assume that both workers and firms consume variable lot sizes. In this context, dispersion, and then agglomeration, arises for the same reasons as in the CP model. However, when the supply of land is very inelastic, or commuting costs are very high, competition for land among firms and workers leads to high urban costs that spark the redispersion of the manufacturing sector for sufficiently low transportation costs. Because several alternative models do suggest the existence of a bell-shaped relationship between economic integration and spatial inequality, we may safely conclude that this relationship has strong theoretical underpinnings (Puga 1999; Fujita and Mori 2005; Combes, Mayer, and Thisse 2008).

The CP model can be used to study the growing geographical concentration of business services in large metropolitan areas. In this context, firms in the *service sector* not only supply consumers and manufacturing firms but also serve each other. This circularity in demand gives the corresponding firms incentives to agglomerate that are very similar to those studied by Krugman. As a result, once the different sectors are properly reinterpreted to account for the new trends emerging in developed economies, the CP model keeps its relevance despite the gradual shift of manufacturers toward smaller cities or even rural areas. This tendency will be strengthened by the growing inclination of business services to work near the headquarters and research laboratories of manufacturing firms, which remain mostly located in large cities.

In Section 8.6, we formalize this idea by considering a large array of more or less tradable intermediate goods and business services as a major cause for agglomeration. So far, indeed, agglomeration has been considered as the outcome of a circular causality process fed by the mobility of workers. Yet, in the international marketplace, it is reasonable to expect this mobility to be low, and thus the core–periphery model cannot be used to explain the agglomeration of industries in the world economy. Consequently, as argued by Venables (1996), dealing with the intermediate sector allows us to explain the possible emergence of a core–periphery structure. However, instead of following Venables (who assumes that both the intermediate and final sectors operate under increasing returns and monopolistic competition), we use a simpler framework. As in Section 4.2.1, we assume that the intermediate sector produces a differentiated good and exhibits increasing returns; however, the final sector produces a homogeneous good and exhibits constant returns. Finally, it is supposed that workers remain in their region. We then show that both sectors coagglomerate within the same region – they are *spatially* integrated – provided that the transport costs of the intermediate goods are sufficiently high (typically when they are nontradable). This is so even when the transport cost of the final good is very low. Indeed, the agglomeration of the intermediate sector firms makes it profitable for the final sector firms to agglomerate with them despite the wage gap generated by the immobility of workers.

8.2 THE CORE-PERIPHERY MODEL

Although we focus on a two-region economy in this chapter, it proves convenient to have a more general framework for subsequent developments.

8.2.1 The Spatial Economy

The economic space is made of $R \geq 2$ regions. There are two production factors, the workers and the farmers; the economy is endowed with H workers and with L farmers. The workers are perfectly mobile between regions while the farmers are immobile. The interpretation of the two production factors is made for expositional convenience. The critical point is that the mobile production factor is related to labor, while the other factor, such as untradable business services, is immobile. The economy has two sectors called agriculture ($\mathbb{A}$) and manufacturing ($\mathbb{M}$). The denomination of these two sectors is conventional. What really matters for our purposes are the market and technological properties of these two sectors, which we now define. In accordance with the principle of differentiation discussed in Section 7.3.1, manufactures produce a continuum of varieties of a horizontally differentiated good under increasing returns using workers as the only input. The agricultural sector produces a homogeneous good under constant returns using farmers as the only input. The share of farmers in region r is fixed and denoted $0 \leq \nu_r \leq 1$ for $r = 1, \ldots, R$. The share of workers in each region r is variable and denoted $0 \leq \lambda_r \leq 1$ for $r = 1, \ldots, R$.

Although both consumption and production take place in a specific region, for the moment it is notationally convenient to describe preferences and technologies without explicitly referring to any particular region.

Consumers. Preferences are identical across all workers and described by a Cobb-Douglas utility:

$$U = Q^{\mu} A^{1-\mu} / \mu^{\mu}(1-\mu)^{1-\mu} \qquad 0 < \mu < 1 \tag{8.1}$$

where Q stands for an index of the consumption of the manufactured good, while A is the consumption of the agricultural good. When the manufacturing sector provides a continuum of varieties of size M, the index Q is given by

$$Q = \left(\int_0^M q_i^{\rho} \mathrm{d}i \right)^{1/\rho} \qquad 0 < \rho < 1 \tag{8.2}$$

where q_i represents the consumption of variety $i \in [0, M]$. Each consumer displays a *preference for variety*: when varieties are equally priced, the consumer's most preferred choice is to spread her consumption of the differentiated good over the whole range of varieties. In (8.2), the parameter ρ stands for the inverse of the intensity of love for variety over the differentiated product. When ρ is close to 1, varieties are close to perfect substitutes; when ρ decreases, the desire to spread consumption over all varieties increases. If we set

$$\sigma \equiv \frac{1}{1-\rho}$$

then σ is the elasticity of substitution between any two varieties, which varies between 1 and ∞.

If Y denotes the consumer income, $p^{\mathbb{A}}$ the price of the agricultural good, and p_i the price of variety i, then the individual demand functions are

$$A = (1-\mu)Y/p^{\mathbb{A}} \tag{8.3}$$

$$q_i = \frac{\mu Y}{p_i}\frac{p_i^{-(\sigma-1)}}{P^{-(\sigma-1)}} = \mu Y p_i^{-\sigma} P^{\sigma-1} \qquad i \in [0, M] \tag{8.4}$$

where P is the price index of the differentiated product given by

$$P \equiv \left(\int_0^M p_i^{-(\sigma-1)} \mathrm{d}i\right)^{-1/(\sigma-1)}. \tag{8.5}$$

Hence, the demand for a variety increases with the price index so that a lower (higher) price index means that the product market is more (less) competitive. In other words, a firm's demand accounts for the aggregate behavior of its competitors via the price index. More generally, $\mu Y P^{\sigma-1}$ acts as a demand shifter.

Introducing (8.3) and (8.4) into (8.1) yields the indirect utility function

$$V(Y, P, p^{\mathbb{A}}) = Y P^{-\mu}(p^{\mathbb{A}})^{-(1-\mu)}. \tag{8.6}$$

Producers. The technology in agriculture is such that one unit of output requires one farmer. Each variety of the differentiated good is produced according to the same technology such that the production of the quantity q_i requires l_i workers:

$$l_i = f + cq_i \tag{8.7}$$

where f and c are, respectively, the fixed and marginal labor requirements. This technology exhibits scale economies. Without loss of generality, we choose the unit of labor in the manufacturing sector such that $c = 1$. Because there are increasing returns but no scope economies, each variety is produced by a single firm. Indeed, any firm obtains a higher share of the market by producing a differentiated variety than by replicating an existing one. In turn, this implies that the mass of firms is identical to the mass of varieties and that the output of a firm equals the demand of the corresponding variety.

The output of the agricultural sector is costlessly traded between any two regions and is chosen as the numéraire so that $p^{\mathbb{A}} = 1$. In contrast, the output of the manufacturing sector is shipped at a positive cost according to the iceberg technology: when one unit of the differentiated product is moved from region r to region s, only a fraction $1/\tau_{rs}$ arrives at destination, where $\tau_{rs} > 1$ for $r \neq s$ and $\tau_{rr} = 1$.[1]

Because varieties are equally weighted in the utility function, we may disregard the variety index and focus upon the region index only. Hence, if a variety is produced in region r and sold at the mill (fob) price p_r, the delivered (cif) price p_{rs} paid by a consumer located in region s ($\neq r$) is

$$p_{rs} = p_r \tau_{rs}. \tag{8.8}$$

If the distribution of firms is $(M_1, \ldots, M_R)$, using (8.5), we obtain the price index P_r in region r:

$$P_r = \left[\sum_{s=1}^{R} \phi_{sr} M_s p_s^{-(\sigma-1)} \right]^{-1/(\sigma-1)} \tag{8.9}$$

where

$$\phi_{sr} = \tau_{sr}^{-(\sigma-1)}$$

can be interpreted as a "spatial discount" factor: the higher the transport cost from s to r, the lower the actual demand from region s faced by a firm located in region r. In other words, ϕ_{rs} measures the freeness of trade: $\phi_{rs} = 0$ means that transport costs from r to s are prohibitive, while $\phi_{rs} = 1$ means that trading the differentiated good is costless.

Let w_r denote the nominal wage rate of a worker living in region r. Because the price of the agricultural good equals 1, the wage of the farmers is also equal to 1 in all regions. Thus, because there is free entry and exit, and therefore zero profit in equilibrium, the income of region r is

$$Y_r = \lambda_r H w_r + \nu_r L. \tag{8.10}$$

[1] One may wonder why shipping the agricultural good is assumed to be costless, whereas shipping the manufactured good is costly. Recall that the primary purpose of the CP model is to investigate how steadily decreases in the cost of shipping manufactured goods affects the structure of the space-economy. To isolate this effect, it is common to work with a setting in which farmers' wages are equalized across space; this is guaranteed by the assumption of zero transport cost for the agricultural good. This assumption is restrictive because decreasing transport costs for manufactured goods below some threshold, whereas keeping constant those of agricultural goods, stops the concentration process and leads to the redispersion of manufacturing firms and population (Fujita and Mori 2005). We return to this problem in Chapter 9.

From (8.4), the *total* demand of a firm located in region r is

$$q_r = \sum_{s=1}^{R} \mu Y_s (p_r \tau_{rs})^{-\sigma} P_s^{\sigma-1} \tau_{rs}$$
$$= \mu p_r^{-\sigma} \sum_{s=1}^{R} \phi_{rs} Y_s P_s^{\sigma-1}. \quad (8.11)$$

This expression requires some comments. The term $\mu Y_s (p_r \tau_{rs})^{-\sigma} P_s^{\sigma-1} \tau_{rs}$ stands for the quantity shipped from the firm located in r to region s. Here, the regional consumption in s, which is equal to $\mu Y_s (p_r \tau_{rs})^{-\sigma} P_s^{\sigma-1}$, must be multiplied by τ_{rs} because the firm's output "melts" on the way, thus implying that the firm must send out a larger quantity of its output for the desired quantity to be delivered. The expression (8.11) has a gravity-like nature. Indeed, each term in (8.11) gives the demand in s for a variety produced in r, which depends positively on the local income, Y_s, and negatively on the accessibility to region s, measured by ϕ_{rs}. Raising ϕ_{rs} implies that region s gets "closer" to region r, which means that the demand stemming from region s for a variety produced in region r is shifted upward. To put it simply, what is going on in region s matters more to region r's firms. Finally, the competitiveness of region s is measured by the value of the price index $P_s^{\sigma-1}$, which depends on the prices charged by the local and foreign firms.

Since there is a continuum of firms, each firm is negligible and the interactions between any two firms are zero, but aggregate market conditions affect each firm. This provides a setting in which firms are not competitive (in the classic economic sense of having infinite demand elasticity), but at the same time they have no strategic interactions with one another. Because each firm has a negligible impact on the market, it may accurately neglect the impact of a price change over consumers' income (Y_r) and other firms' prices and hence on the regional price indices (P_r). Consequently, (8.11) implies that, regardless of the spatial distribution of consumers, each firm faces an isoelastic downward-sloping demand (the price-elasticity equals σ). This very convenient property depends crucially on the assumption of an iceberg transport cost, which affects the level of demand but not its elasticity.

The profit function of a firm in r is

$$\pi_r = p_r q_r - w_r (f + q_r) = (p_r - w_r) q_r - w_r f. \quad (8.12)$$

It is both convenient and relevant to think of the market equilibrium in which the locations of firms and workers are fixed as being a short-run equilibrium. The distinction between short-run and long-run is justified here by the fact that adjustments in the agents' locations are slower than adjustments in market prices. In other words, for a given distribution of population, we determine the equilibrium prices and wages prevailing in all regions. We then study how firms and workers are distributed between the regions.

8.2.1.1 The Short-Run Equilibrium

Solving the first-order condition using (8.11) yields the common equilibrium price

$$p_r^* = \frac{\sigma}{\sigma - 1} w_r \quad r = 1, \ldots, R. \tag{8.13}$$

This means that firms use a relative markup equal to $\sigma/(\sigma - 1)$, which is independent of the firms' and consumers' distributions. Everything else being equal, more product differentiation leads to a higher markup and, therefore, to a higher equilibrium price. However, the equilibrium price depends on the mass of firms and workers established in region r through the local wage w_r.

Substituting (8.13) into the profit function leads to

$$\pi_r = \frac{w_r}{\sigma - 1} q_r - w_r f = \frac{w_r}{\sigma - 1}[q_r - (\sigma - 1)f]. \tag{8.14}$$

Under free entry, profits are zero, and thus the equilibrium output of a firm is a constant given by

$$q^* \equiv q_r^* = (\sigma - 1)f \qquad r = 1, \ldots, R. \tag{8.15}$$

Note that this quantity is independent of the distributions of firms and workers and is the same across regions. As a result, in equilibrium a firm's labor requirement is also unrelated to the firms' distribution:

$$l^* \equiv l_r^* = \sigma f \qquad r = 1, \ldots, R.$$

Thus, the total mass of firms in the manufacturing sector is constant and equal to H/l^*, whereas the corresponding firm distribution

$$M_r = \lambda_r H / l^* = \lambda_r H / \sigma f \qquad r = 1, \ldots, R \tag{8.16}$$

depends only on the distribution of workers. These equalities imply that the CP model allows for the spatial redistribution of the manufacturing sector but not for its growth, for the total number of firms (or varieties) is constant; this issue is addressed in Chapter 11.

Introducing the equilibrium prices (8.13) and substituting (8.16) for M_r in the regional price index (8.9), we obtain:

$$\begin{aligned} P_r &= \left[\sum_{s=1}^{R} \phi_{sr} \frac{\lambda_s H}{\sigma f} \left(\frac{\sigma}{\sigma - 1} w_s \right)^{-(\sigma-1)} \right]^{-1/(\sigma-1)} \\ &= \kappa_1 \left[\sum_{s=1}^{R} \phi_{sr} \lambda_s w_s^{-(\sigma-1)} \right]^{-1/(\sigma-1)} \qquad r = 1, \ldots, R \end{aligned} \tag{8.17}$$

where

$$\kappa_1 \equiv \frac{\sigma}{\sigma - 1} \left(\frac{H}{\sigma f} \right)^{-1/(\sigma-1)}$$

is a bundle of parameters. Clearly, the price index P_r depends on the spatial distribution of workers as well as on the values of transport costs. Note that, from the viewpoint of a firm located in region r, the term $\phi_{sr}\lambda_s H$ may be interpreted as the "effective" number of competitors set up in region s. Indeed, a large number of firms located in a region having a poor access to region r has a low impact on P_r. In contrast, when ϕ_{sr} is close to 1, the effective number of competitors is almost the actual number of firms, $\lambda_s H$.

Although firms' sizes are unaffected when the economy gets larger, there is a scale effect at the market level. It takes the specific form of a growth in the number of varieties. The greater the increase in the number of workers/consumers H, the greater the increase in the number of firms and, consequently, in the number of varieties. The price index then decreases, thus contributing to making all consumers better-off.

Finally, we consider the labor market clearing conditions for a given distribution of workers. The wage prevailing in region r is the highest wage that firms located there can pay under the nonnegative profit constraint. For that, we evaluate the demand (8.11) as a function of the wage through the equilibrium price (8.13):

$$q_r(w_r) = \mu \left(\frac{\sigma}{\sigma - 1} \right)^{-\sigma} w_r^{-\sigma} \sum_{s=1}^{R} \phi_{rs} Y_s P_s^{\sigma-1}. \tag{8.18}$$

Because this expression is equal to $(\sigma - 1)f$ when profits are zero, we obtain the following implicit expression for the equilibrium wages:

$$w_r^* = \kappa_2 \left[\sum_{s=1}^{R} \phi_{rs} Y_s P_s^{\sigma-1} \right]^{1/\sigma} \qquad r = 1, \ldots, R \tag{8.19}$$

where

$$\kappa_2 \equiv \frac{\sigma - 1}{\sigma} \left[\frac{\mu}{(\sigma - 1) f} \right]^{1/\sigma}.$$

Clearly, w_r^* is the equilibrium wage prevailing in region r when $\lambda_r > 0$. It varies positively with the income of region $s \neq r$ because firms in region r face a higher demands there; the equilibrium wage also varies positively with P_s because a higher value of the price index in region s means that the corresponding market is less competitive.

Substituting (8.19) for Y and setting $p^{\mathbb{A}} = 1$ in the indirect utility (8.6), we obtain the *real wage* in region r as follows:

$$V_r = \omega_r = \frac{w_r^*}{P_r^{\mu}} \qquad r = 1, \ldots, R. \tag{8.20}$$

In other words, the indirect utility is equivalent to the real wage.

Finally, the Walras law implies that the agricultural sector market is also in equilibrium provided that the equilibrium conditions above are satisfied.

8.2.1.2 The Long-Run Equilibrium

The equilibrium distribution of workers is obtained from the comparison of the welfare levels that workers can achieve in regions $1, \ldots, R$. The well-being of a worker in a region depends on the wage that she can earn as well as the cost of living prevailing there. A low nominal wage in a region can, indeed, be more than compensated for by low prices for the differentiated product, if this region accommodates a higher number of firms, and vice versa.

Specifically, for a given spatial distribution of workers, we now ask whether there is an incentive for them to migrate and, if so, what direction the flow of migrants will take. A *spatial equilibrium* arises when no worker may get a higher utility level in another region: $(\lambda_1^*, \ldots, \lambda_R^*)$ is a spatial equilibrium if there exists a positive constant ω^* such that

$$\begin{aligned} \omega_r &\leq \omega^* \qquad \text{for } r = 1, \ldots, R \\ \omega_r &= \omega^* \qquad \text{if } \lambda_r^* > 0. \end{aligned}$$

Hence, the zero-profit real wage that local firms could afford to pay in a region containing no workers is lower than (or just equal to) the equilibrium real wage. Since the functions $\omega_r(\lambda_1, \ldots, \lambda_R)$ are continuous in $(\lambda_1, \ldots, \lambda_R)$ over the compact set

$$\Lambda \equiv \left\{ (\lambda_1, \ldots, \lambda_R); \sum_{r=1}^{R} \lambda_r = 1 \quad \text{and} \quad \lambda_r \geq 0 \right\}$$

we can appeal to Schmeidler (1973) to guarantee that such an equilibrium always exists.

Following a now well-established tradition in migration modeling, we focus on a myopic evolutionary process in which workers are attracted (repulsed) by regions providing high (low) utility levels:

$$\dot{\lambda}_r = \lambda_r(\omega_r - \overline{\omega}) \qquad r = 1, \ldots, R$$

where $\dot{\lambda}_r$ is the time-derivative of λ_r, ω_r is the equilibrium real wage corresponding to the distribution $(\lambda_1, \ldots, \lambda_R)$, and $\overline{\omega} \equiv \Sigma_s \lambda_s \omega_s$ is the average real wage across all regions. In other words, workers move from the low-wage regions toward the high-wage ones.

A spatial equilibrium is stable if, for any marginal deviation of the population distribution from the equilibrium, the equation of motion above brings the distribution of workers back to the original one. In doing so, we assume that local labor markets adjust instantaneously when some workers move from one region to another. More precisely, the mass of firms in each region must be such that the labor market clearing conditions (8.16) remain valid for the new distribution of workers. Wages are then adjusted in each region for each firm to earn zero profits in any region having workers because workers move toward high-wage regions.[2]

More than forty years ago, Muth (1971) asked the question: Is the migration of individuals the chicken or the egg of regional and urban development? In NEG, firms are created and destroyed according to a process driven by the locational choices made by workers who vote with their feet. Thus, NEG seems to assume that workers are the chicken. However, preferences for amenities or other givens are not central to the locational choices of individuals in NEG. Migrations are based on real wage differences that stem from the interaction between the product and labor markets in a world where firms produce under increasing returns and bear transportation costs. Furthermore, Picard, Thisse, and Toulemonde (2004) show that Krugman's results remain true when the distribution of activities is driven by the locational decisions made by firms seeking the highest profits, while workers adjust instantaneously. In this event, the equilibrium arises when profits accruing to entrepreneurs, instead of workers' utilities, are equalized across regions. Thus, it seems fair to say that NEG is agnostic about "who" is the egg and the chicken.[3]

8.2.2 The Two-Region Case

The analytical complexity of the CP model has typically constrained its theoretical analysis to stylized settings with two region, 1 and 2. To avoid any exogenous comparative advantage, we assume that farmers are equally split between regions ($\nu_1 = \nu_2 = 1/2$). In order to keep things as symmetric as possible, we also assume that $\tau_{12} = \tau_{21} \equiv \tau$.[4]

[2] Observe here one more justification for working with a continuum of agents (workers and firms): this modeling strategy allows respecting the integer nature of a worker's or firm's location while describing the evolution of the regional share of production by means of differential equations.

[3] Note that in the CP model and its relatives, firms are not anchored in some specific locales for one or several of the reasons discussed in Chapter 4. They can freely substitute one location for another.

[4] The mathematical properties of the CP model are studied in detail by Robert-Nicoud (2005).

In this context, the equilibrium equations are as follows:

$$Y_r = \lambda_r H w_r^* + L/2 \qquad r = 1, 2 \tag{8.21}$$

$$P_r = \kappa_1(\lambda_r (w_r^*)^{-(\sigma-1)} + \tau^{-(\sigma-1)}\lambda_s (w_s^*)^{-(\sigma-1)})^{-1/(\sigma-1)} \qquad s \neq r. \tag{8.22}$$

$$w_r^* = \kappa_2 \left(Y_r P_r^{\sigma-1} + \tau^{-(\sigma-1)} Y_s P_s^{\sigma-1}\right)^{1/\sigma} \qquad s \neq r \tag{8.23}$$

$$\omega_r = w_r^* P_r^{-\mu} \qquad r = 1, 2. \tag{8.24}$$

From now on, we use $\lambda \equiv \lambda_1$ so that $\lambda_2 = 1 - \lambda$. For any given λ, Mossay (2006) shows that there exists a unique short-run equilibrium. Furthermore, it follows from the implicit function theorem that the equilibrium values of Y_r, P_r, and w_r are continuous in λ. Using the equilibrium conditions (8.21)–(8.23), we readily verify that the sum of nominal wages, $\lambda w_1^* + (1-\lambda) w_2^*$, across regions is constant. Since profits are zero, the global income of the economy, $Y_G \equiv Y_1 + Y_2$, is independent of the spatial distribution of the manufacturing sector and the degree of market integration. Therefore, the relocation of agents does not affect the global income. These results show that the price index is the only channel through which workers' welfare is affected by the location of economic activity. By contrast, the relocation of agents affects the income of regions, the additional surplus of a region being just equal to the loss of the other.

A *spatial equilibrium* arises at $\lambda \in (0, 1)$ when

$$\Delta(\lambda) \equiv \omega_1(\lambda) - \omega_2(\lambda) = 0$$

or at $\lambda = 0$ when $\Delta(0) \leq 0$, or at $\lambda = 1$ when $\Delta(1) \geq 0$. Location choices exhibit strategic complementarity (substitutability) if the $\Delta(\lambda)$ is increasing (decreasing).

The stability is studied with respect to the myopic evolutionary dynamics

$$\dot{\lambda} = \lambda \Delta(\lambda)(1 - \lambda) \tag{8.25}$$

defined in Section 8.2.1. If $\Delta(\lambda)$ is positive and $\lambda \in (0, 1)$, workers move from 2 to 1; if it is negative, they go in the opposite direction. Clearly, any spatial equilibrium is a steady-state for (8.25).

The system (8.21)–(8.24) of nonlinear equations cannot be solved analytically. As a consequence, deriving a characterization of its solution in terms of λ is not simple. To derive some insight into the nature of the equilibrium, computational experiments have been performed by Krugman (1991b).[5] The results are displayed in Figure 8.1, where the following results appear. For a large value of τ $(= \tau_1)$, there is only one equilibrium corresponding to the full dispersion of the manufacturing sector ($\lambda = 1/2$), which is stable. When τ takes some

[5] See Fujita Krugman and Venables (1999, chapter 5) for more details.

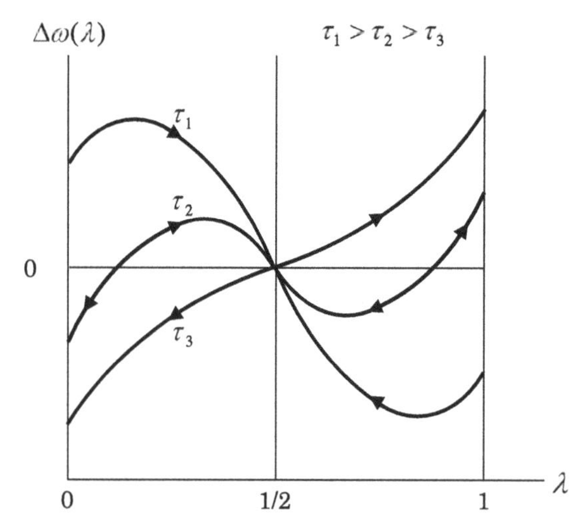

Figure 8.1. Migration dynamics under various values of τ.

intermediate value τ_2, four more equilibria emerge that are all asymmetric. However, the two interior equilibria are unstable. Hence, three stable equilibria now exist: the symmetric configuration and the core–periphery structure with concentration of the manufacturing sector in region 1 or region 2. Finally, when τ takes a sufficiently low value ($= \tau_3$), the symmetric equilibrium becomes unstable, and thus the core–periphery structure is the only stable outcome.

These observations will serve as a guide in the rest of the analysis.

8.2.2.1 The Core-Periphery Structure

Suppose that the manufacturing sector is concentrated in one region, say region 1 so that $\lambda = 1$. To check whether this is an equilibrium, we ask whether a worker could be strictly better off in 2. More precisely, we wish to determine conditions under which the real wage she may obtain in region 2 does not exceed the real wage this worker gets in region 1.

Setting $\lambda = 1$ in (8.21)–(8.24), we get the following equations:

$$Y_1 = Hw_1^* + L/2 \quad \text{and} \quad Y_2 = L/2$$
$$P_1 = \kappa_1 w_1^* \quad \text{and} \quad P_2 = \kappa_1 \tau w_1^*. \tag{8.26}$$

Then, w_1^* is obtained by substituting (8.26) into (8.23) with $r = 1$,

$$w_1^* = \kappa_2 \left[Y_1(\kappa_1 w_1^*)^{\sigma-1} + Y_2(\kappa_1 w_1^*)^{\sigma-1} \right]^{1/\sigma}$$

which yields $w_1^* = (\mu/H)(Y_1 + Y_2)$, or

$$w_1^* = \frac{\mu}{1-\mu}\frac{L}{H}.$$

This shows that the wage within the agglomeration increases with the farmer–worker ratio (L/H) as well as with the share of the manufactured good in consumers' expenditures (μ). Note that there is no mobility between the two sectors. Thus, w_1^* need not exceed farmers' income. Yet, one expects the mobile individuals to have a higher income than those who stay put. This is so if and only if the following condition holds:

$$\mu\left(\frac{L}{H}+1\right) > 1.$$

From (8.13), it is then possible to determine the common equilibrium price of all varieties in terms of the fundamentals of the economy:

$$p_1^* = \frac{\sigma}{\sigma-1}\frac{\mu}{1-\mu}\frac{L}{H}$$

which implies

$$P_1^* = \kappa_1\frac{\sigma}{\sigma-1}\frac{\mu}{1-\mu}\frac{L}{H} \qquad P_2^* = \tau P_1^* > P_1^*.$$

In words, the price index of the manufactured good rises with the degree of product differentiation of this good, the farmer–worker ratio, and the share of the manufactured good in consumers' expenditures.

Finally, when the manufacturing sector is geographically concentrated in 1, the regional nominal incomes are as follows:

$$Y_1^* = \frac{\mu}{1-\mu}L + \frac{L}{2} \quad \text{and} \quad Y_2^* = \frac{L}{2}$$

and thus the global income is given by

$$Y_G = \frac{L}{1-\mu} \tag{8.27}$$

which increases with the mass of farmers.

The equilibrium real wage in region 1 is

$$\omega_1 = \kappa_1^{-\mu}(w_1^*)^{1-\mu} = \left(\frac{\sigma}{\sigma-1}\right)^{-\mu}\left(\frac{H}{\sigma f}\right)^{\mu/(\sigma-1)}\left(\frac{\mu}{1-\mu}\frac{L}{H}\right)^{1-\mu}$$

which is independent of τ because all varieties are produced in region 1.

Agglomeration in region 1 is an equilibrium if and only if ω_1 is larger than or equal to ω_2. Thus, we need to determine what ω_2 would be if some workers were to choose to set up there. To find it, we substitute (8.22) for the price index and (8.23) for the nominal wage into the real wage (8.24) and get:

$$\omega_2 = \kappa_1^{\rho-\mu}\kappa_2(w_1^*)^{\rho-\mu}\tau^{-\mu}\left(Y_1\tau^{-(\sigma-1)} + Y_2\tau^{\sigma-1}\right)^{1/\sigma}.$$

The equilibrium real wage in region 2 does depend on τ because all varieties are imported from region 1.

It is then readily verified that

$$\frac{\omega_2}{\omega_1} = \left[\frac{1+\mu}{2}\tau^{-\sigma(\mu+\rho)} + \frac{1-\mu}{2}\tau^{-\sigma(\mu-\rho)}\right]^{1/\sigma}. \quad (8.28)$$

When shipping is costless ($\tau = 1$), we always have $\omega_2/\omega_1 = 1$: location does not matter. Furthermore, the first term in the right-hand side of (8.28) is always decreasing in τ. Therefore, because the second term is also decreasing when $\mu \geq \rho$, the ratio ω_2/ω_1 always decreases with τ, thus implying that $\omega_2 < \omega_1$ for all $\tau > 1$. This means that the core–periphery structure is a stable equilibrium for all $\tau > 1$ when

$$\mu \geq \rho$$

which is called the *black hole condition*: varieties are so differentiated that firms' demands are not very sensitive to differences in transportation costs, thus making the agglomeration force very strong. In fact, it is so strong that agglomeration can be viewed as a "black hole" attracting any movable activity.

More interesting is the case in which

$$\mu < \rho \quad (8.29)$$

that is, varieties are not very differentiated so that the firms' demands are sufficiently elastic and, hence, the agglomeration force is weaker. If (8.29) holds, then the second term in (8.28) goes to infinity when $\tau \to \infty$, and the ratio ω_2/ω_1 is as depicted in Figure 8.2.

We see that a single value $\tau_s > 1$ exists such that $\omega_2/\omega_1 = 1$. Hence, the agglomeration is a stable equilibrium for any $\tau \leq \tau_s$. In other words, once all firms belonging to the manufacturing sector locate together within a region, they stay there as long as carrying their output to the other region is sufficiently cheap. This occurs because firms can enjoy all the benefits of agglomeration without losing much of their business in the other region. Such a point is called the *sustain point* because, once firms are fully agglomerated, they stay so for all smaller values of τ.[6] On the other hand, when transportation costs are sufficiently high ($\tau > \tau_s$), firms lose much on their exports so that the core–periphery structure is no longer an equilibrium.

[6] This terminology is dictated by the secular fall in transportation costs discussed in Chapter 1.

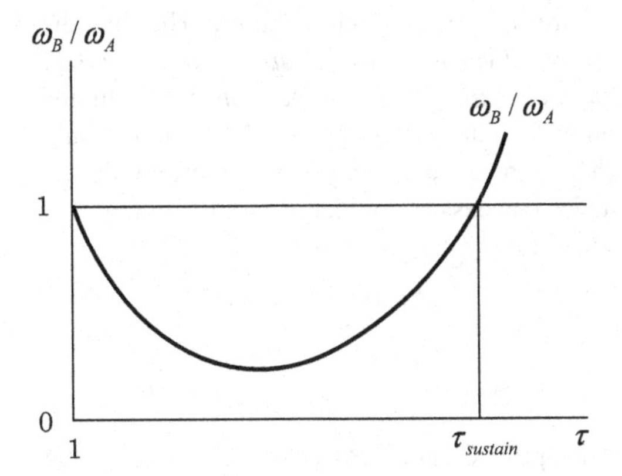

Figure 8.2. The determination of the sustain point.

Summarizing these results, we have the following:

Proposition 8.1. *Consider a two-region economy.*
(i) If $\mu \geq \rho$, then the core–periphery structure is always a stable equilibrium.
(ii) If $\mu < \rho$, then there exists a unique solution $\tau_s > 1$ to the equation

$$\frac{1+\mu}{2}\tau^{-\sigma(\mu+\rho)} + \frac{1-\mu}{2}\tau^{-\sigma(\mu-\rho)} = 1 \tag{8.30}$$

such that the core–periphery structure is a stable equilibrium for any $\tau \leq \tau_s$.

It is remarkable that τ_s depends only upon the degree of product differentiation (σ) and the share of the manufactured good in consumption (μ).

8.2.2.2 The Symmetric Pattern

What we have just seen suggests that the manufacturing sector is geographically dispersed when transportation costs are high and when (8.29) holds. To check this conjecture, we consider the symmetric configuration ($\lambda = 1/2$). In this case, there are only four equilibrium conditions,

$$Y_1 = Y_2 = (H/2)w^* + L/2$$

where w^* is the common equilibrium wage prevailing at the symmetric configuration. Since

$$Hw^* + L = Y_G = L/(1-\mu)$$

we have

$$w^* = \frac{\mu}{1-\mu}\frac{L}{H}$$

which is equal to the wage that prevails under agglomeration. This has the following implication: *locally produced varieties are cheaper in the core than the locally produced varieties in each region under dispersion*. Interestingly, this result is confirmed by the empirical analysis conducted by Handbury and Weinstein (2011) who observe that aggregate grocery prices are lower in larger cities while such cities' residents have access to a wider array of varieties.

The common price index is equal to

$$P^* = \kappa_1 \left[\frac{1}{2}(w^*)^{-(\sigma-1)} + \frac{1}{2}(w^*\tau)^{-(\sigma-1)} \right]^{-1/(\sigma-1)}$$
$$= \kappa_1 2^{1/(\sigma-1)} w^* (1 + \tau^{-(\sigma-1)})^{-1/(\sigma-1)}$$

which is larger (smaller) than the price indices P_1^* (P_2^*) prevailing in the agglomerated configuration for the same value of τ. The common real wage is

$$\omega^* = w^*(P^*)^{-\mu}.$$

Because $\omega_1^* = \omega_2^* = \omega^*$, the symmetric structure is a spatial equilibrium for all $\tau > 1$.

For a given $\tau > 1$, the symmetric equilibrium is stable (unstable) if the slope of $\Delta\omega(\lambda)$ is negative (positive) at $\lambda = 1/2$. Checking this condition requires fairly long calculations using all the equilibrium conditions. However, Fujita, Krugman, and Venables (1999, chapter 5) have shown the following results. First, when (8.29) does not hold, the symmetric equilibrium is always unstable. However, when (8.29) holds, this equilibrium is stable (unstable) if τ is larger (smaller) than some threshold value τ_b given by

$$\tau_b = \left[\frac{(\rho + \mu)(1 + \mu)}{(\rho - \mu)(1 - \mu)} \right]^{1/(\sigma-1)} \tag{8.31}$$

which is clearly larger than 1. This is called the *break point* because symmetry between the two regions is no longer a stable equilibrium for lower values of τ. It is interesting to note that τ_b depends on the same parameters as τ_s. It is apparent from (8.31) that τ_b is increasing with the share of the manufacturing sector (μ) and with the degree of product differentiation ($1/\rho$).

Figure 8.3 represents all stable (unstable) equilibria by solid (broken) lines. It is shown in appendix A that $\tau_b < \tau_s$. Hence, a domain of transport cost values exists over which there is multiplicity of equilibria, namely agglomeration and dispersion. More precisely, for $\tau > \tau_s$, the economy necessarily involves full dispersion. For $\tau < \tau_b$, the core–periphery structure always arises, the winning region depending on the initial conditions: the region with the initially larger share of the manufacturing sector ends up with the whole share. Finally, for $\tau_b \leq \tau \leq \tau_s$, both full agglomeration and full dispersion are stable equilibria. In the corresponding domain, the economy displays some hysteresis because full dispersion still prevails when transport costs fall below the sustain

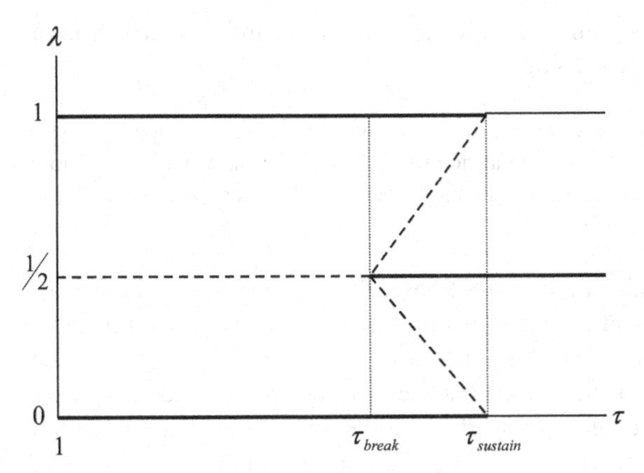

Figure 8.3. Bifurcation diagram for the CP model.

point while staying above the break point. Eventually, as transportation costs decrease sufficiently, sudden agglomeration of the manufacturing sector arises. The catastrophic nature of the bifurcation is an artifact due to the assumption of identical consumers. Once it is recognized that consumers are heterogeneous in their migration behavior, the transition becomes smooth (Tabuchi and Thisse 2002). Therefore, the interest generated by the result of sudden agglomeration is for the most part unwarranted.

Observe that, when region-2 workers start moving to region 1, their nominal wage decreases. Indeed, we have

$$\frac{dY_G}{d\lambda} = w_1^* + \lambda\frac{dw_1^*}{d\lambda} - w_2^* + (1-\lambda)\frac{dw_2^*}{d\lambda} = 0$$

because Y_G is constant. Evaluating this expression at $\lambda = 1/2$, we obtain

$$\left.\frac{dw_1^*}{d\lambda}\right|_{\lambda=1/2} + \left.\frac{dw_2^*}{d\lambda}\right|_{\lambda=1/2} = 0.$$

Thus, when λ slightly exceeds $1/2$, the nominal wage in the region attracting (losing) workers must decrease (increase). However, the price index decreases (increases) even more, and thus offsets the wage drop (hike). In other words, *workers do not move to earn more but to be better off through cheaper varieties.*

The idea that interregional economic integration enhances the geographical concentration of activities may at first sight seem counter-intuitive as agents are less sensitive to the costs of distance.[7] One could thus think that the economic activity can locate anywhere and, therefore, specifically on the periphery.

[7] The two configurations discussed here should not be interpreted literally. Dispersion means that industry is spread over a large number of regions, with small or medium-sized cities. At the other extreme, agglomeration should be seen as a situation in which industry is concentrated in a small number of highly urbanized regions.

Proposition 8.1 does not say anything new, however. It was anticipated by Kaldor (1970, 241) more than 40 years ago:

> When trade is opened up between them, the region with the more developed industry will be able to supply the need of the agricultural area of the other region on more favourable terms: with the result that the industrial centre of the second region will lose its market and will tend to be eliminated.

Furthermore, although firms are footloose, they gradually lose their malleability once the effects of the agglomeration forces associated with increasing returns come into play. This is mapped into a *putty-clay geography*: the regions may be similar at the outset, but they can diverge considerably later on. What makes these forces so powerful is the combination of a drastic fall in transport and communication costs, together with the cumulative nature of the agglomeration process to give rise to a new type of economic geography in which space is "slippery" whereas locations are "sticky." Furthermore, unlike Henderson's model studies in Chapter 4 where cities result from the actions taken by large agents, agglomeration is here the unintentional consequence of individual decisions made by firms and workers pursuing the own interest. In such a context, policy makers seem to have very little influence on the structure of the location of economic activity. Yet, as observed by Krugman (2005), policy can matter a lot because factor mobility magnifies the effects of small differences between regions, while pecuniary externalities allow a small push in the "right" direction at the right time to have lasting effects on the distribution of activities.

In the CP model, agglomeration is not based on increasing returns external to firms but on pecuniary externalities stemming from imperfect competition and increasing returns internal to firms. As competition is imperfect, pecuniary externalities find their origin in the fact that prices do not reflect the social value of individual decisions. Consequently, the move of workers and firms unintentionally affect the welfare of all agents through pecuniary externalities.[8] Another major difference with the models of city formation studied in Sections 4.3 and 4.4 of Chapter 4 is that cities are anchored in the CP model because intercity trade involves positive transport costs. However, this model deals with two locations only. We see in Chapter 10 how the model can be extended to generate several urban agglomerations.

[8] Note that prices do not reflect the social value of goods when technological externalities are at work. However, as seen in Chapter 4, the existence of large agents who base their decisions on social costs and benefits removes this problem and allows the small agents to make the socially optimal migration decisions.

8.2.3 The Manufacturing Sector with Two Factors

8.2.3.1 The Market Outcome

The CP model is unsatisfying in many respects. (i) It is fairly cumbersome to handle and does not lead to an analytical solution: something frustrating for a specific model. (ii) It only accounts for two sectors and two regions. (iii) It overlooks other costs whose origin lies in the space-economy (for example, the congestion costs generated by the emergence of an agglomeration) and, conversely, overlooks other agglomeration benefits, such as those discussed in Chapter 4. (iv) The agricultural sector is given a very restricted role, its main role being to guarantee the equilibrium of the trade balance. Along the same line, it is hard to see why trading the agricultural good is costless in a model seeking to ascertain the overall impact of trade costs on the location of economic activity. Although this list is not exhaustive, it nevertheless seems fair to say that Krugman has identified a major channel explaining why regional disparities exist.

The first difficulty has led Forslid and Ottaviano (2003) to propose a simplified version of the CP model, where firms use unskilled labor to produce the manufactured good. It is, indeed, reasonable to view the factor standing behind the fixed costs as skilled labor, especially when these costs correspond to research and development as well as advertising and sales promotion. Furthermore, a firm belonging to the manufactured sector also uses unskilled labor (or rural workers) to produce its output. Formally, this means that the production of any variety requires a fixed amount f of skilled labor (workers) and a marginal requirement $c = 1$ of unskilled labor (farmers). In this case, the marginal labor requirement is measured in terms of the numéraire. Such a modeling strategy allows us to provide a complete analytical solution for the short-run equilibrium, because the marginal costs, and hence the equilibrium prices, no longer depend on the wages of the skilled and, therefore, on their location. This cancels out some interesting effects but allows for a more detailed treatment of the CP model.

Indeed, (8.12) becomes

$$\pi_r = (p_r - 1)q_r - w_r f \qquad r = 1, 2.$$

Because demands (8.4) are symmetric and isoelastic and the marginal cost is 1 instead of w_r,[9] the equilibrium price is now the same across firms *and* regions:

$$p_1^* = p_2^* = \frac{\sigma}{\sigma - 1}.$$

[9] This is so as long as the agricultural good is produced in both regions. This amounts to assuming that the condition $\max\{H, L\} < (1 - \mu)(1 - \mu/\sigma)(H + L)$ holds. See Baldwin et al. (2003, section 4.2.2).

Thus, the delivered price τp_r^* of imported varieties is also the same in both regions. As a result, the regional price indices are as follows:

$$P_r = \frac{\sigma}{\sigma - 1}\left(\frac{H}{f}\right)^{-1/(\sigma-1)}(\lambda_r + \phi\lambda_s)^{-1/(\sigma-1)} \qquad s \neq r \tag{8.32}$$

where $\phi \equiv \tau^{-(\sigma-1)} \in [0, 1]$.

This expression illustrates in a neat and simple way how spatial frictions transform the actual number of firms competing in region r $(n_r + n_s)$ into the effective number of competitors $(n_r + \phi n_s)$ that determines the level of the price index in region r. For example, lowering transport costs is equivalent to increasing the number of foreign competitors as they both lead to a lower price index.

Under free entry, the output of a firm located in region $r = 1, 2$ is now

$$q_r^* = (\sigma - 1) f w_r \qquad r = 1, 2$$

which, unlike (8.15), increases with the nominal wage prevailing in the region where the firm is located.

From (8.4), the demands in region $s = 1, 2$ for any variety produced in region $r = 1, 2$ are given by

$$q_{rs} = \frac{p_{rs}^{-\sigma}}{M_r p_{rs}^{-(\sigma-1)} + M_s p_{ss}^{-(\sigma-1)}} \mu Y_s$$

in which the regional incomes Y_r are

$$Y_r = L/2 + \lambda_r H w_r \qquad r = 1, 2.$$

Consequently, the market-clearing conditions for the differentiated product become

$$q_r^* = q_{rr} + \tau q_{rs} \qquad s \neq r$$

or

$$w_r = \frac{\mu}{\sigma}\left[\frac{1}{\lambda_r + \phi\lambda_s}\left(\frac{L}{2H} + \lambda_r w_r\right) + \frac{\phi}{\phi\lambda_r + \lambda_s}\left(\frac{L}{2H} + \lambda_s w_s\right)\right].$$

Thus, we have two linear equations in the nominal wages w_r and w_s, the solutions of which are as follows:

$$w_1^*(\lambda) = \frac{\mu/\sigma}{1 - \mu/\sigma}\frac{L}{2H}\frac{2\phi\lambda + [1 - \mu/\sigma + (1 + \mu/\sigma)\phi^2](1 - \lambda)}{\phi[\lambda^2 + (1 - \lambda)^2] + [1 - \mu/\sigma + (1 + \mu/\sigma)\phi^2]\lambda(1 - \lambda)}$$

$$w_2^*(\lambda) = \frac{\mu/\sigma}{1 - \mu/\sigma}\frac{L}{2H}\frac{2\phi(1 - \lambda) + [1 - \mu/\sigma + (1 + \mu/\sigma)\phi^2]\lambda}{\phi[\lambda^2 + (1 - \lambda)^2] + [1 - \mu/\sigma + (1 + \mu/\sigma)\phi^2]\lambda(1 - \lambda)}$$

which both increase with the worker–farmer ratio. Note that $\mu/\sigma < 1$ always holds because $\sigma > 1$ and $\mu < 1$.

As in Section 8.2.2, the global income is constant; it is now given by

$$Y_G = \left[\lambda w_1^*(\lambda) + (1-\lambda)w_2^*(\lambda)\right] H + L = \frac{\mu/\sigma}{1-\mu/\sigma} L + H$$

which is the counterpart of (8.27). The global income increases with both the mass of workers and farmers, which means that a more populated economy generates a higher income.

By deriving the ratio

$$\frac{w_1^*(\lambda)}{w_2^*(\lambda)} = \frac{2\phi\lambda + [1-\mu/\sigma + (1+\mu/\sigma)\phi^2](1-\lambda)}{2\phi(1-\lambda) + [1-\mu/\sigma + (1+\mu/\sigma)\phi^2]\lambda}$$

with respect to λ, we find that the region with the larger number of workers offers a higher wage than the other if and only if

$$\phi > \frac{1-\mu\sigma}{1+\mu\sigma}.$$

In other words, the larger region offers higher nominal wages when the two regions are sufficiently integrated.

Given these two solutions, (8.20) and (8.32) imply that

$$\Omega(\lambda) \equiv \frac{\omega_1(\lambda)}{\omega_2(\lambda)} = \frac{w_1^*/P_1^{\mu}}{w_2^*/P_2^{\mu}} = \left[\frac{\lambda + \phi(1-\lambda)}{(1-\lambda)+\phi\lambda}\right]^{\frac{\mu}{\sigma-1}}$$
$$\times \frac{2\phi(\sigma-1)\lambda + [(\sigma-\mu\rho-1)+\phi^2(\sigma+\mu\rho-1)](1-\lambda)}{2\phi(\sigma-1)(1-\lambda) + [(\sigma-\mu\rho-1)+\phi^2(\sigma+\mu\rho-1)]\lambda}.$$

Since

$$\Delta(\lambda) = \omega_2(\lambda)[\Omega(\lambda) - 1]$$

we have

$$\Delta(\lambda) \gtreqless 0 \qquad \text{if and only if} \qquad \Omega(\lambda) \gtreqless 1.$$

Thus, $\Omega(\lambda)$ allows us to obtain the indirect utility differential as an explicit function of the distribution of skilled workers, which is something that cannot be achieved in the original core–periphery model. As usual, because $\Omega(1/2) = 1$, $\lambda = 1/2$ is always a spatial equilibrium.

By studying $\Omega(\lambda)$ with respect to λ, one can show that the equilibrium configurations are similar to those obtained above. First, let us determine τ_b, which is a hard task in the original model. Because $\Omega(1/2) = 1$, the symmetric configuration is stable for some τ if and only if

$$\Omega'(1/2) < 0$$

for the corresponding value of τ. It can readily be verified that

$$\Omega'(1/2) = 0$$

has two roots in ϕ:

$$\phi_1 = \frac{(\sigma - \mu - 1)(\sigma - \mu)}{(\sigma + \mu - 1)(\sigma + \mu)} \quad \text{and} \quad \phi_2 = 1$$

with $\phi_1 < \phi_2$. When $\mu \geq \sigma - 1$, $\phi_1 < 0$ so that the symmetric equilibrium is never stable. This means that this condition is comparable to the black hole condition $\mu \geq \rho \equiv (\sigma - 1)/\sigma$ obtained in Section 8.2.2. When $\mu < \sigma - 1$, $\partial\Omega/\partial\lambda$ evaluated at $\lambda = 1/2$ and $\phi = 0$ is negative, and thus the symmetric configuration is stable for any $\phi < \phi_1$. In other words, the symmetric configuration is stable provided that τ is larger than

$$\tau_b = \left[\frac{(\sigma + \mu - 1)(\sigma + \mu)}{(\sigma - \mu - 1)(\sigma - \mu)}\right]^{1/(\sigma-1)} > 1 \tag{8.33}$$

which is the counterpart of (8.31). For $\tau < \tau_b$, the symmetric equilibrium ceases to be stable.

Next, setting $\Omega(1) = 1$ yields

$$\frac{1 + \mu/\sigma}{2}\tau^{-(\sigma-1+\mu)} + \frac{1 - \mu/\sigma}{2}\tau^{\sigma-1-\mu} = 1 \tag{8.34}$$

which is the counterpart of (8.30). Solving this equation, we obtain the τ_s such that the core–periphery structure is a stable equilibrium for any $\tau \leq \tau_s$.

We may thus conclude that Forslid-Ottaviano's model displays the main features of Krugman's and is much easier to handle. For this reason, we find it convenient to use it in Chapter 11.

8.2.3.2 Forward-Looking Behavior and the CP Model

So far, we have assumed that workers care only about their current utility level, thus implying that only history matters. This is a fairly restrictive assumption to the extent that migration decisions are typically made on the grounds of current and future utility flows and various costs as a result of search, mismatch, and homesickness. It is therefore important to determine if and how workers' expectations about the evolution of the economy may influence the process of agglomeration. In this section, we want to see how the CP model can be used to shed more light on the interplay between history and expectations in the formation of the economic space when migrants maximize the intertemporal value of their utility flows. Furthermore, we have seen that the CP model displays several spatial equilibria. In such a context, stability is used as a refinement to dismiss unstable equilibria. However, studying stability requires specifying a dynamic adjustment process. As seen in Section 8.2.2, Krugman uses the myopic evolutionary dynamics (8.25). Because workers cannot move all together, this process assumes implicitly the existence of moving costs such as search, mismatch, and homesickness. A myopic evolutionary dynamics is a good approximation when the discount rate is high, migration costs are large, or both. Things become very different, however, when workers care about their future and/or are very mobile.

Oyama (2009a, 2009b) highlights the relationships between these two important issues by using the concept of potential games.[10] The payoff functions are given by the real wages $\omega_1(\lambda)$ and $\omega_2(\lambda)$; they define a game in which a continuum of players choose between two strategies, 1 and 2. A player's payoff is determined by the share λ of workers choosing 1 as well as by her own choice. Since $\omega_1(\lambda)$ and $\omega_2(\lambda)$ are continuous, there exists a function $F(\lambda)$ such that

$$F(\lambda) \equiv \int_0^\lambda \Delta(x)\,dx = \int_0^\lambda [\omega_1(x) - \omega_2(x)]\,\mathrm{d}x$$

for all $\lambda \in [0, 1]$, which is called the *potential function* of the CP model. Being the integral of the indirect utility differential, F may be loosely interpreted as the surplus generated by region 1 relative to region 2. The main interest of this function is that its global maximizers are the equilibria that are stable under the forward-looking dynamics described below.

The equilibria of the CP model are the local maximizers of the potential F and, therefore, solve the first-order condition (Oyama 2009a). As seen in the preceding section, when ϕ is slightly smaller than 1, $\Delta(\lambda)$ has a positive slope, which implies that F is strictly convex over $[0, 1]$. In this case, F has two local maximizers, whence the CP model has two equilibria, $\lambda = 0$ and $\lambda = 1$. In contrast, when ϕ is slightly positive, $\Delta(\lambda)$ has a negative slope, implying that F is strictly concave. Therefore, F is maximized at a unique interior point, which is the unique equilibrium of the CP model. That the potential function is convex (concave) for low (high) transport costs thus provides a neat illustration of the contrasted nature of the equilibria of the CP model obtained for very different transport cost values.

We now turn to the dynamic adjustment process suggested by Krugman (1991c) and applied by Ottaviano (1999) and Oyama (2009b) to the CP model. Workers infinitely live with a rate of time preference equal to $\gamma > 0$. Because we wish to focus on the sole dynamics of migration, we assume that expenditure equals income at each time so that there is no intertemporal arbitrage in the differentiated good. Consider the case in which workers believe that region 1 will eventually attract the $\mathbb{M}$-sector although region 2 is initially larger than 1. Therefore, we want to test the consistency of the belief that, starting from time $\theta = 0$, all workers end up being concentrated in 1 at some future date $\theta = T$,

[10] The reader is referred to Sandholm (2001) for a survey of potential games.

that is, there exists $T > 0$ such that,

$$\begin{aligned} \dot{\lambda}(\theta) &> 0 \qquad \theta \in [0, T) \\ \lambda(\theta) &= 1 \qquad \theta \geq T. \end{aligned} \tag{8.35}$$

Let $\bar{\omega}$ be the utility level incurred in region 1 when $\lambda = 1$. Given workers' expectations, we have

$$\omega_1(\theta) = \bar{\omega} \qquad \theta \geq T.$$

When moving from one region to the other, workers incur a utility loss that depends on the rate of migration inasmuch as a migrant typically imposes a negative externality on the others. Specifically, we assume that the utility loss for a migrant at time θ is equal to $|\dot{\lambda}(\theta)|/\delta$, where $\delta > 0$ is a positive constant whose meaning is given below. Thus, under (8.35), the intertemporal utility at time 0 of a worker who moves from 2 to 1 at time $\theta \in [0, T)$ is assumed to be given by

$$\begin{aligned} U(\theta) &\equiv \int_0^\theta e^{-\gamma s}\omega_2(s)\,\mathrm{d}s + \int_\theta^\infty e_1^{-\gamma s}\omega_1(s)\,\mathrm{d}s - e^{-\gamma\theta}\dot{\lambda}(\theta)/\delta \\ &= \int_0^\theta e^{-\gamma s}\omega_2(s)\mathrm{d}s + \int_\theta^T e^{-\gamma s}\omega_1(s)\mathrm{d}s + e^{-\gamma T}\bar{\omega}/\gamma - e^{-\gamma\theta}\dot{\lambda}(\theta)/\delta \end{aligned}$$

where the first term stands for the utility accumulated in region 2 before moving to 1, the second term for the utility obtained in 1 after migration, and the last represents the migration cost at time θ.

Because in equilibrium workers residing in region 2 do not want to delay their migration beyond T, it follows that[11]

$$\lim_{\theta \to T} \left|\dot{\lambda}(\theta)\right| / \delta = 0.$$

When θ tends toward T, we therefore obtain

$$U(T) = \int_0^T e^{-\gamma s}\omega_2(s)\,\mathrm{d}s + e^{-\gamma T}\bar{\omega}/\gamma.$$

Let

$$W_r(\theta) \equiv \int_\theta^T e^{-\gamma(s-\theta)}\omega_r(s)\,\mathrm{d}s + e^{-\gamma(T-\theta)}\bar{\omega}/\gamma \quad \theta \in [0, T) \tag{8.36}$$

[11] Note that this belief allows for the possibility that migrants will return and remigrate until time T is reached. See Oyama (2009a) for a detailed analysis.

be the discounted sum of future utility flows gross of moving costs of a worker at time θ residing in region $r = 1, 2$. Then, we have

$$U(\theta) - U(T) = \int_{\theta}^{T} e^{-\gamma s}[\omega_1(s) - \omega_2(s)]\mathrm{d}s - e^{-\gamma\theta}\dot{\lambda}(\theta)/\delta$$
$$= e^{-\gamma\theta}\Delta W(\theta) - e^{-\gamma\theta}\dot{\lambda}(\theta)/\delta \qquad (8.37)$$

where $\Delta W(\theta) \equiv W_1(\theta) - W_2(\theta)$. Given that workers are free to choose when to migrate, it follows that

$$U(\theta) = U(T) \qquad \theta \in [0, T)$$

along the equilibrium path, and thus (8.37) becomes

$$\dot{\lambda}(\theta) = \delta\Delta W(\theta) \qquad \theta \in [0, T). \qquad (8.38)$$

Therefore, the private marginal cost of moving equals its private marginal benefit at any time $\theta < T$. In this expression, δ represents the speed of adjustment: the larger δ, the higher the mobility of workers.

Using (8.36), the second law of motion is obtained by differentiating the utility gap $W_A(\theta) - W_B(\theta)$ with respect to θ:

$$\mathrm{d}(\Delta W)\mathrm{d}t = \gamma\Delta W(\theta) - \Delta\omega(\theta) \qquad \theta \in [0, T) \qquad (8.39)$$

where $\Delta\omega(\theta) = 0$ for all $\theta \geq T$ because all workers expect the utility flow $\bar{\omega}$. As argued by Ottaviano (1999), expression (8.39) states that, during the migration process, the "annuity value" of being in 1 rather than in 2 (i.e., $\gamma\Delta W$) equals the "dividend" ($\Delta\omega$) plus the "capital gain" ($\mathrm{d}\Delta W/\mathrm{d}\theta$). As a result, we obtain a system of two differential equations involving the variables λ and W and the terminal conditions $\lambda(T) = 1$ and $\Delta W(T) = 0$.

To show the role played by the potential function in the study of the stable equilibria, we first assume that $\Delta(\lambda) > 0$. When migration decisions are based solely on the current utility difference, a worker has an incentive to migrate from 2 to 1. Her move increases the value of λ by an infinitesimal value $\mathrm{d}\lambda$, which in turn increases the value of the potential F because $\mathrm{d}F/\mathrm{d}\lambda = \Delta(\lambda) > 0$. In other words, under the myopic evolutionary dynamics (8.25), the adjustment process ascends the potential F and reaches one of the *local* maximizers of this function, which is locally stable. Evolutionarily stable equilibria, i.e., the local maximizers of F, are thus distinguished from unstable equilibria, i.e., the local minimizers and saddles of F.

On the other hand, when workers care about the future (γ is small) or are very mobile (δ is large) so that the adjustment process is described by (8.38)–(8.39), regardless of the initial configuration $\lambda(0)$, any path converging to the unique *global* maximizer of the potential F is an equilibrium path.[12] Along such a

[12] It is well known that the potential has two global maximizers when the model is symmetric. When the model is asymmetric, F is neither convex nor concave for intermediate values of ϕ. As

path, at some time t the economy may descend the potential and go through a local minimizer; for t arbitrarily large, however, the economy moves to the point where the potential is globally maximized. In contrast, the economy always ascends the potential under myopic evolutionary dynamics, and thus may converge to a local maximizer of the potential. This shows how using such dynamics may generate fragile results.[13] Thus, the region that becomes the core is determined by workers' expectations and not by history.

When the two regions host initially different numbers of workers, one may wonder whether or not their common belief about the future of the space-economy leads them to agglomerate in the currently smaller region, thus reversing the historically inherited advantage of the larger region. Oyama (2009a) shows that the answer is positive when ϕ is close to 1. Assume that the population of farmers is larger in 1 than in 2. Even when all workers are initially located in region 2, there exist self-fulfilling expectations that lead the economy toward full agglomeration in region 1. The reverse does not hold, however: when more workers and farmers are initially located in region 1, there exist no self-fulfilling expectations that leads the economy toward full agglomeration in region 2. Thus, when transportation costs are low, *expectations may wash out the legacy of history when the region with the smaller initial number of workers has an exogenous and permanent comparative advantage.* This result may be explained as follows. If the evolution of the economy were to change direction, workers would experience falling, instantaneous, indirect utility flows for some time period as long as $\lambda < 1/2$. The instantaneous, indirect utility flows would start growing only after λ became larger than $1/2$. Put differently, workers would first experience utility losses followed by utility gains. Because the losses would come before the gains, they would be less discounted. However, the comparative advantage of region 1 makes the benefits of $\lambda = 1$ sufficiently large to compensate workers for the losses they incur during the transition phase.

By contrast, when ϕ is slightly positive, the potential function F has a unique global maximizer at some interior point $\lambda^* \in (0, 1)$, to which all the equilibrium paths converge. In other words, when transport costs are sufficiently high, the stable distribution of the $\mathbb{M}$-sector reflects the exogenous comparative advantage of region 1, and thus only history matters.

To sum up, the above results show that the multiplicity of stable equilibria in the CP model, a topic that has attracted a lot of attention in the literature (see Baldwin et al. 2003; Davis and Weinstein 2002), arises *only* when workers' migration behavior is myopic or, under forward-looking behavior, when the

a result, F could display several global maximizers. However, this corresponds to a zero-measure configuration of parameters. Thus, we may disregard this case.

[13] In the symmetric model, there are 5 equilibria over the interval $[\tau_{\text{sustain}}, \tau_{\text{break}}]$. The equilibria $\lambda = 0, 1/2, 1$ are local maximizers of the potential function, and therefore stable under the myopic evolutionary dynamics, whereas the other two equilibria are local minimizers.

setting is perfectly symmetric. Otherwise, interior and boundary equilibria are never simultaneously stable. We may thus safely conclude that the multiplicity of stable equilibria that arises within the interval $[\tau_s, \tau_b]$ is mainly an artifact due to the symmetry assumption.[14]

If the reasons explaining why cities exist are now clear, it is much less clear why a specific place should become prosperous and vibrant. This is why the above results are interesting: they lead to predictions about *where* agglomeration arises.

8.3 THE WELFARE ANALYSIS OF THE CORE-PERIPHERY MODEL

The following point has been overlooked in the literature devoted to the design of regional policies: both the planner who seeks to maximize global efficiency and the market work with the same agglomeration and dispersion forces. Since the planning optimum and the market equilibrium depend on the fundamental characteristics of the economy, the agglomeration and dispersion forces discussed above are to be taken into account in both cases. What makes the two solutions different is the institutional mechanism used to solve the trade-off between these forces. Such a difference is often poorly understood, thus leading the public and some policy makers to believe that the socially optimal pattern of activities has nothing to do with what the free play of market forces yields. Yet, we see that agglomeration may be socially efficient. This is so when transport costs are sufficiently low. The reason is simple to grasp: firms are able to take advantage of the larger market created by their concentration to exploit scale economies, while guaranteeing the inhabitants of the periphery a good access to their products. In parallel, a large number of consumers have a direct access to a wide portfolio of differentiated goods and services, which are to be imported by a small number of consumers only.

To ease the burden of notation, we make several normalizations in the CP model of Section 8.2.2. First, we choose the unit of the manufactured good for such that $\sigma f = 1$. We also use the fact that the mass of firms is given by a real number and choose the unit of the real line for M to be such that $c = (\sigma - 1)/\sigma$ in (8.7) instead of $c = 1$. It then follows that

$$p_r^* = w_r \tag{8.40}$$

and that

$$l_r^* = \sigma f = 1.$$

[14] When region 1 is endowed with a much larger number of farmers than region 2, using the myopic evolutionary dynamics Sidorov and Zhelobodko (2013) show that the agglomeration of workers arises only in region 1. When region 1 is weakly larger than region 2, agglomeration in region 1 is sustained over a wider range of transport cost values than agglomeration in region 2 (see also Tabuchi and Thisse 2002).

Thus, (8.16) implies that

$$M_1 = \lambda H \qquad M_2 = (1 - \lambda)H.$$

Let us now show that, at any spatial equilibrium, prices as well as wages are constant regardless of the type of equilibrium – agglomeration (A) or dispersion (D). When the economy is dispersed, we have

$$w_1 = w_2 \equiv w^D = \frac{\mu L}{(1-\mu)H}. \tag{8.41}$$

When the economy is agglomerated in, say, region 1, it follows from Section 8.2.2 that

$$w_1 \equiv w^A = \frac{\mu L}{(1-\mu)H} = w^D.$$

Choosing the units of workers' and farmers' labor such that $H = \mu$ and $L = 1 - \mu$, we then obtain

$$p_r = 1 \qquad w_r = w^D = w^A = 1$$

Hence, in both equilibria, the price of local varieties is the same and equal to 1 in both regions, which implies that the real wage varies only with the spatial distribution of firms through the price index:

$$\omega_r = (\lambda_r + \phi\lambda_s)^{\mu/(\sigma-1)} \qquad r \neq s \tag{8.42}$$

up to a constant factor $\mu^{-\mu/(\sigma-1)}$.

Let q_{rr}^D (q_{sr}^D) be the equilibrium consumption of a worker located in region r of any variety produced in region r ($s \neq r$) under dispersion (D). The expressions of q_{sr}^D and q_{rr}^D are respectively given by

$$q_{rr}^D = \mu P_r^{\sigma-1} = \frac{2}{1+\phi} \qquad q_{sr}^D = \mu P_r^{\sigma-1}\tau^{-\sigma} = \frac{2\tau^{-\sigma}}{1+\phi}$$

which implies $q_{rr}^D = \tau^\sigma q_{sr}^D$. Observe that, when dispersion prevails, workers and farmers consume the same quantity of a local (imported) variety.

When there is agglomeration (A), the equilibrium consumptions of a consumer located in regions 1 and 2 differ:

$$q_{11}^A = \mu P_1^{\sigma-1} = 1 \qquad q_{12}^A = \tau^{-1} q_{11}^A = \tau^{-1}.$$

Since $\tau > 1$, we have the following ranking of the consumption levels:

$$q_{rr}^D > q_{11}^A > q_{12}^A > q_{sr}^D.$$

These inequalities shed light on the consumption structure under A and D, and thus on the respective welfare levels. First, under agglomeration, because of transport costs, workers and farmers living in the core consume more of each variety than those living in the periphery ($q_{11}^A > q_{12}^A$). Second, under dispersion, workers and farmers consume more of each of the locally produced varieties and less of each of those produced abroad ($q_{rr}^D > q_{sr}^D$). The inequality $q_{rr}^D > q_{11}^A$ is less straightforward. Because of transport costs, workers and farmers substitute local varieties to imported varieties and end up consuming more of each of the locally produced varieties under dispersion than under agglomeration. Similarly, due to the absence of substitution effect within varieties, farmers living in the periphery consume more of each imported variety under agglomeration than they do under dispersion ($q_{12}^A > q_{sr}^D$).

8.3.1 Does Agglomeration Pareto Dominate Dispersion or Vice Versa?

Denote by ω_1^A a worker's real wage when there is agglomeration in region 1. When dispersion prevails, the real wage is the same in both regions, $\omega_1^D = \omega_2^D = \omega^D$. Using (8.42), it is readily verified that ω_1^A and ω^D are as follows:

$$\omega_1^A = 1 \qquad \omega^D = \left(\frac{1+\phi}{2}\right)^{\frac{\mu}{\sigma-1}}. \tag{8.43}$$

First, ω^A always exceeds ω^D because $\phi < 1$. As a result, *workers always prefer agglomeration to dispersion*. Consider now farmers' welfare. The utility level of a farmer located in the core is the same as a worker's. Therefore, her well-being increases when agglomeration arises. By contrast, a farmer living in the periphery is worse off. Indeed, a farmer living in region 2 prefers agglomeration to dispersion when $\omega_2^A \geq \omega^D$ where

$$\omega_2^A = \tau^{-\mu}. \tag{8.44}$$

Using (8.43), we readily verify that $\omega_2^A \geq \omega^D$ if and only if $\tau^{-\mu} \geq [(1+\phi)/2]^{\frac{\mu}{\sigma-1}}$, which never holds because $\tau > 1$. Thus, farmers located in the periphery always prefer dispersion to agglomeration.

To sum up, *neither agglomeration nor dispersion is a Pareto-dominant allocation* because $\omega_1^A > \omega^D > \omega_2^A$. Thus, there is a conflict of interest between the two groups of farmers. The agglomeration of firms and workers in one region implies a fall in the price index in this region, but leads to an increase in the price index in the other region because all varieties have to be shipped there. Simply put, when workers move from one region to the other, they impose a positive external effect on the farmers located in the core but a negative external effect on the farmers located in the periphery. As a consequence, market forces left to their own device do not generate a Pareto-dominant distribution of activities.

8.3.2 Compensating Losers

A compensation criterion based on the prevailing equilibrium prices and wages may be used in order to determine whether the level of social welfare rises when agglomeration (A) or dispersion (D) prevails. Restricting ourselves to these two configurations is legitimate because they are the only market equilibria. Without loss of generality, we can compute the compensation schemes in terms of labor units. Indeed, as preferences are homothetic, the compensation paid or received by an individual is equal to the compensation associated with her type of labor times the number of labor units she owns. This computation can be made only within a general equilibrium framework, which is precisely one of the main features of the CP model.

Assume that agglomeration prevails. In order to answer the question "Is A preferred to D?," two approaches must be distinguished. In the former, we follow Kaldor (1939) and say that A is preferred to D when the winners are able to compensate the losers in order to give them the utility level they would reach under dispersion. In the latter, we follow Hicks (1940) and say that A is preferred to D when the losers are not able to compensate the winners by giving them the utility level they would reach under agglomeration, when the economy moves to dispersion. As argued by Scitovsky (1941), both criteria must be satisfied for A to be preferred to D (or vice versa).[15]

In either case, to determine the compensations to be paid, we take as a given the equilibrium prices and wages. Consequently, for the compensations to be feasible, it must be that the individual consumptions of each variety evaluated at the incomes net of compensation add up to the quantity supplied by each firm. In this case, if the material balance conditions hold true, the equilibrium prices remain the same. These conditions must also be satisfied for the firms to be able to pay the equilibrium wages on which the compensations are computed.

1. *Does agglomeration generate a potential Pareto improvement upon dispersion?* More precisely, when agglomeration prevails, can income redistribution from those located in the core keep unchanged the utility level of the farmers residing in the periphery, without making the core consumers worse off?

The argument involves three steps: (i) we compute the transfers needed to compensate those who are in the periphery, (ii) we then check that the material balance conditions still hold after compensation, and (iii) we determine under which condition (if any) the level of welfare net of transfers of each type of worker living in the core must exceed the well-being she would get under dispersion without compensation.

[15] At the agglomerated and dispersed configurations, prices and wages are the same. Therefore, the two compensation mechanisms are non-distortionary. However, this ceases to hold when comparing other configurations because prices and wages differ.

(i) For the farmers in the periphery to be exactly compensated, they must be given an additional income C_A such that their utility level at the agglomerated configuration after compensation is just equal to the utility level they reach at the dispersed configuration, that is,

$$\tau^{-\mu}(1 + C_A) = \omega^D = \left(\frac{1+\phi}{2}\right)^{\frac{\mu}{\sigma-1}}$$

the solution of which is

$$C_A = \left(\frac{1+\phi}{2\phi}\right)^{\frac{\mu}{\sigma-1}} - 1 \tag{8.45}$$

which is positive because $\phi < 1$. As a result, the total compensation paid by the consumers residing in the core must be equal to

$$\frac{1-\mu}{2} C_A$$

which increases with transportation costs.

Because all the core residents have the same welfare level and face the same prices and wage, each one must then pay the same amount T_A given by

$$T_A = \frac{1-\mu}{1+\mu} C_A. \tag{8.46}$$

After compensation, the income of an individual in the core is $1 - T_A > 0$.

(ii) We must now determine if the material balance conditions hold at the consumption pattern corresponding to the total incomes obtained after compensation:

$$Y_1 = \frac{1+\mu}{2}(1 - T_A) \qquad Y_2 = \frac{1-\mu}{2}(1 + C_A).$$

At the agglomerated configuration, the total consumption of every variety *after* compensation is given by the sum of the total consumption of the core consumers augmented by the total consumption of the farmers in the periphery. It follows from (8.40) and (8.41) that the total demand for any variety – which are here all produced in region 1 – is such that

$$q_1 = \mu(P_1^{\sigma-1} Y_1 + \phi P_2^{\sigma-1} Y_2)$$

where, given (8.22),

$$P_1 = \mu^{\frac{1}{1-\sigma}} \qquad P_2 = \tau\mu^{\frac{1}{1-\sigma}}.$$

Substituting in q_1 yields

$$q_1 = \frac{1+\mu}{2}(1 - T_A) + \frac{1-\mu}{2}(1 + C_A) = 1$$

where the second equality stems from (8.45) and (8.46). Thus, q_1 is just equal to the equilibrium production of a firm. In other words, the equilibrium output allows each firm to pay the equilibrium wage ($w_r = 1$) used to calculate the compensation.

It follows from the Walras law that the market clearing condition for the agricultural good holds.

(iii) Finally, every consumer in the core strictly prefers the agglomeration outcome if and only if her welfare level after compensation exceeds the welfare level she would get under dispersion, namely

$$1 - T_A > \left(\frac{1+\phi}{2}\right)^{\frac{\mu}{\sigma-1}}.$$

Using (8.45) and (8.46), this is equivalent to

$$F(\tau) \equiv \left(\frac{1+\phi}{2}\right)^{\frac{-\mu}{\sigma-1}} - \left(\frac{1+\mu}{2} + \frac{1-\mu}{2}\tau^{\mu}\right) > 0. \tag{8.47}$$

As shown in appendix B, there exists a single value of $\tau > 1$, denoted τ_K, such that $F(\tau) = 0$ and $F(\tau) > 0$ if and only if $\tau < \tau_K$. Consequently, when the economy moves from dispersion to agglomeration, the state A is preferred to the state D in the sense of Kaldor as long as $\tau < \tau_K$. In contrast, when $\tau \geq \tau_K$, D is preferred to A.

2. *Does dispersion generate a potential Pareto improvement upon agglomeration?* In other words, when dispersion prevails, can income redistribution from the farmers, who would live in the periphery, keep unchanged the utility level of those who would live in the core, without making those farmers worse off?

The payment of any compensation makes the spatial distribution of income uneven between regions: $Y_1 > Y_2$. This in turn prevents the wages and prices corresponding to the dispersed configuration to balance the product and labor markets. Consequently, when the economy moves from dispersion to agglomeration, farmers in region 2 are unable to compensate the consumers who would be in the core at the market prices and wages prevailing under dispersion. In this case, state A is preferred to state D in the sense of Hicks.

Accordingly, when $\tau < \tau_K$ agglomeration is preferred to dispersion according to both criteria. In contrast, when $\tau \geq \tau_K$, we are in a situation of *indetermination* in the sense of Scitovsky (1941), which means no state of the economy is preferred under the two compensation criteria. We may then conclude as follows:

Proposition 8.2. *When transport costs are sufficiently low, agglomeration is socially preferable to dispersion in the sense of both Kaldor's and Hicks'* *criteria. Otherwise, it is impossible to discriminate between these two configurations.*

Charlot et al. (2006) show that τ_K is lower than τ_b for values of μ and σ that agree with empirical evidence. In this case, the market yields agglomeration for values of the transport costs that exceed the threshold below which it is socially desirable. As a result, no general conclusion may be drawn in the CP model as to whether the market yields excessive and insufficient agglomeration.

This indeterminacy may be resolved by resorting to specific social welfare functions. Charlot et al. consider the CES family that encapsulates different attitudes toward inequality across individuals. In the case of n agents whose utility is $u_i(s)$ when the state of the economy is s, the CES social welfare function is given by

$$W(s) = \begin{cases} \frac{1}{1-\eta} \sum_{i=1}^{n} [u_i(s)]^{1-\eta} & \text{for } \eta \neq 1 \\ \sum_{i=1}^{n} \ln u_i(s) & \text{for } \eta = 1 \end{cases} \tag{8.48}$$

in which $\eta \geq 0$ measures the degree of aversion toward inequality. In particular, when $\eta = 0$ (or zero aversion to inequality) the function W is identical to the *utilitarian* welfare function in which the sum of all workers' (indirect) utilities is maximized. At the other extreme, when $\eta \to \infty$ (or infinite aversion to inequality), we have the *Rawlsian* welfare function, which only values the (indirect) utility of the worst-off worker. Intermediate values of η express different societal attitudes toward economic inequality among individuals, that is, among three groups of workers in our setting: as η rises from zero to infinity, the bias in favor of the disadvantaged increases.

As expected, the relative merit of agglomeration critically depends on societal values, i.e., the value of η. If society does not care much about inequality across individuals, agglomeration (dispersion) is socially desirable once transport costs are below (above) some threshold, the value of which depends on the fundamental parameters of the economy. Even though these results are derived from social preferences defined on individualistic utilities, it is worth noting that they lead to policy recommendations that could be regarded as being region-based. This is because the market yields much contrasted distributions of income in the core–periphery structure.

Furthermore, when varieties are very differentiated, it can be shown that agglomeration is always socially preferred to dispersion. Indeed, as varieties are very poor substitutes, workers have a strong preference for variety, thus implying that the consumption of imported varieties is just slightly below that of local varieties. Agglomeration is then more desirable than dispersion because fewer individuals consume imported varieties under agglomeration than under dispersion. By contrast, when varieties are good substitutes, dispersion is more desirable than agglomeration for sufficiently large values of transport costs because consumers' bias toward local varieties is strong.

8.4 CITY-REGIONS AND THE AGGLOMERATION OF FIRMS AND CONSUMERS

In the CP model, the existence of different equilibrium patterns hinges on the geographical immobility of some production factors, i.e., farmers. Relaxing this ad hoc assumption implies that agglomeration always arises because it allows saving on transport costs since the full agglomeration of agents generates no specific costs. In this section, we tackle the issue from a different perspective and recognize that a human settlement of a sizable scale almost inevitably takes the form of a city in which workers bear urban costs that rise with the size of the urban population (see Chapter 3). In order to account for this, we modify the CP model as follows.

Consider an economy involving two monocentric cities (labeled $r = 1, 2$), one type of labor, and two goods, land and a manufactured good. Each city has a large amount of land and is spread along a one-dimensional space X. There is a unit mass of identical and mobile households/workers ($L = 1$); each worker owns one unit of labor. Let λ denote the fraction of workers residing in city 1 so that the mass of workers in cities 1 and 2 is respectively given by $L_1 = \lambda$ and $L_2 = 1 - \lambda$. The welfare of a worker depends on her consumption of the two goods. As in Section 8.2.2, the manufacturing sector supplies a continuum of varieties of a horizontally differentiated good produced under monopolistic competition and increasing returns. Any variety of this good can be shipped from one city to the other according to the iceberg transportation technology described in Section 8.2.2. The second good is land; it is perfectly immobile. The amount of land available at each location $x \in X$ is equal to 1. Each worker consumes a fixed lot size normalized to 1. All firms located in city r are set up at the CBD situated at $x = 0 \in X$.

At the residential equilibrium, the L_r workers are evenly distributed around the CBD. To capture the idea that the level of commuting costs increases with the wage rate, we assume that these costs have the nature of a time-iceberg, which means that the effective labor supply of a worker living at a distance x from the CBD is given by

$$s(x) = 1 - 2tx < 1 \qquad x \in [0, L_r/2]$$

where $t > 0$ is the time commuting rate per distance unit. For $s(x)$ to be positive regardless of the mass of workers in city r, we assume $t < 1/2$. As a result, the total effective labor supply in city r is given by

$$S_r = 2 \int_0^{L_r/2} s(x)\mathrm{d}x = L_r(1 - tL_r/2) \qquad r = 1, 2. \tag{8.49}$$

Therefore, the effective supply of labor increases at a decreasing rate with the number of workers because commuting costs are longer. This modeling strategy reflects the idea that the growth of a city takes resources away from private consumption to construct new urban infrastructures.

We normalize the opportunity cost of land to zero. Then, if w_r stands for the wage rate paid to the workers at the city-rCBD by analogy with region-1 firm, the wage net of commuting costs earned by a worker residing at $L_r/2$ is such that

$$s(L_r/2)w_r = (1 - tL_r)w_r.$$

Because workers are identical, the wage net of urban costs must be equal across locations. In other words, it must be that

$$s(x)w_r - R_r(x) = s(L_r/2)w_r$$

where $R_r(x)$ is the land rent at a distance x from the CBD. Because $R_r(L_r/2) = 0$, the equilibrium land rent in city r is given by

$$R_r^*(x) = t(L_r - 2x)w_r \qquad r = 1, 2$$

while the aggregate land rent is equal to

$$ALR_r = 2\int_0^{L_r/2} R_r^*(x)\mathrm{d}x = tL_r^2 w_r/2.$$

Each city is an independent jurisdiction in which each worker owns an equal share of land. Accordingly, in addition to her wage, a worker receives a fee equal to $ALR_r/L_r = tL_r w_r/2$, so that her disposable income is given by

$$y_r = (1 - tL_r/2)w_r \qquad r = 1, 2.$$

Consumers' preferences being the same as in Section 8.2, the real wage of a city-r worker is given by

$$\omega_r = \frac{y_r}{P_r} \qquad r = 1, 2 \tag{8.50}$$

where P_r is the price index (8.22) prevailing in city r.

Without loss of generality we may choose the unit of the manufacturing sector good for the marginal requirement to satisfy the condition $c\sigma/(\sigma - 1) = 1$, which implies $p_r^* = w_r$. We also choose the unit of labor for $\sigma f = 1$ to hold. As a result, a firm's demand for labor is

$$l_r^* = \sigma f = 1 \qquad r = 1, 2.$$

8.4.1 The Trade-off between Transportation and Commuting Costs

Let M_r be the mass of firms located in city r, which is equal to the total effective labor supply in this city:

$$M_r = S_r \qquad r = 1, 2. \tag{8.51}$$

Differentiating the total mass of varieties with respect to λ, we have

$$\frac{\mathrm{d}(M_1 + M_2)}{\mathrm{d}\lambda} = \frac{\mathrm{d}(S_1 + S_2)}{\mathrm{d}\lambda} = t(1 - 2\lambda).$$

Consequently, the more symmetric the spatial distribution of workers, the larger the total mass of varieties. Indeed, when the economy gets more dispersed, the aggregate commuting costs decrease, thus implying that more labor is available for the manufactured sector. Consequently, when firms and workers are more concentrated in city 1, *commuting costs are higher and transport costs are lower, while the whole range of varieties is narrower.*

Market clearing conditions for the differentiated good yield the wage equations:

$$w_1^\sigma = P_1^{\sigma-1} S_1 w_1 + \phi P_2^{\sigma-1} S_2 w_2$$
$$w_2^\sigma = \phi P_1^{\sigma-1} S_1 w_1 + P_2^{\sigma-1} S_2 w_2$$

where the corresponding price indices are given by

$$P_1 = \left(S_1 w_1^{-(\sigma-1)} + \phi S_2 w_2^{-(\sigma-1)}\right)^{\frac{-1}{\sigma-1}}$$
$$P_2 = \left(\phi S_1 w_1^{-(\sigma-1)} + S_2 w_2^{-(\sigma-1)}\right)^{\frac{-1}{\sigma-1}}.$$

For any given intercity distribution of workers λ, i.e., for given S_1 and S_2, these four equations have a unique solution $\{P_1, P_2, w_1, w_2\}$.

To uncover how transportation and commuting costs interact, we consider the following three steps.

(i) Let $\psi \equiv w_1/w_2$ be the wage ratio. The trade balance between the two cities is given by

$$B(\psi) = S_1 S_2 \left(\frac{\phi \psi^{-(\sigma-1)}}{S_1 \phi \psi^{-(\sigma-1)} + S_2} - \frac{\phi \psi^\sigma}{S_1 + S_2 \phi \psi^{\sigma-1}} \right).$$

Let

$$\varepsilon \equiv \frac{S_1}{S_1 + S_2} = \frac{\lambda(2 - t\lambda)}{2 - t[\lambda^2 + (1 - \lambda)^2]}$$

be the labor supply ratio. Since $\mathrm{d}\varepsilon/\mathrm{d}\lambda > 0$, there is a one-to-one relationship between ε and λ. Thus, for any given $\varepsilon \in (0, 1)$, the equilibrium value of ψ is the solution to the equation $B(\psi) = 0$, which is implicitly given by the following expression:

$$\varepsilon(\psi) = \frac{1}{\frac{\psi^{1-2\sigma} - \phi\psi^{1-\sigma}}{1-\phi\psi^{-\sigma}} + 1}.$$

Because $\varepsilon(\psi)$ is strictly increasing over the interval (0, 1), this function has an inverse, $\psi(\varepsilon)$, which is also strictly increasing over (0, 1). As a result, because $\psi(1/2) = 1$, *the nominal wage is higher in the larger city than in the smaller city*. Thus, workers living in the larger city have a higher pay and bear higher urban costs.

(ii) Dividing the numerator and denominator by $S_1 + S_2$, the ratio ω_2/ω_1 can be shown to be as follows:

$$\frac{\omega_2}{\omega_1} = \frac{1 - t(1-\lambda)/2}{1 - t\lambda/2} \frac{w_2/P_2}{w_1/P_1}$$

$$= \underbrace{\frac{1 - t(1-\lambda)/2}{1 - t\lambda/2}}_{\mathcal{U}(\lambda)} \underbrace{\left[\frac{\varepsilon + \phi(1-\varepsilon)\psi^{\sigma-1}}{\phi\varepsilon\psi^{-(\sigma-1)} + 1 - \varepsilon}\right]^{\frac{-1}{\sigma-1}}}_{\mathcal{T}(\lambda)}.$$

When λ changes, $\mathcal{U}(\lambda)$ accounts for the impact of commuting, and $\mathcal{T}(\lambda)$ for the impact of shipping, on the relative attractiveness of the two cities. Note that $\mathcal{T}(\lambda)$ is influenced by t through the mass of varieties produced in each city, which decreases with t.

(iii) Because $\psi(\varepsilon)$ is increasing in ε and $\varepsilon(\lambda)$ increasing in λ, it is readily verified that

$$\frac{d\mathcal{U}(\lambda)}{d\lambda} > 0 \qquad \frac{d\mathcal{T}(\lambda)}{d\lambda} < 0.$$

When $\mathcal{U}$ increases, city 1 becomes less attractive than city 2 because the relative share spent on commuting rises. In other words, as λ rises, the dispersion becomes stronger. Since $\mathcal{T} = (w_2/P_2)/(w_1/P_1)$, a decrease in $\mathcal{T}$ means that city 1 becomes more attractive than city 2 in terms of consumption. Therefore, the foregoing two inequalities imply that *a rise in the population of city 1 strengthens both the dispersion force associated with commuting costs and the agglomeration force associated with transportation costs*. This shows that the impact of cheaper commuting is not straightforward.

How the equilibrium outcome is determined is shown by comparing the values of workers' welfare reached at each of the two configurations:

$$V^A = (M^A)^{\frac{\sigma}{\sigma-1}} \qquad V^D = (M^D)^{\frac{\sigma}{\sigma-1}} \left(\frac{1+\phi}{2}\right)^{\frac{1}{\sigma-1}}.$$

By being agglomerated, workers save on the transportation costs of the manufactured good, but have access to a narrower range of varieties. In contrast, when they are dispersed, workers have access to a broader range of varieties but must bear the cost of shipping the varieties produced in the other city.

8.4.2 The Equilibrium Patterns

8.4.2.1 Dispersion

As in the CP model, $\lambda = 1/2$ is always a spatial equilibrium. In this configuration, urban costs are low and the range of varieties is wide, whereas transport costs are large. To study its stability, we must determine the break point at which the symmetric configuration ceases to be stable. Totally differentiating ω_r with respect to L_r and evaluating the resulting expression at $\lambda = 1/2$, we obtain

$$\frac{d\omega_r}{\omega_r} = -\frac{tL_r/2}{1 - tL_r/2}\frac{dL_r}{L_r} + \frac{dw_r}{w_r} - \frac{dP_r}{P_r}. \tag{8.52}$$

Applying the same approach to the wage equations and the price indices yields

$$\left(\frac{\sigma}{\Phi} - 1\right)\frac{dw_r}{w_r}\bigg|_{\lambda=1/2} = (\sigma - 1)\frac{dP_r}{P_r}\bigg|_{\lambda=1/2} + \frac{dS_r}{S_r}\bigg|_{\lambda=1/2} \tag{8.53}$$

and

$$\left(\frac{1-\sigma}{\Phi}\right)\frac{dP_r}{P_r}\bigg|_{\lambda=1/2} = (1 - \sigma)\frac{dw_r}{w_r}\bigg|_{\lambda=1/2} + \frac{dS_r}{S_r}\bigg|_{\lambda=1/2} \tag{8.54}$$

where

$$\Phi \equiv \frac{1-\phi}{1+\phi} < 1. \tag{8.55}$$

Solving the equations (8.53) and (8.54) for dw_r/w_r and dP_r/P_r, we get

$$\frac{dw_r}{w_r}\bigg|_{\lambda=1/2} = \frac{\Phi}{\sigma(\Phi+1) - \Phi}\frac{dS_r}{S_r}\bigg|_{\lambda=1/2} \tag{8.56}$$

$$\frac{dP_r}{P_r}\bigg|_{\lambda=1/2} = -\frac{\sigma\Phi}{(\sigma-1)[\sigma(\Phi+1) - \Phi]}\frac{dS_r}{S_r}\bigg|_{\lambda=1/2}. \tag{8.57}$$

Furthermore, it follows from (8.49) that

$$\frac{dS_r}{S_r} = \frac{1 - tL_r}{1 - tL_r/2}\frac{dL_r}{L_r}. \tag{8.58}$$

Substituting (8.56), (8.57), and (8.58) into (8.52), we can determine the elasticity of ω at $\lambda = 1/2$:

$$\frac{L_r}{\omega_r}\frac{d\omega_r}{dL_r}\bigg|_{\lambda=1/2} = \frac{4-2t}{4-t}\left[\frac{(2\sigma-1)\Phi}{(\sigma-1)[\sigma(\Phi+1) - \Phi]} - \frac{t}{2(2-t)}\right]. \tag{8.59}$$

It follows immediately from this expression that

$$\left.\frac{L_r}{\omega_r}\frac{\mathrm{d}\omega_r}{\mathrm{d}L_r}\right|_{\lambda=1/2} < 0 \iff \frac{(2\sigma-1)\Phi}{(\sigma-1)[\sigma(\Phi+1)-\Phi]} < \frac{t}{2(2-t)}.$$

As a result, the symmetric equilibrium is stable if and only if

$$\Omega(\Phi) \equiv \frac{(2\sigma-1)\Phi}{(\sigma-1)[\sigma(\Phi+1)-\Phi]} < \Gamma(t) \equiv \frac{t}{2(2-t)}.$$

Because $\partial\Omega(\Phi)/\partial\Phi > 0$ and $\Phi \in (0, 1)$, it must be that $\Omega(\Phi) < 1/(\sigma - 1)$. Thus, if $\Gamma(t) < 1/(\sigma-1)$ or, equivalently, if $t < 4/(\sigma+1)$, there exists a unique value of Φ that satisfies

$$\left.\frac{L_r}{\omega_r}\frac{\mathrm{d}\omega_r}{\mathrm{d}L_r}\right|_{\lambda=1/2} = 0 \tag{8.60}$$

(or $\Omega(\Phi) = \Gamma(t)$). Since $\partial\Phi/\partial\tau > 0$, there exists a unique value of τ, denoted τ_{b}, such that (8.60) holds. Solving (8.60) for τ, we obtain (8.61) given below. In addition, $\tau < \tau_{\mathrm{b}}$ implies

$$\left.\frac{L_r}{\omega_r}\frac{\mathrm{d}\omega_r}{\mathrm{d}L_r}\right|_{\lambda=1/2} < 0$$

which means that the symmetric configuration is stable.

Furthermore, when $t \geq 4/(\sigma+1)$, we have

$$\left.\frac{L_r}{\omega_r}\frac{\mathrm{d}\omega_r}{\mathrm{d}L_r}\right|_{\lambda=1/2} < 0$$

for all $\tau \in (1, \infty)$. In this case, there is no break point, which implies that the symmetric configuration is stable regardless of the value of τ.

Summarizing these results, we have the following:

Proposition 8.3. *Consider a two-region economy.*
(i) If $t \in \left[\frac{4}{\sigma+1}, \frac{1}{2}\right)$, then the symmetric equilibrium is always stable.
(ii) If $t \in \left(0, \min\{\frac{4}{\sigma+1}, \frac{1}{2}\}\right)$, there exists a unique break point given by

$$\tau_{\mathrm{b}} = \left\{\frac{(2\sigma-1)+(\sigma-1)\Gamma(t)}{(2\sigma-1)[1-(\sigma-1)\Gamma(t)]}\right\}^{\frac{1}{\sigma-1}} > 1 \tag{8.61}$$

such that the symmetric configuration is stable for any $\tau < \tau_{\mathrm{b}}$.

In other words, when commuting costs are small and transportation costs high, the symmetric configuration is unstable. Indeed, although the whole range of varieties in the economy shrinks when workers are agglomerated, they benefit from a better access to a wider array of local varieties. Therefore, when $\tau \geq \tau_{\mathrm{b}}$, the net benefit of having all varieties locally produced is sufficiently large to outweigh the higher urban costs that workers must bear by being agglomerated. Note, however, that the benefit of a better access to the whole range of varieties is high (low) when varieties are bad (good) substitutes. Thus, varieties must be sufficiently differentiated ($\sigma < 7$) for the break point to exist. By contrast, when commuting costs are large, the symmetric configuration is always stable.

The preceding analysis has focused on transportation costs. Nevertheless, the above proposition may be reinterpreted in terms of commuting costs. Specifically, the following result can be shown to hold: *if $\sigma > 3$, the symmetric configuration is stable if $t > t_b$* where

$$t_b \equiv \frac{4(2\sigma - 1)\Phi}{(\sigma^2 + 2\sigma - 1)\Phi + \sigma(\sigma - 1)}. \tag{8.62}$$

Observe that (8.62) is the inverse relationship of (8.61). Accordingly, the previous result is indeed the counterpart of Proposition 8.2 expressed in terms of commuting costs instead of transportation costs.

8.4.2.2 Agglomeration

We now consider the case of an agglomeration ($\lambda = 1$). In this configuration, the wage paid to the workers and the urban costs are the highest, the range of varieties the narrowest, whereas transport costs are zero because there is no shipping.

The price indices yield the relationship

$$P_2 = \tau P_1$$

while it follows from the wage equations that

$$w_2 = \tau^{\frac{1-\sigma}{\sigma}} w_1.$$

These two relationships imply that the real wage ratio is given by

$$\left.\frac{\omega_2}{\omega_1}\right|_{\lambda=1} = \frac{\tau^{\frac{-(2\sigma-1)}{\sigma}}}{1 - t/2}. \tag{8.63}$$

It follows from (8.63) that

$$\left.\frac{\omega_2}{\omega_1}\right|_{\lambda=1} < 1 \iff \tau > (1 - t/2)^{\frac{-\sigma}{2\sigma-1}}.$$

Hence, we have:

Proposition 8.4. *Consider a two-region economy. There exists a single value*

$$\tau_s \equiv (1 - t/2)^{\frac{-\sigma}{2\sigma-1}} \tag{8.64}$$

such that the agglomerated configuration is a stable equilibrium for any $\tau > \tau_s$.

In other words, workers are willing to agglomerate within a single city, that is, to bear high commuting costs and to consume a narrow range of varieties when importing varieties from the other city is very expensive.

As in the foregoing, Proposition 8.4 can be reinterpreted in terms of commuting costs. Specifically, *the agglomerated configuration is a stable equilibrium for any $t < t_s$ where*

$$t_s = 2\left(1 - \tau^{\frac{-(2\sigma-1)}{\sigma}}\right). \tag{8.65}$$

Note that (8.65) is the inverse of (8.64).

As in Section 8.2.2, the break and sustain points differ. Because their analytical expressions are available, we may directly compare them. To this end, consider the ratio of the sustain and break points. Taking the limit of this ratio when t tends to zero, we obtain

$$\lim_{t \to 0} \frac{\tau_s}{\tau_b} = 1.$$

Differentiating the ratio of the sustain and break points with respect to t yields

$$\frac{d}{dt}\left(\frac{\tau_s}{\tau_b}\right) \equiv \Delta(t) = -8\sigma^2 + (\sigma + 1)(3\sigma - 1)t.$$

Because t must be smaller than $4/(\sigma + 1)$ for a break point to exist, $\Delta(t)$ is increasing. Furthermore, we have

$$\Delta\left(\frac{4}{\sigma + 1}\right) < 0 \qquad \Delta\left(\frac{1}{2}\right) < 0.$$

Consequently, it must be that $\Delta(t) < 0$ for all $t < 4/(\sigma + 1)$. Thus, $\tau_s < \tau_b$ for all admissible values of t. In other words, as in the CP model, when $\tau \in [\tau_s, \tau_b]$ both agglomeration and dispersion are stable equilibria.

The foregoing results bear some resemblance to those derived in Section 8.2.2. There is, however, one fundamental and striking difference: agglomeration is a stable equilibrium when transportation costs are sufficiently large. In addition, a steady decrease in transportation costs leads to the dispersion of the industry because urban costs become the dominant force. In other words, *the sequence of spatial configurations obtained in the CP model is reversed.* The symmetric configuration is stable here for $\tau < \tau_b$, whereas it is stable for $\tau > \tau_b$ in the CP model; likewise, the agglomerated configuration is a stable equilibrium when $\tau > \tau_s$, whereas it is a stable equilibrium in Krugman's model when $\tau < \tau_s$.

In addition, the agglomerated configuration is a stable equilibrium for any $t < t_s$, which agrees with what economic historians have observed (Bairoch 1988; Hohenberg and Lees 1985): the agglomeration of activities is more likely to arise when commuting costs within cities are sufficiently small.

In the CP model, the cost generated by the formation of an agglomeration is related to the provision of the manufactured goods to the – by assumption – immobile farmers residing in the periphery, which is independent of the number of workers in city 1. By contrast, the formation of an agglomeration generates specific costs, i.e., higher commuting costs and a narrower range of varieties, which increase with the number of workers. Thus, the spatial concentration of activities is associated with very different forces in the two models, which implies that the interplay of agglomeration and dispersion forces may vastly change with the nature of the forces at work.

Unlike the CP model, the above results suggest that *a more integrated economy need not be more agglomerated.* Quite the opposite: lower transportation costs lead to the dispersion of economic activities because this allows firms and workers to alleviate the burden of urban costs. Would the number of potential cities be arbitrarily large, the steady decrease in transport costs would eventually generate a more and more dispersed pattern of production, thus leading to the vanishing of cities (Anas 2004). This difference in results needs qualification. The CP model is designed to deal with issues arising at the macro-spatial level, and thus a spatial agglomeration à la Krugman may be formed by a dense network of medium-sized cities such as the Randstadt area of the Netherlands. By contrast, because it focuses on the internal structure of cities, the city-region model developed in this section seems more relevant to study issues at the micro-spatial level. Furthermore, the model above does not take into account the agglomeration economies discussed in Section 4.2, which tend to bind firms together. Likewise, it does not account for sectors producing nontradable business-to-business and business-to-consumer services. Last, the model neglects possible firm relocations to the suburbs of the core metropolitan area rather than the distant periphery.

That said, the two approaches used here and in Section 8.2 are not orthogonal. The city-region model captures some fundamental ingredients of the urban system studied in Section 4.4. As a result, if intercity trade accounts for a large share of interregional and international trade, this model highlights new phenomena that are disregarded by the CP model. This is important because the process of market integration affects the shipping costs of commodities but has no direct impact on workers' commuting costs. Therefore, globalization need not lead to a polarized economic space.

8.5 THE BELL-SHAPED CURVE OF SPATIAL DEVELOPMENT

The CP model and the city-region model developed in the preceeding section lead to opposite conclusions regarding the impact of decreasing transport costs on the location of economic activity. Does it mean that NEG is useless? Not necessarily. Krugman and Venables (1995) have invited us to reconsider the conclusions of the CP model in that the relationship between the agglomeration rate of the manufacturing sector and the level of transportation costs would be ∩-shaped instead of monotone decreasing. The appropriate question is: can the above models and results be reconciled within a more general framework that would yield a *bell-shaped* relationship between economic integration and regional disparities? In other words, as the costs of moving goods go down, economic activities would start to be concentrated in a fairly small number of large urban regions; in a second stage, activities would be redispersed toward a larger number of regions made up of small or medium-sized cities. As in Chapter 6, both workers and firms consume land, and lot sizes are endogenous. However, unlike Section 8.4, there is no commuting. This assumption is made for analytical convenience.

The economy has two consumption goods, land and the manufactured good, and two production factors, land and labor. Preferences are given by

$$U = Q^{\mu} S^{1-\mu} / \mu^{\mu}(1-\mu)^{1-\mu}$$

where S stands for the consumption of land. In other words, the agricultural good is replaced by land in (8.1). If y denotes the consumer income and R the land rent, the individual demand functions are, respectively,

$$Q = \mu y p^{-\sigma} P^{\sigma-1} \qquad S = (1-\mu)y/R$$

and thus the indirect utility (8.6) becomes

$$V(y, P, R) = yP^{-\mu} R^{-(1-\mu)}. \tag{8.66}$$

Each region is endowed with the same amount of land, which is normalized to 1. The total amount of land in the economy being equally owned by households, the aggregate land rent accruing to region r is proportional to its share of total labor. Hence region r's income is given by

$$Y_r = w_r L_r + (R_r + R_s) L_r \tag{8.67}$$

where the total mass of workers is also normalized to 1.

Each variety is produced by a single firm under increasing returns to scale. The fixed requirement is a Cobb-Douglas composite of land and labor where $0 \leq \alpha \leq 1$ is the share of land. The marginal labor requirement is equal to 1. Thus, the total cost of a firm located in region $r = 1, 2$ that produces the quantity q_r is given by

$$C_r(q) = f R_r^{\alpha} w_r^{1-\alpha} + q_r w_r.$$

In this expression, the first term corresponds to the (endogenous) fixed cost; when $\alpha = 0$, this function is identical to the cost function of the CP model.

Using the profit-maximizing price, it is readily verified that the zero-profit condition yields the following relationship between firm output, land rent, and wage in region r:

$$q_r = f(\sigma - 1)\left(\frac{R_r}{w_r}\right)^{\alpha}.$$

Assume that the distribution of labor is fixed with $L_1 \geq L_2 = 1 - L_1$. Let M_r be the number of firms located in region r. Each firm requires a fixed amount of labor and a variable amount of labor, which depends on its output. Market clearing for labor yields

$$L_r = \delta_1 M_r \left(\frac{R_r}{w_r}\right)^{\alpha} \tag{8.68}$$

where $\delta_1 \equiv f(\sigma - \alpha) > 0$. Thus, labor demand is positively related to the number of firms and negatively to the wage.

Market clearing for land leads to a similar relation:

$$1 = \delta_2 M_r \left(\frac{w_r}{R_r}\right)^{1-\alpha} + \frac{\mu Y_r}{R_r} \tag{8.69}$$

where $\delta_2 \equiv f\alpha > 0$. Thus, land demand stemming from firms is positively related to the number of firms and negatively to the land rent.

Without loss of generality, we assume that labor in region 1 is the numéraire so that $w_1 = 1$. Hence w_2 is the relative wage between the two regions.

Using (8.67), (8.68), and (8.69) yields the mass of firms M_1, the land rent R_1, and the income Y_1 in terms of w_2:

$$M_1(w_2) = \delta_1^{\alpha-1} L_1^{1-\alpha} \left\{\frac{\mu}{[(1-\mu)\delta_1 + \delta_2][L_1 + \mu L_2 + (1-\mu)L_2 w_2]}\right\}^{\alpha}$$

$$R_1(w_2) = L_1 \frac{[(1-\mu)\delta_1 + \delta_2][L_1 + \mu L_2 + (1-\mu)L_2 w_2]}{\mu\delta_1}$$

$$Y_1(w_2) = L_1 \frac{\delta_1(L_1 + \mu L_2) + \delta_2 L_1 + [(1-\mu)\delta_1 + \delta_2]L_2 w_2}{\mu\delta_1}.$$

Similar expressions can be obtained for region 2 by permuting L_1 and L_2. Unlike the CP model, the total mass of firms, $M_1(w_2) + M_2(w_2)$, varies with the interregional distribution of the manufacturing sector and the level of transport costs.

The previous model embeds the same forces as the CP model. Its main distinctive feature is the following additional dispersion force: an inflow of workers (and firms) in a region leads to a higher rent therein. As a result, unlike in the CP model, *the agglomeration of firms and workers in a single region*, say 1, *is never a spatial equilibrium*. Indeed, because $Y_2/L_2 > 0$ and $R_2 = 0$, it follows from (8.66) that the indirect utility in region 2 is arbitrarily large. Consequently, there is no vacant land in region 2 and $\lambda = 1$ is never an equilibrium outcome.

As in the CP model, dispersion is always a spatial equilibrium. Thus, when dispersion is not stable, the manufacturing sector is *partially* agglomerated. Pflüger and Tabuchi (2010) show that the derivative of the indirect utility differential with respect to $\lambda \equiv L_1$ evaluated at $\lambda = 1/2$ is given by the following expression:

$$\Lambda(\phi) \equiv A\phi^2 - 2B\phi + D(1 - D)$$

where $D \equiv 1 - \alpha\mu - (1 - \mu)\sigma < 1$, while A and B are two (positive or negative) constants determined by the parameters α, μ, and σ given in Pflüger and Tabuchi. As usual, the symmetric equilibrium is stable (unstable) if $\Lambda(1/2) < 0$ ($\Lambda(1/2) > 0$). Evidently, the sign of $\Lambda(0)$ is given by the sign of D. Furthermore, $\Lambda(1) < 0$ because workers' and firms' locations are driven by land rent considerations only, and thus the manufacturing sector is dispersed as in the preceding section.

Assume that $D < 0$, which means $\Lambda(0) < 0$. For this to happen, σ must be sufficiently large. The equation $\Lambda(\phi) = 0$ has two real roots ($\phi_1 < \phi_2$) if and only if $\Lambda(B/A) > 0$. In this case, ϕ_1 and ϕ_2 belong to the interval (0, 1) if and only if $0 < B/A < 1$.

Proposition 8.5. *Assume $D < 0$. If $0 < B/A < 1$ and $\Lambda(B/A) > 0$, then dispersion prevails when $\phi < \phi_1$; the manufacturing sector is partially agglomerated when $\phi_1 < \phi < \phi_2$; redispersion prevails when $\phi > \phi_2$.*

For completeness, when $\Lambda(0) > 0$, it must be that the locus of Λ goes through the interval (0, 1) once at $\bar{\phi} \in (0, 1)$ because $\Lambda(1) < 0$. Therefore, partial agglomeration prevails for $\phi < \bar{\phi}$, whereas the manufacturing sector is dispersed when ϕ exceeds $\bar{\phi}$. This is so when land is used for housing only.[16] We thus fall back on results similar to Propositions 8.3 and 8.4.

In Proposition 8.5, agglomeration occurs during the second phase of the integration process. The dispersion in the first and third integration phases emerges for very different reasons. In the former phase, like in the CP model the manufacturing sector is dispersed because shipping its output is expensive; in the latter phase, like in the city-region model dispersion occurs because the smaller region develops a comparative advantage in terms of land rent. When shipping the manufactured good is sufficiently inexpensive, the price indices and the wage rates are more or less the same in the two regions. By contrast, the price of land in region 1 exceeds its price in region 2. Therefore, workers and

[16] This result is similar to the one obtained by Helpman (1998) who assumes $\alpha = 0$. In this case, if $(1 - \mu)\sigma < 1$ there is full agglomeration when $\phi = 0$. Furthermore, it can be shown that $A < 0$ and $B > 0$. Therefore, $A/B < 0$ and $\Phi(\phi) = 0$ has a single root belonging to (0, 1). Thus, as ϕ steadily increases, the manufacturing sector gets more dispersed until $\bar{\phi}$ is reached. Beyond this value, dispersion prevails. If $(1 - \mu)\sigma > 1$, dispersion is the only stable equilibrium.

firms move from 1 to 2 where they pay a lower land rent. This process comes to a halt when symmetry is achieved. Simply put, the relationship between economic integration and spatial inequality is not monotone: *while the first stages of economic integration exacerbate regional disparities, once a certain threshold is reached, additional integration starts undoing them*. This amounts to the reindustrialization of the periphery and a simultaneous deindustrialization of the core.

Similar bell-shaped relationships between economic integration and spatial inequality emerge in a number of other contexts, thus endowing this relationship with strong theoretical foundations. For example, Oyama et al. (2011) develop a framework combining (i) two regions having different sizes and (ii) immobile and heterogeneous individuals who are entitled to be either a worker in an existing firm or an entrepreneur producing a new variety. In other words, spatial mobility is replaced by professional mobility. These authors show that the larger region always retains a more than proportional share of firms (see Chapter 9). This does not mean, however, that this region always benefits from lower transport costs. Indeed, the process of economic integration is split into two contrasting phases. In the first one, which occurs when transport costs remain relatively high, the industrial basis of the larger region grows whereas that of the smaller region shrinks. Because consumers living in the smaller region have access to a much wider range of varieties, the local firms lose a substantial market share in their home market, thus reducing the incentives to become entrepreneurs. On the contrary, firms in the larger region benefit from a market expansion effect that leads more individuals to become entrepreneurs. Consequently, during the first phase of the integration process, *regions become more dissimilar and spatial inequality rises*. In the second phase, which is reached when transport costs are sufficiently low, we observe a complete reversal in the foregoing tendencies. On the one hand, transport costs are now sufficiently low for the smaller region firms to benefit from a much larger market, thus inducing more individuals to become entrepreneurs. On the other hand, because foreign competition is exacerbated by lower transport costs, business is less profitable in the larger region. Hence, during the second phase, *economic integration fosters interregional convergence*. Working with richer settings thus leads us to believe that the twin goals of economic efficiency and spatial equality may be pursued simultaneously, at least once a certain level of integration has been reached. This concurs with Fujita, Krugman, and Venables (1999, 260) for whom "declining trade costs first produce, then dissolve, the global inequality of nations."

Williamson (1965) argued that spatial development follows a bell curve. Recent work in economic history seems to bolster this conjecture. For example, computing Gini indices for twenty American industries in 1860, 1914, 1947, 1967, and 1987, Kim (1995) finds a bell-shaped relationship between economic integration and geographical concentration in the manufacturing sector. Using the Theil index for 87 French departments, Combes et al. (2011)

find that employment in the industrial and services sectors in 1860, 1895, 1930, 1983, and 2000 obeys such a curve. Rosès (2003), dividing Spain into eight macro-regions, observes that the most dynamic industrial sectors became more concentrated over the nineteenth century, when Spanish regions started to come together to form an integrated national economy. Rosès, Martínez-Galarraga, and Tirado (2010) extend this analysis and confirm the bell-shaped relationship for Spain. The turning point of this curve occurred after the international integration of the Spanish economy in the mid-1970s. Thus, the empirical evidence seems to be compelling.

It is worth stressing once more that the CP model was designed to cope with macro-regions. A macro-region may accommodate several specialized cities such as those studied in Section 4.4. As a result, the region as a whole may be diversified even when cities are specialized. Furthermore, large cities are often polycentric (Glaeser and Kahn 2004). For example, Baum-Snow (2010) reports that declining commuting costs not only allowed workers to spread out but also allowed firms to benefit from the same agglomerations economies as before but at farther distances. The existence of secondary business centres relaxes the pressures exerted by urban costs, and thus slows down the interregional or international relocation process (Cavailhès et al. 2007). What differs between these two types of dispersion is again the *spatial scale* at which they occur: the intra-urban scale here and the interregional scale for the CP model.

8.6 THE COAGGLOMERATION OF UPSTREAM AND DOWNSTREAM INDUSTRIES

In the CP model, agglomeration is the outcome of a circular causality process in which more people concentrate within the same region because they love variety. However, if workers are sticky, no agglomeration can arise. Instead, each region specializes in the production of differentiated varieties on the basis of their initial endowments, and intra-industry trade occurs for all values of the transportation costs.

However, the agglomeration of industries is a pervasive phenomenon even when labor is immobile. An alternative way to explain the emergence of agglomeration is to recognize that the final sector uses an array of differentiated intermediate goods. In this case, *the agglomeration of the final sector in a particular region can occur because of the concentration of the intermediate sector in that region, and conversely* (Krugman and Venables 1995; Venables 1996). In this section, we show how this process works in a context in which we combine elements belonging to the core–periphery model and to the one presented in Section 4.2.1.[17] The key issue in the approach followed here is how workers living in a given region allocate themselves between the different sectors

[17] We assume here that the final sector uses labor in a Cobb-Douglas production function.

of the regional economy assuming for simplicity that the intersectoral mobility is perfect. For each region, a given allocation of labor generates a certain wage through the labor market clearing condition. At the corresponding wages, firms choose to stay put or to relocate. In equilibrium, no firm of the final or intermediate sector has an incentive to change location.

8.6.1 The Intermediate and Final Sectors

The economy involves three sectors: the final, intermediate, and agricultural ones. Because workers are spatially immobile, love for variety is no longer an agglomeration force, and thus it is convenient to assume that the output of the final sector is homogeneous. Preferences are identical across all workers and described by the utility (8.1):

$$U = Q^{\mu} A^{1-\mu} / \mu^{\mu} (1-\mu)^{1-\mu} \qquad 0 < \mu < 1$$

where Q now stands for the consumption of a homogeneous good produced by the final sector, and A is the consumption of the agricultural sector's output.

Workers being immobile, we may consider a single type of labor. Because the output is homogeneous, the manufacturing sector is assumed to operate under constant returns to scale and perfect competition. The manufactured good is produced according to the Cobb-Douglas production function:

$$X^{\mathrm{M}} = l^{1-\alpha} I^{\alpha} \qquad 0 < \alpha < 1 \tag{8.70}$$

where X^{M} is the output of the manufacturing sector, l the amount of labor, while I represents an index of the consumption of the intermediate varieties defined by

$$I = \left(\int_0^M q_i^{\rho} \mathrm{d}i \right)^{1/\rho} \qquad 0 < \rho < 1 \tag{8.71}$$

in which q_i is now the quantity of the intermediate good i and M the number of intermediate goods. As usual, a smaller ρ means a more differentiated set of intermediate varieties.

By contrast, the intermediate sector exhibits increasing returns and operates under monopolistic competition (as in Section 4.2.1). Each variety of the intermediate sector is produced according to the same technology such that the production of the quantity q_i requires l_i units of labor which is again given by

$$l_i = f + q_i \tag{8.72}$$

where f is the fixed requirement of labor.

Finally, as in Section 8.2, the technology in the agricultural sector is such that one unit of output requires one unit of labor.

The demand functions for the two consumption goods are as follows:

$$A = (1 - \mu)Y/p^{\mathbb{A}} \tag{8.73}$$

$$Q = \mu Y/p^{\mathbb{M}} \tag{8.74}$$

where $p^{\mathbb{M}}$ is the price of the manufactured good.

The price index for the $\mathbb{I}$-sector is as given by (8.5):

$$P \equiv \left(\int_0^M p_i^{-(\sigma-1)} \mathrm{d}i \right)^{-1/(\sigma-1)} \tag{8.75}$$

where $\sigma \equiv 1/(1 - \rho)$ and $p(i)$ is the price of the intermediate good i. Given the wage rate w, the unit production cost in the $\mathbb{M}$-sector is as follows:

$$c^{\mathbb{M}} = \alpha^{-\alpha}(1 - \alpha)^{-(1-\alpha)} w^{1-\alpha} P^{\alpha} \tag{8.76}$$

whereas the input demands of the manufacturing sector corresponding to output $X^{\mathbb{M}}$ are

$$L^{\mathbb{M}} = (1 - \alpha)c^{\mathbb{M}} X^{\mathbb{M}} w^{-1} \tag{8.77}$$

$$q_i = \alpha c^{\mathbb{M}} X^{\mathbb{M}} p_i^{-\sigma} P^{\sigma-1} \qquad i \in [0, M]. \tag{8.78}$$

Consider an economy with two regions 1 and 2, each endowed with $L > 0$ workers. As in Section 8.2, we assume that the $\mathbb{A}$-good can be costlessly shipped from one region to another; this good is used as the numéraire ($p^{\mathbb{A}} = 1$). The output of the manufacturing sector (intermediate sector) is shipped from one region to the other at a positive cost according to the iceberg cost $\tau^{\mathbb{M}} > 1$ ($\tau^{\mathbb{I}} > 1$). Let $L_r^{\mathbb{M}}$, $L_r^{\mathbb{I}}$, and $L_r^{\mathbb{A}}$ be the mass of workers living in region r ($= 1, 2$) and working in the manufacturing, intermediate, and agricultural sectors, respectively.

Using the same argument as in Section 8.2.2, we see that the common equilibrium price of the intermediate varieties produced in region $r = 1, 2$ is

$$p_r^{\mathbb{I}} = \frac{\sigma}{\sigma - 1} w_r$$

and thus the output of an $\mathbb{I}$-sector firm under zero profit is still given by $q^* = (\sigma - 1)f$ and the labor requirement by σf.

The price index for the intermediate goods in region $r = 1, 2$ can be shown to be equal to:

$$P_r = k \cdot \left[L_r^{\mathbb{I}}(w_r)^{-(\sigma-1)} + L_s^{\mathbb{I}}(w_s \tau^{\mathbb{I}})^{-(\sigma-1)} \right]^{-1/(\sigma-1)} \qquad s \neq r \tag{8.79}$$

where

$$k \equiv \frac{\sigma}{\sigma - 1} (\sigma f)^{1/(\sigma-1)}.$$

The common output of an $\mathbb{I}$-firm located in r is

$$q_r = \alpha\left(\frac{\sigma}{\sigma-1}w_r\right)^{-\sigma}\left[c_r^{\mathbb{M}}X_r^{\mathbb{M}}P_r^{\sigma-1} + c_s^{\mathbb{M}}X_s^{\mathbb{M}}(\tau^{\mathbb{I}})^{-(\sigma-1)}P_s^{\sigma-1}\right] \qquad s \neq r \tag{8.80}$$

where $X_r^{\mathbb{M}}$ is the production of the manufactured good in region $r = 1, 2$.

8.6.2 The Spatial Integration of Intermediate and Final Producers

Suppose that both the final and intermediate industries are concentrated in one region, say region 1, so that $L_2^{\mathbb{M}} = L_2^{\mathbb{I}} = 0$ and $L_2^{\mathbb{A}} = L$. Hence, region 1 exports the manufactured good and region 2 the agricultural good. Assume also that workers residing in region 1 work either for the intermediate or for the manufacturing sector so that $L_1^{\mathbb{A}} = 0$. Then, it must be that $w_1^* \geq w_2^* = 1$.

The corresponding regional price indices are obtained from (8.79) as follows:

$$\begin{aligned} P_1 &= k \cdot \left[L_1^{\mathbb{I}}(w_1^*)^{-(\sigma-1)}\right]^{-1/(\sigma-1)} \\ &= k\frac{\mu}{1-\mu}(L_1^{\mathbb{I}})^{-1/(\sigma-1)} \end{aligned} \tag{8.81}$$

$$P_2 = P_1\tau^{\mathbb{I}} \tag{8.82}$$

where we have used (8.83) given below.

Consider first the market clearing condition for the agricultural good. Because $Y_1 = Lw_1^*$ and $Y_2 = L$, regional demands for this good are respectively given by

$$A_1 = (1-\mu)Lw_1^* \quad \text{and} \quad A_2 = (1-\mu)L.$$

Because $X_1^{\mathbb{A}} = 0$ and $X_2^{\mathbb{A}} = L$, the equality of supply and demand implies that

$$w_1^* = \frac{\mu}{1-\mu}. \tag{8.83}$$

For the agricultural sector to be unprofitable in region 1, it must be that $w_1^* \geq 1$, which holds if and only if

$$\mu \geq 1/2. \tag{8.84}$$

Because we have

$$p_1^{\mathbb{M}} = c_1^{\mathbb{M}} \quad \text{and} \quad p_2^{\mathbb{M}} = p_1^{\mathbb{M}}\tau^{\mathbb{M}} = c_1^{\mathbb{M}}\tau^{\mathbb{M}}$$

using (8.74), the regional demands for the $\mathbb{M}$-good are given by

$$Q_1 = \mu Lw_1^*/c_1^{\mathbb{M}} \quad \text{and} \quad Q_2 = \mu L/c_1^{\mathbb{M}}\tau^{\mathbb{M}}.$$

Because the $\mathbb{M}$-good is exported to region 2, market clearing for the manufactured good implies that the aggregate production $X_1^{\mathbb{M}}$ is such that

$$X_1^{\mathbb{M}} = Q_1 + Q_2 \tau^{\mathbb{M}}$$
$$= \frac{\mu}{1-\mu} \frac{L}{c_1^{\mathbb{M}}}$$

from (8.83), or

$$X_1^{\mathbb{M}} c_1^{\mathbb{M}} = \frac{\mu}{1-\mu} L. \tag{8.85}$$

Producing the manufactured good in region 2 is never profitable if and only if

$$c_2^{\mathbb{M}} \geq p_2^{\mathbb{M}} = c_1^{\mathbb{M}} \tau^{\mathbb{M}}$$

which amounts to $c_2^{\mathbb{M}}/c_1^{\mathbb{M}} \geq \tau^{\mathbb{M}}$. Using (8.76), this holds if and only if

$$\tau^{\mathbb{I}} \geq \left(\frac{\mu}{1-\mu}\right)^{(1-\alpha)/\alpha} (\tau^{\mathbb{M}})^{1/\alpha}.$$

It remains to consider the intermediate sector. Given (8.80), (8.85), and $X_2^{\mathbb{M}} = 0$, we have

$$q_1 = \alpha \left(\frac{w_1^*}{\rho}\right)^{-\sigma} c_1^{\mathbb{M}} X_1^{\mathbb{M}} P_1^{\sigma-1}$$
$$= \alpha \rho^{\sigma} k^{\sigma-1} L (L_1^{\mathbb{I}})^{-1}$$

$$q_2 = \alpha \left(\frac{1}{\rho}\right)^{-\sigma} c_1^{\mathbb{M}} X_1^{\mathbb{M}} (\tau^{\mathbb{I}})^{-(\sigma-1)} P_1^{\sigma-1}$$
$$= \alpha \rho^{\sigma} k^{\sigma-1} L (L_1^{\mathbb{I}})^{-1} \left(\frac{\mu}{1-\mu}\right)^{\sigma} \left(\tau^{\mathbb{I}}\right)^{-(\sigma-1)}.$$

The first equilibrium condition is $q_1 = q^* = (\sigma - 1) f$, which yields

$$L_1^{\mathbb{I}} = \alpha L.$$

The second equilibrium condition, that is the non-profitability of region 2 for $\mathbb{I}$-firms, means $q_2 \leq q^*$, which is equivalent to the condition

$$\tau^{\mathbb{I}} \geq \left(\frac{\mu}{1-\mu}\right)^{1/\rho}.$$

To sum up, we have shown:

Proposition 8.6. *Assume $\mu \geq 1/2$. Then, the coagglomeration of the intermediate and final sectors into the same region is an equilibrium if and only if the* *following two conditions are satisfied:*

$$\tau^{\mathbb{I}} \geq \left(\frac{\mu}{1-\mu}\right)^{(1-\alpha)/\alpha} (\tau^{\mathbb{M}})^{1/\alpha} \tag{8.86}$$

$$\tau^{\mathbb{I}} \geq \left(\frac{\mu}{1-\mu}\right)^{1/\rho}. \tag{8.87}$$

Hence, when the transport cost of the intermediate goods is high relative to the transport cost of the final good, or when business services are nontradable, there is complete regional specialization: both the final and intermediate sectors are entirely concentrated in one region, whereas the other region is specialized in agriculture. Condition (8.86) becomes less stringent as the transport cost of the final good declines. In addition, the transport cost of the intermediate goods must also exceed some threshold value (8.87), for $\mu/(1-\mu) \geq 1$. Clearly, this threshold rises when the intermediate goods are more differentiated. The domains of $(\tau^{\mathbb{I}}, \tau^{\mathbb{M}})$ sustaining the core–periphery structure are represented by the shaded areas in Figure 8.4.

Condition (8.86) means that the manufacturing sector does not find it profitable to start operating in region 2 because importing the intermediate goods from region 1 turns out to be costly owing to the high transport costs of these goods, whereas exporting its output from 1 to 2 is less costly because of the relatively low value of $\tau^{\mathbb{M}}$. Condition (8.87) means that no firm of the intermediate sector wants to set up in region 2 because it has to export all its production to region 1 at a high transport cost. It should be stressed that both sectors are trapped within the same region even when shipping the final good becomes cheaper and cheaper ($\tau^{\mathbb{M}}$ approaches 1). To break such a trap, the transport costs of the intermediate goods must fall below some critical value. This is not necessarily easy to implement when the provision of specific intermediate goods requires face-to-face contacts such as for highly specialized services (in which case $\tau^{\mathbb{I}}$ is high).

As long as (8.86) and (8.87) hold, μ can rise. Because $w_1^* = \mu/(1-\mu)$ and $w_2^* = 1$, this rise generates a widening wage gap between the core region and the periphery. It can readily be verified that the real wage gap, in turn, becomes even larger. This agrees with the observation that (8.86) becomes less and less stringent as intermediate goods play a growing role in the economy (α rises). However, the final sector eventually decentralizes some of its activities in the periphery as its share in consumption increases because the cost of labor in region 1 becomes too high.

When transportation costs for the intermediate sector decrease enough for (8.86) not to hold anymore, whereas (8.87) is still valid, one expects the $\mathbb{I}$-firms to remain concentrated in region A, and some share of the final sector now operates in region 2. In this case, the intermediate goods needed by the

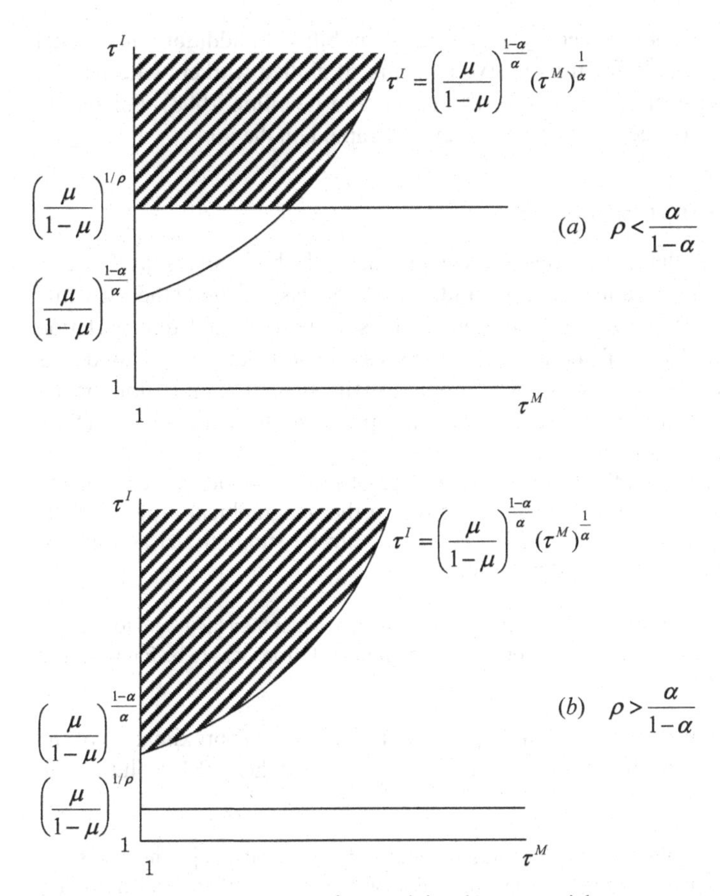

Figure 8.4. Transport cost ranges for sustaining the core–periphery structure.

final sector in region 2 are imported from region 1. Finally, when shipping the intermediate goods becomes very inexpensive (τ^{I} approaches 1), it is reasonable to expect the symmetric configuration to be the only stable equilibrium. These issues are left for further investigation.

Before concluding, note that Toulemonde (2006) has identified another channel conducive to agglomeration, and that bears some strong resemblance to the vertical linkage setting considered in this section. When workers are immobile and unskilled, some of them choose to become skilled in order to be able to work in the manufacturing sector. As a consequence, they earn a higher income and, therefore, have a higher demand for the manufactured good, making their region a larger and more attractive market to firms. At the same time, the installation of new firms within this region gives a stronger incentive to workers to improve their skill. This yields a mechanism of cumulative causality in which spatial mobility is replaced by sector-based mobility. In addition, this model provides a rationale for the observed sorting of skilled workers who tend to gather in a few places (Combes, Duranton, and Gobillon 2008). For this to happen, workers need not to move; they get trained on the job.

8.7 CONCLUDING REMARKS

By focusing on the interactions between product and labor markets in a $2 \times 2 \times 2$ setting, Krugman remains in the tradition of neoclassical trade theory, while combining monopolistic competition, increasing returns, and transportation costs is at the heart of the new trade theories. What makes the CP unique is the interregional mobility of labor, a topic usually studied in migration theory. Therefore, it is fair to say that Krugman has provided the synthesis that Ohlin (1933) called for long ago.

In order to assess the historical relevance of the CP model, we can turn to Pollard (1981), who paid special attention to the geographical aspects of the Industrial Revolution. His main conclusions can be summarized as follows. First, before the Industrial Revolution,

> the gaps between different parts of Europe were much smaller than they were to become later and some industrial activity not unlike that in Inner Europe was to be found almost everywhere. (Pollard 1981, 201)

Thus, the symmetric configuration provides a fairly good approximation of the space-economy in preindustrial societies. After the Industrial Revolution, he observes that

> the industrial regions colonize their agricultural neighbours [and take] from them some of their most active and adaptable labour, and they encourage them to specialize in the supply of agricultural produces, sometimes at the expense of some preexisting industry, running the risk thereby that this specialization would permanently divert the colonized areas from becoming industrial themselves. (Pollard 1981, 11)

In other words, there was a simultaneous move of workers and firms toward the new industrial regions. As in Krugman, a core–periphery structure thus emerged in Europe in the aftermath of the Industrial Revolution.

The decline in transport costs could have suggested that firms would become indifferent about their location. However, footloose activities, which are inherently independent of first nature, rely increasingly on second nature mechanisms. There are at least two reasons behind this phenomenon. First, as transportation costs decrease, firms have an incentive to concentrate their production in a smaller number of sites to better exploit scale economies in production. Second, low transportation costs tend to make price competition fierce, thus inducing firms to differentiate their products to relax price competition. This in turn leads firms to seek locations in which they have the best access to the largest pool of potential customers. In view of the results discussed in Chapter 7, this tendency suggests that product differentiation is a powerful force toward agglomeration.

The core–periphery structure may emerge owing to the migration of workers and the imperfectly competitive nature of the final sector or to the existence of an imperfectly competitive intermediate sector when workers are immobile. This result is very important for the space-economy, and thus it is crucial to know how it depends on the specificities of the framework employed. First, the use of the CES utility and iceberg cost leads to a convenient setting in which demands have a constant elasticity across space. However, such a result conflicts with research in spatial pricing theory in which demand elasticity varies with distance. Second, although the iceberg cost is able to capture the fact that shipping is resource-consuming, such a modeling strategy implies that any increase in the mill price is accompanied with a proportional increase in transport cost, which often seems unrealistic. Finally, although models are based on very specific assumptions, they are often beyond the reach of analytical resolution, forcing authors to appeal to numerical investigations.

This state of affairs has led Ottaviano, Tabuchi, and Thisse (2002) to revisit NEG models using the linear model of monopolistic competition presented in the next chapter. Such a setting takes us far away from the model used by Krugman and offers the advantage of yielding simple analytical solutions. Although the conclusions are not exactly the same as those derived by Krugman, this alternative model also yields a core–periphery structure once transportation costs are sufficiently low. Therefore, the conclusions derived by Krugman seem to be robust against different formulations of preferences. More generally, the main results of this chapter are similar to those obtained when using the linear model rather than the CES model of monopolistic competition (Combes, Mayer, and Thisse 2008, chapter 8).

Unlike the models studied in Chapter 4, using positive transport costs between cities allows placing firms and consumers at specific locations. Yet, extending models of NEG to a variable number of regions/cities appears to be a formidable task. The reason is that stable equilibria may vanish while new stable equilibria may emerge for a marginal decrease in transportation costs. In a very simple model in which cities are equidistant, Tabuchi, Thisse, and Zeng (2005) show that the *number* of cities initially decreases and then increases. Put simply, in the early stages of the integration process, the economy is made of a shrinking number of cities (agglomeration phase). However, once transportation costs are sufficiently low, the market solves the congestion problem induced by the agglomeration of population by redistributing firms and workers among a larger number of cities (dispersion phase). The size of the population being fixed, the agglomeration phase (dispersion phase) is such that existing cities grow (shrink). This result concurs with the bell curve discussed in Section 8.5.

APPENDIX

A Proof that the break point is smaller than the sustain point. The following proof is due to Frédéric Robert-Nicoud. For notational convenience, set

$$\phi \equiv \tau^{-(\sigma-1)} \tag{8A.1}$$

and denote respectively by ϕ_b and ϕ_s the values of ϕ corresponding to τ_b and τ_s. Because $\sigma > 1$, ϕ is inversely related to τ and belongs to the interval (0, 1].

Using (8.30) and (8A.1), it is easy to show that ϕ_s is a solution to the equation

$$\phi^{-\mu\rho-1}[(1+\mu)\phi^2 + 1 - \mu] - 2 = 0.$$

Setting

$$f(\phi) \equiv \phi^{-\mu\rho-1}[(1+\mu)\phi^2 + 1 - \mu] - 2$$

it is straightforward that $f(0) \to \infty$ and $f(1) = 0$. Furthermore, it is readily verified that $f(\phi)$ has a single minimizer given by

$$\phi^* = \left[\frac{(1-\mu)(1+\mu\rho)}{(1+\mu)(1-\mu\rho)}\right]^{1/2} < 1.$$

Finally, it can be shown that $f'(0) < 0$ and $f'(1) > 0$. When ϕ varies from 0 to 1, all these facts put together imply that $f(\phi)$ decreases from arbitrarily large values to reach its minimum at $\phi^* > \phi_s$ because $f(\phi^*) < 0$ and, then, increases but takes negative values to reach the value 0 at $\phi = 1$.

Using (8.31) and (8A.1), we obtain

$$\phi_b = \frac{(\sigma - 1 + \sigma\mu)(1+\mu)}{(\sigma - 1 - \sigma\mu)(1-\mu)}.$$

Evaluating $f(\phi)$ at ϕ_b shows that $f(\phi_b) < 0$. Because $f(\phi_s) = 0$ and $f(\phi)$ decreases over $(0, \phi^*)$, it must be that

$$\phi_b > \phi_s$$

which yields the desired inequality

$$\tau_b < \tau_s.$$

B. The function

$$F(\tau) \equiv \left(\frac{1+\phi}{2}\right)^{\frac{-\mu}{\sigma-1}} - \left(\frac{1+\mu}{2} + \frac{1-\mu}{2}\tau^{\mu}\right)$$

may be rewritten as follows:

$$g(\phi) \equiv \left(\frac{1+\phi}{2}\right)^{\frac{\mu}{1-\sigma}} - \left(\frac{1+\mu}{2} + \frac{1-\mu}{2}\phi^{-\frac{\mu}{\sigma-1}}\right)$$

which is defined on (0, 1). Note first that $g(1) = 0$ whereas $g(\phi) \to -\infty$ when $\phi \to 0$. It is readily verified that $g(\phi)$ has a single extremum at

$$\phi^* = \frac{1}{2(1-\mu)^{-\frac{\sigma-1}{\sigma-1+\mu}} - 1}$$

which belongs to (0, 1). Because

$$\lim_{\phi \to 1} g(\phi) = \frac{\mu^2}{2(1-\sigma)} < 0$$

$g(\phi)$ is decreasing in the left neighborhood of $\phi = 1$. This in turn implies that, as ϕ falls from 1 to 0, $g(\phi)$ first increases, reaches its maximum at ϕ^* and, finally, decreases. As a result, $f(\phi) = 1$ for a single value $\phi_K < 1$ such that $g(\phi) > 0$ if and only if $\phi > \phi_K$. Let τ_K be the value of τ that corresponds to ϕ_K. Hence, $F(\tau) > 0$ if and only if $\tau < \tau_K$.

9

Market Size and Industrial Clusters

9.1 INTRODUCTION

Ever since Adam Smith, it is well known that market size matters for the division of labor, hence for economic development. In this chapter, we want to deal with a related, but different, idea, namely *market size is one of the basic determinants of firms' choices of location*. Both economists and geographers agree that a large market tends to increase the profitability of the firms established in it. First of all, in his location problem where a firm chooses the location minimizing the total transport costs it bears, Weber ([1909] 1927) showed that the market – or input source – that has a weight exceeding the weighted sum of the other markets and input sources is always the firm's optimal location.[1] In the same vein, the gravity equation asserts that locations having a good access to large markets offer firms greater profit opportunities.[2] The profitability of firms is further enhanced by increasing returns because the growth in their volume of production also generates a drop in their average production costs. As a result, it seems reasonable to expect larger markets to attract more firms than smaller markets. This idea agrees with market potential theory, as developed by the American geographer Harris (1954) according to which firms tend to locate where they have the best access to markets in which they can sell their product.[3] That size matters for the development of a country is also emphasized by the economic historian Pollard (1981, 249) for whom, even though there are examples of export-led development, "it is obviously harder to build up an industrial complex without the solid foundation of a home market." That the

[1] Weights are to be interpreted as the quantities shipped from and to the firm multiplied by the transport rate of the corresponding goods (Beckmann and Thisse 1986).

[2] Such profit opportunities may be measured by the share of entrepreneurs located in a region. Sato, Tabuchi, and Yamamoto (2012) show that a 10% increase in population density increases by approximately 1% the share of people who become entrepreneurs in Japanese prefectures.

[3] Recall that Harris defines the *market potential* of a region as the sum of regional GDPs weighted by the inverse of the distance to the region in question. This sum includes the region itself and its internal distance.

home market is big is often explained by the behavior and interactions between households and firms that are located within it.

Under perfect competition and constant returns to scale, country size does not matter, which explains why neoclassical trade models have been built on differences in either countries' productivity or countries' endowments of production factors. On the other hand, once it is recognized that firms operate under increasing returns while shipping goods is costly, things become different (Dixit and Norman 1980; Helpman and Krugman 1985). Indeed, when choosing where to locate, firms face a *proximity-competition trade-off* that lies at the heart of spatial economics. On the one hand, firms benefit from proximity to larger markets, which allows them to exploit scale economies more effectively and to economize on transportation costs; on the other, they face tougher competition when more firms choose to set up in the same location. Because a profit-maximizing firm also minimizes the transport costs it incurs when delivering its output, everything else equal it will locate in the larger market, the counterpart of the market area effect in spatial competition studied in Chapter 7.

Nevertheless, as more firms set up in large markets, competition there is also heightened, which reduces markups and fragments demand. Such competitive pressures typically hold back the tendency for firms to agglomerate, the reason being that positive transportation costs allow firms to relax price competition by locating far from their competitors. This corresponds to the price effect in spatial competition.

The geographical distribution of firms, therefore, is the outcome of the interplay between two opposing forces, that is, a *market-access* effect and a *market-crowding* effect. If the latter effect has been stressed in spatial competition theory (see Chapter 7), the former has been underscored in the New Trade Theories (Dixit and Norman 1980; Helpman and Krugman 1985). Hence, the forces at work are the same as in spatial competition theory, even though we consider a two-location setting. The main difference is that we work here with a general equilibrium-like framework that allows capturing new channels. For example, by changing their investment locations, capital-owners affect the intensity of competition within each country, thus making the penetration of foreign products easier or more difficult, which in turn affects operating profits made in each market. In addition, the spatial distribution of demand, which influences the location of firms, may vary with income, which depends itself on the spatial distribution of firms through the determination of the rental rate of capital.

Starting with Redding and Venables (2004) various empirical studies have confirmed the positive correlation between the economic performance of territories and their market potential. After a careful review of the state of the art, Redding (2011) concludes that "there is not only an association but also a causal relationship between market access and the spatial distribution of economic activity." For example, one of the more remarkable geographical concentration of activities is what is known as the "manufacturing belt," which accommodates around four-fifths of the US manufacturing output for a century or so within an area that comprises one-sixth of the country area. Klein and Crafts (2012, 800) show that "market potential had a substantial impact on the location of manufacturing in the USA throughout the period 1880–1920 and . . . was more important than factor endowments." In the same vein, Head and Mayer (2011, 282) summarize their analysis of the relationship between market proximity and economic development over the 1965–2003 period by saying that "market potential is a powerful driver of increases in income per capita." This is only a seeming paradox: inexpensive shipping of goods makes competition tougher, and thus firms today care more about small advantages than they would in a world in which they were protected by the natural barriers of high transportation costs.

As recognized by the Royal Swedish Academy of Sciences on the occasion of the 2008 Nobel Prize in Economic Sciences, "[t]raditionally, trade theory and economic geography evolved as separate subfields of economics. More recently, however, they have converged to become more and more united through new theoretical insights, which emphasize that the same basic forces simultaneously determine specialization across countries for a given international distribution of factors of production (trade theory) and the long-run location of those factors across countries (economic geography)." The organization of this chapter is a reflection of this evolution.

In Section 9.2, we present the linear model of monopolistic competition developed by Ottaviano, Tabuchi, and Thisse (2002). The CES and linear models should not be viewed as "substitutes" but as "complements." By yielding linear equilibrium conditions, the latter delivers a full analytical solution that captures in a simple way the pro-competitive effects economic integration is supposed to spark. More precisely, the linear model allows one to show how market prices and trade flows are affected by market size and the degree of economic integration. In Sections 9.3 and 9.4, we build on this model to study the location of an industry when the geographical distribution of consumers is fixed, a topic investigated by Lösch (1940, chapter II) and extensively studied in location theory since then. There are differences, however. In standard location theory, space is represented by a line or a plane (Beckmann and Thisse 1986); space is here described by two regions or countries, as in trade theory. Even though poorer from a spatial point of view, the setting used here is richer in terms of microeconomic content.

We first consider the case of homogeneous firms, meaning that firms are equally efficient while their output has the same quality. The main result is the home market effect: *the larger country attracts a more than proportionate share of capital*. This result provides a possible rational to the Lucas (1990) paradox: capital does not necessarily flow from countries in which it is abundant to countries where it is scarce. Furthermore, the home market effect is magnified when transportation costs fall: *market integration widens the gap in the spatial distribution of capital.* This contradicts a second prediction of standard trade theory, which views trade barriers as an obstacle to convergence among countries. All in all, these two results run against the expectation of many trade theorists, Note also that here a steady decrease in transportation costs leads to a smooth agglomeration of firms in the larger market. Unlike what we observe in the CP model studied in Section 8.3, there is no sudden agglomeration of activities because the immobility of consumers prevents a rapid expansion of the larger region's market.

We then study the robustness of the home market effect when firms are heterogeneous. In doing so, we uncover a process of *spatial selection* that does not appear when firms are homogeneous. That is, as transportation costs decrease, the more efficient firms congregate in the larger market whereas the less efficient firms locate in the smaller one, a process that is observed in the data (Syverson 2004; Foster, Haltiwanger, and Syverson 2008). This suggests an additional reason for the growth of regional disparities: the sorting out of heterogeneous firms makes the larger region more productive and the smaller one less productive.

The main pitfall of the linear model of monopolistic competition is the absence of an income effect. In other words, the value of the equilibrium rental rate of capital does not impact the spatial distribution of demand, which depends only on where workers are located. This is why we return to the CES model in Section 9.5 to study the home market effect in a full-fledged general equilibrium model in which wages are endogenous. As shown by Takahashi, Takatsuka, and Zeng (2013), this approach is more involved but delivers a much richer set of results. First, the home market effect still holds. Second, the wage in the larger country exceeds the wage that prevails in the smaller one. Under these circumstances, the price of the varieties produced in the former exceeds the price of those produced in the latter. As a consequence, a firm located in the larger market exports less than a firm located in the smaller one. In this context, the larger country produces a more than proportionate share of varieties and trade is balanced because the smaller region exports capital to the larger one.

In the last section, we turn our attention to industrial clusters. Some industrial districts are engaged in high-tech activities (Saxenian 1994), but others are involved in more traditional, labor-intensive activities, many of which can be found in the "Third Italy" (Pyke et al. 1990, chapters 4 and 5): Sassuolo specializes in ceramic tiles, Prato is known for textiles, shoes are made in Montegranaro, and wooden furniture in Nogara. For example, Hanson (1996, 1266) accurately points out that "the fact that New York City remains a major apparel producer is perhaps the most persuasive evidence one can find of localization economies." Our research strategy is to view localization economies as a black box (see Section 4.2). This shortcut allows exploring the common implications of these economies for the spatial distribution of activities without going into the details of their specification. According to Porter (1998, chapter 7), the formation of an industrial cluster appears to depend on the relative strength of three distinct forces: The magnitude of localization economies, the intensity of price competition, and the level of transport costs. Following Belleflamme, Picard, and Thisse (2000), we highlight how localization economies interact together with the dispersion forces generated by market competition within the global economy to lead to the emergence of asymmetric clusters. Indeed, if localization economies are obviously an agglomeration force, it is also well known that geographical proximity renders price competition on the product market fiercer (Section 7.3). In other words, firms have an incentive to separate from one another to enjoy local market power. Consequently, whereas firms enjoy low costs when they concur in their locational choices, they can sell their products at higher prices when they are dispersed.

This is not the end of the story, however. Even if price competition is relaxed through product differentiation, it is still true that firms want to be far apart when transport costs are high. Because the spatial distribution of demand is supposed to be unaffected by the locations and sizes of clusters, the cost reduction associated with the agglomeration may be more than offset by the fall in exports. By contrast, firms could enjoy higher profits by being local monopolists. Consequently, transport costs have to be low for firms to congregate. In other words, firms must be able to serve almost all markets equally (globalization) to enjoy the local advantages associated with the formation of a cluster (localization). Thus, this section may be viewed as an attempt to reconcile NEG with local interactions among firms, such as those studied in Section 6.3.

The main purpose of Section 9.6 is to identify the conditions under which asymmetric clusters emerge in an economy that is otherwise symmetric. In particular, contrary to the belief of cluster-proponents, we will see that the size and efficiency of clusters does not depend only upon the strength of localization economies. How the local economy is embedded within the global economy matters too. Our secondary objective is to provide additional insights regarding a question that lies at the center of hot political debates: Are the big clusters too big? Our answer is no. Very much like in Chapter 6, the reason is that firms care about the benefit they receive from the other firms, but neglect the efficiency gains they bring to the others. Note, finally, that the distribution of firms is here driven by the supply side of the economy, whereas it is governed by the demand side in the previous sections.

9.2 TRADE UNDER MONOPOLISTIC COMPETITION

Recall that the objective of this chapter is to study how market integration affects the spatial distribution of firms across space. To ease the burden of notation, we normalize the parameters that are of second-order importance for our purpose.

9.2.1 A Linear Model of Monopolistic Competition

We consider a $2 \times 2 \times 2$ setting. The global economy involves two sectors (agriculture and manufacturing), two regions or countries ($r = 1, 2$), and two production factors (capital and labor). The global population has a unit mass. Let region 1 host the larger population and denote by $\theta \in (1/2, 1)$ the share (and mass) of consumers in region 1. Each individual is endowed with one unit of labor and one unit of capital, both of which are supplied inelastically. Thus θ also measures that region's shares (and masses) of labor and capital. In sum, the relative factor endowment is the same in the two regions, which differ only in size. Under these circumstances, there would be no trade in a Heckscher-Ohlin world.

Consumers are immobile and supply labor in the region where they reside. In contrast, they are free to supply capital wherever they want and seek the higher rental rate; the returns on capital investments are repatriated. In other words, the spatial distribution of capital is endogenous and determined as an equilibrium outcome.

In what follows, we isolate the impact of market integration on the spatial distribution of capital by working with a setting in which wages are exogenous and equalized between regions. This is guaranteed by assuming that the agricultural good is produced in both regions and costlessly traded between them. Labor is chosen as the numéraire, and thus the wage w is equal to 1.

The manufacturing sector produces a differentiated good, which is given by a unit continuum of horizontally differentiated varieties indexed by $i \in [0, 1]$. Each variety is produced by a single firm under increasing returns and monopolistic competition. There is no scope economies, and thus a firm produces a single variety. Because consumers have a love for variety, any firm obtains a higher share of the market by producing a differentiated variety than by replicating an existing one. To operate, a firm needs one unit of capital and hires a quantity of labor proportional to its output. The total cost of producing q units of variety i is thus equal to $C(q) = r + cq$ where r is the (endogenous) rental rate of capital and c the marginal production cost. This setting is known in the literature as the "footloose capital" (FC) model.

The utility derived from consuming q_i units of variety $i \in [0, 1]$ is given by

$$u(q_i) = \alpha q_i - \frac{\beta}{2} q_i^2 - \frac{\gamma}{2} q_i \int_0^1 q_j \mathrm{d}j. \tag{9.1}$$

Thus, the marginal utility of variety i decreases with its own consumption as well as with the total consumption of the manufactured good. The presence of this term implies that preferences are not additive. The subutility (9.1) is then nested into a linear utility.

For any given price profile (p_i), a consumer chooses the quantity profile of the manufactured good (q_i) and the consumption q_0 of the numéraire, which maximize his utility

$$U(q_0; q_i, i \in [0,1]) = \alpha \int_0^1 q_i \mathrm{d}i - \frac{\beta}{2} \int_0^1 q_i^2 \mathrm{d}i - \frac{\gamma}{2} \int_0^1 q_i \left(\int_0^1 q_j \mathrm{d}j \right) \mathrm{d}i + q_0 \tag{9.2}$$

subject to the budget constraint:

$$\int_0^1 p_i q_i \mathrm{d}i + q_0 = 1 + r + \bar{q}_0$$

where the right-hand side is the consumer income. The initial endowment $\bar{q}_0$ is sufficiently large for the consumption of the agricultural good to be strictly positive at the market outcome. This assumption is made to capture the idea that consumers have a taste for each good.

The parameters of the utility U may be interpreted as follows. The parameter α captures the intensity of preference for the manufactured good with respect to the numéraire, while $\gamma > 0$ is the degree of substitutability between variety i and any other variety. A higher γ means that varieties are less differentiated, and thus the consumption of close substitutes reduces the utility of consuming variety i. Consider now the parameter β. Suppose that a consumer consumes a total quantity Q of the manufactured good; his consumption of a variety is given by Q/x on $[0, x]$ and zero on $(x, 1]$. Evaluating (9.2) at this consumption pattern yields

$$U(q_0, q_{i \leq x}) = \alpha Q - \frac{\beta}{2x} Q^2 - \frac{\gamma}{2} Q^2 + q_0$$

which is increasing in x and, hence, maximized at $x = 1$ where variety consumption is maximal. As a result, the quadratic utility function exhibits a *love for variety* whose intensity is measured by the value of β: a high value of β means that a consumer is more inclined to equalize his consumption over the entire range of varieties.[4]

Substituting the budget constraint into (9.2), maximizing the resulting expression with respect to q_i and solving yields the individual inverse demand for variety i:

$$p_i = \alpha - \beta q_i - \gamma \int_0^1 q_j \mathrm{d}j. \tag{9.3}$$

[4] The intuition behind this interpretation is very similar to the one that stands behind the Herfindahl index used to measure industrial concentration. If we control for the total amount of the differentiated good consumption, the absolute value of the quadratic term in U increases with the concentration of consumption on fewer varieties, thus decreasing utility.

As previously mentioned, we ease the burden of notation by making a certain number of normalizations. First, by replacing the demand intercept α with $\alpha - c$, we normalize the marginal production cost to zero. Prices and markups are thus equal. Without loss of generality, the unit of the agricultural good is then chosen for the new intercept $\alpha - c$ to be 1 and the unit of the manufactured good for $\beta = 1$ to hold. As a result, the demand function for variety i is given by

$$q_i = \frac{1}{1+\gamma} - p_i + \frac{\gamma}{1+\gamma} P \tag{9.4}$$

where P is the price index defined by

$$P \equiv \int_0^1 p_j \mathrm{d}j.$$

Because there is a unit mass of firms, P is also the average price.[5]

The price index P is to be viewed as a statistics measuring the *aggregate* impact of the price decisions made by all the other firms: the larger (smaller) P, the higher (lower) the demand for variety i because competition is softer (tougher). Thus, (9.4) encapsulates the idea that the demand for a certain variety falls when its own price rises not only in absolute terms (*own price effect*) but also relative to the average price (*differential price effect*). Each firm accurately treats the price index as a given because its price choice does not affect it (*price index–taking assumption*). By contrast, each firm is aware that the market as a whole has a nonnegligible impact on its demand, whence on its behavior, through the value of the price index. In other words, the model leads to a system of demands that encompass pro-competitive effects through endogenous choke prices, $(1+\gamma)(1+\gamma P)$, above which demands are zero. Unlike the CES model of Section 8.2, making competition tougher or softer through some changes in the structural parameters of the model affects the elasticity of the demand for a variety.

Last, shipping one unit of the manufactured good between the two regions requires $t > 0$ units of the numéraire. The transportation cost t is paid by the firm. This modeling strategy is in line with standard location theory.

One may wonder why we need introducing product differentiation in a firm location model, while location theory typically assumes that firms produces homogeneous goods.[6] Though not necessary from the formal point of

[5] A priori using linear demand functions seems to be very restrictive. However, these functions are probably less peculiar than the iso-elastic demands associated with the CES. Furthermore, Greenhut, Norman, and Hung (1987) have shown that many properties holding for a spatial monopoly facing linear demands remain true for demand functions that are concave or less convex than the negative exponential. This is worth noting because a monopolistically competitive firm behaves as if it were a monopolist on its residual demand.

[6] Observe, indeed, that many results in NEG can be derived under oligopolistic competition with quanity-setting firms selling a homogeneous (Thisse 2010). However, this approach has

view, this assumption captures an essential economic phenomenon stressed by Hicks (1969, 56) in his book *A Theory of Economic History*: "[t]he extension of trade does not primarily imply more goods. . . . The variety of goods is increased, with all the widening of life that entails. There can be little doubt that the main advantage that will accrue to those with whom our merchants are trading is a gain of precisely this kind."

As in Chapter 8, we disentangle the various channels through which market integration operates by distinguishing between a short-run equilibrium when firms are immobile, and a long-run equilibrium when they are mobile. In what follows, we focus on region 1. Symmetric expressions hold for region 2.

9.2.2 Market Prices and Trade Flows

The two regions – or countries – having the same relative endowment in capital and labor, trade theory à la Heckscher-Ohlin would predict a no-trade outcome. However, because firms produce under increasing returns and no scope economies, trade allows firms to sell their varieties on both their domestic and foreign markets. Under these circumstances, trade allows firms to produce at a lower average cost. Furthermore, as observed by Hicks, trade allows variety-loving consumers to benefit from a broader range of goods.

Let λ be the share (and mass) of firms located in region 1. These firms play a noncooperative game with a continuum of players. Regional markets are segmented, which means that each firm chooses a price specific to the region in which it sells its variety. Empirical evidence strongly supports this assumption on the international marketplace; less known is the fact that market segmentation also arises within nations (Engel and Rogers 2001; Parsley and Wei 2001). In other words, there is *spatial price discrimination*. Because the iceberg cost enters the profit function multiplicatively in the CP model, demands have the same elasticity across locations, and thus both mill and discriminatory pricing policies yield the same equilibrium prices and outputs. Few people noticed the equivalence between the two policies under the iceberg technology in the spatialized CES model (Greenhut et al. 1987, chapter 2). This equivalence no longer holds in the linear model with additive transport costs. This opens the door to the study of firms' spatial pricing behavior.[7]

Each firm being negligible to the market, it chooses its profit-maximizing prices by treating accurately the regional price indices as parameters. When the product markets clear, equilibrium values of price indices are consistent with all firms' pricing decisions. Because domestic firms are symmetric, they sell

attracted much less attention than monopolistic competition in those two fields because its empirical implications are less interesting.

[7] Note here the existence of a big literature developed in the 1970s and 1980s, which deals with spatial pricing policies (see Greenhut et al. 1987 for a survey). This literature is ignored by most contributors to NEG and applied trade theory.

their varieties at the same price, and thus the variety index i may be dropped. A firm located in region 1 chooses its local price p_{11} to maximize its domestic operating profits given by

$$\pi_{11} = \theta \left(\frac{1}{1+\gamma} - p_{11} + \frac{\gamma}{1+\gamma} P_1 \right) p_{11}$$

where the price index P_1 is given by

$$P_1 = \lambda p_{11} + (1-\lambda) p_{21}$$

p_{21} being the price set by a foreign firm (recall that the marginal cost c has been normalized to zero).

Using (9.4), it is readily verified that maximizing π_{11} with respect to p_{11} yields the best reply function given by

$$p_{11}^*(P_1) = \frac{1+\gamma P_1}{2(1+\gamma)}.$$

Thus, a firm charges a higher price when the local price index is higher because price competition is relaxed. Moreoever, we have a setting in which each firm must know only one aggregate statistics about the market but not its details.

A foreign firm exporting to region 1 chooses its price p_{21} to maximize its operating profit earned abroad:

$$\pi_{21} = \theta \left(\frac{1}{1+\gamma} - p_{21} + \frac{\gamma}{1+\gamma} P_1 \right) (p_{21} - t).$$

Because foreign firms are symmetric, their prices are the same and such that

$$p_{21} = p_{11}(P_1) + \frac{t}{2}.$$

This relationship implies that P_1 is a function of the domestic price p_{11}. As a consequence, the equilibrium price selected by a region-1 firm is determined by the fixed point condition $p_{11}(P_1(x)) = x$, that is,

$$p_{11}^* = \frac{2+\gamma t(1-\lambda)}{2(2+\gamma)}$$

while the price of a foreign variety is

$$p_{21}^* = p_{11}^* + \frac{t}{2}.$$

Unlike the CES, the linear model of monopolistic competition thus yields *variable markups*. In particular, market prices decrease with the number of firms (λ) because local competition is tougher and increases with the unit transportation cost (t) because markets are better protected against external competition. These results are in line with the predictions of spatial competition theory (see Section 4.5).

Furthermore, trade exacerbates competition in each region even though the consumer (delivered) price of imported varieties is higher than that of domestic varieties because foreign firms have to cover the cost of shipping their output. Owing to the trade barriers associated with positive transportation costs, in both regions domestic firms price below the average prices, whereas foreign firms price above average prices. However, the producer (mill) price of imported varieties, $p_{21}^* - t = p_{11}^* - t/2$, is smaller than that of the locally produced varieties, p_{11}^*. In other words, there is *freight absorption* to facilitate the penetration of varieties produced in distant places. Freight absorption thus biases the relative prices of domestic and imported varieties in favor of the latter. In addition, the price differential

$$p_{12}^* - p_{11}^* = \frac{t}{2} + \frac{\gamma t(2\lambda - 1)}{2(2+\gamma)}$$

exceeds $p_{21}^* - p_{22}^*$, which means that a region-2 firm absorbs more freight than a region-1 firm owing to the difference in market size.

For the pro-competitive effect generated by trade to materialize, transportation costs cannot be too high: $p_{12}^* - t > 0$. This condition holds regardless of the value of λ if

$$t < t_{trade} \equiv \frac{2}{2+\gamma}. \tag{9.5}$$

More differentiated varieties make the inequality (9.5) less stringent and, therefore, facilitate exchanges between the two regions, which agrees with Krugman (1979) for whom product differentiation is one of the main drivers of trade.

A region-1 firm supplies the quantity

$$q_{12}^* = \frac{2 + \gamma t\lambda - (2+\gamma)t}{2(2+\gamma)} \tag{9.6}$$

to a region-2 consumer. Thus, though market integration is damaging to a firm's domestic sales, it boosts its exports. Observe that $q_{12}^*(\lambda) > q_{21}^*(\lambda)$, the reason being that consumers in region 1 have access to a broader set of domestic varieties, thus making foreign varieties less attractive.

The aggregate value of region-1 exports is given by

$$X_{12} \equiv \lambda(1-\theta)p_{12}^* q_{12}^* = \lambda(1-\theta)q_{12}^*(q_{12}^* + t)$$

where $q_{12}^* = p_{12}^* - t$ follows from (9.6). Therefore, using (9.4), we obtain

$$\begin{aligned}
\frac{\mathrm{d}}{\mathrm{d}t} q_{12}^*(q_{12}^* + t) &= (2q_{12}^* + t)\frac{\mathrm{d}q_{12}^*}{\mathrm{d}t} + q_{12}^* \\
&= -2\frac{(3-2\lambda)(1+t\lambda) + t\lambda^2}{9} < 0.
\end{aligned}$$

Because the same holds for region-2 exports X_{21}, *the value of global exports* $X_{12} + X_{21}$ *decreases with the level of transportation costs*, a prediction that agrees with the gravity equation.

Finally, the size of a firm located in region 1 being given by

$$q_1^* \equiv \theta q_{11}^* + (1-\theta)q_{12}^* = \theta q_{12}^* + (1-\theta)(q_{22}^* - t/2)$$

we have

$$q_1^* - q_2^* = (2\theta - 1)\frac{t}{2} > 0.$$

As a consequence, the size of a firm set up in the larger region exceeds that of a firm located in the smaller region.

Before proceeding, observe that the linear model leads to finite choke prices. This makes it suitable to discuss the relationships between the intensity of competition and the nature of trade, which in turn affects the interregional distribution of firms and capital, and vice versa. For example, a higher concentration of firms in the larger region intensifies competition therein, which lowers the corresponding choke price and makes penetration of foreign varieties more difficult. Eventually, this might result in a trade pattern involving one-way trade from the larger to the smaller region, which reinforces the attractiveness of the former region at the expense of the latter (Behrens 2005a).[8] By contrast, the standard CES model used in Chapter 9 imposes non-zero trade flows for all goods.

9.3 THE HOME MARKET EFFECT

We now study how capital is allocated between regions that have different market sizes. To simplify, we assume that each region is endowed with a sufficiently high number of potential entrepreneurs who seek to attract physical capital. In a competitive capital market, the capital return is determined by the entrepreneurs' bidding process for capital, which comes to an end when no firm can earn a strictly positive profit. That is, firms' operating profits are entirely absorbed by the capital return. In other words, although the total number of active firms is exogenous, everything works as if there were free entry since equilibrium profits are zero.

Before proceeding, it is worth stressing a major difference with the models discussed in the previous chapter. In the approach developed here, *human* capital is replaced with *physical* capital. The latter seeks the highest *nominal* return, whereas the former cares about *real* income. This difference vastly simplifies the analysis of the models. As seen, the mobility of these two production factors also has different consequences for the way the space-economy is organized.

[8] See also Melitz and Ottaviano (2008) for a rich analysis of the determinants of trade flows when firms are heterogeneous.

9.3.1 The Location of Firms

Let r_1 be the return of one unit of capital invested in region 1. For any given allocation of capital λ, the profits earned by a region-1 firm are given by $\pi_1 - r_1$ where π_1 are the operating profits defined by

$$\pi_1 = \pi_{11} + \pi_{21} = \theta \left(p_{11}^*\right)^2 + (1-\theta)(p_{12}^* - t)^2.$$

The previously mentioned bidding process for capital comes to an end when no firm can earn a strictly positive profit. That is, firms' operating profits are entirely absorbed by the capital return:

$$r_1(\lambda) = \pi_1(\lambda).$$

Capital market clearing implies that no capital-owner can earn a higher return by relocating his capital to another region. Formally, at an *interior* equilibrium $\lambda^* \in (0, 1)$, we have $r_1^* = r_2^* = r^*$; there is a *corner* equilibrium at $\lambda^* = 1$ when r_1 exceeds r_2 for all values of λ.

Since capital-owners seek the highest rate of return, the relocation incentives are given by the profit differential $\pi_1 - \pi_2$. This expression has a unique zero given by

$$\lambda^* - \frac{1}{2} > \theta - \frac{1}{2} > 0 \tag{9.7}$$

owing to (9.5). Two types of spatial equilibria may arise.

Partial agglomeration. There is partial agglomeration in region 1 with two-way trade when $\lambda^* < 1$. This condition is equivalent to

$$\frac{\theta}{1-\theta} < \frac{2(2-t)+\gamma t}{2(2-t)-\gamma t}. \tag{9.8}$$

The following comments are in order. First, *the larger region hosts a more than proportionate share of firms*. Indeed, we have

$$\lambda^* - \frac{1}{2} > \theta - \frac{1}{2} \iff t < \frac{4}{2+\gamma} \tag{9.9}$$

which holds under (9.5). This result, which is due to Helpman and Krugman (1985), has been coined the *home market effect* (HME). It says that the smaller region is a capital exporter.

To gain further insight about the reasons for the HME, we rewrite (9.9) as follows:

$$2(2-t)(\theta - 1/2) - t\gamma(\lambda^* - 1/2) = 0.$$

This equality shows that the equilibrium distribution of firms is determined by the interaction between two terms. The first one depends on the spatial distribution of consumers θ. Since the coefficient of $(\theta - 1/2)$ is positive, this term measures the *market-access* advantage of the larger region in the presence of transportation costs. The second term depends on the interregional or international distribution of firms λ^*. Since the coefficient of $(\lambda^* - 1/2)$ is negative, the second term measures the *market-crowding* disadvantage of the region that hosts the larger number of firms. More product differentiation (a lower γ) decreases the weight of market crowding and leads more firms to gather within the larger region. In the limit case of monopoly ($\gamma = 0$), only market access considerations matter since a firm's operating profits are independent from other firms' locations.

Observe also that transportation costs t affect both market access and crowding effects. In particular, lower t strengthens the former and weakens the latter. As a result, $d\lambda^*/dt > 0$, which reveals the magnification of the HME generated by a deeper market integration: *lowering transport costs leads to a stronger concentration of firms in the larger region*. This can be understood as follows. On the one hand, a higher degree of economic integration makes exports to the smaller market easier, thus allowing firms to exploit their scale economies more intensively; on the other hand, the deepening of integration reduces the advantages associated with geographical isolation in the smaller market, where competition is softer. These two effects push toward more agglomeration, thus implying that, as transportation costs go down, the smaller region gets deindustrialized to the benefit of the larger one. In a nutshell, small permanent shocks to relative demands may give rise to larger differences in interregional specialization. Note that the magnification of the HME is not a priori obvious because increasing the number of firms in the larger region makes local competition tougher, a force that could deter outside firms to locate therein. The HME also agrees with one of the key results we have encountered on many occasions in this book: low transport costs foster the geographical concentration of activities.

Using (9.6) and $\lambda^* > \theta$, we can readily verify that $\lambda^*(1-\theta)p_{12}^*q_{12}^*$ exceeds $(1-\lambda^*)\theta p_{21}^*q_{21}^*$. Consequently, we have:

Proposition 9.1. *The larger region is a net exporter of the good produced under increasing returns.*

Thus, the HME generates a demand-driven trade pattern in which two regions are partially specialized: the larger one in producing the manufactured good and the smaller one in the agricultural good. This pattern of trade owes nothing to a Ricardian comparative advantage, the nature of the forces at work here being totally different. They rest on the interplay between the market-access and the market-crowding effects. This proposition, which was first obtained by Krugman (1980), is one of the channels through which the size advantage of a region materializes. The sector producing the homogeneous good absorbs the trade imbalance caused by the home market effect.

Full agglomeration. When

$$\frac{\theta}{1-\theta} > \frac{2(2-t)+\gamma t}{2(2-t)-\gamma t}$$

there is full agglomeration ($\lambda^* = 1$). In other words, when the two regions are very dissimilar in size, transportation costs are very low, or both *all* firms set up in the larger region. This has an important welfare implication. Because the cost of living in region 1 is lower than in region 2, workers living in the former are better off than those residing in the latter. The welfare differential is the "price" region-2 workers pay for living there.

To sum up, we have shown the following result:

Proposition 9.2. *If (9.8) holds, the equilibrium distribution of capital involves a more than proportionate share of capital in the larger region. Furthermore, when (9.8) does not hold, capital is agglomerated in the larger region.*

The HME is obtained in a market governed by monopolistic competition. However, we want to stress that, despite differences in market structure, the HME bears some strong resemblance with the models discussed in Section 7.3. In both sections, consumers are dispersed and firms are lured to the location with the highest potential for demand: the larger market in NEG and the market center – or the median – in spatial competition theory. The HME also provides a rational for the fact that larger countries export a wider array of products/varieties than smaller countries (Hummels and Klenow 2005).

Observe, finally, that in the present setting there is no cumulative process similar to the one we have found in the CP model, the reason being that all factor-owners are immobile though capital as a production factor is mobile. As a consequence, a region's market size cannot grow as it does in the CP model. The HME reflects here the given asymmetry between regions. Indeed, this effect vanishes when regions are symmetric ($\theta = 1/2$): the capital distribution is then the mirror image of the labor distribution ($\lambda^* = \theta$).

9.3.2 Does the Large Region Host Too Many Firms?

When firms move from one region to another, they impose negative pecuniary externalities on the whole economy. More precisely, firms neglect the impact of their move on product and capital markets in both destination and origin regions. Consequently, the HME may lower the social surplus because location decisions are based on market prices that do not reflect the true social costs. In particular, does the concentration of firms in the larger market generate a waste of resources? To answer this question, we develop a first-best analysis in which a welfare-maximizing planner is able (i) to assign any number of firms to a specific region, (ii) to use lump sum transfers from workers to pay for the loss firms incur while pricing at marginal cost ($p_{11}^o = 0$ and $p_{12}^o = t$ owing to the normalization of the marginal production cost), and (iii) to use interpersonal transfers across workers. The supply of capital being perfectly inelastic, the first-best value of the rental rate of capital is zero.

Since individual preferences are quasi-linear, the relevant welfare measure is the sum of regional consumer surpluses. The individual consumer surplus is given by the following expression:

$$CS = \int_0^1 q_i \mathrm{d}i - \frac{1}{2}\int_0^1 q_i^2 \mathrm{d}i - \frac{\gamma}{2}\left(\int_0^1 q_i \mathrm{d}i\right)^2 - \int_0^1 p_i q_i \mathrm{d}i$$

$$= \frac{1}{2}\int_0^1 q_i^2 \mathrm{d}i + \frac{\gamma}{2}\left(\int_0^1 q_i \mathrm{d}i\right)^2$$

where we have used (9.3). Consequently, the consumer surplus in region 1 is equal to

$$CS_1 = \frac{\theta}{2}\left[\lambda(q_{11}^o)^2 + (1-\lambda)(q_{21}^o)^2\right] + \frac{\theta\gamma}{2}\left[\lambda^2(q_{11}^o)^2 + (1-\lambda)^2(q_{21}^o)^2 + 2\lambda(1-\lambda)q_{11}^o q_{21}^o\right] \quad (9.10)$$

where

$$q_{11}^o = \frac{1}{1+\gamma} + \frac{\gamma t}{1+\gamma}(1-\lambda) \qquad q_{21}^o = \frac{1}{1+\gamma} - t + \frac{\gamma t}{1+\gamma}(1-\lambda).$$

The planner engages in trade as long as consumers are willing to buy the foreign varieties (q_{12}^o and q_{21}^o are positive). This is so if and only if t is smaller than $t_{opt} \equiv 1/(1+\gamma)$, which is smaller than t_{trade}. Indeed, the price differential $p_{21}^o - p_{11}^o = t$ reflects the exact cost of shipping one unit of the differentiated good, whereas firms pass on to consumers a fraction of this cost at the market outcome, thus facilitating trade. As a consequence, the market may generate wasteful trade.

Maximizing the social welfare function $W = CS_1 + CS_2$ with respect to λ yields the first-best distribution of capital:

$$\lambda^o = \frac{1}{2} + \frac{2-t}{2\gamma t}(2\theta - 1).$$

Very much like the market outcome, *the first-best solution features an HME*. However, as long as $\lambda^o < 1$, *there are too many firms located in the larger region* since λ^o is smaller than λ^*. Why is it so? The answer is provided by Ottaviano and Van Ypersele (2005). Observe, first, that a profit-maximizing firm chooses the location that minimizes the transportation costs it bears to serve the foreign market. Therefore, since firms absorb more freight when exporting from the smaller to the larger region than vice versa, firms have incentive to locate in the larger region (see Section 9.2.2). Tougher competition there holds back the agglomeration process but this dispersion force is not strong enough for a sufficiently large number of firms to set up in the smaller region.

Note, however, that it is efficient to concentrate *all* firms in the larger region when

$$\theta > \frac{1}{2} + \frac{\gamma t}{2 - t}$$

which holds when transportation costs are very low, varieties are bad substitutes, or both. In this case, the market delivers the efficient solution. Meanwhile, lowering transportation costs exacerbates the deindustrialization of the smaller regions since $\lambda^* - \lambda^o$ increases with t.

Proposition 9.3. *Unless agglomeration is socially optimal, the HME leads to an excessive concentration of firms in the larger region.*

9.3.3 The Location of Nontradables

The share of the manufacturing sector has dramatically shrunk in developed economies. So one may wonder what the HME becomes when we consider the location of services, the main feature of which is that they must be consumed where they are produced. In other words, unlike most goods *services are nontradables*. In what follows, we reinterpret the framework of Section 9.2 by assuming that the differentiated product describes a range of differentiated services while the manufactured good is now homogeneous and tradable at negligible transportation costs.

In this case, no demand stems from region 2, and thus a region-1 firm competes with λ firms only. The equilibrium price in region 1 is then given by

$$p_{11}^* = \frac{1}{2 + \gamma\lambda}.$$

Location incentives are given by $\pi_{11} - \pi_{22}$ instead of $(\pi_{11} + \pi_{12}) - (\pi_{22} + \pi_{21})$. The unique zero of this expression is equal to

$$\lambda^* = \frac{1}{2} + \frac{1}{2}\frac{\sqrt{\theta} - \sqrt{1-\theta}}{\sqrt{\theta} + \sqrt{1-\theta}}\frac{4+\gamma}{\gamma} \geq \frac{1}{2}.$$

Therefore, the interregional allocation of capital remains biased toward the larger region. However, the HME need not hold anymore. Indeed, there is a

HME if and only if

$$\lambda^* - \frac{1}{2} > \theta - \frac{1}{2} \iff \left(\sqrt{\theta} + \sqrt{1-\theta}\right)^2 < 1 + \frac{4}{\gamma}.$$

Clearly, the left-hand side of the second inequality decreases from 2 to 1 as θ increases from $1/2$ to 1, whereas the right-hand side takes values exceeding 2 if and only if $\gamma < 4$. In other words, when varieties are bad substitutes, there is always a HME.

By contrast, if $\gamma > 4$, the above inequality holds provided that θ is sufficiently large. Specifically, there is an HME if and only if

$$\theta > \frac{1}{2} + \frac{1}{2}\sqrt{1 - \left(\frac{4}{\gamma}\right)^2}.$$

In this event, region 1 is big enough to overcome the competition effect triggered by the low degree of product differentiation. On the contrary, when the two regions have fairly similar sizes, there is a *reverse HME*. The larger region no longer provides a sufficiently big outlet to host a more than proportionate share of firms. Hence, as observed by Behrens (2005b), *trade is neither necessary nor sufficient for the HME to arise.*

9.4 HETEROGENEOUS FIRMS

9.4.1 Cost Heterogeneity

There is mounting empirical evidence that firms selling similar goods use different technologies, have different size, and display different degrees of efficiency (Bernard et al. 2007; Mayer and Ottaviano 2007). It is, therefore, natural to ask what the HME becomes in such a context. In this section, we assume that firms have different marginal costs: *high-cost* firms ($v = h$) requires $m > 0$ units of labor to produce one unit of the manufactured good, while *low-cost* firms ($v = l$) require a lower amount of labor units, which we normalize to zero. If q denotes the volume of production, high-cost and low-cost firms incur the following costs:

$$C^h(q) = r + mq \qquad C^\ell(q) = r.$$

Let the mass of low-cost and high-cost firms in the global economy be respectively denoted by μ and $1 - \mu$, where $0 \leq \mu \leq 1$. In the previous sections, we have $\mu = 1$.

In the short run, the interregional distribution of capital and the shares of low-cost and high-cost firms in each region are fixed. So, let $0 \leq \lambda \leq 1$ be the mass of capital invested in region 1, while the share of v-firms in region 1 is denoted by $0 \leq s^v \leq 1$ with $v = h, \ell$. Evidently, we have $\lambda = \mu s^\ell + (1 - \mu)s^h$.

High- and low-cost firms located in the same region do not set the same price. This means that the price index in region 1 is now given by

$$P_1 = \mu s^\ell p_{11}^\ell + \mu(1-s^\ell)p_{21}^\ell + (1-\mu)s^h p_{11}^h + (1-\mu)(1-s^h)p_{21}^h.$$

In the short-run equilibrium, consumers maximize utility, firms maximize profits, and product and factor markets clear. Since ν-firms located in region 1 are symmetric, they charge the same prices and earn the same profits π_1^ν defined as follows:

$$\pi_1^\ell = \theta p_{11}^\ell q_{11}^h + (1-\theta)(p_{12}^\ell - t)q_{12}^\ell$$

and

$$\pi_1^h = \theta(p_{11}^h - m)q_{11}^h + (1-\theta)(p_{12}^h - m - t)q_{12}^h.$$

The equilibrium prices in region 1 charged by the domestic and foreign firms are given by

$$p_{11}^\ell = \frac{1+\gamma P_1^*}{2(1+\gamma)} \qquad p_{21}^\ell = p_{11}^\ell + \frac{t}{2}$$

and

$$p_{11}^h = p_{11}^\ell + \frac{m}{2} \qquad p_{21}^h = p_{11}^\ell + \frac{m+t}{2}$$

where the equilibrium price index is equal to

$$P_1^* = \frac{1+(1+\gamma)[(1-\mu)m + t(1-\lambda)]}{2+\gamma}.$$

The following remarks are in order. (i) All prices decrease with the mass of domestic firms λ because competition in region 1 is tougher. (ii) A higher number of low-cost firms (μ) leads to lower prices in the two regions because both markets become more competitive. (iii) Lowering transportation costs (t) leads to lower prices in both markets for the same reason as in the homogeneous firm case. (iv) The price charged by the domestic low-cost firms (p_{11}^ℓ) is the lowest price prevailing in region 1, whereas the highest one is the price set by the foreign high-cost firms (p_{21}^h).

Very much like in the above section, there is two-way trade if m and t are not too large:

$$t + m < \frac{2}{2+\gamma} \tag{9.11}$$

a condition that boils down to (9.5) when firms are homogeneous ($m = 0$). In this case, the operating profits earned by each type of firm located in region 1 are defined as follows:

$$\pi_1^\ell = \theta(p_{11}^\ell)^2 + (1-\theta)\left(p_{22}^h - \frac{t}{2}\right)^2$$

$$\pi_1^h = \theta\left(p_{11}^\ell - \frac{m}{2}\right)^2 + (1-\theta)\left(p_{22}^h - \frac{m+t}{2}\right)^2.$$

By studying the behavior of the profit differentials $\pi_1^h - \pi_2^h$ and $\pi_1^\ell - \pi_2^\ell$ with respect to s^h and s^ℓ in [0, 1], Okubo, Picard, and Thisse (2010) determine which configuration is a long-run equilibrium. Their results may be summarized as follows.

(i) When the two regions have very different sizes, all firms agglomerate in the larger region because the proximity benefit outweighs the competition effect ($s^\ell = s^h = 1$). Region 1 is so large that the access to its market is always the dominant force. For the opposite reason, agglomeration in the smaller region is never an equilibrium.

(ii) As the difference in market size becomes smaller, some high-cost firms relocate in the smaller region, which offers them better protection against the competition of low-cost firms while benefiting from a bigger local market in region 2 ($s^\ell = 1$ and $0 < s^h < 1$).

(iii) High-cost firms completely sort out when asymmetry in size declines further. The long-run equilibrium then involves *perfect selection*, with all high-cost firms being located in the smaller region and all low-cost firms in the larger one ($s^\ell = 1$ and $s^h = 0$).

(iv) Last, as market size asymmetries become sufficiently small, some low-cost firms find it profitable to set up in the smaller region. They do so to soften competition with the bulk of low-cost firms located in the larger region while benefiting from their cost-advantage in region 2 whose market is almost as large as that of region 1 ($0 < s^\ell < 1$ and $s^h = 1$).

Does the HME still hold in such a context? To answer this question, we consider in turn the above four equilibrium configurations.

(i) In the agglomerated configuration, $\lambda^* - 1/2$ is equal to $1/2$ while $\theta - 1/2$ is less than $1/2$, and thus the former exceeds the latter.

(ii) In the configuration involving partial selection of high-cost firms, we have

$$\lambda^* - \frac{1}{2} = \frac{2 - t - m(2+\gamma\mu)}{\gamma t}(2\theta - 1). \tag{9.12}$$

Under (9.11), the term multiplying $(2\theta - 1)$ is always larger than $1/2$. Note that (9.12) is identical to (9.7) when firms are homogeneous ($m = 0$).

(iii) In the configuration with perfect selection, we have

$$\lambda^* - \frac{1}{2} = \mu - \frac{1}{2}.$$

Using (9.11), this expression exceeds $\theta - 1/2$.

(iv) Last, in the configuration involving partial selection of low-cost firms, we have

$$\lambda^* - \frac{1}{2} = \frac{2 - t + \gamma m(1-\mu)}{\gamma t}(2\theta - 1).$$

The term multiplying $(2\theta - 1)$ exceeds the corresponding term in (9.12), so that it must also exceed $1/2$. To sum up, in all equilibrium configurations, we have

$$\lambda^* > \theta.$$

Hence, we have:

Proposition 9.4. *The HME holds regardless of the degree of firms' heterogeneity. Furthermore, the larger region always accommodates a higher share of low-cost firms than the smaller one.*

Decreasing transport costs affects the location and selection of firms as increasing market size asymmetries does. In particular, as market integration gets deeper, low-cost firms sort completely out of the smaller region before high-cost firms begin to sort out. In other words, lowering transport costs first entices more low-cost firms to locate in the larger region and then, after all of them have relocated, it entices high-cost firms to move away from the smaller market. Consequently, the share of low-cost firms in the larger region always exceeds the share of high-cost firms, whereas the opposite holds in the smaller region. Thus, as transport costs fall, low-cost firms leave the smaller region before any high-cost firms also start to leave that region.

These results have an important implication about the relative competitiveness of different territories, namely *the larger market is always more productive than the smaller market*, which agrees with the empirical studies mentioned in the introduction. However, trade liberalization does not always exacerbate interregional disparities. Indeed, the relationship between trade liberalization and the interregional productivity gap is bell-shaped. As transportation costs fall from very high values, the productivity gap widens because low-cost firms relocate to the larger region. In contrast, the average productivity of each region does not change when there is perfect sorting. Finally, when transportation costs fall further, high-cost firms move to the larger region, thus reducing the productivity of this region and, therefore, diminishing the productivity gap.

Dealing with more than two types of firms generates technical difficulties. However, the main result still holds the spatial selection of firms across markets obeys a cascade-like process based on their respective productivity. In the limited case of a continuum of types, there is always perfect sorting (Nocke 2006).

9.4.2 Quality Heterogeneity

The assumption of horizontally differentiated varieties is shared by most NEG models. In doing so, NEG disregards the fact that varieties available in different regions and cities are also differentiated by their quality. The model studied above can be easily modified to deal with varieties that are both horizontally and vertically differentiated. Recall that two varieties are vertically differentiated when all consumers agree on their ranking. Vertical differentiation is then captured by assuming that the intensity of preference across varieties is described by a quality distribution, which, for a given set of prices, maps into heterogeneous demands. This can be achieved by replacing the subutility (9.1) by

$$u(q_i) = \alpha^{\nu} q_i - \frac{\beta}{2} q_i^2 - \frac{\gamma}{2} q_i \int_0^1 q_j \mathrm{d}j$$

where α^{ν} is the quality parameter. It is readily verified that the maximum price that a consumer is willing to pay for a variety increases with its quality parameter α^{ν}.

To use the approach developed in the subsection above, we assume that varieties can be divided between high- and low-quality varieties. In this case, the utility (9.2) is replaced by

$$U(q_0; q_{\nu i}, \nu = h, \ell \text{ and } i \in [0,1]) = \alpha^h \int_0^{\mu} q_i \mathrm{d}i + \alpha^{\ell} \int_{\mu}^1 q_i \mathrm{d}i - \frac{\beta}{2} \int_0^1 q_i^2 \mathrm{d}i$$
$$- \frac{\gamma}{2} \int_0^1 q_i \left(\int_0^1 q_j \mathrm{d}j \right) \mathrm{d}i + q_0$$

where $\alpha^h > \alpha^{\ell}$ while μ is the share of high-quality varieties. The difference between α^h and α^{ℓ} translates into demand functions given by

$$q_i^h = \frac{\alpha^h}{1+\gamma} - p_i + \frac{\gamma}{1+\gamma} P \qquad q_i^{\ell} = \frac{\alpha^{\ell}}{1+\gamma} - p_i + \frac{\gamma}{1+\gamma} P$$

where the demand for a high-quality variety is always higher than the demand for a low-quality variety because $\alpha^h > \alpha^{\ell}$. This endows the high-quality firms with more market power, and thus leads them to charge higher prices, very much as low-cost firms set prices lower than high-cost firms.

If both types of firms share the same cost function ($C^{\nu} = r$), setting $\alpha^h = 1$ and $\alpha^{\ell} = 1 - m$ shows that a high-quality (low-quality) firm is formally equivalent to a low-cost (high-cost) firm. As a consequence, quality heterogeneity and cost heterogeneity lead to similar results. In particular, Proposition 9.4 holds true. Thus, the larger region does not only get access to more varieties (HME); *the larger region also hosts a higher share of firms producing high-quality varieties than the smaller one.* This result confirms the empirical evidence reported in Berry and Waldfogel (2010) and Handbury and Weinstein (2011).

Note, however, that the sorting of firms results in a smaller number of firms in the larger market when vertical differentiation is present. This is because low-quality firms seek protection against high-quality firms by setting up in the smaller region.[9]

9.5 THE HOME MARKET EFFECT IN GENERAL EQUILIBRIUM

One of the main drawbacks of the analysis conducted in Section 9.3 is that the cost of shipping the agricultural good is zero. Though convenient in the first stages of development of NEG, such an assumption is weird in a setting that aims to capture the impact of the various impediments to trade on the location of firms. In addition, because preferences are quasi-linear, the level of capital returns has no impact on the demand for the manufactured good, hence on the interregional distribution of firms. All of this endows the linear model with a strong partial equilibrium flavor. There are two ways to obviate the former problem: either we assume that the economy has a single sector or we recognize that shipping the agricultural good is costly. In both cases, wages differ between regions. As for the latter, we return to the preference structure used in Chapter 8. Because preferences are no longer quasi-linear and the income generated by investments is repatriated where the capital-owners live and consume, the level of the rental rate of capital now affects the demand for the manufacturing good in both regions, whence the location of this sector. As a consequence, the location of capital-owners now matters. The absence of a Heckscher-Ohlin-type comparative advantage is critical for the analysis developed in this section because it neutralizes the impact that the location of capital-owners could have on the interregional distribution of income, hence on the spatial distribution of firms. Unless explicitly mentioned, the notation is the same as in the previous sections.

9.5.1 The One-Sector Economy

Following Takahashi et al. (2013), we assume that the economy involves only the manufacturing sector. Preferences are given by

$$U = \left(\int_0^M q_i^\rho \, \mathrm{d}i \right)^{1/\rho}$$

and the demand for variety i by

$$q_i = Y p_i^{-\sigma} P^{\sigma - 1}$$

where P is the price index given by (8.5).

[9] Picard and Okubo (2012) developed a richer setting in which firms selling the higher added value goods sort out into the region hosting the larger number of consumers. However, the spatial distribution of firms crucially depends on the properties of the taste distribution. In particular, a reverse HME may arise.

Each manufacturing firm has a unit fixed requirement of capital and a marginal requirement of labor equal to $(\sigma - 1)/\sigma$. Labor in region 2 is chosen as the numéraire, and thus $w_2 = 1$ while $w_1 = w$ is endogenous. Recall that $w_1 = w_2 = 1$ in Section 9.3.

The profits of a region r-firm are

$$\pi_1 = \left(p_1 - \frac{\sigma - 1}{\sigma} w\right) q_1 - r_1 \qquad \pi_2 = \left(p_2 - \frac{\sigma - 1}{\sigma}\right) q_2 - r_2$$

where q_r is given by (8.11). Applying the first order condition yields $p_1^* = w$ and $p_2^* = 1$.

Let $\phi = \tau^{-(\sigma-1)} > 1$. Plugging the equilibrium consumptions (8.11) and prices into the profit functions, we obtain the rental rates of capital:

$$r_1(\lambda) = \frac{1}{\sigma}\left[\frac{w^{1-\sigma} Y_1}{\lambda w^{1-\sigma} + \phi(1-\lambda)} + \frac{\phi w^{1-\sigma} Y_2}{\lambda \phi w^{1-\sigma} + (1-\lambda)}\right] \tag{9.13}$$

$$r_2(\lambda) = \frac{1}{\sigma}\left[\frac{\phi Y_1}{\lambda w^{1-\sigma} + \phi(1-\lambda)} + \frac{Y_2}{\lambda \phi w^{1-\sigma} + (1-\lambda)}\right] \tag{9.14}$$

where the regional incomes are endogenous and given by

$$Y_1 = \theta\left[\lambda r_1 + (1-\lambda) r_2 + w\right] \tag{9.15}$$

$$Y_2 = (1-\theta)\left[\lambda r_1 + (1-\lambda) r_2 + 1\right]. \tag{9.16}$$

These expressions show that the regional incomes depend on the rental rates of capital – recall that returns on investments are repatriated – but also on the wage rate prevailing in region 1. As a consequence, both capital returns and wages affect the demand for the manufactured good in each region, hence firms' gross profits. This general equilibrium effect generated by the income effect was absent in Section 9.2.2.

Using (9.13)–(9.16), capital market clearing implies

$$r = r_1 = r_2 = \frac{Y_1 + Y_2}{\sigma}.$$

Substituting this expression in (9.15) and (9.16) yields the equilibrium regional incomes and capital return as functions of the wage rate w:

$$Y_1 = \frac{\theta[\sigma w + (1-\theta)(1-w)]}{\sigma - 1} \qquad Y_2 = \frac{(1-\theta)[\sigma - \theta(1-w)]}{\sigma - 1}$$

and

$$r = \frac{\theta w + 1 - \theta}{\sigma - 1}.$$

Adding first (9.15) and (9.16), then substituting r yields the labor income in region 1:

$$\lambda \frac{\sigma - 1}{\sigma}(Y_1 + Y_2) = \lambda(\theta w + 1 - \theta)$$

which is also equal to θw. Solving the equation $\lambda(\theta w + 1 - \theta) = \theta w$, we obtain the relationship between the equilibrium wage rate and mass of firms in region 1:

$$\lambda^* = \frac{\theta w^*}{\theta w^* + 1 - \theta}$$

or, equivalently,

$$w^* = \frac{\lambda^*(1 - \theta)}{(1 - \lambda^*)\theta}.$$

These relationships show that both *the size of the manufacturing sector and the wage rate in the larger region are positively related*. Indeed, the supply of labor being perfectly inelastic, competition on the local labor market intensifies as firms congregate in the larger region, which leads these firms to pay a higher wage to their workers. This in turn generates a higher demand for the manufactured good, thus making region 1 attractive to region-2 firms. This process of cumulative causality bears some resemblance to the one that fuels the CP model. However, it is likely to stop before the manufacturing sector is fully agglomerated in the larger region. The wage hike associated with the establishment of more firms puts a break on the relocation process. As a consequence, the equalization of profits can be reached at an interior equilibrium at which higher wages offset the greater market advantage provided by region 1. Note that $w^* = 1$ if and only if $\lambda^* = \theta$, that is, wage equalization prevails when the geographical distribution of capital is the same as the geographical distribution of labor.

It remains to determine the equilibrium wage rate in region 1. Labor market clearing in this region means

$$\theta = \lambda \frac{\sigma - 1}{\sigma} q_1.$$

Substituting a firm's equilibrium output q_1^* into this expression yields the following implicit wage equation:

$$\mathcal{F}(w) \equiv \mathcal{G}_0(w) + \mathcal{G}_1(w)\phi + \mathcal{G}_2(w)\phi^2 = 0$$

where

$$\mathcal{G}_0(w) = (w - 1)\theta(1 - \theta)$$
$$\mathcal{G}_1(w) = w^{2-\sigma}[(1 - \theta)w^{2\sigma-3} - \theta]\sigma$$
$$\mathcal{G}_2(w) = \theta(\sigma - 1 + \theta)w - (1 - \theta)(\sigma - \theta).$$

The preceding wage equation has no analytical solution except when $\sigma = 2$. However, Takahashi et al. have shown that for any given value of ϕ in $(0, 1)$, this equation has a unique solution w^* and this solution is such that $w^* > 1$. In other words, *the wage rate in the larger region exceeds the wage rate in the smaller region.*

Note that

$$\lambda^* - \theta = \frac{\theta w^*}{\theta w^* + 1 - \theta} - \theta = \frac{\theta(1 - \theta)(w^* - 1)}{\theta w^* + 1 - \theta}$$

which is positive because $w^* > 1$. As a consequence, λ^* exceeds θ. In other words, even when the wage paid in the larger region exceeds that paid in the smaller one, market access remains a critical variable in determining factor prices and the location of economic activity.

By studying the behavior of $\mathcal{F}(w)$, Takahashi et al. (2013) show that the magnification of the HME obtained in Section 9.3 no longer holds: both the equilibrium share of capital and wage follow the bell-shaped curve of spatial development discussed in Section 8.5. In other words, once workers are immobile, a higher concentration of firms within a region translates to an increase in wages for this region. This gives rise to two opposite forces. On the one hand, final demand in the core region increases because consumers enjoy higher incomes. As in Krugman (1991b), final demand is an agglomeration force; however, it is no longer sparked by an increase in population size, but by an increase in wages. On the other hand, an increase in the wage level generates a new dispersion force, which lies at the heart of many debates regarding the deindustrialization of developed countries, i.e., their high labor costs. In such a context, firms are induced to relocate their activities to the periphery when lower wages there more than offset lower demand.

In the linear model used in Sections 9.2 and 9.3, capital returns are spent on the homogeneous good, and thus the interregional distribution of capital-ownership does not matter for the location of firms. Things are very different here because capital returns affect the demand for the manufactured good. If the relative endowment of capital-owners in the larger region were higher (lower) than θ, more (fewer) firms would be located in this region while the wage rate would be higher (lower). Hence a small but rich country such as Switzerland may attract a relatively large share of firms at the expense of the large country.

In closing, trade between the two regions is not balanced. The smaller region imports more than it exports because consumers living in the former benefit from the returns on investments made in the latter. To put it simply, its gross national product exceeds its gross domestic product. The pre-crisis Ireland was a good case in point.

9.5.2 Shipping the Agricultural Good Is Costly

Consider a two-sector economy such as that discussed in Section 8.2.2 in which each manufacturing firm has a unit fixed requirement of capital and a unit marginal requitement of labor. However, we now assume that shipping the agricultural good from one region to the other requires scarce resources. Specifically, $\tau^{\mathbb{M}} > 1$ ($\tau^{\mathbb{A}} > 1$) units of the manufactured (agricultural) good must be shipped for one unit of this good to reach the other region. As in the foregoing, wages need not be equal across regions: $w_1 = w$ and $w_2 = 1$. Because the agricultural good is produced under constant returns and perfect competition, its price in region 1 is $p_1^{\mathbb{A}} = w$ while its price in region 2 is $p_2^{\mathbb{A}} = 1$. Furthermore, repeating the argument developed in Section 8.2.1, we can readily verify that the equilibrium outputs are such that

$$q_1^* = \frac{(\sigma - 1)r_1}{w} \qquad q_2^* = (\sigma - 1)r_2. \tag{9.17}$$

Under which conditions may we expect the HME to hold? If region 1 imports the agricultural good, this is because there is not enough labor available there to produce this good. In this event, it must be that $p_1^{\mathbb{A}} = w = \tau^{\mathbb{A}} > 1$ since $p_2^{\mathbb{A}} = 1$.[10] As shown by (9.17), $\tau^{\mathbb{A}} > 1$ implies that region-1 firms are smaller than region-2 firms, which implies that they hire fewer workers. For these two observations to be consistent, region 1 must accommodate a more than proportionate share of manufacturing firms. As long as shipping the agricultural good is not too expensive ($\tau^{\mathbb{A}} < \bar{\tau}$), Takatsuka and Zeng (2012a) show that the higher wage paid in the larger region does not prevent the HME from arising. Moreover, region 2 exports the agricultural good to region 1, while both regions exchange the manufactured good. In other words, there is both intra-industry and intersectoral trade.

When shipping the agricultural good is expensive ($\tau^{\mathbb{A}} > \bar{\tau}$), this good ceases to be imported. Otherwise the wage in region 1 would become sufficiently high for the manufacturing firms in region 1 to reduce substantially their output due to the high wage, thus making more workers available for the agricultural sector. In this case, we have $p_1^{\mathbb{A}} = w^* = \bar{\tau} > 1$. However, the individual income ratio $(r + \bar{\tau})/(r + 1)$ is smaller than the wage ratio $\bar{\tau}$. Therefore, in the $\mathbb{A}$-sector the share of region-1 workers is smaller than the share of region-2 workers. As a

[10] This is formally equivalent to working with a setting in which labor in region 1 is more efficient than region 2, thus implying a higher wage in the former than in the latter.

consequence, the share of labor used in the manufacturing sector is larger in region 1 than in region 2. Since firms are smaller in 1 than in 2, the mass of firms located in region 1 must exceed θ; thereby the HME still holds (Takatsuka and Zeng 2012a). To sum up, regardless of the value of the transportation cost τ^{A}, the larger region always accommodates a more than proportionate share of the manufacturing sector.

Putting together the results of the above two subsections shows that the HME does not depend on the presence or absence of a homogeneous good traded at zero cost. More important is the difference between the one-factor and two-factor models. In the former the total number of firms is variable whereas it is constant in the latter because the capital supply is perfectly inelastic. In addition, capital mobility allows trade imbalance, the deficit being covered by the transfer of numéraire generated by foreign direct investment. Note, however, that in the two-factor model the rental rate of capital is endogenous and affects the demand for the manufactured good through the income effect, which is absent in the model used in Sections 9.2 and 9.3.

9.5.3 Notes on the Literature

We have studied in Section 4.5, the location of an industry selling a homogeneous good to consumers uniformly distributed in a one- or two-dimensional space. In this model, which is often refereed to as the spatial model of monopolistic competition, the supply of capital is perfectly elastic and the interest rate exogenous, whereas the supply of capital is perfectly inelastic and the interest rate endogenous in the FC model. Consequently, the fixed cost is exogenous in the former and endogenous in the latter. As shown by Proposition 4.4, the market outcome involves too many firms, which means that the interfirm distance is too small. This echoes the excessive concentration of firms in the larger region highlighted by Proposition 9.3. To the best of our knowledge, the connections between the FC model and the spatial model of monopolistic competition have not been explored.

In his pioneering paper, Krugman (1980) considered a one-factor – labor – model in which the mass of firms in each region is determined by the zero-profit condition. In such a context, potential firms choose whether or not to enter; they do not choose location because labor is immobile. In other words, the number of firms operating in each region stems from the profit opportunities generated by the difference in market size and the degree of market integration. Helpman and Krugman (1985, chapter 10) added the agricultural sector to this model and assumed that its output can be traded costlessly between the two regions, which assures wage equalization between regions. In this case, as in Section 9.3, the HME holds. By contrast, Davis (1998) established that there is no HME when the transport costs of the agricultural and manufactured goods are the same. Takatsuka and Zeng (2012b) have generalized the model to deal with any positive transport cost. They showed that the HME holds if and only if the cost of shipping the agricultural good is not too large for this good to be traded from the smaller to the larger region. Otherwise, the agricultural good is not traded, and thus export and import of the manufactured good are equal. Under these circumstances, there is no HME: the distribution of firms mirrors the distribution of labor.

The idea of working with a two-factor model in which capital is mobile and labor immobile is developed by Martin and Rogers (1995). They assume that preferences are given by (8.1), and thus the level of the rental rate of capital affects the demand for the manufactured good; the linear version is due to Ottaviano and Thisse (2004). The FC model, which is more in line with standard location theory where firms choose their location, has been extensively studied in Baldwin et al. (2003). It has been used as a building block in various public policy questions, especially those related to fiscal competition such as Baldwin and Krugman (2004), Ottaviano and van Ypersele (2005), Behrens et al. (2007), and Behrens and Picard (2008). Most of the recent literature is empirical and focuses on the wage equation of Section 9.4. Head and Mayer (2004) and Redding (2011) provide rich and detailed surveys of the main contributions.

Two applications of the above models are worth mentioning. First, although transport costs are a key ingredient in economic geography, the transport sector is abstracted away from the analysis. Put differently, freight rates are taken as parametric and are not set by the market. Behrens, Gaigné, and Thisse (2009) show that the demand for transport services becomes less elastic as the degree of spatial agglomeration rises, thus increasing carriers' market power. When manufacturing firms are free to relocate in response to changes in transport costs, an increasing number of carriers, falling marginal costs in transportation, or both, trigger a gradual agglomeration of industry. When carriers must commit to capacities and offer transport services in both shipping directions, trade imbalances lead to asymmetric freight rates. The resulting freight rate differentials create an additional dispersion force that may strongly attenuate the HME (Behrens and Picard 2011).

Second, the models presented in the above sections can be extended to multinational enterprises, which choose to operate either one or two plants. In the former case, firms bear the fixed production cost of a single plant, and thus concentration prevails. In the latter, firms save the cost of shipping their output to the other region, and thus proximity prevails. Using the CES, Toulemonde (2008) shows that (i) for low transportation costs, all firms have one plant, (ii) for intermediate transportation costs, single-plant and multiplant firms coexist, and (iii) for large transportation costs, all firms run two plants. Hence, market integration leads to the concentration of production within fewer but larger plants as well as to a higher extensive and intensive margins of trade.

Last, a few papers have proposed a new research strategy to study the relationship between market proximity and economic development: they investigate the impact of unanticipated historical events that have generated the disruptions of prior trade relationships. Redding and Sturm (2008) and Nakajima (2008) showed that the post–World War II loss of accessibility to East Germany and North Korea, respectively, has been detrimental to German and Japanese cities located near to the new border.

9.6 INDUSTRIAL CLUSTERS

9.6.1 When Do Clusters Emerge?

The HME highlights the attractiveness of large markets but it does not explain why some markets are larger than others. In this section, we return to the linear model of Section 9.2 and show how localization economies operating within the same industry may generate an asymmetric distribution of firms in a global economy that is otherwise symmetric ($\theta = 1/2$). In other words, once it is recognized that firms may benefit from their technological proximity by forming a cluster, we will identify conditions under which firms choose to be (partially) agglomerated in one region in the absence of market size differences. By the same token, this approach allows us to combine global pecuniary and local technological externalities. Thus, we recognize that the difference in the economic performance of regions is explained by the behavior and interactions between firms that are located within them as well as by their market potential. Note also that models of monopolistic competition is especially well suited to study the emergence of industrial clusters involving a large number of small firms.

In modeling the idea of localization economies, we follow Chipman (1970) and assume that the marginal production cost c_r prevailing in region r decreases with the number of manufacturing firms located therein. Though incomplete, this black-box approach captures the presence of localization economies such as those discussed in Section 4.2. We use this modeling strategy not only because of its convenience in view of the difficulty of studying the interplay between competition *across* locales and nonmarket interactions *within* each locale, such as those studied in Section 6.3, but also because clusters cannot be understood without explicit reference to competition and to the role played by specific location in the global economy.

Being negligible to the market, a firm accurately treats the marginal cost c_r as a parameter. However, it is aware that its locational choice affects its production cost. Thus firms located in different regions are heterogeneous. The other difference with Section 9.4 is that the degree of heterogeneity is endogenous since it varies with the way firms are distributed between the two regions.

For any given λ, a firm located in region 1 maximizes its operating profits, which are now defined by

$$\pi_1 = (p_{11} - c_1)q_{11} + (p_{12} - c_1 - t)q_{12}.$$

Applying the method described in Section 9.2 yields the equilibrium prices:

$$p_{11}^* = \frac{c_1}{2} + \frac{2 + [\lambda c_1 + (1-\lambda)(c_2 + t)]}{2(2+\gamma)}$$

$$p_{12}^* = \frac{c_1 + t}{2} + \frac{2 + [\lambda(c_1 + t) + (1-\lambda)c_2]}{2(2+\gamma)}.$$

Two-way trade arises if the condition

$$t + \max\{c_1, c_2\} < \frac{2}{2+\gamma} \tag{9.18}$$

holds. In this case, the equilibrium operating profits of a region-1 firm are given by

$$\pi_1(\lambda) = \frac{1}{4(2+\gamma)^2}\{[2(1-c_1) - \gamma(1-\lambda)(c_1 - c_2) - t]^2 + [1 + \gamma(1-\lambda)]^2 t^2\}.$$

In what follows, it is assumed that localization economies obey the same linear law:

$$c_r(\lambda) = c - \alpha\lambda$$

where $0 < \alpha < c$ measures the intensity of these economies: the higher the former, the stronger the latter.

We can take advantage of the symmetry of the problem by setting $\Delta\lambda \equiv 2\lambda - 1$. Thus, $c_1(\Delta\lambda) + c_2(\Delta\lambda) = 2c - \alpha$ and $c_1(\Delta\lambda) - c_2(\Delta\lambda) = -\alpha(\Delta\lambda)$. Consequently, the operating profits can be rewritten as follows:

$$\pi_1(\Delta\lambda) = \frac{1}{16(2+\gamma)^2}\{[4 - 2(2c + t - \alpha) - \alpha\gamma(\Delta\lambda)^2 + \alpha\gamma(\Delta\lambda)]^2 + [2 + \gamma - \gamma(\Delta\lambda)]^2 t^2\}.$$

Accordingly, the equilibrium condition

$$r_1 - r_2 = \pi_1(\Delta\lambda) - \pi_2(\Delta\lambda) = \Delta\pi(\Delta\lambda) = 0$$

is given by

$$\Delta\pi(\Delta\lambda) = \frac{\Delta\lambda}{4(2+\gamma)}\{\alpha[4 - 2(2c + t - \alpha) - \alpha\gamma(\Delta\lambda)^2] - \gamma t^2\} = 0$$

which can be rewritten as the following cubic function of $\Delta\lambda$:

$$\Delta\pi(\Delta\lambda) = \frac{\alpha^2\gamma}{4(2+\gamma)}\Delta\lambda[\Lambda - (\Delta\lambda)^2] = 0 \tag{9.19}$$

where Λ is a constant given by

$$\Lambda \equiv \frac{\alpha[4 - 2(2c + t - \alpha)] - \gamma t^2}{\alpha^2\gamma} \tag{9.20}$$

while its slope is:

$$\frac{\mathrm{d}(\Delta\pi)}{\mathrm{d}(\Delta\lambda)} = -\frac{\alpha^2\gamma}{2(2+\gamma)}[3(\Delta\lambda)^2 - \Lambda].$$

Given (9.19), the symmetric configuration ($\Delta\lambda = 0$) is always an equilibrium. As in Chapter 8, in the presence of multiple equilibria we use stability as a selection device. In the present context, the dynamics is fairly natural. If firms observe that a region offers higher profits than the other, they want to move to that region. In other words, as in the previous sections, the driving force is the profit differential between regions 1 and 2. If $\Delta\pi$ is positive and if $0 < \lambda < 1$, some firms will move from 2 to 1; if it is negative, some will go in the opposite direction. An equilibrium is stable if, for any marginal deviation from the equilibrium, the equation of motion above brings the distribution of firms back to the original one. An agglomerated configuration is always stable when it turns out to be an equilibrium, while an interior equilibrium is stable if and only if the slope of $\Delta\pi(\Delta\lambda)$ is negative in a neighborhood of this equilibrium.

Several stable equilibria may arise in the present setting. Either all firms agglomerate in one region (corner solution) or they distribute themselves between the two regions (interior solution) in a way that equalizes operating profits. In the latter case, firms can spread evenly ($\Delta\lambda = 0$) or unevenly across regions.

Using (9.19), the equilibria can be determined as follows. (i) When $\Lambda < 0$, the equation $\Delta\pi = 0$ has a single real solution $\Delta\lambda = 0$ at which the slope is negative. Thus, $\Delta\lambda = 0$ is the only stable equilibrium. (ii) When $\Lambda > 0$, the equation $\Delta\pi = 0$ has three real solutions $\Delta\lambda = 0$ and $\Delta\lambda = \pm\sqrt{\Lambda}$. In this case, one of the following two cases must arise. (iii) The asymmetric solutions $\Delta\lambda = \pm\sqrt{\Lambda}$ are equilibria if and only if $0 < \Lambda < 1$. They are stable since the slope of $\Delta\pi$ evaluated at $\Delta\lambda = \pm\sqrt{\Lambda}$ is negative as $0 < \Lambda < 1$. By contrast, the symmetric equilibrium is unstable since $\Delta\pi(0) > 0$. (iv) When $\Lambda > 1$, there is no asymmetric interior equilibrium and the only stable equilibria are such that $\Delta\lambda = \pm 1$ since either $\Delta\pi(1) > 0$ or $\Delta\pi(-1) > 0$.

This is summarized in the following proposition.

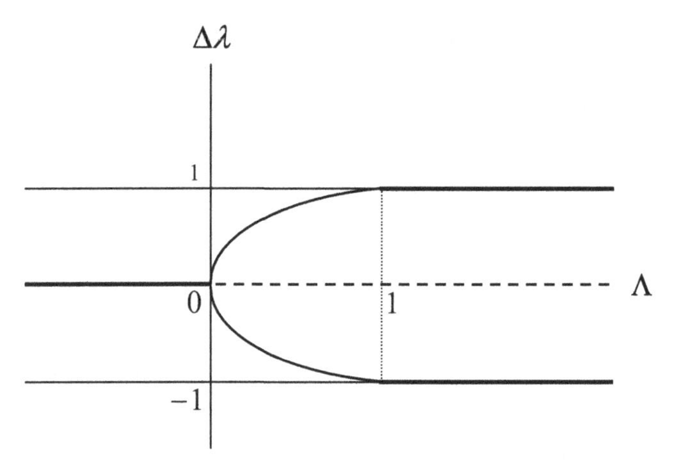

Figure 9.1. Stable equilibria.

Proposition 9.5. *The two-region economy has always a single (up to a permutation) stable spatial equilibrium. This one involves:*
(i) dispersion ($\Delta\lambda = 0$) *if and only if* $\Lambda \leq 0$;
(ii) partial agglomeration ($\Delta\lambda = \pm\sqrt{\Lambda}$) *if and only if* $0 < \Lambda < 1$;
(iii) agglomeration ($\Delta\lambda = \pm 1$) *if and only if* $1 \leq \Lambda$.

The stable equilibria are represented by the bold lines and the unstable ones by the dotted lines in Figure 9.1.

In spite of the symmetry of the economy, *industrial clusters involving different numbers of firms may emerge in equilibrium.* In this case, the number of firms in region 1 is

$$\lambda^* = \frac{1 \pm \sqrt{\Lambda}}{2} > \theta = \frac{1}{2}.$$

The region that ends up with the larger number of firms is the one that has the larger initial share of firms, however small the difference. This result illustrates what seems to be one of the main spatial features of modern economies, namely the emergence of a *putty-clay economic geography*. More precisely, the fall in transportation and communication costs allows for a great deal of flexibility on where particular activities can locate, but once spatial differences develop, locations tend to become quite rigid. Actually, a small shock arising near the bifurcation displayed in Figure 9.1 may be enough to pick up one region instead of the other. Hence, *regions that were once similar may end up having very different production structures*.

Since λ^* depends only upon Λ, the impact of a parameter on the spatial equilibrium can be analyzed through Λ as given by (9.20). First, we have:

$$\frac{\partial \Lambda}{\partial t} = -\frac{2(\alpha + \gamma t)}{\alpha^2 \gamma} < 0$$

which implies that a decrease in transportation costs leads to more asymmetry between clusters. In other words, *lowering transportation costs drives the economy toward more agglomeration in one region at the expense of the other*. It is worth pointing out that this process is smooth unlike what is observed in the CP model we studied in Chapter 8.

Furthermore

$$\frac{\partial \Lambda}{\partial \alpha} = -\frac{\Lambda}{\alpha} + 2\frac{1}{\alpha(2+\gamma)} + \frac{t^2}{\alpha^3}$$

which shows that an increase in the intensity of localization economies strengthens the tendency toward agglomeration provided that α is small enough, that is,

$$\alpha < \frac{2(2+\gamma)t^2}{4(1-c)-t} \tag{9.21}$$

where the right-hand side is positive by (9.18). By contrast, when (9.21) does not hold stronger localization economies generate more dispersion. This surprising result may be explained as follows. When production costs are not too high, firms in the smaller cluster price in the inelastic part of their demands, whereas firms in the larger cluster price in the elastic part. By reducing production costs, an increase in α thus intensifies competition much more in the larger cluster than in the smaller one, leading some firms to move from the former to the latter. In sum, *stronger localization economies do not necessarily foster the growth of the big cluster*. The size of clusters is indeed determined by a much richer set of interactions, which also involves the working of global markets.

9.6.2 Are the Big Clusters too Big or too Small?

We have seen that the social welfare function is here defined by the sum of the consumer surpluses in the two regions. After having replaced prices and quantities by their first-best values in the consumer surplus (9.10), we obtain

$$W = CS_1 + CS_2 = -\frac{A}{4}(\Delta\lambda)^4 + \frac{A}{2}\Gamma(\Delta\lambda)^2 + B$$

where

$$A \equiv \frac{\alpha^2 \gamma}{1+\gamma} > 0$$

and B are constants and where

$$\Gamma \equiv \frac{1+\gamma}{2\gamma} + \frac{\Lambda}{2}. \tag{9.22}$$

The first-best locational pattern is then obtained by maximizing W with respect to $\Delta\lambda$.

As in Proposition 9.5, the proof involves three steps. Firstly, when the maximum is interior, we have:

$$\frac{\mathrm{d}W}{\mathrm{d}(\Delta\lambda)} = -A\Delta\lambda\left[(\Delta\lambda)^2 - \Gamma\right] = 0$$

and

$$\frac{\mathrm{d}^2 W}{\mathrm{d}(\Delta\lambda)^2} = -A\left[3(\Delta\lambda)^2 - \Gamma\right] < 0.$$

When $\Gamma \leq 0$, there is a unique maximizer given by $\Delta\lambda = 0$ because the second-order condition is satisfied. Secondly, when $0 < \Gamma < 1$, W reaches a minimum at $\Delta\lambda = 0$ and is maximized at $\Delta\lambda = \pm\sqrt{\Gamma}$ where the second-order condition holds. Finally, when $1 \geq \Gamma$, the social welfare function is maximized at $\Delta\lambda = \pm 1$.

To sum up, we have:

Proposition 9.6. *The first-best allocation involves:*
(i) dispersion if and only if $\Gamma \leq 0$;
(ii) partial agglomeration if and only if $0 < \Gamma < 1$;
(iii) agglomeration if and only if $1 \leq \Gamma$.

Thus, the first-best solution displays a pattern similar to that arising when firms are free to choose prices and locations at the market equilibrium. In the case of asymmetric clusters, the socially optimal distribution of firms is given by

$$\lambda^0 = \frac{1 \pm \sqrt{\Gamma}}{2}.$$

It follows from (9.22) that Γ exceeds Λ when $0 < \Lambda \leq 1$, while $\Gamma > 0$ when $\Lambda = 0$. Furthermore, Γ is a strictly decreasing function of t so that lower transport costs yield more asymmetry between optimal clusters.[11] Consequently, we have the following result:

Proposition 9.7. *The market equilibrium is never more concentrated than the first-best optimum.*

[11] Using (9.22), it is readily verified that the impact of α on Γ is similar to the impact on Λ as previously discussed.

Thus, regardless of the intensity of localization economies, the larger cluster never involves too many firms in equilibrium from the efficiency viewpoint. In particular, the planner sets up more asymmetric clusters than arise at the market solution unless the market outcome corresponds to full agglomeration or the first-best solution involves full dispersion. This requires some explanation. At the first-best optimum, prices are set at the marginal cost level whereas locations are chosen to maximize the difference between the benefits of agglomeration and total transport costs. By contrast, at the market equilibrium, firms take advantage of their spatial separation to relax price competition and, hence, to make higher profits. These two effects combine to generate the discrepancy between the market and optimal solutions. This confirms what we saw in Section 7.3, that is, price competition is a strong dispersion force.

Unlike what many regional planners would argue, the optimal configuration tends to involve a more unbalanced distribution of firms than the market outcome. If localization economies become increasingly important in advanced economic sectors, as suggested by the growing role played by knowledge spillovers in research and development, the observed regional imbalances in the geographical distribution of high-tech activities may not signify a wasteful allocation of resources. On the contrary, the size of the existing clusters could well be too small.

However, unless dispersion corresponds to both the equilibrium and the optimal outcomes, the difference between regional surpluses generates a conflict between regions about firms' locations, which might give rise to fiscal competition. Indeed, the region with the larger cluster benefits from larger localization economies, and thus lower prices, as well as from lower transportation costs on its imports. This occurs because the planner focuses only on global efficiency and not on spatial equity. This policy is a sensible one when lump-sum transfers compensating the consumers of the less industrialized regions are available. However, when such redistributive instruments are not available, a trade-off between global efficiency and spatial equity arises.

9.7 CONCLUDING REMARKS

This chapter has highlighted three different aspects associated with a size advantage: (i) the larger region accommodates a more than proportionate share of firms, (ii) the larger region is a net exporter of the good produced under increasing returns, and (iii) the wage prevailing in the larger region exceeds that of the smaller one. These three properties need not be equivalent. Therefore, *how a size advantage translates into an economic advantage is multiform and ambivalent.*

One of the most striking implications of the results presented in this chapter is that, during the process of economic integration, *a small initial advantage may lead to the emergence of a strongly polarized space*. Such an advantage is magnified when the mobility of factors or the transportability of products are high, or both. Even in the absence of size differences, localization economies suffice to generate asymmetric clusters that emerge endogenously.

Several remarks are in order. First, market potential affects positively the economic performance of a region or country at the macro-spatial level. This is less clear at the micro-level. Indeed, once market accessibility is maintained through high-quality transport infrastructure, distance matters much less in shipping commodities, and thus the market potential would become less significant (Combes, Duranton, and Gobillon 2011). In this case, local interactions such as those discussed in Chapter 6 are likely to be more relevant (Fingleton 2011). Owing to the strong distance-decay effect that characterizes spillover effects, localization economies appear to be a strong agglomeration force at the intraregional level. This is especially true when transport costs between regions are low. In this event, (partial) agglomeration occurs because firms are able to enjoy a high level of localization economies while they are able to sell a substantial fraction of their output on distant markets. Thus, as in previous chapters, but not necessarily for the same reasons, lower transportation costs are associated with a more concentrated pattern of activities.

That more product differentiation also fosters more agglomeration is not new either. This fact agrees with what we have seen in Chapters 7 and 8. The reason is always the same: a higher degree of product differentiation allows firms to relax price competition, thus permitting any existing agglomeration force to dominate the dispersion force. This agglomeration force appears to be crucial in very different spatial settings and is likely to be strong in modern economies. Thus, the same causes lead to the same effects, although the geographical scale as well as the forces at work are very different. Interestingly, the same tendency holds at the first best optimum.

We have argued repeatedly that product differentiation provides a natural framework for studying interregional trade and the mobility of production factors. Though both elegant and relevant, this should not conceal one fundamental feature of the NEG models studied here: all the results obtained are driven by the combination involving increasing returns and *imperfect* competition, and not necessarily monopolistic competition. For example, Cournotian firms producing a homogeneous good and competing in quantities have positive markups that allow them to cover their fixed production costs. Not surprisingly, therefore, the main results obtained in this chapter and in the previous one also hold in this context (Thisse 2010).

Furthermore, despite being indisputably valuable, NEG-like models such as those used in this chapter suffer from a major drawback, which has been brushed away in most of the literature: they are built on a two-location setting. Yet, it is well known that a firm's location is the balance of a system of forces pulling the firm in various directions. The new fundamental ingredient that a multi-location setting brings about is that spatial frictions between any two cities are likely to be different. As a consequence, the *relative position* of a city within the whole network of interactions matters (Behrens et al. 2009; Combes, Mayer, and Thisse 2008).

Another key insight one can derive in a multi-location economy is that any change in the underlying parameters has in general complex impacts that vary in non-trivial ways with the properties of the graph representing the spatial economy. When there are only two locations, any change in structural parameters necessarily affects directly either one of the two cities, or both. On the contrary, when there are more than two locations, any change in parameters that directly involves only two cities now generates spatial spillover effects that are unlikely to leave the remaining cities unaffected. More work is called for here but one should not expect the answer to be simple.

A last word, in closing. We have seen that pecuniary externalities lead to an excessive concentration of firms, whereas there is insufficient agglomeration under technological externalities. This difference in results shows how important it is to distinguish these two types of externalities. As already mentioned, they do not operate at the same spatial scale as stressed by the intuition behind these contrasting results. How to combine them in an encompassing model is a task that remains out of (our) reach as long as we do not understand better the spatial aggregation problem.

PART IV

URBAN SYSTEMS, REGIONAL GROWTH, AND THE MULTINATIONALIZATION OF FIRMS

10

Back to von Thünen

The Emergence of Cities in a Spatial Economy

10.1 INTRODUCTION

Thus far, we have studied cities from several different perspectives, for they constitute the most visible and important facet of the phenomenon of economic agglomeration. However, we have left untouched one important issue, namely, the location of cities. Under the assumption of costless intercity trade, cities are like floating islands, and their location is irrelevant. For many purposes, this has been a convenient simplifying assumption. However, because the central concern of this book is to bring back space into economics in its many aspects and dimensions, we cannot end our quest without exploring the question of where cities are established, and why. More important, such issues are likely to be crucial for the future of our economies. In an increasingly borderless world economy, the location of prosperous and growing cities should increasingly become a critical factor in the determination of people's well-being.

If the location of cities in the real world were arbitrary, it would be hopeless (and useless) to develop a theory about the location of cities. The reality, however, is quite the opposite. In fact, over the past century, economic geographers and historians have tirelessly advocated the surprising regularity in the actual structure of urban systems observed throughout the world, and so at different time periods (see, J. Marshall 1989, chapter 5; Hohenberg and Lees 1985, chapter 2). This effort has culminated in what is called "central place theory," as pioneered by Christaller ([1933] 1966) and Lösch ([1940] 1954). The aim of these authors was to explain the spatial distribution of economic activities within *a hierarchical system of urban centers.* Specifically, different goods, characterized by nested market areas and indexed accordingly by $i = 1, \dots, n$, are supplied by different firms. The goal is then to show that a location where good i is available also accommodates firms supplying all goods of order lower than i. The bulk of central place theory has been directed toward identifying conditions under which such a superposition of regular structures is possible. However, this theory has focused far too much on geometric considerations.

Indeed, there are no economic forces in these models that lead firms selling different goods to cluster, and thus it is hard to see why central places should emerge.

To the best of our knowledge, Eaton and Lipsey (1982) were the first to model multipurpose shopping as an economic foundation for the existence of clusters in which different goods are supplied by different firms.[1] Indeed, it is a well-documented fact that consumers organize their trips to satisfy various needs. For example, on the same trip, a consumer buys different goods, meets friends, visits a movie theater, goes to the post office, or just wanders and looks around. That consumers group their purchases to reduce travel costs creates demand externalities that firms can exploit by locating with firms selling other goods.

Eaton and Lipsey have identified a set of conditions under which the only equilibria involve clusters in which firms selling good 1 or good 2, each bought at a different frequency, are located together. Using the same framework, Quinzii and Thisse (1990) have proven that the socially optimal configuration of firms always involves the clustering of firms selling goods 1 and 2. These results therefore confirm the initial intuition. However, the spatial competition approach to the formation of central places taken in such articles becomes very quickly intractable. The reason is that trip-chaining implies a particular structure of substitution between outlets. This structure is such that it is hard for a consumer to determine her optimal spatial structure of purchases because this requires solving a particularly difficult combinatorial problem. It is accordingly easy to imagine how firms' demands become complex and intricate. Hence, a need exists for other approaches. Furthermore, although central place theory offers several fundamental insights about the organization of the space-economy (Mulligan 1984), it is fair to say that it has been largely descriptive. In this chapter, we intend to develop a microeconomic approach to the formation of urban systems in which the location of cities matters.

To this end, we go back to the origin of spatial economics, that is, Thünen's *Isolated State*. As discussed in Chapter 3, Thünen (1826) started his work by making the following the following assumption:

> Imagine a very large town at the center of a fertile plain which is crossed by no navigable river or canal. Throughout the plain the soil is capable of cultivation and of the same fertility. Far from the town, the plain turns into an uncultivated wilderness which cuts off all communication between this state and the outside world.

[1] Once more, this idea has been anticipated by Thünen ([1826] 1966): "For instance, a countryman may visit the capital to sell his products, and decide to buy some liquor. It will be cheaper for him to buy this in the capital, even if it costs him half a thaler more than he would pay in the provincial town two miles from his farm, because he would have to make a special journey to fetch the local alcohol (p. 287 of the English translation).

There are no other towns on the plain. The central town must therefore supply the rural areas with all manufactured products, and in return will obtain all its provision from the surrounding countryside (p. 7 of the English translation).

Although countless variations of the Thünian model have appeared since then, the literature has left aside a fundamental issue: Why should all manufactured goods be produced in a single city? To the best of our knowledge, Fujita and Krugman (1995) were the first to offer a model in which city and agricultural land use are endogenously determined, thus making the analysis of Thünen complete. This work not only fills in a gap in the literature but, more important, it also suggests a microeconomic approach that allows one to study the emergence of an urban system in the spatial economy. Indeed, the identification of conditions under which a monocentric economy is sustainable as an equilibrium leads quite naturally to the fundamental question: Where and when do new cities emerge?

In Section 10.2, we present the results obtained by Fujita and Krugman for the monocentric economy. The underlying structure is closely related to that of the core–periphery model studied in Section 8.2. That is, agglomeration arises from love for variety on the consumer side (see also Section 7.2). However, here all workers are assumed to be identical and perfectly mobile between locations and sectors (typically, agriculture and industry). The centrifugal force now lies in the existence of a land market in the agricultural sector, for producing the agricultural goods requires both land and labor, thus leading to the spatial dispersion of demand for the manufactured goods because farmers are also consumers of such goods. In addition, the location space is continuous and one-dimensional (the same assumption is made throughout this chapter). Such a setting allows a synthesis of the Thünian model and the Dixit-Stiglitz model of monopolistic competition used in NEG. We see that a monocentric economy is a spatial equilibrium provided that the population size does not exceed some threshold value depending on the parameters of the economy.

Ellison et al. (2010) have highlighted the empirical relevance of input-output linkages in explaining the collocation of different industries. In Section 10.3, love for variety on the consumer side is, therefore, replaced by product variety in intermediate goods as in Section 8.6. Using the work of Fujita and Hamaguchi (2001), we will show that a monocentric economy in which both the final and intermediate sectors are established within a single city emerges as a spatial equilibrium provided that the cost of shipping intermediate commodities is high relative to the cost of transporting the consumption goods. Although they bear some resemblance, this setting and the one studied in Section 10.2 are not identical, and we discuss the main analogies and differences. By contrast, once the intermediate inputs become cheaper to move relative to the output of the final sector, but not too much, the intermediate sector remains agglomerated, whereas the final output is locally produced and consumed when the population of workers does not exceed some level. In this case, the process of agglomeration with intermediate commodities becomes almost the same as the one studied in Section 10.2. In both cases, the city is *diversified* because it hosts firms belonging to different sectors linked through vertical linkages.

Hence, in Sections 10.2 and 10.3, the total population cannot be too large for a monocentric configuration to occur. This suggests that, as the population grows, new cities emerge when some critical population threshold is reached. When the population keeps rising, still more cities will appear, and so on. Using the framework of Section 10.2, we make this idea more precise in Section 10.4 by proposing an evolutionary approach to central place theory, which has been proposed by Fujita and Mori (1997). The main result is that *similar cities are created at (more or less) equal distances as the population increases continuously.* This provides a formal proof of one of the key ideas of central place theory:

> The normal pattern of human settlements . . . is one in which town growth is primarily a response to the needs of an agricultural population. (Marshall 1989, p. 15)

Our emphasis on population growth as a major reason for urbanization is justified by historical examples, such as the urbanization of Western Europe and the United States in the twelfth and nineteenth centuries, respectively, which were both accompanied by a substantial population increase. As expected, we will see that population growth not only fosters the development of incumbent cities but also provides incentives to found new cities. In Section 10.5, we return to the standard thought experiment of NEG and focus on the work of Tabuchi and Thisse (2011) to find out how the number and size of cities vary with the level of transport costs. As in the CP model, lowering transport costs leads to a shrinking number of cities that host a growing population of consumers and firms. However, the set of outcomes being broader, the spatial process is richer than in the CP model.

In this chapter, a city is considered to be a clustering of firms and workers that has no spatial extension. This means that workers do not bear any urban costs because the land market plays a role in the agricultural sector only. This is a severe restriction. We believe, however, that the models presented here may be viewed as a first attempt at synthesizing various aspects of a spatial economy that have been studied in previous chapters. Such a progressive synthesis is needed to put our understanding of the space-economy on solid ground. Furthermore, unlike what we saw in Chapters 4 and 5, there is no agent, such as a land developer or a local government, whose job it is to organize a new city by coordinating the actions of firms and workers. City formation is the outcome of a process involving agents who do not plan a priori to create a city but rather pursue their own interests. In other words, a city appears here as a complex system whose existence is the result of a self-organizing process.

Throughout, we consider only one group of differentiated goods (either for consumption or for use as intermediate inputs). Consequently, all cities produce the same type of goods and have similar sizes. To generate a hierarchical urban system à la Christaller, one needs to introduce different groups of differentiated goods with (i) different preference intensities, (ii) different transport costs, and (iii) different technologies. This extension will be discussed in our concluding section.

10.2 CITY FORMATION UNDER PREFERENCE FOR VARIETY

To study the formation of cities in a continuous space, we modify accordingly the model described in Section 8.2. More precisely, because all workers are now assumed to be perfectly mobile, we introduce a new immobile factor, *land*, which is used as an input in the agricultural sector.

10.2.1 The Framework

Consider an unbounded, one-dimensional location space X along which land has the same fertility and the same unit density. Because space is continuous, all variables are now described by continuous functions of locations. For example, the nominal wage rate at location r is denoted $w(r)$ instead of w_r.

As in Section 8.2, there are two sectors, the manufacturing ($\mathbb{M}$) and the agricultural ($\mathbb{A}$) sectors. Unlike Section 8.2, all workers in the economy are assumed to be identical and free to choose their location and occupation. Each worker is endowed with one unit of labor that can be used indifferently in the agricultural or manufacturing sector. There are L workers in the economy and a group of landowners who, for simplicity, are assumed to live on their land holdings. This implies that land rents are consumed where they are created. All consumers (workers and landowners) have the same utility function given by (8.1), so that the demand functions are still given by (8.3) and (8.4). The agricultural good is produced using both land and labor by means of fixed technological coefficients; both are normalized to 1 by choosing appropriately the units of land and of the agricultural good. Hence, the distribution of farmers is uniform over the hinterland surrounding the city. In the manufacturing sector, the technology of a firm is given by (8.7); the unit of the good is such that $c\sigma/(\sigma - 1) = 1$.

Though their formal definitions differ from those used in the previous two chapters, we have chosen to use the letter τ to describe transport parameters. No confusion should arise. Transport costs are assumed to be positive for both agricultural and manufactured goods. If one unit of the agricultural good is shipped from $r \in X$ to $s \in X$, only a fraction, given by $\exp(-\tau^{\mathbb{A}}|r - s|)$, arrives at its destination; this fraction decreases as the distance to the destination point

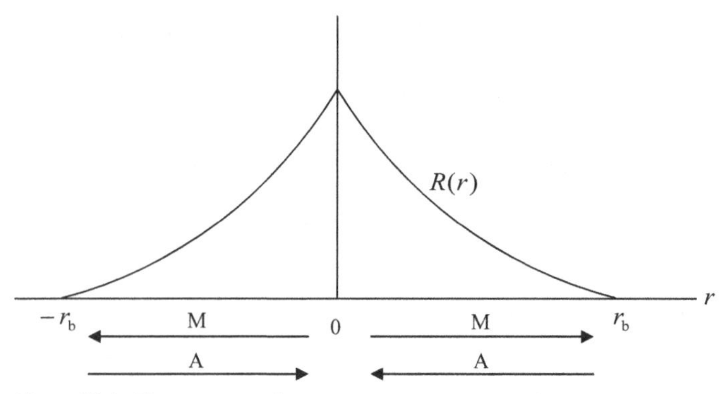

Figure 10.1. The monocentric economy.

increases. For the manufacturing sector, we similarly have $\exp(-\tau^{\mathbb{M}}|r-s|)$. These costs can be reinterpreted to cope with the case in which farmers have to go to the city to trade their output against the manufactured good.[2]

10.2.2 The Formation of a Monocentric Economy

Recalling Thünen, let us imagine a monocentric economy such as the one depicted in Figure 10.1. In such a setting, the production of all industrial goods occurs in a single city located, by convention, at $r = 0$, and the agricultural area surrounding the city expands from $-r_b$ to r_b, where r_b stands for the frontier distance to be determined. The city exports all the industrial goods to its agricultural hinterland and imports all the produce needed by its inhabitants. The question we want to solve is: Under which conditions is this configuration a spatial equilibrium? To answer this question, we proceed in two steps. First, we determine the equilibrium prices of all goods, factors, and land rents, assuming that all firms are located in the city. Then, we determine the conditions to be satisfied such that no firm wants to locate away from the city. Because everything is symmetric, we restrict our analysis to the domain in which $r \geq 0$.

10.2.2.1 Equilibrium Prices

Let $p^{\mathbb{A}}$ and $p^{\mathbb{M}}$ be respectively the price of the agricultural good and the common price of the differentiated varieties in the city. For the trade pattern between the city and its agricultural hinterland just described to arise, the price

[2] For notational simplicity, we keep using τ as the transport parameter. However, the formal definitions are different. In Chapters 8 and 9, $\tau = 1$ means costless transportation. Here, zero transport costs imply $\tau = 0$ because the exponential of 0 is 1.

of each good at location $r \in X$ must be such that

$$p^{\mathbb{A}}(r) = p^{\mathbb{A}} \exp(-\tau^{\mathbb{A}} r) \tag{10.1}$$

$$p^{\mathrm{M}}(r) = p^{\mathrm{M}} \exp(\tau^{\mathrm{M}} r). \tag{10.2}$$

Let $R(r)$ and $w(r)$ be the land rent and wage rate prevailing at r. Inside the agricultural area, the land rent is equal to the price of the agricultural good minus the wage bill paid to the farmer needed to produce one unit of output (see Section 3.2):

$$R^{*}(r) = p^{\mathbb{A}}(r) - w(r). \tag{10.3}$$

Thus, the evolution of the land rent depends on how the price and the wage vary with distance.

At the agricultural border r_{b}, the land rent equals zero, and thus

$$w^{*}(r_{\mathrm{b}}) = p^{\mathbb{A}} \exp(-\tau^{\mathbb{A}} r_{\mathrm{b}}). \tag{10.4}$$

Without loss of generality, we may choose the unit of labor for the wage in the city to be equal to one:

$$w^{*} = 1.$$

Turning to the manufacturing sector and restating (8.13) within the present context, we see immediately that, in the city, the equilibrium price of each variety is given by $p^{\mathrm{M}} = 1$. Let L^{M} be the mass of individuals working for the urban manufacturing sector. Because an agricultural area of size $2r_{\mathrm{b}}$ requires $2r_{\mathrm{b}}$ workers, it must be that

$$L^{\mathrm{M}} = L - 2r_{\mathrm{b}}.$$

Furthermore, given that the manufactured good is produced in the city only, applying (8.17) in which $\tau_{rs} = \exp(\tau^{\mathrm{M}} |r - s|)$, we see that the price index of the manufactured good at location $r \in X$ is such that:

$$P(r) = \left(\frac{L - 2r_{\mathrm{b}}}{\sigma f}\right)^{-1/(\sigma-1)} \exp(\tau^{\mathrm{M}} r) \tag{10.5}$$

which increases with distance from the city because of the increasing transport costs.

We are now ready to determine all the equilibrium prices. This can be achieved by using the following equilibrium conditions: (i) market clearing for the agricultural good and (ii) the equality of the real wages at each location for all workers.

First, we notice that the income generated within the city equals $w^* L^{\mathbb{M}} = L - 2r_{\mathrm{b}}$. Hence, using (8.3), the demand for the agricultural good in the city is

$$D^{\mathbb{A}} = (1 - \mu)\frac{L - 2r_{\mathrm{b}}}{p^{\mathbb{A}}}$$

which increases with the total population. On the supply side, one unit of land at location r generates a gross return equal to $p^{\mathbb{A}}(r)$, thus giving rise to a demand for the agricultural good given by $(1 - \mu)$. Hence μ units of the agricultural good are shipped to the city. Because only a fraction, $\exp(-\tau^{\mathbb{A}} r)$, of this amount reaches the city, the total supply of the agricultural good at the city place is:

$$S^{\mathbb{A}} = 2\mu \int_0^{r_{\mathrm{b}}} \exp(-\tau^{\mathbb{A}} r) \mathrm{d}r$$

which increases with the size of the hinterland. Thus, market clearing yields the following expression for the equilibrium price of the agricultural good at the city place:

$$p^{\mathbb{A}} = \frac{1 - \mu}{2\mu} \frac{L - 2r_{\mathrm{b}}}{\int_0^{r_{\mathrm{b}}} \exp(-\tau^{\mathbb{A}} r) \mathrm{d}r}. \tag{10.6}$$

Next, we move to the equality of real wages between farmers and workers. Equation (10.4) gives the nominal wage earned by a farmer residing at the agricultural frontier. Using (10.1), (10.4), and (10.5), the farmer's real wage is then as follows:

$$\begin{aligned} \omega(r_{\mathrm{b}}) &= w(r_{\mathrm{b}})[P(r_{\mathrm{b}})]^{-\mu}[p^{\mathbb{A}}(r_{\mathrm{b}})]^{-(1-\mu)} \\ &= P^{-\mu} \left(p^{\mathbb{A}}\right)^{\mu} \exp\left[-\mu(\tau^{\mathbb{A}} + \tau^{\mathbb{M}}) r_{\mathrm{b}}\right]. \end{aligned}$$

Because $w^* = 1$, the real wage of a city worker is

$$\omega = P^{-\mu} \left(p^{\mathbb{A}}\right)^{-(1-\mu)}. \tag{10.7}$$

Hence, the equality of real wages between workers and farmers requires that

$$p^{\mathbb{A}} = \exp\left[\mu(\tau^{\mathbb{A}} + \tau^{\mathbb{M}}) r_{\mathrm{b}}\right]. \tag{10.8}$$

Putting (10.6) and (10.8) together shows that

$$L - 2r_{\mathrm{b}} = \frac{2\mu}{1 - \mu} \frac{1 - \exp(-\tau^{\mathbb{A}} r_{\mathrm{b}})}{\tau^{\mathbb{A}}} \exp[\mu(\tau^{\mathbb{A}} + \tau^{\mathbb{M}}) r_{\mathrm{b}}]. \tag{10.9}$$

Because the left-hand side of this expression decreases with r_{b}, whereas the right-hand side increases with r_{b}, it can readily be verified that (10.9) has a unique solution. It also follows from (10.9) that the equilibrium value of r_{b} increases from 0 to ∞ as the population L keeps rising from 0. As a result, when the population grows the rural hinterland expands, and thus the two goods are traded over longer distances. In addition, (10.6) implies that the price of the agricultural good drops relative to the price of the manufactured one, which means that the terms of the rural hinterland are deteriorate.

Finally, introducing (10.5) and (10.8) into (10.7) and using (10.9), we obtain the equilibrium real wage common to farmers and workers:

$$\omega^* \equiv k_1[1 - \exp(-\tau^{\mathbb{A}} r_b)]^{\mu/(\sigma-1)} \exp[\mu\rho(\mu - \rho)(\tau^{\mathbb{A}} + \tau^{\mathrm{M}})r_b] \quad (10.10)$$

where

$$k_1 \equiv \rho^{\mu} \left(\frac{2\mu}{(1-\mu)\sigma f \tau^{\mathbb{A}}} \right)^{\mu/(\sigma-1)}.$$

Because $\omega^* = w^*(r)[P(r)]^{-\mu}[p^{\mathbb{A}}(r)]^{-(1-\mu)}$ must hold in equilibrium, the equilibrium nominal wage is as follows:

$$w^*(r) = \exp[\mu\tau^{\mathrm{M}} - (1-\mu)\tau^{\mathbb{A}}]r. \quad (10.11)$$

Thus, the wage gradient is negative if and only if $\tau^{\mathrm{M}}/\tau^{\mathbb{A}}$ exceeds $(1-\mu)/\mu$, which is likely to hold when the consumption share of the manufactured good is small. Once this share becomes sufficiently large, farmers must be compensated for the higher transport costs they bear to acquire the manufactured good.

10.2.2.2 Sustainability of the Monocentric Configuration

So far, we have assumed that all firms are located within the city. However, for the monocentric configuration to be a spatial equilibrium, we must show that no firm has an incentive to move away from the city and to set up in the countryside.

Let $w^{\mathrm{M}}(r)$ be the zero-profit wage rate that stands for the highest wage that a firm located at r is willing to pay given that the rest of the economy remains unchanged (this wage was formally introduced in Section 8.2 for a finite location space). Then, no firm in the city has an incentive to move at r if $w^{\mathrm{M}}(r) \leq w^*(r)$. Instead of working directly with these two variables, it appears to be more convenient to use a monotonic transformation of their ratio.

Specifically, we define a firm's *potential function* as

$$\Omega(r) = \left[\frac{w^{\mathrm{M}}(r)}{w^*(r)} \right]^{\sigma} \qquad \text{for all } r \geq 0. \quad (10.12)$$

The monocentric configuration is then a spatial equilibrium if and only if

$$\Omega(r) \leq 1 \qquad \text{for all } r \geq 0$$

because there is no alternative location at which a firm making zero profits is able to offer more than what workers actually earn. Since $w^*(r)$ is given by (10.11), it remains to determine $w^{\mathrm{M}}(r)$.

Let Y be the total income generated by the manufacturing sector in the city and $Y(r)$ the total income generated by the farming activities at $r \leq r_b$. Then, using (8.19), we obtain

$$w^{\mathbb{M}}(r) = \kappa_2 \left\{ Y P^{\sigma-1} \exp[-(\sigma - 1)\tau^{\mathbb{M}} r] + 2 \int_0^{r_b} Y(s)[P(s)]^{\sigma-1} \exp[-(\sigma - 1)\tau^{\mathbb{M}} |r - s|] ds \right\}^{1/\sigma} \quad (10.13)$$

where κ_2 is the same as in (8.19). Clearly, we have $Y = w^* L^{\mathbb{M}} = L - 2r_b$ and $Y(r) = p^{\mathbb{A}}(r) = p^{\mathbb{A}} \exp(-\tau^{\mathbb{A}} r)$, in which $p^{\mathbb{A}}$ is given by (10.8). Thus, using (10.5) for the price index $P(r)$ as well as (10.9) for Y, we may rewrite (10.13) as follows:

$$w^{\mathbb{M}}(r) = \kappa_2 \left(\frac{\sigma f}{\rho^{\sigma-1}} \right)^{1/\sigma} \left\{ \exp[-(\sigma - 1)\tau^{\mathbb{M}} r] + \frac{1-\mu}{2\mu} \cdot \frac{2\tau^{\mathbb{A}}}{1 - \exp(-\tau^{\mathbb{A}} r_b)} \times \int_0^{r_b} \exp\left[-\tau^{\mathbb{A}} |s| - (\sigma - 1)\tau^{\mathbb{M}} (|r - s| - |s|)\right] ds \right\}^{1/\sigma}. \quad (10.14)$$

Substituting (10.11) and (10.14) into (10.12) yields

$$\Omega(r) = \mu \exp\left\{-\sigma[\mu\tau^{\mathbb{M}} - (1 - \mu)\tau^{\mathbb{A}}] r\right\} \cdot \left\{ \exp[-(\sigma - 1)\tau^{\mathbb{M}} r] + \frac{1-\mu}{2\mu} \cdot \frac{2\tau^{\mathbb{A}}}{1 - \exp(-\tau^{\mathbb{A}} r_b)} \times \int_0^{r_b} \exp\left[-\tau^{\mathbb{A}} |s| - (\sigma - 1)\tau^{\mathbb{M}} (|r - s| - |s|)\right] ds \right\}^{1/\sigma}. \quad (10.15)$$

As shown in the appendix, this expression can be rewritten in a more convenient way as follows:

$$\Omega(r) = \exp(-\eta r) \left\{ 1 + (1 - \mu)(\sigma - 1)\tau^{\mathbb{M}} \times \int_0^{r} \left(\exp[2(\sigma - 1)\tau^{\mathbb{M}} s]\right) \left(1 - \frac{1 - \exp(-\tau^{\mathbb{A}} s)}{1 - \exp(-\tau^{\mathbb{A}} r_b)} \right) ds \right\} \quad (10.16)$$

in which r_b appears only once, while

$$\eta \equiv \sigma[(\mu + \rho)\tau^{\mathbb{M}} - (1 - \mu)\tau^{\mathbb{A}}]. \quad (10.17)$$

Expression (10.16) is depicted in Figure 10.2 for the following values: $\sigma = 4$, $\mu = 0.5$, $\tau^{\mathbb{A}} = 0.8$, and $\tau^{\mathbb{M}} = 1$. For any given value of r_b, (10.16) is represented by a curve called the potential curve. Because r_b is uniquely determined by the population size L, this amounts to saying that each potential curve is associated with a single value of L.

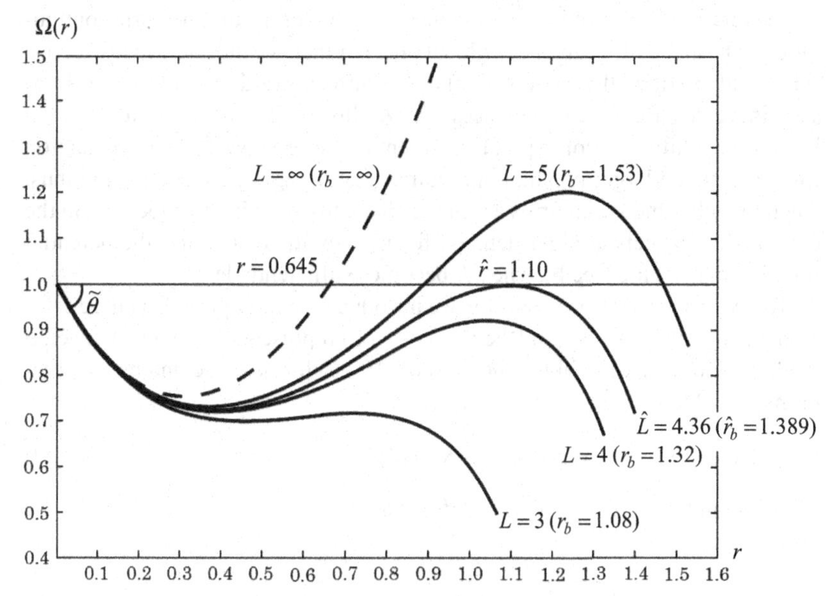

Figure 10.2. Potential curves for the monocentric configuration.

For the monocentric configuration to be an equilibrium, the potential function associated with the corresponding value of L should never exceed 1. To determine when this is so, we must study the behavior of (10.16). First, it is apparent that $\Omega(0) = 1$, which means that firms located within the city pay a wage equal to the zero-profit wage at $r = 0$. Thus, for the function $\Omega(r)$ not to exceed 1 in a neighborhood of $r = 0$, the slope of $\Omega(r)$ at $r = 0$ given by

$$\Omega^{'}(0) = \sigma[(1-\mu)\tau^{\mathrm{A}} - \mu(1+\rho)\tau^{\mathrm{M}}] \tag{10.18}$$

must be nonpositive, that is,

$$\frac{1-\mu}{\mu(1+\rho)}\tau^{\mathrm{A}} \leq \tau^{\mathrm{M}}. \tag{10.19}$$

Observe that (10.18) is independent of L and is, therefore, the same for all potential curves.

If (10.19) holds as a strict inequality, the potential function has a cusp at $r = 0$ (see Figure 10.2), which corresponds to the *lock-in effect* generated by the agglomeration of firms and workers in the city. In this case, no firm finds it profitable to move a short distance away from the city because a sufficiently large share of its demand comes from there. As shown by (10.19), this happens when (i) the transport cost of the manufactured good is high relative to that of the agricultural good, (ii) varieties are good substitutes, and (iii) the expenditure share on the manufactured good is large.

However, (10.19) is a local sufficient condition for the monocentric configuration to be an equilibrium, not a global one. For that, we must return to (10.16). It is readily verified that the potential curve shifts upward (except at the origin) as r_b increases. Because r_b increases with L, this implies that an increase in the labor force shifts the corresponding potential curve upward. The explanation for this is that a larger population requires a larger agricultural area, and thus, when the other industrial firms are in the city, a firm moving to a location in the countryside expects a larger demand for its output. As a result, the potential function may well exceed 1 when L becomes sufficiently large.

To investigate such a possibility, we introduce the limit potential curve $\bar{\Omega}(r)$ associated with $r_b \to \infty$ (and, hence, $L \to \infty$) representing the upper envelop of all potential curves. Taking the limit of (10.16) for $r_b \to \infty$ and rearranging terms, we obtain

$$\bar{\Omega}(r) = (1 - K)\exp(-\eta r) + K\exp(\gamma r) \tag{10.20}$$

where K and γ are two constants defined as:

$$K \equiv \frac{\rho(1-\mu)\tau^{\mathrm{M}}}{\rho(1-\mu)\tau^{\mathrm{M}} + (\rho - \mu)(\tau^{\mathrm{A}} + \tau^{\mathrm{M}}) - \Omega'(0)/\sigma}$$

$$\gamma \equiv \sigma(\rho - \mu)(\tau^{\mathrm{A}} + \tau^{\mathrm{M}})$$

in which we have used (10.17) rewritten as follows:

$$\eta \equiv (1-\mu)(\sigma - 1)\tau^{\mathrm{M}} - \Omega'(0).$$

Because $\bar{\Omega}'(0) = \Omega'(0)$ and we consider only the case in which $\Omega'(0) \leq 0$, the limit potential curve slopes down at the origin. Furthermore, since $\bar{\Omega}(r)$ is the sum of two exponential functions, it has at most one turning point (at which $\bar{\Omega}'(r) = 0$). Accordingly, $\bar{\Omega}(r)$ exceeds 1 for some $r > 0$ if and only if $\bar{\Omega}(\infty) > 1$. Because $\Omega'(0) \leq 1$ implies $\eta > 0$, it follows from (10.20) that $\bar{\Omega}(\infty) = K\exp(\gamma\infty)$, and thus $\bar{\Omega}(r)$ exceeds 1 for some positive r if and only if $K\exp(\gamma\infty) > 1$.

If $\rho < \mu$, then $\gamma < 0$ and, hence, $K\exp(\gamma\infty) = 0$. If $\rho = \mu$, then $\gamma = 0$ and $K \leq 1$, so that $K\exp(\gamma\infty) = K \leq 1$. Hence, when

$$\rho \leq \mu \tag{10.21}$$

it follows that $\bar{\Omega}(r) \leq 1$ for all $r > 0$. This in turn implies that $\Omega(r) < 1$ for all $r > 0$. Condition (10.21) holds when either the industrial goods are very differentiated (ρ is small) or a large fraction of the labor force works in the city. In either case, the city is the most profitable site for the industrial sector however large the population L of the economy is. Note that (10.21) corresponds to the black hole condition discussed in Section 8.2.3: the city attracts all industrial activities and corresponds to *the* megalopolis.

Conversely, and more interestingly, if

$$\rho > \mu \tag{10.22}$$

then $\gamma > 0$, whereas $0 < K$ so that $K \exp(\gamma\infty) = \infty$, thus implying that $\bar{\Omega}(r)$ exceeds 1 for some value $r > 0$. In this case, as L keeps rising, the potential function $\Omega(r)$ will exceed 1 for some $r > 0$. Therefore, when varieties are not very differentiated, the city population is relatively small, or both, the agricultural area generates a sufficiently high demand for the industrial goods once L is large enough. This in turn implies that a firm finds it profitable to locate away from the city to benefit from some monopoly power in its local market.

Figure 10.2 illustrates the case in which the potential function is just equal to 1 at some critical distance $\hat{r}$ when $L = \hat{L}$. Any further increase in the population size above $\hat{L}$ makes the location $\hat{r}$ more profitable than the city for any single firm, thus suggesting that a new city might well emerge there. However, we postpone the analysis of this transition to Section 10.4. It is also worth noting the existence of an area of *urban shadow* in which the potential function never exceeds 1. This means that a new city never appears within this area.

Putting all these results together, we may conclude as follows:[3]

Proposition 10.1. *For a monocentric economy to be a spatial equilibrium, it must be that*

$$\frac{1-\mu}{\mu(1+\rho)}\tau^{A} \leq \tau^{M}.$$

(i) *If the foregoing condition holds and if $\rho \leq \mu$, then the monocentric configuration is an equilibrium regardless of the population size.*
(ii) *If the foregoing condition holds and if $\rho > \mu$, then there exists a critical population level $\hat{L}$ such that the monocentric configuration is an equilibrium for all $L \leq \hat{L}$, whereas it is no longer an equilibrium as soon as $L > \hat{L}$.*

Thus, a monocentric economy does not emerge when the cost of shipping the manufactured good is low relative to that of the agricultural good. Note, however, that τ^{M} need not be higher than τ^{A} for a monocentric economy to be a spatial equilibrium. In addition, although urbanites bear no residential costs, a sufficiently large population may be incompatible with the agglomeration of firms. For example, this is so when the share of the manufacturing sector is low, varieties are close substitutes, or both. Under such circumstances, the benefits generated by the agglomeration of manufactures are offset by the higher costs of shipping manufactured goods over longer distances. In other words, scale economies can be exploited with dispersed firms since farmers cannot cluster.

[3] We see in Section 10.4 that the spatial equilibrium identified in the proposition is also stable in a sense that is explained there.

By contrast, when μ is large and/or σ small, competition is sufficiently relaxed and/or the demand stemming from the urban population large enough for a megalopolis to exist.

The foregoing setting allows for some interesting comparative statics results studied by Fujita and Krugman (1995). Assume that technological progress in agriculture has led to the development of a labor-saving technology, such as those observed in the nineteenth century in the United Kingdom and later on, in the twentieth century, in the United States and then in Europe. This means that the price of the agricultural good decreases. Such a technological change thus fosters migration from the rural hinterland toward the city. This in turn leads to an increase in the urban population as well as to an expansion of the manufacturing sector through a wider product range and a larger number of firms. Such *rural-urban migrations* not only concur with historical evidence but also agree with what we observe today in developing countries.

Last, consider a decrease in transport cost for either type of good (either $\tau^{\mathbb{M}}$ or $\tau^{\mathbb{A}}$ decreases). This renders distant locations more attractive, thus inducing reverse migration from the urban center of the economy toward the agricultural frontier that moves farther away. To some extent, this provides a rationale for the westward expansion of the United States economy in the second half of the nineteenth century, during which transport costs fell dramatically as railways and waterways were built and developed.

10.2.3 Welfare in a Monocentric Economy

We now come to the impact of the population growth on the economy's welfare. In this perspective, one must keep in mind that the economy involves two different groups of agents, that is, workers and landlords. Workers' welfare is represented by their equilibrium real wage, as given by (10.10). Differentiating this expression with respect to r_b, we obtain

$$\frac{d\omega^*}{dr_b} = \frac{\mu\omega^*}{\sigma - 1}\left[\sigma(\mu - \rho)(\tau^{\mathbb{A}} + \tau^{\mathbb{M}}) + \frac{\tau^{\mathbb{A}}}{\exp(\tau^{\mathbb{A}} r_b) - 1}\right]. \quad (10.23)$$

Regarding the landlords' welfare, we know that they receive per unit of land a rent equal to $R(r) = p^{\mathbb{A}}(r) - w(r)$ for all $r \leq r_b$. As a result, their real income $\omega^L(r)$ is given by

$$\omega^L(r) = [p^{\mathbb{A}}(r) - w^*(r)][P(r)]^{-\mu}[p^{\mathbb{A}}(r)]^{-(1-\mu)}.$$

Because

$$\omega^* = w^*(r)[P(r)]^{-\mu}[p^{\mathbb{A}}(r)]^{-(1-\mu)}$$

it follows that

$$\omega^L(r) = \omega^*\left(\frac{p^{\mathbb{A}}(r)}{w^*(r)} - 1\right). \quad (10.24)$$

Substituting (10.1) and (10.11) into (10.24) and using (10.8) yields

$$\omega^L(r) = \omega^* \left\{\exp[\mu(\tau^{\mathbb{A}} + \tau^{\mathbb{M}})(r_{\mathrm{b}} - r)] - 1\right\}. \tag{10.25}$$

If the black hole condition holds ($\rho \leq \mu$), it is obvious from (10.23) that workers are always better off when the population rises. Furthermore, on the right-hand side of (10.25), the second factor increases with r_{b} and, therefore, with L. Consequently, the welfare of both workers and landlords always increases with the population size. This is because the population growth leads to a wider array of varieties that dominates the higher transportation costs associated with a larger agricultural area (recall that varieties are very differentiated).

When the black hole condition does not hold ($\rho > \mu$), then the first term on the right-hand side of (10.23) is negative, whereas the second term decreases continuously with r_{b} (hence, with L) from infinity to zero. Accordingly, ω^* is $\cap$-shaped, thus implying that the real wage of workers first increases and then decreases with the population size. The highest welfare level is achieved for a particular population size L^o associated with the fringe distance

$$r_{\mathrm{b}}^o = \frac{1}{\tau^{\mathbb{A}}}\left[\log\left(1 + \frac{1}{\sigma(\rho-\mu)}\frac{\tau^{\mathbb{A}}}{\tau^{\mathbb{A}} + \tau^{\mathbb{M}}}\right)\right] \tag{10.26}$$

which is obtained by setting the right-hand side of (10.23) equal to zero. This is so because the varieties are not sufficiently differentiated to prevent the increase in transportation costs caused by the enlargement of the agricultural hinterland from becoming predominant. In this case, L^o is the worker-optimal population size. Because (10.26) decreases with ρ, the worker-optimal population size increases with product differentiation.

When L rises above L^o, the welfare of landlords may continue to increase, for their income, which comes from land rent, keeps rising as the agricultural area expands. More precisely, using (10.23) and (10.24), we find that

$$\begin{aligned}\frac{1}{\omega^L(r)}\frac{\mathrm{d}\omega^L(r)}{\mathrm{d}r_{\mathrm{b}}} &= \frac{\mu}{\sigma-1}\left[\sigma(\mu-\rho)(\tau^{\mathbb{A}}+\tau^{\mathbb{M}}) + \frac{\tau^{\mathbb{A}}}{\exp(\tau^{\mathbb{A}}r_{\mathrm{b}})-1}\right] \\ &\quad + \frac{\mu(\tau^{\mathbb{A}}+\tau^{\mathbb{M}})}{1-\exp[-\mu(\tau^{\mathbb{A}}+\tau^{\mathbb{M}})(r_{\mathrm{b}}-r)]} \\ &> \frac{\mu(\mu-\rho)}{\rho}(\tau^{\mathbb{A}}+\tau^{\mathbb{M}}) + \mu(\tau^{\mathbb{A}}+\tau^{\mathbb{M}}) \\ &= \frac{\mu^2}{\rho}(\tau^{\mathbb{A}}+\tau^{\mathbb{M}}) \\ &> 0\end{aligned} \tag{10.27}$$

which holds for all r_{b} and, therefore, for all L.

We may then summarize the foregoing discussion as follows:

Proposition 10.2. *Consider a monocentric economy. Then, if the population size increases*

(i) the welfare of the landlords always increases within the rural area;
(ii) when $\rho \leq \mu$, workers' welfare always increases;
(iii) when $\rho > \mu$, workers' welfare rises up to some population level and declines beyond.

Hence, workers' welfare displays a pattern similar, although not identical, to that of the equilibrium described in Proposition 10.1. When the city is not a black hole ($\rho > \mu$), increasing the population beyond L^o entails a conflict between workers' and landlords' interests because a rising population yields a decrease in workers' individual welfare. Since people are free to move, some workers will eventually be induced to move away from the city to create new cities together with some farmers, an issue that is analyzed in Section 10.4.

10.3 COAGGLOMERATION OF THE INTERMEDIATE AND FINAL SECTORS

In this section, we focus on the role of *intermediate goods* in city formation by combining the ideas of Sections 8.6 and 10.2. To this end, we modify the model of Section 8.6 as we did with the model of 8.2 in the previous section. Thus, the resulting model is essentially the counterpart to that presented in Section 10.2. Land is an immobile input for the agricultural sector. The industry is formed by two sectors vertically linked, that is, the final sector producing the homogeneous manufactured good for consumption and the intermediate ($\mathbb{I}$) sector supplying a range of intermediate goods to the final sector. Such a setting yields a richer set of outcomes than before. In particular, we see that two types of monocentric configurations exist involving very different patterns of trade. In the first, both sectors are coagglomerated and form a diversified city, which exports the final good to the agricultural hinterland. In the second, the intermediate sector is concentrated within a city. As for the final sector, it is partially concentrated and supplies the city consumers; the rest is mixed with the agricultural sector such that each place produces the manufactured good for its own needs. The city exports intermediate goods only, whereas the manufactured good is consumed where it is produced. The first pattern is called an *integrated city*, and the second one a *specialized city*. Not surprisingly, the former (the latter) tends to arise when the transport costs of the intermediate goods are high (low). We also show that, when the economy involves the coagglomeration of the two sectors, the growth of the population alone can never destroy this pattern as an equilibrium. By contrast, in the case of a specialized city, population growth eventually leads to the formation of new cities. After having described this new framework, we proceed by studying the integrated and specialized cities in turn.

10.3.1 The Framework

The approach taken here is fairly similar to that followed in the previous section. In particular, space is given by a unbounded, linear space X, whereas land has the same fertility and density across locations. The agricultural sector produces one unit of the agricultural good using one unit of labor and one unit of land. The manufacturing sector now produces a homogeneous good under constant returns using labor and a continuum of intermediate inputs supplied by the $\mathbb{I}$-sector. The production function of this sector is given by (8.70), yielding the unit production cost (8.76) as well as the input demands (8.77) and (8.78). As in Section 8.6, each intermediate variety is produced by using labor only according to the technology (8.72), which thus exhibits scale economies.

The variable Q in the utility (8.1) now stands for the homogeneous output of the manufacturing sector; consumers' demands for the agricultural and manufacturing goods are given, respectively, by (8.73) and (8.74). As in the Section 10.2, we assume that transport costs have the iceberg form: if one unit of the agricultural good (the manufactured good or the intermediate good) is shipped from $r \in X$ to $s \in X$, only a fraction, given by $\exp(-\tau^{\mathbb{A}}|r - s|)$ ($\exp(-\tau^{\mathbb{M}}|r - s|)$ or $\exp(-\tau^{\mathbb{I}}|r - s|)$), arrives at destination, where $\tau^{\mathbb{A}}$ ($\tau^{\mathbb{M}}$ or $\tau^{\mathbb{I}}$) is a positive constant. Finally, as in the Section 10.2, all workers are identical and free to choose their job in any of the three sectors as well as their location, either in the city or in the countryside.

The two equilibria we want to analyze share several similar features that are now described. Because scale economies arise only in the intermediate sector, we restrict ourselves to the case in which this sector is established within the city. The agricultural area is assumed to surround the city symmetrically from $-r_{\mathrm{b}}$ to r_{b}. In both equilibria, let $p^{\mathbb{A}}(r)$ and $p^{\mathbb{M}}(r)$ be, respectively, the price of the agricultural good and the price of the manufactured good at distance r from the city, whereas ω^* is the common equilibrium real wage earned by the workers in the two industrial sectors as well as by the farmers. Then, the equilibrium nominal wage at r is as follows:

$$w^*(r) = \omega^*[p^{\mathbb{M}}(r)]^{\mu}[p^{\mathbb{A}}(r)]^{(1-\mu)}. \tag{10.28}$$

Using the normalization $w^* = 1$, from (10.28) we obtain

$$\omega^* = \left(p^{\mathbb{M}}\right)^{-\mu}\left(p^{\mathbb{A}}\right)^{-(1-\mu)} \tag{10.29}$$

$$w^*(r) = \left(p^{\mathbb{M}}(r)/p^{\mathbb{M}}\right)^{\mu}\left(p^{\mathbb{A}}(r)/p^{\mathbb{A}}\right)^{(1-\mu)}. \tag{10.30}$$

Through a now standard argument, it is easy to show that the common equilibrium price of the intermediate good produced in the city is $p^{\mathbb{I}} = 1$.

Hence, its delivered price at r is:

$$p^{\mathbb{I}}(r) = \exp(\tau^{\mathbb{I}} r). \tag{10.31}$$

Let $L^{\mathbb{I}}$ be the mass of workers in the intermediate sector. Then, because the labor requirement of each firm under the zero-profit condition equals σf, $L^{\mathbb{I}}/\sigma f$ varieties are produced in the city. Using (8.75) and (10.31), the price index of the $\mathbb{I}$-varieties at location r can be obtained as (10.5) and is given by the following expression:

$$P^{\mathbb{I}}(r) = \left(\frac{L^{\mathbb{I}}}{\sigma f}\right)^{-1/(\sigma-1)} \exp(\tau^{\mathbb{I}} r). \tag{10.32}$$

Using (8.76), the marginal production cost of the manufactured good at location r is now given by

$$\begin{aligned} c^{\mathbb{M}}(r) &= \alpha^{-\alpha}(1-\alpha)^{-(1-\alpha)}[w^*(r)]^{1-\alpha}\left[P^{\mathbb{I}}(r)\right]^{\alpha} \\ &= \kappa_3 (L^{\mathbb{I}})^{-\alpha/(\sigma-1)}[w^*(r)]^{1-\alpha}\exp(\alpha\tau^{\mathbb{I}} r) \end{aligned} \tag{10.33}$$

where

$$\kappa_3 \equiv \alpha^{-\alpha}(1-\alpha)^{-(1-\alpha)}(\sigma f)^{\alpha/(\sigma-1)}.$$

Let $L^{\mathbb{M}}$ be the labor force working for the manufacturing sector in the city and $L^{\mathbb{M}}(r)$ the density of workers in this sector at $r \neq 0$. It is then clear that the total city income equals $L^{\mathbb{M}} + L^{\mathbb{I}}$ since $w^* = 1$, whereas the total income per unit of land at $r \neq 0$ is $p^{\mathbb{A}}(r) + w^*(r)L^{\mathbb{M}}(r)$. As a consequence, the demand for the manufactured good in the city and at $r \neq 0$, respectively, are given by

$$Q^{\mathbb{M}} = \mu(L^{\mathbb{M}} + L^{\mathbb{I}})/p^{\mathbb{M}} \tag{10.34}$$

$$Q^{\mathbb{M}}(r) = \mu\left[p^{\mathbb{A}}(r) + w^*(r)L^{\mathbb{M}}(r)\right]/p^{\mathbb{M}}(r). \tag{10.35}$$

On the supply side, using (8.74), the output of the manufacturing sector produced in the city and at $r \neq 0$ are as follows:

$$X^{\mathbb{M}} = L^{\mathbb{M}}/(1-\alpha)c^{\mathbb{M}} \tag{10.36}$$

$$X^{\mathbb{M}}(r) = w^*(r)L^{\mathbb{M}}(r)/(1-\alpha)c^{\mathbb{M}}(r). \tag{10.37}$$

Because the final sector is characterized by constant returns, the following two conditions hold:

$$L^{\mathbb{M}} > 0 \Rightarrow p^{\mathbb{M}} = c^{\mathbb{M}}$$

$$L^{\mathbb{M}}(r) > 0 \Rightarrow p^{\mathbb{M}}(r) = c^{\mathbb{M}}(r).$$

The market clearing condition for the manufactured good depends on the type of equilibrium; so its study is postponed to the next two sections.

We now turn to the market clearing condition for labor. We have

$$2r_b + L^M + 2\int_0^{r_b} L^M(r)dr + L^{\mathbb{I}} = L. \tag{10.38}$$

It turns out to be convenient to rewrite this expression. For that, note that free entry in the intermediate sector implies that its total cost, $L^{\mathbb{I}}$, is equal to its total revenue, which in turn is given by the total expenditure of the manufacturing sector on the intermediate good:

$$\alpha\left[c^M X^M + 2\int_0^{r_b} c^M(r)X^M(r)dr\right]$$

which, using (10.36) and (10.37), is equal to

$$\alpha\left[\frac{L^M}{1-\alpha} + 2\int_0^{r_b} \frac{w^*(r)L^M(r)}{1-\alpha}dr\right].$$

Therefore, it follows that

$$L^{\mathbb{I}} = \frac{\alpha}{1-\alpha}\left[L^M + 2\int_0^{r_b} w^*(r)L^M(r)dr\right]. \tag{10.39}$$

Substituting (10.39) into (10.38), we may then rewrite the labor market clearing condition as follows:

$$2r_b + \frac{L^M}{1-\alpha} + 2\int_0^{r_b}\left[1 + \frac{\alpha}{1-\alpha}w^*(r)\right]L^M(r)dr = L. \tag{10.40}$$

Regarding the equilibrium conditions for the manufacturing sector that is perfectly competitive, we have

$$p^M(r) \leq c^M(r). \tag{10.41}$$

In order to obtain the equilibrium conditions for the $\mathbb{I}$-firms, as in (10.12), we follow the same approach as in the previous section and define the potential function for an $\mathbb{I}$-firm as

$$\Omega(r) = \left[\frac{w^{\mathbb{I}}(r)}{w^*(r)}\right]^{\sigma} \tag{10.42}$$

in which $w^{\mathbb{I}}(r)$ stands for the highest, i.e., zero-profit, wage rate that an $\mathbb{I}$-firm located at r can pay. Then, as in 10.2.2, the agglomeration of the $\mathbb{I}$-firms in the city is a location equilibrium if and only if

$$\Omega(r) \leq 1 \qquad \text{for all } r \geq 0.$$

To obtain the zero-profit wage $w^{\mathbb{I}}(r)$, we reformulate (10.13) as follows. The total expenditure on the $\mathbb{I}$-good in the city is equal to $\alpha c^M X^M$, whereas that at

$r \neq 0$ it is equal to $\alpha c^{\mathbb{M}}(r)X^{\mathbb{M}}(r)$. Consequently, replacing in (10.13) Y with $c^{\mathbb{M}}X^{\mathbb{M}}$, $Y(r)$ with $c^{\mathbb{M}}(r)X^{\mathbb{M}}(r)$, $\tau^{\mathbb{M}}$ with $\tau^{\mathbb{I}}$, and μ with α yields

$$w^{\mathbb{I}}(r) = \kappa_2' \left\{ c^{\mathbb{M}}X^{\mathbb{M}} \exp[-(\sigma - 1)\tau^{\mathbb{I}}r] \left(P^{\mathbb{I}}\right)^{\sigma-1} + 2\int_0^{r_b} c^{\mathbb{M}}(s)X^{\mathbb{M}}(s) \exp[-(\sigma - 1)\tau^{\mathbb{I}}|r - s|][P^{\mathbb{I}}(s)]^{\sigma-1} \mathrm{d}s \right\}^{1/\sigma}$$

where $P^{\mathbb{I}}(s)$ is given by (10.32) and

$$\kappa_2' \equiv \rho[\alpha/(\sigma - 1)f]^{1/\sigma}.$$

Furthermore, in the foregoing expression for $w^{\mathbb{I}}(r)$, we may set $c^{\mathbb{M}}X_o^{\mathbb{M}} = L_o^{\mathbb{M}}/(1-\alpha)$, and $c^{\mathbb{M}}(r)X^{\mathbb{M}}(r) = w^*(r)L^{\mathbb{M}}(r)/(1-\alpha)$ by using (10.36) and (10.37), so that the potential function of an $\mathbb{I}$-firm (10.42) becomes

$$\Omega(r) = \frac{\alpha}{(1-\alpha)L^{\mathbb{I}}[w^*(r)]^{\sigma}} \left\{ L_o^{\mathbb{M}} \exp[-(\sigma - 1)\tau^{\mathbb{I}}r] + 2\int_0^{r_b} w^*(s)L^{\mathbb{M}}(s) \exp\left[-(\sigma - 1)\tau^{\mathbb{I}}(|r - s| - |s|)\right] \mathrm{d}s \right\}. \quad (10.43)$$

10.3.2 The Integrated City

10.3.2.1 Equilibrium

We consider here the configuration in which the entire production of both industrial sectors takes place within the city, thus implying that the city exports the manufactured good to farmers and imports the agricultural good. Hence, it must be that

$$X^{\mathbb{M}}(r) = 0 \quad \text{and} \quad L^{\mathbb{M}}(r) = 0 \qquad \text{for all } r \neq 0 \quad (10.44)$$

and thus the market clearing condition for the manufactured good can be written as follows:

$$X^{\mathbb{M}} = Q^{\mathbb{M}} + 2\int_0^{r_b} Q^{\mathbb{M}}(r) \exp(\tau^{\mathbb{M}}r)\mathrm{d}r.$$

Using (10.34), (10.35), and (10.44), this expression becomes

$$X^{\mathbb{M}} = \mu\frac{L^{\mathbb{M}} + L^{\mathbb{I}}}{p^{\mathbb{M}}} + 2\int_0^{r_b} \mu\frac{p^{\mathbb{A}}(r)}{p^{\mathbb{M}}(r)} \exp(\tau^{\mathbb{M}}r)\mathrm{d}r. \quad (10.45)$$

Furthermore, to support the trade pattern, the equilibrium prices, $p^{\mathbb{A}}(r)$ and $p^{\mathbb{M}}(r)$, and the land rent, $R^*(r)$, must satisfy the relations (10.1), (10.2), and (10.3), respectively. Therefore, the wage at the agricultural border r_b is also given by (10.4).

Finally, because the final sector is characterized by constant returns the equilibrium condition for the manufacturing sector in the city implies

$$p^{\mathbb{M}} = c^{\mathbb{M}}. \tag{10.46}$$

Using these conditions together with (10.29), (10.30), (10.32), (10.33), (10.39), and (10.40), it is easy to solve the corresponding system for all the variables as functions of the single unknown r_b. We thus obtain:

$$L^{\mathbb{I}} = \alpha(L - 2r_b) \tag{10.47}$$

$$L^{\mathbb{M}} = (1 - \alpha)(L - 2r_b) \tag{10.48}$$

$$p^{\mathbb{A}}(r) = \exp(\mu(\tau^{\mathbb{M}} + \tau^{\mathbb{I}})r_b)\exp(-\tau^{\mathbb{A}}r) \tag{10.49}$$

$$p^{\mathbb{M}}(r) = \kappa_3\alpha^{-\alpha/(\sigma-1)}(L - 2r_b)^{-\alpha/(\sigma-1)}\exp(\tau^{\mathbb{M}}r) \tag{10.50}$$

$$w^*(r) = \exp[\mu\tau^{\mathbb{M}} - (1 - \mu)\tau^{\mathbb{A}}]r \tag{10.51}$$

$$P^{\mathbb{I}}(r) = \left(\frac{\sigma f}{\alpha}\right)^{1/(\sigma-1)}(N - 2r_b)^{-1/(\sigma-1)}\exp(\tau^{\mathbb{I}}r). \tag{10.52}$$

To find r_b, we substitute (10.36), (10.47), and (10.48) into (10.45) and use (10.1), (10.2), and (10.46). This leads to the relation

$$L - 2r_b = \frac{2\mu}{1-\mu}\frac{1 - \exp(-\tau^{\mathbb{A}}r_b)}{\tau^{\mathbb{A}}}\exp[\mu(\tau^{\mathbb{A}} + \tau^{\mathbb{M}})r_b] \tag{10.53}$$

which is identical to (10.9)

Therefore, when the total population L is the same, both the monocentric economy equilibrium studied in Section 10.2 and the integrated city equilibrium considered here yield the same agricultural border and, hence, the same agricultural population. The number of workers in the industry is therefore the same in both equilibria. It can also be readily verified that the equilibrium nominal wages, (10.11) and (10.51), are the same, as well as the equilibrium prices of the agricultural good. The reason for these seemingly surprising results is as follows. As long as the final and intermediate sectors are coagglomerated, the economy as a whole looks essentially like an economy with a single manufacturing sector involving increasing returns. Indeed, we have seen in Section 4.4 that, in the aggregate, the increasing returns appearing in the intermediate sector are transferred to the final sector.

This analogy, however, does not carry over to all the microeconomic aspects of the economy. In particular, the equilibrium real wages are different. To obtain ω^* in the present context, we substitute (10.49) and (10.50) into (10.29) and use (10.52) as well as (10.53). We then find that

$$\omega^* = k_2[1 - \exp(-\tau^{\mathbb{A}}r_b)]^{\alpha\mu/(\sigma-1)}\exp\{\mu[\alpha\mu/\rho - (1 - \mu(1 - \alpha))](\tau^{\mathbb{A}} + \tau^{\mathbb{M}})r_b\} \tag{10.54}$$

in which

$$k_2 \equiv \alpha^{\alpha\mu/\rho}(1-\alpha)^{(1-\alpha)\mu}\rho^{\alpha\mu}\left(\frac{2\mu}{(1-\mu)\sigma f\tau^{\mathbb{A}}}\right)^{\alpha\mu/(\sigma-1)}$$

which is different from (10.10). Both expressions, however, have the same structure and are identical when $\alpha = 1$.[4]

Next, we turn to the sustainability of the integrated city as an equilibrium. First, we must check the equilibrium location conditions (10.41) for the manufacturing sector. Substituting (10.50) for $p^{\mathbb{M}}(r)$ while solving (10.33), (10.47), and (10.51) for $c^{\mathbb{M}}(r)$, we may rewrite (10.41) as follows:

$$\exp(\tau^{\mathbb{M}}r) \leq \left\{\exp(1-\alpha)[\mu\tau^{\mathbb{M}} - (1-\mu)\tau^{\mathbb{A}}]r\right\}\exp(\alpha\tau^{\mathbb{I}}r)$$

or, equivalently,

$$\frac{(1-\alpha)(1-\mu)}{\alpha}\tau^{\mathbb{A}} + \frac{1-\mu(1-\alpha)}{\alpha}\tau^{\mathbb{M}} \leq \tau^{\mathbb{I}}.$$

Considering now the equilibrium location condition for the $\mathbb{I}$-firms, we can evaluate the potential function (10.43) by using (10.44), (10.47), (10.48), (10.51), (10.52), and (10.53) to obtain

$$\Omega(r) = \exp\left\{-\sigma[\mu\tau^{\mathbb{M}} - (1-\mu)\tau^{\mathbb{A}} + \rho\tau^{\mathbb{I}}]r\right\}.$$

Hence, the equilibrium condition, $\Omega(r) \leq 1$, holds if and only if

$$(1-\mu)\tau^{\mathbb{A}} - \mu\tau^{\mathbb{M}} \leq \rho\tau^{\mathbb{I}}.$$

Therefore, we have shown the following:

Proposition 10.3. *An integrated city is a spatial equilibrium if and only if the transport costs $\tau^{\mathbb{A}}$, $\tau^{\mathbb{M}}$ and $\tau^{\mathbb{I}}$ satisfy the following two conditions:*

$$\frac{(1-\alpha)(1-\mu)}{\alpha}\tau^{\mathbb{A}} + \frac{1-\mu(1-\alpha)}{\alpha}\tau^{\mathbb{M}} \leq \tau^{\mathbb{I}} \tag{10.55}$$

and

$$\frac{1-\mu}{\rho}\tau^{\mathbb{A}} - \frac{\mu}{\rho}\tau^{\mathbb{M}} \leq \tau^{\mathbb{I}}. \tag{10.56}$$

The parameter range in which these two conditions hold is described by the shaded area in Figure 10.3 for the case in which $(1-\alpha)/\alpha > \sigma/(\sigma-1)$.[5]

[4] In order to show this, it is sufficient to set $0^0 = 1$ in (10.54), which is then identical to (10.10). Indeed, when $\alpha = 1$ in the production function (8.70) it does not make any difference in the aggregate whether the differentiated varieties are directly assembled by the consumers or through the perfectly competitive $\mathbb{M}$-sector.

[5] When the opposite inequality holds, the two intercepts along the vertical axis are reversed. This difference, however, is not important for our discussion of the equilibrium.

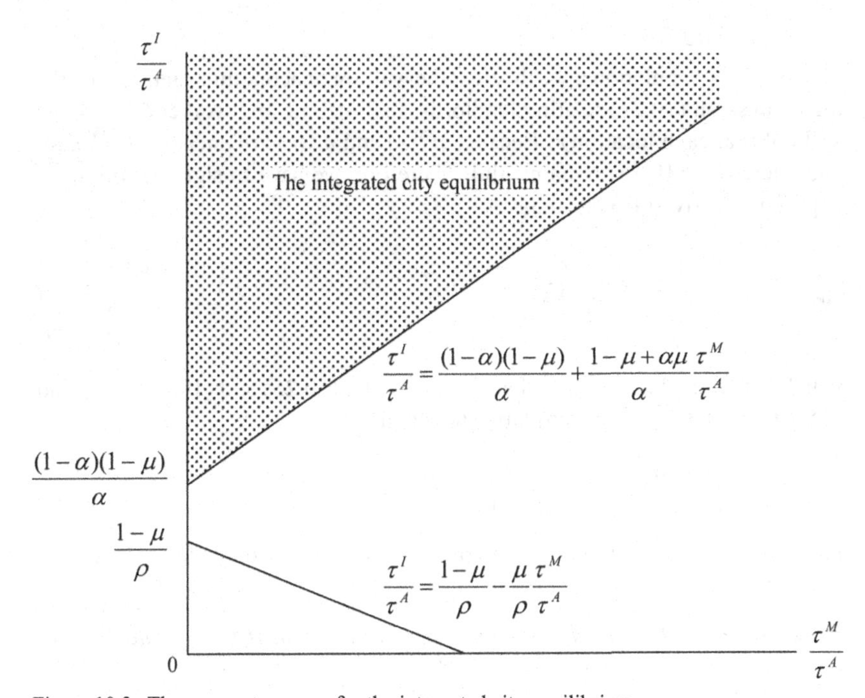

Figure 10.3. The parameter range for the integrated city equilibrium.

The figure reveals that, for the integrated city to be an equilibrium, the transport costs of the intermediate commodities must be sufficiently high relative to those of the consumption goods. This is because the vertical linkages between the two sectors create a strong agglomeration force, a result that agrees with what we saw in Section 8.6. Yet, as shown by the wage function (10.51), any location in the countryside has a comparative advantage in labor cost for both sectors when $\mu\tau^{\mathrm{M}} < (1 - \mu)\tau^{\mathrm{A}}$, that is, when shipping the manufactured good is sufficiently cheap relative to the cost of shipping the agricultural good. However, when shipping the intermediate good is costly enough, this advantage turns out to be more than outweighed by the manufacturing sector's having a high accessibility to its suppliers, which are all located in the city, once it is itself concentrated within the city.

Observe also that conditions (10.55) and (10.56) are independent of L. As a result, increasing the population size does not affect the spatial pattern of the economy but results in a growing city and a larger agricultural area and never in the formation of new cities. Although the conditions stated in Proposition 10.3 differ from those given in Proposition 10.1, they can be viewed as the intermediate-good counterpart of the black hole condition (10.21) found in Section 10.2. However, their respective welfare implications differ.

10.3.2.2 Welfare

How does population growth affect the welfare of economic agents? Clearly, the expression (10.24) relating landlords' real income and workers' real wage still holds at each location r. Because $p^{\mathbb{A}}(r)$ and $w^*(r)$ are unchanged, (10.24) and, therefore, (10.25) remain valid. Therefore, we have to sign the following expression derived from (10.54):

$$\frac{d\omega^*}{dr_b} = \frac{\mu\omega^*}{\sigma - 1}\left\{\sigma\left[\alpha\mu - \frac{\sigma - 1}{\sigma}(1 - \mu(1 - \alpha))\right](\tau^{\mathbb{A}} + \tau^{\mathbb{M}}) + \frac{\alpha\tau^{\mathbb{A}}}{\exp(\tau^{\mathbb{A}} r_b) - 1}\right\} \tag{10.57}$$

which is identical to (10.23) when $\alpha = 1$. Using (10.25) and (10.57) as we did in Section 10.2.3, we can similarly show that

$$\frac{1}{\omega^L(r)}\frac{d\omega^L(r)}{dr_b} > \frac{\mu^2(\alpha + \sigma - 1)}{\sigma - 1}(\tau^{\mathbb{A}} + \tau^{\mathbb{M}}) > 0$$

regardless of the value of r_b. As in Proposition 10.2, we may then conclude as follows:

Proposition 10.4. *Consider the integrated city. Then, if the population size increases,*

(i) the welfare of the landlords always increases within the agricultural area;

(ii) when

$$\rho \le \alpha\mu/[1 - \mu(1 - \alpha)] \tag{10.58}$$

workers' welfare always increases;

(iii) when

$$\rho > \alpha\mu/[1 - \mu(1 - \alpha)] \tag{10.59}$$

workers' welfare rises up to some population level and declines beyond.

It is worth noting that this proposition is very similar to Proposition 10.2 obtained in the case of a monocentric economy based on love for variety (they are even identical in the special case where $\alpha = 1$). By contrast, the sustainability conditions stated in Propositions 10.1 and 10.3 are very different. In particular, we know that raising the population size never destroys the integrated city equilibrium, although, beyond some threshold level, workers' welfare starts declining. In this case, the economy is in a situation of "primacy trap" in which workers' welfare declines with the growth of the metropolis whereas no other major city emerges. Today, some urban giants in developing countries (think of Manilla or Nairobi) may be examples of such large primate cities.

The primacy trap never arises, however, in the setting considered in 10.2. On one hand, when $\rho \leq \mu$, the monocentric configuration remains an equilibrium when L increases, but the welfare of all agents also rises. On the other hand, when $\rho > \mu$, the welfare of workers declines beyond some population size; however, the monocentric configuration ceases to be an equilibrium when the population is sufficiently large, implying that new cities emerge and, hence, that workers' welfare starts increasing again.

Such a difference in results occurs because, in the love for variety model of Section 10.2, the consumers themselves put together the varieties of the differentiated product, whereas here this is done by the manufacturing sector that sells a homogeneous product to consumers. In the former case, the producers of the differentiated varieties sell their output directly to the consumers, who are themselves dispersed, whereas, in the latter, the producers of the differentiated inputs sell their output to the manufacturing sector, which is entirely concentrated within the city. Hence, not surprisingly, the lock-in effect of an integrated city with intermediate commodities is much stronger than that of a monocentric economy based on love for variety.

10.3.3 The Specialized City

10.3.3.1 Equilibrium

We now come to the case of the specialized city in which only the intermediate sector is completely agglomerated within the city. By contrast, the production of the manufactured good is decentralized across locations in a way such that each place is self-sufficient. Thus, the city exports the $\mathbb{I}$-varieties toward the hinterland, from which the agricultural good is imported.

The self-sufficiency of each location in the manufactured good implies that

$$X^{\mathbb{M}} = Q^{\mathbb{M}}$$
$$X^{\mathbb{M}}(r) = Q^{\mathbb{M}}(r).$$

The equilibrium prices of the manufactured good are determined by the zero-profit condition:

$$p^{\mathbb{M}}(r) = c^{\mathbb{M}}(r).$$

For the agricultural good, the equilibrium price is given by (10.1), whereas the wage at the fringe of the inhabited area is (10.4).

As before, we may use these conditions together with those stated in Section 10.3.1 to determine all the variables as functions of the single unknown r_b:

$$L^{\mathbb{I}} = \frac{2\alpha\mu}{1-\mu}\left[1 - \exp(-\tau^{\mathbb{A}} r_b)\right] \exp\left\{[\alpha\mu(\tau^{\mathbb{A}} + \tau^{\mathbb{I}})r_b/[1 - \mu(1-\alpha)]\right\} \tag{10.60}$$

$$L^{\mathbb{M}} = \frac{\mu(1-\alpha)}{1-\mu(1-\alpha)} L^{\mathbb{I}} \tag{10.61}$$

$$L^{\mathbb{M}}(r) = \frac{\mu(1-\alpha)}{1-\mu(1-\alpha)} \exp\left\{\alpha\mu(\tau^{\mathbb{A}} + \tau^{\mathbb{I}})(r_b - r)/[1-\mu(1-\alpha)]\right\} \tag{10.62}$$

$$p^{\mathbb{A}}(r) = \exp[\alpha\mu(\tau^{\mathbb{A}} + \tau^{\mathbb{I}})r_b/(1-\mu(1-\alpha))]\exp(-\tau^{\mathbb{A}}r) \tag{10.63}$$

$$p^{\mathbb{M}}(r) = \kappa_3(L^{\mathbb{I}})^{-\alpha/(\sigma-1)} \exp\left\{[\alpha\tau^{\mathbb{I}} - (1-\alpha)(1-\mu)\tau^{\mathbb{A}}]r/[1-\mu(1-\alpha)]\right\} \tag{10.64}$$

$$w^*(r) = \exp\left\{[\alpha\mu\tau^{\mathbb{I}} - (1-\mu)\tau^{\mathbb{A}}]r/[1-\mu(1-\alpha)]\right\} \tag{10.65}$$

$$P^{\mathbb{I}}(r) = \left(\frac{\sigma f}{L^{\mathbb{I}}}\right)^{1/(\sigma-1)} \exp(\tau^{\mathbb{A}}r).$$

To obtain r_b, we substitute (10.61), (10.62), and (10.65) into the labor market clearing condition (10.40):

$$L - 2r_b = \frac{2\mu}{1-\mu+\alpha\mu}\left\{\frac{\alpha}{1-\mu}\frac{1-\exp(-\tau^{\mathbb{A}}r)}{\tau^{\mathbb{A}}} + (1-\alpha)\frac{1-\exp(-\varkappa r_b)}{\varkappa}\right\}\exp(\varkappa r_b)$$

where

$$\varkappa \equiv \alpha\mu(\tau^{\mathbb{A}} + \tau^{\mathbb{I}})/[1-\mu(1-\alpha)].$$

As in 10.2.2.2, it is readily verified that r_b is uniquely determined and strictly increasing with L.

For the specialized city configuration to be a spatial equilibrium, two additional conditions must be met. First, the assumption of no trade in the manufactured good holds if and only if the rate of variation in the equilibrium prices of this good never exceeds the transport cost of this good. That is,

$$\frac{\left|\mathrm{d}p^{\mathbb{M}}(r)/\mathrm{d}r\right|}{p^{\mathbb{M}}(r)} \leq \tau^{\mathbb{M}}.$$

Given (10.64), this condition amounts to

$$\frac{\left|\alpha\tau^{\mathbb{I}} - (1-\alpha)(1-\mu)\tau^{\mathbb{A}}\right|}{1-\mu(1-\alpha)} \leq \tau^{\mathbb{M}}$$

or,

$$\frac{(1-\alpha)(1-\mu)}{\alpha}\tau^{\mathbb{A}} - \frac{1-\mu(1-\alpha)}{\alpha}\tau^{\mathbb{M}} \leq \tau^{\mathbb{I}} \leq \frac{(1-\alpha)(1-\mu)}{\alpha}\tau^{\mathbb{A}} + \frac{1-\mu(1-\alpha)}{\alpha}\tau^{\mathbb{M}}.$$

Second, the potential function of the $\mathbb{I}$-firms must never exceed 1. Substituting (10.60), (10.61), (10.62), and (10.65) into (10.43), we obtain the following expression for the potential function:

$$\Omega(r) = \frac{\alpha\mu}{1-\mu(1-\alpha)}\left\{\exp -\sigma\left[\frac{\alpha\mu\tau^{\mathbb{I}}-(1-\mu)\tau^{\mathbb{A}}}{1-\mu(1-\alpha)}\right]r\right\}\cdot\left\{\exp[-(\sigma-1)\tau^{\mathbb{I}}r]+\right.$$
$$\left.\frac{2(1-\mu)\tau^{\mathbb{A}}}{\alpha\mu\left(1-\exp(-\tau^{\mathbb{A}}r_{\mathrm{b}})\right)}\int_0^{r_{\mathrm{b}}}\exp\left[-\tau^{\mathbb{A}}|s|-(\sigma-1)\tau^{\mathbb{I}}(|r-s|-|s|)\right]\mathrm{d}s\right\}.$$

Following the approach developed in the appendix, we may rewrite this expression as follows:

$$\Omega(r) = \exp(-\tilde{\eta}r)\left\{1+\frac{(1-\mu)(\sigma-1)\tau^{\mathbb{I}}}{1-\mu(1-\alpha)}\int_0^r\exp[2(\sigma-1)\tau^{\mathbb{I}}s]\right.\tag{10.66}$$
$$\left.\times\left(1-\frac{1-\exp(-\tau^{\mathbb{A}}s)}{1-\exp(-\tau^{\mathbb{A}}r_{\mathrm{b}})}\right)\mathrm{d}s\right\}$$

where

$$\tilde{\eta} \equiv \frac{\sigma\left\{[\alpha\mu+\rho(1-\mu(1-\alpha))]\tau^{\mathbb{I}}-(1-\mu)\tau^{\mathbb{A}}\right\}}{1-\mu(1-\alpha)}.$$

Comparing (10.16) and (10.66), we see that the two expressions have essentially the same structure (when $\alpha = 1$ they are even identical). Accordingly, the location of the $\mathbb{I}$-firms may be studied as in 10.2.2.2. The following results are then obtained. First, since

$$\Omega'(0) = \sigma[(1-\mu)\tau^{\mathbb{A}} - \alpha\mu(1+\rho)\tau^{\mathbb{I}}]/[1-\mu(1-\alpha)]$$

a nonpositive slope at the origin requires that

$$\frac{1-\mu}{\alpha\mu(1+\rho)}\tau^{\mathbb{A}} \le \tau^{\mathbb{I}}.$$

Next, using the limit potential curve $\bar{\Omega}(r)$ associated with $r_{\mathrm{b}} \to \infty$, it can be shown that $\rho \le \alpha\mu/[1-\mu(1-\alpha)]$ implies $\Omega(r) < 1$ for all r regardless of the positive value of r_{b}. By contrast, when $\rho > \alpha\mu/[1-\mu(1-\alpha)]$, the potential curves display the same patterns as those represented in Figure 10.2. This means that a critical value $\hat{L}$ exists such that the potential function is just equal to 1 at a particular location $\hat{r}$. Hence, for any value of L exceeding $\hat{L}$, $\Omega(r) > 1$ for a sufficiently large r and the specialized city configuration ceases to be a spatial equilibrium. Therefore, putting all these results together, we have:

Proposition 10.5. *For a specialized city to be a spatial equilibrium, it must be that*

$$\frac{(1-\alpha)(1-\mu)}{\alpha}\tau^{\mathbb{A}} - \frac{1-\mu(1-\alpha)}{\alpha}\tau^{\mathbb{M}} \leq \tau^{\mathbb{I}} \leq \frac{(1-\alpha)(1-\mu)}{\alpha}\tau^{\mathbb{A}} + \frac{1-\mu(1-\alpha)}{\alpha}\tau^{\mathbb{M}} \quad (10.67)$$

and

$$(1-\mu)\tau^{\mathbb{A}} \leq [1-\mu(1-\alpha)]\tau^{\mathbb{I}}. \quad (10.68)$$

(i) *If the conditions (10.67) and (10.68) hold and if*

$$\rho \leq \alpha\mu/[1-\mu(1-\alpha)] \quad (10.69)$$

then the specialized city is an equilibrium regardless of the population size.

(ii) *If the conditions (10.67) and (10.68) hold and if*

$$\rho > \alpha\mu/[1-\mu(1-\alpha)] \quad (10.70)$$

then there exists a critical population level $\hat{L}$ such that the specialized city is an equilibrium for all $L \leq \hat{L}$, whereas it is no longer an equilibrium when $L > \hat{L}$.

In Figure 10.4, we represent the domains of transport cost values for which the two equilibrium conditions hold.

This figure reveals that the specialized city configuration is a spatial equilibrium when the transport cost of the intermediate varieties is sufficiently low when compared to that of the manufactured good. However, it should not be too low either, for otherwise $\mathbb{I}$-firms would move into the hinterland where they can benefit from the lower wages prevailing there. But this is not yet the end of the story. When the intermediate inputs are good substitutes (that is, [10.70] holds), then this configuration is an equilibrium only when the population does not become too large. Thus, *the specialized city displays an equilibrium pattern very similar to that of the monocentric economy* described in Proposition 10.1. In particular, the condition (10.69) is the new black hole condition, which reduces to the previous one, $\rho \leq \mu$, when $\alpha = 1$.

10.3.3.2 Welfare

We study again the impact of population growth on workers' and landlords' welfare. To this end, we first substitute (10.63) and (10.64) into (10.29) and then use (10.60) in order to obtain the equilibrium real wage:

$$\omega^* = k_2[1-\exp(-\tau^{\mathbb{A}} r_{\mathrm{b}})]^{\alpha\mu/(\sigma-1)} \exp\left[\frac{\alpha\mu/\rho - (1-\mu(1-\alpha))}{1-\mu(1-\alpha)}\alpha\mu(\tau^{\mathbb{A}}+\tau^{\mathbb{I}})r_{\mathrm{b}}\right]. \quad (10.71)$$

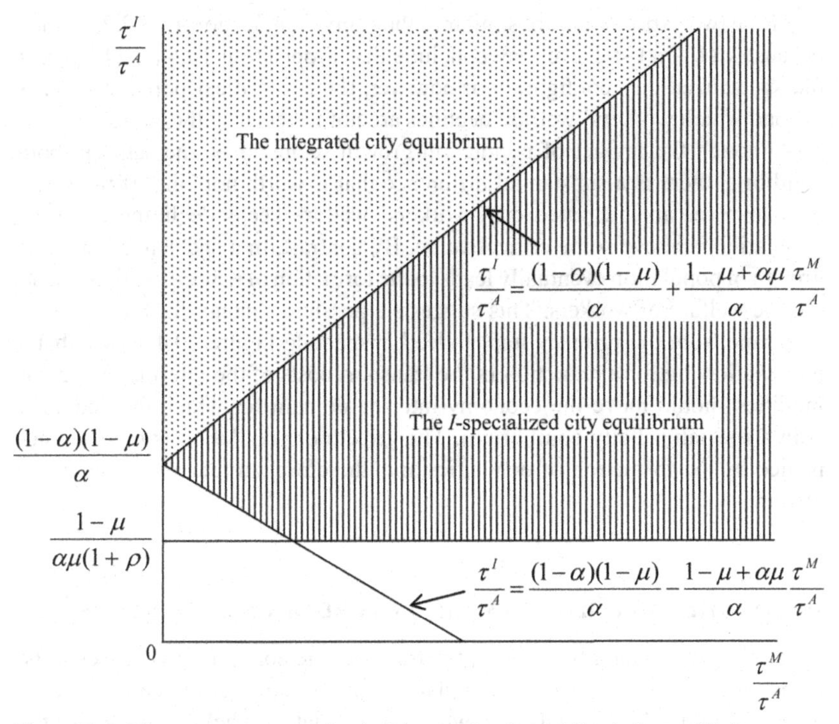

Figure 10.4. The parameter ranges for the integrated and specialized city equilibria.

Furthermore, because (10.24) still holds, substituting (10.63) and (10.64) into (10.24) and using (10.60) leads to the equilibrium real income of the landlords:

$$\omega^L(r) = \omega^* \left\{ \exp\left[\frac{\alpha\mu(\tau^{\mathbb{A}} + \tau^{\mathbb{I}})}{1-\mu(1-\alpha)}(r_{\mathrm{b}} - r)\right] - 1 \right\}.$$

Differentiating (10.71) with respect to r_{b} yields

$$\frac{d\omega^*}{dr_{\mathrm{b}}} = \frac{\mu\omega^*}{\sigma - 1}\left\{\frac{\alpha}{1-\mu(1-\alpha)}\sigma[\alpha\mu - \rho(1-\mu(1-\alpha))](\tau^{\mathbb{A}} + \tau^{\mathbb{M}}) + \frac{\alpha\tau^{\mathbb{A}}}{\exp(\tau^{\mathbb{A}} r_{\mathrm{b}}) - 1}\right\}.$$

Using the same approach as in 10.3.2.2, we also obtain:

$$\frac{1}{\omega^L(r)}\frac{d\omega^L(r)}{dr_{\mathrm{b}}} > \frac{\alpha}{1-\mu(1-\alpha)}\frac{\mu^2(\alpha+\sigma-1)}{\sigma-1}(\tau^{\mathbb{A}} + \tau^{\mathbb{M}}) > 0$$

regardless of the value of r_{b}.

These two expressions are similar to those given in Section 10.3.2.2. In fact, because $\mu(1-\alpha) < 1$, we may conclude that Proposition 10.4 also holds for the specialized city configuration; however, the two critical population sizes beyond which workers' welfare declines are not necessarily the same.

Although the impact of population growth seems to be the same in both equilibria, there is a substantial difference that is worth noticing. If the economy involves an integrated city, workers' welfare keeps declining once the population is above some critical value. By contrast, in a specialized city, the growth of population eventually leads to the formation of new cities, thus boosting the welfare of workers. This suggests a possible strategy for the economy to escape from the primacy trap. Indeed, inspecting Figure 10.4 shows that a policy allowing for a reduction in the transport costs of the intermediate commodities should move the economy into the domain for which the economy is in a specialized city equilibrium. The growth of population is then accompanied by the formation of new cities and, therefore, an increase in workers' welfare.

10.4 ON THE EMERGENCE AND STRUCTURE OF URBAN SYSTEMS

When the city is not a black hole, the monocentric configuration ceases to be a spatial equilibrium once the population size becomes sufficiently large. A glance at Figure 10.2 reveals that, when the population reaches the level $\hat{L}$, the potential curve just hits the value 1 at location $\hat{r}$. Even though no agglomeration exists there, this location becomes as attractive as the incumbent city because firms now have direct access to a large local market situated deep inside the hinterland. This suggests that the relocation of an arbitrary small (but positive) mass of firms at $\hat{r}$ is able to trigger a mechanism of agglomeration that leads to the creation of a new city. Simultaneously, a mechanism of contraction is at work in the existing city, but the lock-in effect prevents this city from disappearing. Hence, the new city does not capture the whole population of the incumbent city. By symmetry, the same arises for $r < 0$, and thus the economy actually moves from a one-city configuration to a three-city system. However, for the moment, we focus on the area $r > 0$.

When the population keeps rising, the agricultural frontier moves farther and farther away from the new city because a growing population must be supported. Accordingly, for the same reason as before, when the population reaches some threshold level, a potential curve similar to the original one hits the value 1 at a new location. This leads to the emergence of an additional city there. With a growing population and an unbounded space, a new city will be created periodically at a certain distance from the nearest existing city. In this way, a system of cities is formed in which cities are located at (more or less) equal distances.

In this section, we use the framework of Section 10.2 to make the foregoing ideas more precise. When the monocentric pattern described in Proposition 10.1 ceases to be a stable equilibrium, the economy moves to a new stable equilibrium involving the formation of a new city. This is achieved through the decisions made by myriads agents motivated only by their own interests. The contrast with the approach taken in Chapter 4 is, therefore, striking.

However, to study stability, we must describe the behavior of economic agents when the economy is not at equilibrium. Our first step is, therefore, to describe how the transition works, using an adjustment process followed by the agents. We then use this process to show how the combination of a growing population and of a homogeneous space leads to the formation of a regular network of cities. Because the formal analysis is long and complex and details can be found in the cited references, we will refrain from trying to be complete and will restrict ourselves to the presentation of the main ideas.

10.4.1 The Adjustment Process

We assume, again, that the total population grows slowly. Our purpose is to study how the spatial economy evolves as a consequence of this growth. As previously discussed, changes in the spatial configuration take the form of new cities, which appear once the existing spatial system becomes unstable. To assess stability, we must specify an adjustment process. The intuition behind this process is similar to the one used in Chapter 8, which is driven by workers' migration toward locations offering higher real wages. There are, however, several differences. First, the set of potential locations for new cities is now infinite, thus making the set of possible spatial configurations much larger than before. Furthermore, as the population grows, the economy entails a sequence of changes in the spatial distribution of industry that correspond to different spatial equilibria (by contrast, we focused on a single transition in Chapter 8).

Our research strategy is to use the "structural stability" of spatial equilibria as a selection device at each time t. Accordingly, when studying the stability of the spatial equilibrium prevailing at any given time t, we first assume that the population $L(t)$ is momentarily fixed and then analyze the impact of small perturbations of the population distribution equilibrium over what we call "fictitious time" denoted by ξ. To this end, consider a set with any number K of sites, which includes the actual cities, whereas the remaining sites represent potential locations for new cities. During the adjustment process, the population of the kth city is denoted by $L_k(\xi) \geq 0$. At the fixed time t, the workers' equation of motion over ξ is as follows:

$$\frac{\mathrm{d}L_k(\xi)}{\mathrm{d}\xi} = L_k(\xi)\,[\omega_k(\xi) - \bar{\omega}(\xi)]\,L(t) \qquad k = 1, \ldots, K \tag{10.72}$$

in which $\omega_k(\xi)$ is the temporary-equilibrium real wage prevailing in city k, whereas $\bar{\omega}(\xi)$ is the average real wage across all workers and farmers in the economy:

$$\bar{\omega}(\xi) = \left\{ \sum_{k=1}^{K} L_k(\xi)\omega_k(\xi) + \left[L(t) - \sum_{k=1}^{K} L_k(\xi) \right] \omega^{\mathbb{A}}(\xi) \right\} / L(t)$$

where $\omega^{\mathbb{A}}(\xi)$ is the equilibrium real wage common to all agricultural workers at time ξ. Because the total population of workers and farmers is equal to $L(t)$, the mass of farmers, $L^{\mathbb{A}}(\xi)$, must obey the following equation:

$$\frac{dL^{\mathbb{A}}(\xi)}{d\xi} = L^{\mathbb{A}}(\xi) \left[\omega^{\mathbb{A}}(\xi) - \bar{\omega}(\xi) \right] L(t). \tag{10.73}$$

Equations (10.72) and (10.73) describe the migration of workers and farmers across the whole inhabited area; this area is itself variable because the fringe moves with ξ.

Stability of a spatial equilibrium at time t requires the following condition: for any number K (such that K is never lower than the number of actual cities in equilibrium) of sites at any possible locations (but in which the locations of actual cities are unchanged), the spatial equilibrium is stable under the system (10.72) and (10.73). This definition is proposed to accommodate the infinite number of possible city locations.

At first sight, checking stability looks like a formidable task. However, given a spatial equilibrium, it can be shown that if the associated potential curve is strictly less than 1 but at the locations of existing cities, the spatial system is stable, thus implying that no new city is viable at any location (Fujita and Mori 1995; 1997). Intuitively, this can be understood as follows. When the economy is in equilibrium, workers' real wage in each city and farmers' real wage are equal across all locations. Because

$$\Omega(r) = \left(\frac{w^{\mathbb{M}}(r)}{w^*(r)} \right)^{\sigma} = \left(\frac{\omega^{\mathbb{M}}(r)}{\omega^*(r)} \right)^{\sigma}$$

and $\Omega(r) < 1$ at any r that does not host a city, there is no place, other than the incumbent cities, at which firms can offer workers the prevailing equilibrium real wage while making nonnegative profits.

10.4.2 The Urban System as a Network of Cities

Consider an economy having a monocentric configuration associated with a small population (so that the potential curve is lower than 1 for all $r \neq 0$). In this case, the equilibrium configuration is stable and new cities cannot emerge.

However, as seen in Section 10.2, increasing the population size shifts the potential curve up. Eventually, this curve hits the value 1 at some location $\hat{r}$ when the population size reaches the level $\hat{L}$, thus making this location as profitable as the city. If the population slightly rises above $\hat{L}$, then the potential curve exceeds 1 at $\hat{r}$. Hence, $\hat{r}$ is now more profitable than the city, which leads some firms to set up there. In other words, a new city is forming at $\hat{r}$. Of course, the same arises at location $-\hat{r}$. Thus, at the population level $\hat{L}$, the monocentric equilibrium is transformed into a symmetric tricentric pattern. If the multiplier effect encapsulated in the agglomeration mechanism is sufficiently powerful, the resulting change will be catastrophic, resulting in the emergence of two fairly large flanking cities. In this respect, Fujita, Krugman, and Venables (1999, 168) have shown that sufficient conditions for such a catastrophic transition are as:

$$\mu\tau^{\mathbb{M}} \geq (1-\mu)\tau^{\mathbb{A}} \tag{10.74}$$

and

$$\mu \geq \frac{\rho}{1+\rho}. \tag{10.75}$$

Equation (10.74) means that transport costs of the industrial goods, weighted by their expenditure share, are to be large enough when compared with those of the agricultural goods, and thus being located in a city allows consumers to raise their real income markedly. Equation (10.75) states that the share of the industrial goods in consumption must be above some threshold that depends negatively on the degree of product differentiation. Indeed, a weak share in consumption would not provide enough incentive for firms and consumers to form a large agglomeration. Of course, μ cannot be larger than ρ, for otherwise the agglomeration force is so strong that the incumbent city acts as a black hole and no new city can emerge.

It appears to be very problematic to derive analytical results when the equilibrium involves more than three cities. We thus restrict ourselves to a discussion of the numerical results obtained by Fujita and Mori (1997). The parameters of the economy take the values corresponding to Figure 10.2; they satisfy (10.74) and (10.75).

Figure 10.5 describes the evolution of the urban system as L keeps rising. Figure 10.5(a), drawn when $L = 3$, shows that the monocentric configuration is a stable equilibrium. In Figure 10.5(b), drawn when L takes the critical value 4.36, the monocentric configuration becomes structurally unstable because the corresponding potential curve hits the value 1 at $r = 1.10$. At this particular value of L, the spatial economy experiences a catastrophic transition from a monocentric to a tricentric pattern. As shown by the corresponding potential curve depicted in Figure 10.5(c), this new equilibrium is stable.

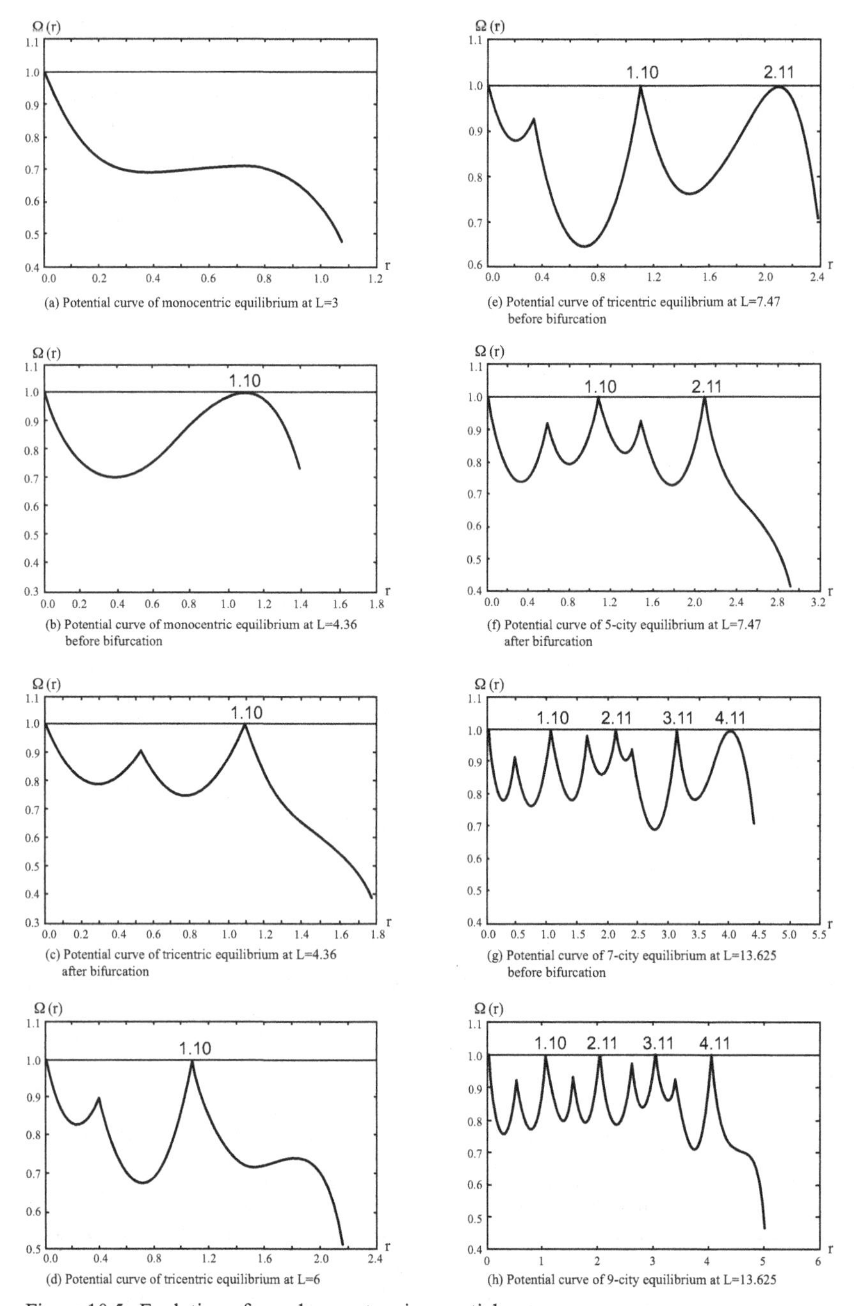

Figure 10.5. Evolution of an urban system in a spatial economy.

In Figure 10.5(d), the tricentric equilibrium is shown to be stable for $L = 6$, that is, a value of L that lies between the first and second bifurcations. In Figure 10.5(e), L takes the new critical value 7.47 and the corresponding potential curve hits the value 1 at $r = 2.11$, which indicates that the tricentric pattern becomes structurally unstable. Again, there is a catastrophic bifurcation such that the tricentric pattern is transformed into a pentacentric configuration. Figure 10.5(f) describes the potential curve after the transition.

In a similar manner, as L continues to rise, a pair of frontier cities emerge periodically as a result of a catastrophic transition of the spatial economy. Figures 10.5(g) and (h) describe another example of such a bifurcation from a heptacentric to a nonacentric configuration in which the new city arises at $r = 4.11$.

These diagrams suggest that, as the number of cities increases, the urban system approaches a highly regular network of cities, as conjectured in central place theory.

10.4.3 On the Number and Size of Cities

In the foregoing, we studied the impact of a growing population on the formation of an urban system. In this section, we follow Tabuchi and Thisse (2011) and return to the standard thought experiment of NEG: how decreasing transport costs affects the number and size of cities hosting the manufacturing sector.

Space is given by a circle $(0, 1]$ of unit length and there is one industry producing a differentiated manufactured good under increasing returns, monopolistic competition, and positive transport costs.[6] As in the CP model, the size of the workforce is fixed and split according to given shares between farmers and workers. Each farmer/worker supplies one unit of labor. Farmers are immobile and uniformly distributed across space, whereas workers are mobile across cities. A city arises provided that it accommodates a positive mass of workers and firms. By implication, the number and size of cities distributed along the circle $(0, 1]$ are variable.

Consumers' preferences are quasi-linear and given by

$$U = \alpha \log Q + A$$

where

$$Q = \left(\int_0^M q_i^\rho \mathrm{d}i \right)^{1/\rho} \qquad 0 < \rho < 1$$

[6] Tabuchi and Thisse also discuss the case of several industries.

while $\alpha > 0$ is the expenditure on the manufactured good. Denoting by C the number of cities, the budget constraint of a consumer living at $x \in (0, 1]$ is as follows:

$$\sum_{c=1}^{C} n_c p(x_c, x) q(x_c, x) + A = w(x) + \bar{A}$$

where n_c is the number of firms producing the manufactured good in city c, $q(x_c, x)$ the individual consumption at $x \in (0, 1]$ of a variety produced in city c at $x_c \in (0, 1]$, $p(x_c, x)$ the delivered price of this variety, $w(x)$ the income she earns at location x, and $\bar{A}$ the initial endowment in the agricultural good.

Let $\tau(x_c, x) \equiv \tau^{\min\{|x_c - x|, 1 - |x_c - x|\}}$ be the cost that a manufacturing firm located in the city located at x_c has to bear to produce and ship one unit of its output to location $x \in (0, 1]$. In this expression, the marginal production cost is normalized to 1. The iceberg transport cost is now a power function of the distance between the firm and the consumer instead of an exponential function.

For different lattices of cities to be nested, an integer number n must exist for the number of cities of order k to be just n times the number of cities of order $k - 1$ and $1/n$th the number of cities of order $k + 1$. Therefore, it is convenient to focus on the special case in which $n = 2$, so that a central place configuration emerges for power values of 2.

Consider first the case of equidistant configurations involving C cities, each having the same size. Tabuchi and Thisse show that, for all $C = 2^n$, there exists a threshold $\tau_h(C) > 0$ such that, when the equilibrium involves $2C$ equidistant cities for $\tau > \tau_h(C)$, the equilibrium number of cities is equal to C when τ falls slightly below $\tau_h(C)$. To put it differently, if there are 2^n equidistant cities for some value of τ, the number of cities is halved once τ has sufficiently decreased. In other words, the symmetric equilibrium path (if any) involves a decreasing number of cities whose size increases when transport costs steadily decline.

Tabuchi and Thisse also show the existence of a symmetry-breaking threshold τ_b such that, when τ steadily decreases, the urban system is described by the sequence formed by the following two patterns: (i) when $\tau_h\left(2^{n-1}\right) < \tau < \tau_b\left(2^n\right)$, there is an equilibrium involving 2^n cities in which a small city alternates with a big city; (ii) when $\tau_b\left(2^{n-1}\right) < \tau < \tau_h\left(2^{n-1}\right)$, the equilibrium is formed by 2^{n-1} equidistant and symmetric cities. To illustrate, consider a pattern with $C = 16$ symmetric cities and let the transport rate τ decrease steadily. First, the urban system remains the same until the break point $\tau_b(16)$ is reached. When τ falls slightly below $\tau_b(16)$, the symmetric configuration becomes unstable, so that the urban system now involves 16 cities that alternate in size. As τ keep falling, the big cities grow whereas the small cities shrink. Once $\tau_h(16)$ is reached, the small cities disappear and the urban system involves only 8 bigger and identical cities; both the inter-city distance and the city size have doubled. The same pattern is repeated with 4 and 2 cities, until τ reaches the threshold $\tau_h(1)$.

In sum, the urban system displays a sequence of bifurcations in which small cities disappear gradually from the space-economy, whereas a decreasing number of cities accommodate a growing range of activities. Furthermore, the resulting geography is of the putty-clay type: workers and firms are free to launch a city anywhere but, once it exists, a city has a well-defined location that does not change, even in the absence of durable infrastructure such as roads, housing, and public facilities. Last, cities gaining primacy in the urban hierarchy retain their high rank during the whole process, whereas the low-rank towns gradually enter the urban shadow of large cities and, eventually, vanish. All of this is in accordance with the fact that "cities show remarkable resilience" (Hohenberg 2004).

10.5 CONCLUDING REMARKS

We have seen in this chapter that the addition of a land market to the canonical model of Chapter 8, together with the assumption of mobile workers, allows for the study of a process of urbanization in which firms balance the advantages of being close to concentrated output markets against those associated with a low degree of competition in rural areas. Despite severe limitations, such a process captures some of the basic forces stressed by geographers and historians. Not surprisingly, it appears that the number of cities expands with the size of the total population. Our emphasis on population growth as a major factor for urbanization agrees with economic history as well as with the observations made by early scholars such as Adam Smith ([1776] 1965, 17), who observed:

> In the lone houses and very small villages which are scattered about in so desert a country as the Highlands of Scotland, every farmer must be butcher, baker and brewer for his own family.

Stated differently, population must become dense enough for the division of labor to expand through the emergence of new cities. The finer division of labor is expressed here through a larger variety of goods available to consumers.

More surprisingly perhaps, new cities distribute themselves according to a (fairly) regular network in which differentiated varieties are traded. This is in accordance with some of the main principles of central place theory. It is worth noting, however, that if cities serve as a basis for the agricultural area, they are also engaged in trade because they are specialized in the production of different varieties. This implies that *a city has a twofold function, namely serving its agricultural hinterland and trading with other cities,* as suggested by the work of many economic historians (see Hohenberg and Lees 1985, chapter 2).

However, only one type of city emerges in this urbanization process. Thus, the model considered fails to grasp the fundamental aspect of an urban hierarchy. It is our contention, however, that the approach developed in this chapter may be enriched to address this difficult question. A first step in this direction was taken by Fujita, Krugman, and Mori (1999), who introduced several manufactured goods into the utility (8.1), each having different elasticities of substitution. They assumed that transport costs are equal across goods and that

$$\sum_{k=1}^{K} \frac{\mu_k}{\rho_k} \geq 1$$

which boils down to the black hole condition $\mu \geq \rho$ when $K = 1$ (see Section 8.2.3). As the population size increases, these authors have shown that a (more or less) regular hierarchical central place system, reminiscent of Christaller's, emerges within the economy. In this urban system, "higher-order cities" provide a larger number of groups of manufactured goods. However, there is two-way trade between cities because cities are specialized in the production of differentiated goods. This leads to a more intricate pattern of trade in which horizontal relations are superimposed on the pyramidal structure of central place theory. As expected, higher-order cities export more varieties than lower-order cities. However, horizontal relations between cities of the same order may be more important than trade with lower-order cities. Thus, the urban hierarchy obtained here displays a richer trade pattern than in Christaller.

Following a similar approach, Tabuchi and Thisse (2011) have solved numerically the model presented in Section 10.5 in the case of several industries. Their main conclusions may be summarized as follows. When transport costs decrease, the small cities lose one industry at a time. Furthermore, industries get agglomerated in the order of increasing elasticities of substitution. Indeed, firms facing tougher competition choose to relax competition by being more dispersed, whereas firms facing softer competition get clustered in bigger cities where they can exploit scale economies. Hence, as economic integration gets deeper, the relative size of cities changes in the sense that big cities attract more firms and workers, whereas small cities lose them. Structural changes in the urban system arise when one industry moves away from the small cities to set up in the big ones. Eventually, when transport costs are sufficiently low, small cities disappear from the space-economy, which is formed by a few big cities.

APPENDIX

We may rewrite (10.15) as follows:

$$\Omega(r) = \mu A(r) \exp(-\eta r) \tag{10A.1}$$

where η is defined by (10.17), whereas

$$A(r) \equiv 1 + \frac{1-\mu}{2\mu} \frac{\tau^{\mathbb{A}} \exp[(\sigma - 1)\tau^{\mathrm{M}} r]}{1 - \exp(-\tau^{\mathbb{A}} r_{\mathrm{b}})}$$

$$\times 2 \int_0^{r_{\mathrm{b}}} \exp\left[-\tau^{\mathbb{A}} |s| - (\sigma - 1)\tau^{\mathrm{M}} (|r - s| - |s|)\right] \mathrm{d}s$$

$$= 1 + \frac{1-\mu}{2\mu} \frac{\tau^{\mathbb{A}}}{1 - \exp(-\tau^{\mathbb{A}} r_{\mathrm{b}})} \left\{ \int_{-r_{\mathrm{b}}}^{r} \exp\left[-\tau^{\mathbb{A}} |s| + (\sigma - 1)\tau^{\mathrm{M}} (s + |s|)\right] \mathrm{d}s \right.$$

$$\left. + \exp[2(\sigma - 1)\tau^{\mathrm{M}} r] \int_r^{r_{\mathrm{b}}} \exp(-\tau^{\mathbb{A}} s) \mathrm{d}s \right\}.$$

Taking the logarithm of (10A.1) and differentiating both sides of the resulting expression with respect to r, we obtain:

$$\frac{\Omega'(r)}{\Omega(r)} = -\eta + \frac{A'(r)}{A(r)}$$

or, using (10A.1),

$$\Omega'(r) = -\eta \Omega(r) + \mu \exp(-\eta r) A'(r) \tag{10A.2}$$

where

$$A'(r) = \frac{1-\mu}{\mu} \frac{(\sigma - 1)\tau^{\mathrm{M}}}{1 - \exp(-\tau^{\mathbb{A}} r_{\mathrm{b}})} \exp[2(\sigma - 1)\tau^{\mathrm{M}} r] \int_r^{r_{\mathrm{b}}} \exp(-\tau^{\mathbb{A}} s) \mathrm{d}s.$$

Solving the differential equation (10A.2) under the initial condition $\Omega(0) = 1$ leads to the expression

$$\Omega(r) = \exp(-\eta r) \left[1 + \mu \int_0^r A'(s) \mathrm{d}s \right]$$

which is identical to (10.16).

11

Globalization, Growth, and the Geography of the Supply Chain

11.1 INTRODUCTION

Globalization is a multifaceted process. This chapter aims to address two of them that we consider as central for the future of our economies. Firstly, we build on the idea that knowledge spillovers are an important channel in the spatial diffusion of technological progress. Our goal is to understand how these spillovers affect the growth of various regions, especially through their spatial extent. Secondly, it is recognized that the contemporary and spectacular decrease in communication costs deeply affects the organization of firms through the spatial fragmentation of the supply chain. This in turn has a knock-on effect on the way the space-economy is organized. The common thread of this chapter therefore is to find out how the transfer of knowledge and information across space affects the location of economic activity. Note a major difference between spillover and communication: in the former, the information learned from others is the involuntary consequence of activities undertaken by some agents; in the latter, communication costs arise because geographically separated agents choose to exchange information.

As seen in Chapter 8, market integration might well be accompanied by the appearance of some core regions whose wealth is, in part, obtained at the expense of peripheral regions: the average welfare in the region accommodating the manufacturing sector rises but it decreases in the other. So far, however, such a result has been obtained in the context of static models in which the total number of firms and varieties is constant. It is, therefore, fundamental to figure out what the core–periphery property becomes in a dynamic setting where the number of firms grows over time. In other words, we want to deal with the following question: *How do growth and location affect each other?* More precisely, we want to know whether regional discrepancies widen or fall over time, and what are the main reasons for such a possible divergence or convergence? Because in the context of human history, the current disparities between rich and poor regions are recent (Bairoch 1993, chapter 9), it is important to understand how they may change over time. As regional discrepancies are often considered as socially undesirable, the issue is indeed critical from a policy standpoint. If one finds strong reasons for the existing disparities to persist or, worse, for growth and agglomeration to make those living in the periphery worse off, governments and international bodies should become more active in designing policies fostering a more equitable distribution of wealth across countries and regions.

It has long been argued that growth is *localized*, the reason being that technological and social innovations tend to be clustered while their diffusion across places is slow. For example, Hirschman (1958, 183) claimed that

> we may take it for granted that economic progress does not appear everywhere at the same time and that once it has appeared powerful forces make for a spatial concentration of economic growth around the initial starting points

Hohenberg and Lees (1985, 179) similarly argued:

> Despite the rapid growth of urban industries in England, Belgium, France, Germany and northern Italy after 1840 or so, economic development was a spatially selective process. Some regions deindustrialized while others were transformed by new technologies.

Once it is recognized that the accumulation of knowledge is central to economic growth, the role of urban agglomeration in this process becomes clear. In the words of Sachs (2000),

> innovation shows increasing returns to scale, meaning that regions with advanced technologies are best placed to innovate further. New ideas are typically produced from a recombination of existing ideas . . . so environments rich in ideas produce chain reactions of innovation.

Glaeser (2011, 8) accurately stressed the resilience of this phenomenon:

> the spread of knowledge from engineer to engineer, from designer to designer, from trader to trader is the same as the flight of ideas from painter to painter, and urban density has long been at the heart of that process.

The congruence of talents is rarely natural; rather, it is generally due to the attractive power of prosperous cities, such as Venice, Amsterdam, and Edo in the past, and New York, London, and Shanghai today. And, indeed, Feldman and Florida (1994) observed that in the late twentieth century innovations clustered geographically in areas where research and development (R&D)-oriented firms or universities were established. These authors also observed that concentrations of such specialized resources reinforce a region's capacity to innovate and to grow.

Thus, the connection between growth and geography would become even stronger when regional specialization in innovation activity is viewed as the outcome of the combination of specific capabilities and capacities developed in those regions: innovation and agglomeration would go hand in hand. In particular, the role of cities in economic growth since the second half of the nineteenth century has been emphasized by economic historians (Hohenberg and Lees 1985, chapters 6 and 7). Cities are the main social institutions in which both technological and social innovations are developed through market and non-market interactions, thus strengthening the fact that growth is localized. To put it differently, agglomeration is the geographical counterpart of economic growth.

Space and time are thus intrinsically mixed in the process of economic development. However, the study of their interaction is a formidable task. Because either agglomeration or growth is a complex phenomenon by itself, one should expect any integrated analysis to face many conceptual and analytical hurdles. Not surprisingly, therefore, the field is still in its infancy, and relevant contributions have been few. Even so, it is beyond the reach of this chapter to provide a complete survey of the field of regional growth. Instead, we have chosen to present some results that are strongly linked to previous chapters in the hope of shedding light on the main factors in play and encouraging future research in this important domain. Because both modern theories of growth and new economic geography share the same basic framework of monopolistic competition, a solid foundation for cross-fertilization exists between the two fields. And, indeed, the few existing contributions that have recently explored the mutual influences between growth and location exploit this formal analogy; see Baldwin and Martin (2004) for a detailed survey. In the same spirit as in Chapter 8, we assume here that skilled people working for the R&D sector are mobile, whereas unskilled people working in the manufacturing and agricultural sectors are immobile. Regional growth models typically put aside the migration of workers whereas economic geography often relies on myopic migration processes. Therefore, connecting the two fields requires dealing with the migration issue in a sophisticated way because the skilled workers' consumption and location decisions now depend on the beliefs they have about the way the economy is going to evolve. Despite those difficulties, it is possible to derive some tentative conclusions that appear to be reasonable.

Growth. In Section 11.2, we propose a simple model of endogenous growth for a two-region economy that represents a natural combination of a Krugman-type core–periphery model and a Grossman-Helpman-Romer-type model of endogenous growth with horizontally differentiated products. Growth is driven by the increase in the number of varieties, whereas the skilled workers create the blueprints that are necessary for the production of new varieties. To be precise, the fixed cost of a firm producing a given variety is equal to the cost of acquiring the corresponding patent and is, therefore, expressed in terms of skilled labor, which is mobile. By contrast, the marginal cost of a firm belonging to the modern sector is expressed in terms of unskilled labor, which is immobile. Specifically, this means that we add to the core–periphery model a research and development sector that uses skilled labor to create new varieties for the manufacturing sector so that the number of firms producing in this sector is variable.

This model may be viewed as an attempt at integrating several issues addressed in previous chapters. More precisely, it combines (i) the demand effect generated by the migration of skilled workers, as in Chapter 8, and (ii) the cost effect generated by the existence of spillovers, such as those studied in Chapters 6 and 9. These two effects are in turn associated with the growth in the number of varieties, which gives rise to a second demand effect. Hence, this model provides a "general" framework of reference, which is amenable to a complete analytical solution. For simplicity, we focus on a steady-state spatial equilibrium in which the spatial distribution of skilled workers is time-invariant while the total number of patents/varieties/firms grows at a constant rate, both being determined at the equilibrium outcome. One of the most stimulating results obtained in this chapter is that the growth rate, measured by the variation in the number of varieties, changes with the equilibrium spatial distribution of skilled workers. In other words, *the growth of the economy depends on the spatial organization of the innovation sector across regions*.

In Section 11.3, we assume that patents developed in one region are not transferable to the other region. It is, indeed, well documented that there exist various social and cultural barriers to the adoption of new ideas and technologies, which prevent a particular region from producing at the technological frontier. For example, a firm applying for a patent must mention all previous patents that it uses. This makes it possible to reconstruct the approximate path followed by flows of knowledge (Jaffe et al. 1993). Peri (2005), using a sample of 147 regions in 18 countries, shows that crossing one regional border reduces the flow of patent citations by 80 percent. As observed by Prager and Thisse (2012, 39), "transferring knowledge is effective only if at least two conditions are met: first, those who possess knowledge must be willing to share it, which will inevitably happen but can take time; and second, lagging regions must be able to assimilate the new knowledge, that is, to imitate and subsequently transform it." Moreover, there are additional problems that hamper the effective implementation of blueprints in a foreign region owing to the tacit knowledge embodied in individuals, which is hard to transfer abroad (Teece 1977). In such a sticky world, very much like in the CP model, the core–periphery structure in which both the innovation and the manufacturing sectors are entirely agglomerated into the same region is stable when the transportation costs of the manufactured good are sufficiently low.

Thus, the existence of a R&D sector appears to be a strong centripetal force at the interregional-international level, thus amplifying the circular causality that lies at the heart of the CP model. Such a result seems to confirm the idea that *growth and agglomeration go hand in hand*, even though we recognize that the relationship is influenced by other factors (Henderson 2003b). We find it interesting to observe that this result lies at the heart of economic policy debates that take place in several industrialized countries. Indeed, our equilibrium analysis seems to give credit to the existence of a trade-off between growth and equity. However, our welfare analysis also supports the idea that the additional growth spurred by agglomeration may lead to a Pareto-dominant outcome. Specifically, when the economy moves from dispersion to agglomeration, innovation follows a faster pace. As a consequence, *even those who live in the periphery are better off than under dispersion provided that the growth effect triggered by the agglomeration is strong enough*. It should be stressed that this Pareto-optimal property does not require any transfer whatsoever: it is a pure outcome of market interaction.

To be sure, the unskilled who live in the core of the economy enjoy a higher level of well-being than those in the periphery. Thus, what appears here is a situation in which everybody can be made better off because agglomeration generates more growth. However, the gap between those who live, respectively, in the core and in the periphery enlarges. Put differently, *the rich get richer and so may the poor, but without ever catching up* (Moretti 2012). Hence, according to Rawls' principle of justice, there would be no conflict between growth and equity since all workers, even the unskilled residing in the periphery, can be made better off. In our setting, *the regional income discrepancy reflects the spatial distribution of skills*, a result that concurs with various empirical studies (Combes, Duranton, and Gobillon 2008; Mion and Naticchioni 2009; Moretti 2012). The welfare gap between the core and the periphery arises because of the additional gains generated by a faster growth that the skilled are able to spur by being agglomerated. This in turn makes the unskilled residing in this region better off, even though their productivity is the same as those living in the periphery.

Globalization. A major facet of the process of globalization, which also generates harsh political debates, is the fragmentation of the firm associated with *vertical* foreign investments. Vertical investments arise when firms choose to break down their production process into various stages spread across different countries or regions. Specifically, the modern firm organizes and performs discrete activities in distinct locations, which altogether form a *supply chain* starting at the conception of the product and ending at its delivery. This spatial fragmentation of production aims at taking advantage of differences in technologies, factor endowments, or factor prices across places (Feenstra 1998). Some policy makers and the general public in rich countries tend to view vertical investments as the main force driving the growing wage inequality between skilled and unskilled workers through the relocation of routinized production activities in low-wage countries. For various groups and nongovernmental organizations, the liberalization of trade and capital flows, which go hand in hand with fragmentation, would also be detrimental to undeveloped countries, by fostering more international economic inequality. Our purpose is to show that vertical investments and the existence of multinational enterprises need not have such detrimental implications for low-income people and countries.

Besides transportation costs, geographical separation generates another type of spatial friction, namely *communication costs*. Indeed, coordinating activities within the firm is more costly when the headquarters and its production plants are physically separated because the transmission of information remains incomplete and imperfect. Furthermore, more uncertainty about production plants' local environment is associated with conducting a business at a distance. Again, this implies higher coordination costs, hence higher communication costs between the headquarters and its plants. Last, it should be clear that monitoring the effort of a plant manager is easier when the plant is located near the headquarters than across borders. Put differently, communication costs are now to be interpreted as a reduced form for the informational rent that accrues to the plant manager. In sum, lower communication costs make the coordination between headquarters and plants easier and, therefore, facilitates the process of fragmentation.

In Section 11.4, we use the CP model in which firms are formed by two units, i.e., a headquarters and a production plant, which need not be located under the same roof. How does the spatial division of labor change when both communication and transportation costs become lower, and what are the corresponding implications for the various groups of workers, are the topics studied in Section 11.5. It is assumed that headquarters are established in large urban agglomerations for the reasons discussed in Chapters 4 and 6. In such a context, for international fragmentation to arise, the intrafirm coordination costs must be sufficiently low so that operating a plant at a distance is not too costly, whereas transportation costs must decrease substantially to permit the supply of large markets at low delivery costs from distant locations. In order to make low-wage areas more accessible and attractive for the establishment of their production, firms therefore need the development of new information and communication technologies as well as a substantial fall in transportation costs. Interestingly, this is precisely what we have witnessed during the last decades.

When communication costs are high, we show that all plants are located together with their headquarters. In this case, all firms are national and established in the core. Once communication costs steadily decrease, the industry moves toward a configuration in which *some firms are multinational whereas others are national*. Note that an equilibrium involving the two types of firms does not suggest itself because firms are a priori identical. The difference in attitudes toward foreign investment comes about as lowering the level of communication costs raises firms' incentives to become multinational. Eventually, when communication costs have reached a sufficiently low level, the economy ends up with a deindustrialized core that retains only firms' strategic functions.

Interestingly, a steady drop in transportation costs leads to contrasted patterns of production that depend on the level of communication costs. When these are high, reducing transportation costs leads to a growing agglomeration of plants within the core, very much like in the CP model. However, the agglomeration process is here gradual instead of exhibiting bang-bang behavior. Things are totally different when communication costs are low. For high transportation costs, most plants are located within the core. However, once transportation costs fall below some threshold, the relocation process unfolds and the core loses a growing share of plants. All in all, *our model supports the idea that globalization triggers the deindustrialization of the core*, unless this one accommodates a R&D sector able to develop new and competitive products (see Sections 11.2 and 11.3).

As more plants move into the periphery, the unskilled workers residing there are better off whereas the unskilled living in the core are worse off. Totally unexpected (at least to us) is the outcome that the skilled workers located within the core are also hurt by the fragmentation of firms. In sum, both types of workers living in the core are worse off when firms gradually relocate their plants into the periphery. Although each firm gets fragmented in the pursuit of its own interest, such a strategy might hurt them all, as if "going multinational" were to obey a large prisoner's dilemma. Hence, once it is recognized that the market economy is imperfectly competitive, the process of fragmentation can be harmful to both the skilled and unskilled workers living in the core. By contrast, it would be beneficial to the workers located in the periphery. As a result, *fragmentation contributes to narrowing the gap between rich and poor countries*.

Therefore, the geographical fragmentation of the supply chain might well have redistributive consequences that vastly differ from those expected by the anti-globalization demonstrators. It also runs against the popular idea that the geographical fragmentation of the supply chain lies at the origin of the growing inequality between skilled and unskilled workers in developed countries. However, our results confirm another popular idea, i.e., *the IT revolution leads to job creation in the periphery and job destruction in the core regions.* Instead of generating unemployment, this takes the form of lower real wages for the workers living in the core.

In the last section, we show how the setting developed in Section 11.4 can be modified to accommodate most of the main organization forms adopted by firms operating on global markets. To be precise, we find conditions for firms to export or to offshore part of their production through horizontal and/or vertical investment, together with the corresponding implications for trade such as one- or two-way intrafirm trade. In particular, we show that firms choose to have several plants when transport costs are high and communication costs low. Whereas the literature stresses the importance of productivity heterogeneity to understand the way firms conduct their business in foreign markets (Helpman

2011), we provide a unified framework that allows explaining the coexistence of different forms of spatial organization when firms share the same technology. Our analysis also shows that coping with both communication and transport costs is needed to disentangle the various effects at work in the process of globalization.

From the methodological viewpoint, the two models used in this chapter build on the CP model with a two-factor manufacturing sector.

11.2 REGIONAL GROWTH AND KNOWLEDGE SPILLOVERS

Our purpose is to analyze a simple setting in which growth is driven by the increase in the number of varieties, whereas the skilled workers who create the blueprints necessary for the production of the new varieties are free to move across regions. We use a model similar to the one presented in Section 8.2.3 in which the fixed cost of a manufacture is expressed in terms of skilled labor, whereas its marginal cost is expressed in terms of unskilled labor. The main difference is an R&D sector in which patents for new varieties are developed. In turn, the fixed cost of a firm producing a given variety is equal to the cost of acquiring the corresponding patent. Throughout this chapter we denote time by t, although this symbol has been used so far to describe transport costs.

11.2.1 Firms and Consumers

The economy consists of two regions, 1 and 2, and three production sectors, namely the agricultural sector ($\mathbb{A}$), the manufacturing sector ($\mathbb{M}$), and the innovation sector ($\mathbb{R}$). There are two production factors, the low-skilled workers (L) and the high-skilled workers (H). Both the agricultural and manufacturing sectors use unskilled workers, while the R&D sector uses skilled workers. Each unskilled worker is endowed with one unit of labor per unit of time and is immobile. Every region has the same number of unskilled ($L/2$) over time, where L is a constant. Each skilled worker is endowed with one unit of labor and can move between regions at some positive cost (see Section 11.2.3). The total number of skilled workers in the economy is constant over time; without loss of generality, this number is normalized to 1 so that L may be interpreted as the relative size of the unskilled to the skilled. Although the total number of workers is constant over time, we show how growth is made possible through another variable, the *knowledge capital*, which rises together with the number of patents. Both skilled and unskilled workers infinitely live with a rate of time preference equal to $\gamma > 0$ common to all individuals.

All workers have the same instantaneous utility function given by (8.1):

$$u = Q^{\mu} A^{1-\mu} / \mu^{\mu} (1-\mu)^{1-\mu} \qquad 0 < \mu < 1$$

where A is the consumption of the agricultural good, while Q stands for the index of the consumption of the manufactured good given by

$$Q = \left(\int_0^M q_i^\rho \mathrm{d}i \right)^{1/\rho} \qquad 0 < \rho < 1.$$

The agricultural good is produced under constant returns and perfect competition. Furthermore, this good is costlessly shipped between the two regions, thus enabling us to normalize its price to one across time and location. Hence, if ε denotes the expenditure of a consumer while p_i is the price of variety i, then his demand functions are as follows:

$$A = (1 - \mu)\varepsilon$$

$$q_i = \mu \varepsilon p_i^{-\sigma} P^{\sigma - 1} \qquad i \in [0, M]$$

where $\sigma = 1/(1 - \rho)$ is the elasticity of substitution between any two varieties and P the price index in the manufactured sector given by

$$P \equiv \left(\int_0^M p_i^{-(\sigma-1)} \mathrm{d}i \right)^{-1/(\sigma-1)}.$$

Thus, the indirect utility function is

$$v = \varepsilon P^{-\mu}.$$

Compared with the corresponding expressions obtained in Section 8.2.1, we see that the individual income Y is replaced throughout by the expenditure ε. Because they are supposed to live indefinitely, consumers need not any longer equalize income and expenditure at each time t.

We now describe the behavior of an arbitrary consumer in space and time. If this consumer chooses an expenditure path, $\varepsilon(t)$ for $t \in [0, \infty)$ such that $\varepsilon(t) \geq 0$, and a location path, $r(t)$ for $t \in [0, \infty)$ such that $r(t) \in \{1, 2\}$, then this consumer's indirect utility at time t is given by

$$v(t) = \varepsilon(t)[P_{r(t)}(t)]^{-\mu} \tag{11.1}$$

where $P_{r(t)}(t)$ is the price index of the manufactured good in region $r(t)$ at time t.[1] If $r(t_-) \neq r(t)$, then he relocates at time t and we denote by t_h $(h = 1, 2, \ldots)$ the sequence of such moves.[2]

Moving between regions imposes various psychological adjustments that negatively affect a migrant. Hence, when the consumer relocates at time t he bears a cost $C_m(t)$ – or a utility loss – expressed in terms of his lifetime utility. Following a standard approach in endogenous growth theory, the lifetime utility

[1] If the consumer is an unskilled worker, then $r(t)$ is either 1 or 2 for all t.
[2] If the consumer is a skilled worker, he is allowed to move back and forth several times.

of this consumer at time 0 is defined by

$$U(0) = V(0) - \sum_h e^{-\gamma t_h} C_m(t_h) \tag{11.2}$$

where

$$V(0) \equiv \int_0^\infty e^{-\gamma t} \ln \nu(t) \mathrm{d}t \tag{11.3}$$

is the lifetime utility gross of migration costs (hence, preferences are intertemporally CES with unit elasticity of intertemporal substitution).

We now describe a consumer's budget constraint. In an intertemporal context, a consumer can spend more (less) than his income at time t by borrowing (lending) some numéraire on a global and perfectly competitive capital market in which bonds, bearing an interest rate equal to $\upsilon(t)$, are traded. The interest rate is common to both regions because the capital market is fully integrated and equally accessible to all consumers and firms, wherever they reside. We now specify the consumer's intertemporal budget constraint, that is, the present value of expenditure equals wealth. Let $w_{r(t)}(t)$ be the wage rate the consumer receives when he resides in region $r(t)$ at t. Then, the present value of labor income is given by

$$W(0) = \int_0^\infty e^{-\int_0^t \upsilon(s)\mathrm{d}s} w_{r(t)}(t)\mathrm{d}t. \tag{11.4}$$

Using the budget flow constraint, the consumer's intertemporal budget constraint may be written as follows:

$$\int_0^\infty e^{-\int_0^t \upsilon(s)\mathrm{d}s} \varepsilon(t)\mathrm{d}t = A + W(0) \tag{11.5}$$

where A is the value of the consumer's initial assets.

Consider an arbitrary location path $r(\cdot)$. Then, if $\varepsilon(\cdot)$ stands for an expenditure path that maximizes (11.2) subject to (11.5), the first order condition implies that

$$\dot{\varepsilon}(t)/\varepsilon(t) = \upsilon(t) - \gamma \qquad t \geq 0 \tag{11.6}$$

where $\dot{\varepsilon}(t) \equiv \mathrm{d}\varepsilon(t)/\mathrm{d}t$. Since (11.6) must hold for every consumer, it is clear that the following relation must hold:

$$\dot{E}(t)/E(t) = \upsilon(t) - \gamma \qquad t \geq 0 \tag{11.7}$$

where $E(t)$ stands for the total expenditure in the global economy at time t.

We now turn to the production side of the economy. As in the CP model, the $\mathbb{A}$-sector operates under constant returns: one unit of the homogeneous good is produced using one unit of unskilled labor, which can be costlessly traded between the two regions and is chosen as the numéraire. We also assume that the expenditure share $(1 - \mu)$ on the agricultural good is sufficiently large for the agricultural good to be always produced in both regions.[3] In this case, at any time t the wage rate of the unskilled is equal to 1 in each region:

$$w_1^L = w_2^L = 1 \qquad t \geq 0. \tag{11.8}$$

In the manufacturing sector, the production of a variety requires the use of the patent specific to this variety, which has been developed in the R&D sector. Once a firm has acquired the patent at the market price (which corresponds to this firm's fixed cost), it can produce one unit of this variety by using one unit of unskilled labor. When the variety is moved from one region to the other, only a fraction $1/\tau$ arrives at destination, where $\tau > 1$. Hence, if variety i is produced in region $r = 1, 2$ and sold at the mill price p_r, then the price p_{rs} paid by a consumer located in region $s \neq r$ is $p_{rs} = \tau p_r$.

Let E_r be the total expenditure in region r at the time in question and P_r be the price index of the manufactured good in this region. As seen in Section 8.2.1, the total demand for a variety produced in region r equals

$$q_r = \mu E_r p_r^{-\sigma} P_r^{\sigma-1} + \mu\phi E_s p_r^{-\sigma} P_s^{\sigma-1} \tag{11.9}$$

where $r, s = 1, 2$ and $r \neq s$, while $\phi \equiv \tau^{-(\sigma-1)}$ is the now-familiar spatial discount factor. Profits are given by

$$\pi_r = (p_r - 1)q_r$$

which yields the equilibrium price common to all varieties produced in region r:

$$p_r^* = \frac{\sigma}{\sigma - 1}.$$

Thus, if M_r denotes the number of varieties produced in region r at the time in question (which may differ from the number of patents developed in this region), we have

$$P_r = \frac{\sigma}{\sigma - 1}(M_r + \phi M_s)^{-1/(\sigma-1)} \tag{11.10}$$

where $r, s = 1, 2$ and $r \neq s$. Accordingly, the equilibrium output of any variety produced in region r is equal to

$$q_r^* = \frac{\sigma - 1}{\sigma}\mu\left(\frac{E_r}{M_r + \phi M_s} + \frac{\phi E_s}{\phi M_r + M_s}\right) \tag{11.11}$$

whereas the equilibrium profit is given by

$$\pi_r^* = q_r^*/(\sigma - 1). \tag{11.12}$$

We now study the labor market clearing conditions for the unskilled. If L_r^M denotes the demand of the unskilled by the manufacturing sector in region r,

[3] A sufficient condition for this to hold is that $1 - \mu > \rho/(1 + \rho)$.

then

$$L_r^M = M_r q_r^*$$

and, by (11.11),

$$L_1^M + L_2^M = \frac{\sigma - 1}{\sigma}\mu(E_1 + E_2)$$

or, because $E = E_1 + E_2$,

$$L_1^M + L_2^M = \frac{\sigma - 1}{\sigma}\mu E. \tag{11.13}$$

Because the total demand for the agricultural good is $A = (1 - \mu)E$, the demand of unskilled labor in the $\mathbb{A}$-sector is equal to

$$L^T = (1 - \mu)E. \tag{11.14}$$

In equilibrium, we must have

$$L^T + L_1^M + L_2^M = L$$

and thus (11.13) and (11.14) imply that, in equilibrium, the total expenditure

$$E^* = \frac{L}{1 - \mu/\sigma}$$

is time-invariant because L is constant. Therefore, we may conclude from (11.7) that the equilibrium interest rate is equal to the subjective discount rate over time

$$\upsilon^*(t) = \gamma \qquad \text{for all } t \geq 0. \tag{11.15}$$

As a result, using (11.6), a consumer's expenditure is also a constant, which is readily obtained from (11.5) and (11.15):

$$\varepsilon = \gamma[A + W(0)]. \tag{11.16}$$

11.2.2 The R&D Sector

Turning to the innovation sector, the patents for the new varieties are produced by perfectly competitive laboratories that use skilled workers and benefit from technological spillovers. Following the literature on endogenous growth theory (Romer 1990; Grossman and Helpman 1991, chapter 3), we assume that the productivity of a researcher increases with the total capital of past ideas and methods and that this capital has the nature of a (possibly local) public good.

Very much as in Chapter 6 where firms are identical but own different pieces of information, we assume that the knowledge capital is determined as the outcome of the interactions among skilled workers because each one has something to learn from the others. More precisely, when a region accommodates a mass $\lambda \leq 1$ of skilled workers and a worker $j \in [0, \lambda]$ has a personal knowledge capital given by h_j (e.g., his human capital or the number of papers he has read), the total knowledge capital K is given by the following CES-aggregate:

$$K = \left(\int_0^\lambda h_j^\beta \mathrm{d}j \right)^{1/\beta} \qquad 0 < \beta < 1$$

where $1/\beta$ is a measure of skilled workers' complementarity in knowledge creation: the lower β, the higher K. This statistic is reminiscent of the aggregate intermediate input considered in Section 4.2.1. That β is constant means that skilled workers have the same capacity to absorb knowledge and innovation.

For simplicity, we assume that the level of knowledge is the same across skilled workers and equal to the total stock of patents:

$$h_j = M. \tag{11.17}$$

In this case, we have

$$K = M\lambda^{1/\beta}$$

which rises at an increasing rate with the mass λ of skilled workers. In other words, the R&D sector displays increasing returns with respect to λ.

Once we recognize the existence of a distance-decay effect in the spatial diffusion of knowledge, the knowledge capital need not be the same in the two regions. More precisely, if λ_r denotes the share of skilled workers residing in region r, this region has a knowledge capital given by

$$K_r = \left(\int_0^{\lambda_r} h_j^\beta \mathrm{d}j + \eta \int_0^{1-\lambda_r} h_j^\beta \mathrm{d}j \right)^{1/\beta} \qquad 0 \leq \eta \leq 1 \tag{11.18}$$

where the parameter η is a measure of the "spatial extent" of the knowledge spillover. It depends on the degree of access to knowledge and the capacity to absorb new knowledge and ideas displayed by region r's skilled workers. When $\eta = 1$, there is no distance-decay effect in knowledge diffusion, and thus knowledge is a *pure* public good. By contrast, when $\eta = 0$, knowledge is a *local* public good. To sum up, η has the nature of a spatial discount factor associated with the diffusion of knowledge across space. The empirical literature documents the existence of such spillovers as well as their localized nature (Peri 2005; Henderson 2007).

Expressions (11.17) and (11.18) imply

$$K_r = M[\lambda_r + \eta(1 - \lambda_r)]^{1/\beta}. \tag{11.19}$$

If $\eta = 1$, we have $K_r = M$, whereas $K_r = M\lambda_r$ when $\eta = 0$. We assume that the productivity of a skilled worker in region r is equal to this region's knowledge capital K_r. Hence, the number of patents developed per unit of time in region r is given by

$$m_r = K_r\lambda_r. \tag{11.20}$$

For the results presented below to hold, it is not necessary to consider a specific functional form such as (11.19). We may assume a more general form given by

$$K_r = Mk[\lambda_r + \eta(1 - \lambda_r)] \tag{11.21}$$

where $k(\cdot)$ is a strictly increasing and convex function, such that

$$k(0) = 0 \quad \text{and} \quad k(1) = 1.$$

Expression (11.21) implies that both regions are in a symmetric relationship in the sense that their own knowledge capital depends only on the distribution of the skilled and not upon their specific attributes. Substituting (11.21) into (11.20) yields the patent production function in region r:

$$m_r = Mk(\lambda_r)\lambda_r \tag{11.22}$$

where k_r is given by (11.21).

The length of patents is assumed to be infinite, and thus a firm that produces a particular variety enjoys a monopoly position forever. This yields the following equation of motion for the number of varieties (or, equivalently, of patents) in the global economy:

$$\dot{M} = m_1 + m_2 = M[\lambda k_1(\lambda) + (1 - \lambda)\, k_2(\lambda)]$$

where $\lambda \equiv \lambda_1$ $(1 - \lambda \equiv \lambda_2)$ and $k_1(\lambda) \equiv k[\lambda + \eta(1 - \lambda)]$ $(k_2(\lambda) \equiv k(1 - \lambda + \eta\lambda))$.

Setting

$$g(\lambda) \equiv \lambda k_1(\lambda) + (1 - \lambda)\, k_2(\lambda)$$

the preceding equation of motion becomes

$$\dot{M} = g(\lambda)M \tag{11.23}$$

where $g(\lambda)$ is the *growth rate* of the number of patents and varieties in the economy when the distribution of skilled workers is λ. The growth rate of the economy thus depends on the knowledge capital of the entire economy as well as on the spatial distribution of the R&D sector.

It can readily be verified that $g(\lambda)$ is symmetric about $1/2$ and such that

$$g(0) = g(1) = 1$$

while, for $\eta < 1$

$$g'(\lambda) \gtreqless 0 \text{ as } \lambda \gtreqless \frac{1}{2} \quad \text{and } g''(\lambda) > 0 \qquad \lambda \in (0, 1).$$

This implies that, for any given $\eta < 1$, the number of varieties grows at an increasing rate when the innovation sector gets more agglomerated in one region, whereas it falls at an increasing rate when this sector gets more dispersed.

When spillovers are global ($\eta = 1$), we have

$$g(\lambda) = 1 \qquad \lambda \in [0, 1]$$

in which case the spatial distribution of the R&D sector does no longer matter. Furthermore, $g(\lambda)$ is shifted upward when η rises and reaches its maximum value when $\eta = 1$. In sum, the growth rate reaches its highest value when the spillovers are global ($\eta = 1$) or when the R&D sector is agglomerated in one region ($\lambda = 1$); it is minimized when both $\eta = 0$ and $\lambda = 1/2$ hold. Hence, the existence of a distance-decay effect in the spatial diffusion of knowledge slows down the growth of the global economy.

We now turn to the formation of wages for the skilled workers. In the patent production function (11.22), each $\mathbb{R}$-firm located in region r takes the local knowledge capital K_r as given because its contribution to this stock is negligible. Hence, from a firm's viewpoint, the marginal productivity of skilled labor in region r is equal to $K_r = Mk_r(\lambda)$, which is here equal to the average productivity of skilled labor. If the wage of a skilled worker is denoted by w_r, then the cost of a new patent in region r is given by

$$w_r / Mk_r(\lambda).$$

Firms enter freely into the R&D sector. Hence, if Π_r denotes the market price of a patent developed in region r, i.e., the asset value of the firm that produces the corresponding variety, the zero-profit condition implies that

$$\Pi_r = w_r / Mk_r(\lambda)$$

and thus

$$w_r^* = \Pi_r Mk_r(\lambda). \qquad (11.24)$$

In addition, free entry in the manufacturing sector implies that Π_r equals the asset value of an $\mathbb{M}$-firm that starts producing a new variety by using a new patent. This value, however, cannot be determined without specifying the conditions that govern the interregional mobility of patents and, therefore, that of the manufacturing firms. These conditions are discussed in the next two sections.

It remains to determine the individual expenditure for each type of worker. We assume that all manufacturing firms at time zero are equally owned by the skilled workers.[4] Hence, the initial endowment of an unskilled is zero. Furthermore, (11.8) implies

$$W(0) = \int_0^\infty e^{-\gamma t} \mathrm{d}t = 1/\gamma.$$

[4] When the $\mathbb{M}$-firms at time 0 are equally owned by both types of workers, our results remain essentially the same.

As a result, the expenditure of an unskilled worker is constant and given by

$$\varepsilon^* = 1. \tag{11.25}$$

On the other hand, for each skilled worker, we have

$$\varepsilon^* = \gamma[A_H + W(0)] \tag{11.26}$$

where the initial endowment A_H of a skilled worker is given by

$$A_H = M_1(0)\Pi_1(0) + M_2(0)\Pi_2(0) \tag{11.27}$$

(recall that the mass of skilled workers is equal to 1) where $M_r(0) \geq 0$ is the initial number of manufacturing firms in region r. The value of $W(0)$ is determined through (11.4) and (11.24) under the specific location path followed by the skilled worker.

11.2.3 Migration Behavior

As in section 8.2.3, the migration cost is given by

$$C_m(t) = \left|\dot{\lambda}(t)\right| / \delta \tag{11.28}$$

where $\dot{\lambda}(t)$ represents the flow of skilled workers moving from one region to the other at time t, while $\delta > 0$ is the speed of adjustment in workers' migration; $\dot{\lambda}(t)$ is positive (negative) when skilled workers move from 2 to 1 (from 1 to 2).

Consider a steady-state equilibrium such as $\tilde{\lambda} \in (0, 1]$. Without loss of generality, let the initial distribution λ_0 of skilled workers be lower than $\tilde{\lambda}$. In this case, the common expectation is that $\tilde{\lambda} - \lambda_0$ skilled workers gradually move from region 2 to region 1. More precisely, $T > 0$ exists such that a flow of skilled workers from 2 to 1 starts at 0 and stops at T. Hence, we have

$$\begin{aligned} &\dot{\lambda}(t) > 0 \qquad t \in (0, T) \\ &\lambda(t) = \tilde{\lambda} \qquad t \geq T. \end{aligned} \tag{11.29}$$

In this case, all the skilled workers residing in region 2 are identical except for their migration time. As a result, we can identify them on the basis of their migration time t: for each $t \in [0, T)$, denote by $W(0;t)$ the lifetime wage of a skilled worker who migrates from 2 to 1 at time t, that is,

$$W(0;t) = \int_0^t e^{-\gamma s} w_2(s) ds + \int_t^\infty e^{-\gamma s} w_1(s) ds. \tag{11.30}$$

Then, using (11.2) and (11.28), the lifetime utility of such a migrant is given by

$$U(0;t) = V(0;t) - e^{-\gamma t}\dot{\lambda}(t)/\delta \tag{11.31}$$

where $V(0;t)$ is the lifetime utility gross of migration costs. Using (11.1) and (11.3), $V(0;t)$ may be determined as follows:

$$V(0;t) = \frac{1}{\gamma}\ln\gamma + \frac{1}{\gamma}\ln[A_H + W(0;t)] \\ -\mu\left[\int_0^t e^{-\gamma s}\ln P_2(s)\mathrm{d}s + \int_t^\infty e^{-\gamma s}\ln P_1(s)\mathrm{d}s\right]. \quad (11.32)$$

Furthermore, since in equilibrium the skilled workers residing in region 2 do not want to delay their migration beyond T (Fukao and Bénabou 1993), it must be that

$$\lim_{t\to T} C_m(t) = 0.$$

Taking the limit of (11.31), we therefore obtain

$$U(0;T) = V(0;T) \\ = \frac{1}{\gamma}\ln\gamma + \frac{1}{\gamma}\ln[A_H + W(0;T)] \\ -\mu\left[\int_0^T e^{-\gamma s}\ln P_2(s)\mathrm{d}s + \int_T^\infty e^{-\gamma s}\ln P_1(s)\mathrm{d}s\right]. \quad (11.33)$$

Because, in equilibrium, all migrants are indifferent about their migration time, it must be that $U(0;t) = U(0;T)$ for all $t \in (0, T)$. Therefore, using (11.31), (11.32), and (11.33), we get

$$\dot{\lambda}(t) = \delta e^{\gamma t}[V(0;t) - V(0;T)] \\ = \frac{\delta}{\gamma}e^{\gamma t}\ln\left[\frac{A_H + W(0;t)}{A_H + W(0;T)}\right] + \delta\mu e^{\gamma t}\int_t^T e^{-\gamma s}\ln\left[\frac{P_2(s)}{P_1(s)}\right]\mathrm{d}s \quad (11.34)$$

for any $t \in (0, T)$. This expression describes the equilibrium migration dynamics of skilled workers under the expectation (11.29).

11.3 AGGLOMERATION AND GROWTH

In this section, we first study the dynamics of the regional and global economy; then, we turn to its welfare implications for the various groups of workers. We consider the case in which the development and production of a variety must occur within the same region; thus, λ describes the share of both the R&D and manufacturing sectors in region 1. We proceed in two steps. In the first one, we characterize the steady-state growth path (in short, the ss-growth path) of the model when the regional share of skilled workers is given. In the second step, we determine which ss-growth path is an equilibrium, which means that the ss-growth path must be migration-proof.

11.3.1 The Growth Dynamics

The number of $\mathbb{M}$-varieties produced in region r at each time t is equal to the cumulative number of patents previously developed in this region. Choose any fixed $\lambda \in [0, 1]$. Thus, using the patent production function (11.22), we get

$$\dot{M}_r(t) = k_r(\lambda)\lambda_r M(t). \tag{11.35}$$

Given (11.23), the total number of patents at time t is such that

$$M(t) = M_0 e^{g(\lambda)t} \tag{11.36}$$

where M_0 is the initial number of patents in the economy. Hence, (11.35) may be rewritten as follows:

$$\dot{M}_r = k_r(\lambda)\,\lambda_r M_0 e^{g(\lambda)t}.$$

Solving this differential equation, we obtain

$$M_r(t) = [M_r(0) - \theta_r(\lambda)\,M_0] + \theta_r(\lambda)\,M_0 e^{g(\lambda)t} \tag{11.37}$$

where

$$\theta_r(\lambda) \equiv \frac{k_r(\lambda)\,\lambda_r}{g(\lambda)}$$

represents the share of region r's contribution to the growth in the total number of patents. Because $\theta_1(\lambda) + \theta_2(\lambda) = 1$, it follows from (11.37) that

$$\lim_{t\to\infty} \frac{M_r(t)}{M(t)} = \theta_r(\lambda) \quad \text{and} \quad \lim_{t\to\infty} \frac{\dot{M}_r(t)}{M_r(t)} = g(\lambda) \tag{11.38}$$

where the convergence process is monotonic.

Because λ is fixed, the growth rate is constant if and only if

$$M_r(0) = \theta_r(\lambda)\,M_0. \tag{11.39}$$

In this case, and only in this case, we have

$$\frac{M_r(t)}{M(t)} = \theta_r(\lambda) \quad \text{and} \quad \frac{\dot{M}_r(t)}{M_r(t)} = g(\lambda) \tag{11.40}$$

so that

$$M_r(t) = \theta_r(\lambda)M(t) = \theta_r(\lambda)\,M_0 e^{g(\lambda)t}. \tag{11.41}$$

In other words, under any fixed $\lambda \in [0, 1]$, there exists an ss-growth path if and only if the initial number of patents in each region is given by (11.39). When (11.39) does not hold, (11.38) implies that the growth path under a fixed λ approaches the corresponding ss-growth path when $t \to \infty$.

11.3.1.1 The ss-Growth Path When Migration Is Not Allowed

Determining the ss-growth paths under a fixed λ requires finding the asset value of a manufacturing firm at time t. Substituting (11.41) into (11.10) and (11.11) yields

$$P_r = \frac{\sigma}{\sigma - 1}\{M[\theta_r(\lambda) + \phi\theta_s(\lambda)]\}^{-1/(\sigma-1)} \tag{11.42}$$

$$q_r^* = \frac{\sigma - 1}{\sigma}\frac{\mu}{M}\left[\frac{E_r}{\theta_r(\lambda) + \phi\theta_s(\lambda)} + \frac{\phi E_s}{\phi\theta_r(\lambda) + \theta_s(\lambda)}\right]. \tag{11.43}$$

It then follows from (11.12) and (11.43) that

$$\begin{aligned}\Pi_r(t) &= \int_t^{\infty} e^{-\gamma(s-t)}\pi_r^*(s)\,\mathrm{d}s \\ &= \frac{\mu}{\sigma[\gamma + g(\lambda)]M(t)}\left[\frac{E_r}{\theta_r(\lambda) + \phi\theta_s(\lambda)} + \frac{\phi E_s}{\phi\theta_r(\lambda) + \theta_s(\lambda)}\right]\end{aligned} \tag{11.44}$$

where, from (11.25) and (11.26), E_r is given by

$$E_r = \frac{L}{2} + \lambda_r\gamma[A_H + W_r(0)] \tag{11.45}$$

which is time-invariant because λ is fixed. Hence, using (11.41) and (11.44), we obtain

$$M_r(t)\,\Pi_r(t) = \frac{\mu}{\sigma}\frac{\theta_r(\lambda)}{\gamma + g(\lambda)}\left[\frac{E_r}{\theta_r(\lambda) + \phi\theta_s(\lambda)} + \frac{\phi E_s}{\phi\theta_r(\lambda) + \theta_s(\lambda)}\right] \tag{11.46}$$

which is also time-invariant.

It remains to determine the equilibrium values of $A_H(\lambda)$ and $W_r(0;\lambda)$ conditional upon λ. Substituting (11.46) into the wage equation (11.27) yields the equilibrium asset value of a skilled $A_H^*(\lambda)$ as a function of λ:

$$A_H^*(\lambda) = \frac{\mu}{\sigma}\frac{E^*}{\gamma + g(\lambda)}. \tag{11.47}$$

Furthermore, plugging (11.40) and (11.46) into (11.24) leads to

$$\begin{aligned}w_r(t) &= \Pi_r(t)M(t)k_r(\lambda) = \Pi_r(t)M_r(t)k_r(\lambda)/\theta_r(\lambda) \\ &= \frac{\mu}{\sigma}\frac{k_r(\lambda)}{\gamma + g(\lambda)}\left[\frac{E_r}{\theta_r(\lambda) + \phi\theta_s(\lambda)} + \frac{\phi E_s}{\phi\theta_r(\lambda) + \theta_s(\lambda)}\right]\end{aligned} \tag{11.48}$$

which is time-invariant. As a result, we have

$$W_r(0;\lambda) = \int_0^\infty e^{-\gamma t} w_r(t)\,dt$$
$$= \frac{\mu}{\sigma}\frac{k_r(\lambda)}{\gamma[\gamma+g(\lambda)]}\left[\frac{E_r}{\theta_r(\lambda)+\phi\theta_s(\lambda)}+\frac{\phi E_s}{\phi\theta_r(\lambda)+\theta_s(\lambda)}\right]. \quad (11.49)$$

Substituting (11.47) and (11.49) into (11.45) yields the total expenditure in each region:

$$E_r = \frac{L}{2}+\frac{\mu}{\sigma}\frac{\lambda_r}{\gamma+g(\lambda)}\left\{\gamma E^* + k_r(\lambda)\left[\frac{E_r}{\theta_r(\lambda)+\phi\theta_s(\lambda)}+\frac{\phi E_s}{\phi\theta_r(\lambda)+\theta_s(\lambda)}\right]\right\}.$$

Solving these two linear equations for E_r and E_s and substituting the solutions into (11.48) yields the equilibrium wage in region r as a sole function of λ:

$$w_r^*(\lambda) = \frac{\mu}{\sigma}\frac{k_r(\lambda)}{\gamma+g(\lambda)}\left[\frac{E_r^*(\lambda)}{\theta_r(\lambda)+\phi\theta_s(\lambda)}+\frac{\phi E_s^*(\lambda)}{\phi\theta_r(\lambda)+\theta_s(\lambda)}\right] \quad (11.50)$$

which gives the equilibrium lifetime wage in region r:

$$W_r^*(0;\lambda) = \frac{w_r^*(\lambda)}{\gamma}. \quad (11.51)$$

In turn, plugging (11.47) and (11.51) into (11.16) yields the equilibrium expenditure of a skilled worker living in region r:

$$\varepsilon_r^H(\lambda) = \gamma[A_H^*(\lambda) + W_r^*(0;\lambda)]. \quad (11.52)$$

11.3.1.2 The ss-Growth Path When Migration Is Allowed

We now determine the equilibrium ss-growth path along which no skilled worker has an incentive to move at any time $t \geq 0$. To achieve this goal, we have to compare not only the ratio of utility levels but also the nominal wage rate and price indices in the two regions. Indeed, if one region has a higher nominal wage rate while the other has a lower price index along an ss-growth path, a skilled worker could improve his intertemporal utility by residing in one region for some period of his life and in the other for the rest of the time.

For any chosen value of λ, applying (11.1) together with the expenditure function (11.52), we can obtain the indirect utility of each skilled worker in region r at time t:

$$v_r(t;\lambda) = \gamma[A_H^*(\lambda) + W_r^*(0;\lambda)][P_r(t)]^{-\mu}. \quad (11.53)$$

Let $p_{1/2}(\lambda)$ be the price index ratio defined by

$$p_{1/2}(\lambda) \equiv \frac{P_1(t)}{P_2(t)} = \left[\frac{\phi\theta_1(\lambda)+\theta_2(\lambda)}{\theta_1(\lambda)+\phi\theta_2(\lambda)}\right]^{1/(\sigma-1)} \quad (11.54)$$

which is time-invariant. Using (11.42), we get

$$\Phi(\lambda) \equiv \frac{v_1(t;\lambda)}{v_2(t;\lambda)} = \frac{A_H^*(\lambda) + W_1^*(0;\lambda)}{A_H^*(\lambda) + W_2^*(0;\lambda)} \left[p_{1/2}(\lambda)\right]^{-\mu}$$

which is time-invariant. Hence, we have

$$V_1(0;\lambda) - V_2(0;\lambda) = \frac{1}{\gamma} \ln \Phi(\lambda)$$

and, hence,

$$V_1(0;\lambda) \gtreqless V_2(0;\lambda) \quad \text{as } \Phi(\lambda) \gtreqless 1.$$

Therefore, for the ss-growth path under a fixed λ to be migration-proof, it must be that $\Phi(\lambda) = 1$ when $\lambda \in (0, 1)$, whereas $\Phi(\lambda) \geq 1$ when $\lambda = 1$. However, for the reasons previously discussed, this necessary condition is not sufficient for an ss-growth path to be migration-proof. To find such a condition, we must consider every possible location path of a skilled worker: let $\varphi(\cdot)$ be a piecewise continuous function on $[0, \infty)$ such that either $\varphi(t) = 1$ or $\varphi(t) = 0$ for each $t \geq 0$, where $\varphi(t) = 1$ means that the skilled worker in question resides in region 1 at time t, whereas $\varphi(t) = 0$ implies that he resides in region 2. Given the ss-growth path under some fixed $\lambda \in [0, 1]$, let $V(\lambda, \varphi(\cdot)) \equiv V(0; \lambda, \varphi(\cdot))$ be the lifetime utility of a skilled worker when he chooses the location path $\varphi(\cdot)$ (a single worker who migrates does not affect the value of λ). Using (11.1), (11.3), and (11.16), we then obtain

$$\begin{aligned} V(\lambda, \varphi(\cdot)) &= \frac{1}{\gamma} \ln \gamma + \frac{1}{\gamma} \ln[A_H^*(\lambda) + W(\lambda, \varphi(\cdot))] \\ &\quad - \mu \left\{ \ln \left[p_{1/2}(\lambda)\right] \int_0^\infty e^{-\gamma t} \varphi(t)\, dt + \int_0^\infty e^{-\gamma t} \ln P_2(t)\, dt \right\} \end{aligned}$$

where the lifetime wage income $W(\lambda, \varphi(\cdot))$ is defined by

$$\begin{aligned} W(\lambda, \varphi(\cdot)) &\equiv W(0; \lambda, \varphi(\cdot)) \\ &= \int_0^\infty e^{-\gamma t} \varphi(t)\, w_1^*(\lambda)\, dt + \int_0^\infty e^{-\gamma t} [1 - \varphi(t)] w_2^*(\lambda)\, dt. \end{aligned}$$

For notational convenience, let

$$\bar{\varphi} \equiv \gamma \int_0^\infty e^{-\gamma t} \varphi(t)\, dt$$

be the amount of "effective time" spent in region 1. Denoting $V(\lambda, \bar{\varphi}) \equiv V(\lambda, \varphi(\cdot))$ and $W(\lambda, \bar{\varphi}) \equiv W(\lambda, \varphi(\cdot))$, we may rewrite these two functions as follows:

$$V(\lambda, \bar{\varphi}) \equiv \frac{1}{\gamma} \ln \gamma + \frac{1}{\gamma} \ln[A^*(\lambda) + W(\lambda, \bar{\varphi})] \\ - \frac{\mu}{\gamma} \bar{\varphi} \ln[p_{1/2}(\lambda)] - \mu \int_0^{\infty} e^{-\gamma t} \ln P_2(t)\, dt \tag{11.55}$$

and

$$W(\lambda, \bar{\varphi}) = \frac{1}{\gamma} [\bar{\varphi} w_1^*(\lambda) + (1 - \bar{\varphi}) w_2^*(\lambda)]. \tag{11.56}$$

Finally, substituting (11.56) into (11.55) yields

$$V(\lambda, \bar{\varphi}) = \frac{1}{\gamma} \ln[\gamma A_H^*(\lambda) + \bar{\varphi} w_1^*(\lambda) + (1 - \bar{\varphi}) w_2^*(\lambda)] \\ - \frac{\mu}{\gamma} \bar{\varphi} \ln[p_{1/2}(\lambda)] - \mu \int_0^{\infty} e^{-\gamma t} \ln P_2(t)\, dt. \tag{11.57}$$

Hence, for a skilled worker, choosing the optimal location path amounts to choosing the proportion of the time to be spent in region 1 that maximizes (11.57).

By definition, we have $0 \leq \bar{\varphi} \leq 1$. Furthermore, $\bar{\varphi} = 1$ if and only if $\varphi(t) = 1$ for all $t \geq 0$; likewise, $\bar{\varphi} = 0$ if and only if $\varphi(t) = 0$ for all $t \geq 0$. Hence, because

$$V_r(0; \lambda) = \int_0^{\infty} e^{-\gamma t} \ln[v_r(t; \lambda)] dt$$

we have $V(\lambda, 1) = V_1(0; \lambda)$ and $V(\lambda, 0) = V_2(0; \lambda)$. Therefore, for any given interior distribution $\lambda \in (0, 1)$, the ss-growth path under λ is migration-proof if and only if

$$V(\lambda, 1) = V(\lambda, 0) = \max_{\bar{\varphi} \in [0,1]} V(\lambda, \bar{\varphi}) \tag{11.58}$$

whereas the ss-growth path under a core–periphery distribution $\lambda = 1$ (say) is migration-proof if and only if

$$V(1, 1) = \max_{\bar{\varphi} \in [0,1]} V(1, \bar{\varphi}). \tag{11.59}$$

In order to find out when condition (11.58) or (11.59) holds, we differentiate twice (11.57) with respect to $\bar{\varphi}$:

$$\frac{\partial V(\lambda, \bar{\varphi})}{\partial \bar{\varphi}} = \frac{1}{\gamma} \frac{w_1^*(\lambda) - w_2^*(\lambda)}{\gamma A_H^*(\lambda) + \bar{\varphi} w_1^*(\lambda) + (1 - \bar{\varphi}) w_2^*(\lambda)} - \frac{\mu}{\gamma} \ln[p_{1/2}(\lambda)] \tag{11.60}$$

and

$$\frac{\partial^2 V(\lambda,\bar{\varphi})}{\partial\bar{\varphi}^2} = -\frac{1}{\gamma}\frac{[w_1^*(\lambda) - w_2^*(\lambda)]^2}{[\gamma A_H^*(\lambda) + \bar{\varphi}w_1^*(\lambda) + (1-\bar{\varphi})w_2^*(\lambda)]^2} \leq 0. \quad (11.61)$$

Let us first examine the case of an interior ss-growth path. Given any $\lambda \in (0, 1)$, it must be that $V(\lambda, \cdot)$ is not strictly concave on $[0, 1]$ for (11.58) to hold. Given (11.61), this is so only when

$$w_1^*(\lambda) = w_2^*(\lambda)$$

which implies that $V(\lambda, \cdot)$ is constant on $[0, 1]$. This, in turn, means that (11.58) holds if and only if (11.60) is zero on $[0, 1]$, thus implying that

$$p_{1/2}(\lambda) = 1 \quad (11.62)$$

namely, the two regions have the same price index. It is readily verified that (11.62) holds if and only if $\lambda = 1/2$. We may thus conclude as follows:

Proposition 11.1. *Any interior equilibrium ss-growth path is symmetric.*

In short, when $\lambda \neq 1/2$ and $V(\lambda, 0) = V(\lambda, 1)$, the wage rate is higher in one region while the price index is lower in the other region. In this case, skilled workers are able to increase their lifetime utility by "changing places" (formally, they "convexify" their location choices) rather than staying put forever. Such an incentive to change places arises not only from the forward-looking behavior of workers, but also from the presence of saving opportunities, which lead to the averaging of consumption expenditures over time as expressed in (11.16).

Next, we come to the study of the ss-growth path under $\lambda = 1$ (i.e., a core–periphery configuration). Since (11.61) implies that $V(1, \bar{\varphi})$ is concave on $[0, 1]$, (11.59) holds if and only if

$$\left.\frac{\partial V(1,\bar{\varphi})}{\partial\bar{\varphi}}\right|_{\bar{\varphi}=1} \geq 0$$

or, using (11.60), if and only if

$$\frac{w_1^*(1) - w_2^*(1)}{\gamma A_H^*(1) + w_1^*(1)} \geq \mu \ln[p_{1/2}(1)]. \quad (11.63)$$

Note that when $\lambda = 1$, we have

$$\theta_1(1) = 1 \qquad \theta_2(1) = 0 \qquad g(1) = 1 \qquad k_1(1) = 1 \qquad k_2(1) = k(\eta).$$

Hence, using (11.47), (11.50), (11.54), and the equilibrium regional expenditures when $\lambda = 1$ ($E_1^* = L/2 + \mu L/(\sigma - \mu)$ and $E_2^* = L/2$), we obtain

$$w_1^*(1) = A_H^*(1)$$

$$w_2^*(1) = A_H^*(1)k(\eta)[(\sigma + \mu)\phi + (\sigma - \mu)\phi^{-1}]/2\sigma$$

$$p_{1/2}(1) = \phi^{1/(\sigma-1)}.$$

Substituting these expression into (11.63) yields

$$\frac{1 - [k(\eta)/2\sigma]\,[(\sigma + \mu)\phi + (\sigma - \mu)\phi^{-1}]}{\gamma + 1} \geq \frac{\mu}{\sigma - 1} \ln \phi$$

or, equivalently,

$$\Gamma(\phi) \equiv 1 - k(\eta)\left[\frac{1 + \mu/\sigma}{2}\phi + \frac{1 - \mu/\sigma}{2}\phi^{-1}\right] + \frac{\mu(\gamma + 1)}{\sigma - 1} \ln \phi^{-1} \geq 0. \tag{11.64}$$

The existence of knowledge-spillovers implies $\eta > 0$ and, hence, $k(\eta) > 0$. Under these circumstances, it is readily verified that $\Gamma'(\phi) = 0$ has a unique solution $\bar{\phi}_s$ belonging to (0, 1). Because $\Gamma(0) = -\infty$ and $\Gamma(1) > 0$, we have $\Gamma(\phi) > 0$ for $\phi \in (\bar{\phi}_s, 1)$ while $\Gamma(\phi) < 0$ for $\phi < \bar{\phi}_s$. Thus, we may conclude as follows:

Proposition 11.2. *There always exists a unique sustain point, $\bar{\phi}_s < 1$, such that the ss-growth path under a core–periphery structure is an equilibrium if and only if $\phi \geq \bar{\phi}_s$.*

This result is similar to what we have obtained in Section 8.2.3, namely the R&D and manufacturing sectors are agglomerated provided that transport costs are low enough. By contrast, the symmetric ss-growth path is an equilibrium under any transport cost value. Observe also that $k(\eta)$ increases with η. It then follows from (11.64) that

$$\frac{d\bar{\phi}_s}{d\eta} > 0.$$

In other words, when the spatial extent of the spillover widens, the disadvantage of the periphery in R&D is reduced and, accordingly, the core–periphery structure is sustainable for a narrower range of transport costs.

Note, finally, that the self-fulfilling nature of the migration process makes the concept of stability more difficult to define. Indeed, the model may yield several perfect-foresight solutions under the same initial distribution of skilled labor. Consequently, for a given ss-growth path under $\lambda \in \{0, 1/2, 1\}$, a neighborhood Λ of λ may exist such that, for each $\lambda_0 \in \Lambda$, an equilibrium path based on a certain expectation converges to this ss-growth path, whereas another equilibrium path based on another expectation diverges from the same ss-growth path. In this case, is the ss-growth path stable or unstable? A natural way to escape from such a difficulty is to impose a priori some plausible restriction on the expectations that must be satisfied when an equilibrium path converges to the ss-growth path in question. Because there is perfect foresight, this is equivalent to imposing a restriction on the equilibrium path itself. Fujita and Thisse (2003) have suggested a simple condition that is in the spirit of (11.29): let $\tilde{\lambda} \in [0, 1]$ and $\lambda_0 \in [0, 1]$ such that $\lambda_0 \neq \tilde{\lambda}$. If $\lambda(t)$ is an equilibrium path satisfying the initial condition $\lambda(0) = \lambda_0$, this path satisfies the *monotonic convergence hypothesis under* $\tilde{\lambda}$ when there exists $0 < T \leq \infty$ such that

$$\text{when } \lambda_0 < \tilde{\lambda} \quad \begin{array}{ll} \dot{\lambda}(t) > 0 & \text{for } t \in (0, T) \\ \lambda(t) = \tilde{\lambda} & \text{for } t \geq T \end{array}$$

$$\text{when } \lambda_0 > \tilde{\lambda} \quad \begin{array}{ll} \dot{\lambda}(t) < 0 & \text{for } t \in (0, T) \\ \lambda(t) = \tilde{\lambda} & \text{for } t \geq T. \end{array}$$

Then, the ss-growth path under $\tilde{\lambda}$ is said to be stable if there exists a neighborhood Λ of $\tilde{\lambda}$ such that, for any $\lambda_0 \in \Lambda$ with $\lambda_0 \neq \tilde{\lambda}$, there exists an equilibrium path that satisfies the monotonic convergence hypothesis under $\tilde{\lambda}$. Otherwise, the ss-growth path is said to be unstable.

Under these circumstances, whenever $\phi \geq \bar{\phi}_s$, the ss-growth path under the core–periphery structure can be shown to be stable. By contrast, the stability analysis of the symmetric ss-growth path is much more involved. For example, if

$$\frac{\mu}{\sigma - 1}\left(1 + \frac{\gamma}{g(1/2)}\right) \geq 1$$

the symmetric ss-growth path is unstable regardless of the level of transport costs. In this case, if the ss-growth path under a core–periphery structure is not an equilibrium, there exists a path along which the cross-migration of skilled workers occurs cyclically even though the overall distribution of skilled workers is constant over time.

Before proceeding, one may wonder what the previous results become in the opposite case, that is, where patents can be transferred costlessly between regions. In this event, the agglomeration forces generated within the R&D sector turn out to be so strong that this sector is always concentrated into a single region. In addition, the manufacturing sector is partially (fully) agglomerated in the same region as the R&D sector when shipment costs are high (low). The reader is referred to Fujita and Thisse (2003) for more details.

11.3.2 Should We Mind the Gap?

The foregoing analysis shows that the pace of growth is faster when agglomeration arises. It is therefore tempting to conclude that there is a conflict between economic growth and spatial equity because the peripheral region would be a loser when growth is boosted by the agglomeration of mobile activities. This would be so in a zero-sum game, but ours is not. Quite the contrary. As we see, there might be only gainers in our game, although some regions would gain more than others. This is because global growth may be strong enough for everybody, including the unskilled who live in the peripheral region, to be better off.

To study the main aspects of the trade-off between growth and equity, we compare the following two equilibrium configurations: dispersion ($\lambda = 1/2$) and the core-periphery structure ($\lambda = 1$). From the spatial equity standpoint, dispersion is the best possible outcome because both types of workers reach respectively the same utility level regardless of the region in which they live. Although this outcome can be unstable, one could imagine enforcing it by controlling the mobility of the skilled.

Consider now the core–periphery structure ($\lambda = 1$). There are three groups of individuals to consider: the unskilled residing in regions 1 and 2, respectively, as well as the skilled. For the unskilled, since $w_r^L = \varepsilon_r^L = 1$ for $r = 1, 2$, (11.1) becomes

$$v_r^L(t; \lambda) = [P_r(t)]^{-\mu}.$$

Using (11.10) and (11.41) implies

$$\frac{v_1^L(t;1)}{v_1^L(t;1/2)} = \left(\frac{2}{1+\phi}\right)^{\mu/(\sigma-1)} \exp\left\{\frac{\mu}{\sigma-1}\left[1-k\left(\frac{1+\eta}{2}\right)\right]t\right\}$$

which always exceeds 1 because $k \leq 1$. Hence,

$$V_1^L(0;1) - V_1^L(0;1/2) = \frac{\mu}{\gamma(\sigma-1)}\left[\frac{1-k\left(\frac{1+\eta}{2}\right)}{\gamma} + \ln\left(\frac{2}{1+\phi}\right)\right] > 0$$

because $k \leq 1$ and $\phi < 1$. Thus, the unskilled residing in the core region always prefer agglomeration to dispersion.

Regarding the unskilled living in the periphery, we have

$$\frac{v_2^L(t;1)}{v_2^L(t;1/2)} = \left(\frac{1+\phi}{2\phi}\right)^{-\mu/(\sigma-1)} \exp\left\{\frac{\mu}{\sigma-1}\left[1-k\left(\frac{1+\eta}{2}\right)\right]t\right\}$$

so that

$$V_2^L(0;1) - V_2^L(0;1/2) = \frac{\mu}{\gamma(\sigma-1)}\left[\frac{1-k\left(\frac{1+\eta}{2}\right)}{\gamma} - \ln\left(\frac{1+\phi}{2\phi}\right)\right].$$

The first term inside the brackets stands for the *growth effect* associated with the agglomeration of the R&D sector. More precisely, given that $g(1) = k(1) = 1$ and $g(1/2) = k[(1+\eta)/2]$, the numerator of the first term represents the increase in the growth rate of varieties in the economy due to the R&D sector agglomeration into the core region; thus, the first term represents the lifetime impact of agglomeration on consumers' welfare. It is strictly positive if and only if $\eta < 1$, that is, spillovers are not global. The second term represents the disadvantage of being located in the peripheral region, which is measured by the relative increase in the price index of the manufactured good in region 2.

Clearly, the unskilled living in the periphery prefer agglomeration to dispersion if and only if

$$\frac{1-k\left(\frac{1+\eta}{2}\right)}{\gamma} > \ln\left(\frac{1+\phi}{2\phi}\right)$$

namely, when the extra growth boosted by agglomerating the R&D sector in one region is sufficiently large. Thus, *the unskilled residing in the lagging region prefer a core–periphery structure to a dispersed one when the former leads to a sufficiently high rate of growth in the global economy*. This is the more likely, the lower the discount rate (γ), the weaker the spillover effect (η), and the lower the transport costs.

It remains to consider the skilled workers. Using (11.47), (11.50), (11.51), and (11.53), we obtain

$$\frac{v_1^H(t;1)}{v_1^H(t;1/2)} = \frac{v_1^L(t;1)}{v_1^L(t;1/2)}$$

and thus

$$V_1^H(0;1) - V_1^H(0;1/2) = V_1^L(0;1) - V_1^L(0;1/2)$$
$$= \frac{\mu}{\gamma(\sigma-1)}\left[\frac{1-k\left(\frac{1+\eta}{2}\right)}{\gamma} + \ln\left(\frac{2}{1+\phi}\right)\right] > 0.$$

Hence, when the skilled are agglomerated in the core, their well-being increases by the same amount as the unskilled residing in the core.

Summarizing the preceding results, we may conclude as follows.

Proposition 11.3. *The welfare levels of the three groups of workers under the core–periphery growth path Pareto-dominates the symmetric growth path if* *and only if the inequality*

$$\frac{1 - k\left(\frac{1+\eta}{2}\right)}{\gamma} > \ln\left(\frac{1+\phi}{2\phi}\right)$$

holds.

This configuration implies the existence of a welfare gap between the unskilled located in the core and the periphery. Indeed, when $\lambda = 1$, we have

$$\frac{v_1^L(t;1)}{v_2^L(t;1)} = \phi^{-\mu/(\sigma-1)} = \tau^{\mu}$$

and thus the welfare gap is

$$V_1^L(0;1) - V_2^L(0;1) = \frac{\mu}{\gamma}\ln\tau > 0.$$

Hence, *a high growth rate generates inequalities among the unskilled workers* who are treated differently according to the region in which they live. Note that the welfare gap widens as the manufactured good gets more differentiated and more difficult to transport.

11.4 GLOBALIZATION AND OFFSHORING

Following Caves (1971), it is common to distinguish between horizontal and vertical outward investments. Firms undertake *horizontal* investment when several plants produce the same good at different locations. The cost of being a horizontal multinational firm is the loss in the returns to scale economies, whereas the benefit is direct access to each market. By contrast, the investment is *vertical* when the firm organizes and performs discrete activities in distinct locations, which altogether form a supply chain starting at the conception of the product and ending at its delivery. The spatial fragmentation of production aims to take advantage of differences in technologies, factor endowments, or factor prices across space. Therefore, horizontal and vertical models should not be viewed as competitors because they address different issues (Navaretti and Venables 2004). In what follows, we study vertical investment through the geographical fragmentation of the supply chain.

The economy is made of two countries, 1 and 2, two production factors, the high-skilled and low-skilled workers, and two sectors, the manufacturing and agricultural sectors. The manufacturing sector produces a horizontally differentiated product under increasing returns. Each variety is produced by a single firm, which is made of two distinct units, a *headquarters* (HQ) and a production *plant*. HQs use skilled labor to produce services that are firm-specific assets à la Williamson, whereas plants use HQ-services and unskilled workers to produce the variety. The HQ and production facility of a firm need not be located together. When both are located in the same country, the firm is *national* (or geographically integrated); when they are not, the firm is *multinational* (or geographically disintegrated). Hence, the spatial fragmentation of the firm (if any) is only vertical. Shipping the output of the manufactured sector is described by an iceberg cost $\tau_M > 1$. Each manufacturer weighs the cost of offshoring the production of its product against the cost saving from producing abroad.

The agricultural sector produces a homogeneous good under constant returns, using unskilled labor as the only input. One unit of output requires $a_r \geq 1$ units of unskilled labor in country r. Without loss of generality, we set $a_1 = 1$ and $a_2 \geq 1$, thus allowing unskilled workers in the agricultural sector to be more productive in country 1 than in country 2. More generally, this assumption aims to reflect the productivity difference between the two countries. Let L_1 and L_2 be the number of unskilled workers in countries 1 and 2. For the standard assumption of symmetry between the two countries to hold, the spatial distribution of unskilled workers is such that both countries have the same amount of efficiency units of unskilled labor, which is normalized to $1/2$:

$$L_1 = \frac{L_2}{a_2} = \frac{1}{2}. \tag{11.65}$$

The output of the agricultural sector is costlessly traded between any two regions, and thus its price is the same in the two regions. It is chosen as the numéraire so that $p^{\mathbb{A}} = 1$. The expenditure share on the agricultural good is sufficiently large for this good to be always produced in both countries. In this case, the equilibrium wages of the unskilled are:

$$w_1^L = 1 \quad \text{and} \quad w_2^L = \frac{1}{a_2} \leq 1. \tag{11.66}$$

Thus, there is a factor-price motive that may explain spatial fragmentation. However, we see that factor price differential is not sufficient to trigger the multinationalization of firms.

Though firms are assumed to be vertically integrated, they may be geographically disintegrated. This is to be contrasted with the pattern studied in Section 8.5 where vertically related parties are independent but located together. Because HQs benefit from a wide range of agglomeration economies (Davis and Henderson 2008), one of the most commonly observed patterns of cross-border fragmentation of the supply chain is the one where a certain number of firms *offshore* their production activities in low-wage countries (here country 2), while keeping their strategic functions (e.g., management, R&D, marketing, and finance) concentrated in a few affluent urban regions where the high-skilled workers and specialized services they need are available (here country 1). For this to happen, skilled workers are to be located in country 1. As a consequence, this country may be viewed as the core of the global economy and country 2 as its periphery.[5]

The setting of a HQ requires a fixed amount f of skilled labor. Because each firm has a HQ, the total number of firms in the economy is given by $m = 1/f$, where the mass of skilled workers is normalized to 1. Production plants operate under constant returns.[6] To be precise, when a firm's plant is located in country r, producing q units requires l_r units of unskilled labor:

$$l_r = c_r q \qquad r = 1, 2$$

where $c_r > 0$ is the plant's marginal labor requirement in unskilled labor. The value of c_r decreases with the effectiveness of the services provided by the HQ to its plant. In particular, it is negatively affected by the distance between the HQ and its plant because the relevant information need not be codifiable, more uncertainty about the plant's local environment is associated with conducting a business at a distance, or both. In addition, it is easier to monitor the effort of the plant manager when the plant is located near the HQ than across borders. All of this implies higher coordination costs, hence higher communication costs, between the HQ and its plant.

When the plant is located in country 1 with its HQ, we have

$$c_1 = 1$$

whereas, when the plant is located in country 2, the unit requirement is given by

$$c_2 = \tau_C > 1$$

which accounts for all the impediments to communication within the firm.[7] This specification has two important implications. First, for the reasons previously explained the physical separation of HQs and plants generates an additional cost borne by firms. In other words, operating a foreign plant is more costly than a home plant. Second, as long as the supply of HQ-services is the same, unskilled workers are equally productive in home and foreign plants. This is because firms are able to organize their production in the same way whatever the plant's location.[8]

[5] In Krugman and Venables (10995) and in Section 8.6, labor is immobile whereas firms belonging to the intermediate and final sectors are mobile. Here, labor is immobile whereas production plants are mobile.

[6] Note that the model can be extended to account for country-specific fixed production costs f_1 and f_2. It can be shown that more (fewer) firms choose to become multinational when $f_1 > f_2$ ($f_1 < f_2$).

[7] The model could be extended to cope with differentiated HQ-services that can be transferred at different cost, maybe because they are characterized by different degrees of complexity.

[8] Thus, firms are a priori identical. Alternatively, we could assume that they are heterogeneous. We prefer to work with homogeneous firms because it is less clear that such firms choose to operate under different organizational forms.

When all firms are national, country 1 exports the manufactured good while country 2 exports the agricultural good, as in the CP model. When all firms are multinational, there is intrafirm trade from country 1 to country 2, while the latter exports the manufactured good to the former; which country exports the agricultural good depends on the relative values of these two types of exports. In between these two extreme cases, the trade pattern is very rich as it involves *all* types of trade, i.e., intra-industry trade, intrafirm trade, and intersectoral trade.

Let w_1 be the wage earned by skilled workers in country 1. Then, (11.65) and (11.66) imply that national incomes are such that

$$Y_1 = w_1 + \frac{1}{2} \quad \text{and} \quad Y_2 = \frac{1}{2}. \tag{11.67}$$

Thus, country 1 is richer than country 2, which means that the global economy displays a core–periphery structure. Replacing E_1 and E_2 with Y_1 and Y_2 in (11.9), the total demand for a variety produced in country r is given by

$$q_r = \mu Y_r p_r^{-\sigma} P_r^{\sigma-1} + \mu\phi_M Y_s p_s^{-\sigma} P_s^{\sigma-1}$$

where P_r (P_s) stands for the price index of the manufactured good in country r (s), while

$$\phi_M \equiv \tau_M^{-(\sigma-1)}.$$

The profit of a national firm located in country 1 is as follows:

$$\pi_{11} = p_1 q_1 - w_1 f - q_1$$

and thus the equilibrium price charged by such a firm is

$$p_1^* = \frac{\sigma}{\sigma - 1}. \tag{11.68}$$

Similarly, the profit of a multinational firm that has a HQ in country 1 and a plant in country 2 is:

$$\pi_{12} = p_2 q_2 - w_1 f - \frac{\tau_C}{a_2} q_2$$

so that the equilibrium mill price charged by the plant located in country 2 is

$$p_2^* = \frac{\sigma}{\sigma - 1} \frac{\tau_C}{a_2}. \tag{11.69}$$

Comparing (11.68) with (11.69) reveals that the equilibrium prices of the same variety produced in either of the two countries differ not only because of the wage differential for the unskilled workers, but also because of the higher communication costs (τ_C) of the HQ-services that a firm must incur when it decentralizes its production.

Let θ be the share of national firms. It is readily verified that the equilibrium price indices in countries 1 and 2 are given by

$$P_1^* = \frac{\sigma}{\sigma - 1} m^{-1/(\sigma-1)} [\theta + (1-\theta)\phi_C \phi_M]^{-1/(\sigma-1)} \tag{11.70}$$

$$P_2^* = \frac{\sigma}{\sigma - 1} m^{-1/(\sigma-1)} [\theta \phi_M + (1-\theta)\phi_C]^{-1/(\sigma-1)} \tag{11.71}$$

where

$$\phi_C \equiv \left(\frac{\tau_C}{a_2}\right)^{-(\sigma-1)} \tag{11.72}$$

with ϕ_C varying from 0 (prohibitive communication costs) to $a_2^{\sigma-1} > 1$ (zero communication costs) for a fixed value of $a_2 > 1$. Hence, ϕ_C accounts for two different effects, namely the factor price difference and the intrafirm communication costs. This parameter may be interpreted as an index that captures both the impediments to and the advantages of offshoring production. Observe that w_2^L must be sufficiently small for ϕ_C to exceed 1. When $w_1^L = w_2^L$, ϕ_C is always smaller than 1.

For a given distribution of plants θ between the two countries, the equilibrium profits may be obtained as follows:

$$\pi_{11}^* = \frac{\mu f}{\sigma} \left[\frac{w_1 + L/2}{\theta + (1-\theta)\phi_C \phi_M} + \frac{L/2}{\theta + (1-\theta)\phi_C \phi_M^{-1}} \right] - w_1 f \tag{11.73}$$

$$\pi_{12}^* = \frac{\mu f}{\sigma} \left[\frac{w_1 + L/2}{\theta \phi_C^{-1} \phi_M^{-1} + (1-\theta)} + \frac{L/2}{\theta \phi_C^{-1} \phi_M + (1-\theta)} \right] - w_1 f. \tag{11.74}$$

The zero-profit condition is given by

$$\max \left\{ \pi_{11}^*, \pi_{12}^* \right\} = 0.$$

Hence, the wage paid to skilled workers stems from the operating profits earned by plants. The spatial fragmentation of the firm therefore gives rise to an international transfer of profits from the periphery to the core.

We start by describing the mixed configuration involving both national and multinational firms ($0 < \theta^* < 1$). The cases in which all firms are national or multinational may then be treated as two limiting cases (see Section 6.3 for a similar approach in a different context). For a mixed configuration to be an equilibrium both national and multinational firms must earn zero profits, that is, $\pi_{11}^* = \pi_{12}^* = 0$. For any $\theta \in (0, 1)$, the condition $\pi_{11}^* = 0$ yields:

$$w_1 = \frac{\mu}{\sigma} \frac{\theta + (1-\theta)\phi_C(\phi_M + \phi^{-1})/2}{[\theta + (1-\theta)\phi_C\phi_M - \mu/\sigma][\theta + (1-\theta)\phi_C\phi_M^{-1}]} \tag{11.75}$$

whereas the condition $\pi_{11}^* = \pi_{12}^*$ leads to

$$2w_1 + 1 = \frac{\phi_C\phi_M^{-1} - 1}{1 - \phi_C\phi_M} \cdot \frac{\theta + (1-\theta)\phi_C\phi_M}{\theta + (1-\theta)\phi_C\phi_M^{-1}}. \tag{11.76}$$

Substituting (11.75) into (11.76) and solving for θ, we obtain

$$\theta(\phi_C, \phi_M) \equiv \frac{\frac{1+\mu/\sigma}{2}\phi_M^{-1} + \frac{1-\mu/\sigma}{2}\phi_M - \phi_C}{\phi_M^{-1} + \phi_M - (\phi_C^{-1} + \phi_C)} \tag{11.77}$$

which is well defined provided that the denominator is nonzero. Under these circumstances, (11.77) describes the share of firms that are national when transport and communication costs are given by ϕ_M and ϕ_C. Although they are a priori identical, firms choose to conduct their business in different ways. As a consequence, the organizational heterogeneity that characterizes many industries does not require the ex ante heterogeneity of firms' productivity.

Fujita and Thisse (2006) show how the positive quadrant of the plane (ϕ_M, ϕ_C) can be partitioned in three domains each corresponding to one type of equilibrium. In the lower-right corner of Figure 11.1, communication costs are high enough for all firms to be national, whereas, in the upper-right corner, communication costs are sufficiently low for all firms to be multinational. Between them, both *national and multinational firms coexist.* By offshoring their production, the multinationals become more competitive than the nationals in the periphery because they supply this market at a lower production cost and zero transport costs. However, not all firms choose to be multinational because the national firms can supply the larger market, i.e., the core, without bearing transport and communication costs. Put differently, a certain number of firms choose to become multinational as offshoring allows production to be split between different countries, which in turn relaxes competition. This is in accordance with the principle of differentiation discussed in Section 7.3. Firms will adopt the same mode of operation only in fairly extreme cases in which there exists a unique dominant strategy.

Thus, contrary to general belief, there is no need to assume productivity differences for firms to adopt different modes of organization. A clarifying point is in order, however. That firms are heterogeneous in productivity is an unquestionable fact. Though we would be the last to claim that heterogeneity does not matter for the study of trade, it is our contention that a lot may be learned without appealing to this fact. Evidently, in empirical studies, accounting for productivity differences is critical.

The two lines separating the corner domains ($\theta^* = 0$ and $\theta^* = 1$) from the interior one ($0 < \theta^* < 1$) are obtained by solving the equations $\theta(\phi_C, \phi_M) = 0$

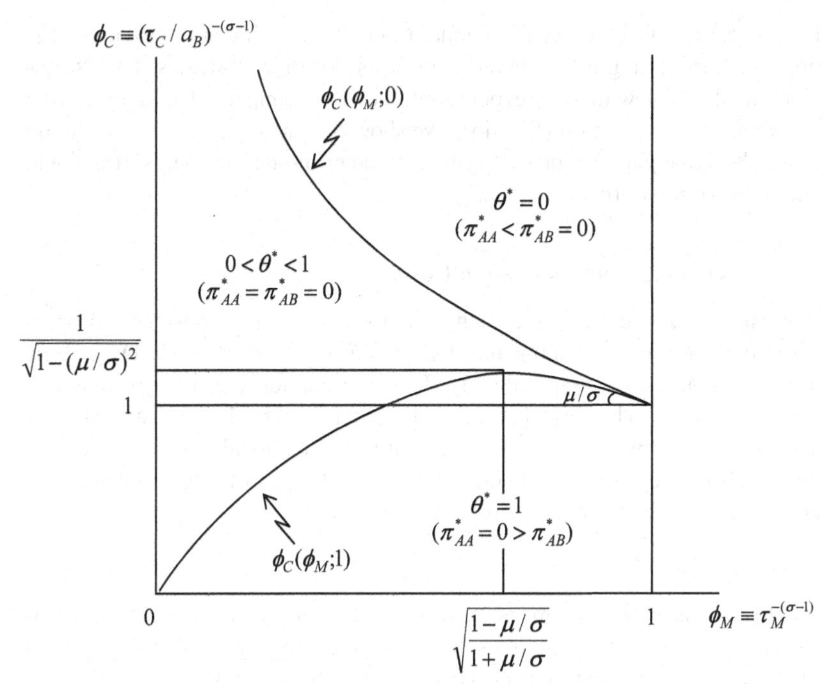

Figure 11.1. The parameter domains of plant distributions.

and $\theta(\phi_C, \phi_M) = 1$ with respect to ϕ_C:

$$\phi_C(\phi_M; \theta = 0) = \frac{1+\mu/\sigma}{2}\phi_M^{-1} + \frac{1-\mu/\sigma}{2}\phi_M$$

$$\phi_C(\phi_M; \theta = 1) = \left(\frac{1-\mu/\sigma}{2}\phi_M^{-1} + \frac{1+\mu/\sigma}{2}\phi_M\right)^{-1}.$$

The previous discussion suggests that the industrial structure of a given area may take the form of either many specialized firms or of a small number of vertically integrated firms (McLaren 2000). Inasmuch as transport and communication costs correspond to a particular type of transaction cost, globalization should be accompanied with a move toward more offshoring and less spatial integration. Because firms tend to relocate or offshore a great deal of intermediate activities and to concentrate on their core competencies, the local supply of specialized business services becomes more important to them, thus making this trend relevant for the industrial structure of cities.

11.5 THE SPATIAL FRAGMENTATION OF THE FIRM

In this section, we consider the standard thought experiment of NEG, i.e., the impact of decreasing transport costs on firms' location strategies. This is supplemented by a new thought experiment, that is, the impact of communication costs on firms' multinationalization. We show that the level of communication costs, the wage gap, or both are critical in determining the shares of national and multinational firms.

11.5.1 Reducing Communication Costs

Assume that ϕ_C and ϕ_M are such that $0 < \theta^* < 1$ and consider a drop in communication costs. Taking the distribution of plants $\theta^* \in (0, 1)$ as fixed, the rise in ϕ_C has a simple direct effect: multinational firms now charge a lower price (11.69) because their marginal cost is lower, whereas national firms stick to the same price (11.68). Consequently, multinational firms increase their market share in each country at the expense of national firms. Profits being zero before the drop in communication costs, this implies

$$\pi^*_{11} < 0 < \pi^*_{12}.$$

In other words, national firms now make negative profits, whereas multinationals earn positive profits. Moving some plants into country 2 restores the profits of the national firms but reduces those of the multinationals:

$$\frac{\partial \pi^*_{11}}{\partial \theta} < 0 \quad \text{and} \quad \frac{\partial \pi^*_{12}}{\partial \theta} > 0.$$

Indeed, national firms increase their profits when there are fewer of them because competition is softened in the core, thus firms that remain national have higher demands in the core, hence higher profits. Similarly, multinational firms' profits decrease when more firms are fragmented because competition in the periphery is tougher, and thus multinationals have a lower demand therein, hence lower profits. As a result, for any given value of ϕ_M *reducing communication costs leads to a gradual increase in the share of plants located in the periphery* (Fujita and Thisse 2006).

As shown by panel A of Figure 11.2, when communication costs are sufficiently high, all plants are set up in the core. However, steadily decreasing communication costs trigger the gradual relocation of plants into the periphery where they can produce at a lower unit cost. This process is progressive because the population size of country 2 does not change. Eventually, very low communication costs magnifies the wage gap, and all plants end up being located in the periphery. As shown by Figure 11.2, the domain in which $\theta^* = 0$ is a subset of $\{0 < \phi_M < 1; 1 < \phi_C < a_2^{\sigma-1}\}$, and thus the agglomeration of plants in the periphery occurs only if there exists a wage gap.

The following proposition comprises a summary.

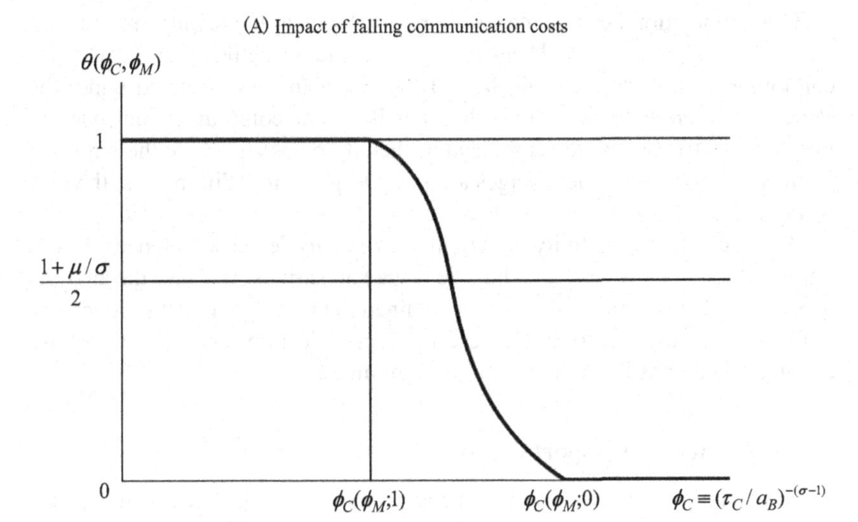

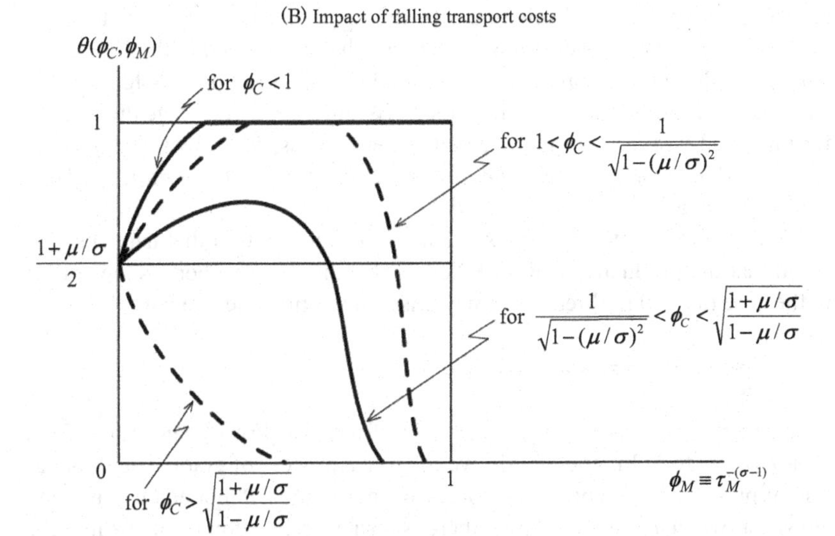

Figure 11.2. Impact of falling communication and transportation costs on plant distribution.

Proposition 11.4. *Consider any given positive value of transport costs. When communication costs are sufficiently high, all plants are located with their headquarters. When these costs become sufficiently low, the share of plants located in the core starts decreasing. If communication costs keep decreasing, the relocation process goes on monotonically until all firms are multinational.*

This proposition bears some strong resemblance to the results presented in Section 6.6. There, front and back offices are located together at the CBD when communication costs are high; here, HQs and plants are grouped under the same roof when these costs are high. Likewise, when communication costs are low, some activities are decentralized to the city outskirts where the land rent is low or to countries where wages are low. Despite some differences, the idea is the same.

If country 2's productivity in agriculture rises, a_2 decreases. Hence, (11.66) implies that w_2^L increases, and thus the wage gap shrinks. Because the analysis in Section 11.4 depends only upon ϕ_C defined in (11.72), a higher productivity is formally equivalent to an increase in communication costs. In either case country 2 becomes less attractive to foreign investors.

11.5.2 Reducing Transport Costs

The impact of a decrease in transport costs is more involved because it depends on the value of communication costs in a nonlinear way. The various cases are depicted in panel B of Figure 11.2. When $\phi_C < 1$, it is readily verified that reducing transport costs leads to a growing agglomeration of plants together with their HQs. This result is reminiscent of what is obtained in the CP model, but the agglomeration process is now gradual (see the upper bold curve in panel B of Figure 11.2 for an illustration). When $a_2 = 1$ (no wage differential for unskilled workers), it must be that $\phi_C < 1$. Thus, *in the absence of wage differential, economic integration always fosters the agglomeration of plants within the core.*

Things become more complex when $\phi_C > 1$, a situation that happens provided that the productivity of unskilled workers in the periphery is lower than in the core ($a_2 > 1$). Three cases may arise. In the first one, we have

$$1 < \phi_C < \frac{1}{\sqrt{1 - (\mu/\sigma)^2}}.$$

When transport costs decrease, the share of national firms keeps rising from $(1 + \mu/\sigma)/2$ to 1. In other words, we observe a process of gradual agglomeration of plants into the core as the forces at work in the CP model are dominant. However, when ϕ_M is very large, there is a sharp relocation of plants into the periphery as the ϕ_C-domain over which transition occurs is very small (see the upper broken curve in panel B of Figure 11.2). This is because transport costs become so low that it is optimal for the firms to take advantage of the lower wage prevailing in country 2 by locating there.

In the second case, we have

$$\frac{1}{\sqrt{1 - (\mu/\sigma)^2}} < \phi_C < \sqrt{\frac{1 + \mu/\sigma}{1 - \mu/\sigma}}.$$

Again, as transport costs decrease, plants progressively agglomerate in country 1 until θ reaches the value for which $\phi_C[\phi_M(\theta);\theta] = \phi_C$ holds. However, further decreases in transport costs now lead to a gradual fall in the plant share in the core until all plants are established in the periphery (see the lower bold curve in panel B of Figure 11.2). In the third case, we have

$$[(1+\mu/\sigma)/(1-\mu/\sigma)]^{1/2} < \phi_C.$$

Then, when transport costs are prohibitive, the mass of plants concentrated in 1 is just equal to $(1+\mu/\sigma)/2$. As transport costs start falling, more and more plants set up in the periphery until they are all clustered there, i.e., when ϕ_M hits the horizontal axis (see the lower broken curve in panel B of Figure 11.2).

These results may be summarized as follows.

Proposition 11.5. *When $\phi_C \geq 1$, a steady decrease in transport costs leads to a gradual agglomeration of plants in the core. When $\phi_C < 1$, two subcases may arise. If ϕ_C is not too small, a steady decrease in transport costs leads, first, to a gradual agglomeration of plants in the core and, then, to a relocation of plants into the periphery. If ϕ_C is sufficiently small, reducing transport costs triggers immediately the relocation process of plants into the periphery.*

Thus, once we account for the existence of communication costs, market integration has a non-monotonic impact on the spatial fragmentation of the supply chain.

11.5.3 Who Gains and Who Loses from Offshoring Production?

It should be clear from the foregoing that the process of globalization may have very contrasted implications for the various groups of workers involved. In this section, we distinguish between the unskilled working in the core, the unskilled residing in the periphery, and the skilled who live in the core. Although reducing communication and transport costs may not have the same impact on the well-being of the different groups of workers, we restrict ourselves to a fall in communication costs caused by the development of the new information and communication technologies, which is the novel ingredient of the present setting.

Unskilled workers' nominal wages being independent of ϕ_C, the welfare impact of decreasing communication costs is driven by the changes in price indices. Using (11.70), we have

$$\frac{\partial P_1^*}{\partial \phi_C} = -\frac{P_1^*}{\sigma - 1}\frac{(1-\theta^*)\phi_M + (1-\phi_C\phi_M)\partial\theta^*/\partial\phi_C}{\theta^* + (1-\theta^*)\phi_C\phi_M}.$$

As long as there is no overseas plant, reducing communication costs has no impact on the price index in country 1. When ϕ_C rises sufficiently for θ^* to belong to $(0, 1)$, the analysis is less straightforward because two opposite effects are at work. The direct effect is that varieties made in the periphery are produced at a lower unit cost because of the decreasing communication costs. The indirect effect is that more varieties are produced in the periphery, thus making them more expensive for country 1's workers. The net effect is thus a priori unclear. However, it turns out to be possible to show that the latter effect dominates the former. The argument goes as follows. Evidently,

$$\frac{\partial P_1^*}{\partial \phi_C} \lesseqgtr 0 \qquad \text{if and only if} \qquad -\frac{\partial \theta^*(\phi_C, \phi_M)}{\partial \phi_C} \lesseqgtr \frac{(1-\theta^*)\phi_M}{1-\phi_C\phi_M}.$$

Some tedious calculations show that

$$-\frac{\partial \theta(\phi_C, \phi_M)}{\partial \phi_C} > \frac{(1-\theta^*)\phi_M}{1-\phi_C\phi_M}.$$

Therefore, we have

$$\partial P_1^*/\partial \phi_C > 0 \qquad \text{when } 0 < \theta^* < 1.$$

Finally, when all firms are multinational, we have

$$\frac{\partial P_1^*}{\partial \phi_C} = -\frac{P_1^*}{(\sigma-1)\phi_C} < 0.$$

Regarding the price index of country 2, we use (11.71) to show that

$$\frac{\partial P_2^*}{\partial \phi_C} = -\frac{P_2^*}{\sigma-1}\frac{(1-\theta^*) - (\phi_C - \phi_M)\partial\theta^*/\partial\phi_C}{\theta^*\phi_M + (1-\theta^*)\phi_C}.$$

Noting that $\partial\theta^*/\partial\phi_C = 0$ at $\theta^* = 1$ and setting $\theta^* = 1$ in the above expression, we see immediately that $\partial P_2^*/\partial\phi_C = 0$ as long as $\theta^* = 1$. When the configuration is mixed, we have

$$\frac{\partial \theta^*}{\partial \phi_C} = \frac{\partial \theta^*(\phi_C, \phi_M)}{\partial \phi_C}$$

which has been shown to be negative. Hence, we get

$$\partial P_2^*/\partial \phi_C < 0 \qquad \text{when } 0 < \theta^* < 1.$$

Finally, when $\theta^* = 0$, we have

$$\frac{\partial P_2^*}{\partial \phi_C} = -\frac{P_2^*}{(\sigma-1)\phi_C} < 0.$$

Because nominal wages are independent of ϕ_C, real wages are determined only by the evolution of the price indices of the manufactured good. Consider, first, the unskilled in the periphery. As long as $\theta^* = 1$, their real wage is unaffected by a decrease in communication costs. When $\theta^* \in (0, 1)$, $\partial P_2^*/\partial\phi_C < 0$ and thus the unskilled living in the periphery are better off. Finally, when all firms are multinational, $\partial P_2^*/\partial\phi_C < 0$ still holds, thus implying that the real wage of the unskilled living in country 2 keeps rising. Thus, we may conclude that a fall in communication costs leaves the unskilled in the periphery unaffected as long as all plants remain in the core. By contrast, when the relocation process starts, any further drop in communication costs makes the unskilled workers in the periphery better off. This should not come as a surprise. When these costs keep decreasing, more and more varieties are produced in the periphery because the unit production cost decreases. Hence, the domestic price index must also decrease.

Consider now the unskilled workers living in the core. When there is no overseas plant, lower communication costs have no impact on the price index in country 1 and, therefore, on the well-being of the unskilled residing there. When $\theta^* \in (0, 1)$, we have seen that $\partial P_1^*/\partial \phi_C > 0$ so that the unskilled are worse off. Finally, when all plants are located overseas, the unskilled living in the core benefit from further decreases in communication costs because plants operate at lower cost. As a result, the unskilled workers in country 1 are now better off.

It remains to investigate the impact of decreasing communication costs on the welfare of the skilled workers. First, we have to determine their nominal wage. Substituting (11.77) in (11.73) yields after tedious calculations:

$$w_1^* = \frac{\mu/\sigma}{1-\mu/\sigma}. \tag{11.78}$$

Setting $\theta^* = 1$ in (11.75) yields (11.78), whereas setting $\theta^* = 0$ in (11.69) and solving for w_1 also yields (11.78). Therefore, regardless of the pattern of plant distribution, the nominal wage of the skilled workers is given by (11.78), which is independent of the transport and communication costs. This somewhat unexpected result may be explained as follows. First, because the nominal wage of unskilled labor in efficiency units is normalized to one in both regions, nominal incomes are given by (11.67), which do not depend directly on ϕ_M and ϕ_C. Second, when communication costs decrease, (11.69) implies that a firm with a plant in country 2 becomes more competitive. But, as the same holds for all multinational firms, the reduction in communication costs also makes the firm in question less competitive. In the present context, these two opposite effects just cancel out, thus implying that firms' operating profits are unaffected. Because the same argument applies to a decrease in transport costs, we may conclude the level of operating profits are unaffected by changes in transport and communication costs. This in turn implies that the zero-profit equilibrium wage of the skilled workers remains constant. Therefore, what we have seen about the unskilled living in the core also applies to the skilled. In sum, we may conclude that *welfare in the core goes down as plants move into the periphery*.

The foregoing discussion may be summarized as follows.

Proposition 11.6. *Assume that communication costs fall. First, all workers are unaffected as long as firms are integrated. Once some firms start relocating* *their production facilities into the periphery, the skilled and unskilled in the core are worse off, whereas the unskilled living in the periphery are better off. Last, when all plants are located overseas, all workers benefit from further decrease in communication costs.*

As the offshoring of routine tasks occupies center stage in political debates, the preceding results deserve some further discussion. Indeed, our last proposition runs against the widespread idea that only the unskilled living in the core are negatively affected by globalization. We view the reason for this divergence in the fact that each firm accurately neglects the general equilibrium effects its relocation triggers because it is negligible to the market. As each firm does the same, after the communication cost drop, all firms end up in a situation in which they make operating profits that are lower than those made before the communication cost decrease. As a result, the skilled workers may also lose from the spatial fragmentation of firms. Though the spatial scales are very different, the same phenomenon arose a long time ago with the relocation of activities at the city outskirts, which has often been harmful to the inner city.

This is not yet the end of the story. In various developed countries, some policy makers want to make it more difficult for firms to relocate their production activities and, thus, to cut unskilled jobs. This argument disregards the fact that adopting such a policy may incentivize firms to relocate *both* their HQs and plants into the periphery. In this case, consumers living in the core would be worse-off than when firms offshore their production activities only (Robert-Nicoud 2008).

11.6 ALTERNATIVE STRATEGIES OF MULTINATIONALIZATION

In the previous two sections, we have discussed a special type of foreign direct investment (FDI) strategy. It is, therefore, important to figure out whether the propositions established in Section 11.5 are robust against alternative strategies implemented by firms (Helpman 2011). In what follows, we show that the model above displays enough versatility to accommodate a wide range of observed situations, thus endowing our main results with a practical relevance that goes far beyond the specific context considered in the previous sections. Indeed, a fair amount of recent research zooms in on different microeconomic underpinnings that yield a reduced form akin to what we call communication costs. Therefore, the ultimate impacts are similar.

11.6.1 Offshoring an Intermediate Input

In Section 11.4, production takes place either at home or abroad. This corresponds to an extreme form of spatial fragmentation. In practice, firms may choose instead to offshore part of their supply chain, that is, an intermediate input is produced in a foreign subsidiary, which is then used to produce the final good in a home unit. In this event, a firm has one HQ and two plants, one plant producing at home the final good and one plant producing abroad an intermediate. The trade structure then involves intrafirm trade from country 2 to country 1, while the final good is exported only from country 1.

Assume that producing one unit of the final good requires α units of the same good used as an intermediate input. When q units of the final good are produced at home, (11.66) implies that the total cost of a firm offshoring the production of its intermediate input is given by

$$C(q) = \alpha \frac{\tau_C}{a_2} q + q = \left(\alpha \frac{\tau_C}{a_2} + 1 \right) q$$

where τ_C now stands for both the communication cost between the HQ and its foreign subsidiary and the shipment cost of the intermediate from the latter to the former. By contrast, the total cost of a geographically integrated firm is

$$C(q) = (\alpha + 1)q.$$

Choosing the unit of the product for $\alpha + 1$ to be replaced by 1 and setting

$$\frac{\alpha \frac{\tau_C}{a_2} + 1}{\alpha + 1} \equiv \Upsilon_C$$

the analysis of Sections 11.4 and 11.5 can be repeated once τ_C / a_2 is replaced by Υ_C. Because τ_C and Υ_C move together, Propositions 11.4, 11.5, and 11.6 hold true in this new setting.

A growing number of firms adopt an offshoring strategy when both the cost of shipping the intermediate and the communication cost between firms' units keep decreasing. In other words, lower transport and communication costs facilitate intrafirm trade, and thus vertical investment (Egger 2008). Furthermore, intrafirm trade is now bidirectional: the parent firm imports the intermediate good from its subsidiary while the latter imports HQ-services from the former.

11.6.2 Horizontal Investment

Armchair evidence shows that some firms export, while others supply foreign markets from subsidiaries built or acquired abroad. Evidently, high transport costs foster horizontal investment whereas they deter vertical investment. Fewer firms choose to become multiplant when the fixed cost associated with the opening of a second plant gets higher. Evidently, we encounter here the proximity/concentration trade-off: (i) the multiplant firm saves the cost of shipping its output to a foreign market and (ii) the single-plant firm saves the fixed cost of acquiring a second plant (Markusen 1984). Furthermore, as the size of the foreign market grows horizontal investment becomes more attractive, the reason being that firms can spread the second plant's fixed cost over a larger volume of sales. All of this explains why American car manufacturers invested in Europe soon after the launching of the Common Market in 1958: they accessed an integrating and growing market while obviating high trade costs by being located within the tariff wall.

Section 11.4 shows that firms face a wider set of options when communication costs and factor price differential are taken into account. This generates three categories of firms: (i) the firm has one plant and is geographically integrated, (ii) it has one plant and is geographically disintegrated, and (iii) the firm has two plants, one located together with the HQ and the other abroad, each plant supplying its host country's market with similar goods or services.[9] Fujita and Gokan (2005) extend the model presented in Section 11.4 to study the impact of decreasing transport and communication costs on the number and location of plants. Assume first that transport costs are high. Then, when communication costs steadily decrease, the pattern of production is described by the following sequence: first, all firms are geographically integrated in the core, then some firms choose to operate two plants and, eventually, all firms are multiplant. This is because high transport costs incentivize firms to be multiplant. However, firms will choose to do so only when communication costs are sufficiently low. This pattern is consistent with the supply chain that characterizes the car industry. Observe that homogeneous firms may choose different modes of operation. By implication, although firms have the same productivity, *exports and FDI can coexist within the same industry*.

By contrast, when transport costs are low, the trade-off between increasing returns and transport costs implies that all firms operate a single plant. In this event, as seen above when communication costs steadily decrease, production plants are moved gradually from the core to the periphery. Such an evolution explains the growing concentration of production of consumer electronics in China and Southeast Asia.

Last, firm-level data sets that became available in the 1990s reveal that, within the same sector, firms vary greatly in productivity. Accounting for this fact gives rise to new and important results. In this respect, it is worth mentioning the work by Helpman, Melitz, and Yeaple (2004). These authors show that the least productive firms only serve their domestic market; firms with a higher average productivity export, whereas the most productive firms engage in foreign direct investment. In other words, *firms' attitude toward trade and FDI is sorted by their degree of productivity*.

11.6.3 Complex Integration

It is well documented that modern multinational firms develop *complex integration strategies* that combine different forms of foreign investment (Yeaple

[9] If exporting involves a fixed cost as in Melitz (2003), a fourth category of firms may emerge: those supplying only their domestic market.

2003). To see how this works, consider a global economy formed by three countries. Firms located in country 1 may choose to engage in horizontal investment in, say, country 2 and vertical investment in country 3. This is so when shipping the final good is relatively more expensive than shipping the intermediate good, communication costs are low, and countries 1 and 2 are high-wage countries whereas 3 is a low-wage country. Under these circumstances, there is intrafirm trade from country 3 to countries 1 and 2, and trade in the final good from country 1 or 2 to country 3. Such a strategy may explain investment flows between developed countries as well as investment flows from high-wage to low-wage countries.

Observe that the two types of investment are interdependent in that firms are able to cover the additional fixed cost associated with the opening of a second production plant because they may offshore the production of the intermediate to a low-wage country. In the absence of offshoring, firms could find it more profitable to be spatially integrated and to export to countries 2 and 3.

11.6.4 Outsourcing

So far, firms have been assumed to be vertically integrated: the foreign unit is owned by the parent firm. However, firms may licence a nonaffiliated company to produce the final product or may purchase the intermediate input from an independent party established in the foreign country. The "make-or-buy" decision, which defines the boundaries of the firm, is relevant for foreign and domestic investment alike. As usual, the firm has to weigh the costs and benefits of internalization. To illustrate, consider the typical example of a firm outsourcing the production of a firm-specific intermediate input to a unique independent supplier. In this event, the firm becomes a hostage of its supplier, and vice versa. Put differently, the relationship between the two parties has the nature of a bilateral monopoly in which they bargain for the payment the supplier receives from the firm. It is well known that the solution to this problem depends on the bargaining power of each party and the values of their outside options. The solution to the bilateral monopoly may also be analyzed within the principal-agent framework when the firm has less information than the supplier on how to produce the intermediate input.

Those various considerations are important for the study of the organizational forms chosen by firms because they influence the nature and intensity of trade (Helpman 2011).[10] However, for our purpose selecting a particular solution to the outsourcing problem often generates effects that are essentially equivalent to a hike or a drop in the transport and/or communication costs. Therefore, the make-or-buy decision does not seem to add much to what we have shown above.

[10] Note that the industrial organization literature had highlighted long ago the possible co-existence of firms having different organizational forms within the same industry.

11.7 CONCLUDING REMARKS

The results presented in the first part of this chapter support Myrdal's (1957, 26) claim: "the main idea I want to convey is that the play of the forces in the market normally tends to increase, rather than to decrease, the inequalities between regions." When transport costs are sufficiently low, both the manufacturing and the innovation sectors concentrate within the same region, whereas the other region specializes in the production of the agricultural good. This is so even though the number of firms operating in the manufacturing sector keeps rising over time. In fact, our analysis strongly supports the idea that *agglomeration and growth reinforce each other*. An interesting implication of our analysis is that policies fostering dispersion are likely to hurt global economic growth.

Nevertheless, the increase of regional disparities does not necessarily imply the impoverishment of the peripheral regions. When agglomeration does not succeed in boosting enough growth, the transfer of more economic activities into the core region does hurt those who keep living in the periphery. In the opposite case, it is not so clear that agglomeration, growth, and equity do conflict: Those residing in the periphery are better off in the core–periphery structure than under dispersion. There is a conflict only when a fairly narrow interpretation of justice, that is, egalitarianism, is considered because the unskilled living in the core region are better off than those in the periphery. At this stage of the debate, we do not have much to say: the answer depends on societal values. But whatever the answer, it is our contention that understanding regional and urban growth is crucial for improving our knowledge of how modern economies do or may develop.

The second part of this chapter points in a different, but complementary, direction. In the absence of a strong R&D sector, the steady drop in transport costs, compounded by the decline of protectionism in the post–World War II era and, more recently, by the near-disappearance of communication costs might well be detrimental to the core region. The gradual relocation of production activities in low-wage countries is a powerful trend that will hurt the old industrialized countries if they do not provide a regular flow of innovations.

Evidently, investment and trade flows are intermingled through the modes of operation chosen by firms. These choices, which need not be the same across a priori identical firms, are in turn affected by the transport costs of the intermediate and final goods, the communication costs between firms' units, factor price differences, and sales in each country. As a consequence, the market outcome results from the interplay between very distinct variables. This may explain a certain proliferation of papers focusing on the details of the relationships between trade and the way multinational firms operate. We also want to stress a fact frequently unnoticed in the literature, that is, what is accomplished at the international level may be repeated mutatis mutandis at the city level, and vice versa. The factor price difference that matters in the former case is the wage rate, whereas differences in land rents drive the relocation of activities in the latter (see Chapter 6). In both cases, the development of information technologies is key to the fragmentation of the supply chain.

According to Helpman (2011), "to understand globalization, one needs first to understand what shapes international trade and the organization of production across national boundaries." We agree with Helpman but we believe that one ingredient is missing in his argument: space. Globalization affects regions and cities even more than nations because growth is a localized process while new ideas influencing the pace of innovation blossom only in a few places. The spatial diffusion effects being limited in space and hampered by great inequalities in knowledge absorption capacity, lasting and sizable economic gaps arise between and within nations. To understand fully the implications of globalization, we must also take into account the spatial distribution of economic activities at different spatial scales.

A word, in closing. No doubt, the growth of intangible trade and the development of computer-aided technologies will change our way of thinking about the structure of the supply chain as well as the factors influencing the competitiveness of cities, regions, and countries (*The Economist* 2012). Yet, we concur with Krugman (2007, 33) for whom "the spaceless, borderless world is still a Platonic ideal, a long way from coming into existence." Although, as always in economics, everything depends on everything else, the results presented in this book and the overwhelming empirical evidence reported in the literature support the idea that, on all geographical scales, *what is near has more influence than what is far*.

To illustrate, we would like to appeal to our own experience. In revising this book we have exchanged files for several months through the Internet and made significant progress. Yet, quite a few issues remained unsettled. After a while, we decided to discuss them face-to-face in one of our favorite cities, i.e., Paris. There, it took us a few days to find solutions to the unsolved problems and to complete the second edition. This is in accordance with Glaeser (2011, 248) who writes: "The Internet is a wonderful tool, but it works best when combined with knowledge gained face-to-face." Therefore, there seems to be a broad agreement in recognizing that distance and location still matter.

References

[1] Abdel-Rahman, H. (2000). City systems: general equilibrium approaches. In: J.-M. Huriot and J.-F. Thisse (eds.). *Economics of Cities. Theoretical Perspectives*. Cambridge: Cambridge University Press, 109–37.

[2] Abdel-Rahman, H., and Anas, A. (2004). Theories of systems of cities. In: J.V. Henderson and J.-F. Thisse (eds.). *Handbook of Regional and Urban Economics. Cities and Geography*. Amsterdam: North-Holland, 2293–339.

[3] Abdel-Rahman, H., and Fujita, M. (1990). Product variety, Marshallian externalities, and city sizes. *Journal of Regional Science* 30: 165–83.

[4] Abdel-Rahman, H., and Fujita, M. (1993). Specialization and diversification in a system of cities. *Journal of Urban Economics* 33: 189–222.

[5] Acemoglu, D. (1996). A microfoundation for social increasing returns in human capital accumulation. *Quarterly Journal of Economics* 111: 779–804.

[6] Alesina, A., and Spolaore, E. (1997). On the number and size of nations. *Quarterly Journal of Economics* 112: 1027–55.

[7] Allais, M. (1943). *A la recherche d'une discipline économique*. Reprinted as: *Traité d'économie pure*. Paris: Imprimerie nationale, 1952.

[8] Alonso, W. (1960). Theory of the urban land market. *Papers and Proceedings of the Regional Science Association* 6: 149–57.

[9] Alonso, W. (1964). *Location and Land Use*. Cambridge, MA: Harvard University Press.

[10] Alonso, W. (1994). Comment on 'Interaction between regional and industrial policies: evidence from four countries'. *Proceedings of World Bank Annual Conference on Development Economics*, 299–302.

[11] Anas, A. (1983). Discrete choice theory, information theory, and the multinomial logit and gravity models. *Transportation Research B* 17: 13–23.

[12] Anas, A. (1990). Taste heterogeneity and spatial urban structure: the logit model and monocentric theory reconciled. *Journal of Urban Economics* 28: 318–35.

[13] Anas, A. (2004). Vanishing cities: what does the new economic geography imply about the efficiency of urbanization? *Journal of Economic Geography* 4: 181–99.

[14] Anas, A., Arnott, R., and Small, K.A. (1998). Urban spatial structure. *Journal of Economic Literature* 36: 1426–64.

[15] Anderson, J., and van Wincoop, E. (2004). Trade costs. *Journal of Economic Literature* 42: 691–751.

[16] Anderson, S.P., and Braid, R.M. (1999). Spatial competition, monopolistic competition, and optimum product diversity. William Vickrey. *International Journal of Industrial Organization* 17: 953–63.

[17] Anderson, S.P., and de Palma, A. (1988). Spatial price discrimination under heterogeneous products. *Review of Economic Studies* 55: 573–92.

[18] Anderson, S.P., de Palma, A., and Thisse, J.-F. (1992). *Discrete Choice Theory of Product Differentiation.* Cambridge, MA: MIT Press.

[19] Anderson, S.P., and Neven, D. (1991). Cournot competition yields spatial agglomeration. *International Economic Review* 32: 793–808.

[20] Arnott, R.J. (1979). Optimal city size in a spatial economy. *Journal of Urban Economics* 6: 65–89.

[21] Arnott, R. (1981). Aggregate land rents and aggregate transport costs. *Economic Journal* 91: 331–47.

[22] Arnott, R. (1995). Time for revisionism on rent control. *Journal of Economic Perspectives* 14 Winter: 99–120.

[23] Arnott, R., and Stiglitz, J. (1979). Aggregate land rent, expenditure on public goods, and optimal city size. *Quarterly Journal of Economics* 93: 471–500.

[24] Arrow, K., and Debreu, G. (1954). Existence of an equilibrium for a competitive economy. *Econometrica* 22: 265–90.

[25] Arthur, W.B. (1994). *Increasing Returns and Path Dependence in the Economy.* Ann Arbor: The University of Michigan Press.

[26] Asami, Y. (1990). A determination of bid rents through bidding procedures. *Journal of Urban Economics* 27: 188–211.

[27] Asami, Y., Fujita, M., and Smith, T.E. (1990). On the foundations of land use theory: discrete versus continuous population. *Regional Science and Urban Economics* 20: 473–508.

[28] Asami, Y., Fujita, M., and Thisse, J.-F. (1993). A land capitalization approach to the efficient provision of urban facilities. *Regional Science and Urban Economics* 23: 487–522.

[29] Au, C.C., and Henderson, J.V. (2006). Are Chinese cities too small? *Review of Economic Studies* 73: 549–76.

[30] Audretsch, D.B., and Feldman, M.P. (2004). Knowledge spillovers and the geography and innovation. In: J.V. Henderson and J.-F. Thisse (eds.). *Handbook of Regional and Urban Economics. Cities and Geography*. Amsterdam: North-Holland, 2713–39.

[31] Aumann, R.J. (1964). Markets with a continuum of traders. *Econometrica* 32: 39–50.

[32] Bacolod, M., Bull, B.S., and Strange, W.C. (2009). Skills in the city. *Journal of Urban Economics* 65: 136–53.

[33] Bairoch, P. (1988). *Cities and Economic Development: From the Dawn of History to the Present.* Chicago: University of Chicago Press.

[34] Bairoch, P. (1993). *Economics and World History: Myths and Paradoxes.* Chicago: University of Chicago Press.

[35] Bairoch, P. (1997). *Victoires et déboires. Histoire économique et sociale du monde du XVIe siècle à nos jours*. Paris: Editions Gallimard.

[36] Baldwin, R.E., Forslid, R., Martin, P., Ottaviano, G.I.P., and Robert-Nicoud, F. (2003). *Economic Geography and Public Policy*. Princeton, NJ: Princeton University Press.

[37] Baldwin, R.E., and Krugman, P.R. (2004). Agglomeration, integration and tax harmonization. *European Economic Review* 48: 1–23.

[38] Baldwin, R.E., and Martin, P. (2004). Agglomeration and regional growth. In: J.V. Henderson and J.-F. Thisse (eds.). *Handbook of Regional and Urban Economics. Cities and Geography*. Amsterdam: North-Holland, 2671–711.

[39] Baumeiter, R.F., and Leary, M.R. (1995). The need to belong: desire for interpersonal attachments as a fundamental human motivation. *Psychological Bulletin* 117: 497–529.

[40] Baumont, C., and Huriot, J.-M. (2000). Urban economics in retrospect: continuity or change? In: J.-M. Huriot and J.-F. Thisse (eds.). *Economics of Cities. Theoretical Perspectives*. Cambridge: Cambridge University Press, 74–107.

[41] Baum-Snow, N. (2010). Changes in transportation infrastructure and commuting patterns in US metropolitan areas, 1960–2000. *American Economic Review: Papers & Proceedings* 100: 378–82.

[42] Becattini, G. (1990). The Marshallian industrial district as a socio-economic notion. In: F. Pyke, B. Becattini, and W. Sengenberger (eds.). *Industrial Districts and Inter-firm Cooperation in Italy*. Geneva. International Institute for Labour Studies, 37–51.

[43] Beckmann, M.J. (1957). On the distribution of rent and residential density in cities. Yale University, mimeo.

[44] Beckmann, M.J. (1969). On the distribution of urban rent and residential density. *Journal of Economic Theory* 1: 60–8.

[45] Beckmann, M.J. (1972a). Von Thünen revisited: a neoclassical land use model. *Swedish Journal of Economics* 74: 1–7.

[46] Beckmann, M.J. (1972b). Spatial Cournot oligopoly. *Papers and Proceedings of the Regional Science Association* 28: 37–47.

[47] Beckmann, M.J. (1973). Equilibrium models of residential land use. *Regional and Urban Economics* 3: 361–8.

[48] Beckmann, M.J. (1976). Spatial equilibrium in the dispersed city. In: Y.Y. Papageorgiou (ed.). *Mathematical Land Use Theory*. Lexington, MA: Lexington Books, 117–25.

[49] Beckmann, M.J., and Thisse, J.-F. (1986). The location of production activities. In: P. Nijkamp (ed.). *Handbook of Regional and Urban Economics, Volume 1*. Amsterdam: North-Holland, 21–95.

[50] Behrens, K. (2005a). How endogenous asymmetries in interregional market access trigger regional divergence. *Regional Science and Urban Economics* 35: 471–92.

[51] Behrens, K. (2005b). Market size and industry location: traded vs non-traded goods. *Journal of Urban Economics* 58: 24–44.

[52] Behrens, K., and Picard, P. (2011). Transportation, freight rates, and economic geography. *Journal of International Economics* 85: 280–91.

[53] Behrens, K., Gaigné, C., and Thisse, J.-F. (2009). Industry location and welfare when transport costs are endogenous. *Journal of Urban Economics* 65: 195–208.

[54] Behrens, K., Lamorgese, A.R., Ottaviano, G.I.P., and Tabuchi, T. (2009). Beyond the home market effect: market size and specialization in a multi-country world. *Journal of International Economics* 79: 259–65.

[55] Belleflamme, P., Picard, P., and Thisse, J.-F. (2000). An economic theory of regional clusters. *Journal of Urban Economics* 48: 158–84.

[56] Ben-Akiva, M., de Palma, A., and Thisse, J.-F. (1989). Spatial competition with differentiated products. *Regional Science and Urban Economics* 19: 5–19.

[57] Bénabou, R. (1994). Working of a city: location, education and production. *Quarterly Journal of Economics* 106: 619–52.

[58] Berglas, E. (1976). On the theory of clubs. *Papers and Proceedings of the American Economic Association* 66: 116–21.

[59] Berliant, M. (1985). Equilibrium models with land: a criticism and an alternative. *Regional Science and Urban Economics* 15: 325–40.

[60] Berliant, M., and Fujita, M. (1992). Alonso's discrete population model of land use: efficient allocation and land use. *International Economic Review* 33: 535–66.

[61] Bernard, A., Jensen, J., Redding, S. and Schott, P. (2007). Firms in international trade. *Journal of Economic Perspectives* 21/3: 105–30.

[62] Berry, S., and Waldfogel, J. (2010). Product quality and market size. *Journal of Industrial Economics* 48, 1–31.

[63] Blaug, M. (1985). *Economic Theory in Retrospect.* Cambridge: Cambridge University Press.

[64] Borukhov, E., and Hochman, O. (1977). Optimum and market equilibrium in a model of a city without a predetermined center. *Environment and Planning A* 9: 849–56.

[65] Brakman, S., and Heijdra, B.J. (2004). *The Monopolistic Competition Revolution in Retrospect.* Cambridge: Cambridge University Press.

[66] Braudel, F. (1979). *Civilisation matérielle, économie et capitalisme, XVe–XVIIIe siècle: le temps du monde.* Paris: Armand Colin. English translation: *Civilization and Capitalism 15th–18th Century: The Perspective of the World.* New York: Harper Collins (1985).

[67] Brueckner, J.K., Thisse, J.-F., and Zenou, Y. (1999). Why is Central Paris rich and Downtown Detroit poor? An amenity-based theory. *European Economic Review* 43: 91–107.

[68] Buchanan, J.M. (1965). An economic theory of clubs. *Economica* 33: 1–14.

[69] Cantillon, R. (1755). *Essai sur la nature du commerce en général.* London: Fletcher. English translation by H. Higgs. Reprinted in 1964. New York: A.M. Kelley.

[70] Casetti, E. (1971). Equilibrium land values and population density in an urban setting. *Economic Geography* 47: 16–20.

[71] Cavailhès, J., Gaigné, C., Tabuchi, T., and Thisse, J.-F. (2007). Trade and the structure of cities. *Journal of Urban Economics* 62: 383–404.

[72] Cavailhès, J., Peeters, D., Sekeris, E., and Thisse, J.-F. (2004). The periurban city. Why to live between the suburbs and the countryside? *Regional Science and Urban Economics* 34: 681–703.

[73] Caves, R.E. (1971). International corporations: the industrial economics of foreign investment. *Economica* 38: 1–27.

[74] Chamberlin, E. (1933). *The Theory of Monopolistic Competition*. Cambridge, MA: Harvard University Press.

[75] Charlot, S., and Duranton, G. (2004). Communication externalities in cities. *Journal of Urban Economics* 56: 581–613.

[76] Charlot, S., Gaigné, C., Robert-Nicoud, F., and Thisse, J.-F. (2006). Agglomeration and welfare: the core-periphery model in the light of Bentham, Kaldor, and Rawls, *Journal of Public Economics* 90: 325–47.

[77] Chipman, J.S. (1970). External economies of scale and competitive equilibrium. *Quarterly Journal of Economics* 85: 347–85.

[78] Christaller, W. (1933). *Die Zentralen Orte in Süddeutschland*. Jena: Gustav Fischer Verlag. English translation: *The Central Places of Southern Germany*. Englewood Cliffs, NJ: Prentice-Hall (1966).

[79] Ciccone, A., and Hall, R.E. (1996). Productivity and the density of economic activity. *American Economic Review* 86: 54–70.

[80] Coase, R. (1937). The nature of the firm. *Economica* 4: 386–405.

[81] Combes, P.-P., Duranton, G., and Gobillon, L. (2008). Spatial wage disparities: sorting matters! *Journal of Urban Economics* 63: 723–42.

[82] Combes, P.-P., Duranton, G., and Gobillon, L. (2011). The identification of agglomeration economies. *Journal of Economic Geography* 11: 253–66.

[83] Combes, P.-P., Duranton, G., Gobillon, L., Puga, D., and Roux, S. (2012). The productivity advantages of large cities: distinguishing agglomeration from firm selection. *Econometrica* 80: 2543–94.

[84] Combes, P.-P., Lafourcade, M., Thisse, J.-F., and Toutain, J.-C. (2011). The rise and fall of spatial inequalities in France. A long-run perspective. *Exploration in Economic History* 48: 243–71.

[85] Combes, P.-P., Mayer, T., and Thisse, J.-F. (2008). *Economic Geography. The Integration of Regions and Nations*. Princeton, NJ: Princeton University Press.

[86] Cournot, A. (1838). *Recherches sur les principes mathématiques de la théorie des richesses*. Paris: Hachette. English *Researches into the Mathematical Principles of the Theory of Wealth*. New York: Macmillan (1897).

[87] Cremer, H., de Kerchove, A.-M., and Thisse, J.-F. (1985). An economic theory of public facilities in space. *Mathematical Social Sciences* 9: 249–62.

[88] Darnell, A.C. (1990). *The Collected Economics Articles of Harold Hotelling*. Heidelberg: Springer-Verlag.

[89] d'Aspremont, C., Gabszewicz, J.J., and Thisse, J.-F. (1979). On Hotelling's "Stability in Competition." *Econometrica* 47: 1045–50.

[90] Davis, D.R. (1998). The home market, trade and industrial structure. *American Economic Review* 88: 1264–76.

[91] Davis, D.R., and Weinstein, D. (2002). Bones, bombs, and break points: the geography of economic activity. *American Economic Review* 92: 1269–89.

[92] Davis, J.C., and Henderson, J.V. (2008). The agglomeration of headquarters. *Regional Science and Urban Economics* 38: 445–60.

[93] Deardorff, A.V. (1984). Testing trade theories and predicting trade flows. In: R.W. Jones and P.B. Kenen (eds). *Handbook of International Economics. Volume 1*. Amsterdam: North Holland, 467–517.

[94] Debreu, G. (1959). *Theory of Value*. New York: Wiley.

[95] De Fraja, G., and Norman, G. (1993). Product differentiation, pricing policy and equilibrium, *Journal of Regional Science* 33: 343–63.

[96] de Palma, A., Ginsburgh, V., Labbé, M., and Thisse, J.-F. (1989). Competitive location with random utilities. *Transportation Science* 23: 244–52.

[97] de Palma, A., Ginsburgh, V., Papageorgiou, Y.Y., and Thisse, J.-F. (1985). The principle of minimum differentiation holds under sufficient heterogeneity. *Econometrica* 53: 767–81.

[98] de Palma, A., Lindsey, R., Quinet, E., and Vickerman, R. (2011). *A Handbook of Transport Economics*. Cheltenham, UK: Edward Elgar.

[99] Diamond, J. (1997). *Guns, Germs, and Steel. The Fate of Human Societies*. New York: W. W. Norton.

[100] Dixit, A.K. and Norman, V. (1980).*Theory of International Trade*. Cambridge: Cambridge University Press.

[101] Dixit, A.K., and Stiglitz, J.E. (1977). Monopolistic competition and optimum product diversity. *American Economic Review* 67: 297–308.

[102] Dos Santos Ferreira, R., and Thisse, J.-F. (1996). Horizontal and vertical differentiation: the Launhardt model. *International Journal of Industrial Organization* 14: 485–506.

[103] Dunn, E.S. (1954). The equilibrium of land-use pattern in agriculture. *Southern Economic Journal* 21: 173–87.

[104] Duranton, G., and Puga, D. (2000). Diversity and specialization in cities: why, where and when does it matter? *Urban Studies* 37: 533–55.

[105] Duranton, G., and Puga, D. (2001). Nursery cities: urban diversity, process innovation, and the life-cycle of products. *American Economic Review* 91: 1454–63.

[106] Duranton, G., and Puga, D. (2004). Micro-foundations of urban increasing returns: theory. In: J.V. Henderson and J.-F. Thisse (eds.). *Handbook of Regional and Urban Economics. Cities and Geography*. Amsterdam: North-Holland, 2063–117.

[107] Duranton, G., and Puga, D. (2005). From sectoral to functional urban specialization. *Journal of Urban Economics* 57: 343–70.

[108] Eaton, B.C., and Lipsey, R.G. (1977). The introduction of space into the neoclassical model of value theory. In: M. Artis and A. Nobay (eds.). *Studies in Modern Economics*. Oxford: Basil Blackwell, 59–96.

[109] Eaton, B.C., and Lipsey, R.G. (1979). Comparison shopping and the clustering of homogeneous firms. *Journal of Regional Science* 19: 421–35.

[110] Eaton, B.C., and Lipsey, R.G. (1982). An economic theory of central places. *Economic Journal* 92: 56–72.

[111] Eaton, B.C., and Lipsey, R.G. (1997). *On the Foundations of Monopolistic Competition and Economic Geography*. Cheltenham: Edward Elgar.

[112] *The Economist* (2012). The Third Industrial Revolution, April 21st.

[113] Egger, P. (2008). On the role of distance for outward FDI. *Annals of Regional Science* 42: 375–89.

[114] Ekelund Jr., R.B., and Hébert, R.F (1999). *Secret Origins of Modern Microeconomics. Dupuit and the Engineers*. Chicago: The University of Chicago Press.

[115] Ellison, G., and Glaeser, E.L. (1999). The geographic concentration of industry: does natural advantage explain agglomeration? *American Economic Review: Papers & Proceedings* 89: 311–16.

[116] Ellison, G., Glaeser, E.L., and Kerr, W.R. (2010). What causes industry agglomeration? Evidence from coagglomeration patterns. *American Economic Review* 100: 1195–213.

[117] Engel, C., and Rogers, J. (2001). Deviations from purchasing power parity: causes and welfare costs. *Journal of International Economics* 55: 29–57.

[118] Enke, E. (1951). Equilibrium among spatially separated markets: solution by electric analogue. *Econometrica* 19: 40–7.

[119] Ethier, W. (1982). National and international returns to scale in the modern theory of international trade. *American Economic Review* 72: 389–405.

[120] Feldman, M.P., and Audretsch, D.B. (1999). Innovation in cities: science-based diversity, specialization and localized competition. *European Economic Review* 43: 409–29.

[121] Feldman, M.P., and Florida, R. (1994). The geographic sources of innovation: technological infrastructure and product innovation in the United States. *Annals of the Association of American Geographers* 84: 210–29.

[122] Fingleton, B. (2011). The empirical performance of the NEG with reference to small areas. *Journal of Economic Geography* 11: 267–79.

[123] Fischer, C. (1982). *To Dwell Among Friends: Personal Networks in Town and City*. Chicago: University of Chicago Press.

[124] Flatters, F., Henderson, V., and Mieszkowsi, P. (1974). Public goods, efficiency, and regional fiscal equalization. *Journal of Public Economics* 3: 99–112.

[125] Florian, M., and Los, M. (1982). A new look at static spatial price equilibrium models. *Regional Science and Urban Economics* 12: 579–97.

[126] Forslid, R. and Ottaviano, G.I.P. (2003). An analytical solvable core-periphery model. *Journal of Economic Geography* 3: 229–40.

[127] Foster, L., Haltiwanger, J., and Syverson, C. (2008). Reallocation, firm turnover, and efficiency: Selection on productivity or profitability? *American Economic Review* 98: 394–425.

[128] Fujita, M. (1988). A monopolistic competition model of spatial agglomeration: a differentiated product approach. *Regional Science and Urban Economics* 18: 87–124.

[129] Fujita, M. (1989). *Urban Economic Theory. Land Use and City Size*. Cambridge: Cambridge University Press.

[130] Fujita, M. (2012). Thünen and the new economic geography. *Regional Science and Urban Economics* 42: 907–12.

[131] Fujita, M. and Gokan, T. (2005). On the evolution of the spatial economy with multi-unit . multi-plant firms: the impact of IT development. *Portuguese Economic Review* 4: 93–105.

[132] Fujita, M., and Hamaguchi, N. (2001). Intermediate goods and the spatial structure of an economy. *Regional Science and Urban Economics* 31: 79–109.

[133] Fujita, M., and Krugman, P. (1995). When is the economy monocentric? von Thünen and Chamberlin unified. *Regional Science and Urban Economics* 25: 505–28.

[134] Fujita, M., Krugman, P., and Mori, T. (1999). On the evolution of hierarchical urban systems. *European Economic Review* 43: 209–51.

[135] Fujita, M., Krugman, P., and Venables, A.J. (1999). *The Spatial Economy. Cities, Regions and International Trade*. Cambridge, MA: MIT Press.

[136] Fujita, M., and Mori, T. (1995). Structural stability and evolution of urban systems, Working Paper N°171, Department of Regional Science, University of Pennsylvania.

[137] Fujita, M., and Mori, T. (1997). Structural stability and evolution of urban systems. *Regional Science and Urban Economics* 27: 399–442.

[138] Fujita, M., and Mori, T. (2005). Transport development and the evolution of economic geography. *Portuguese Economic Journal* 4: 129–59.

[139] Fujita, M., and Ogawa, H. (1982). Multiple equilibria and structural transition of non-monocentric urban configurations. *Regional Science and Urban Economics* 12: 161–96.

[140] Fujita, M., and Smith, T.E. (1987). Existence of continuous residential land-use equilibria. *Regional Science and urban Economics* 17: 549–94.

[141] Fujita, M., and Thisse, J.-F. (1991). Spatial duopoly and residential structure. *Journal of Urban Economics* 30: 27–47.

[142] Fujita, M., and Thisse, J.-F. (2003). Does geographical agglomeration foster economic growth? And who gains and loses from it? *Japanese Economic Review* 54: 121–45.

[143] Fujita, M., and Thisse, J.-F. (2006). Globalization and the evolution of the supply chain: who gains and who loses? *International Economic Review* 47: 811–36.

[144] Fujita, M., Thisse, J.-F., and Zenou, Y. (1997). On the endogenous formation of secondary employment centers in a city. *Journal of Urban Economics* 41: 337–57.

[145] Fujita, M. and Tokunaga, S. (1993). Impact of landownership on residential land use equilibria. In: T.R. Lakshmanan and P. Nijkamp (eds.). *Structure and Changes in the Space Economy: Festschrift in Honor of Martin J. Beckmann*. Berlin: Springer-Verlag.

[146] Fukao, K., and Bénabou, R. (1993). History versus expectations: a comment. *Quarterly Journal of Economics* 108: 535–42.

[147] Gabszewicz, J.J., and Thisse, J.-F. (1986). Spatial competition and the location of firms. In: J.J. Gabszewicz, J.-F. Thisse, M. Fujita, and U. Schweizer. *Location Theory*. Chur: Harwood Academic Publishers, 1–71.

[148] Gabszewicz, J.J., and Thisse, J.-F. (1992). Location. In: R.E. Aumann and S. Hart (eds.). *Handbook of Game Theory with Economic Applications, Volume 1*. Amsterdam: North-Holland, 281–304.

[149] Garretseen, H., and Martin, R. (2010). Rethinking (new) economic geography models: taking geography and history seriously. *Spatial Economic Analysis* 5: 127–60.

[150] Gaspar, J., and Glaeser, E.L. (1998). Information technology and the future of cities, *Journal of Urban Economics* 43: 136–56.

[151] Gehrig, T. (1998). Competing exchanges. *European Economic Review* 42: 277–310.

[152] Glaeser, E.L. (1998). Are cities dying? *Journal of Economic Perspectives* 12: 139–60.

[153] Glaeser, E.L. (2011). *Triumph of the City*. London: Macmillan.

[154] Glaeser, E.L., and Gottlieb, J.D. (2009). The wealth of cities: agglomeration economies and spatial equilibrium in the United States. *Journal of Economic Literature* 47: 983–1028.
[155] Glaeser, E.L., and Kahn, M.E. (2004). Sprawl and urban growth. In: J.V. Henderson and J.-F. Thisse (eds.). *Handbook of Regional and Urban Economics. Cities and Geography*. Amsterdam: North-Holland, 2481–527.
[156] Glaeser, E.L., Kallal, H.D., Scheinkman, J.A., and Shleifer, A. (1992). Growth in cities. *Journal of Political Economy* 100: 1126–52.
[157] Glaeser, E. L., and Kohlhase, J. E. (2004). Cities, regions and the decline of transport costs. *Papers in Regional Science* 83: 197–228.
[158] Glaeser, E.L., Kolko, J., and Saiz, A. (2001). Consumer city. *Journal of Economic Geography* 1: 27–50.
[159] Goldstein, G.S., and Gronberg, T.J. (1984). Economies of scope and economies of agglomeration. *Journal of Urban Economics* 16: 91–104.
[160] Goldstein, G.S., and Moses, L.N. (1975). Interdependence and the location of economic activities. *Journal of Urban Economics* 2: 63–84.
[161] Greenhut, M.L., Norman, G., and Hung, C.-S. (1987). *The Economics of Imperfect Competition. A Spatial Approach*. Cambridge: Cambridge University Press.
[162] Grossman, G., and Helpman, E. (1991). *Innovation and Growth in the World Economy*. Cambridge, MA: MIT Press.
[163] Gupta B., Pal, D., and Sarkar, J. (1997). Spatial Cournot competition and agglomeration in a model of location choice. *Regional Science and Urban Economics* 27: 261–82.
[164] Hägerstrand, T. (1953). *Innovation Diffusion as a Spatial Process*. Chicago: University of Chicago Press.
[165] Hamilton, B.W. (1980). Indivisibilities and interplant transportation cost: do they cause market breakdown? *Journal of Urban Economics* 7: 31–41.
[166] Handbury, J., and D. Weinstein. (2011) Is New Economic Geography right? Evidence from price data. NBER Working Paper n°17067.
[167] Hanson, G.H. (1996). Localization economies, vertical organization, and trade. *American Economic Review* 86: 1266–78.
[168] Harris, C. (1954). The market as a factor on the localization of industry in the United States. *Annals of the Association of American Geographers* 64: 315–48.
[169] Hartwick, J., Schweizer, U. and Varaiya, P. (1976). Comparative statics of a residential economy with several classes. *Journal of Economic Theory* 13: 396–413.
[170] Heffley, D.R. (1972). The quadratic assignment problem: a note. *Econometrica* 40: 1155–63.
[171] Heffley, D.R. (1976). Efficient spatial allocation in the quadratic assignment problem. *Journal of Urban Economics* 3: 309–22.
[172] Helpman, E. (1998). The size of regions. In: D. Pines, E. Sadka, and I. Zilcha (eds.). *Topics in Public Economics. Theoretical and Applied Analysis*. Cambridge: Cambridge University Press, 33–54.
[173] Helpman, E. (2011). *Understanding Global Trade*. Cambridge, MA: Harvard University Press.

[174] Helpman, E., and Krugman, P.R. (1985). *Market Structure and Foreign Trade*. Cambridge, MA: MIT Press.

[175] Helpman, E., Melitz, M., and Yeaple, S. (2004). Export versus FDI with heterogeneous firms. *American Economic Review* 94: 300–16.

[176] Helsley, R.W., and Strange, W.C. (1990). Matching and agglomeration economies in a system of cities. *Regional Science and Urban Economics* 20: 189–212.

[177] Helsley, R.W., and Strange, W.C. (1997). Limited developers. *Canadian Journal of Economics* 30: 329–48.

[178] Helsley, R.W., and Strange, W.C. (2004). Knowledge barter in cities. *Journal of Urban Economics* 56: 327–45.

[179] Henderson, J.V. (1974). The sizes and types of cities. *American Economic Review* 64: 640–56.

[180] Henderson, J.V. (1977). *Economic Theory and the Cities*. New York: Academic Press.

[181] Henderson, J.V. (1985). The Tiebout model: bring back the entrepreneurs. *Journal of Political Economy* 93: 248–64.

[182] Henderson, J.V. (1987). Systems of cities and inter-city trade. In: P. Hansen, M. Labbé, D. Peeters, J.-F. Thisse, and J.V. Henderson. *Systems of Cities and Facility Location*. Chur: Harwood Academic Publishers, 71–119.

[183] Henderson, J.V. (1988). *Urban Development. Theory, Fact and Illusion*. Oxford: Oxford University Press.

[184] Henderson, J.V. (1997a). Medium size cities. *Regional Science and Urban Economics* 27: 583–612.

[185] Henderson, J.V. (1997b). Externalities and industrial development. *Journal of Urban Economics* 42: 449–70.

[186] Henderson, J.V. (2003a). Marshall's scale externalities. *Journal of Urban Economics* 53: 1–28.

[187] Henderson, J.V. (2003b). Urbanization and economic growth: the so-what question. *Journal of Economic Growth* 8: 47–71.

[188] Henderson, J.V. (2007). Understanding knowledge spillovers. *Regional Science and Urban Economics* 37: 497–508.

[189] Henderson, J.V., Kuncoro, A., and Turner, M. (1995). Industrial development in cities. *Journal of Political Economy* 103: 1066–90.

[190] Henderson, J.V., and Mitra, A. (1996). The new urban landscape: developers and edge cities. *Regional Science and Urban Economics* 26: 613–43.

[191] Henderson, J.V., and Thisse, J.-F. (2001). On strategic community development. *Journal of Political Economy* 109: 546–69.

[192] Herbert, J.D., and Stevens, B.H. (1970). A model of the distribution of residential activity in urban areas. *Journal of Regional Science* 2: 21–36.

[193] Hicks, J. (1940). The valuation of social income. *Economica* 7: 105–24.

[194] Hicks, J.H. (1969). *A Theory of Economic History*. Oxford: Clarendon.

[195] Hildenbrand, W. (1974). *Core and Equilibria in a Large Economy*. Princeton, NJ: Princeton University Press.

[196] Hirschman, A.O. (1958). *The Strategy of Development*. New Haven, CN: Yale University Press.

[197] Hochman, O., Pines, D., and Thisse, J.-F. (1995). On the optimal structure of local governments. *American Economic Review* 85: 1224–40.

[198] Hohenberg, P. (2004). The historical geography of Europe: an interpretative essay. In: J.V. Henderson and J.-F. Thisse (eds.). *Handbook of Regional and Urban Economics. Cities and Geography*. Amsterdam: North-Holland, 3021–52.
[199] Hohenberg, P., and Lees, L.H. (1985). *The Making of Urban Europe (1000–1950)*. Cambridge, MA: Harvard University Press.
[200] Hoover, E.M. (1936). *Location Theory and the Shoe and Leather Industries*. Cambridge, MA: Harvard University Press.
[201] Hoover, E.M. (1937). Spatial price discrimination. *Review of Economic Studies* 4: 182–91.
[202] Hoover, E.M. (1948). *The Location of Economic Activity*. New York: McGraw-Hill.
[203] Hotelling, H. (1929). Stability in competition. *Economic Journal* 39: 41–57.
[204] Hotelling, H. (1938). The general welfare in relation to problems of taxation and of railway and utility rates. *Econometrica* 6: 242–69.
[205] Hummels, D., and Klenow, P.J. (2005). The variety and quality of a nation's exports. *American Economic Review* 95: 704–23.
[206] Imai, H. (1982). CBD hypothesis and economies of agglomeration. *Journal of Economic Theory* 28: 275–99.
[207] Ingram, G.K. and Carroll, A. (1981). The spatial structure of Latin American cities. *Journal of Urban Economics* 9: 257–73.
[208] Ioannides, Y.M. (2012). *From Neighborhoods to Nations: The Economics of Social Interactions*. Princeton, NJ: Princeton University Press.
[209] Irmen, A., and Thisse, J.-F. (1998). Competition in multi-characteristics spaces: Hotelling was almost right. *Journal of Economic Theory* 78: 76–102.
[210] Isard, W. (1949). The general theory of location and space-economy. *Quarterly Journal of Economics* 63: 476–506.
[211] Isard, W. (1956). *Location and Space-Economy*. Cambridge, MA: MIT Press.
[212] Jacobs, J. (1969). *The Economy of Cities*. New York: Random House.
[213] Jackson, M.O. (2008). *Social and Economic Networks*. Princeton, NJ: Princeton University Press.
[214] Jackson, M.O., and Wolinsky, A. (1996). A strategic model of social and economic networks. *Journal of Economic Theory* 71: 44–74.
[215] Jaffe, A.B., Trajtenberg, M., and Henderson, R. (1993). Geographic localization of knowledge spillovers as evidenced by patent citations. *Quarterly Journal of Economics* 108: 577–98.
[216] Jofre-Monseny, J., Marín-López, R., and Viladecans-Marsal, E. (2011). The mechanisms of agglomeration: evidence from the effect of interindustry relations on the location of new firms. *Journal of Urban Economics* 70: 61–74.
[217] Jones, C.I., and Romer, P.M. (2010). The new Kaldor facts: ideas, institutions, population, and human capital. *American Economic Journal: Macroeconomics* 2: 224–45.
[218] Jovanovic, M. (2009). *Evolutionary Economic Geography. Location of Production and the European Union*. London: Routledge.
[219] Kaldor, N. (1935). Market imperfection and excess capacity. *Economica* 2: 35–50.
[220] Kaldor, N. (1939). Welfare propositions of economics and interpersonal comparisons of utility. *Economic Journal* 49: 549–51.

[221] Kaldor, N. (1970). The case for regional policies. *Scottish Journal of Political Economy* 17: 337–48.
[222] Kaldor, N. (1985). *Economics without Equilibrium*. Armonk, NY: M.E. Sharpe.
[223] Kanemoto Y. (1980). *Theory of Urban Externalities*. Amsterdam: North-Holland.
[224] Kim, S. (1995). Expansion of markets and the geographic distribution of economic activities: the trends in U.S. regional manufacturing structure, 1860–1987. *Quarterly Journal of Economics* 110: 881–908.
[225] Klein, A., and Crafts, N. (2012). Making sense of the manufacturing belt: determinants of U.S. industrial location, 1880–1920. *Journal of Economic Geography* 12: 775–807.
[226] Koopmans, T.C. (1957). *Three Essays on the State of Economic Science*. New York: McGraw-Hill.
[227] Koopmans, T.C., and Beckmann, M.J. (1957). Assignment problems and the location of economic activities. *Econometrica* 25: 1401–14.
[228] Krugman, P.R. (1979). Increasing returns, monopolistic competition, and international trade. *Journal of International Economics* 9: 469–79.
[229] Krugman, P.R. (1980). Scale economies, product differentiation, and the pattern of trade. *American Economic Review* 70: 950–59.
[230] Krugman, P. (1991a). *Geography and Trade*. Cambridge, MA: MIT Press.
[231] Krugman, P. (1991b). Increasing returns and economic geography. *Journal of Political Economy* 99: 483–99.
[232] Krugman, P. (1991c). History versus expectations. *Quarterly Journal of Economics* 106: 651–67.
[233] Krugman, P. (1995). *Development, Geography, and Economic Theory*. Cambridge MA: MIT Press.
[234] Krugman, P. (1998). Space: the final frontier. *Journal of Economic Perspectives* 12: 161–74.
[235] Krugman, P. (2007). The new economic geography: where are we? In: M. Fujita (ed.). *Regional Integration in East Asia from the Viewpoint of Spatial Economics*. London: Macmillan, 23–34.
[236] Krugman, P., and Venables, A.J. (1995). Globalization and the inequality of nations. *Quarterly Journal of Economics* 110: 857–80.
[237] Labbé, M., Peeters, D., and Thisse, J.-F. (1995). Location on networks. In: M. Ball, T. Magnanti, C. Monma, and G. Nemhauser (eds.). *Handbook of Operations Research and Management Science: Networks*. Amsterdam: North-Holland, 551–624.
[238] Labys, W.C., and Yang, C.W. (1997). Spatial price equilibrium as a foundation to unified spatial commodity modeling. *Papers in Regional Science* 76: 199–228.
[239] Launhardt, W. (1885). *Mathematische Begründung der Volkswirtschaftslehre*. Leipzig: B.G. Teubner. English translation: *Mathematical Principles of Economics*. Aldershot: Edward Elgar (1993).
[240] Lederer, P.J., and Hurter, A.P. (1986). Competition of firms: discriminatory pricing and location. *Econometrica* 54: 623–40.
[241] Lerner, A., and Singer, H.W. (1937). Some notes on duopoly and spatial competition. *Journal of Political Economy* 45: 145–86.
[242] Liu, H.-L., and Fujita, M. (1991). A monopolistic competition model of spatial agglomeration with variable density. *Annals of Regional Science* 25: 81–99.

[243] Lösch, A. (1940). *Die Räumliche Ordnung der Wirtschaft*. Jena: Gustav Fischer. English translation: *The Economics of Location*. New Haven, CT: Yale University Press (1954).
[244] Lucas, R.E. (1988). On the mechanics of economic development. *Journal of Monetary Economics* 22: 3–22.
[245] Lucas, R.E. (1990). Why doesn't capital flow from rich to poor countries? *Papers of the American Economic Association* 80: 92–6.
[246] Lucas, R.E. (2001). Externalities and cities. *Review of Economic Dynamics* 4: 245–74.
[247] Lucas, R.E., and Rossi-Hansberg, E. (2002). On the internal structure of cities. *Econometrica* 70: 1445–76.
[248] Magrini, S. (2004). Regional (di)convergence. In: J.V. Henderson and J.-F. Thisse (eds.). *Handbook of Regional and Urban Economics. Cities and Geography*. Amsterdam: North-Holland, 2243–92.
[249] Manne, A. (1964). Plant location under economies of scale – Decentralization and computation. *Management Science* 11: 213–35.
[250] Manski, C. (2000). Economic analysis of social interactions. *Journal of Economic Perspectives* 14/3: 115–36.
[251] Marchand, B. (1993). *Paris, histoire d'une ville*. Paris: Editions du Seuil.
[252] Markusen, J.R. (1984). Multinationals, multi-plant economies and the gain from trade. *Journal of International Economics* 16: 205–16.
[253] Marshall, A. (1890). *Principles of Economics*. London: Macmillan. 8th edition published in 1920.
[254] Marshall, J.U. (1989). *The Structure of Urban Systems*. Toronto: University of Toronto Press.
[255] Martin, P., and Rogers, C.A. (1995). Industrial location and public infrastructure. *Journal of International Economics* 39: 335–51.
[256] Martin, R. (1999). Editorial: The "new" economic geography: challenge or irrelevance. *Transactions of the Institute of British Geographers* 24: 389–91.
[257] Matsuyama, K. (1995). Complementarities and cumulative process in models of monopolistic competition. *Journal of Economic Literature* 33: 701–29.
[258] Mayer, T., and Ottaviano, G.I.P. (2007). *The Happy Few: The Internationalisation of European Firms*. Brussels: Bruegel Blueprint Series.
[259] McFadden, D. (1974). Conditional logit analysis of qualitative choice behavior. In: P. Zarembka (ed.). *Frontiers in Econometrics*. New York: Academic Press, 105–42.
[260] McLaren, J. (2000). "Globalization" and vertical structure. *American Economic Review* 90: 1239–54.
[261] McMillan, J., and Rothschild, M. (1994). Search. In: R.J. Aumann and S. Hart (eds.). *Handbook of Game Theory with Economic Applications, Volume 2*. Amsterdam: North-Holland, 905–27.
[262] Meade, J.E. (1972). The theory of labour-managed firms and of profit-sharing. *Economic Journal* 62: 402–28.
[263] Melitz, M. (2003). The impact of trade on intraindustry reallocations and aggregate industry productivity. *Econometrica* 71: 1695–725.
[264] Melitz, M., and Ottaviano, G.I.P (2008). Market size, trade, and productivity. *Review of Economic Studies* 75: 295–316.

[265] Mills, E.S. (1967). An aggregative model of resource allocation in a metropolitan area. *American Economic Review* 57: 197–210.
[266] Mills, E.S. (1970). The efficiency of spatial competition. *Papers and Proceedings of the Regional Science Association* 25: 71–82.
[267] Mills, E.S. (1972a). *Studies in the Structure of the Urban Economy*. Baltimore: The Johns Hopkins University Press.
[268] Mills, E.S. (1972b). *Urban Economics*. Glenview, IL: Scott, Foresman and Company.
[269] Mion, G., and Naticchioni, P. (2009). The spatial sorting and matching of skills and firms. *Canadian Journal of Economics* 42: 28–55.
[270] Mirrlees, J. (1972). The optimum town. *Swedish Journal of Economics* 74: 114–35.
[271] Mirrlees, J. (1995). Welfare economics and economies of scale. *Japanese Economic Review* 46: 38–62.
[272] Mohring, H. (1961). Land values and measurement of highway benefits. *Journal of Political Economy* 49: 236–49.
[273] Moretti, E. (2012). *The New Geography of Jobs*. New York: Houghton Mifflin Harcourt.
[274] Mossay, P. (2006). The core-periphery model: a note on the existence and uniqueness of short-run equilibrium. *Journal of Urban Economics* 59: 389–93.
[275] Mossay, P., and Picard, P. (2011). On spatial equilibria in a social interaction model. *Journal of Economic Theory* 146: 2455–77.
[276] Mulligan, G. (1984). Agglomeration and central place theory: a review of the literature. *International Regional Science Review* 9: 1–42.
[277] Murata, Y., and Thisse, J.-F. (2005). A simple model of economic geography à la Helpman-Tabuchi. *Journal of Urban Economics* 58: 137–55.
[278] Muth, R.F. (1961). The spatial structure of the housing market. *Papers and Proceedings of the Regional Science Association* 7: 207–20.
[279] Muth, R.F. (1969). *Cities and Housing*. Chicago: University of Chicago Press.
[280] Muth, R.F. (1971). Migration: chicken or egg? *Southern Economic Journal* 37: 295–306.
[281] Myrdal, G. (1957). *Economic Theory and Underdeveloped Regions*. London: Duckworth.
[282] Nagurney, A. (1993). *Network Economics: A Variational Inequality Approach*. Dordrecht: Kluwer Academic Publishers.
[283] Nakajima, K. (2008). Economic division and spatial relocation: The case of postwar Japan. *Journal of the Japanese and International Economies* 22: 383–400.
[284] Navaretti, G.B., and Venables, A.J. (2004). *Multinational Firms in the World Economy*. Princeton, NJ: Princeton University Press.
[285] Nelson, P. (1970). Information and consumer behavior. *Journal of Political Economy* 78: 311–29.
[286] Nerlove, M.L., and Sadka, E. (1991). Von Thünen's model of the dual economy. *Journal of Economics* 54: 97–123.

[287] Nocke, V. (2006). A gap for me: entrepreneurs and entry. *Journal of the European Economic Association* 4: 929–55.

[288] Norman, G., and Thisse, J.-F. (1996). Product variety and welfare under soft and tough pricing regimes. *Economic Journal* 106: 76–91.

[289] Ogawa, H., and Fujita, M. (1980). Equilibrium land use patterns in a non-monocentric city. *Journal of Regional Science* 20: 455–75.

[290] O'Hara, D.J. (1977). Location of firms within a square central business district. *Journal of Political Economy* 85: 1189–207.

[291] Ohlin, B. (1933). *Interregional and International Trade.* Cambridge, MA: Harvard University Press). Revised version published in 1968.

[292] Ohmae, K. (1995). *The End of the Nation State*. New York: The Free Press.

[293] Okubo, T., Picard, P., and Thisse, J.-F. (2010). The spatial selection of heterogeneous firms. *Journal of International Economics* 82: 230–37.

[294] Ota, M., and Fujita, M. (1993). Communication technologies and spatial organization of multi-unit firms in metropolitan areas. *Regional Science and Urban Economics* 23: 695–729.

[295] Ottaviano, G.I.P. (1999). Integration, geography, and the burden of history. *Regional Science and Urban Economics* 29: 245–56.

[296] Ottaviano G.I.P., and Robert-Nicoud, F. (2006). The "genome" of NEG models with vertical linkages: a positive and normative synthesis. *Journal of Economic Geography* 6: 113–39.

[297] Ottaviano G.I.P., Tabuchi, T., and Thisse, J.-F. (2002). Agglomeration and trade revisited. *International Economic Review* 43: 409–36.

[298] Ottaviano, G.I.P., and Thisse, J.-F. (2004). Agglomeration and economic geography. In: J.V. Henderson and J.-F. Thisse (eds.). *Handbook of Regional and Urban Economics. Cities and Geography*. Amsterdam: North-Holland, 2563–608.

[299] Ottaviano, G.I.P., and van Ypersele, T. (2005). Market size and tax competition. *Journal of International Economics* 67: 25–46.

[300] Oyama, D. (2009a). History versus expectations in economic geography reconsidered. *Journal of Economic Dynamics & Control* 33: 394–408.

[301] Oyama, D. (2009b). Agglomeration under forward-looking expectations: potentials and global stability. *Regional Science and Urban Economics* 39: 696–713.

[302] Oyama, D., Sato, Y., Tabuchi, T., and Thisse, J.-F. (2011). On the impact of trade on the industrial structures of nations. *International Journal of Economic Theory* 7: 93–109.

[303] Papageorgiou, G.J., and Casetti, E. (1971). Spatial equilibrium residential land values in a muticentric city. *Journal of Regional Science* 11: 385–89.

[304] Papageorgiou, Y.Y., and Pines, D. (1990). The logical foundations of urban economics are consistent. *Journal of Economic Theory* 50: 37–53.

[305] Papageorgiou, Y.Y., and Pines, D. (1999). *An Essay in Urban Economic Theory*. Dordrecht: Kluwer Academic Publishers.

[306] Papageorgiou, Y.Y., and Smith, T.R. (1983). Agglomeration as local instability of spatially uniform steady-states. *Econometrica* 51: 1109–19.

[307] Papageorgiou, Y.Y., and Thisse, J.-F. (1985). Agglomeration as spatial interdependence between firms and households. *Journal of Economic Theory* 37: 19–31.

[308] Parsley, D.C., and Wei, S.-J. (2001). Explaining the border effect: the role of exchange rate variability, shipping costs and geography. *Journal of International Economics* 55: 87–105.

[309] Peri, G. (2005). Determinants of knowledge flows and their effects on innovation. *Review of Economics and Statistics* 87: 308–22.

[310] Perroux, F. (1955). Note sur la notion de pôle de croissance. *Economique appliquée* 7: 307–20.

[311] Pflüger, M., and Tabuchi, T. (2010). The size of regions with land use for production. *Regional Science and Urban Economics* 40: 481–89.

[312] Picard, P.M., and Okubo, T. (2012). Firms' locations under demand heterogeneity. *Regional Science and Urban Economics* 42: 961–74.

[313] Picard, P.M., Thisse, J.-F., and Toulemonde, E. (2004). Economic geography and the distribution of profits. *Journal of Urban Economics* 56: 144–67.

[314] Pirenne, H. (1925). *Medieval Cities*. Princeton, NJ: Princeton University Press.

[315] Polèse, M. (2010). *The Wealth and Poverty of Regions. Why Cities Matter*. Chicago: University of Chicago Press.

[316] Pollard, S. (1981). *Peaceful Conquest: The Industrialization of Europe 1760–1970*. Oxford: Oxford University Press.

[317] Ponsard, C. (1983). *History of Spatial Economic Theory*. Heidelberg: Springer-Verlag.

[318] Porter, M.E. (1998). *On Competition*. Cambridge, MA: A Harvard Business Review Book.

[319] Prager, J.-C., and Thisse, J.-F. (2012). *Economic Geography and the Unequal Development of Regions*. London: Routledge.

[320] Puga, D. (1999). The rise and fall of regional inequalities. *European Economic Review* 43: 303–34.

[321] Puga, D. (2010). The magnitude and causes of agglomeration economies. *Journal of Regional Science* 50: 203–19.

[322] Pyke, F., Becattini, B., and Sengenberger, W., eds. (1990). *Industrial Districts and Inter-firm Cooperation in Italy*. Geneva, International Institute for Labour Studies.

[323] Quigley, J.M., and Raphael, S. (2004). Is housing unaffordable? Why isn't it more affordable? *Journal of Economic Perspectives* 18/1: 191–214.

[324] Quinzii, M., and Thisse, J.-F. (1990). On the optimality of central places. *Econometrica* 58: 1101–19.

[325] Rappaport, J., and Sachs, J.D. (2003). The United States as a coastal nation. *Journal of Economic Growth* 8: 5–46.

[326] Redding, S. (2011). Economic geography: a review of the theoretical and empirical literature. In: D. Bernhofen, R. Falvey, D. Greenaway, and U. Kreickemeie (eds.). *The Palgrave Handbook of International Trade*. London: Palgrave Macmillan.

[327] Redding, S., and Sturm, D. (2008). The cost of remoteness: evidence from German division and reunification. *American Economic Review* 98: 1766–97.

[328] Redding, S., and Venables, A. J. (2004). Economic geography and international inequality. *Journal of International Economics* 62: 53–82.

[329] Reilly, W.J. (1931). *The Law of Retail Gravitation*. New York: Pilsbury.

[330] Rice, P., and Venables, A.J. (2003). Equilibrium regional disparities: theory and British evidence. *Regional Studies* 37: 675–86.

[331] Roback, J. (1982). Wages, rents, and the quality of life. *Journal of Political Economy* 90: 1257–78.

[332] Robert-Nicoud, F. (2005). The structure of simple "New Economic Geography" models (or, On identical twins). *Journal of Economic Geography* 5: 201–34.

[333] Robert-Nicoud, F. (2008). Offshoring of routine tasks and (de)industrialisation: Threat or opportunity – And for whom? *Journal of Urban Economics* 63: 517–35.

[334] Romer, P. (1986). Increasing returns and long-run growth. *Journal of Political Economy* 94: 1002–37.

[335] Romer, P. (1990). Endogenous technological change. *Journal of Political Economy* 98: S71–S102.

[336] Romer, P. (1992). Increasing returns and new developments in the theory of growth. In: W.A. Barnett, B. Cornet, C. d'Aspremont, J.J. Gabszewicz, and A. Mas-Colell (eds.). *Equilibrium Theory with Applications*. Cambridge: Cambridge University Press, 83–110.

[337] Rosenstein-Rodan, P.N. (1943). Problems of industrialization of Eastern and South-Eastern Europe. *Economic Journal* 53: 202–11.

[338] Rosenthal, S.S., and Strange, W.C. (2004). Evidence on the nature and sources of agglomeration economies. In: J.V. Henderson and J.-F. Thisse (eds.). *Handbook of Regional and Urban Economics. Cities and Geography*. Amsterdam: North-Holland, 2119–71.

[339] Rosès, J.R. (2003). Why isn't the whole of Spain industrialized? New economic geography and early industrialization, 1797–1910. *Journal of Economic History* 63: 995–1022.

[340] Rosès, J.R., Martinez-Galarraga, J., and Tirado, D.A. (2010). The upswing of regional income inequality in Spain (1860–1930). *Exploration of Economic History* 47: 244–57.

[341] Sachs, J. (2000). A new map of the world. *The Economist* June 24, 2000, 99–101.

[342] Salop, S.C. (1979). Monopolistic competition with an outside good. *Bell Journal of Economics* 10: 141–56.

[343] Samuelson, P.A. (1939). The gains from international trade. *Canadian Journal of Economics* 5: 195–205.

[344] Samuelson, P.A. (1952). Spatial price equilibrium and linear programming. *American Economic Review* 42: 283–303.

[345] Samuelson, P.A. (1954a). The transfer problem and transport cost, II: analysis of effects of trade impediments. *Economic Journal* 64: 264–89.

[346] Samuelson, P.A. (1954b). The pure theory of public expenditures. *Review of Economics and Statistics* 36: 387–89.

[347] Samuelson, P.A. (1962). The gains form international trade once again. *Economic Journal* 72: 820–29.

[348] Samuelson, P.A. (1983). Thünen at two hundred. *Journal of Economic Literature* 21: 1468–88.

[349] Sandholm, W.H. (2001). Potential games with continuous player sets. *Journal of Economic Theory* 97: 81–108.

[350] Sato, Y., Tabuchi, T., and Yamamoto, K. (2012). Market size and entrepreneurship. *Journal of Economic Geography* 12: 1139–66.
[351] Saxenian, A. (1994). *Regional Advantage: Culture and Competition in Silicon Valley and Route 128*. Cambridge, MA: Harvard University Press.
[352] Schmeidler, D. (1973). Equilibrium points of nonatomic games. *Journal of Statistical Physics* 7: 295–300.
[353] Schulz, N., and Stahl, K. (1989). Good and bad competition in spatial markets for search goods: the case of linear utility function. *Annales d'Economie et de Statistique* 15/16: 113–36.
[354] Schulz, N., and Stahl, K. (1996). Do consumers search for the highest price? equilibrium and monopolistic optimum in differentiated products markets. *Rand Journal of Economics* 27: 542–62.
[355] Schweizer, U. (1986). General equilibrium in space. In: J.J. Gabszewicz, J.-F. Thisse, M. Fujita, and U. Schweizer, *Location Theory*. Chur, Switzerland: Harwood Academic Publishers, 151–85.
[356] Schweizer, U., and Varaiya, P.V. (1976). The spatial structure of production with a Leontief technology. *Regional Science and Urban Economics* 6: 231–51.
[357] Schweizer, U., Varaiya, P.V., and Hartwick, J. (1976). General equilibrium and location theory. *Journal of Urban Economics* 3: 285–303.
[358] Scitovsky, T. (1941). A note on welfare propositions in economics. *Review of Economic Studies* 9: 77–88.
[359] Scitovsky, T. (1954). Two concepts of external economies. *Journal of Political Economy* 62: 143–51.
[360] Scotchmer, S. (1986). Local public goods in an equilibrium: how pecuniary externalities matter, *Regional Science and Urban Economics* 16: 463–81.
[361] Scotchmer, S. (2002). Local public goods and clubs. In: A. Auerbach and M. Feldstein (eds.). *Handbook of Public Economics, Volume 4*. Amsterdam: North-Holland, 1997–2042.
[362] Serk-Hanssen, J. (1969). The optimal number of factories in a spatial market. In: H.C. Bos (ed.). *Towards Balanced International Growth*. Amsterdam: North-Holland, 269–81.
[363] Sidorov, A., and Zhelobodko, E. (2013). Agglomeration and spreading in an asymmetric world. *Review of Development Economics*, 17: 201–19.
[364] Smith, A. (1776). *An Inquiry into the Nature and Causes of the Wealth of Nations*, London: Straham and Cadell. Fifth edition reprinted in 1965. New York: The Modern Library.
[365] Smith, H., and Hay, D. (2005). Streets, malls, and supermarkets. *Journal of Economics and Management Strategy* 14: 29–59.
[366] Smith, W.D. (1984). The function of commercial centers in the modernization of European capitalism: Amsterdam as an information exchange in the seventeenth century. *Journal of Economic History* 44: 985–1005.
[367] Solow, R.M. (1956). A contribution to the theory of economic growth. *Quarterly Journal of Economics* 70: 65–94.
[368] Solow, R.M. (1973). On equilibrium models of urban locations. In: J.M. Parkin (ed.). *Essays in Modern Economics*. London: Longman, 2–16.
[369] Spence, M. (1976). Product selection, fixed costs, and monopolistic competition. *Review of Economic Studies* 43: 217–35.

[370] Spulber, D.F. (2007). *Global Competitive Strategy*. Cambridge: Cambridge University Press.

[371] Sraffa, P. (1926). The laws of return under competitive conditions. *Economic Journal* 36: 535–50.

[372] Stahl, K. (1982). Differentiated products, consumer search, and locational oligopoly. *Journal of Industrial Economics* 31: 97–114.

[373] Stahl, K. (1987). Theories of urban business location. In: E.S. Mills (ed.). *Handbook of Regional and Urban Economics, Volume 2*. Amsterdam: North-Holland, 759–820.

[374] Starrett, D. (1974). Principles of optimal location in a large homogeneous area. *Journal of Economic Theory* 9: 418–48.

[375] Starrett, D. (1978). Market allocations of location choice in a model with free mobility. *Journal of Economic Theory* 17: 21–37.

[376] Starrett, D. (1988). *Foundations of Public Economics*. Cambridge: Cambridge University Press.

[377] Stern, N. (1972). The optimal size of market areas. *Journal of Economic Theory* 4: 154–73.

[378] Stigler, G.J. (1961). The economics of information. *Journal of Political Economy* 69: 213–25.

[379] Stiglitz, J. (1977). The theory of local public goods. In: M.S. Feldstein and R.P. Inman (eds.). *The Economics of Public Services*. London: Macmillan, 273–334.

[380] Stollsteimer, J.F. (1963). A working model for plant numbers and locations. *Journal of Farm Economics* 45: 631–45.

[381] Storper, M. (2013). *Keys to the City: How Economics, Institutions, Social Interactions and Politics Affect Regional Development*. Princeton, NJ: Princeton University Press.

[382] Streeten, P. (1993). The special problems of small countries. *World Development* 21: 197–202.

[383] Stuart, C. (1979). Search and the spatial organization of trading. In: S. Lipman and J.J. McCall (eds.). *Studies in the Economics of Search*. Amsterdam: North-Holland, 17–33.

[384] Syverson, C. (2004). Market structure and productivity: a concrete example. *Journal of Political Economy* 112: 1181–222.

[385] Tabuchi, T. (1986). Urban agglomeration economies in a linear city. *Regional Science and Urban Economics* 16: 421–36.

[386] Tabuchi, T. (1998). Agglomeration and dispersion: a synthesis of Alonso and Krugman. *Journal of Urban Economics* 44: 333–51.

[387] Tabuchi, T., and Thisse, J.-F. (2002). Taste heterogeneity, labor mobility and economic geography. *Journal of Development Economics* 69: 155–77.

[388] Tabuchi, T., and Thisse, J.-F. (2011). A new economic geography model of central places. *Journal of Urban Economics* 69: 240–52.

[389] Tabuchi, T., Thisse, J.-F., and Zeng, D.-Z. (2005). On the number and size of cities. *Journal of Economic Geography* 5: 423–48.

[390] Takahashi, T., Takatsuka, H., and Zeng, D.-Z. (2013). Spatial inequality, globalization, and footloose capital. *Economic Theory* 53: 213–38.

[391] Takatsuka, H., and Zeng, D.-Z. (2012a). Mobile capital and the home market effect. *Canadian Journal of Economics* 45: 1062–82.

[392] Takatsuka, H., and Zeng, D.-Z. (2012b). Trade liberalization and welfare: differentiated-good versus homogeneous-good markets. *Journal of the Japanese and International Economies* 26: 308–25.

[393] Takayama, T., and Judge, G.G. (1971). *Spatial and Temporal Price and Allocation Models*. Amsterdam: North-Holland.

[394] Tauchen, H., and Witte, A.D. (1984). Socially optimal and equilibrium distributions of office activity: models with exogenous and endogenous contacts. *Journal of Urban Economics* 15: 66–86.

[395] Teece, D.J. (1977). Technology transfer by multinational firms: the resource cost of transferring technological know-how. *Economic Journal* 87: 242–61.

[396] Teitz, M.B. (1968). Towards a theory of urban facility location. *Papers and Proceedings of the Regional Science Association* 21: 35–52.

[397] Thisse, J.-F. (2010). Toward a unified theory of economic geography and urban economics. *Journal of Regional Science* 50: 281–96.

[398] Thisse, J.-F., and Zoller, H.G. (1983). *Locational Analysis of Public Facilities*. Amsterdam: North-Holland.

[399] Thünen, J.H. von (1826). *Der isolierte Staat in Beziehung auf Landwirtschaft und Nationalökonomie*. Hamburg: Perthes. English translation: *The Isolated State*. Oxford: Pergammon Press (1966).

[400] Tiebout, C.M. (1956). A pure theory of local public expenditures. *Journal of Political Economy* 64: 416–24.

[401] Tiebout, C.M. (1961). An economic theory of fiscal decentralization. In: National Bureau of Economic Reseach, *Public Finances: Needs, Sources and Utilization*. Princeton, NJ: Princeton University Press.

[402] Toulemonde, E. (2006). Acquisition of skills, labor subsidies, and agglomeration of firms. *Journal of Urban Economics* 59: 420–39.

[403] Toulemonde, E. (2008). Multinationals: too many or too few? The proximity-concentration trade-off. *Open Economies Review* 19: 203–19.

[404] Toulemonde, E. (2011). The proximity–concentration trade-off with asymmetric countries. *The Manchester School* 79: 972–93.

[405] Venables, A.J. (1996). Equilibrium locations of vertically linked industries. *International Economic Review* 37: 341–59.

[406] Vickrey, W. (1977). The city as a firm. In: M.S. Feldstein and R.P. Inman (eds.). *The Economics of Public Services*. London: Macmillan, 334–43.

[407] Warsh, D. (2006). *Knowledge and the Wealth of Nations*. New York: Norton.

[408] Weber, A. (1909). *Über den Standort der Industrien*. Tübingen: J.C.B. Mohr. English translation: *The Theory of the Location of Industries*. Chicago: Chicago University Press, (1929).

[409] Wheaton, W.C. (1974). A comparative static analysis of urban spatial structure. *Journal of Economic Theory* 9: 223–37.

[410] Wheaton, W.C. (1977). Income and urban residence: an analysis of consumer demand for location. *American Economic Review* 67: 620–31.

[411] Whitaker, J.K. (1998). Henry George on the location of economic activity. In: M. Bellet and C. L'Harmet (eds.). *Industry, Space and Competition*. Cheltenham: Edward Elgar, 174–84.

[412] Wildasin, D.E. (1986). *Urban Public Finance*. Chur, Switzerland: Harwood Academic Publishers.

[413] Wildasin, D. (1987). Theoretical analysis of local public economics. In: E.S. Mills (ed.). *Handbook of Regional and Urban Economics, Volume 2*. Amsterdam: North-Holland, 1131–78.

[414] Wilson, A.G. (1967). A statistical theory of spatial distribution models. *Transportation Research* 1: 253–69.

[415] Wolinsky, A. (1983). Retail trade concentration due to consumers' imperfect information. *Bell Journal of Economics* 14: 275–82.

[416] Yeaple, S.R. (2003). The complex integration strategies of multinationals and cross country dependencies in the structure of foreign direct investment. *Journal of International Economics* 60: 293–314.

[417] Young, A. (1928). Increasing returns and economic progress. *Economic Journal* 38: 527–42.

[418] Zenou, Y. (2009). *Urban Labor Economics*. Cambridge: Cambridge University Press.

Author Index

Subject Index

Printed in the United States
By Bookmasters